THE CHURCH AND GALILEO

Studies in Science and the Humanities
from the Reilly Center for Science, Technology, and Values

Ottavio Leoni, portrait of Galileo, chalk, Biblioteca Marucelliana, Florence.
Scala/Art Resource, New York.

THE
CHURCH
AND

Galileo

edited by

ERNAN McMULLIN

University of Notre Dame Press   Notre Dame, Indiana

Manufactured in the United States of America

Library of Congress Cataloging-in-Publication Data
The church and Galileo / edited by Ernan McMullin.
       p.   cm.
    (Studies in science and the humanities from the Reilly Center for Science,
Technology, and Values)
    Includes bibliographical references and index.
    ISBN 0-268-03483-4 (alk. paper)
    ISBN 0-268-03484-2 (pbk. : alk. paper)
    1. Galilei, Galileo, 1564–1642.   2. Religion and science—Italy—History—17th century.
3. Catholic Church—Italy—Rome—History—17th century.   4. Astronomy—Religious
aspects—Christianity—History of doctrines—17th century.   5. Catholic Church—
Doctrines—History—17th century.   6. Italy—Church history—17th century.
7. Science, Renaissance.   I. McMullin, Ernan, 1924–   II. Series.
    QB36.G2C48   2005
    520'.9'032—dc22

                                                                    2005002602

CONTENTS

LIST OF AUTHORS

Mariano Artigas: Professor of Philosophy of Science and former Dean of the Ecclesiastical Faculty at the University of Navarra, Spain. Author of *The Mind of the Universe: Understanding Science and Religion* (2000) and coauthor, with William Shea, of *Galileo in Rome: The Rise and Fall of a Troublesome Genius* (2003).

Francesco Beretta: Chargé de recherche at the CNRS (Laboratoire de recherche historique Rhone-Alpes, Lyon). Author of *Galilée devant le Tribunal de l'Inquisition* (1998) and articles based on research at the recently opened archival records of the Holy Office (e.g. "Le procès de Galilée et les archives du Saint-Office," 1999).

George V. Coyne, S.J.: Director of the Vatican Observatory. Head of one of the four divisions of the Galileo Commission (1981–92). Co-editor, with Michael Heller and Jósef Zycinski, of *The Galileo Affair: A Meeting of Faith and Science* (1985) and coauthor, with Ugo Baldini, of *The Louvain Lectures (Lectiones Lovanienses) of Bellarmine* (1984).

Annibale Fantoli: Adjunct Professor in the Department of History at the University of Victoria (Canada). Author of *For Copernicanism and for the Church* (1994), now in its third edition (2003), and *Galileo and the Catholic Church: A Critique of the "Closure" of the Galileo Commission's Work* (2002).

Stéphane Garcia: Doctor in History at the University of Lausanne, Switzerland. Author of *Galilée-Elie Diodati: Naissance d'une réseau scientifique dans l'Europe du xviie siècle* (2004).

John L. Heilbron: Formerly Professor of History and Vice-Chancellor, University of California, Berkeley; now Senior Research Fellow at Worcester College, Oxford. Author of *The Sun in the Church* (1999); editor-in-chief of *The Oxford Companion to the History of Modern Science* (2003).

Irving A. Kelter: Associate Professor and Chair, Department of History, University of St. Thomas, Houston. Author of "Paolo Foscarini's *Letter to Galileo:* The Search for Proofs of the Earth's Motion" (1992) and "A Catholic Theologian Responds to Copernicanism: The Theological *Judicium* of Paolo Foscarini's *Lettera*" (1997).

Michel-Pierre Lerner: Research Director at the Centre nationale de la recherche scientifique. Attached to the History of Astronomy Division at the Observatoire de Paris. Author of *Le monde des sphères* (1996–97); editor and translator of Tommaso Campanella's *Apologia pro Galileo/Apologie de Galilée* (2001).

Rafael Martínez: Associate Professor of Philosophy of Science at the Pontifical University of the Holy Cross (Rome). Coauthor, with Mariano Artigas, Lucas F. Mateo-Seco, and William Shea, of "Un inedito sul caso Galilei" (2001).

Ernan McMullin: Professor Emeritus of Philosophy and former Director of the Program in History and Philosophy of Science at the University of Notre Dame. Editor of and contributor to *Galileo, Man of Science* (1967); author of "The Conception of Science in Galileo's Work" (1978) and "Galileo on Science and Scripture" (1998).

Michael H. Shank: Professor, Department of History of Science, and Senior Member of the Institute for Research in the Humanities at the University of Wisconsin. Author of "How Shall We Practice History? The Case of Mario Biagioli's Galileo, Courtier" (1996); editor of *The Scientific Enterprise in Antiquity and the Middle Ages* (2000).

Michael Sharratt: Lecturer in Philosophy at Ushaw College, affiliated with the University of Durham, England. Author of *Galileo: Decisive Innovator* (1994) and "Copernicanism at Douai" (1974).

William R. Shea: Galileo Professor of the History of Science at the University of Padua. Author of *Galileo's Intellectual Revolution* (1972); coauthor, with Mariano Artigas, of *Galileo in Rome: The Rise and Fall of a Troublesome Genius* (2003); coeditor, with Trevor H. Levere, of *Nature, Experiment, and the Sciences: Essays on Galileo and the History of Science* (1990).

PREFACE

In 1964, the University of Notre Dame played host to an international Galileo Quatercentenary Congress celebrating the four hundredth anniversary of the birth of Galileo Galilei as well as the first centenary of the founding of the university's own College of Science. From that congress came a sizable volume, *Galileo: Man of Science* (New York: Basic Books, 1967), which included not only papers from the congress but also six additional commissioned papers from notable Galileo scholars in the United States and in Europe, as well as four classic papers in translation from the leading Galileo scholars of an earlier generation. And there was a continuation of the official Carli-Favaro-Boffito *Bibliografia Galileiana,* covering the period 1940–64 and containing more than 2,100 items.

Many people noted at the time the absence from this massive collection of any papers dealing with what, in the public mind at least, may be Galileo's principal claim to contemporary interest, his long and ultimately unsuccessful attempt to bring his Church around to an acceptance of the new and revolutionary Copernican worldview, his trial and condemnation by the Holy Office on suspicion of heresy, and his confinement under strict house arrest for his last years. The exclusion of this broad topic was deliberate: the intention was to honor Galileo's scientific achievement in the light of a great deal of new scholarship in this general area appearing at that time. Research on Galileo's relations with the Church, on the other hand, had not progressed much in scholarly terms in the decades immediately preceding, and it still evoked a degree of partisanship that made scholarly assessment more than usually difficult. But there was an implicit promise that one day the other side of the tumultuous life of the great Florentine would receive the same attention when the conditions would be right.

The present volume is the fulfillment of that promise. Once again, thanks must go to the University of Notre Dame for support of a major conference in April 2002, this time on Galileo and the Church, as well as for the secretarial and other aid it afforded in later stages of the project. The university's Reilly Center for Science, Technology, and Values and its College of Science have aided in substantial ways.

And generous grants from the Templeton Foundation and the Vatican Observatory enabled the conference to accomplish much more than it would otherwise have done.

One of the most successful features of the conference was the imaginative production of Bertolt Brecht's *Life of Galileo* by the university's Department of Film, Television, and Theater under the direction of Holger Teschke, with the aid of Wendy Arons. Each performance was followed by a discussion between members of the production, Galileo scholars, and members of the audience. Dava Sobel, author of the immensely popular *Galileo's Daughter,* and Regine Lutz (who had played the part of Virginia, Galileo's daughter, in the original Berliner Ensemble production of the play in 1958, under Brecht's own direction) contributed in indirect but very real ways to this splendid production, much enjoyed by those who attended the conference.

A special thanks goes to Annibale Fantoli, whose encyclopedic knowledge of the scholarship of the field was indispensable to the planning of the original conference and of this volume. Francesco Beretta was extremely helpful as a guide to the liveliest sectors of the abundant current European scholarship on the Galileo affair. Above all, the entire project owes much to the inspiration of George Coyne, S.J., director of the Vatican Observatory, whose steady support has meant so much at every stage.

Several people contributed in essential ways to the hard work of putting together the volume itself. Ryan MacPherson labored long and intelligently on matters of format and bibliography. Ryan Truesdell aided in the translation of a number of the essays. Cheryl Reed took untidy manuscript copy and transformed it patiently into orderly print. Elisabeth Magnus proved to be a copy editor beyond compare.

To all of these, much thanks! I hope that the volume itself will serve as adequate reward for the many who have helped to shape it, most particularly the authors whose work appears here. They have given of their best.

The Editor

THE CHURCH AND GALILEO

INTRODUCTION

Ernan McMullin

No other figure in the history of the natural sciences catches the imagination as Galileo Galilei does. Within the last decade, a new opera (Philip Glass's *Galileo Galilei*), a best-selling biography (Dava Sobel's *Galileo's Daughter*), a new play (Richard Godwin's *The Hinge of the World*), a NASA spacecraft (the Galileo orbiter, surveying Jupiter's four "Medicean" moons), and a *Nova* TV special ("Galileo's Battle for the Heavens") confirm his fascination for yet another generation. He lived at a time when great wheels were turning, when an old world was passing away and the new was still in the making. He saw farther than anyone had before him: his telescope extended the human reach out into the cosmos beyond where the unaided human senses could penetrate, to realms where the imagination could turn the old sense-bound world-system upside down. Galileo could not bring his Church to imagine with him, to share his vision of a whirling earth, so clearly at odds with the familiar cosmos of the Bible. A century before, Luther and Calvin, in their drive to reform the Church, had proclaimed the Bible as their standard; defenders of the older order had called likewise on the Bible for support. Each side launched proof-texts at the other; each side insisted on theirs being the proper interpretation of ambiguous language. It was not a time to challenge the cosmos of the Bible or of the common man.

Why another book on a topic already so often rehearsed as the Church and Galileo? The time seems right, for a number of reasons. First, the recent opening of the archives of the Holy Office to scholars has already allowed the filling up of gaps that have long hampered those who tried to reconstruct the lines of the Galileo story. Further, the contention that remains has lost some, at least, of the polemic edge that

1

marked historical writing on the Galileo affair (as it has come to be called) for too long. An obvious target for critics of the Church and their "warfare" metaphors, a rampart to be held at all costs for the Church's defenders, it was a topic where partisanship too often ruled. The stakes, after all, were high, and the drama of the Galileo story, however presented, was irresistible. But the tone of the discussion is much less strident now than it was. Careful historical research has brought to light complexities that have transmuted the simplicities of black and white into more realistic (though not much less dramatic!) shades of gray.

However, one particular development, more than any other, called into life this book and the conference from which it originated. In 1979, the new pope, John Paul II, addressing the Pontifical Academy of Sciences in one of the first major speeches of his pontificate, called for a new inquiry into the Church's treatment of Galileo, one that would, he hoped, help "to dispel the mistrust . . . between science and faith."[1] In 1981, a commission was established, consisting of four research groups representing science, law, exegesis, and culture. It was a promising start. But after eleven years, when the commission was finally wound up in 1992, its achievements fell far short of what had been expected from it. There were some achievements, to be sure, but they were meager in light of what was needed and clearly possible. The commission, it has to be said, did not live up to the mandate it had been given by the pope, who had wanted a thorough and unbiased scholarly inquiry in all four areas of interest.

More troubling still, the final report delivered to the Pontifical Academy of Sciences and the speech prepared for the pope for delivery on the same occasion were plainly inadequate from the historical standpoint. They did acknowledge fault on the part of the Church's theologians in dealing with the Copernican challenge; they did praise Galileo's contributions to science and to exegesis. But they also perpetuated some of the defensive stratagems employed by apologists of an earlier time, stratagems easily discredited on historical grounds. And they passed over in silence the trial of Galileo, the topic over which more ink had been spilt than over any other aspect of the Galileo affair. But rather than belabor the inadequacies of those disappointing documents and the missed opportunity that they represented, it seemed that a more constructive approach was called for.

Hence the conference at the University of Notre Dame in April 2002 and the present collection of essays, many of them revised versions of papers presented at the conference, others chosen from the abundance of recent Galileo scholarship in European journals, reworked by the authors and translated for inclusion here. An effort has been made to cover the three different stages into which the Galileo affair can be divided, paying special attention to those topics that have all along been the occasion of deep division among commentators. In some cases, new research has made it possible to close these divisions or at least bring them much nearer to closing. In other cases, the incompleteness of the surviving historical record, the daunting complexity of the factors involved, and the differing value preferences of the historians themselves make division still inevitable—but that is both the frustration and the fascination of history. The two concluding essays reflect from the Catholic viewpoint on some of the theological lessons to be learnt from the Galileo affair. They acknowledge with sadness the failed outcome of the recent Galileo Commission from which so much had been expected and offer the hope that the present volume may help to bring the fabled affair a little nearer to closure.

BY WAY OF A MORE specific introduction to the book's contents, it seems best simply to characterize in broad outline the different stages of the Galileo affair, leaving the details to be filled in by the essays that follow.

Prelude

As early as the 1590s, twenty years before Galileo turned his telescope to the skies, several of the Church's most prominent biblical scholars were already reacting to the Copernican innovation. Reflecting the prevailing post-Reformation literalism in biblical interpretation, they set aside the possibility that the language in which sun and earth were described in the early books of the Bible could have been accommodated to the capacities of those for whom it was originally intended, an accepted exegetic principle in earlier theology. They therefore rejected the Copernican ordering of earth and sun as contrary to Scripture, whose literal interpretation carried with it (they insisted) the sanction of divine revelation.

The Index Decree in 1616

Galileo's telescopic discoveries drew attention to the Copernican challenge as never before. The rapidly escalating debate about its theological status prompted Galileo to devise first a set of commonsense exegetical arguments as to why Scripture ought not to be invoked in matters of this nature and later a more elaborate treatise in which he drew on the authority of the Church fathers, notably St. Augustine, to make his case. Though his treatise was probably not generally circulated at the time and did not play any part, so far as we know, in the Roman discussions that ensued, it is of value in outlining for us the case that those discussions should have taken seriously.

Disturbed by the growing conflict, Pope Paul V decided that action was called for. In early 1616, the Church's top doctrinal body, the Congregation of the Holy Office, called on the advice of a body of consultors, who reported back that the

Copernican propositions were "false and absurd in philosophy" (that is, in the science of nature), a view that would in all probability have been shared by the great majority of the natural philosophers and astronomers of the day, Kepler being a notable exception. With natural philosophy apparently on their side, the consultors went on to the more properly theological (and much more far-reaching) judgment that the suspect propositions were, in the case of the sun's being at rest, formally heretical and, in the case of the earth's motion, at least erroneous in the faith.

In the decree subsequently issued by the Congregation of the Index, the term 'formally heretical' was dropped, and 'altogether contrary to Scripture' was substituted as the Church's judgment on the Copernican ordering of earth and sun. On this basis, the work of Copernicus was banned "until corrected," and a short Copernican work by the theologian P. A. Foscarini was prohibited entirely. Galileo was not mentioned in the decree, but the pope had already personally intervened to instruct Cardinal Bellarmine to order Galileo privately to abandon the condemned Copernican view. If he proved recalcitrant, he was to receive a formal injunction not to teach or even discuss the prohibited ideas. Whether this injunction was, in fact, delivered has long been debated; the document registering it is problematic in certain respects. It seems likely that it *was* delivered, but if it was, it fairly clearly should not have been. As far as one can tell from the (admittedly incomplete) evidence, the conditions laid down for its administration were not satisfied.

The Trial and Condemnation of Galileo, 1633

When Maffeo Barberini, a friend and admirer of Galileo, became Pope Urban VIII in 1623, he allowed Galileo to take up again the Copernican issue, apparently on condition that it be treated "hypothetically," by which the pope would have meant that it should not make any definitive claim to physical reality. In his *Dialogue on Two Chief World-Systems,* however, Galileo presented Copernicanism as a "hypothesis" for which one could make the best arguments for its truth that one could find. He managed, with considerable difficulty, to get an imprimatur (permission to print) for the work, and it appeared in 1632.

Almost immediately the alarm was raised in Rome, and an angry pope, feeling betrayed by his friend, ordered that Galileo be brought to trial. There was, first of all, the problem that Galileo had, after all, received permission to print. But the prosecutor claimed that he had obtained the imprimatur fraudulently by not letting the censors know that he had secretly been given a formal injunction "not to hold, defend, or teach" the Copernican view in any way whatever. Galileo responded by producing a certificate later given him by Cardinal Bellarmine that seemed to imply that no such injunction had, in fact, been given.

In response to the prosecutor's questions (and perhaps to an offer that would today be called a plea bargain), he admitted that he had, in fact, presented arguments in favor of the prohibited doctrine and expressed his contrition, even offering to add a new section to the *Dialogue* refuting those earlier arguments. There is evidence that at this point the prosecutor hoped for a "lenient" solution of the affair, a hope that would be dashed. When the prosecution concluded, an evidence summary was presented to the cardinal-judges of the Holy Office; from surviving documents, it can be shown that the summary is seriously deficient. Galileo was found to be "vehemently suspect of heresy," namely of "having held and believed a doctrine which is false and contrary to Holy Scripture" according to the decree of 1616. He was then required to abjure the "Copernican opinion" publicly. The sentence and abjuration, with their emphasis on heresy, went significantly beyond the decree of 1616. Urban VIII was personally involved in the court's decision and took the unusual step of having the texts of the sentence and abjuration proclaimed across Catholic Europe. Galileo's sentence was commuted to house arrest, which was maintained until his death in 1642.

Aftermath

The Galileo affair, however, did not end there; "Galileo and the Church" might be over, but "The Church and Galileo" was only just beginning. In the immediate aftermath, there was some disagreement as to what the exact theological status of the prohibited Copernican view had become in light of the trial sentence and abjuration. Had it been effectively declared to be heretical or not? The uncertainty was exploited by, among others, Descartes and Gassendi in the years that followed. The leading Jesuit astronomers, when proclaiming the merits of the Copernican alternative, as many did, fell back on the notion of hypothesis whose ambiguity had earlier betrayed Galileo. Or they opted for the Tychonic geocentric alternative, which retained the observational merits of the Copernican system without incurring the theological censure imposed on Copernicanism.

As the century wore on and a new century dawned, the case for the heliocentric option strengthened steadily. Though lip service was paid to the ban, Catholic astronomers tended to find their way around it more and more. By the accession of Pope Benedict XIV in 1740, the discrepancy between the decree and the by then almost universal affirmation of the heliocentric system among astronomers was beginning to be viewed as a real embarrassment for the Church.

A realist in such matters, the new pope clearly favored a change. In 1741, Galileo's *Dialogo* received an imprimatur as part of a collected edition of Galileo's works. But there was a catch. It had to be prefaced with a disclaimer (like the one Osiander had inserted as preface of Copernicus's *De revolutionibus*): the work was to be regarded as no more than a "mathematical hypothesis." It also had to contain the texts of the sentence and abjuration and had to substitute the "earth's apparent motion" for "the earth's motion" in the marginal postils. It was thus far from a revocation of the 1616 ban on the *Dialogue;* indeed, it effectively changed nothing with regard to the theological status of Copernicanism.

Benedict evidently kept the discussion going, but the most that the Holy Office would concede, apparently, was to omit the general prohibition of Copernican works from the 1758 edition of the *Index*—while retaining the works of Copernicus and Galileo on the prohibited list. This inconsistency reflects the fact that what had begun to weigh on the Church's decision at this point was no longer the theological arguments that had prompted the original ban (these had been effectively undermined by astronomers' rejection on scientific grounds of the geocentrism on which the ban had indirectly depended) but the fact of the ban itself and even more the later condemnation of Galileo on suspicion of heresy. To reverse these publicly would be to admit errors on the part of those responsible, the Holy Office and the popes who had sanctioned the decisions. And this the Holy Office was not prepared to do.

This ambiguous situation persisted until a dramatic incident forced the Roman authorities to confront the awkward issue once again. In 1820, a priest-professor in Rome, Giuseppe Settele, was refused permission by the Dominican censor, Filippo Anfossi, to publish an explicitly Copernican textbook on the grounds that the decree of 1616 and the sentence of 1633 had never been revoked. Nor did Anfossi, for that matter, believe that so definitive a doctrinal decision *could* be changed. It took the intervention of the pope, Pius VII, to override Anfossi's logic and to prod the Holy Office to decide (though not to publish their decision) that Copernicanism was no longer theologically objectionable. The decision could be changed, it was argued, because now the heliocentric alternative had been, in effect, demonstrated, so the situation was no longer what it had been for the theologians of 1616 and 1633. That those earlier decisions had implicitly excluded the possibility of such a turn of events could be quietly ignored. The works of Copernicus and Galileo were finally dropped, without comment, from the next edition of the *Index of Prohibited Books,* which did not appear until 1835. After two centuries, the *Dialogue* was at last free from censure.

But the Galileo affair was still not really over. The Church authorities evidently believed that they had done all that was called for and without the embarrassment of a public declaration of error. But unfinished business clearly remained. The bit-by-bit publication of the Galileo file from the Holy Office archives over the later decades of the century (enforced by the seizure of those archives by Napoleon in 1810) ensured that the issue would not go away. The new materials set off a duel of opposing interpretations of the original Galileo affair, engaging critics and defenders of the Church in partisan battle. It was a time when the authority of the Church and in particular the newly defined papal infallibility were the center of dispute, and the Galileo affair was seized on by critics as a test case of both.

In 1893, Pope Leo XIII published an encyclical on the interpretation of Scripture, *Providentissimus Deus,* which could not very well avoid the issues that had engaged Galileo and the theologians all those years before. The encyclical acknowledged the validity of most (not all) the exegetic principles that Galileo had called on, even citing some of the very passages in Augustine on which Galileo had relied. But, significantly, Galileo himself and the Galileo affair were nowhere mentioned. The matter was, evidently, still too sensitive.

In 1941, the Pontifical Academy of Sciences commissioned a new biography of Galileo from Pio Paschini, a priest-professor of Church history in Rome. The occasion was the impending third centenary of Galileo's death. It was to be a work both "scientific and historical." But when Paschini submitted the finished work to the academy three years later, it was rejected by the academy and by the Holy Office as unduly favorable to Galileo. Twenty years later, under a new Pope, Paul VI, and with the impetus of the Second Vatican Council, the manuscript was brought forth again for possible publication. Though the author meanwhile had died, it was decided that the manuscript could be revised to remove what had originally been regarded as its blemishes. This was done by the Jesuit historian Edmond Lamalle, and the book was published. The editor's note acknowledging the substantial revisions that had been carried out was omitted from the separate edition of the work published by the academy. In preparing the council's document "The Church in the Modern World" (*Gaudium et Spes*), a proposal to acknowledge the Church's error with regard to Galileo was made but was rejected finally as "inopportune." It would "ask the Church to say: I have been wrong."[2] The final version of the council document limited itself to a footnote reference to the (reworked) Paschini book.

Against this background, Pope John Paul's call in 1979 "to go beyond the stand taken by the council" and to initiate a major collaborative study of the Galileo affair "in loyal recognition of wrongs from whatever side they come" sounded a welcome new note. There has admittedly been disappointment, grave disappointment indeed, in the interim. But it is in the spirit of that original invitation that this collection of essays was first conceived and is now presented.

Notes

1. John Paul II, "Faith, Science, and the Search for Truth," Einstein Centenary, *Origins* 9 (1979): 389–92.

2. From the summary of the proceedings of the Commission charged with the preparation of the Council document, Monsignor Pietro Parente, co-president of the Commission, speaking. See Michele Maccarrone, "Mons. Paschini e la Roma ecclesiastica," in *Atti del convegno di studio su Pio Paschini* (Udine: Tipographia Vaticana, 1980), 49–93, at 91; Annibale Fantoli, *Galileo: For Copernicanism and for the Church* (Vatican City: Vatican Observatory Publications, 1996), 503–6.

PART ONE

THE STORM GATHERS

ONE

THE HELIOCENTRIC "HERESY"

From Suspicion to Condemnation

Michel-Pierre Lerner

Before 1543: Rheticus

In 1540, a doctor, Achilles Pirmin Gasser, of Lindau, sent to his colleague Georg Vögeli a certain *Narratio prima,* the work of a "young mathematician," recently published in Prussia. With it he sent a letter that began as follows:

> I am sending you, most excellent friend, as if you were a Heraclean touchstone, this little treatise; not only is it new and unknown to our contemporaries, but you will find it, if I am not utterly mistaken, admirable and absolutely riveting because it goes against common sense. My fellow countryman and best friend, Georg Joachim Rheticus, a Master of Arts and one-time professor of mathematics at Wittenberg, sent it to me a few days ago from Gdansk [Danzig] with a letter all about these matters. Although it does not follow the methods of teaching in use up till now and can be held to contradict, on more than one point, the theories usually defended in the schools and can be judged heretical (as the monks might say), this book seems truly to propose the restoration or even the rebirth of an astronomy that besides being new is completely in conformity with the truth.[1]

Gasser's text, placed by Rheticus as a preface to the second edition of the *Narratio prima* published in Basel in 1541, and reprinted in 1566 and 1596, contains, if we are not mistaken, the first printed mention of the term 'heretical' associated with the new astronomy that Copernicus himself, after much hesitation, expounded in a detailed manner two years later in his *De revolutionibus orbium coelestium.*

The contents of the letter (lost) sent by Rheticus, with his book, to his friend Gasser are not known to us. However, it would not be going too far to suggest that the young and enthusiastic disciple of Copernicus had brought up in it the worrying question of the way in which the philosophers and theologians were likely to take the propositions on which heliocentric astronomy was based, propositions that were quite unheard of in the schools. One finds proof of this concern in the letter that Rheticus sent, with several copies of the *Narratio prima,* to Andreas Osiander (1498–1552), a Lutheran theologian, well versed in mathematics, who occupied an important position in Nuremberg—the city where the *De revolutionibus* was to be printed. In the same letter Rheticus told Osiander of Copernicus's reluctance to publish.[2] Copernicus himself wrote on July 1, 1540, letting Osiander know of his perplexity. The following year the latter suggested to him, as well as to Rheticus, the following strategy: since he feared the adverse reaction of the philosophers and the theologians, he might be able to disarm their opposition beforehand by presenting his heliocentric hypothesis as a simple method of calculation, without claiming that "this was how it actually worked."[3]

Copernicus did not follow this prudent advice. He was probably encouraged by Rheticus and Tiedeman Giese to refuse such an expedient. Tiedeman Giese (1480–1550) had been a longtime colleague of his at the Warmia (Ermland) chapter, becoming bishop of Chelmno (Kulm) from 1537. Giese, convinced of the truth of heliocentrism and one of the most ardent among those who urged the publication of the *De revolutionibus,* had already written before 1536 *Hyperaspisticon* (Supershield). In this work, now lost, he claimed that Scripture was compatible with the new astronomy.[4] As for Rheticus, he too composed, probably before September 1541, a little work in which he showed "very clearly . . . that the motion of the earth does not contradict the Holy Scriptures."[5] In this short work, considered lost until recently brought to light by Reyer Hooykaas, Rheticus assumed that "since . . . the motion of the earth may be considered as demonstrated truth, we need not fear that more balanced and learned judges will ascribe the marks of impiety to us."[6] Just as Copernicus had done, he rejected the categories of Aristotelian physics within which the glossers of Scripture, for whom the motion of the earth was "monstrous," wished to constrain the power of the God of the Creation:

> Furthermore, there will not be lacking those who will bellow that it is monstrous to attribute movements to the earth, and who will take occasion to draw on and display their wisdom taken from the philosophers of nature. They are ridiculous, as if God's power could be measured by our capacities or our intellect.

Are we to think that anything is impossible for God, who, by his Word, made the whole natural order out of nothing? Are we to tie God to the disputations of the Peripatetics?[7]

It is clear, then, that for Rheticus Scripture could not provide any confirmation of the geocentric thesis. This did not, however, prevent him from "accommodating" a certain number of passages in the Bible with the main thesis of the *De revolutionibus* by declaring Copernicus's attempt to be orthodox: "From all this it is plain that it cannot be proved from the sacred writings that the earth is immobile. Therefore, he who assumes its mobility in order to provide a reliable calculation of times and motions is not acting against Holy Scripture."[8]

What is at first sight paradoxical, if not contradictory, in Rheticus's approach should be emphasized here. For, taking his cue from Saint Augustine, he declares that, in the passages where Scripture speaks of the earth, the heavens, the stars, and the like, it "borrows a style of discourse and idiom of speech or a method of teaching from popular usage." He can thus deny to theologians of Aristotelian persuasion the right to draw from the texts of Scripture a confirmation of the geocentrism that Aristotle and Ptolemy defended.[9] This does not prevent him further on, however, from seeking to impose a heliocentric interpretation on certain passages of Scripture; here he sometimes goes well beyond the limits of the plausible.[10] Appealing in this way to Scripture ran contrary, of course, to the principle of accommodation that he had himself first called upon in his defense against the critics of Copernicanism. Rheticus does recognize, however, that the passages of Scripture quoted by him as implicitly heliocentric contain only *"obscure allusions"* to the motion of the earth.[11]

Copernicus and Osiander: Contrasting Positions

Apparently persuaded that he was not imperiling the salvation of his soul by placing the sun in the center of the world, Copernicus, as already noted, adopted a different strategy from that followed by Osiander, different also from that proposed by his friends Giese and Rheticus. He aimed high by dedicating his work directly to the head of the Church and, to use Kepler's language, by deciding "with the steadfastness of his Stoic soul" not to hide anything of his thoughts, even if the doctrine that he propounded were to suffer.[12] Convinced that "the learned and ingenious mathematicians"—the only readers who counted in his eyes—would not fail to adopt his hypothesis once they had thoroughly examined his demonstrations, Copernicus addressed himself to the pope, both by reason of the latter's "love of all learning and even of mathematics"[13] and, perhaps above all, because, as he wrote, "by your influence and judgment you can restrain the stings of false accusers, although it is proverbial that there is no remedy against the sting of the sycophant."[14] Copernicus further added: "There may be prattlers who, though wholly ignorant of mathematics, nevertheless arrogate to themselves the right to make judgments about it because of some passage in Scripture wrongly twisted to their purpose, and will dare to criticize and censure this undertaking of mine. I waste no time on them, and indeed I despise their judgment as thoughtless."[15]

This warning was addressed to the theologians. It was especially for them that Copernicus mentioned the error of Lactantius in denying the existence of the Antipodes.[16] The warning was directed also to the reader who sought to invoke Scripture to mock, or even to condemn, mathematical works destined, Copernicus insisted, for mathematicians alone: this was the famous "Mathematics is written for mathematicians" (mathemata mathematicis scribuntur). These remarks would hardly have been well received by the supreme theologian occupying the throne of Saint Peter! In a warning, "*Ad lectorem:* To the Reader on the Hypotheses of This Work," placed at the beginning of the *De revolutionibus* before Copernicus's letter to the pope, Osiander, in an unsigned text written on his own initiative and without Copernicus's knowledge, presented the heliocentric hypothesis as a convenient fiction without any real cosmological relevance.[17] Did Osiander's text have, in Rome, the effect of an antidote to the assertive wording of Copernicus's dedication to the pope? The question remains open.

The First Catholic Attack on Heliocentrism: Tolosani

In any case and almost certainly on account of Copernicus's warning against the ill-intentioned misuse of Scripture—a warning that inevitably drew attention to his heliocentric hypothesis—but also on account of his work having been printed on the presses of a Lutheran printer who had published the works of heretical authors, among whom it is enough to mention those of Philipp Melanchthon,[18] the *De revolutionibus* was handed for examination to Bartolomeo Spina, the Master of the Sacred Palace, whose authority also covered printed works liable to be banned.[19] Bartolomeo Spina's conclusions are known to us. In his view Copernicus's work should be condemned. But because of his death in 1547, he was unable to carry out his intention. The theologian Giovanmaria Tolosani,[20] a Dominican co-worker and friend of Spina's, from whom we know this important fact concerning the first reception of the *De revolutionibus* by the Master of the Sacred Palace at the time, took it upon himself to examine Copernicus's work after Spina's death and to compose a detailed report justifying its being banned.

Two works of Tolosani are known to us: a *Compendio di sphera et machina del mondo nuovamente composto,* which contains a chapter on the correction of the calendar,[21] and an *Emendationes temporum in duas partes divise* (Venice 1537), published under the pseudonym of Iohannes Lucidus Samotheus and reissued in 1546 under the title *Opusculum de emendationibus temporum ab orbe condito ad hanc usque nostram aetatem*.[22] These texts, the only ones to appear during Tolosani's lifetime, show his interest in the problems of the calendar and more generally in astronomy. But Tolosani had also composed several important little works that remained unpublished because of his death at the beginning of 1549. The National Library in Florence today holds a collection of these works. The first group is entitled "On the Absolutely Pure Truth of Divine Scripture against Human Errors: An Excellent Work Containing Inquiries into the Old and New Testaments Together with Their Resolutions, by Brother Giovanni Maria Tolosani, Florentine of Colle Vallis Else, also Professor of the Reformed Dominican Order, Inquisitor of the Catholic Truth, and Evangelical and Apostolic Preacher of God's Word, for the Common Usage of the Faithful."[23] It is preceded by a letter of approval from Bartolomeo Spina, Master of the Sacred Palace, dated August 6, 1546, and by a dedication to Pope Paul III.[24] The second part of the manuscript includes more especially an *Opusculum quartum* entitled "On the Highest Immobile Heaven and the Lowest Stable Earth, and All Other Movable Heavens and Intermediate Elements" (De coelo supremo immobili et terra infima stabili, ceterisque coelis et elementis intermediis mobilibus), in which Tolosani vigorously denounced the danger to faith posed, in his view, by Copernicus's doctrine.[25]

The essence of Tolosani's thesis was contained in the first two chapters of his text. In the first, Tolosani referred to the constitution of the world as it appeared in the Bible's references to the subject of cosmology. In his exposition he also incorporated knowledge taken from the astronomical science of his day. Especially to be noted is the importance he accorded to the highest immobile heaven, or the Empyrean—to which there was no reference in Scripture—as the crowning piece of the Creation as this had been understood by Christian theologians since the early Middle Ages.[26] The pagan Aristotle, for evident reasons, was unaware of the existence of such a heaven, but on the other hand he correctly placed the earth in the center of the world. In this respect (Tolosani went on) Aristotle followed the majority of the philosophers of the ancient world, who like him were guided by the light of nature alone. Exceptions were the Pythagoreans, who, misled by a false conception, had set the earth in motion round a central fire. But they had been thoroughly refuted by Aristotle in his *De caelo* and St. Thomas Aquinas's commentary on it, texts to which Tolosani referred the reader: "For everything that is written there coincides with what is said in Holy Scripture."[27]

Only the first book of the *De revolutionibus* (the work contains six in all) was analyzed by Tolosani in chapter 2 of the *Opusculum quartum*. Copernicus was presented as a reviver of the absurd opinion of the Pythagoreans, fallen into oblivion after Aristotle's refutation of it. On this point it should be noted that Tolosani carefully distinguished Copernicus's "realist" approach from that of the writer of the warning *Ad lectorem.*[28] To explain how Copernicus could have defended such a doctrine, Tolosani, in his criticism, pointed to an inhibiting defect in Copernicus's method. Though incontestably competent in mathematics and in astronomy, Copernicus was gravely lacking in the knowledge of the "higher" sciences such as physics, dialectics, and the study of the Scriptures. His ignorance of dialectics, in particular, deprived him of an essential capacity: that of distinguishing the false from the true. But anyone who did not follow the first principles of the sciences put himself outside the field of rational discourse; one could therefore rightly deny him the capacity to pass sound judgment.

Tolosani's argument reduced, then, to this. Since the Pythagorean doctrine of Copernicus had already been refuted in a demonstrative manner by the philosopher Aristotle, by the astronomer Ptolemy, and finally by Saint Thomas, a most erudite logician, philosopher, and theologian, all the arguments that Copernicus could bring forward were already undermined in advance and did nothing to excuse the untenable character of the paradox he had dared to defend. How could an intelligent reader accept the violence to which Copernicus had subjected the divine Creation by placing the sun in the middle of the universe, where in fact the immobile earth had been placed?[29] No one could arrogate to himself the right to change, by his imagination alone or by any other invention, any single thing in the system of the universe created by God. And when Copernicus claimed that the heaven of the fixed stars, which he called the "first and highest of all the spheres," was immobile, he went not against reason but against the theologians. For these, as already mentioned, had invented the so-called *coelum empyreum,* an immobile new heaven containing the outermost movable sphere (*primum mobile*). Lacking any astronomical role, this heaven had a double function: a supercelestial realm reserved to the elect, it was also deemed to contain, in the form of an immobile place, all the moving celestial spheres.[30] A further confirmation that the Copernican doctrine was obviously contrary to reason and to Holy Scripture was the warning "To the reader" at the beginning of the *De revolutionibus.* Its author was the first to reject Copernicus's doctrine, while at the same time bringing it before the public.[31]

The conclusion of chapter 2 of the *Opusculum quartum* fully brought out the seriousness of the challenge offered by Copernicus's book to the philosophers as well as to the theologians of the day. According to Tolosani, Copernicus's doctrine "could easily provoke discord between Catholic commentators on Holy Scripture and those who have resolutely decided to follow this false opinion. It is in order to avoid such scandal that we have written this short work."[32]

Tolosani's denunciation had no immediate consequences. The first *Index of Prohibited Books,* published at Rome in 1557, made no mention of Copernicus or of his work. It was, however, implicitly banned for a few years (between 1557 and 1564) together with all other books published by Johann Petreius, a printer of heretical works (a point that is usually overlooked). By contrast, all of Rheticus's works (including, therefore, the openly Copernican *Narratio prima*) were banned in the different editions of the *Index librorum prohibitorum* published at Rome between 1559 and 1593 on the grounds that their author was "a disciple of Oswald [Myconius] and a schoolfellow of Conrad Gesner."[33] As a direct consequence of this general prohibition of Rheticus's works, a suppression was ordered in 1598 of his *Narratio prima,* according to a recently discovered document from the Archepiscopal Curia of Naples. The edition concerned is the one published in 1566, after the *De revolutionibus.*[34]

In the six decades following the appearance of Tolosani's work, no new examination of Copernicus's case seems to have been undertaken in Rome, so far as can be judged from the documents available to us today. How can this apparent silence on the part of the Roman authorities be explained? It is no doubt related to the fact that the *De revolutionibus* had only a limited circulation in Italy, as well as to the undoubted effect sought, and in part obtained, by Osiander's *Ad lectorem,* though a few rare alert readers like Tolosani (and Giordano Bruno)[35] were not taken in by it. In any event, between 1570 and 1610 Catholic theologians seem to have shown a greater propensity than before to emphasize the contradiction between the idea of the earth's motion, considered, as a rule, in regard to rotation on its axis only, and the literal teachings of Scripture. In keeping with this, astronomers and authors of texts in natural philosophy, whether religious or secular, seem also to have been prompter than their predecessors to emphasize the possible agreement or the disagreement between the assertion of the earth's motion and certain passages of the Bible. I shall limit myself here to examining the reaction of some of the theologians who occupied positions of first importance in the discipline of exegesis at the turn of the sixteenth century.

An Exception

The Platonic philosopher Francesco Patrizi (1529–97) had to face numerous censures during the last years of his life. When his hypothesis of the earth's rotation on its axis and its location at the center of the universe, which he had formulated in his *Nova de universis philosophia* (Ferrara, 1591), was denounced as contrary to Scripture, Patrizi was called to explain himself before the Holy Office. In the defense that he prepared to answer the censures of the Master of the Sacred Palace, Patrizi stated that he did not make the earth move *de medio suo et naturali loco* (implicitly, move around the sun) and that he thus considered it possible to save all the passages in Scripture that were brought up against him. But he prudently added that he would suppress the passage if he were ordered to (Delebo tamen si iubetis).[36]

Particularly interesting in the context of these censures is the mention of Copernicus (whom Patrizi had quoted in his *Pancosmia*)[37] by another censor, the theologian Benedetto Giustiniani (ca. 1550–1622), and in terms of quite surprising benevolence.[38]

This Jesuit priest, who had been chosen in 1593 by the general of the Society of Jesus to write for the Congregation of the Index an expert opinion on Patrizi's *Nova de universis philosophia,* does not seem to have had the same principled aversion that the Aristotelians had for the earth's motion. He was aware that the Copernican hypothesis had been proposed by some interpreters to explain the famous passage in Job 9:5–7, "Qui movet terram de loco suo. . . ." Having definitely here in mind Diego de Zúñiga's commentary on Job (Toledo, 1584),[39] Giustiniani held that the Copernican hypothesis could, without difficulty, be accorded (*accomodari*) with the passage in Ecclesiastes 1:4 ("Terra autem in aeternum stat"). For this enlightened censor of Patrizi, the question of the motion of the earth was a matter for debate between philosophers; the passage quoted from Ecclesiastes, which offered no evidence against such motion, could not be used against them.[40] Such a concordism, rare in favor of what had regularly been held to be a "paradox" springing out of Copernicus's brain, appears the very opposite of labeling Patrizi's views as heresy. Although it is not clear that Giustiniani had fully grasped the nature of the earth's movements in Copernicus's thought, this reaction on Giustiniani's part deserves to be emphasized in that it went against the attitude generally adopted by his fellow theologians at the time (and later by himself).[41]

Christoph Clavius and His Followers

The tendency of Catholic theologians to reject heliocentrism was, in significant measure, determined by the position taken, from 1570 onwards, by the Jesuit Christoph Clavius (1537–1612) in his *Commentary on the Sphere of Sacrobosco,* a manual that retained its authority over some fifty years, going through numerous editions.[42] After briefly recalling the essentials of the Copernican hypothesis, Clavius wrote in the first edition of his commentary:

> We conclude, then, in accordance with the common doctrine of the astronomers and the philosophers, that the earth lacks any local motion, either rectilinear or circular, and that the heavens themselves revolve continually round it. . . . Holy Scripture is also in favor of this doctrine, stating in a great number of places that the earth is stationary. It also bears witness to the fact that the sun and the other heavenly bodies are in motion. [There follow, by way of confirmation, certain passages of Scripture, such as Psalm 103, Ecclesiastes 1, and Psalm 18.][43]

Clavius, as the Jesuits' uncontested authority on the subject of astronomy, having thus opened the way, it remained only to follow his example, and this is what his fellow Jesuits did, one after another, using him to refute Copernicus and Diego de Zúñiga. The first of these was Juan de Pineda (1558–1637) in his *Commentaria in Job libri tredecim* (Cologne, 1600),[44] followed by Jean Lorin (1559–1634) in his *In Acta Apostolorum commentarii* (Lyons, 1605). Lorin had long held office as examiner of books and as theologian for the master general of the Company of Jesus.[45]

But the Jesuit who went furthest in his condemnation of Copernicus was Nicolas Serarius (1555–1609). In a text published in 1609–10, Serarius wrote that Copernicus's two basic theses—that the sun was in the center of the world and that the earth lay together with the moon's orbit in the fifth (*sic*) heaven—were refuted by everyone (ab omnibus), adding:

> Although in order to escape reprobation Copernicus dedicated his revolutions to the pope, nevertheless, in so far as his hypotheses are supposed to be held to be true, I do not see how they can avoid being tainted with heresy [non video quemadmodum ab haeresi esse possent immunes]. For Scripture always keeps the earth *at rest* and gives *motion* to the sun and to the moon, so that when these heavenly bodies stand still one can see that it is on account of a great miracle.[46]

These condemnations of Copernicanism on scriptural grounds were probably very significant in forming Catholic theological opinion during this period, especially because of the unambiguous attitude they expressed and continued to express. But they did not commit the Holy See on the subject of heliocentrism. Rome's silence concerning Copernicus, which some in the past have tended to interpret as a sign of benevolence, in contrast to the supposedly more hostile attitude of the Protestant theologians, together with the relative lack of polemical texts denouncing heliocentrism, could give an author like Justus Lipsius (1547–1606) the impression, in 1604, that the Copernican "heresy" was dead and buried with its author.[47] The same might be said of Kepler, who also had to take account of the hostility of the Lutheran theologians toward heliocentrism.[48] In 1609, he wrote in praise of the Roman Church that it had shown proof of wisdom in not condemning Copernicus: "All the popes since 1542 . . . have interpreted Scripture in such a way that none of them have so far accused Copernicus—even apart from the fact that Copernicus dedicated his work *De revolutionibus* to Paul III—of *error* or of *heresy*."[49]

After 1610: Open Attack on Heliocentrism and Galileo's Reply

The publication in 1610 of the *Sidereus nuncius,* in which Galileo made public his support for the Copernican system, brought about a rapid change leading to an official condemnation of Copernicanism by the Church of Rome. Paolo Gualdo, one of Galileo's correspondents, had foreseen that the whole troop of astronomers, philosophers, and theologians would hasten to reject the Copernican hypothesis as contrary to the universally held belief in a geocentric universe.[50] This prophecy essentially came true; however, two theologians, to whom we shall return, proved exceptions to the rule.

At the end of 1610, the philosopher, mathematician, and poet Lodovico delle Colombe (1565–post 1615) set the tone for the way in which the Copernicans were to be received.[51] Showing no hesitation in venturing out of the field of his own competence, in his *Trattato contro il moto della terra* he wrote, taking as his authority the Dominican theologian Melchior Cano, that any proposition contrary to the general sentiment of the Church fathers was rash and that it was a universal rule for theologians that a great error in philosophy was also suspect in theology. The theory of the Pythagoreans, which Copernicus had followed, deserved to be so qualified, as Pineda had declared in his *Commentary on Job*.[52]

Delle Colombe was the first writer to attack Galileo in the name of Scripture, a terrain where Galileo would place himself with a degree of audacity. Although not himself a theologian—any more than delle Colombe was—Galileo proposed, as Rheticus had done some seventy years earlier, an exegesis intended to go beyond the simple defense of the assertion that the Copernican claims and Scripture were not in contradiction with one another.

In his letter to Castelli of December 21, 1613, and again in his longer letter to Christina of Lorraine, Galileo declared that the sacred writers had no "thought of teaching the people the order and motion of the celestial bodies." On this basis, he went on to dispute those of his adversaries who claimed to find Scripture's bare words in conformity with the (erroneous) system of Ptolemy. Then, in an apparent contradiction, he developed the idea that a physical truth, after having been demonstrated, could give a clue to the correct interpretation of Scripture, and he illustrated this thesis with a clever "explanation" of the miracle of Joshua, which would show the literal wording of the Bible to be in conformity with heliocentrism.[53]

Galileo made this point particularly clear in his letter to Monsignor Pietro Dini of March 23, 1615. Having learned from Dini two weeks before that Cardinal Robert Bellarmine considered the passage of Psalm 18:5–6 to be entirely contrary to the motion of the earth advocated by the Copernicans,[54] he rejected such a conclusion. Answering Bellarmine indirectly, he developed a long commentary on the same passage in Psalm 18 intended to confirm philosophically the truth of heliocentrism: "I would venture to say that between some passages of the Sacred Writings and this structure of the world, many agreements are to be found which are not recognized, it seems to me, by the common philosophy." In this way he was implicitly rejecting the common theological exegesis of this passage of Psalm 18 (and other biblical texts) in terms of classical geocentrism. On the contrary, according to him, Scripture would here support, with high probability, the conclusion that the sun, in which the spirit and the light of the entire world came together and were united, and from which they diffused again with more strength, was therefore "located in the center of the Universe."[55]

This unconventional interpretation on the part of one who did not hesitate to make incursions onto a terrain that theologians considered their preserve[56] stemmed from his conviction that the truth of God's two books—the Bible and the world—was one and the same. The intention of the Holy Spirit was assuredly not to teach men physics or astronomy but to lead them to salvation ("to teach us how one goes to heaven and not how heaven goes").[57] Nevertheless, the real structure of the *machina mundi* discovered by Copernicus "in the garb of a philosopher," and confirmed according to Galileo on the basis of "sensory experiences" and "necessary demonstrations," could not, in principle, be contrary to the Bible as long as the true meaning of the latter had been grasped (tutta volta che si sia penetrato il suo vero sentimento). The revealed truths in Scripture necessarily agreed with natural demonstrated truths,[58] one of these truths being the location of the sun in the center of the world. And this cosmological reality was already known by all the sacred authors, as Galileo wrote in an unpublished comment on Bellarmine's response to Foscarini: "We believe that Solomon, and also Moses and all the sacred authors, knew the constitution of the world perfectly" (obviously heliocentric!).[59] This being so, we think that Galileo's efforts to interpret some key passages of the Scripture, and even a church hymn, in terms of heliocentrism, were not for him a mere rhetorical or diplomatic expedient.

Campanella and Foscarini: Two Independent Minds

Galileo was a philosopher and mathematician. Among the theologians, most of them denouncing heliocentrism as contrary to God's revelation, two emerged who were ready to admit a new reading of scriptural passages that could bring the Bible into accord with the Pythagorean conception of the world revived by Copernicus. They were the Dominican Tommaso Campanella (1568–1639) and the Carmelite friar Paolo Antonio Foscarini (ca. 1562–1616).

As early as January 1611, Campanella had foreseen that the reaction of religious figures to the cosmological implications that Galileo thought could be drawn from his recent discoveries was likely to be hostile. This led this future defender of the "Messenger of the Stars" to write:

> Let us rejoice if the theologians protest; the Fathers of Theology [i.e., of the Church] will defend you with their prophecies: Chrysostom and his master, Theodore, the Bishop of Tarsus, and Procopius of Gaza, who taught that the heaven is motionless. . . . Augustine taught that this opinion had been proven

according to the rules of the astronomers of his day and said we should not challenge it by relying on Holy Scripture and so become the laughingstock of the
astronomers. This is a principle he himself ought to have followed when he denied the antipodes. You have on your side Origen, who taught that the earth and
all the heavenly bodies are alive and who praised and proved the teachings of
the Pythagoreans with the aid of the Scriptures.[60]

At the beginning of 1616, in a text composed at the request of Cardinal Bonifacio Caetani (1568–1617), a member of the Congregation of the Index, Campanella
defended Galileo at length, who at this time had already been denounced to the Tribunal of the Inquisition. This text was drawn up in the form of a dispute allowing
weight to both sides (ad utramque partem), "where it is asked whether the philosophical method advocated by Galileo is in accordance with the Holy Scriptures or
goes against them" (ubi disquiritur, utrum ratio philosophandi, quam Galileus cele-
brat, faveat sacris scripturis, an adversetur). In this work, published in 1622 at Frankfurt under the title *Apologia pro Galileo,* Campanella tried to persuade his fellow theologians to refrain from condemning heliocentrism as contrary to the faith. Following
the format of a scholastic exercise, he upheld the thesis that it was possible to adopt
the Copernican doctrine without falling into heresy and that in any case this danger
was less than if one held to Aristotelian doctrine.[61]

To argue that Galileo's doctrine, which was not really new but of respectable antiquity, going back to the Pythagorean teachings, could not be—if demonstrated—
contrary to Scripture, Campanella referred to the celebrated formula of the Council
of Lateran V. Relying on it, the theologians could not help but approve of that doctrine, since "one truth does not contradict another truth."[62] This formula had the force
of dogma as much for theologians attached to the traditional geocentric conception,
like Pereira, Bellarmine, and Inchofer, as for the defenders of the new doctrine, like
Galileo and Foscarini. In the language of Campanella, this principle became "The
book of wisdom by God the creator does not contradict the book of wisdom by God
the revealer."[63]

Second, Campanella postulated that the divine wisdom spread through Creation was interpreted correctly in Galileo's natural philosophy—of which Campanella spoke prudently, however, in the conclusion of his text in terms of probability,
not of physical truth.[64] Relying on this presupposition, he applied the principle, expressed in book 3 of his *Theologia,* that determined the development and the conclusion of the dispute: "[T]he Sacred Scripture is always certain and trustworthy,
whatever hypothesis is sustained" (ab omnibus opinionibus S. Scriptura ostenditur
tuta et verax semper).[65] In other words, he claimed that Scripture could be saved in
terms of different physical interpretations. These were merely opinions, some more
or less close to the real truth contained in the Bible. And just as in the *Philosophia sen-
sibus demonstrata* (Naples, 1591), where he had upheld the possibility of bringing Tele-

sio's philosophy into accord with Scripture, so in the *Apologia* he upheld a similar possibility concerning the doctrine of the Pythagoreans together with that of Galileo.[66]

In short, Campanella (a) denounced the idea, held in his time by the great majority of Catholic theologians, that there existed a unity of doctrine among the
Church fathers and the scholastics concerning the question of the structure of the
universe (the respective positions of the earth and the sun, the shape and motion of
the heavens); (b) defended the value of the literal wording of the text over mystical
and allegorical interpretations leading to false philosophical doctrines concerning the substance of the heavens (Galileo's discoveries had in this context enabled
a clear historical and literal reading of the text of Genesis); and (c) refused on the
other hand the principle of an exclusively literal interpretation of the biblical passages that went against heliocentrism on the triple grounds that this system had in
its favor a philosophical tradition stemming from antiquity, that it gave a satisfactory explanation of celestial phenomena, and that it in no way concerned the Christian faith directly.[67]

Campanella composed his disputation in the theological manner (*more theologico*)
at the request of a cardinal who sought enlightenment on a complex subject on which
he was to make a judgment. At the same time he took the opportunity of addressing
in his text another Church dignitary whom he knew would have a determining role
in the affair: Cardinal Bellarmine. Twice in the *Apologia,* he alerted Bellarmine to the
"political" dangers to which a condemnation of Galileo's *modus philosophandi* would,
according to him, expose the Roman Church:

> I think that this philosophical method should not be condemned. One reason for
> this is that it will be embraced even more enthusiastically by the heretics and
> they will laugh at us. For we know how greatly those who live north of the Alps
> complained about some of the decrees adopted at the Council of Trent. What
> will they do when they hear that we have attacked the physicists and the as-
> tronomers? Will they not immediately proclaim that we have done violence to
> both nature and the Scriptures? Cardinal Bellarmine is well aware of this.[68]

Campanella repeated this warning in his conclusion: "In my judgment . . . ,
it is not possible to prohibit Galileo's investigations and to suppress his writings
without causing either damaging mockery of the Scriptures, or a strong suspicion
that we reject the Scriptures along with the pagans, or the impression that we detest great minds (especially since in our day the heretics disagree with everything
said by the Roman theologians, as Bellarmine has pointed out)."[69]

When Campanella's text reached Rome about mid-March 1616,[70] the Roman
Church had already taken up an official position against Copernicus and had forbidden Galileo to propagate his doctrines as a physical truth. However, it is hardly
likely in any event that Bellarmine would have lent an attentive ear to the counsels

of prudence offered by the author of the *Apologia*. From April of the previous year, Bellarmine had clearly expressed his rejection of heliocentric cosmology and his refusal to change the traditional interpretation of Scripture in order to bring it into accord with the "Pythagorean" doctrine.[71]

The occasion for taking up this position was given to Bellarmine by his reading of a text composed in Italian and published in Naples in 1615, the *Lettera sopra l'opinione de'Pittagorici e del Copernico* by the Carmelite friar Paolo Antonio Foscarini, a well-known theologian who had sided with Galileo in claiming the compatibility of the Scriptures with Copernicus's renewal of ancient astronomy.[72] Rapidly submitted to examination, the *Lettera* became the subject of a report that has reached us under the title of *Judicium de epistola F. Pauli Foscarini de mobilitate terrae*. For the anonymous censor who wrote this report, Foscarini's treatise "excessively favors the rash opinion of the motion of the earth and the immobility of the sun." But an opinion that was "clearly contrary to Sacred Scripture" (evidenter contra sacras litteras) could not be "obviously probable" (evidenter probabile). Among the objections put forward by the censor as proof of the certainty of the traditional geocentric doctrine was the forthright affirmation that "in those texts [Psalms 92:1 and 103:5], the Holy Spirit *assigns the reason* for the immobility of the earth, when he says that it is established on its own foundation."[73] In this context, to say, as Foscarini did in his *Lettera,* that this passage in Scripture was to be understood not "in itself and as in nature" (secundum se et naturam ipsam) but only "in respect to us, in relation only to us, and according to the appearances" (secundum nos, et respectu nostri tantum, et secundum apparentiam)[74] distorted "the Sacred Scriptures, and explain them contrary to the common explication of the holy fathers, which agreed with the more common, indeed the most common, and most true opinion of almost all the astronomers."[75]

In a text written in haste for Bellarmine[76] and attached to the *Lettera* submitted to the judgment of the cardinal, Foscarini denied having propounded a "rash" opinion in developing his argument and buttressing it with citations to the effect that there was no consensus among the Church fathers in support of the generally accepted opinion regarding the earth's immobility.[77] But the reasons given by Foscarini do not seem to have convinced Bellarmine, who, in his well-known response of April 12, 1615, warned Foscarini against his audacious interpretation and in particular warned him of the danger in giving an interpretation to the Scriptures "contrary to all the holy fathers and to all the Greek and Latin commentators" (un senso contrario a tutti li santi padri et tutti li espositori greci e latini).[78]

In his answer to Foscarini, Bellarmine rightly remarked that the Copernican hypothesis was not *demonstrated,* and he suggested for form's sake that the question of the interpretation of Scripture would be quite different if the truth of the Copernican hypothesis were ever to be established. The great courtesy of tone should not mislead as to what was at the back of his mind. He remained unmoved by Foscarini's arguments and underlined the seriousness of what was at stake. Applying the principle that any word of Scripture concerned the faith, whether *ex parte objecti* (because of the subject matter) or *ex parte dicentis* (because of who said it), Bellarmine insisted that it was impossible for a Catholic to reject the literal meaning of a text such as Ecclesiastes 1:5 on the daily motion of the sun round the earth. It was clear to Bellarmine that Solomon (who was inspired by God) had here laid down a truth that no philosopher or astronomer—and *a fortiori* no theologian!—had the right to place in doubt.[79] And he warned Foscarini of the risk he ran in being stubborn: that of falling into heresy. There is confirmation that such had been Bellarmine's thinking on the question of heliocentrism in the lines that Prince Federico Cesi wrote to Galileo on January 12, 1615, some three months before Bellarmine's answer to Foscarini: "Concerning Copernicus's opinion, Bellarmine, who is one of the eminent members of the congregations who deal with these matters, has told me himself that he holds it to be heretical and that the motion of the earth is without any doubt contrary to Scripture."[80]

Galileo, who commented on Bellarmine's letter of April 12, 1615, did not accept the exegetical principles formulated by him. Focusing on the limited domain where, according to him, the rules for the interpretation of Scripture defined by the Council of Trent operated—the domain of matters relating to faith and morals—Galileo left it to be clearly understood that in his view to deny Solomon's words concerning the motion of the sun *"non sia heresia."*[81] And convinced of the justness of his judgment, he composed the *Letter to Christina of Lorraine* as an indirect answer to Bellarmine. But neither Galileo's arguments nor Foscarini's vigorous *Defensio* nor finally Campanella's *Apologia pro Galileo* was able to change the course of events leading first to the decree of March 5, 1616,[82] and then, seventeen years later, to the placing on the Index of Galileo's *Dialogo sopra i due massimi sistemi del mondo* and to the sentence on its author that he be made to abjure on the grounds of "strong suspicion of heresy." The Jesuit Melchior Inchofer was given the task of promptly producing a theological legitimation of the condemnation in the form of a *Tractatus syllepticus* (Rome, 1633), the composition of which he was called upon to undertake by Pope Urban VIII, who was directly responsible for the punishment inflicted on Galileo.[83]

Conclusion

Thus the "monks" had finally judged the heliocentric opinion to be heretical, just as Achille Pirmin Gasser had foreseen long ago before in 1540, and as Copernicus, Campanella, and Galileo had feared. The English poet John Donne (1572–1631) had glimpsed the possibility of this decision five years before the *De revolutionibus* was placed on the Index. In his *Ignatius his Conclave*,[84] an anti-Jesuit satire, he claimed that "the *Papists* have extended the name & the punishment of Heresie, almost to everything."[85] A reader of Kepler's *De stella nova* and Galileo's *Sidereus nuncius,* Donne envisioned the possibility that the pope might one day anathematize the Copernican system after the immobility of the earth had been "defined as a matter of faith."[86]

There remains the basic question: In what sense can one speak of a heliocentric *heresy?* One would probably have to look very carefully at the answers to this question given by a number of Galileo's contemporaries after the publication of the decree of March 1616 and then in the months and years that followed the condemnation and the abjuration of June 22, 1633. One would also then have to look at a number of authors who for a long time after Galileo's death still worried about whether the condemnation of the *Dialogo* and, through it, heliocentrism was indeed a matter of faith.[87]

Notes

This chapter is a partially modified version of a study that appeared in *Sciences et religions de Copernic à Galilée (1540-1610): Actes du Colloque International organisé par l'Ecole Française de Rome, Dec. 1996* (Rome: École française de Rome, 1999), 69–91. I am grateful to W. G. L. Randles for the English translation of my text and to Ernan McMullin for his care in editing it.

1. "En mitto ad te, vir excellentissime, *hosper pros ton herakleion lithon,* libellum hunc non modo novum, nostrisque hominibus ignotum, sed tibi quoque, ni plane fallor, admirabilem, et undiquaque ad stuporem usque *paradoxôtaton.* Quem Georgius Ioachimus Rheticus artium liberalium Magister, mathematumque apud Vuitebergam aliquando Professor, Civis, et amicus meus summus, superioribus diebus, una cum epistola harum rerum refertissima, ex Gedano ad me dedit. Qui liber, licet consuetae hactenus docendi methodo non respondeat, possitque non unico themate usitatis scholarum theoricis contrarius, et (ut Monachi dicerent) haereticus existimari: Videtur tamen novae, et verissimae astronomiae restitutionem, imo *tèn palinggenesian* haud dubie prae se ferre." Latin text in K. H. Burmeister, *Georg Joachim Rheticus, 1514-1574: Eine Bio-Bibliographie,* 3 vols. (Wiesbaden: Pressler, 1968), 3:15; French translation in G. J. Rheticus, *Narratio prima* (hereafter *NP*), ed. and trans. H. Hugonnard-Roche and J.-P. Verdet, with the collaboration of Michel-Pierre Lerner and Alain Segonds, Studia Copernicana 20 (Wrozlaw: Ossolineum, 1982), Appendix I, no. 1, 197–98. The text of Gasser's letter to Vögeli can also be found republished in 1596 by Michael Maestlin with Rheticus's *Narratio prima* in Johannes Kepler, *Gesammelte Werke* (hereafter *KGW*), ed. M. Caspar and F. Hammer (Munich: Beck, 1937–93), 1: 86–87. On Gasser, see K. H. Burmeister, *Achilles Pirmin Gasser (1505-1577), Artz und Naturforscher, Historiker und Humanist,* 3 vols. (Wiesbaden: Pressler, 1970–75).

2. Letter of Mar. 13, 1540, in Andreas Osiander D. Ae, *Gesamtausgabe,* vol. 7, *Schriften und Briefe, 1539 bis März 1543,* ed. G. Muller and G. Seebass (Gütersloh: Mohn, 1988), letter no. 262, 278–80.

3. Copernicus's letter is lost. Its existence is known from the reply that Osiander sent to him, Apr. 20, 1541, in Osiander D. Ae, *Schriften und Briefe,* letter no. 275, 333–36. The same day

he also wrote to Rheticus on the same subject (*Schriften und Briefe,* letter no. 276, 337–38; Fr. translation in *NP,* Appendix II, no. 1, 208). See also, for these two letters of Osiander, Nicolaus Copernicus, *Briefe, Texte und Uebersetzung,* ed. Andreas Kühne, vol. 6, pt. 1 of *Nicolaus Copernicus Gesamtausgabe,* ed. Heribert M. Nobis, Documenta Copernicana (Berlin: Akademie, 1994), letters no. 158–59, 302–4.

    4. On Giese, also the author of a *De Regno Christi* (unpublished), in which he showed an irenic spirit in relation to Lutheranism close to that of Erasmus, see A. Kempfi, "Erasme et la vie intellectuelle en Warmie au temps de Nicolas Copernic," in *Colloquia Erasmiana Turonensia,* 2 vols. (Paris: Vrin, 1972), 1:397–406.

    5. These are the terms used by Giese in his letter to Rheticus, July 26, 1543, in Copernicus, *Briefe, Texte,* letter no. 194, 359: "opusculum tuum, quo a sacrarum scripturarum dissidentia aptissime vindicasti telluris motum"; French translation in *NP,* Appendix II, no. 5, 217.

    6. Rheticus's text was published in 1651 at Utrecht by Johannes van Waersberge under the title *Cujusdam anonymi epistola de terrae motu* (hereafter *CAE*), at the end of David Gorlaeus's *Idea physica* (1591–1612). Reyer Hooykaas has published Rheticus's Latin text with an English translation and notes under the title *G. J. Rheticus' Treatise on Holy Scripture and the Motion of the Earth* (hereafter *GJRT*) (Amsterdam: North-Holland, 1984). For the passage quoted, see *CAE,* 15; *GJRT,* 48 (Latin) and 72 (English).

    7. *CAE,* 44; *GJRT,* 57 and 91 (modified): "Porro non deerunt, qui monstrosum esse vociferabuntur, terrae motus attribuere, et hic suam sapientiam ex Physicis proferent et ostentabunt. Ridiculi, quasi potentia DEI ex nostris viribus ac nostro intellectu sit metienda. An putabimus DEO, qui ex nihilo totam rerum naturam verbo condidit, quicquam esse impossibile? An alligabimus Deum Peripateticis disputationibus de gravi et levi . . . ?"

    8. *CAE,* 52; *GJRT,* 60 and 95 (modified): "Ex his patet non probari ex sacris literis, terram esse immobilem. Non igitur contra S. Scripturam facit . . . qui ejus mobilitatem assumit." In his *Epistola,* Rheticus insists on his attachment to the "Catholic" faith. On how this declaration should be understood, see *GJRT,* 144–46.

    9. *CAE,* 8–13; *GJRT,* 45–47 and 68–71. This apparent contradiction can be found among the Copernicans, Foscarini and Galileo.

    10. After suggesting that Job 9:6 and Isaiah 51:6 referred respectively to the annual motion and the daily motion of the earth, Rheticus goes so far as to claim that in Psalm 73:17 — "Thou [God] hast made all the ends of the earth, summer and spring" (Tu fecisti omnes terminos terrae, aestatem et ver tu plasmasti ea) — a confirmation can be seen of the *motus declinationis,* the third motion of the earth postulated by Copernicus; see *CAE,* 21–26; *GJRT,* 50–52 and 76–79.

    11. "These are some passages of Scripture, by which we may say that, if the earth moves, something of this, albeit obscurely, is contained in the Bible" (Hi sunt fere loci Scripturae, quibus si terra movetur, aliquid de hac re, *sed obscure in bibliis possemus dicere contineri*) (emphasis mine); see *CAE,* 27; *GJRT,* 52 and 79. For a carefully balanced analysis of Rheticus's position in general on this point, see Kenneth J. Howell, *God's Two Books: Copernican Cosmology and Biblical Interpretation in Early Modern Science* (Notre Dame: University of Notre Dame Press, 2002), 63–67; see also Isabelle Pantin, "Science et religion au temps de la 'révolution scientifique': Les coperniciens et les règles de l'exégèse," *Archives des Sciences et Comptes Rendus des Séances de la Société de Physique et d'Histoire Naturelle de Genève* 55 (2002): 107–22, esp. 113–16.

12. Johannes Kepler, *Apologia pro Tychone contra Ursum,* in *The Birth of History and Philosophy of Science: Kepler's* A Defence of Tycho against Ursus *with Essays on Its Provenance and Significance,* ed. Nicholas Jardine (Cambridge: Cambridge University Press, 1984), 97, 152: "In fact, Copernicus, steadfast in his Stoic resolution, believed that he should declare his opinions openly even to the detriment of his science" (Copernicus quidem Stoica rigiditate obfirmatus, animi sensa candide sibi profitenda putavit, etiam cum dispendio hujus scientiae).

13. The term *mathematices* should be understood here as mainly referring to astronomy. In fact, Pope Paul III was principally interested in the problem of calendar reform. Five years before the publication of the *De revolutionibus,* Jerome Fracastor had dedicated his *Homocentrica* to Paul III—a work that Copernicus does not seem to have known. Fracastor also sought to arouse the pope's interest in astronomy: "Post religionis, & Christianae Reipublicae curas nullo alio magis tenetur [*scil.* Paul III] studio quam totius Philosophiae, praecipue illius quae circa sydera, & coelestes orbes versatur." See Jerome Fracastor, *Hieronymi Fracastorii opera omnia,* 3d ed. (Venice, 1584), fol. 2A.

14. Nicholas Copernicus, *De revolutionibus orbium coelestium libri VI* (Nuremberg, 1543), fol. IIIIv; English translation, *On the Revolutions of the Heavenly Spheres,* trans. A. M. Duncan (New York: Barnes and Noble, 1976), 26. The proverb cited by Copernicus was translated into Latin for the first time by Erasmus, who had found it in Aristophanes (*Ploutos,* line 885) and had incorporated it into his edition of the *Chiliades adagiorum* published at Venice in 1508.

15. Copernicus, *On the Revolutions,* 26 (modified). The Greek word *mataiologoi* (rendered by the Vulgate as *vaniloqui* and here by 'prattlers') is a rare word that Copernicus probably took from the New Testament, Titus 1:10, where St. Paul denounces the false doctors.

16. It is not surprising that this passage was censured by the commission (composed of theologians!) who were given the task of emending the *De revolutionibus.* The text of the *Monitum ad Nicolai Copernici lectorem, eiusque emendatio,* published in 1620, is now easily accessible in the work of Massimo Bucciantini, *Contro Galileo: Alle origini dell'Affaire* (Florence: Leo S. Olschki, 1995), doc. 3, 211–12; see 211: "in praefatione, circa finem. Ibi 'Si fortasse' dele omnia usque ad verba 'hi nostri labores' et sic accomoda: 'Cœterum hi nostri labores'" (In the preface near the end: delete everything from "perhaps" to the words "my works," and accommodate in this way: "moreover these works of mine"); see also Pierre-Noël Mayaud, S.J., *La condamnation des livres coperniciens et sa révocation à la lumière de documents inédits de Congrégations de l'Index et de l'Inquisition,* Miscellanea Historicae Pontificiae 64 (Rome: Editrice Pontificia Università Gregoriana, 1997), 77–84; and now Owen Gingerich, *An Annotated Census of Copernicus' "De revolutionibus" (Nuremberg, 1543 and Basel, 1566)* (Leiden: E. J. Brill, 2002), Appendix III; see also the map of Europe (p. xxv) with the location of the currently known censored copies of *De revolutionibus* according to the decree of 1620.

17. It was Kepler who first identified the author of this "Warning to the Reader" as Andreas Osiander. Cf. *Astronomia nova* (1609) in *KGW,* 3:6. Kepler had already in about 1601 revealed the identity of the author in his *Apologia pro Tychone contra Ursum,* 96–98. This text of Kepler's, however, remained unpublished until the nineteenth century. Giese reacted violently to Osiander's initiative, which he considered treasonous toward Copernicus. See his letter to Rheticus, July 1543, in *NP,* Appendix II, no. 5, 216–18.

18. For a list of the works published by Petreius (1497–1550), see J. C. Shipman, "Johannes Petreius, Nuremberg Publisher of Scientific Works, 1524–1550, with a Short-Title List of His

Imprints," in *Homage to a Bookman: Essays on Manuscripts, Books and Printings Written for Hans P. Kraus on His Sixtieth Birthday, Oct. 12, 1967,* ed. H. Lehmann-Haupt (Berlin: Mann, 1967), 146–62. See also Noel M. Swerdlow, "Annals of Scientific Publishing: Johannes Petreius's Letter to Rheticus," *Isis* 83 (1992): 270–74.

19. On Bartolomeo Spina (1479–1547), see the entry by Klaus-Bernard Springer in *Biographisch-Bibliographisches Kirchenlexikon,* ed. F. W. Bautz and T. Bautz, 23 vols. (Nordhausen: Bautz, 1975–2003), vol. 14, cols. 1506–9. Spina is better known for the polemic he engaged in against Pomponazzi and Cardinal Cajetan on the question of the immortality of the soul, as well as for his writings against witchcraft. He was Master of the Sacred Palace from 1542 to his death in April 1547.

20. See Salvatore I. Camporeale, O.P., "Giovanni Tolosani O.P. e la teologia antiumanistica agli inizi della Riforma: L'*Opusculum* antivalliano *De Constantini Donatione,*" in *Xenia Medii Aevi Historiam Illustrantia, oblata Thomae Kaeppeli O.P.,* ed. R. Greytens and P. Kunzle, 2 vols. (Rome: Edizioni di Storia e Letteratura, 1978), 2:809–31, and "Giovanmaria dei Tolosani O.P. 1530–1546: Umanesimo, riforma e teologia controversista," in *Fede e controversia nel '300 e '500,* ed. Centro Riviste della Provincia Romana, Memorie Domenicane, n.s. 17 (Pistoia: Centro Riviste della Provincia Romana, 1986), 145–252.

21. Giovanni Tolosani, *Compendio di sphera* (BnF, Rés. V 1030), Libro Primo, Membro Tertio, "Transcorso del Chalendario," fol. 8v, col. 2, to 9r, col. 2.

22. The pseudonym used by Tolosani for this essay, composed in the context of the work on calendar reform begun during the Council of Trent, was not immediately divulged.

23. Biblioteca Nazionale di Firenze, Conv. soppr. J. 1, 25, fol. 339r–342r: *De purissima veritate divine scripture adversus errores humanos: opus egregium, in quo continentur inquisitiones ac resolutiones veteris et novi testamenti, auctore fratre Joanne Maria de Tholosanis Florentino ex Colle Vallis Else nec non et Dominicani ordinis reformati professore atque catholice veritatis inquisitore ac verbi dei predicatore evangelico et apostolico, ad communem fidelium utilitatem.*

24. Camporeale, "Giovanmaria dei Tolosani," 149.

25. Latin text and French translation in Michel-Pierre Lerner, "Aux origines de la polémique anticopernicienne I. L'*Opusculum quartum* [1547–1548] de Gio. Maria Tolosani O.P.," *Revue des Sciences Philosophiques et Théologiques* 86 (2002): 681–721.

26. We shall return in a moment to this notion of an "Empyrean."

27. Lerner, "Aux origines," 700.

28. The Dominican did not, of course, know that this text was, as we have seen, the work of the Lutheran theologian Andreas Osiander (1496 or 1498–1552). It was Osiander who, in 1542, took over from Georg Joachim Rheticus the printing of Copernicus's book in Nuremberg.

29. It did not escape Tolosani's notice that the Pythagoreans placed a central fire in the middle of the world, round which the sun was supposed to revolve, together with the earth, an anti-earth, and other planets. That is why he said Copernicus "partly" imitated the Pythagoreans (cf. Lerner, "Aux origines," 704).

30. Edward Grant, *Planets, Stars, and Orbs: The Medieval Cosmos, 1200–1687* (Cambridge: Cambridge University Press, 1994), 317–89; see also Michel-Pierre Lerner, *Le monde des sphères,* vol. 1, *Genèse et triomphe d'une représentation cosmique* (Paris: Les Belles Lettres, 1996), 215–21, and W. G. L. Randles, *The Unmaking of the Medieval Christian Cosmos, 1500–1760: From Solid Heavens to Boundless Æther* (Brookfield, Vt.: Ashgate, 1999), 38–39, 133–50. To the best of my

knowledge, Tolosani was one of the rare theologians to have emphasized the theological difficulty posed by Copernicus's immobile heaven of the fixed stars. For Copernicus said not a word about the existence of any other heaven beyond the astronomical one of the fixed stars. Copernicus's heaven of the fixed stars thus took, as it were, the place of the immobile heaven of the theologians.

31. Cf. Lerner, "Aux origines," 708.

32. Ibid., 709: "Ex qua [doctrina] facile possent oriri dissensiones inter divinae scripturae catholicos expositores et eos qui huic falsae opinioni pertinaci animo adhaerere vellent. Ad cuius vitandum scandalum, hoc nostrum opusculum scripsimus."

33. See J. M. de Bujanda, *Index des livres interdits,* vol. 8, *Index de Rome 1557, 1559, 1564* (Sherbrooke, Québec: Centre d'études de la Renaissance, Université de Sherbrooke, 1990), 38; see 751 and 786 for the presence of Johann Petreius in the Indexes of 1557 and 1559. The Index of 1564 does not repeat this banning, of a general character, concerning sixty-one printers of heretical works, whether the works in question treated of matters religious or not. See 93 and 131–34. For Rheticus, see 478 (no. 331) and 840, and J. M. de Bujanda, *Index des livres interdits,* vol. 9, *Index de Rome 1590, 1593, 1596* (Sherbrooke, Québec: Centre d'études de la Renaissance, Université de Sherbrooke, 1994), 816 and 877 (no. R 331).

34. Archives of the Congregation for the Doctrine of the Faith (ACDF), Index, XXIII. 1, fol. 64v: "Ex operibus Nicolai Caprearij [sic] Volutionibus [sic] orbium Basileae Henrici et deleatur 1566. Dele narratio per Georgium Ioachimum Reticum Ereticum" (my thanks to Leen Spruit for the transcription of this document; see also Leen Spruit, "Giordano Bruno eretico: Le imputazioni del processo nel contesto storico-dottrinale," in *Cosmologia, teologia y religion en la obra y en el proceso de Giordano Bruno,* ed. M. A. Granada (Barcelona: Publicacions de la Universitat de Barcelona, 2001), 113 n. 5. This passage mentions only a work of the "heretic" Rheticus, not that of Copernicus himself (whose name and the title of whose book are distorted), nor is heliocentrism named. Gingerich, in *An Annotated Census,* xxiii n. 16, mentions "a number of copies of the 1566 edition with the *Narratio prima* cut out, or simply with the names of Rheticus and Schöner [the dedicatee of the book] altered, excised with ink, or pasted over." Though Rheticus disappeared from the Indexes published in Rome from the seventeenth century on, he remained listed in the Spanish Indexes (where he was included in 1584) at least until 1707, together with Tycho Brahe, Kepler, Mulerius, Reinhold, and Rothmann. On this point, see J. Pardo Tomás, *Ciencia y censura: La inquisición española y los libros científicos en los siglos XVI y XVII* (Madrid: Consejo Superior de Investigaciones Científicas, 1991), 183–89, 352–68. On the presence of Brahe in the Spanish Indexes, see Michel-Pierre Lerner, "Tycho Brahe Censured," in *Tycho Brahe and Prague: Crossroads of European Science,* ed. John R. Christianson et al., Acta Historica Astronomiae 16 (Frankfurt am Main: Deutsch, 2002), 95–101.

35. Giordano Bruno suggests that the *Ad lectorem* was written by "a conceited ass . . . (as if he wanted to support the author by excusing him, or for the benefit of other asses who, finding greens and small fruit, would not put down a book without having eaten)." See Giordano Bruno, *La cena de le ceneri/Le souper des cendres,* in vol. 2 of *Oeuvres complètes* (Paris: Les Belles Lettres, 1994), 126–27. I have cited the English translation: *The Ash Wednesday Supper,* ed. and trans. E. A. Gosselin and L. S. Lerner (Hamden, Conn.: Archon, 1977), 137.

36. See Francesco Patrizi de Cherso, "Emendatio in libros suos novae philosophiae (a cura di Paul Oskar Kristeller)," *Rinascimento* 10 (1970): 218.

37. See Michel-Pierre Lerner, "L'Achille des coperniciens," *Bibliothèque d'Humanisme et Renaissance* 42 (1980): 313–27, and *Le monde des sphères,* vol. 2, *La fin du cosmos classique* (Paris: Les Belles Lettres, 1997), 104–8.

38. On this figure, see C. Sommervogel, *Bibliothèque de la compagnie de Jésus,* 12 vols., (Brussels: Schepens, 1890–1939), vol. 3, cols. 1489–91; see also Francesco Patrizi de Cherso, *Nova de universis philosophia: Materiali per un'edizione emendata,* ed. A. L. Puliafito Bleuel (Florence: Leo S. Olschki, 1993), xxii–xxiii.

39. A convincing clue to this can be seen in the fact that Giustiniani quotes ancient and modern authors in favor of the rotation of the earth in exactly the same order as that followed by Diego de Zúñiga, *In Job commentaria* (1584; reprint, Rome, 1591), 140. On this author, who, it should be noted, rejected his own pro-Copernican interpretation in a later work entitled *Philosophiae prima pars* (Toledo, 1596), see chap. 2 of this volume and Victor Navarro Brotóns, "The Reception of Copernicus in Sixteenth-Century Spain: The Case of Diego de Zúñiga," *Isis* 86 (1995): 52–78.

40. Benedetto Giustiniani, *Admonitio in novam Francisci philosophiam,* in Patrizi de Cherso, *Nova de universis philosophia,* xxxii: "Res ergo philosophis disputanda relinquatur. Nam quamvis scriptura dicat solem oriri ac occidere, tamen ea loquendi ratio potest etiam accomodari huic sententiae, certe eam non aperte refellit."

41. Twenty-five years later, Giustiniani's open-mindedness was to remain but a distant memory. In signing, on Feb. 24, 1616, the censure of the two Copernican propositions submitted for examination to the qualifiers of the Holy Office, of which he had been appointed a member, Benedetto Giustiniani no longer judged the question of the earth's motion to belong solely to the competence of philosophers. Galileo Galilei, *Opere di Galileo Galilei* (hereafter *OGG*), ed. Antonio Favaro (1890–1909; reprint, Florence: Giunti Barbèra, 1968), 19:312, 419.

42. On the different editions of this text, which became a veritable best-seller among the manuals of astronomy, and more generally on the work of this renowned professor of mathematics at the Collegio Romano, see J. M. Lattis, *Between Copernicus and Galileo: Christoph Clavius and the Collapse of Ptolemaic Cosmology* (Chicago: University of Chicago Press, 1994); see also Michel-Pierre Lerner, "L'entrée de Tycho Brahe chez les jésuites ou le chant du cygne de Clavius," in *Les jésuites à la Renaissance: Système éducatif et production du savoir,* ed. Luce Giard (Paris: Presses Universitaires de France, 1995), 145–85.

43. Christoph Clavius, *In Sphaeram Ioannis de Sacrobosco Commentarius* (Rome, 1570), 247–48: "Concludimus igitur cum communi Astronomorum, atque philosophorum sententia, terram esse omnis motus localis tam recti, quam circulari, expertem; cœlos autem ipsos continue circa ipsam circumagi. . . . FAVENT huic quoque sententiæ sacræ literæ, quæ plurimis in locis terram esse immobilem affirmant, Solemque ac cætera astra moveri testentur"; quoted from the extract in the very rare 1570 edition of the *Commentarius* reproduced by Z. Wardeska in his *Teoria heliocentryczna w interpretacji teologów XVI wieku,* Studia Copernicana 12 (Wroclaw: Ossolineum, 1975), doc. no. 6 a–b. These lines from the first edition of Clavius's *Commentarius* are also quoted and analysed by Corrado Dollo in his important study "Le ragioni del geocentrismo nel Collegio Romano (1562–1612)," in *La diffusione del copernicanesimo in Italia, 1543-1610,* ed. Massimo Bucciantini and Maurizio Torrini (Florence: Leo S. Olschki, 1997), 99–167, esp. 154–55. Clavius's criticism of Copernicus, only summarily developed in the 1570 edition of his *Commentary,* was carried much further in the 1581 and other succeeding editions.

44. Juan de Pineda, *Commentaria in Job libri tredecim,* cap. IX, v. 6, text cited in Wardeska, *Teoria,* doc. no. 31. On Juan de Pineda, see Sommervogel, *Bibliothèque,* vol. 6, cols. 796 ff. In his *In Ecclesiasten commentaria liber unus* (Seville, 1619), Pineda quotes with approval the criticism of Copernicus developed by his fellow Jesuit Christoph Scheiner in the latter's *Disquisitiones mathematicae de controversiis et novitatibus astronomicis* (Ingoldstadt, 1614), an approval that Scheiner took the trouble to reproduce textually in his notice in Leone Allaci's *Apes urbanae* (Rome, 1633); see the facsimile reprint by Michel-Pierre Lerner (Lecce: Conte, 1999), 70.

45. Wardeska, *Teoria,* doc. no. 22; in the extract reproduced, Lorin quotes Clavius and Pineda. On Jean Lorin (1559–1634), see Sommervogel, *Bibliothèque,* cols. 1–5; see also, on Juan de Pineda and Jean Lorin, chap. 2 of this book and Dollo, "Le ragioni," 112–17.

46. Nicolai Serari, S.J., *Josue ab utero ad ipsum usque tumulum . . . tomus posterior* (Maguntiae, 1610), cap. X, quaestio 14, 238: *"Stare naturaliter an possint sol, & luna?"* (There is another edition of this commentary in a volume published in Paris in 1610; see cols. 1005–6). Tommaso Caccini, O.P., invoked the authority of this Jesuit author's passage in his evidence given before the Holy Office on Mar. 20, 1615; see Sergio M. Pagano and Antonio G. Luciani, eds., *I Documenti del processo di Galileo Galilei* (Vatican City: Pontifical Academy of Sciences, 1984), doc. no. 8, 81; translation in Maurice E. Finocchiaro, *The Galileo Affair: A Documentary History* (hereafter *GA*) (Berkeley: University of California Press, 1989), 137. On Nicolas Serarius, a prolific author, see Sommervogel, *Bibliothèque,* vol. 7, cols. 1134 ff; see also Rinaldo Fabris, *Galileo Galilei e gli orientamenti esegetici del suo tempo* (Vatican City: Pontifical Academy of Sciences, 1986), 40–41. On his *Prolegomena biblica et commentaria in omnes epistulas canonicas* (Maguntiae, 1612), see Fabris, *Galileo Galilei,* 33–34.

47. Justus Lipsius, *Physiologiae Stoicorum libri tres* (Antwerp, 1604), bk. 2, p. 122: "etsi (tantus Paradoxorum amor est) etiam patrum aevo nobilis mathematicus hanc haeresim excitavit, sed cum ipso sepultam." Copernicus is not named by Justus Lipsius, but it is clearly Copernicus whom he has in mind, as Giorgio Polacco rightly noted, deploring moreover that Justus Lipsius here did not speak the truth. See *Anticopernicus Catholicus, seu de terrae statione, et de solis motu, contra systema Copernicanum, Catholicae assertiones* (Venice, 1644), assertio I, p. 2: "quod utinam verum esset."

48. One can probably hear an echo of the criticisms of heliocentrism formulated by the theologian Matthias Haffenreffer and his colleagues in the formula used by Kepler in a letter of October 1597 to Maestlin to characterize Galileo's cosmological beliefs: "est . . . et ipse (scil. Galileus) in *Copernicana haeresi* inde a multis annis" (cf. *KGW,* 13:143, letter no. 75, line 122 (emphasis mine). On the rejection of heliocentrism by Protestant theologians, see Edward Rosen, "Kepler and the Lutheran Attitude towards Copernicanism in the Context of the Struggle between Science and Religion," in *Kepler: Four Hundred Years,* ed. A. Beer and P. Beer (Oxford: Pergamon Press, 1975), 317–38; see also Howell, *God's Two Books.*

49. Johannes Kepler, *Antwort auf Roeslini Diskurs,* in *KGW,* 4:106, lines 18–20: "alle Päpste von 1542 an, die haben die schrifft also ausgelegt, das sie Copernicum, unangesehen derselbig sein Opus Revolutionum Paulo III. dedicirt, noch nie eins *irthumbs* oder *ketzeren* beschuldiget" (emphasis mine). But already in a letter to Herwart von Hohenburg of Mar. 28, 1605, Kepler praised the Roman Church for having abstained from condemning Copernicus: "sapienter factum ab Ecclesia Romana puto, quod . . . illam Copernicj philosophiam in medio suspensam relinquit." *KGW,* 15:183, letter no. 340, lines 95–102.

50. Gualdo to Galileo, May 6, 1611: "Che la terra giri, sinhora non ho travato nè filosofo, nè astrologo che se voglia sottoscrivere all'opinione di V. S., e molto meno lo vorrano fare i theologi . . . massime quando s'ha l'opinione universale di tutti contra, imbibita, si può dire, *ab orbe condito.*"(As to the matter of the Earth turning around, I have found hitherto no philosopher nor astronomer who is willing to ascribe to the opinion of Your Honor, and much less would a theologian wish to do so . . . especially when the contrary opinion is held by everyone, imbibed so to speak, since the foundation of the world.) *OGG,* 11:100; English translation (slightly modified) by George V. Coyne in Annibale Fantoli, *Galileo: For Copernicanism and for the Church,* Studi Galileiani 3 (Vatican City: Vatican Observatory Publications, 1994), 117.

51. On this author, see the notice by M. Mucillo in *Dizionario biografico degli Italiani* (Rome: Istituto della Enciclopedia Italiana 1960–), 38:29–31.

52. The *Trattato,* which circulated in manuscript, is reproduced and annotated by Galileo in *OGG,* vol. 3, pt. 1, 254–90, esp. 289–90. Lodovico delle Colombe quotes the following passage from Pineda which in his view speaks for itself: "According to others, this doctrine [Copernicanism] is foolish, frivolous, rash, and dangerous to the faith, and Copernicus and Celio Calcagnini have revived it from the dead remains of those ancient philosophers more as a figment of their own imagination than as something good and useful for philosophy and astronomy." (Alii certe scientiam hanc deliram, nugatoriam, temerariam et in fide periculosam dicunt, atque ex ore antiquorum illorum philosophorum a Copernico et Caelio Calcagnino revocatam, potius ad ingenii specimen, quam ad philosophiae atque astrologiae bonum et utilitatem aliquam.) English translation (modified) in Richard J. Blackwell, *Galileo, Bellarmine and the Bible* (hereafter *GBB*) (Notre Dame: University of Notre Dame Press, 1991), 26–27. On the Dominican Melchior Cano (1509–60), author of a *De locis theologicis* that was to go into many editions and was quoted as an authority by Foscarini in the *Defensio* of his *Lettera* of 1615, see B. Körner, *Melchior Cano: De locis theologicis. Ein Beitrag zur theologischen Erkenntnislehre* (Graz: Styria-Medienservice, 1994); see also *GBB,* 15–20, 100–101, 255–58.

53. *OGG,* 5:284, 286: "Io dico che questo luogo [Joshua 10:12] ci mostra manifestamente la falsità e impossibilità del mondano sistema Aristotelico e Tolemaico, e all'incontro *benissimo s'accomoda co'l Copernicano*" (emphasis mine). On this letter, see A. Battistini, "Scienza come retorica: La lettera copernicana a Benedetto Castelli," in *Galileo e i gesuiti: Miti letterari e retorica della scienza* (Milan: Vita e Pensiero, 2000), 88–124. The argument is taken up and developed in the *Letter to Christina of Lorraine* (*OGG,* 5:343–48).

54. Dini to Galileo, Mar. 7, 1615, *OGG,* 12:151; translation in *GBB,* Appendix V B, 207. Bellarmine had published in 1611 an *Explanatio in Psalmos* (a text that Galileo might have known); and Clavius, as we have seen above, also quoted Psalm 18 in favor of the diurnal motion of the sun. Bellarmine would give the same interpretation of this passage in Scripture in his opusculum *De ascensione mentis in Deum* published four years later; see below. The glosses on the verses "et ipse [sol] tanquam sponsus procedens de thalamo suo. Exultavit ut gigas ad currendam viam," proposed respectively by Bellarmine and Galileo, can be compared in E. Festa, *L'erreur de Galilée* (Paris: Austral, 1995), 244–52. On the Galilean exegesis of the biblical passages in question, see in particular P. Rossi, "Galileo Galilei e il libro dei Salmi," *Rivista di Filosofia* 10 (1978): 45–71.

55. Galileo to Dini, Mar. 23, 1615, *OGG,* 5:301 and 302; translation in *GBB,* Appendix V C, 212 and 213 16). Galileo seeks a scriptural confirmation of his heliocentric exegesis when

commenting on Psalm 73:16 (where he appeals to the meaning of the original Hebrew, obviously after consulting someone with a knowledge of Hebrew) and citing a passage of the *De divinis nominibus* of Blessed Dionysius the Areopagite to support his thesis. He reproduces the same text in the *Letter to Christina* (*OGG* 5:45–46; translation in *GA,* 116–17).

56. At the end of his *Letter to Christina,* Galileo cites the first eight verses of a Gregorian hymn, then attributed to Saint Ambrose (*Hymni ad Vesperas,* "Feria quarta," in *Poésie latine chrétienne du Moyen Age IIIe-XVe siècle,* ed. H. Spitzmuller [Paris: Desclée de Brouwer, 1971], 208–9), whose meaning would suggest the heliocentric conception (*OGG,* 5:348; translation in *GA,* 118). On the cosmological import here given to the Church's hymns—obviously with divergent conclusions—by Galileo, as well as by Bellarmine and by Francesco Ingoli in his *De situ et quiete terrae contra Copernici systema disputatio* (1616), see Tommaso Campanella, *Apologia pro Galileo/Apologie de Galilée,* ed. Michel-Pierre Lerner, Latin text with French translation and notes (Paris: Les Belles Lettres, 2001), 246–47. For an English translation, see Tommaso Campanella, *A Defense of Galileo, the Mathematician from Florence,* trans. Richard Blackwell (Notre Dame: University of Notre Dame Press, 1994).

57. There is an abundant bibliography on the metaphor of God's two books: see Howell, *God's Two Books.* The idea that the Bible teaches "come si vadia al cielo, non come vadia il cielo," heard by Galileo "from an ecclesiastical person in a very eminent position," is generally attributed to Cardinal Cesare Baronio (*OGG,* 5:319; translation in *GA,* 96).

58. *OGG,* 5:315–17; translation in *GA,* 92–93. Pierre Duhem insisted on Galileo's conviction in this regard, speaking as a theologian. Pierre Duhem, *To Save the Phenomena: An Essay on the Idea of Physical Theory from Plato to Galileo,* trans. E. Doland and C. Maschler (French original, 1908; Chicago: University of Chicago Press, 1969), 105, 109.

59. *OGG,* 5:369; *GBB,* 272: "Noi crediamo che e Salomone e Moisè e tutti gli altri scrittori sacri *sapessero perfettamente la costituzione del mondo*" (emphasis mine). We shall return to this letter of Bellarmine to Foscarini. R. Amerio rightly considers that for Galileo the sacred authors were "Copernicans," although excused from revealing this knowledge because the main purpose of Scripture is to lead men to salvation, not to teach them the world's constitution. See R. Amerio, "Galileo e Campanella: La tentazione del pensiero nella filosofia della riforma cattolica," in *Nel terzo centenario della morte di Galileo Galilei,* ed. Università Cattolica del Sacro Cuore (Milan: Vita e Pensiero, 1942), 321.

60. Tommaso Campanella, *Lettere,* ed. V. Spampanato (Bari: Laterza, 1927), no. 31, 166–67: "Gaudeamus: si murmuraverint theologi, prophetizantes defendent te patres theologiae, Chrysostomus et Theodorus episcopus tarsensis magister eius et Procopius gazaeus, qui caelum stare . . . docent; et Augustinus hanc opinionem suo tempore a mathematicis rite demonstratam fuisse docet, neque per sacras literas evertendam esse nobis, ne simus irrisui mathematicis: quod debuisset ipse observare cum antipodas negavit. Habes Origenem qui terram esse animal et sidera omnia docuit, et pythagorica dogmata laudat et ex Scripturis probat."

61. In the lines that follow, we repeat the analysis developed in our recent edition of Campanella's *Apologia pro Galileo.* See also Michel-Pierre Lerner, "Le moine, le cardinal et le savant: À propos de l'*Apologia pro Galileo* de Tommaso Campanella," *Les Cahiers de l'Humanisme* 2 (2001): 71–94.

62. Blackwell, *Defense of Galileo,* 71. This formula comes from the decree *Apostolici regiminis,* promulgated in 1513. On this decree, which affirms the subordination of philosophy to

theology and on the use that was made of it in the seventeenth century, see Alain Segonds, "Le retour en Italie de Giordano Bruno, philosophe," Michel-Pierre Lerner, "Vérité des philosophes et vérité des théologiens selon Tommaso Campanella, O.P.," and Francesco Beretta, "*Magno Domino & Omnibus Christianae, Catholicaeque Philosophiae amantibus. D. D.:* Le *Tractatus syllepticus* du jésuite Melchior Inchofer, censeur de Galilée," in *Freiburger Zeitschrift für Philosophie und Theologie* 48 (2001): 269–80, 281–300, and 301–27, respectively.

63. Campanella, *Apologia pro Galileo*, 61; Blackwell, *Defense of Galileo*, 69.

64. Campanella, *Apologia pro Galileo*, 147–49; Blackwell, *Defense of Galileo*, 118.

65. Tommaso Campanella, *Theologiae liber III*, ed. R. Amerio (Rome: Centro Internazionale di Studi Umanistici, 1964), cap. 7, a. 2, 142. (The composition of this text goes back to 1614.) St. Thomas Aquinas says practically the same thing. See, for example, *Quaestiones quodlibetales*, Quodlibet IV, art. 3: "And so, whichever opinion is considered, the truth of the Sacred Scripture can be saved in different ways. *In consequence of which one should not constrain the meaning of the Sacred Scripture to just one of these interpretations*" (Sic ergo secundum quamcumque opinionem potest veritas sacrae scripturae salvari diversimode. *Unde non est coarctandus sensus sacrae scripturae ad aliquid horum*) (emphasis mine).

66. See Michel-Pierre Lerner, introduction to Campanella, *Apologia pro Galileo*, lvi ff.

67. Ibid., cii–cxiii.

68. Campanella, *Apologia pro Galileo*, 79: "Arbitror, non debere hunc modum philosophandi vetari; tum quia auidius ab hæreticis amplexabitur, & nos irridebimur; scimus quantopere conquesti sint Vltramontani ob determinationes quasdam in Concilio Tridentino factas: Quid facient, cum contra physicos & astronomos nos insurgere audient? Nonne statim acclamabunt, quod naturæ, nedum scripturæ, vim inferamus. Scit hæc Cardinalis Bellarminus." In Blackwell, *Defense of Galileo*, 79 (translation slightly modified).

69. Campanella, *Apologia pro Galileo*, 157: "Arbitror . . . non absque periculo irrisionis scripturarum vel potius suspicionis, quasi nos contra scripturas cum ethnicis sentiamus, vel sublimibus ingeniis invideamus (præsertim cum hæretici nihil hoc tempore in theologis Romanis non reprehendant, teste Bellarmino), studium Galilei prohiberi posse, scriptaque eius supprimi." In Blackwell, *Defense of Galileo*, 122–23 (translation slightly modified).

70. Lerner, introduction to Campanella, *Apologia pro Galileo*, xxvi.

71. It is hardly necessary to recall that in the first of the *Opuscula quinque*, entitled *De ascensione mentis in Deum per scalas rerum creatarum* (Rome, 1615), Bellarmine described the ascension of the soul to the celestial kingdom by placing himself in a strictly geocentric context. See, in particular, Gradus II, III and VII, respectively: "Ex consideratione mundi majoris," "Ex consideratione orbis terrae," and "Ex consideratione solis, lunae et stellarum" (where he returns at length to Psalm 18).

72. Paolo Antonio Foscarini's *Lettera* has been reprinted in facsimile by L. Romero (Montalto Uffugo, CS, 1992). It is now also accessible in P. Ponzio's edition of Campanella's *Apologia per Galileo* (Milan: Rusconi, 1997), 199–237. There is an English translation (as well as the anonymous censure quoted below, together with Foscarini's *Defensio*), in *GBB*, Appendices VI and VII A, B.

73. *GBB*, 253–54 (emphasis mine).

74. See Foscarini, *Lettera*, in Campanella, *Apologia per Galileo* (ed. Ponzio), 211–12; English translation in *GBB*, Appendix VI, 228–29 (emphasis mine).

75. *GBB,* 254. For the original text of this *Judicium,* see Domenico Berti, "Antecedenti al processo galileano e alla condanna della dottrina copernicana," *Atti della R. Acc. dei Lincei* (Rome), 3d ser., 10 (1883): 72–73, English translation in *GBB,* 253–54. On this censure, see Irving A. Kelter, "A Catholic Theologian Responds to Copernicanism: The Theological *Judicium* of Paolo Foscarini's *Lettera,*" *Renaissance and Reformation* 21 (1997): 59–70.

76. In 1883, Berti published an abbreviated version by Foscarini with the title "Defensio epistolae . . . super mobilitatem terrae," in Berti, *Antecedenti,* 73–78.

77. A longer preliminary draft can now be read of Foscarini's *Defensio* in a text in his own handwriting, found and published by Emanuele Boaga, "Annotazioni e documenti sulla vita e sulle opere di Paolo Antonio Foscarini teologo 'copernicano' (*ca.* 1562–1616)," *Carmelus* 37 (1990): 205–14; English translation in *GBB,* 255–63. On the different versions (short and long) of the *Defensio,* see S. Caroti, "Un sostenitore napoletano della mobilità della terra: Il padre Paolo Antonio Foscarini," in *Galileo e Napoli,* ed. Fabrizio Lomonaco and Maurizio Torrini (Naples: Guida Editori, 1987), 81–121, esp. 113–21.

78. Cited from the transcription of the original text in Bellarmine's handwriting, in Boaga, "Annotazioni," 215; cf. *GBB,* 266.

79. In his *Lectiones Lovanienses* composed between 1570 and 1572, Bellarmine had not hesitated to reject the received doctrine of almost all the philosophers and astronomers of his time, according to whom each of the heavenly bodies had its own orb, carrying it along as the orb revolved round the earth. Since, in his view, Scripture spoke forthrightly in favor of the planets moving by themselves, the Bible spoke the truth on this point against the specialists, who would thus be well advised not to contradict the plain meaning of the sacred text: "It is certain that the true sense of Scripture does not conflict with any other truth, whether philosophical or astronomical" (Certum enim est verum sensum Scripturae cum nulla alia veritate sive philosophica sive astrologica pugnare). Bellarmine, "In primam partem D. Thomae lectiones," in "Opera nostrorum," 234, fol. 231v, Archivium Romanum Societatis Iesu, unpublished transcription by P. Tromp, 521–22; see Lerner, *Le monde des sphères,* 2:17–20.

80. *OGG,* 12:129, no. 1071: "Quant'all'opinione di Copernico, Bellarmino istesso, ch'è de' capi nelle congregationi di queste cose, m'ha detto che l'ha per heretica, e che il moto della terra, senza dubio alcuno, è contro la Scrittura." This assertion ties in with what Bellarmine clearly insinuated in his letter to Foscarini. Although according to Mayaud (*La condamnation des livres coperniciens,* 50–51, 260–61) Bellarmine showed in the letter that he was truly open to the possibility of a demonstrative proof of the earth's motion, so that as late as 1615 a revision of the theologians' judgment on heliocentrism was possible, the letter cannot be taken to imply this.

81. The notes referred to are part of a group of texts collected by Antonio Favaro under the general title *Considerazioni circa l'opinione copernicana* in *OGG,* vol. 5. The text in ten points published there, 367–70, examines Bellarmine's arguments against Foscarini, one after the other. In the passage to which we refer, 367–68, Galileo rejected the distinction between that which is *de fide ratione dicentis* and that which is *de fide ratione objecti,* a distinction that enabled the theologians to place the whole field of Scripture "under their control" (see English translation in *GBB,* 269–70). On Galileo's and Bellarmine's different interpretations of the scope of the second decree of the Fourth Session of the Council of Trent, see W. Reinhard, "Il Concilio di Trento e le scienze naturali: La controversia fra Bellarmino e Galilei come paradigma," in *Il Concilio di Trento e il moderno,* ed. P. Prodi and W. Reinhard (Bologna: Il Mulino, 1996), 485–501.

82. On this decision, and on the correction of Copernicus's *De revolutionibus* published in 1620 by the Roman authorities, see Michel-Pierre Lerner, "Copernic suspendu et corrigé: Sur deux décrets de la Congrégation Romaine de l'Index (1616–1620)," *Galilaeana: Journal of Galilean Studies* 1 (2004): 21–89.

83. The complete title of the work is *Tractatus syllepticus, In quo, quid de terrae, solisque motu, vel statione, secundum S. Scripturam, & Sanctos Patres sentiendum, quave certitudine alterutra sententia tenenda sit, breviter ostenditur;* see Beretta, "*Magno Domino.*"

84. John Donne, *Ignatius his Conclave* (London, 1611). The work first appeared in Latin at the beginning of the year 1611 but without the author's name (*Conclave Ignati: sive Eius in nuperis Inferni comitiis inthronisatio . . .*), then some months later, still anonymously, in an English translation by the author himself, under the title *Ignatius his Conclave: or, his Inthronisation in a late Election in Hell . . .* These two versions are accessible in John Donne, *Ignatius His Conclave,* ed. T. S. Healy, S.J. (Oxford: Clarendon Press, 1969).

85. Ibid., 13.

86. Ibid., 17. Donne made Loyola refuse to allow Copernicus to be put in hell, on the grounds that the doctrine of the earth's motion "may well be true." It was rather Clavius, he said, who deserved to remain in hell for being opposed to it! But he then made Loyola say that Copernicus's provisionally favorable situation could not endure "if hereafter the Fathers of our order can draw a *Cathedral Decree* from the Pope, by which it may be defined as a matter of faith: *That the earth doth not move; & an Anathema inflicted upon all which hold the contrary*" (19); see C. M. Coffin, *John Donne and the New Philosophy* (1937; reprint, New York: Humanities Press, 1958), 195–213, and Healy's introduction to Donne, *Ignatius His Conclave,* xi–xlii.

87. For attempted answers to this question of the kind that the theologians of the Holy See have tried to give, up to the twentieth century, see Francesco Beretta, "Le siège apostolique et l'affaire Galilée: Relectures romaines d'une condamnation célèbre," *Roma Moderna e Contemporanea* 7 (1999): 421–61.

———

TWO

THE REFUSAL TO ACCOMMODATE

Jesuit Exegetes and the Copernican System

Irving A. Kelter

Prelude: The Seeming End of the Affair: The Condemnation of 1616

On March 5, 1616, the Roman Catholic Church's Sacred Congregation of the Index issued a decree concerning the new Copernican cosmology and current works defending it. The edict prohibited, until corrected, Nicholas Copernicus's classic work *On the Revolutions of the Heavenly Spheres* (1543) and the *Commentaries on Job* (1584), by the Spanish theologian Didacus à Stunica (Diego de Zúñiga). The Carmelite Paolo Foscarini's *Letter . . . on the Opinion of the Pythagoreans and of Copernicus on the Mobility of the Earth and the Stability of the Sun* (1615) was prohibited absolutely for attempting to reconcile Copernicanism with the Bible and for attempting to prove Copernicanism to be consonant with the truth. All other books of this nature were similarly condemned. This condemnation, which expressed the judgment that the new heliocentric and geokinetic cosmology was contrary to Scripture, also led to the later, far more famous personal condemnation of Galileo.[1]

Copernicus and the Catholic Exegetical Community: The Case of Didacus à Stunica

In his study of the condemnation of Copernicanism, R. J. Blackwell properly directed our attention to the problem of biblical objections to the heliocentric cosmology and to the standards of biblical exegesis current in the Counter-Reformation Church.[2] To understand the condemnation of Copernicanism in 1616 and its role in the condemnation of Galileo in 1633, one must determine how the Copernican theory was received by the Catholic exegetical community at the time of the condemnation.

To gauge this reception, one must go back to the sixteenth century and to the first figure in this tale, Didacus à Stunica (1536–ca. 1600), a member of the Augustinian Order and professor of Holy Scripture at Osuna and Toledo, whose work on Job was included in the condemnation of March 5, 1616. Stunica was the first Catholic exegete to examine the Copernican theory in a printed biblical commentary. Stunica's earliest examination of Copernican theory, his 1584 *In Iob commentaria* (Toledo; reprint, Rome, 1591), has become justly famous in the annals of Copernicanism. It is the only printed work of Catholic biblical exegesis between Copernicus's *On the Revolutions* (1543) and Foscarini's *Letter* (1615) that attempts to reconcile scriptural passages with the new system of the universe. Strictly speaking, Foscarini's *Letter* is a short treatise couched in the form of a letter and not a work of biblical commentary at all. In discussing the reception of Copernican ideas in Spain, Victor Navarro Brotóns asserts that Stunica's work may be the only Catholic theological one to defend Copernicus's ideas in the sixteenth century.[3] Stunica's work on *Job* is, in fact, the only pro-Copernican Catholic biblical commentary as such known from the early modern period.[4]

Medieval and early modern exegetes routinely incorporated philosophical and scientific material into their works. Stunica was no exception, so it is not surprising that in discussing Job 9:6, "Who shaketh the earth out of her place, and the pillars thereof tremble," which seems to speak of the motion of the earth, Stunica entered into a detailed astronomical discourse. He argued that the mystery of this passage could be wiped away by employing the Pythagorean opinion of the motion of the earth, revived in early modern times by Copernicus. According to Stunica, Copernicus's theory enabled professional astronomers to resolve problems such as the determination of the length of the year (the problem of calendar reform) and the rate of the precession of the equinoxes. Consequently, Copernicus's theory was the best scientific one available.[5]

Stunica then turned to reconciling anti-Copernican biblical passages with the new astronomy. He resolved the problem of Ecclesiastes 1:4, "One generation passeth away, and another generation cometh, but the earth standeth for ever"—a classic anti-Copernican passage—by arguing that this passage dealt, not with terrestrial immobility, but only with the earth's remaining unchanged in contrast to the vagaries of human existence. Stunica contended that no passage of Scripture contradicted Copernicus if interpreted correctly and that any passage speaking of the motion of the sun, such as Ecclesiastes 1:5–6, "The sun riseth, and goeth down, and returneth to his place: and there rising again, Maketh his round by the south, and turneth again to the north," could be understood as speaking in the language of the people and not in the language of physical truth.[6] This theory of accommodation was standard for later Catholic Copernicans, notably Galileo and Foscarini.

As proof of his commitment to Copernicanism, Stunica argued that the biblical passages that asserted the earth's immobility were far outweighed by Job 9:6's assertion of the earth's mobility. Indeed, he concluded his exegesis by remarking that Job 9:6 demonstrated the miraculous power and wisdom of God, which could imbue the excessively heavy earth with motion.[7] Such a declaration implies that Stunica, at least in 1584, was leaning toward accepting the physical truth of the Copernican theory of the motion of the earth.

But in his later work of philosophy, the *Philosophiae prima pars* (Toledo, 1597), Stunica came to reject the mobility of the earth, not on exegetical and theological grounds, but on physical ones.[8] In book 4, chapter 5 of that work, the chapter devoted to "the constitution of the entire universe," he included a substantial discussion and examination of the Copernican theory. He divided his analysis of Copernicanism into two sections, the first dealing with the location of the earth and the second dealing with the status of the earth and its motion.[9] Such a distinction between the heliocentric and geokinetic aspects of Copernicus's theory was common at the time and can also be found in the decisions of the theologians who condemned Copernicus, Stunica, and Foscarini in 1616.

Stunica acknowledged that most learned men, such as Aristotle and Ptolemy, had endeavored to demonstrate that the earth was at the center of the universe. He then catalogued some of the traditional observational arguments in favor of placing the earth at the center of the universe. Yet he countered all of these arguments in his discussion and stated that Copernicus had demonstrated in his great work that many of these observations would be the same if we removed the earth from the center of the universe. Stunica was undecided on this question, stating that "certainty cannot be had concerning it."

Certainty could, however, be had about the second aspect of Copernicanism, the motion of the earth. Among the multiple motions that Copernicus assigned to the earth, Stunica targeted the daily rotation of the earth for his special concern and criticism: "The motion that is most difficult to accept and that makes the opinion of the motion of the earth seem absurd to me is that whereby the whole earth is turned in rotation in the space of twenty-four hours." This exceptionally fast motion evidently created problems for him, problems for which he had no solutions. He revealed his own position in the debate between Aristotle and Copernicus over the rotation of the earth by both labeling the motion absurd and stating at the outset that he followed the opinions of Aristotle, Ptolemy, and the wisest of astronomers on this question. Nevertheless, he gave a fair hearing to Copernicus and incorporated quotations and paraphrases from the *De revolutionibus* in his own text.

Stunica raised some of the standard objections to the rotational motion in his discourse. He argued that if the earth were rotating from west to east, then the air, the clouds, the birds, and all other bodies moving through the air would be left suspended and everything would appear to be propelled into the west. Therefore, it would take a greater force to hurl a missile or stone to the east than to the west. Finally, if heavy bodies were thrown upward off a moving earth, they could not fall back in a straight line to the spot from which they were thrown, as that spot would have moved with the rotation of the earth.

He was well aware of Copernicus's answers to these objections, and he included them in his work. He presented Copernicus's argument that the air shared in the rotational motion of the earth and consequently that clouds, birds, and other bodies in the air would not be affected by the rotational motion. He was also aware of Copernicus's statement that all bodies at or near the surface of the earth shared in the earth's motions, so that heavy bodies thrown upward had a circular as well as a rectilinear motion. This explained why these bodies returned in a rectilinear motion to the same spot when they fell.

Stunica respected these arguments but did not find them of sufficient weight. He consistently rejected Copernicus's suggestions and instead pointed to insurmountable obstacles to the acceptance of terrestrial rotation. One example, found in many early modern critiques of Copernicanism, was linked to the phenomenon of the winds. He argued that, as wind was nothing more than the motion of the air, any rotation of the earth shared in by the air would generate a tremendously powerful wind. As no such wind was experienced, there was a serious flaw in Copernicus's reasoning.

Another objection came from the field of ballistics. Stunica argued that missiles and bullets moving at high speeds heated up and eventually melted down. As the earth had a fragile nature, it would not be able to withstand the rapid motion of the rotation that Copernicus ascribed to it. In fact, Stunica concluded this line of reasoning by saying that if the earth had been subjected to the rotational motion for any length of time it would have been destroyed by fire. Obviously, as this had not happened, the earth did not rotate.[10]

How is Stunica's apparent change of heart to be explained? In the absence of any evidence of external pressures on him to adopt an anti-Copernican stance in the *Philosophiae prima pars,* the answer must be sought in his own intellectual development. In his *In Iob commentaria,* he demonstrated a concern with some of the most vexing problems of observational and mathematical astronomy. In that context he was very impressed by the superiority of the Copernican theory and how it could be applied to solve the problems of calendar reform and the precession of the equinoxes. This, I think, explains his support for Copernicus in 1584. However, in his last work, when he turned to examine in depth the *physics* of the earth's motion, he was unable, given the science of his time, to answer some of the standard objections to Copernicanism. Add to that Brotóns's intriguing suggestion that Stunica may have been aware of the growing hostility to Copernicus among Catholic exegetes,[11] and it is no surprise that the Spanish exegete and philosopher came to reject the revolutionary message of Copernicus that the earth really did move.

Copernicus and the Catholic Exegetical Community: The Case of the Jesuits

In the late sixteenth and early seventeenth centuries, Catholic exegetes paid more attention to the astronomy of Copernicus. This attention, however, was mainly negative. Nicolaus Serarius (Niccolo Serario, 1555–1609), Johannes Lorinus (Jean Lorin, 1559–1634), and Johannes de Pineda (Juan de Pineda, 1557–1637), all members of the scientifically prestigious Society of Jesus and exegetes of distinction, knew something of Copernicus's theories and harshly rejected them.

For twenty years, Serarius occupied the chairs of theology and Sacred Scripture at Wurtzburg and Mainz and was called by Cardinal Baronio "the light of the Church of Germany." Lorinus taught philosophy, theology, and Sacred Scripture in Rome, Paris, and Milan; during one part of his life, he was also theologian to the father general of the Society. Pineda first lectured on Aristotle in Seville and Cordova and then made a particular study of the Bible, which he taught for eighteen years in Cordova, Seville, and Madrid.[12] All three wrote numerous biblical commentaries and were Bible authorities to be reckoned with. Stunica's commentary and the response to it inaugurated what Zofia Wardeska has called a new stage in the religious reception of Copernicanism, one of a theological, semiofficial polemic.[13]

Lorinus, in his commentaries on the *Acts of the Apostles* and *Ecclesiastes*, attacked the theory of the motion of the earth, defended by Copernicus and Stunica among others. He supported his arguments by citing the writings of "our Clavius," the famed Jesuit astronomer at the Collegio Romano, and the exegetical writings of the Spanish Jesuit Pineda. Before Lorinus's objections to Copernicanism are detailed, the importance of the works of Clavius should be underscored. Edward Grant has pointed out that Christoph Clavius's *In sphaeram Ioannis de Sacro Bosco commentarius* (Rome, 1570), a best-selling astronomical textbook, was an immediate source for at least three biblical passages used against heliocentrism and geokineticism, namely Ecclesiastes 1:4–5, Psalm 18:6–7, and Psalm 103:5.[14] The use of biblical passages to support the idea of the earth's immobility also appeared in the Coimbra Jesuits' influential *Commentarii . . . In quatuor libros De coelo Aristotelis Stagiritae* (Coimbra, 1592).[15] According to Grant, these passages were of great import; for Catholic Aristotelians, they became "the most potent weapon in defense of the traditional geocentric cosmology."[16]

In his *In Acta Apostolorum commentarii* (Lyon, 1605), Lorinus denounced the supporters of the theory of the mobility of the earth as supporting falsehood. The theory was proclaimed to be "dangerous and repugnant to the faith," as shown in Ecclesiastes 1:4. Although Lorinus admitted that this passage could be interpreted plausibly in the manner of Stunica, referring to the earth's ability to preserve its own nature in contrast to the changing generations of human beings, he rejected such a reading. He argued for a fuller and deeper interpretation in which the Latin term *stat,* used in this passage, might also be taken to mean terrestrial immobility.[17] Similar arguments reappeared in his *Commentarii in Ecclesiasten* (Lyon, 1606).[18]

Nicolaus Serarius considered the Copernican theory at length in his massive *Iosue, ab utero ad ipsum usque tumulum* (questioning "[w]hether the Sun and Moon can be motionless by nature").[19] He described Copernicus as "the renowned astronomer of our age, called by some another Ptolemy," and noted that Copernicus had been praised by Catholic astronomers such as Clavius and Magini. Still Serarius rejected Copernicus's revolutionary ideas. Distinguishing between "hypotheses" and "truths" in astronomy, Serarius contended that if one seriously asserted Copernicus's "hypotheses" to be true, one could not possibly be immune from the charge of heresy. "Truly, Scripture always attributes quietude to the earth and motion to the sun and moon, and when the latter stars are said to be stationary this is signified as having been accomplished by a great miracle." Serarius concluded this denunciation of the new cosmology by arguing that "this opinion has been destroyed by all philosophers, save for Nicetas [read Hicetas] and a few Pythagoreans and their disciples, and all the fathers [of the Church] and the theologians of every school have spoken out against it." Of course, he buttressed his denunciation by citing the now standard anti-Copernican texts Ecclesiastes 1:4 and Psalm 103:5.[20] Tommaso Caccini, the Dominican friar, cited this particular biblical commentary in the inflammatory sermon he delivered in Florence against Galileo and his followers on December 20, 1614.[21]

Johannes de Pineda, to whom Lorinus referred as an authority, was the first to take up the cudgels against Stunica and Copernicus. Pineda attacked both in his *Commentariorum in Iob libri tredecim tomis duobus distincti* (1597, 1600, 1612) and *In Ecclesiasten commentariorum liber unus* (1619, 1620).[22] His denunciation grew in force until, in the first edition of the work on Ecclesiastes (1619), Pineda criticized Stunica, a fellow Spaniard, as having been "clearly deluded" (perspicue hallucinatus est) when he had offered his pro-Copernican exegesis. Pineda admitted, as a number of Catholic exegetes had already done, that the true intention and meaning of Ecclesiastes 1:4 appeared to be satisfied if it was understood to refer to the earth's withstanding destruction and change caused by generation and corruption. Nonetheless, he went on to affirm that the use of *stat* in this most crucial passage meant "not only incorruptible but truly immobile and fixed" (sed stet non solum incorrupta, sed etiam immota et fixa). At the very end of his discussion of Ecclesiastes 1:4, after attacking Stunica and citing the anti-Copernican Jesuit astronomer Christopher Scheiner, Pineda derided the Copernican system as "absurd and false." Such words echoed those used by Clavius in his astronomical textbook and possibly those of the Church theologians who had by that time officially condemned the new cosmology in 1616.[23]

A denunciation of Stunica and Copernicus thereafter remained a commonplace of Jesuit exegesis. As examples of other rejections, one can cite the *Commentarius in Ecclesiasten* (Antwerp, 1638) by Cornelius à Lapide (Cornelius van den Steyn, 1567–1637), christened the "universal commentator of the Baroque age,"[24] and the *Iob elucidatus* (Antwerp, 1646) of Balthasarus Corderus (Balthasar Cordier, 1592–1650). In his commentary on Ecclesiastes, Lapide again argued that the literal sense of *stat* must be that of terrestrial immobility and fixity and went on to cite explicitly the condemnation of Copernicanism under Paul V in 1616.[25]

In Corderus's elucidation of Job 9:6, one finds again the appeal to Clavius's text and to biblical passages such as Ecclesiastes 1:4. Corderus roundly rejected the Copernican interpretation given by Stunica and instead proposed that the motion of the pillars of the earth referred to in the passage from Job could be understood either as the motion of the earth's mountains or as motions in the earth's subterranean depths.[26] This exegesis simply continued that of Thomas Aquinas in his own *Literal Exposition on Job*,[27] and Corderus acknowledged Aquinas's authority in this regard, as had Pineda in his earlier commentary of 1612. It must be remembered that the Jesuits had taken Aquinas to their hearts as a teacher in theology, although, according to Rivkha Feldhay, Jesuit Thomism, as distinct from Dominican Thomism, was neither uncritical nor all-encompassing.[28]

Conclusions: What Was the Fuss All About?

What conclusions can be drawn from this exploration of Catholic exegetes and the Copernican system prior to the condemnation of 1616? Certainly these Counter-Reformation Jesuit exegetes held tightly to what they conceived to be the readily apparent "literal" sense of the biblical passages being debated. This emphasis on the simple literal interpretation of the Bible was a growing tendency in the Catholic exegetical community at this time. The literal sense was in fact for them the foundation of all scriptural exegesis. In his study of Genesis commentaries of the early modern era, Arnold Williams discerns not only a decrease in the spiritual exegesis common in the Middle Ages but also a shift in the treatment of it to that of an "application" rather than a true "interpretation."[29] Historians of exegesis have noted the growth among Catholics at this time of what is called the "theory of dictation," which taught that God had dictated not only the ideas present in the Bible but also all the words and verbal expressions.[30]

The distinguished Jesuit theologian and opponent of Copernicanism Robert Cardinal Bellarmine exhibited such an extreme devotion to the words of the Bible. As he wrote in one of his major theological works: "[N]ot the propositions alone [of the Bible], but each and every word pertains to the faith. We believe that no word in Scripture is unnecessary, nor is it incorrectly placed." This statement, coupled with

Bellarmine's belief that every biblical passage had a simple, literal interpretation but that all did not have a "figurative" or "spiritual" interpretation, led him to conclude that "at least some of the passages implying geocentrism had a simple (*simplex*) literal sense and were, therefore, explicit divine teachings."[31] As Ugo Baldini and George Coyne have shown so well, this devotion to the words of the Bible and their "literal" interpretation led Bellarmine to deny such tenets of traditional cosmology/astronomy as the perfect heavenly ether and the use of eccentrics and epicycles. Such devotion also led him to uphold, against the Copernicans, geocentrism and terrestrial immobility.[32]

The Jesuit critics of Copernicus, however, did not denounce the theory of accommodation and the explication of biblical passages according to appearances in toto, but only their specific applications in pro-Copernican works. Indeed, they themselves admitted that in certain cases the pro-Copernican exegesis of passages such as Ecclesiastes 1:4 was quite acceptable. One example of the Jesuit use of the principle of accommodation was the discussion of the heavenly spheres in yet another biblical commentary, the *Commentariorum et disputationum in Genesim, tomi quatuor* (Rome, 1589–98), by Benedictus Pererius (Benito Pereyra, 1535–1610). Pererius was, at various times, a professor of philosophy, theology, and Sacred Scripture at the Collegio Romano and was the author of a number of important works on science and philosophy, as well as on the Bible. Both Alistair Crombie and William Wallace have pointed to Pererius's lectures in Rome as influential in the formation of the young Galileo.[33] In the *Commentariorum et disputationum in Genesim,* which has been called the most popular Christian commentary on Genesis of the early modern period,[34] Pererius analyzed the nature of the heavens and the supposed heavenly spheres. He utilized the theory of accommodation and exegesis *secundum apparentiam* to reconcile biblical passages that seemed to ascribe motion to the planets on their own with the Aristotelian idea of invisible spheres that carried them.[35] Here accommodation was used to uphold Aristotle and traditional cosmological ideas, not to oppose them.

How firmly wedded Pererius was to the Aristotelian worldview is revealed by his *Commentariorum et disputationum in Genesim.* He never mentioned the Copernican theory in his commentary, and Copernicus's name appeared only in a discussion of when the world would end.[36] However, in a discussion of Joshua 10:12, "Move not, O sun, toward Gabaon," Pererius treated the traditional exegesis as unquestionable and spoke of Joshua as "ruling" (*imperaret*) the sun and the moon.[37] In his analysis of the nature of the sun, Pererius pointed to Ecclesiastes 1:5 as proof that, according to Solomon, the sun moved in a circle in the heavens.[38] In a rather lengthy section on "the position and immobility of the earth," Pererius included citations to standard philosophical and biblical texts (Aristotle's *De coelo*, Psalm 103, Ecclesiastes 1:4) that argued against the motion of the earth, and he insisted on the earth's centrality and its lack of motion.[39]

Pererius's devotion to such scientific ideas as the earth's centrality and immo-bility leads to another conclusion concerning these Jesuit exegetes and their rela-tionship to Copernican cosmology. The Jesuits were indisputably the educators of Counter-Reformation Europe. In their ideas and methods they were not hide-bound traditionalists, and they were receptive to new ideas in the humanities and the sci-ences.[40] Yet in the end they saw themselves as the defenders of the old intellectual order. "The Jesuits," in the words of Richard Westfall, "sought to employ the new learning to bolster the old. In natural philosophy, they were wedded to Aristotle, whose philosophy they saw as the foundation of Scholastic theology, the intellec-tual rampart of the Catholic religion."[41]

Finally, more important than the details of the reception of the Copernican cos-mology by these Jesuit exegetes and more important than their devotion to Aristotle was their conception of the proper relationship between science and religion. Their entire approach to the problem of Copernicanism was the reverse of that taken by Stu-nica, Foscarini, and Galileo. Whereas the latter tended to argue that the interpreta-tion of biblical passages about the natural world should take into account philosophi-cal and scientific truths, a Jesuit exegete such as Pineda would argue that physical claims should be judged against biblical passages, literally understood.

What can be more revealing of this approach than the very beginning of Pineda's exegesis of Ecclesiastes 1:4: "Physical truths have been very carefully revealed by this judgment from Solomon" (Physica dogmata subtiliter hac sententia a Salomone in-dicata)? Pineda then listed seven fundamental propositions about the physical world that were confirmed by biblical passages, all of which dealt with the centrality and immobility of the earth.[42] A similar attitude is also evident in Lapide's *Commentarium in Pentateuchum Mosis* (1617), which asserted that "one must adapt philosophy and physics to Sacred Scripture and the word of God. . . . It is forbidden on the contrary to subordinate Sacred Scripture to the words of the philosophers or to the light of nature."[43]

What was at stake here was not only a matter of differing interpretations of the Bible or even of warring cosmologies. What was at stake was the proper relationship of the emerging natural sciences—among them astronomy—to theology. Were these sciences to be subordinate to theology, "queen of the sciences," as it was called in the Middle Ages, or were they to be independent of its control? Copernicus had al-ready called for this independence when, in his preface to Pope Paul III, he asked for protection from "babblers" who would use biblical passages against his theory and who were ignorant of astronomy.[44] Such a call for independence must certainly have antagonized the professional theologians and exegetes of the Counter-Reformation Church.

Intertwined with this independence movement was the contemporary debate concerning the status of the mathematical sciences, including astronomy. Contrary to the claims of a number of Aristotelian philosophers of the day, certain mathematicians and mathematical astronomers had made expanded claims for the nobility of their science and for the physical truth of its assertions. Such a debate between the philosophers and the mathematicians was raging within the Jesuit Society, Clavius being the most prominent defender of the dignity and worth of mathematics.[45]

Was the Jesuit struggle between the philosophers and the mathematicians in some way behind this rejection of Copernicus? It is certainly no accident that none of the Jesuit exegetes under examination had any close connection to the mathematical sciences, although several taught and wrote philosophy. Was the refusal to accept the new worldview based also on Clavius's inability to raise the status of the mathematical disciplines to that of "true sciences" that could claim certain knowledge? Was this defeat within the Jesuit Society itself a by-product of the Jesuits' return to "solid and uniform doctrine," as ordered by its general, Claudio Acquaviva, in the years immediately preceding the condemnation of 1616? Motivated by concerns of internal philosophical differences and external criticisms, notably by Dominican theologians, Acquaviva reaffirmed the stipulation that all Jesuits were to teach according to the authority of Aristotle in philosophy and Aquinas in theology. By creating "solid and uniform doctrine," Acquaviva intended to restore unity, strengthen the Society, and authenticate its orthodoxy. Contemporary Aristotelianism and Thomism allowed the mathematical sciences (including mathematical astronomy) to claim "methodological autonomy" but only probable knowledge.[46]

This form of Aristotelian-Thomist criticism of the mathematical sciences was evident as early as 1544 in the *De veritate sacrae scripturae,* by the Dominican friar Giovanni Maria Tolosani. Tolosani sharply rebuked Copernicus, an expert in mathematics and astronomy, for being deficient in physics and logic. The Dominican friar also rebuked Copernicus for being ignorant of the Bible and for wrongly placing the mathematical science of astronomy over physics and even over theology.[47]

Is not this the key to understanding Serarius's statement that if one asserted Copernicus's "hypotheses" to be true one could not be immune from the charge of heresy? Is this not behind the famous warning issued by Bellarmine to Foscarini in April 1615 to speak of Copernicanism solely in a hypothetical sense lest it conflict with philosophy and the Bible?[48] Are not these all important factors behind the Jesuits' response to Copernicus and their refusal to accommodate?

Notes

This essay is a revised version of the work first published in *Sixteenth Century Journal* 26 (1995): 273–83. I thank Ernan McMullin for inviting me to contribute it to this volume and for his careful reading and advice concerning revising it. I also thank the editors of that journal for allowing me to use it and Ms. Pamela Clesi, my student assistant, for her invaluable aid. Unless otherwise indicated, all translations are my own.

1. For the text of the condemnation, see Sergio M. Pagano and Antonio G. Luciani, eds., *I documenti del processo di Galileo Galilei* (Vatican City: Pontifical Academy of Sciences, 1984), 102–3. An English translation of the decree can be found in Maurice A. Finocchiaro, ed. and trans., *The Galileo Affair: A Documentary History* (hereafter *GA*) (Berkeley: University of California Press, 1989), 148–50. For the final results of the papal investigation of the "Galileo affair," see John Paul II, "Lessons of the Galileo Case," *Origins* 22 (1992): 369, 371–75. For useful guides to the condemnation and some of the issues involved, see Ernan McMullin, "Galileo on Science and Scripture," and Richard J. Blackwell, "Could There Be Another Galileo Case?" in *The Cambridge Companion to Galileo,* ed. Peter Machamer (Cambridge: Cambridge University Press, 1998), 271–347 and 348–66, respectively. Mention must also be made of the learned treatment of this subject in Annibale Fantoli, *Galileo: For Copernicanism and for the Church,* 2d ed. (Notre Dame: University of Notre Dame Press, 1996), 169–270.

2. Richard J. Blackwell, *Galileo, Bellarmine, and the Bible* (hereafter *GBB*) (Notre Dame: University of Notre Dame Press, 1991), which includes new translations of many valuable texts, including the work of Foscarini. For my review of this book, see *Modern Schoolman* 69 (Jan. 1992): 149–52. Two recent analyses of the historiography of the "Galileo affair," both of which include a discussion of Blackwell's positions, are Rivkha Feldhay, "Recent Narratives on Galileo and the Church; or: The Three Dogmas of the Counter-Reformation," in *Galileo in Context,* ed. Jürgen Renn (Cambridge: Cambridge University Press, 2001), 219–37, and Maurice A. Finocchiaro, "Science, Religion, and the Historiography of the Galileo Affair: On the Undesirability of Oversimplification," *Osiris* 16 (2001): 114–32. Feldhay is markedly hostile to the views of a number of interpreters of the "Galileo affair," including Blackwell. The most recent book-length treatment of the matter of biblical interpretation and the Copernican cosmology is Kenneth J. Howell's *God's Two Books: Copernican Cosmology and Biblical Interpretation in Early Modern Science* (Notre Dame: University of Notre Dame Press, 2002). Although Howell examines a number of Catholic authors, he pays no specific attention to professional Catholic biblical exegetes.

3. Victor Navarro Brotóns, "The Reception of Copernicus in Sixteenth-Century Spain: The Case of Diego de Zúñiga," *Isis* 86 (1995): 60. This essay is the best treatment of Stunica available in English.

4. The case of Marin Mersenne's *Quaestiones celeberrimae in Genesim* (1623) must be mentioned here. In that work Mersenne extensively treated the arguments for and against Copernicanism and seems to have been disposed favorably to some aspects of the new astronomy. Still, he argued that no proof was available to substantiate it. Therefore, those who propounded Copernicanism were judged correctly by the Church to have been guilty of temerity in supporting it. However, he left the door open for a change if and when proof was available. See the important study of William L. Hine, "Mersenne and Copernicanism," *Isis* 64 (1973): 18–32. Peter Dear, *Mersenne and the Learning of the Schools* (Ithaca: Cornell University Press, 1988), 32–34, argues that Mersenne's position on this issue was governed by his "probabilistic" understanding of the status of astronomical theories. When he wrote his *Quaestiones,* Mersenne viewed the Ptolemaic system as having the weight of probability behind it. Later, the "probabilities" shifted in favor of Copernicanism.

5. See Zofia Wardeska, *Teoria heliocentryczna w interpretacji telogów xvi wieku* (Wroclaw: Ossolineum, 1975), photoreproduction 47a, for a convenient reproduction of this section of

Stunica's commentary. Also see Grant McColley, ed., "A Facsimile of Salusbury's Translation of Didacus a Stunica's *Commentary upon Job,*" *Annals of Science* 2 (1937): 179–82. For new translations, see *GBB,* 185–86, and Navarro Brotóns, "Reception of Copernicus," 67–69. This essay is the best treatment of Stunica available in English. For Stunica, see also Francesco Barone, "Diego de Zuniga e Galileo Galilei: Astronomia eliostatica ed esegesi biblica," *Critica Storica* 19 (1982): 319–34. All translations of biblical passages supplied by the author are from the Rheims-Douay English translation.

6. See Wardeska, *Teoria,* photoreproduction 47b, for this portion of the commentary. Interpretations of Ecclesiastes 1:4 similar to that of Stunica go back as far as the writings of Gregory the Great; for this, see Thomas Aquinas, *Catena Aurea,* as given in M. E. Toal, ed. and trans., The *Sunday Sermons of the Great Fathers* (Chicago: Regnery, 1958), 1:8.

7. Wardeska, *Teoria,* 47b.

8. Didacus à Stunica, *Philosophiae prima pars* (Toledo, 1597), bk. 4, chap. 5. Stunica's argument was against the diurnal rotation of the earth; he contended that he could come to no conclusive statement concerning the annual revolution of the earth.

9. The following discussion of Stunica's work comes from my own reading of the *Philosophiae prima pars,* fol. 228–31. This was delivered in an unpublished paper, Irving A. Kelter, "Diego de Zuñiga: A Sixteenth-Century Theologian and the Reception of Copernicus," at the History of Science Society's annual meeting, Raleigh, N.C., Oct. 31, 1987. I am happy to see that my reading of Stunica corresponds quite closely to that of Navarro Brotóns.

10. Some of the same physical problems bothered the Copernican theologian Paolo Antonio Foscarini. See Irving A. Kelter, "Paolo Foscarini's *Letter to Galileo:* The Search for Proofs of the Earth's Motion," *Modern Schoolman* 70 (1992): 31–44.

11. Navarro Brotóns, "Reception of Copernicus," 76–78.

12. For basic bio-bibliographical information on these Jesuits, see Augustin de Backer, *Bibliothèque des écrivains de la Compagnie de Jésus ou Notices bibliographiques* (Liège, 1872), 2:807–9, 1981–83; 3:761–66. Robert S. Westman, "The Copernicans and the Churches," in *God and Nature: Historical Essays on the Encounter between Christianity and Science,* ed. David C. Lindberg and Ronald L. Numbers (Berkeley: University of California Press, 1986), 93–95, briefly discusses the reception of Copernicanism by some Jesuit thinkers.

13. Wardeska, *Teoria,* 137.

14. Edward Grant, "In Defense of the Earth's Centraiity and Immobility: Scholastic Reaction to Copernicanism in the Seventeenth Century," *Transactions of the American Philosophical Society* 74 (1984): 61; see Wardeska, *Teoria,* 6b, for this section of Clavius's text. The most detailed treatment of Clavius's response to Copernicus is James M. Lattis, *Between Copernicus and Galileo: Christoph Clavius and the Collapse of Ptolemaic Cosmology* (Chicago: University of Chicago Press, 1994), 106–44. Lattis observes that when mentioning biblical passages against a heliocentric, geokinetic cosmology, Clavius never coupled these citations with the name of Copernicus.

15. Wardeska, *Teoria,* 7.

16. Grant, "In Defense," 63. Grant offers the reader a detailed treatment of the scholastic Aristotelian debate over the mobility of the earth and the centrality of the sun after Copernicus in his magisterial *Planets, Stars, and Orbs: The Medieval Cosmos, 1200-1687* (Cambridge: Cambridge University Press, 1994), 647–53.

17. Wardeska, *Teoria,* 22. Such arguments concerning the term *stat* in Ecclesiastes 1:4 appear in the anonymous theological judgment of the *Lettera* of Paolo Foscarini. On this judgment, see Irving A. Kelter, "A Catholic Theologian Responds to Copernicanism: The Theological *Judicium* of Paolo Foscarini's *Lettera,*" *Renaissance and Reformation* 21 (1997): 59–70.

18. Wardeska, *Teoria,* 23.

19. Nicolaus Serarius, S.J., *Iosue, ab utero ad ipsum usque tumulum . . . , Tomus prior gesta eius usque ad bella, tomus posterior bella omnia ab eo gesta . . .* (Paris, 1610), vol. 1, pt. 2, q. 14.

20. Nicolaus Serarius, S.J., *Iosue, ab utero ad ipsum usque tumulum,* cols. 1004–6. For a careful study of the use of the term 'heresy' in relationship to the Copernican cosmology, see chap. 1 of this book.

21. James Brodrick, S.J., *The Life and Work of Blessed Robert Francis Cardinal Bellarmine, S.J., 1542-1621* (London: Burns, Oates and Washbourne, 1928), 2:352–53. On the use of Serarius, also see Caccini's deposition of Mar. 20, 1615, to the Inquisition in *GA,* 137.

22. Hartmann Grisar, S.J., *Galileistudien: Historische-theologische Untersuchungen über die Urtheile des Römischen Congregationen im Galilei-process* (Regensburg: Pustet, 1882), 264, and Wardeska, *Teoria,* 31, provide references to Pineda's 1597 and 1600 commentaries on Job. For the later commentaries on Job and Ecclesiastes, see Juan de Pineda, S.J., *Commentariorum in Iob libri tredecim tomis duobus distincti* (Antwerp, 1612), 415–17, *Commentarii in Ecclesiasten* (Antwerp, 1619), fol. 128–31, and *Commentarii in Ecclesiasten* (Antwerp, 1620), fol. 111–14.

23. Pineda, *Commentarii in Ecclesiasten* (1619), fol. 131, and (1620), fol. 114. In defense of his geocentric and geostatic cosmology, Pineda cited Clavius, *In sphaeram Ioannis de Sacro Bosco commentarius,* and the work of Christopher Scheiner, S.J., whom Pineda took to be the author of the *Disquisitiones mathematicae* (Ingolstadt, 1614). For an excellent summary of Pineda's exegesis, see Carlo M. Martini, "Gli esegeti del tempo di Galileo," in *Nel quarto centenario della nascita di Galileo Galilei,* ed. Università Cattolica de Sacro Cuore (Milan: Vita e Pensiero, 1966), 115–24. A briefer notice is found in Rinaldo Fabris, *Galileo Galilei e gli orientamenti esegetici del suo tempo* (Vatican City: Pontifical Academy of Sciences, 1986), 39. Pineda's relationship to the condemnation of 1616 is difficult to determine. Although the first edition of his *In Ecclesiasten commentariorum liber unus* appeared in 1619, Pineda made no mention of the earlier condemnation. Martini ("Gli esegeti") argued that Pineda was probably unaware of the ruling; otherwise he would have cited it. This may not have been the case. It is important to note that Pineda was the author of the Spanish version of the *Index of Prohibited Books,* which should have contained the amended edition of Copernicus's *Revolutions,* as required by the condemnation of 1616. As shown by Owen Gingerich, "The Censorship of Copernicus' *De revolutionibus,*" *Annali dell' Istituto e Museo di Storia della Scienza di Firenze* 6 (1981): 57–59, no changes were required in Copernicus's masterpiece according to the *Index* printed in Seville in 1632. Gingerich contends that Pineda and other Spaniards took the condemnation of 1616 to have been purely an Italian affair, seemingly not binding on Catholics in other countries. Consequently, the fact that Pineda made no mention of the condemnation in his work on Ecclesiastes does not mean that he was unaware of the ruling. However, José Pardo Tomás, in his *Ciencia y censura: La Inquisición Española y los libros científicos en los siglos XVI y XVII* (Madrid: Consejo Superior de Investigaciones Científicas, 1991), 183–89, indicates that Copernicus's work was missing from the Seville *Index* because of a "mistake" and that the required corrections to it are included in later *Indexes* under the heading of "Rheticus, a Disciple of Copernicus." My review of Pardo Tomás's excellent work can be found in *Isis* 84 (1993): 795.

24. F. J. Crehan, S.J., "The Bible in the Roman Catholic Church from Trent to the Present Day," in *The Cambridge History of the Bible,* 2d ed., ed. S. L. Greenslade (Cambridge: Cambridge University Press, 1976), 3:216.

25. Cornelius à Lapide, S.J., *Commentaria in Vetus et Novum Testamentum* (Venice, 1761), 5:21–23; the New York Public Library's copy of this work has the volume number marked as 4.

26. Jacques-Paul Migne, ed., *Scripturae Sacrae cursus completus* (Paris, 1839), 13:822–24. Such was the reading of Mersenne, as demonstrated by Hine, "Mersenne and Copernicanism," 25. Mersenne also was suspicious of the use of the principle of accommodation in the manner recommended by the Copernicans. It is worth observing that thirteen years after the condemnation of Galileo and of Copernicanism, the work of Corderus contains no mention of those crucial events in the history of the relationship between Catholicism and modern astronomy.

27. Thomas Aquinas, *Literal Exposition on Job: A Scriptural Commentary Concerning Providence,* trans. A. Damico (Atlanta: Scholars Press, 1989), 168.

28. Rivkha Feldhay, "Knowledge and Salvation in Jesuit Culture," *Science in Context* 1 (1987): 198–201. Feldhay has more on this distinction and on the rivalry between the Jesuits and the Dominicans in her *Galileo and the Church: Political Inquisition or Critical Dialogue* (Cambridge: Cambridge University Press, 1995).

29. Arnold Williams, *The Common Expositor: An Account of the Commentaries on Genesis, 1527-1633* (Chapel Hill: University of North Carolina Press, 1948), 20–21. However, Raymond E. Brown and Sandra M. Schneiders argue in "Hermeneutics," in *The New Jerome Biblical Commentary,* ed. Raymond E. Brown, J. A. Fitzmyer, and R. E. Murphy (Englewood Cliffs, N.J.: Prentice Hall, 1990), 1155, that this decrease in Catholic "spiritual exegesis" was an immediate result of the Protestant Reformation and that after the immediate threat had passed, spiritual exegesis returned.

30. On the theory of "dictation" among Catholic theologians and exegetes during this period, see R. F. Collins, "Inspiration," in Brown et al., *New Jerome Biblical Commentary,* 1027; Bruce Vawter, *Biblical Inspiration* (Philadelphia: Westminster Press, 1972), 58–63.

31. The statement by Bellarmine is taken from his *Prima controversia generalis de concilis, et ecclesia militante.* The Latin text and its analysis are in Ugo Baldini and George V. Coyne, S.J., eds. and trans., *The Louvain Lectures (Lectiones Lovanienses) of Bellarmine and the Autograph Copy of His 1616 Declaration to Galileo* (Vatican City: Vatican Observatory Publications, 1984), 40 n. 92.

32. Ibid., 18–22, 38–43 nn. 83–94.

33. For basic bio-bibliographical information, see de Backer, *Bibliothèque des écrivains,* 2:1861–66; for material on Pererius and the young Galileo, see Alistair C. Crombie, "The Sources of Galileo's Early Natural Philosophy," in *Reason, Experiment, and Mysticism in the Scientific Revolution,* ed. Maria L. Righini-Bonelli and William R. Shea (New York: Science History Publications, 1975), 162–66; William A. Wallace, ed. and trans., *Galileo's Early Notebooks: The Physical Questions* (Notre Dame: University of Notre Dame Press, 1977), 13–15 and passim.

34. Williams, *Common Expositor,* 8.

35. Ibid., 186. Pererius was aware of astronomical observations, such as those of the nova of 1572, which cast doubt on the traditional system of the heavens. As Williams, *Common Expositor,* 189, observes: "He [Pererius] offers three possible explanations [of the nova of 1572]: that it was generated and corrupted in the heavens, that it was another wandering planet in addition to the seven already known, and that the supposedly fixed stars are not fixed but also have their proper courses. Any one of these explanations tears a hole in the approved system.

Pererius apparently did not see their bearing, for instance, on the theory of the solid spheres."
On this matter, see also Baldini and Coyne, *Louvain Lectures,* 34 n. 40.

36. Williams, *Common Expositor,* 189.

37. Benedictus Pererius, S.J., *Commentariorum et disputationum in Genesim,* 4 vols. (Cologne, 1601), 3:962.

38. Ibid., 1:92.

39. Benedictus Pererius, S.J., *Prior tomus commentariorum et disputationum in Genesim* (Ingolstadt, 1590), 66–67. The relative length of Pererius's section on the centrality and immobility of the earth may very well reflect his knowledge of, and opposition to, the Copernican theory. I thank Professors Thomas Settle and Nancy Siraisi for this suggestion.

40. George E. Ganss, S.J., *Saint Ignatius' Idea of a Jesuit University* (Milwaukee: Marquette University Press, 1956), is a good study of Jesuit education and how it related to medieval and Renaissance educational ideas and practices. John W. O'Malley, S.J., *The First Jesuits* (Cambridge, Mass.: Harvard University Press, 1993), 243–64, has perceptive remarks on the Jesuit adoption of both scholasticism and humanism. On the scientific interests and activities of the Jesuits, see the introductory studies by John L. Heilbron, "Science in the Church," and Steven J. Harris, "Transposing the Merton Thesis: Apostolic Spirituality and the Establishment of the Jesuit Scientific Tradition," *Science in Context* 3 (1989): 9–28 and 29–65 respectively, and Rivkha Feldhay, "The Cultural Field of Jesuit Science," in *The Jesuits: Cultures, Sciences, and the Arts, 1540-1773,* ed. John W. O'Malley, S.J., et al. (Toronto: University of Toronto Press, 1999), 107–30.

41. Richard S. Westfall, "Galileo and the Jesuits," in *Metaphysics and Philosophy of Science in the Seventeenth and Eighteenth Centuries: Essays in Honor of Gerd Buchdahl,* ed. R. S. Woolhouse (Dordrecht: Kluwer, 1988), 58. This essay is reprinted in Richard S. Westfall, *Essays on the Trial of Galileo* (Notre Dame: University of Notre Dame Press, 1989), 31–57.

42. Pineda, *Commentarii in Ecclesiasten,* (1619), fol. 128, and (1620), fol. 111.

43. F. Laplanche, "Herméneutique biblique et cosmologie mosaïque," in *Les églises face aux sciences du Moyen Age au XXe siècle,* ed. O. Fatio (Geneva: Droz, 1991), 34, quotes and translates into French this passage from the Paris, 1621, edition of Lapide's commentary. The Latin passage is in Migne, *Scripturae Sacrae cursus completus,* 5:81.

44. Nicholas Copernicus, *On the Revolutions,* ed. J. Dobryzycki, trans. and comm. Edward Rosen (Baltimore: Johns Hopkins University Press, 1978), 5.

45. On this important issue, see Ugo Baldini, "*Legem impone subactis:* Teologia, filosofia e scienze matematiche nella didattica e nella dottrina della Compagnia di Gesu (1550–1630)," in his *Legem impone subactis: Studi sul filosofia e scienza dei gesuiti in Italia, 1540-1632* (Rome: Bulzoni, 1992), 19–73; William A. Wallace, *Galileo and His Sources: The Heritage of the Collegio Romano in Galileo's Science* (Princeton: Princeton University Press, 1984), 126–48; Lattis, *Between Copernicus and Galileo,* 30–38; Rivkha Feldhay, "The Use and Abuse of Mathematical Entities: Galileo and the Jesuits Revisited," in Machamer, *Cambridge Companion to Galileo,* 80–145. L. M. Carolino offers an important and nuanced analysis of the "tense relationship" between Jesuit philosophers and mathematicians in early modern Portugal in his "Philosophical Teaching and Mathematical Arguments: Jesuit Philosophers versus Jesuit Mathematicians on the Controversy of Comets in Portugal (1577–1650)," *History of Universities* 16 (2000): 65–95. For another analysis of this struggle in the context of Galileo's career, see Mario Biagioli, *Galileo, Courtier: The Practice of Science in an Age of Absolutism* (Chicago: University of Chicago Press, 1993), 211–44.

46. The relationship between the adoption of Aristotelianism and Thomism and the critique of the mathematical sciences is developed by Feldhay, "Knowledge and Salvation," 195–213; Rivkha Feldhay and M. Heyd, "The Discourse of Pious Science," *Science in Context* 3 (1989): 109–42, esp. 123–27; and Feldhay, *Galileo and the Church.* For details on the return to "solid and uniform doctrine" under Acquaviva, see Ugo Baldini, "*Uniformitas et soliditas doctrinae:* Le censure *librorum* e *opinionum,*" in his *Legem impone subactis,* 75–119; GBB, 135–64. Blackwell discerns a sharp conflict between obedience to traditional positions and anti-Aristotelian science and presents evidence suggesting that certain "anti-Copernican" Jesuit scientists, such as Clavius and Scheiner, were more attracted to the new astronomy than has been thought. The spread of new cosmological ideas in the Society of Jesus is charted in three excellent studies by Ugo Baldini: "La *nova* del 1604," "Dal geocentrismo alfonsino al modello di Brahe: La discussione Grienberger-Biancani," and "Nuova astronomia e vecchia fisica: La reazione dei filosofi del Collegio Romano alla nuova cosmologia (1604–1618)," all in his *Legem impone subactis,* 155–82, 217–81. Also see the more recent works by Michel-Pierre Lerner, "L'entrée de Tycho Brahe chez les jésuites ou le chant du cygne de Clavius," in *Les jésuites a la Renaissance: Système éducatif et production du savoir,* ed. Luce Giard (Paris: Presses Universitaires de France, 1995), 145–85; W. G. L. Randles, *The Unmaking of the Medieval Christian Cosmos, 1500-1760: From Solid Heavens to Boundless Aether* (Brookfield, Vt.: Ashgate, 1999), esp. 90–99; and Alfredo Dinis, "Was Riccioli a Secret Copernican?" in *Giambattista Riccioli e il merito scientifico dei gesuiti nell'età barocca,* ed. M. T. Borgato (Florence: Leo S. Olschki, 2002), 49–77.

47. Edward Rosen, *Copernicus and the Scientific Revolution* (Malabar, Fla.: Krieger, 1984), 188–91, and Westman, "Copernicans and the Churches," 88–89. Another example of Dominican criticism of the Copernican theory is a work published in 1616 in which Paul Minerva, O.P., of Bari argued that the motion of the earth contradicts reason, sense, and the Bible. On Minerva and Copernicanism, see Lynn Thorndike, *A History of Magic and Experimental Science* (New York: Columbia University Press, 1941), 6:63–64.

48. GBB, 103–6, 265–67. As Westman points out (in "Copernicans and the Churches," 95 and 109 nn. 62–63), it appears significant that Bellarmine knew Lorinus personally and had a copy of Pineda's *Commentariorum in Iob libri tredecim* in his library. It is also undeniable that Bellarmine was influenced by the unsigned letter to the reader in Copernicus's masterpiece, a letter authored by Andreas Osiander. This letter argues that astronomers' theories do not assert anything concerning physical reality but are only mathematical constructions designed to "save the phenomena." If other Jesuits examined Copernicus's work directly, they were probably influenced by this letter. On Osiander's letter, see Edward Rosen, "The Exposure of the Fraudulent Address to the Reader in Copernicus' *Revolutions,*" *Sixteenth Century Journal* 14 (1983): 283–91.

PART TWO

THE STORM BREAKS

THREE

SETTING THE STAGE

Galileo in Tuscany, the Veneto, and Rome

Michael H. Shank

Galileo belongs not only to world history but also to the world of symbols. Indeed, when playwrights and composers recreate their own lives of Galileo to help their audiences work through the problems of our time, we can be sure that this Galileo has transcended his historical time and place.[1] Even though part of him has escaped forever from the historical box, our challenge as historians is to temper the iconic and universal Galileo—the first physicist, the symbol of the conflict of science and religion—with a more concrete one. My task in this essay is to set the stage for the more specific discussions that follow. Because the allotted space permits only a few soundings of Galileo's world, I will pass quickly or in silence over many favorite achievements, tribulations, and episodes. Instead I will try to frame those achievements and tribulations with brief attention to the three primary political contexts in which Galileo lived and moved. Recapturing Galileo's strong regional roots and loyalties—seeing him as a Tuscan and a Florentine citizen in now familiar, now alien settings—will attune us more keenly to his own changing context, particularly to the political opportunities and snares that he encountered when he travelled about the peninsula.

The point I wish to illustrate briefly is simple. Not only did the differences between the longer-term political structures of the Grand Duchy of Tuscany, the Venetian Republic, and the Papal States matter to Galileo's life, as he moved from one context to another, but also the shorter-term contingencies within these political contexts made a difference. Galileo knew the ways of the Grand Duchy of Tuscany best, and he learned much from his years in the Venetian Republic, but these experiences evidently did not fully prepare him to read the contingencies he would face among the Tuscans who ran Rome under Urban VIII.

The Problem of Galileo as Italian

The word 'Italy' nowadays blends a geographical designation (the Italian peninsula) with a unified political entity (the Republic of Italy) to which we often ascribe much more cultural unity than we probably should. To treat Galileo as an Italian in this modern sense, however, is to miss political and cultural distinctions that mattered greatly to him and his contemporaries.

In terms of his self-consciousness, it is significant that Galileo never crossed the Alps. He therefore probably never experienced the full force of the culture shock that would drive a Venetian, a Roman, and a Florentine traveling abroad to overlook their differences and embrace their similarities as fellow inhabitants of the peninsula. He may have glimpsed such kinship in Venice, a cosmopolitan city with thousands of Greek and German residents, or even in Padua, where he interacted with many foreign students. But I would wager that Galileo thought of himself as an Italian—if at all—only in a basic geographical sense, by contrast with the "transalpines."[2] In most circumstances, differences, not similarities, would have been of paramount concern south of the Alps.

And with good reason: Italy is far from homogenized even now, though it has been united for almost a century and a half. In the age of Galileo, Italy was emphatically not united. The peninsula was divided into many competing, often warring, territories controlled by different political regimes, even as individual cities within the same territory retained some autonomy in law and the administration of justice.[3] Galileo was involved primarily with three of these regimes: the Grand Duchy of Tuscany, where he was born, lived most of his life, and died; the Venetian Republic, where he spent eighteen years in midlife; and the Papal States, where he spent a number of months, some exhilarating, others harrowing, that changed the course of his life and gave him the symbolic afterlife that we all know. I will briefly discuss each regime in turn. For the sake of specificity, and to keep the political in tension with the personal, I will associate each regime with a leading individual with whom Galileo had an important interaction—the Grand Duchess of Tuscany, Christina of Lorraine, whose actions and family started off his academic career, developed his patronage trajectory, and provided the stimulus to his first clash with Rome; Fra Paolo Sarpi of the Venetian Republic, a powerful intellect and political activist who led Venice in defying a papal interdict and proved to be one of Galileo's most stimulating conversation partners; and Maffeo Barberini/Urban VIII of Rome, a friend and

Figure 3.1.   The Italian peninsula in the seventeenth century. Courtesy of the University of Wisconsin Cartography Laboratory.

fellow Tuscan who tried to meet the political challenges of ruling the Papal States during the Thirty Years' War on the battlefield of astrology and natural magic.

The broader context for all these happenings was a Europe still working through the aftershocks of the Protestant Reformation (figure 3.1).[4] In the sixteenth and seventeenth centuries, it was far from clear how things would settle out. Territorially and politically, the Spanish and Austrian Habsburgs cast the longest shadow over European politics. Nominally, and often in fact, they controlled much of the territory from the Danube to the North Sea, as well as the Iberian peninsula, Lombardy, and southern Italy. Portions of this territory were contested, often along both political and religious lines, and not only in Germanic lands. Most notably, the northern portion of the Low Countries revolted against the Habsburgs in the late sixteenth century and became independent in the early seventeenth century, fighting Spain for eighty years. Under the circumstances, France worried with good cause about encirclement and pursued vigorous anti-Habsburg policies. France, Spain, and the Holy Roman Empire each had strong interests on the Italian peninsula, which became their open battleground in the early seventeenth century.

Amid papal worries that a general council of the Church might seek to limit the power of the pontiff, the Council of Trent had first convened in 1545 to respond to the Protestant Reformation, finally completing its substantive work almost twenty years later.[5] Meanwhile the wars of religion tore France apart (the St. Bartholomew's Day massacre of Huguenots, instigated by Queen Catherine of Medici, occurred in 1572). Religious tensions would continue throughout Galileo's life. He never knew the Thirty Years' War by the name that we give it. Begun in 1618, this series of devastating political and religious conflicts involving most of Europe would outlast Galileo by six years. Throughout the entire era, a larger-scale politico-religious war threatened with more or less seriousness in the East, as the Ottoman Empire consolidated its hold on the Balkans.

South of the Alps, Habsburg Spain controlled the greater part of the Italian peninsula and the nearby islands: not only all of southern Italy and Sicily but also Sardinia, Genoa, and the Duchy of Milan. France continued to have designs on some of these territories as well. The papacy controlled central Italy and was encroaching northward: under Urban VIII, the Papal States would annex Urbino in an anti-Habsburg (and anti-Medici) move. The Duchy of Tuscany was expanding, not only in dignity (by becoming a grand duchy after 1569), but also in territory (notably by taking over Siena). Even so, Spain still controlled two seaport enclaves in Tuscany. From one ruler to the next, Tuscany would lean now toward the Habsburgs, now toward the French.[6]

Venice in the late sixteenth and seventeenth centuries was no longer the leading European power that it had been in the fifteenth century, but it was still a formidable regional power. (It had supported Pisa's efforts, ultimately unsuccessful, to throw off the Florentine yoke in 1499, a reminder of the tenuous unity of Tuscany.) As Venice lost more outposts in the Mediterranean and saw the spice trade from overland Levantine routes disappear, it expanded its hold on the nearby mainland, the Veneto. Even in decline, the trappings of its former grandeur and its attitude were still everywhere in evidence. In an age of absolute rulers, Venice was almost the sole voice of republican freedom and vigorously fought all attempts—especially those of the papacy—to encroach on its liberties. Suspicious of both pope and emperor, Venice tended to ally itself with France.[7]

Although they were nearly contiguous, the three regimes that concern us here had dramatically different political cultures. Since their aspirations for the peninsula conflicted, the interest of each often lay in limiting its neighbors' influence, and therefore in seeking alliances with its neighbors' enemies. After all, these regimes dealt with one another through ambassadors.

For reasons such as these, we should think of Galileo, not as an Italian who never left his country, but as a Tuscan and Florentine citizen who, without leaving Italy, lived and traveled abroad and had to feel his way in a difficult political landscape. Pisan by his birth and Florentine by paternity, upbringing, and self-designation, he was a subject of the Grand Duke of Tuscany and was closely linked to the two cities in which the Medici court spent most of its time. He was deeply devoted to his own Tuscan vernacular as a literary language.[8]

Galileo was marked as a Florentine citizen when he moved to the Veneto or visited Rome. The rolls of the University of Padua listed the citizenship of its professors as a matter of course, as did trial documents. When Galileo became embroiled in lawsuits in the Veneto, he was always identified as a Florentine citizen: that is, as a foreigner. Since the *Operations of the Geometrical and Military Compass* (1606) and the *Sidereal Messenger* (1610) were both printed in Padua, both were dedicated from abroad to Cosimo, as heir to the Tuscan throne in the first case, as grand duke in the other. The title page of each work identifies Galileo as a "Florentine gentleman" in uppercase letters, but the point here goes beyond the matter of personal pride. "Florentine citizen" was Galileo's legal status while he was serving abroad, as "public mathematician" in a republic with its own publication laws and a long history of tensions with the papacy. Indeed, the *Geometrical Compass* was published during the papal interdict discussed below.[9] When he would publish in Rome or Florence, different laws applied. Where we typically see regional differences, Galileo and his contemporaries saw strongly marked political and legal differences, to say nothing of cultural ones.

The Grand Duchess Christina and Cultural Politics in Tuscany

As Galileo's homeland and the jurisdiction in which he spent most of his life, Tuscany has the first claim on our attention. The territory, in flux for more than a century, was a duchy when Galileo was born in Pisa in 1564. Five years later, Cosimo I of Medici was elevated to Grand Duke of Tuscany—a spectacular, century-long trajectory for a family that had made its wealth in banking when Florence was a republic run by a city council. Crucial to the transformation were the two Medici who had become pope in the early sixteenth century. The first, Leo X (1513–21), not only supervised the Fifth Lateran Council but also gave such extravagant patronage to the arts that the indulgences supplying his need for money kicked off the Reformation. The second, Clement VII (1523–34), was the first pope to hear, apparently with approbation, a detailed exposition of the Copernican system[10] and the pope who would end the Florentine Republic by appointing a Medici relative Duke of Tuscany.

When the seventeen-year-old Cosimo I of Medici took up the succession in 1537, few suspected that he would end his reign several decades later as grand duke, ruling over a more centralized Tuscany expanded by annexation, thinking grand thoughts about the role of the Medici in European affairs. He built alliances by marriage, starting with his own: Eleanor of Toledo, daughter of the Spanish viceroy of Naples, came from a family closely allied with the Habsburg emperor, Charles V.[11] Such Medici alliances with the Habsburgs would worry all subsequent non-Medici popes who, in their role as territorial princes, fretted about finding the Papal States completely encircled.

Like his forebears, Cosimo I was a leading patron of the arts whose many commissions celebrated his Augustan aspirations (he shared with Emperor Augustus a horoscope in which Saturn ruled Capricorn).[12] Cosimo's cultural politics also included the reopening of the university in Pisa with new statutes consonant with absolutism: the grand duke effectively controlled the administration through an appointed overseer who reported vacancies and other items requiring a ducal decision.[13] At Cosimo's death, the senate of forty-eight members had clearly become acculturated as well: this republican ghost of Florence's past rubber-stamped the Medici succession by electing Cosimo's son Francesco as the new grand duke.[14]

If, in looking around Pisa and Florence as a youth, Galileo had somehow missed the message that patronage was a viable option in Tuscany, he would have picked up clues at home. His father Vincenzio was a musician, a musical theorist, and a composer who headed a household dependent on the patronage of Giovanni de' Bardi. It was to Bardi, the head of a Florentine Camerata heavily involved in the upper levels of musical culture, that Vincenzio Galilei had dedicated his *Dialogo* of 1581. Galileo was evidently drawn into the circle too: in 1585, soon after dropping out of the University of Pisa as a twenty-year-old, he built an organ for Jacopo Corsi, another aristocratic member of the Camerata who would take over the patronage of the Camerata after Bardi's departure.[15]

The Corsi connection concretely illustrates Galileo's ties to the highest strata of cultural life in Tuscany. The Florentine Camerata was one of the main providers of theatrical displays for the Medici in the late sixteenth and early seventeenth centuries, and associates of this group continued to be heavily involved in Medici productions. Although the aged Vincenzio Galilei (d. 1591) seems to have been cut out of the event, all other members of the Camerata were involved in planning celebrations for the 1589 Medici wedding, the most spectacular politico-cultural event of late-sixteenth-century Tuscany.[16]

In 1589, Cosimo I's son, Ferdinand I de' Medici, a former cardinal burdened by the unexpected duty of perpetuating the family line, was married in France (by proxy) to Christine de Lorraine, the favorite granddaughter of the notorious Queen Mother of France, Catherine de Medicis.[17] The pageantry associated with the celebration lasted from late April to early June, from Christina's arrival in Tuscany through the five weeks of festivities following her meeting with her husband in Florence. The scale of the festivities remains unprecedented in the annals of Tuscany. The twenty-five-year-old Galileo must have taken in some of the events: beyond the impossibility of avoiding the processions, tournaments, and displays, his father's associates in the Florentine Camerata, like Jacopo Peri and Giovanni de' Bardi, were heavily involved in writing the text and music of the *intermedi* performed between the acts of the plays. These initial efforts would lead directly to Peri's composition in 1597 and 1600 of the earliest extant operas.[18]

It was on the occasion of the 1589 celebration that Galileo, like the rest of Florence, probably first laid eyes on the Grand Duchess Christina (figure 3.2). Although historians of science pay little attention to her, she helped set the stage for at least three turning points in his life. Her arrival in Tuscany coincides with the beginning of a long patronage relationship with the Medici. Since celebratory events are among the most opportune occasions to seek favors, it was perhaps fortunate that a vacancy in mathematics at Pisa occurred in the early summer of 1589. Thanks to Guidobaldo del Monte's intervention, Grand Duke Ferdinand appointed Galileo, who did not have a degree, to the professorship.[19] He had just become a beneficiary of Cosimo I's policy of academic centralization, and he would again. The Medici appointment, which allowed him to compile a proper academic track record, began a lifelong association with universities, initially in Pisa, then in Padua, and finally with a thirty-year Pisa sinecure once again arranged by grand ducal fiat. A second turning point was Christina's search for a tutor for her young Cosimo in the early 1600s, which led Galileo to a more intimate involvement with the family. Beginning in the summers of his Padua years, it would extend nearly four decades into the reigns of Christina's son, Cosimo II (1609–21), and her grandson, Ferdinand II (1621–70), ending with Galileo's death in 1642. Precipitating the third turning point was the grand duchess's intellectual curiosity about the apparent tension between the moving earth of Copernicanism and the stationary earth of the Bible. Galileo learned at second hand about Christina's question from his friend Castelli, a Pisa professor and Benedictine monk.[20] He therefore answered her in writing, first indirectly in the *Letter to Castelli* and eventually in the much longer *Letter to the Grand Duchess Christina*. His layman's foray into biblical interpretation would change his life forever, drawing denunciations to the Roman Inquisition under Pope Paul V and helping to set in motion the 1616 censure of Copernicanism as a physical theory.

Longevity would also characterize Galileo's relationships with several of his father's patrons, associates, and their families. Long after Vincenzio's death, the ties with Jacopo Corsi were still alive: in 1598, even though he was in Padua, Galileo

CHRISTINA LOTARINGIA MAGNA DVC. ETRVRIÆ.

Figure 3.2.   Grand Duchess Christina of Lorraine. From Rafael Gualterotti, *Della descrizione del regale apparato fatto . . . per le nozze della serenissima Madama Cristina di Lorena . . .* (Florence, 1589), frontispiece.

succeeded in borrowing from his father's old patron two hundred scudi, slightly more than his professor's salary for that year.[21] Vincenzio Galilei's associate Jacopo Peri took charge of Medici court music after 1591. Galileo knew not only him but also his son Dino very well. The fact that the surviving correspondence between Galileo and the two Peri occurs during Galileo's visits to Rome (in 1624 and in 1630) suggests that the families saw each other regularly when they were together in Florence.[22] Peri's son Dino, who had studied law at Pisa, eventually became a mathematician under Galileo's tutelage. He was also one of the people summoned by the Inquisition to hear the sentence against Galileo in 1633. Thanks to Galileo's sponsorship, whose postcondemnation touch was not entirely leaden, the grand duke appointed Dino Peri to the chair of mathematics at Pisa in 1636.[23] Those events were still far in the future. In the fall after the celebration of the 1589 Medici wedding, Galileo was just beginning his own academic career in mathematics.

Galileo Tastes Republicanism: Padua, Venice, and Fra Paolo Sarpi

Within three years of his Pisa appointment, Galileo had a better job, but it was much farther from home. Just the same, the invitation to join the university in Padua as lecturer in mathematics was a signal recognition of his competence. In September 1592, the Venetian senate received Padua's recommendation for Galileo's appointment: he had earned the highest praise for his work at Pisa and was reputedly "the first in this profession." The Venetian senators thought they were getting the best mathematician available when they voted nearly unanimously (149 to 8) to appoint him.[24] The contrast between this vote and the grand ducal fiat that led to the position in Pisa must have been particularly salient as Galileo took leave of Tuscany: he "requested and obtained permission from the grand duke at Florence to accept the [Padua] position."[25]

The invitation to join the University of Padua was both a significant and a foreign accolade. When Galileo traveled from Tuscany to Padua, he was not only leaving the land of his birth by crossing the Apennines but also leaving a territory governed by an absolute ruler for one governed by a republic. He may have encountered some sneering. Florence, according to some later-sixteenth-century Venetian analysts, was a former republic undone by its flaws: the excessive individualism of its citizens, its tendency to put artisans in charge of government, and its servility to the pope. The Florentines richly deserved the grand ducal fate that had befallen them.[26] There may have been some resentment too: Venice had been steadily losing its wool trade to the Florentines.[27] Galileo's move also traded one system of law for another, one set of relations with the papacy for another—to say nothing of other aspects of culture: the Paduan and Venetian vernaculars would replace his beloved Tuscan, while the Florentine musical world would make way for the Venetian one that his father had attacked.[28]

There were compensations, however. His teaching load at Padua was exceedingly light by comparison with that of American academics—the equivalent of thirty hours of lectures a year.[29] These focused frequently on elementary introductions to astronomy (the *Sphere* and the *Theorica planetarum*) and also on Euclid. More rarely, he lectured on Ptolemy's *Almagest* and the *Mechanical Questions* attributed to Aristotle.[30]

At the beginning of his appointment, Galileo expressed delight at the free time he enjoyed,[31] some of which permitted exploratory work in natural philosophy and astronomy. During these years, Galileo came to see the "Copernican opinion" as a particularly fruitful premise for new physical explanations of difficult problems (notably the tides), and he devoted increasing attention to the physics of motion.[32]

Following the births of his three children after 1600,[33] Galileo's grumbling about money problems and about the long hours spent in tutoring well-to-do students grew louder. Retrospectively, one gets the sense that Galileo had always considered the move to Padua temporary. He certainly had never burned his bridges to Tuscany. Throughout the Paduan period, the Medici court continued to show interest in him and brought him back to Tuscany when it needed him. Already in late 1601 Galileo was contacted about teaching the young heir to the Tuscan throne, the future Cosimo II. In 1608 the Grand Duchess Christina renewed a request for summer tutoring and let Galileo know that in her eyes he was "the most highly prized mathematician in Christendom."[34]

Padua had said as much, of course, but compliments like these kept alive Galileo's hope of returning to Tuscany, perhaps with an appointment free of all obligations save that of writing books. Even though his salary jumped between 60 and 75 percent every seven years,[35] Galileo complained to the Florentine court several times, in letters on behalf of himself as well as the renowned anatomist Girolamo Fabricio d'Aquapendente, about the constraints inherent in a Paduan appointment. It is not customary, he said, "to obtain from a republic, however splendid and generous, a stipend without serving the public. . . . In the end, I cannot hope for such an accommodation from anyone other than an absolute prince."[36]

Was republicanism standing in his way? In fact, Padua was not so bad, as Galileo demonstrated when he turned down a non-Tuscan absolute ruler. In 1604, a patronage arrangement with the Gonzaga court in Mantua fell through when Galileo demanded 40 percent more money than they were offering and 30 percent more household support.[37] That year, Galileo also had his first documented brush with the Inquisition, and Venetian republicanism showed its colors. In April, Galileo's former scribe, Silvestro Pagnoni, denounced him for casting horoscopes and telling clients that the predictions were indubitable—an accusation nicely tailored to the condemnations of astrological determinism by the Council of Trent and the papal bull of 1586.[38] Galileo's friend and colleague, the prominent Aristotelian natural philosopher, Cesare Cremonini, was also denounced—for the second time.[39] Informed of the charges, the Venetian government discounted the testimony of Pagnoni as that of a mortal enemy. The rectors of Padua were accordingly upset when they discovered that someone had forwarded to Rome the charges that they had dismissed. Nothing came of the denunciations, which ended up on the desk of Cardinal Camillo Borghese, head of the Roman Inquisition and, within the year, Pope Paul V.[40]

THE EFFIGIES
of Father Paul the
Venetian.

Figure 3.3. Fra Paolo Sarpi. From *The Letters of the Renowned Father Paul*, translated by Edward Brown (London: Chiswell, 1693), frontispiece. Courtesy of the Department of Special Collections, General Library System, University of Wisconsin–Madison.

The pope would soon have bigger—and more political—fish to fry, notably Fra Paolo Sarpi (figure 3.3). One of the most stimulating and compromising of Galileo's friends in the Veneto, Sarpi was a Servite friar, a man of extraordinarily wide-ranging interests and one of the finest critical minds of his generation. Among historians of science, he is famous for receiving the 1604 letter in which Galileo sketched his approach to free fall and for telling Galileo in 1608 that a Dutchman had built a new spyglass. Among his compatriots, however, Sarpi was most admired for his intellectual leadership in defending the Venetian Republic against Rome.

In the spring of 1606, Pope Paul V had excommunicated the Venetian senate and placed the entire Veneto under interdict for failing to rescind laws that the papacy considered injurious to its prerogatives. This was not merely a severe ecclesiastical censure; it was also an international political incident that drew the attention of Europe, often with sympathy for the Venetian cause.[41] The interdict, which Rome blamed on Sarpi's heretical advice to the republic, deprived an entire territory of the sacraments, as the papacy forbade the clergy from offering the mass or administering other sacraments. The move assumed that the fear of nefarious eternal consequences would force the prelates and the faithful to place unbearable pressure on the rulers to comply with the papal will.

Sarpi interpreted the interdict as a political act rather than an ecclesiastical censure. To defend this position, he published anonymously a vernacular version of the fifteenth-century conciliar theologian Jean Gerson's argument that excommunication, if used abusively, should be resisted. The Jesuit Cardinal Bellarmine immediately wrote a refutation from Rome, unleashing a small pamphlet war.[42] The republic's heavy-handed threats ensured that almost all prelates in the Veneto, using Gerson's rationale and Sarpi's advice, would disobey the pope. The churches remained open and the clergy continued to administer the sacraments, including the baptism of a baby named Vincenzio, the son of Marina Gamba and an "unknown father" in the summer of 1606.[43] Sarpi, whom the pope excommunicated for failing to appear before the Inquisition in Rome, was hated in the Vatican and among the Jesuits, and he returned the favor. Bellarmine's fellow Jesuits, whom Sarpi considered duplicitous papalists likely to betray the republic, were expelled from the Veneto. Urban VIII would later mention the expulsion as one of three events that had caused him "unspeakable grief."[44]

The resistance that Sarpi spearheaded proved unprecedented and had an unprecedented result. A century earlier, Julius II's interdict on Venice had forced the city to give in. This time, it became clear after a year that Venice would continue to resist, forcing the papacy to lift the interdict unilaterally in April 1607.[45] That fall, a dagger blow to the temple nearly dispatched Sarpi. The would-be assassins took refuge in Rome before receiving a pension from the pro-Habsburg viceroy of Naples.[46]

Sarpi recovered, and his news about the spyglass in 1608 unwittingly set the stage for events that catapulted Galileo into fame, out of the Veneto, and back to Tuscany, where the Florentine professor would get the appointment he wanted. His friends worried that he would also get more than he wished. There was much hand-wringing at the news of Galileo's departure—not least on the part of Cesare Cremonini: "*Il signor* Galileo would do well not to leave the freedom of Padua."[47] Galileo's Venetian friend Sagredo made a similar point about the unique freedom of his republic in a letter, adding: "I am much disturbed by your being in a place where the authority of the friends of the Jesuits counts heavily."[48] It is this quip that Brecht turned into the lines: "*Sagredo:* Don't go to Florence, Galileo. / *Galileo:* Why not? / *Sagredo:* Because it's run by monks." (Scene 3)—presumably to be understood generically as the members of religious orders.

How jarring this remark sounds when one knows that the antipapal religious policies of the Veneto were framed by Fra Paolo Sarpi, Servite friar, official theologian of the Venetian Republic and anti-Jesuit extraordinaire. Soon after Galileo left Padua for good, Sarpi wrote to a French Huguenot: "The most important thing is to destroy the Jesuits; if they are defeated, Rome is lost, and if they are out of the way, religion will 'reform' itself of its own accord."[49] Indeed, Sarpi remained an advocate of a strong antipapal alliance between Venice and France, and even with Protestant powers.[50] Whether or not Galileo sympathized with Sarpi's tactics or stance toward Rome, the interdict certainly set the stage for accusations against him. A Dominican in Florence would later use Galileo's friendship and correspondence with Sarpi to impugn his loyalty to the Church.[51]

While Galileo's friends seemed to sense trouble ahead, he did not. His appointment letter was most attractive: it named him "primary mathematician of the University of Pisa and philosopher of the Most Serene Grand Duke of Tuscany, without obligation of lecturing or residing at the university, with a stipend of one thousand Florentine *scudi* a year and the conditions to give him every opportunity to pursue his studies and to complete his writings."[52] His second Medici appointment to Pisa had improved dramatically upon the first: the grand duke had not only matched his (recently doubled) Paduan salary but also removed all the pesky teaching and residency obligations that republican Venice imposed on its professors. On the map, Galileo had come full circle; in most other respects, he was spiraling upwards.

Rome and the Papal States

Oddly, Galileo never returned to Padua or Venice—not once.[53] When he traveled abroad in subsequent years, which was not often, his destination was Rome, a thriving center of European politics and culture. It had not always been so. The city had fallen on terrible times during the mid–fourteenth century, when the popes lived in Avignon and drew the lucrative pilgrim trade away from Rome. One of the low points of papal power likewise occurred during the Great Schism, which ended with the Council of Constance in 1417. The council had deposed three simultaneous popes and elected a new one, drawing justifications from a conciliar theory that, in an emergency, subordinated the authority of the papacy to that of a council (similar arguments would appeal to Sarpi two centuries later). After the council, the papacy returned to Rome and sought to restore power to the office, including its many temporal aspects. The winds of absolutism were blowing briskly in the late fifteenth and sixteenth centuries, and the papacy found them congenial. Popes were most visibly secular princes in the early sixteenth century, when the Borgias ruled and when Julius II returned to Rome a victor after leading his troops in battle. Disgusted, Erasmus thought Julius II was behaving like Julius Caesar. The pope disagreed only with Erasmus's affect: he had a commemorative medal struck with his portrait and the inscription "Julius Caesar Pontifex II."[54]

The territorial prerogatives of the papacy added considerable turmoil to politics in the Italian peninsula. First, they put Rome in the fray, not above it, making its possessions vulnerable to competing territorial interests. Indeed, German and Spanish troops had sacked Rome twice in 1527—a humiliating event that Urban VIII would live in fear of seeing repeated during his own reign. In addition, for the leading families whose sons were cardinals, papal elections provided an opportunity to use the clout, the territories, and the wealth of the Holy See for their families' political interests, ostensibly for the good of the Church. Even the best-intentioned of cardinals could not, once elected, avoid the entanglements of temporal power, or the temptation to use whatever power was available to meet whatever need seemed most pressing. The pope's duties to the Papal States and to his family sometimes overrode any regional loyalties, as was arguably the case for Urban VIII and Tuscany.

The temporal power of the papacy also served to justify nepotism. To protect himself from political intrigue and plots, the pope needed trusted advisors. Who could be more reliable than one's own nephews and brothers in the College of Cardinals and in high administrative positions?[55] For seventeenth-century observers, the excesses of nepotism and the accoutrements of the temporal ruler culminated under the two long-lived popes who were the key actors in the Galileo affair, Paul V (of Villa Borghese and Venetian interdict fame) and especially Urban VIII. It is to the latter that we now turn to illustrate the blend of absolute rule, international politics, astrology, and intrigue that set the stage for Galileo's final decade.

Maffeo Barberini (1568–1644), the future Urban VIII, came from the minor nobility of Florence. Like Galileo, he grew up in the heady environment of an expanding Tuscany suffused with the legacy of Cosimo I's attempts to centralize and celebrate his power.[56] Unlike Galileo, however, Barberini was a product of Jesuit education, first in Florence and later at the Jesuit Collegio Romano, where he acquired his excellent humanist education.[57] After studying law at Pisa, he returned to Rome, where a rich uncle bought him a post in the papal administration just as Galileo started teaching at Pisa. Barberini's own skills helped him rise through the bureaucracy: he proved himself a competent administrator, who, for a time, specialized in flood and drainage problems and got a taste of diplomacy as an envoy to France.

When Galileo returned to Tuscany in 1610, Maffeo Barberini had already been a cardinal for several years. The two men first interacted at a Medici banquet in 1611 when Galileo was at the height of his fame.[58] They developed a very positive relationship that stood Galileo in good stead in 1616, when his *Letter to Castelli* came under scrutiny. Although Cardinal Bellarmine surely resented the ongoing banishment of his own Jesuit order from the Veneto, and Pope Paul V had imposed an interdict on Venice, they did not tar Galileo with Sarpi's brush, as one of Galileo's accusers hoped they would. Cardinal Barberini nevertheless weighed in as a moderating influence in the theological and procedural discussions. On the one hand, he cautioned Galileo in 1616 to confine himself to the bounds of physics and mathematics and to avoid theology, which was not his domain.[59] On the other hand, Barberini reportedly helped temper the wording of the 1616 censure of Copernicanism and later took credit for keeping Galileo's name out of the official decree.[60] The episode did not affect the warm feelings between the two men; on the contrary, during his final years as cardinal, Barberini signed his last letters to Galileo *come fratello,* "as a brother."[61]

Barberini became Pope Urban VIII in 1623, raising high hopes in many quarters but not among the supporters of Spain, who feared Urban's sympathies for France. Galileo was delighted. Although his polemical *Assayer* was already in press, he managed to get his "brother" to accept the dedication and to commission a splendid new title page featuring Urban's papal coat of arms.[62] Many thought Barberini a man of integrity; and he certainly was a man of culture, a scholar, a poet, and a skilled diplomat, even if he had a hot temper. Significantly for the Galileo affair, the Venetian envoys noticed that the pope took pleasure in contradicting his interlocutors. After expressing their views, the Venetians would proceed to offer objections to their own proposals so that the pope himself would leap to the defense of the course of action they really favored.[63] *Pace* Brecht (Scene 9), Urban was probably not a mathematician, in either our own or the seventeenth century's sense of the term.[64] Whether or not he cast his own horoscopes, he did believe in astrology, however, especially after becoming pope, and he used it as a political tool to predict the deaths of cardinals.[65] His election had been the surprising result of a long and polarized conclave, in which the political divisions of the Thirty Years' War were much in evidence. Being only in his mid-fifties, Barberini had not pressed his case: at one point in the balloting, he had even withdrawn in deference to more senior cardinals. Since he was decisively elected in the end (50 to 5), Urban came to believe that God had destined him for the Holy See (figure 3.4).[66]

Fortified by the heavenly confirmations in his own horoscope, those of his relatives, and that of his election, he set about celebrating the Barberini destiny in stylish manner and became the epitome of nepotism. He made his brother Antonio and his nephews Francesco and Antonio (the younger) cardinals; he gave to a third nephew, Taddeo, the job of producing descendants and of ruling the principality of Palestrina, and to a second brother, Carlo, various secular honors. His deathbed query about the propriety of channeling so many riches to his relatives suggests that even he had qualms about the matter.[67]

Figure 3.4.   Ballot for the election of Urban VIII. Maffeo Barberini, center-left, points to the ballot that had been missing in the first tally but that, being found, sealed the legitimacy of his election as pope. Fabio Cristofani, tapestry, Musei Vaticani. Courtesy of the Istituto Centrale per il Catalogo e la Documentazione, Rome.

Part of the wealth Urban passed on to his nephews paid for the Barberini Palace, where Urban VIII's divine election and his family's destiny are celebrated in some notable frescoes. The building was the old Sforza Palace, which Urban's nephews lavishly redecorated as a residence suitable for Taddeo and the Barberini progeny. The palace contains some of baroque Rome's most splendid ceiling frescoes, which express pictorially the Barberini's sense that, upstarts or not, God wanted them to have a place among the old Roman nobility and papal families. The *Divine Wisdom* ceiling fresco painted by Andrea Sacchi between 1629 and 1631 offers a striking blend of astrological symbolism and allusions to the biblical Book of Wisdom (figure 3.5).[68] In the fresco, the sun occupies the central position, in front of which sits Divine Wisdom, an enthroned female figure surrounded by the solar halo. The globe of the earth (with a vast Antarctic landmass attached to Asia) is off-center, in the foreground. It is hard to miss the presence of the constellation Leo on the upper left. The sun in Leo was the central feature of key Barberini horoscopes. In the nativities of both Urban VIII and his nephew Taddeo, Leo (ruled by the sun) was ascending;

Figure 3.5.   Andrea Sacchi, *Divine Wisdom,* fresco, Palazzo Barberini, Rome. Photograph courtesy of John Beldon Scott.

in Urban's election horoscope, the sun—the lord of the ascendant in his nativity—was not only in Leo but also in conjunction with the beneficent Jupiter.[69]

Scott has made the most compelling recent case for seeing in the unique concept of the fresco the fingerprints of Tommaso Campanella, the controversial Dominican friar who had written widely on politics, religion, and Christian astrology and is perhaps most famous for his *Defense of Galileo* (1622) and the utopian *City of the Sun* (1623).[70] At first glance, a connection between Campanella and the Barberini seems odd indeed. The Spaniards had jailed Campanella in Naples for some twenty-seven years. Two months after they released him in May 1626, he was brought to Rome as a prisoner of the Holy Office (the Inquisition) at the behest of Cardinal Antonio Barberini.[71] Once in Rome, however, Campanella's hopes, Urban VIII's fears, and their common anti-Spanish politics drove the two men together. Campanella's blend of natural philosophy, religion, and politics had by this time identified the pope as the best hope for the reunification of Christendom, and he got the pope's attention during a time of great political and personal insecurity, just as the Thirty Years' War inaugurated its most serious fighting on Italian soil.

In this phase, known as the War of Mantuan Succession, France, which supported the heir of Mantua, for the first time went into open battle against the empire, which sought to replace him. Urban VIII, who was taking an anti-Habsburg, pro-French stance for the good of the Papal States, felt both personally under attack and hard-pressed politically on several fronts. His relations with the Holy Roman Empire had never been cozy. Between 1628 and 1631, they were seriously strained. Emperor Ferdinand II did not trust any of Urban's moves or motives, and his statesmen had even threatened to invade the Papal States. Spain, which Urban—and nearly everyone else—tried to contain, wanted to move troops north from Naples through the Papal States in order to join the fray and was prepared to do so without permission. Spain's ambassador argued vociferously against the pope's visit to the Spanish national church in Rome, outraging Urban, who placed it under interdict. Cardinal Richelieu—his subordinate in religion—was putting strong pressure on Urban to join an anti-Spanish military league. In May 1629, imperial troops were seizing the Alpine passes into Italy, and its mercenaries were talking openly about another sack of Rome. The threat worried Urban into sleeplessness. By July, he had armed seven thousand infantry and eight hundred cavalry to resist them.[72]

The Spanish faction in Rome had long had excellent reasons to wish for a new pope favorable to its cause. Since eclipses portended the deaths of important persons, the Spanish used forthcoming eclipses to give credibility to the rumors of the pro-French Pope's impending demise. Their goal, according to D. P. Walker, was to scare the pope to death.[73] Although Urban had survived several earlier eclipses, he seems to have been especially frightened of those predicted for the years 1628 (lunar in January, solar in December) and 1630 (solar in June). To neutralize these nefarious influences, especially the moon's extinction of the sun that was so important in the Barberini horoscopes, the pope used the services of Campanella, who was still a prisoner of the Inquisition. In 1628, the two men sequestered themselves in the pope's apartments.[74] To compensate for the defective heavens, they resorted to the rituals of Marsilio Ficino's astral and natural magic by lighting candles and torches that substituted for the luminaries and planets. Walker describes part of the ritual as follows: "There was Jovial and Venereal music, which was to disperse the pernicious qualities of the eclipse-infected air and, by symbolizing good planets, to expel the influences of bad ones. For the same purpose, they used stones, plants, colours and odours, belonging to the good planets (that is, Jupiter and Venus). They drank astrologically distilled liquors."[75]

In 1629, when anonymous conspirators printed Campanella's descriptions of these rituals without his consent, he was embarrassed—and Urban VIII was furious.[76] Campanella returned to jail, and his book was examined for heresy. When his book was cleared of suspicion, the pope freed him in 1629. The incident undermined Campanella's bid for a post as adviser to the Inquisition,[77] but it did not remove him from the pope's entourage—at least not until the pope helped him flee to France in 1635—much later than Campanella's enemies had hoped.

The identities of the conspirators did not surface until several years later, but their names are familiar ones in the Galileo affair: they included Campanella's fellow Dominicans Niccolò Ridolfi, the Florentine former Master of the Sacred Palace (i.e., book censor) and head of the order after 1629; Niccolò Riccardi, a consultor to the Inquisition who would replace Ridolfi as Master of the Sacred Palace in June 1629 and serve as censor of Galileo's *Dialogue;* and Raffaello Visconti, a mathematician who served as an aide to Riccardi and would offer to soften the pope's opposition to Galileo's tidal argument for the motions of the earth.[78] With the help of Riccardi, Ridolfi proceeded to embarrass both the pope and Campanella by publishing book 7 of the *Astrologica,* which the author had withheld.

If Campanella's plausible reconstruction of the plot can be believed, his fellow Dominicans were part of a much larger pro-Spanish conspiracy. These men had access to a new horoscope predicting the death of the pope for February 1630. They circulated this open secret to the Spaniards, who sent their cardinals back to Rome for the anticipated conclave.[79] The well-kept secret was that, after Urban's death, Ridolfi would ascend the papal throne, as his powerful horoscope indicated (a western conjunction of all seven planets in Scorpio). He was not yet cardinal, but he expected that the emperor would get him the post.[80] For the pope personally, such rumors and activities were, of course, most unpleasant. Much farther-reaching, however, were their political consequences. Clearly, if the pope's counterparts in his many negotiations took his imminent death seriously, they would have every reason to stall until they could deal with a new, perhaps pro-Spanish pontiff. Like their Spanish counterparts, the German and—no doubt most unsettling to Urban— the French cardinals soon traveled to Rome as well. The preparations for a conclave were in vain: in February 1630, Urban VIII did not die, even if his brother Carlo did.[81]

It was against the backdrop of these political and personal intrigues that Galileo stepped onto the Roman scene in May 3, 1630. He had published his *Assayer* in Rome without a snag right after Urban's election. He was now seeking permission to publish a new work on the tides, which we now know as the *Dialogue.* The book involved some risks because it not only broached Copernicanism but also argued that the motion of the earth was the only sensible explanation for the sloshing of the tides. Although Galileo knew that Urban's insistence on divine omnipotence and omniscience made him skeptical of definitive accounts of the cosmic order,[82] he remained optimistic about obtaining the requisite permissions.

On May 18, the very day on which he had a friendly preliminary meeting with Urban VIII, a handwritten newsletter announced that the mathematician and astrologer of the Grand Duke of Tuscany, who was in town to get a book against the Jesuits published, had predicted that the pope and his nephew Taddeo would die.[83] When Galileo heard about "his" prediction toward the end of the month, he was horrified and, through an intermediary, immediately contacted the pope. It is a testimony to both Urban's savvy about Roman intrigues and the strength of their friendship that the pope discounted the rumor, to Galileo's immense relief.[84]

Meanwhile, on May 24, 1630, before the solar eclipse predicted for June, Galileo received an invitation from an old correspondent, Orazio Morandi, the learned Florentine abbot of Santa Prassede in Rome. The two men were to dine together two days later, along with a representative of the Florentine Inquisition and Raffaello Visconti, the Dominican aide to Riccardi.[85] Like most everyone else, Galileo had no idea that Morandi was behind Urban's February death horoscopes (and many other astrological predictions),[86] or that Visconti—in addition to being part of the pro-Spanish conspiracy against Campanella—was also associated with Morandi's astrological activities.[87]

Within two weeks, belief in the predictions of the pope's death had produced two victims. Among the condemned executed on the Campo dei Fiori on June 9 were a Bolognese priest "favored by many cardinals" and his female accomplice. The priest had been so convinced of the pope's imminent death and of his own promotion to cardinal under Urban's successor that he had performed necromantic rituals with the woman to accelerate the event. After the two had abjured, the authorities hanged him and immured her.[88]

For Galileo, by contrast, things were looking up. His negotiations seemed to be going well. He had not yet received Niccolò Riccardi's signature, which was required to make printing arrangements. But Raffaello Visconti, the recent dinner companion who had tried to soften the pope's opposition to Galileo's tidal argument for the motion of the earth, reported that permission to publish the book now seemed to depend on only a few minor corrections. Galileo left Rome for Florence in late June.[89] The June eclipse had also passed; the pope had survived once again. The summer was marred by the arrival of plague in Florence (until the fall of 1632) and by the death of Federico Cesi. With the prospective Roman publisher of his new book gone, Galileo started to think about publishing in Florence, which he had not done before.

Two weeks after Galileo's departure, in mid-July 1630, the emperor's troops entered Mantua, which they plundered, while the Protestant king, Gustavus-Adolphus II of Sweden, invaded Germany. Urban counted the conjunction of these events, according to Pastor, as a source of "unspeakable grief."[90] In Rome, the authorities had now identified Morandi as the source of the death horoscopes. In mid-July, Urban had Morandi arrested and put on trial. After several months of revealing testimony, the abbot would die in jail, from illness according to the official report, from poisoning according to rumor.[91]

The Barberini family continued to use Campanella's services. Print and embarrassment had not invalidated his natural magic: the friar performed his astral rituals once more, this time to "ward off an influx that threatened the son of Don Taddeo" in December 1630. On the legal front, Urban was cracking down on the subculture of papal prognostication that the Morandi trial had uncovered. Campanella reportedly was helping the pope draft an antiastrological bull.[92] By March 1631, Morandi's friend

Visconti, the assistant to Niccolò Riccardi and advocate for Galileo's tidal argument, had been banished from Rome.[93]

On April 1, 1631, Urban VIII issued the bull *Inscrutabilis,* whose opening sentence reads:

> The inscrutable height of the judgments of God does not suffer that the human intellect, enchained by the dark prison of the body, raising itself above the stars, should with abominable curiosity presume not only to explore the arcana [that are] hidden in the divine mind and unknown to the most blessed spirits themselves, but also, by an arrogant and dangerous example, to peddle them as [already] explored, in contempt of God, to the disturbance of the commonwealth and the danger of princes.[94]

These words articulate, with the full force of papal power, the familiar Barberini theme of the limitations of human knowledge before God's omniscience and power. Here they are not part of an epistemological discussion among friends; rather, they form the doctrinal foundation for a condemnation of astrological practices that threatened the pope, the Papal States, and hence all of Christendom. After reiterating Sixtus V's condemnation of judiciary astrology, Urban's bull turned its focus to predictions made by "mathematicians, diviners, haruspices, prophets, or others who practice judicial astrology" about "the status of the Christian Republic, or the Apostolic See, or the life or death of the sitting Roman Pontiff, including his blood relatives to the third degree inclusive" (i.e., Taddeo Barberini's son). The bull banned all "judgments, prognostications, or precognitions and predictions based upon the foregoing" as well as their transmission orally or in writing.[95] In Walker's summary, "[T]hese are to be considered crimes of *lèse-majesté,* punishable by death and confiscation of goods."[96]

During these months, Urban's international political situation grew even worse. In early 1631, Cardinal Richelieu drew up an alliance between France and the Protestant king of Sweden, Gustavus-Adolphus II, causing the pope great distress and placing him in a very damaging political situation. To an uncharitable eye, Urban's past support of France looked as if it had favored the Protestants, as did his refusal to fund the Habsburgs' Catholic League.

Back in Florence, Galileo still did not have Riccardi's permission to publish, so he contacted the Tuscan secretary of state to put pressure on the Roman Inquisition's censor. Even then Riccardi proved slow and reticent.[97] Finally he insisted on reviewing only the preface and conclusion, with responsibility for the imprimatur resting with the Florentine inquisitor. Three weeks after the bull, he claimed to be worried about the pope's intentions, and he probably had even better reasons for diffidence. While Riccardi's involvement with the Spanish and Morandi was still a secret, he had lost Visconti.[98]

Galileo's politically astute friends in the Veneto sensed trouble brewing long before he did. In 1631, upon learning of Galileo's problems in getting the *Dialogue* approved, they interceded on his behalf: astonishingly, Padua offered to reappoint him.[99] If Galileo's friends in the Veneto thought that grand ducal protection would mean little in case of conflict, they would have been right. Various clues suggest that the pope had little respect for the twenty-year-old grand duke, Ferdinand II, and that his own Tuscan origins did not translate into pro-Tuscan decisions. In 1630, for example, Urban excommunicated all magistrates of public health in Florence during the recent plague: their emergency measures infringed upon clerical prerogatives.[100] More telling yet, Urban VIII in 1631 completed the annexation of the Duchy of Urbino to the Papal States, while Grand Duke Ferdinand II, recently married to the Duke of Urbino's daughter, passively stood by.[101] The Medici now regretted their support of Barberini's election: the grand duke would soon block the policies of Urban and his nephews.[102] In short, Urban VIII had no political grounds for favoring either Ferdinand II or his protégé—quite the contrary. Indeed, 'protégé' was a misnomer: Ferdinand, who had not lifted a finger to keep Urbino from Urban, was not likely to put up a fight for Galileo, whose friendship with the pope, not his patron's protection, was his main asset in Rome.

Meanwhile, Spain was putting exceptional pressure on Urban to give financial support to the emperor against France and placing the worst interpretation on the pope's allegiances. In January 1632, Cardinal Borgia, who headed the Spanish faction, accused the pope of not caring for the Catholic religion. In March, speaking for the king of Spain, Borgia laid the blame for any injury to the Catholic religion at the feet of the pope.[103] Cardinal Borgia made these serious charges—effectively accusations of betrayal—with such disrespect that he and Cardinal Barberini almost came to blows.

It was against the background of these threats and insecurities that Galileo's newly published book arrived in Rome in early March of 1632. Its new title, *Dialogue on the Two Chief World-Systems, Ptolemaic and Copernican,* avoided all reference to the tides as an argument for Copernicanism, as the pope had recommended. The book also reproduced verbatim the preface that Riccardi had sent to Galileo. While complying with these Roman instructions, however, the book's typography seemed to wink at the reader. The front matter contained, as expected, the imprimaturs of the Florentine authorities (in italic font). On the same page were also (in roman font) two imprimaturs by Roman authorities—oddly, since Florence was not in their jurisdiction—including one with Riccardi's name, against his explicit instructions.[104] With such roman/italic coding, the roman font of the preface hinted at its non-Florentine origin. Indeed, except for the dedication to the grand duke, the rest of the book was printed in italic.

The *Dialogue* also had a conclusion that no one in Rome had seen. Galileo had been told to add, as a final peroration consistent with Riccardi's preface, "the reasons pertaining to divine omnipotence which Our Master [the pope] gave him."[105] He had in fact complied on the last page of the *Dialogue*. While he had the good sense not to set these words in roman type, what he did was not much better: he had the dim-witted Simplicio mention God's "infinite power and wisdom" and specifically refer to the inability of the human intellect to conceive of all the ways divine power and knowledge could proceed. As the Special Commission's investigative report would note in its indictment of September 1632, however, Galileo had "put the medicine of the end in the mouth of the fool."[106] This "medicine of the end" was much more than a doctrine personally favored by Maffeo Barberini. After April 1631, it had become the highly public "medicine of the beginning" in the bull *Inscrutabilis*—the very ratio-nale with which Urban VIII tried to counter the threats that astrological predictions of his death posed to his papacy, his family, his negotiations, and his foreign policy.

These circumstances make it much easier to understand why, according to the Tuscan ambassador, "His Holiness exploded into great anger and suddenly told me that even our Galilei had dared to enter where he should not have, into the most serious and dangerous subjects which could be stirred up at this time."[107] This last phrase is far from univocal, but we can eliminate many sources of ambiguity. The *Dialogue* was not advocating Lutheran theology or an alliance with Gustavus Adol-phus; it was not plotting against the pope with the Spanish or imperial causes in Rome. The pope's phrase applies poorly to a discussion of Copernican theory. Con-versely, Urban had issued the bull *Inscrutabilis* of 1631 precisely to parry what he con-sidered "one of the most serious and dangerous subjects . . . at this time." Although the *Dialogue* contained no horoscopes that predicted the death of the pope or a mem-ber of his family to the third degree of consanguinity, it implicitly endorsed a view opposed to the theoretical preamble of the emergency bull. Galileo's book did sug-gest that the divine mind was not *inscrutabilis*: it not only placed the omnipotence ar-gument "in the mouth of the fool" but also declared "a certain equality between the human and the divine intellect in the understanding of geometrical propositions," as another indictment alleged.[108] The dangerous attitude that stood behind the con-demned astrological practices concerned not only the exploration of the divine ar-cana but the treatment of them "as explored": that is, as a settled matter rather than one inscrutably remote from the human intellect. In the tension of the current politi-cal situation, secular rulers were opposing Urban, and cardinals like Richelieu and Borgia were manipulating him or treating him with outright contempt. Now even Galileo had betrayed him, not only mocking him but also undermining his bull. So was the stage set for Galileo's last and most difficult trip to Rome.[109]

Epilogue

The height of God's judgments may have been inscrutable for nonpapal astrologers and mere mortals, but the divine plan for the Barberini was revealed for posterity in the family's horoscopes and palazzo ceilings. By 1632, Sacchi's *Divine Wisdom* fresco in the Barberini Palace had been dry for a year, a graphic reminder of both Campanella's influence with the pope and his nephews and the omnipresence of astrology in baroque Rome. Horoscopes and celestial signs were double-edged swords, however, and Urban VIII discovered that his enemies in the Spanish faction could wield them as deftly as he could. But for every ill, there was a remedy. Thanks to Campanella's astral-magical rituals, the eclipses had passed harmlessly. And thanks to the harsh penalties of Urban VIII's bull, the threats posed by future predictors, if not future predictions, had also passed.

As we have seen, these local events fit into larger matrices of Roman, Italian, and European politics against which we can appreciate how crucially the Galileo affair hinged on the contingencies of its context. One can imagine situations in which Galileo's chiding of the pope's theological views would have had innocuous consequences. While it is more difficult to imagine a layman within reach of Rome jesting in print about the premise of a recently promulgated bull, the Veneto was a territory in which he might have done so with impunity.

Galileo, however, had left the Veneto long ago. Building on a relationship with the Medici that began with Grand Duke Ferdinand I and continued with Grand Duchess Christina, Galileo had returned to Tuscany to become their son Cosimo II's mathematician and philosopher, funded by an absentee professorship in the University of Pisa. Twenty years later, these arrangements were still intact, and, as originally promised, Galileo was still writing books. His latest, in progress during Christina's regency for her grandson Ferdinand, was ready for the press during the youthful apprenticeship of Galileo's third grand duke.

In 1631, when Cesi's death, Riccardi's reticence about approving the book, and the plague in Tuscany raised obstacles to printing the book in Rome, Galileo considered Genoa but finally settled on Florence. Venice was evidently not in the running. After issuing several books in the Veneto and in Rome, it seemed fitting, perhaps, finally to publish in the grand duchy. In the early 1630s, however, with Urban VIII personally and politically threatened from several quarters, Galileo would discover what it meant to treat the pope with Venetian flippancy under the nominal protection of an inexperienced grand duke instead of the backing of the Venetian Republic.

The last decade of Galileo's life further sharpened the political contrasts between the three regimes. Paolo Sarpi had been far more dangerous to Rome than Galileo ever would be. Yet, following his excommunication, Sarpi had walked about the Veneto freely and continued to serve as a priest in defiance of Rome. Galileo, who had abjured but never been excommunicated, had to endure the rest of his life under house arrest in Arcetri; he would not re-enter Florence alive. During those years, Galileo would have occasion to remember Venice, notably as he was finishing his *Discourses on Two New Sciences* and worried about the fate of his manuscript. He contacted Fra Fulgenzio Micanzio, Sarpi's aide during the interdict and successor as consultant to the Venetian Republic. In the end, the manuscript traveled across the Alps to be printed by Elsevier in Leyden, in another republic with even more heretics than Venice.

Politics ruled not only life but also death. Of the main characters discussed in this paper, Sarpi was the first to die, in 1623. The Venetians buried the old excommunicated patriot near the west door of San Michele in Isola. The Grand Duchess Christina died in 1636. When Galileo died in 1642, Urban was still alive and still felt betrayed: the pope personally denied Florence's request for a burial with honor. As if to confirm the sixteenth-century Venetians' judgment about the Medici's excessive deference to Rome, it would take almost a century for Galileo's body to make it into Santa Croce. For his part, Urban VIII vindicated the disgraced Visconti's astrological prowess by dying in 1644, as the Dominican mathematician had predicted in 1630.[110] For the Barberini nephews, Urban's death was the beginning of the end: they no longer plucked their judgment from the stars. After reading the eyes of the Romans, they fled to France, as Campanella (d. 1639) had done, and like him, they died in exile. The books and the frescoes are still with us.

Notes

This essay is a revised and expanded version of an illustrated talk. For comments and criticisms useful to the transformation, I thank especially Carla Bagnoli, Tom Broman, Ernan McMullin, David Lindberg, Jonathan Seitz, Domenico Sella, and Carol Troyer-Shank.

1. Bertolt Brecht, *The Life of Galileo,* trans. John Willett (London: Methuen, 1986); Phillip Glass, *Galileo Galilei,* opera with libretto by Mary Zimmerman (2001); see Jay Pasachoff, "Nevertheless, It Moves Us," *Science* 298 (2002): 1557–58.

2. The note to the reader that prefaces the *Dialogo,* in the words of the Roman censor Niccolò Riccardi, draws a distinction between Rome, Italy, and foreign nations. See Galileo Galilei, *Dialogo sopra i due massimi sistemi del mondo tolemaico e copernicano,* ed. Libero Sosio (Turin: Einaudi, 1970), 8; for Riccardi's suggestion, see Galileo Galilei, *Opere di Galileo Galilei* (hereafter *OGG*), ed. Antonio Favaro (1890–1909; reprint, Florence: Giunti Barbèra, 1968), 19:329. See also John Dickie, "Imagined Italies," in *Italian Cultural Studies: An Introduction,* ed. David Forgacs and Robert Lumley (Oxford: Oxford University Press, 1996), 19–23, esp. 19–20. One of the first uses of 'Italy' to designate a political entity (twelfth century) is counterintuitive to modern ears: it refers to fourteen cities north of Rome. See Harold Berman, *Law and Revolution: The Formation of the Western Legal Tradition* (Cambridge, Mass.: Harvard University Press, 1983), 388.

3. Gaetano Cozzi, "Considerazioni sull' amministrazione della giustizia nella Repubblica di Venezia," in *Florence and Venice: Comparisons and Relations,* vol. 2, *Cinquecento,* ed. Sergio Bertilli, N. Rubinstein, and Craig Smyth (Florence: La Nuova Italia, 1980), 101–33, esp. 105–8.

4. For an excellent introduction and overview, see Domenico Sella, *Italy in the Seventeenth Century* (London: Longman, 1997).

5. Richard J. Blackwell, *Galileo, Bellarmine, and the Bible* (hereafter *GBB*) (Notre Dame: University of Notre Dame Press, 1991), chap. 1.

6. John R. Hale, *Florence and the Medici: A Pattern of Control* (London: Thames and Hudson, 1977), 164–65.

7. William J. Bouwsma, *Venice and the Defense of Republican Liberty: Renaissance Values in the Age of the Counter Reformation* (Berkeley: University of California Press, 1968), 108, 246.

8. Dante della Terza, "Galileo, Man of Letters," in *Galileo Reappraised,* ed. Carlo Golino (Berkeley: University of California Press, 1966), 1–22.

9. For Cosimo and for Rome, the inscription "Printed at Padua in the author's house" (the house of a Florentine citizen) may have carried more weight than "With license of the Superiors," since the latter were all under interdict.

10. About Clement and Copernicus, see Annibale Fantoli, *Galileo: For Copernicanism and for the Church,* 2d ed., Studi Galileiani 3 (Vatican City: Vatican Observatory Publications, 1996), 24–25.

11. Hale, *Florence and the Medici,* 12–13, 104–6, 118–22, 138.

12. Janet Cox-Rearick, *Dynasty and Destiny in Medici Art: Pontormo, Leo X, and the Two Cosimos* (Princeton: Princeton University Press, 1984), esp. 276–79. Against the evidence in Cox-Rearick on which he relies, Mario Biagioli's *Galileo, Courtier: The Practice of Science in an Age of Absolutism* (Chicago: University of Chicago Press, 1993) contrives an argument for Jupiter as the planet of the Medici dynasty (chap. 2). See also Mario Biagioli, "Playing with the Evidence," *Early Science and Medicine* 1 (1996): 69–105; and Michael H. Shank, "How Shall We Practice History? The Case of Mario Biagioli's *Galileo, Courtier,*" *Early Science and Medicine* 1 (1996): 106–50.

13. Paul Grendler, *The Universities of the Italian Renaissance* (Baltimore: Johns Hopkins University Press, 2002), 74–75; Michael Segre, *In the Wake of Galileo* (New Brunswick: Rutgers University Press, 1991), 6–7.

14. Hale, *Florence and the Medici,* 144.

15. Howard Mayer Brown, "How Opera Began: An Introduction to Jacopo Peri's *Euridice* (1600)," in *The Late Italian Renaissance, 1525-1630,* ed. Eric Cochrane (New York: Macmillan, 1970) 405, 412; Tim Carter, "Music and Patronage in Late Sixteenth-Century Florence: The Case of Jacopo Corsi (1561–1602)," *I Tatti Studies: Essays in the Renaissance* 1 (1985): 71, 98.

16. Brown, "How Opera Began," 411–12; James Saslow, *The Medici Wedding of 1589: Florentine Festival as Theatrum Mundi* (New Haven: Yale University Press, 1996), 27–29.

17. Catherine had arranged the marriage, witnessed the contract, and provided the dowry, including all of her own Florentine possessions. She died just before the wedding itself, leaving Christina nearly all of her wealth. See Paul Van Dyke, *Catherine de Médicis,* 2 vols. (New York: Scribner's, 1924), 2:356–58; and Jean Héritier, *Catherine de Médicis* (Paris: Librairie Académique Perrin, 1985), 543, 555.

18. Brown, "How Opera Began," 416–17; Saslow, *Medici Wedding,* 2–3, 19. In 1597, Jacopo Peri (1561–1633) set to music the *Daphne* of Ottavio Rinuccini (1564–1621). The latter's *Euridice* of 1600, the only early opera to survive entire, was written for the wedding of King Henry IV of France and Maria de' Medici. Mary Zimmerman's libretto for Phillip Glass's opera *Galileo Galilei* gives Vincenzio Galilei (d. 1591) too much credit for the birth of the genre: the libretto ends with an imaginary opera composed by Vincenzio, performed for the Medici court, with a

youthful Galileo and the grand duchess in attendance. See Claude Palisca, *The Florentine Camerata: Documentary Studies and Translations* (New Haven: Yale University Press, 1989).

19. Fantoli, *Galileo,* 54.

20. Eric Cochrane, "The Florentine Background of Galileo's Work," in *Galileo, Man of Science,* ed. Ernan McMullin (New York: Basic Books, 1967), 119; *GBB,* chap. 3.

21. Carter, "Music and Patronage," 70, 97. For Galileo's salary, see Antonio Favaro, *Galileo e lo studio di Padova,* 2 vols. (Padua: Antenore, 1966), 2:109.

22. See Jacopo Peri's greetings to Galileo in 1624 in *OGG,* 13:176. Jacopo also relayed message about the costs of Galileo's son's doctoral celebration; *OGG,* 13:424. In 1630, one of Dino's letters recounts in detail his father Jacopo's near-mortal illness and sudden recovery (*OGG,* 14:100–102).

23. Summary in *OGG,* 20:283–84, 505. Galileo had chosen Dino Peri as one of the witnesses to his will in 1638 (*OGG,* 19:523), but it was the younger man who preceded Galileo in death in 1640.

24. "[S]i puo dir che sia il principale de questa professione." Favaro, *Galileo e lo studio,* 2:107; Manlio Pastore Stocchi, "Il periodo veneto di Galileo Galilei," in *Storia della cultura veneta,* ed. Girolamo Arnaldi and Manlio Pastore Stocchi, 6 vols. (Vincenza: Neri Pozza Editore, 1984), 4:37.

25. Ludovico Geymonat, *Galileo Galilei: A Biography and Inquiry into His Philosophy of Science,* trans. Stillman Drake (New York: McGraw-Hill, 1965), 16.

26. Bouwsma, *Venice,* 168–71.

27. Domenico Sella, "The Rise and Fall of the Venetian Wool Industry," in Cochrane, *Late Italian Renaissance,* 340.

28. On the tensions between Tuscany and Padua concerning the Florentine language, see Michael Sherberg, "The Accademia Fiorentina and the Question of Language: The Politics of Language in Ducal Florence," *Renaissance Quarterly* 56 (2003): 26–55. "In music, Florence and Venice were as different as they were in politics and economics." James Haar, "Music in 16th Century Florence and Venice: Some Points of Comparison and Contrast," in Bertilli, Rubinstein, and Smyth, *Florence and Venice,* 2:268. On Vincenzio Galilei's polemics against the Venetian Zarlino, see Claude Palisca, *Humanism in Italian Renaissance Musical Thought* (New Haven: Yale University Press, 1985), 265–79. On Galileo and the Tuscan vernacular, see della Terza, "Galileo, Man of Letters," 1–22, at 21. The Florentine Academy, which had the goal of promoting and standardizing the Florentine language, had invited the twenty-four-year-old Galileo to present a paper on the geography of Dante's hell. He later became a member in his own right and made lifelong friends, including the painter Cigoli. On Cigoli, see Sarah E. Booth and Albert Van Helden, "The Virgin and the Telescope: The Moons of Cigoli and Galileo," in *Galileo in Context,* ed. Jürgen Renn (Cambridge: Cambridge University Press, 2001), 193–216.

29. Eric Cochrane, *Florence in the Forgotten Centuries, 1527-1800* (Chicago: University of Chicago Press, 1973), 171.

30. *OGG,* 19:119–20 (1592–1604).

31. Cochrane, *Florence,* 171.

32. Fantoli, *Galileo,* 68–72. On the tides, Paolo Sarpi, on whom more below, was probably the chief stimulus; see Libero Sosio, "Il copernicanismo di Sarpi," in *Fra Paolo Sarpi dei Servi di Maria,* ed. Pacifico Branchosi and Corrado Pin (Venice: Comune di Venezia, 1986), 171–78.

33. Galileo and Marina Gamba (d. 1607; *OGG,* 19:425) conceived two daughters and a son between 1600 and 1606. Galileo kept his name off of all three baptismal records. Pagnoni, Galileo's nasty former live-in employee, called Marina a whore before the Inquisition. See *OGG,* 19:218; and Antonino Poppi, *Cremonini e Galileo inquisiti a Padova nel 1604* (Padua: Antenore, 1992), 59 n. On the matter of the two Marinas, see Fantoli, *Galileo,* 87–88.

34. *OGG,* 10:214–15. Claims about the low status of mathematicians in this period should be treated with skepticism.

35. He started at 180 florins (1592–98), jumped to 320 (1599–1606), and then to 520 (1607); Favaro, *Galileo e lo studio,* 2:108–10.

36. Ibid., 1:352, citing *OGG,* 6:77; see also *OGG,* 10:164–66.

37. Galileo probably had misgivings about the reliability of Vincenzio Gonzaga as well. See Favaro, *Galileo e lo studio,* 2:96–99.

38. Poppi, *Cremonini e Galileo,* 55–61; on Trent, see D. P. Walker, *Spiritual and Demonic Magic from Ficino to Campanella* (1958; reprint, Notre Dame: University of Notre Dame Press, 1975), 219; Germana Ernst, "Astrology, Religion, and Politics in Counter-Reformation Rome," in *Science, Culture, and Popular Belief in Renaissance Europe,* ed. Stephen Pumphrey, Paolo Rossi, and Maurice Slawinski (Manchester: University of Manchester Press, 1991), 249–50. Pagnoni also testified that Galileo had attended mass only once in a year and a half and that Galileo's mother, for whom Pagnoni was monitoring her son's behavior, had denounced him to the Inquisition in Florence, claiming that he did not go to confession. For an excellent overview of the Inquisition in Venice, see Brian Pullan, *The Jews of Europe and the Inquisition of Venice, 1550-1670* (Oxford: Blackwell, 1983), chaps. 1–4.

39. The 1599 inquest had charged Cremonini with explicating Aristotle's *De anima* along the lines of Alexander of Aphrodisias, thus violating the decrees of the Fifth Lateran Council of 1513, which specifically ordered the confutation of those opinions. Poppi, *Cremonini e Galileo,* 70.

40. Ibid., 65–69. In 1611, however, someone initiated an Inquisition procedure to see if Galileo was mentioned in an earlier Cremonini inquiry. Sergio Pagano and Antonio G. Luciani, eds., *I Documenti del processo di Galileo Galilei* (Vatican City: Pontifical Academy of Sciences, 1984), 219.

41. The controversial laws extended to the mainland legislation that had long been in place in Venice proper. They dealt with the republic's control of Church land, new buildings, ecclesiastical appointments, and civil court jurisdiction over priests—sore points all. Bouwsma, *Venice,* 340, 344–47, 401–4.

42. Ibid., 395–98, 631.

43. *OGG,* 19:220.

44. Ludwig von Pastor, *The History of the Popes from the Close of the Middle Ages,* trans. E. Graf, 40 vols. (London: Hodges and Kegan Paul, 1891–1953), 28:259.

45. Bouwsma, *Venice,* 412–13.

46. David Wootton, *Paolo Sarpi: Between Renaissance and Enlightenment* (Cambridge: Cambridge University Press, 1983), 10.

47. Favaro, *Galileo e lo studio,* 1:361.

48. *OGG,* 11:170–72; Stillman Drake, *Discoveries and Opinions of Galileo* (New York: Doubleday, 1957), 66–68.

49. Pastor, *History of the Popes,* 26:26.

50. Wootton, *Paolo Sarpi,* 11.

51. See the deposition of Tommaso Caccini, O.P., before the Roman Inquisition; *OGG,* 19:309–10; and *GBB,* 116.

52. *OGG,* 10:369.

53. When Galileo tried to resume direct communication with Sarpi on February 12, 1611, the first letter to his friend since he had left the Veneto was also his last (*OGG,* 10:46–50).

54. Charles Stinger, *The Renaissance in Rome* (Bloomington: Indiana University Press, 1985), 235–37. Not surprisingly, Venice had clashed with Julius II, who had also excommunicated the senate and imposed the interdict, eventually forcing the city to capitulate; Bouwsma, *Venice,* 97–101.

55. John Beldon Scott, *Images of Nepotism: The Painted Ceilings of Palazzo Barberini* (Princeton: Princeton University Press, 1991), 4.

56. Cox-Rearick, *Dynasty and Destiny,* 188–98.

57. Pastor, *History of the Popes,* 28:26–28.

58. Fantoli, *Galileo,* 136.

59. Ibid., 179–80.

60. Pastor, *History of the Popes,* 29:44; Fantoli, *Galileo,* 262–63.

61. *OGG,* 13:48–49, 118–19.

62. Nicely reproduced in Pietro Redondi, *Galileo Heretic,* trans. Raymond Rosenthal (Princeton: Princeton University Press, 1987), fig. 1 facing p. 150.

63. Pastor, *History of the Popes,* 28:37.

64. The pope thought he had some competence in astrology and was so considered by nonspecialists; Germana Ernst, "Scienza, astrologia e politica nella Roma barocca: La biblioteca di Don Orazio Morandi," in *Bibliothecae selectae da Cusano a Leopardi,* ed. Eugenio Canone (Florence: Leo S. Olschki, 1993), 246, and *Religione, ragione e natura: Ricerche su Tommaso Campanella e il tardo Rinascimento* (Milan: Franco Angeli, 1991), 218. Giambattista Riccioli's designation of Urban as "most learned in astronomical matters" (astronomicarum rerum scientissimus), which Pastor cites as evidence (*History of the Popes,* 29:43), is suspect as a description: Riccioli's evidence consists of Urban's condemnation of Copernicanism, which Riccioli endorses. See *Almagestum novum* (Bologna, 1651), vol. 1, pt. 2, bk. 9, sec. 4, p. 488.

65. Walker, *Spiritual and Demonic Magic,* 205.

66. He was not alone in seeing the outcome as miraculous; Pastor, *History of the Popes,* 28:1–24, esp. 18, 23–24.

67. Ibid., 28:37–47; Scott, *Images of Nepotism,* 3.

68. Scott, *Images of Nepotism,* 4–5, 41–44, and chap. 5, esp. 81–86.

69. Ibid., 70, 75–80.

70. George Lechner, followed by Scott, sees an ironic Copernican message in the fresco. See George Lechner, "Tommaso Campanella and Andrea Sacchi's Fresco of Divina Sapienza in the Palazzo Barberini," *Art Bulletin* 58 (1976): 97–1108, esp. 108, and the letter in *Art Bulletin* 59 (1977): 309; also Scott, *Images of Nepotism,* 38. To be sure, Campanella did ascribe central importance to the sun in his utopia (and in his program for the Sacchi fresco) and also defended Galileo's right to inquire into Copernicanism (Campanella appreciated a powerful anti-Aristotelian weapon in any guise). Despite assertions to the contrary in the secondary literature, there is no good evidence that Campanella ever became a heliocentrist in an astronomical sense; the fresco, in the absence of other evidence, does not decide the issue. He wrote to Galileo in 1611—before any condemnations—that he had "written four books, in the physical

rather than the mathematical manner, on the motions of the stars against Ptolemy and Copernicus." Later pronouncements suggest that he remained undecided. See Germana Ernst, ed., *Campanella* (Rome: Istituto Poligrafico e Zecca dello Stato, 1999), 102; Thomas Campanella, *A Defense of Galileo, the Mathematician from Florence,* trans. Richard J. Blackwell (Notre Dame: University of Notre Dame Press, 1994), 26–28; Bernardino Bonansea, "Campanella's Defense of Galileo," in *Reinterpreting Galileo,* ed. William A. Wallace (Washington, D.C.: Catholic University of America Press, 1986), 205–39, esp. 213; John Headley, *Tommaso Campanella and the Transformation of the World* (Princeton: Princeton University Press, 1997), 82–83, 167.

71. Léon Blanchet, *Campanella* (1920; reprint, New York: Burt Franklin, 1971), 54–55.

72. Pastor, *History of the Popes,* 28:219–60, esp. 220–21, 236–37, 243, 259.

73. Walker, *Spiritual and Demonic Magic,* 206.

74. Ernst, "Scienza, astrologia," 220; Scott, *Images of Nepotism,* 73–75.

75. Walker, *Spiritual and Demonic Magic,* 207, 205–10; the rationale for the procedures appears on 223.

76. The "De siderali fato vitando" was book 7 of his *Astrologica* (Lyon [?], 1629). The relevant section (chap. 4, art. 1) appears in Ernst, *Campanella,* 660–61; summary in Ernst, "Scienza, astrologia," 218–20.

77. Pastor, *History of the Popes,* 29:40, 420; Walker, *Spiritual and Demonic Magic,* 207–8.

78. *OGG,* 16:113 (June 3, 1630).

79. Ernst, "Scienza, astrologia," 220–21; Fantoli, *Galileo,* 334. Campanella's letter to Urban VIII, written from Paris in April 1635, lays out the details; see Ernst, *Campanella,* 125–34, esp. 128–29.

80. Ernst, *Campanella,* 127–29; Ernst, "Scienza, astrologia," 221.

81. Ernst, "Astrology," 266–67.

82. Fantoli, *Galileo,* 322. Urban's view was not an aberration: Sarpi held a similar, possibly more pervasive, skepticism about all human conclusions. See Luisa Cozzi, "I *Pensieri* di Fra Paolo Sarpi," in Branchosi and Pin, *Fra Paolo Sarpi,* 146.

83. Scott, *Images of Nepotism,* 72 n.; *OGG,* 14:103; Fantoli, *Galileo,* 336–37.

84. Fantoli, *Galileo,* 336–37 (June 3).

85. *OGG,* 14:107; 10:555. On the five letters between the two men (1613–30), see Ernst, "Scienza, astrologia," 227–29.

86. Morandi's horoscopes of Campanella (Ernst, *Religione, ragione,* 158). Galileo, and Urban VIII (Ernst, "Astrology in Counter-Reformation Rome," 266–67) consist of handwritten astrological data entered on copies of the same *printed* blank—a small hint of the large-scale production of such things in Rome.

87. Brendan Dooley, *Morandi's Last Prophecy and the End of Renaissance Politics* (Princeton: Princeton University Press, 2002), offers much useful information on Morandi and his context despite its sometimes speculative narration. He suggests with some plausibility that Ridolfi and Riccardi may have obtained a manuscript of the last book of the *Astrologica* from Morandi's abbey library (p. 164), allowing them to print the book in Rome with a false Lyon imprint.

88. Ernst, *Religione, ragione,* 274; Ernst, "Astrology," 265–66 (where the date should read "1630" instead of "1600").

89. Fantoli, *Galileo,* 337–39; *OGG,* 14:113.

90. Pastor, *History of the Popes,* 28:259–60.

91. Ernst, "Scienza, astrologia," 229.

92. Walker, *Spiritual and Demonic Magic,* 209–10; Ernst, however, argues that Campanella was too terrified to be involved; Ernst, *Religione, ragione,* 279.

93. Fantoli, *Galileo,* 372; Dooley, *Morandi's Last Prophecy,* 181.

94. *Bullarum, diplomatum et privilegiorum Sanctorum Romanorum Pontificum . . . Editio,* 25 vols. (Turin: Sebastian Frank and Henrico Dalmazzo, 1857–72), 14: 211–14, esp. 211. Dooley's translation is unreliable (Dooley, *Morandi's Last Prophecy,* 177–78).

95. *Bullarum, diplomatum,* 14: 212.

96. Walker, *Spiritual and Demonic Magic,* 206, 209–10.

97. Fantoli, *Galileo,* 339–43.

98. Maurice Finocchiaro, ed., *The Galileo Affair: A Documentary History* (hereafter *GA*) (Berkeley: University of California Press, 1989), 206–10.

99. Favaro, *Galileo e la studio,* 2:16–17. Frajese has argued that Galileo's interactions with the Roman Inquisition in 1633 "would not have been *technically possible*" had he stayed in the Venetian Republic. In Venice, the permission to publish had shifted largely to Venice's secular Council of Ten and an extradition based on a book approved by this body and the Venetian inquisitor "would have been, to say the least, rather difficult." The most famous counterexample to Venetian reluctance to extradite is no doubt Giordano Bruno in 1593; Vittorio Frajese, "Venezia e la chiesa durante i decenni galileiani," in *Galileo Galilei e la cultura veneziana,* ed. Istituto Veneto di Scienze, Lettere ed Arti (Venice: Istituto Veneto di Scienze, Lettere ed Arti, 1995), 120–21; Pullan, *Jews of Europe,* 46.

100. Jacopo Riguccio Galluzzi, *Istoria del Granducato di Toscana . . . ,* 2d ed., 8 vols. (Livorno: G. T. Masii, 1781), 6:30–31; Carlo Cipolla, *Faith, Reason, and the Plague in Seventeenth-Century Tuscany* (New York: Norton, 1979), 6.

101. Furio Diaz, *Il Gran Ducato di Toscana: I Medici,* ed. Giuseppe Galasso (Turin: Unione Tipografica Editrice Torinse, 1976), 378.

102. "Beyond his open actions in diplomatic and military matters, he did not fail to operate covertly by means of the party of cardinals hostile to the Barberini." Ibid., 381.

103. Pastor, *History of the Popes,* 28:287–89.

104. *GA,* 209–10.

105. Pagano and Luciani, *I documenti,* 112; *GA,* 354 n. 57.

106. *GA,* 221.

107. *GA,* 229 (slightly modified).

108. *GA,* 222.

109. Galileo's behavior makes one wonder if he never expected to live with the consequences of the *Dialogue.* Perhaps we should take more seriously what looks at first glance like a rhetorical flourish, namely his plea of Mar. 7, 1631, to the Tuscan secretary of state for a swift permission to publish "so that, *while I am still alive,* I may know the outcome of my long and hard work" (*GA,* 208, emphasis mine).

110. A. Bertolotti, "Giornalisti, astrologi e negromanti in Roma nel secolo XVIII," *Rivista Europea,* n.s. 9, vol. 5 (1878): 466–514, esp. 496.

FOUR

GALILEO'S THEOLOGICAL VENTURE

Ernan McMullin

In 1613, as the fame of Galileo's astronomical discoveries spread, Galileo for the first time faced the real possibility that the Church would, on theological grounds, oppose the Copernican alignment of earth and sun that the new discoveries seemed to confirm. In a worried letter to his friend Benedetto Castelli, he marshaled some more or less commonsense considerations that he thought should deter the Church authorities from acting precipitately in regard to the new cosmology. The letter later came into the hands of the theologians of the Holy Office in Rome, so they would have been aware of the arguments it contained against banning the Copernican earth/sun theses. But ban them they did in early 1616. His arguments had obviously not deterred them from making more fateful a decision than they could ever at the time have imagined.[1]

As the debate in Rome over the theological acceptability of the new ideas grew ever more intense in 1614 and early 1615, Galileo set himself down to a more serious attempt at exegesis. His critics had already made it known that, in line with the decrees of the recently concluded Council of Trent, they were emphasizing the authority of the fathers of the Church, who, according to the critics, were unanimous in holding the earth to be at rest in the center of the world with the sun and planets circling it, as a number of texts in the earlier books of the Bible clearly took for granted. So Galileo, probably alerted by some theologian friends to the possibility of finding support for his case in the fathers themselves, turned to the composition of a more considered essay that would lay out the case in a manner that would, he hoped, convince the Roman theologians to draw back from what he regarded as a disastrous mistake on the Church's part.

Formally titled as a letter to the dowager Grand Duchess Christina of Lorraine, mother of his patron and former pupil Cosimo II de Medici, the document (so far as we can tell) never came to the notice of the Roman authorities in the crucial months leading up to the decision to ban the Copernican innovation on the grounds of its being "contrary to Scripture." So the arguments it so ably advances did not directly affect the discussions of the Holy Office and its consultors. Nevertheless, its interest to us is great because, together with the letter to Castelli, it presents the case that the Roman *periti* (theological experts) could have considered before taking the action they did. For the exegetical principles that Galileo proposed were not entirely novel. Each of them found a specific precedent in the writings of the fathers, most notably in a work that the Roman theologians should have known (and that at least one of them did know well). That was the commentary on *Genesis*, the *De Genesi ad litteram*, of St. Augustine. In assessing the responsibility of the Holy Office for the objective error it made in 1616, the case that Galileo makes in opposition thus takes on a singular importance.

In this essay, I will lay out first in some detail the exegetical principles implicit in Augustine's treatment of an early version of an apparent conflict between Scripture and the findings of "sense or reason." Then I will analyze Galileo's two major discussions of the issue, first in his *Letter to Castelli,* and then, much more significantly, in his *Letter to the Grand Duchess,* touching on Foscarini's ill-fated *Letter* in between. I will turn then to an internal tension that many commentators have perceived within the exegetic principles that Galileo deploys in meeting the theological challenge to Copernicanism. The tension was, broadly speaking, between two rather different strategies for dealing with that challenge.

According to one, the more radical choice, the strategy would be to deny the relevance of Scripture to our knowledge of the natural world, especially to issues in astronomy, and to emphasize, besides, the likelihood in the context of astronomical phenomena that the authors of Scripture would have accommodated their language to the understanding of their hearers. The alternative, more conservative, strategy would be to allow that the authority of divine revelation extended to passages in Scripture describing features of the natural world but also to admit that where this description clashed with something that could be demonstrated through "sense or reason," an alternative to the literal, everyday, meaning of the Scripture passage should be sought.[2] This latter proviso would imply that even in this, the most conservative, approach, theology is not being given absolute priority over natural philosophy. *Only* when the content of the disputed doctrine is itself a matter of faith and the issue is not one of interpreting Scripture passages that, in principle, could yield alternative interpretations is such priority asserted.

Augustine: Reading the De Genesi ad litteram

First, then, to Augustine. The young Augustine went through two conversions, the first from the traditional Christianity of his childhood to the fashionable Manichaeism that had some time before swept through the Mediterranean world, and the second back to Christianity again, now professed as a reflective and confident choice. The Manichaeans mocked the Christian Scriptures as primitive and incoherent and offered an entirely different account of cosmic and human origins. The Creator pictured in Genesis they saw as impossibly anthropomorphic, and the notion of creation itself left no room for the great struggle between the rival forces of Good and Evil that they saw everywhere in evidence around them.

Augustine, as a Manichaean, would have known the force of their criticisms of Genesis. Not surprisingly, then, the task of responding to them was one of the first he took on as a Christian convert, even before he was ordained priest. The task, he discovered, was not going to be easy. Indeed, it was one to which he returned again and again throughout the course of his immensely productive life. The focus would be the Book of Genesis, the principal target of the Manichaean attack. How was it to be understood? In particular, could it be taken in a literal historical sense, or ought it to be read in some more figurative way? His first attempt to answer this question, crucial to the Manichaean challenge, was his *De Genesi contra Manichaeos libri duo* (A commentary on Genesis against the Manichaeans in two books), c. 388 A.D. He later remarked about this youthful work that as he attempted to find a credible literal interpretation of the first chapters of Genesis describing the Creation, he found the task nearly impossible.[3] A few years later, he tried again but gave up, leaving the work incomplete, though he decided to preserve the manuscript; this was the *De Genesi ad litteram imperfectus liber* (The literal meaning of Genesis: An unfinished book). Again in books 12 and 13 of his *Confessions* (397–401 A.D.), he attempted to provide both a literal and an allegorical interpretation for the first chapter of Genesis.

At this point, however, he evidently decided that he was now ready for the full-scale work that was clearly called for. The *De Genesi ad litteram* (The literal meaning of Genesis) would take him fourteen years (401–415 A.D.) and was one of his major works. He was still not entirely satisfied, however, remarking that in his effort to find the "proper historical sense" of the enigmatic chapters, he had found more questions than answers, "and of the answers found, not many have been established for certain."[4] He returned to the topic one last time in his great *City of God*. This long effort, extending through much of his life, must have convinced him, if any convincing was needed, that the discovery of the literal meaning of Scripture could be an exceedingly difficult matter and that this difficulty would be heightened where there was an apparent conflict between this literal sense and some finding of "sense or reason," as the Manichaeans claimed regarding many passages in the Creation chapters of Genesis.

I have used the expression 'literal meaning' above as though it were unproblematic. But, unfortunately, that is far from the case. When we use that phrase today, it is usually to contrast the "literal" meaning of some expression with a metaphorical one. But interpreting a text *ad litteram* (according to the letter) meant something much broader in Augustine's day; indeed, exegetes have been at pains to point out that Augustine himself used the phrase in different ways in different contexts, ranging from a usage not unlike the modern one, especially in his earlier works on Genesis, to "a highly sophisticated interpretation that is quite metaphysical and not what we would ordinarily call the literal sense" in the *De Genesi ad litteram.*[5]

John Taylor takes Augustine to mean primarily by 'literal' the sense intended by the author, which could well be metaphorical. (One would also need to specify whether God or the human author is in question.) Its primary sense for Augustine may well have been the negative one, meaning simply "not allegorical." In the case of historical narrative (and Augustine, unlike the neo-Platonists of his day, was quite firm in holding that the Genesis story of Creation *could* be given a broadly historical interpretation), the sense of 'literal' that comes closest to his usage might be "conveying the historical fact, telling us what actually happened." What complicates matters, of course, is that the language in which God's action in creating the world is described cannot possibly, in the nature of the case, be literal in the modern sense of that term.[6] So we have to be content with a "literal meaning of Genesis" that aims to be "literal-historical" but makes no effort to be literal in the usual sense. In this essay, I will use the term in its contemporary, more limited sense.

Long before Augustine's day, two schools had formed regarding the proper interpretive approach to Scripture. The school of Alexandria, whose most notable members were Origen, Clement, and Cyril, favored a highly allegorical interpretation of the Old Testament, seeing it as prefiguring the New. The allegorical meaning was not the intended meaning of the human author, nor was it what the first readers would have seen in the text. Rather, it was the meaning intended by God for later readers, who would grasp in this way the deeper coherence of the story of human salvation. The school of Antioch (John Chrysostom, Theodore of Mopsuestia, Theodoret of Cyr), less influential, preferred a more literal and historical reading, avoiding the imaginative flights of the Alexandrians.

Augustine was thoroughly familiar with this rich literature. In general, he took the middle ground, seeking first the literal or "proper" sense and then, where appropriate, an allegorical (or figurative or prophetic) sense. In the *De Genesi ad litteram,* Augustine's imagination soars as he reads the six days of the Creation narrative not as days in the ordinary sense (how could they be, since, as the Manichaeans had objected, the sun was not made until the fourth "day"?) but as progressions in angelic knowledge of the Creation.

This interpretation of the text, he insists, is still a "literal," not an allegorical, one. Even though it differs from our ordinary understanding of the term 'day,' it is a "truer," deeper sense, of which our ordinary sense is an echo (*LMG*, 1.4.28). He acknowledges, however, that others may find a different meaning here, and he encourages the search. Indeed, he remarks, he may himself still hit on another, and more plausible, interpretation. Interpretive though it may be, however, this is still for him the "literal" sense, that which the text tells us actually happened. What prompts the search for alternatives here is that the normal sense of the term 'day' *cannot* be correct. This is the unequivocal testimonial of human reason and the human senses. In the circumstances, another interpretation of the six-day succession *must* be found.

We are now ready to look more closely at the text of the *De Genesi*. How does Augustine deal with apparent conflicts of this sort between the findings of sense and reason and the literal reading (in *our* sense of that term: i.e., where the component words are taken in their normal usage) of particular scriptural texts? Since he nowhere provides a systematic answer to this question, we have to examine those passages in his commentary where he is dealing with this issue and see what we can infer about the principles that seem to guide him in each case. We may in this way be able to formulate a set of hermeneutic guidelines covering apparent conflicts while keeping in mind that we are imposing system on a context to which it is foreign. Augustine sets down these maxims usually without supporting argument, as though they would be obvious to his readers.

First, he takes for granted throughout the work that both Scripture and human reason are sources of truth; both come from God. They cannot, therefore, truly conflict. If they appear to, this can only be because one or the other has been misunderstood or its claim to truth overstated. This might be called:

> *The Principle of Consistency* (PC): The proper meaning of Scripture cannot be in true conflict with the findings of human sense or reason.[7]

When an apparent conflict arises, what one should ask, then, is how secure the claim on the side of the senses or the reason really is:

> But someone may ask: "Is not Scripture opposed to those who hold that the heavens are spherical, when it says [of God] 'who stretches out the heavens like a skin'?" Let it be opposed indeed, if what they say is false. The truth is rather in what God reveals than in what groping men surmise [humana infirmitas conicit]. But if they are able to establish their doctrine with proofs that cannot be denied [si forte illud talibus illi documentis probare potuerint, ut dubitari inde non debeat], we must show that this statement of Scripture about the skin is not opposed to the truth of their conclusions. (*LMG*, 2.9.21)

"Proofs that cannot be denied"—a demanding condition. And Augustine repeats it, for good measure: the scriptural passages about the shape of the heavens (stretched out like a skin; suspended like a vault) must be shown "not to contradict the theories that may be supported by true evidence, by which heaven is said to be curved on all sides in the shape of a sphere, *provided only that this is proved*" (*LMG,* 2.9.21, emphasis mine). He is not entirely convinced that the spherical shape *has* been proved— "it may be only a man-made theory" (*LMG,* 2.9.22)—but he evidently thinks that it comes close enough that another interpretation of the stretched skin should be sought. And it should not be allegorical, else a "literal-minded interpreter" will remind him that a variant *literal* interpretation should also be forthcoming (*LMG,* 2.9.22). And indeed one is: Why should the skin not be stretched in a *spherical* shape? After all, he says, with just a trace of complacency, "[A] leather bottle and an inflated ball are both made of skin" (*LMG,* 2.9.22).

Augustine has enough confidence in human reason, then, to allow him to require, as a constraint on scriptural interpretation,

> *The Principle of Priority of Demonstration* (PPD): When there is a conflict between a proven truth about the physical world and a particular reading of Scripture, an alternative reading should be sought.

His general approach in the *De Genesi* is to retort to the Manichaean critics of Scripture that whatever they "could demonstrate about the nature of things by means of reliable evidence [quidquid ipsi de natura rerum veracibus documentis demonstrare potuerint], we shall show that it is not contrary to our Scripture" (*LMG,* 1.21.24).[8] He adds a caveat, however. If the Manichaeans "produce from their books" something that is (definitely) contrary to the Catholic faith,[9] "we shall either by some means or other show, or else without a shadow of doubt believe, that it is absolutely false."[10]

His long struggle with the Genesis text had brought home to him how obscure the text of Scripture could be. It was this that allowed him to propose the priority of demonstrated truths in the natural order; given the multiplicity of alternative possible "literal" interpretations of at least some biblical texts, PPD simply helps the reader to narrow the field of permissible interpretations when searching for the genuine "literal" one, the one that conveys the historical truth. But Augustine reminds his readers that the priority given to philosophical/scientific demonstration is limited by a more general principle, one no longer directed to the context of exegesis only:

> *The Principle of Priority of Faith* (PPF): An apparent demonstration on the side of philosophy of something that is contrary to a doctrine of the faith must be set aside.

The absolute priority given to doctrines of the faith became a central issue in medieval theology: Did it extend, for example, to specific theological formulations of those doctrines, even if these had not been declared to be *de fide?* The relevance of PPF to our inquiry here is that Augustine proposes it as a bound on PPD. Where a conflict appears between the literal reading of Scripture and an apparently demonstrated finding on the side of philosophy, this latter ought to be denied any weight in the exegesis of the disputed passage if it is known to be contrary to a doctrine of the faith.

Augustine frequently resorts to another principle, more explicitly exegetical, in his Scripture commentaries: "Sacred Scripture in its customary style is speaking within the limitations of human language in addressing men of limited understanding, while at the same time teaching a lesson to be understood by the reader who is able" (*LMG,* 5.6.19). Or again: "We must hold to the pronouncement of St. Paul [I Corinthians, 15:41] that . . . 'star differs from star in glory [brightness].' But, of course, one may reply, without attacking St. Paul: 'they differ in glory to the eyes of men on earth'" (*LMG,* 2.16.33)." Long before Augustine, theologians had been at pains to point out that the authors of Scripture had to accommodate their expressions to their prospective audience. Sometimes this would be because of the inadequacy of human language to convey their message, as when they described God in anthropomorphic terms. At other times, as here, it might be because of the limitations of human ways of knowing. Both sorts of accommodation could be important in interpreting the Genesis narrative of the Creation. Hence:

> *The Principle of Accommodation* (PA): The choice of language in the scriptural writings is necessarily accommodated to the capacities of the intended audience.

Several times in his commentary on Genesis, when Augustine encounters moderately technical issues regarding the makeup of the natural world, he betrays some impatience. This is not what they should be looking for in the Scriptures, he reminds his readers. Regarding the shape of the heavens, for example, the writers of Scripture gave it no special attention:

> Such subjects are of no profit to those who seek beatitude, and what is worse, they take up precious time that ought to be given to what is spiritually beneficial. What concern is it of mine whether heaven is like a sphere and the earth is enclosed by it and suspended in the middle of the universe, or whether heaven, like a disk above the earth, covers it on one side? . . . I must say briefly that in the matter of the shape of the heaven, the sacred writers knew the truth but the Spirit of God, who spoke through them, did not wish to teach men such things as would be of no avail for their salvation. (*LMG,* 2.9.20)

Augustine is irritated with those who seek detailed knowledge of the natural world in Scripture: "There is a great deal of subtle and learned inquiry into these questions for the purpose of arriving at a true view of the matter; but I have no further time to go into these questions and discuss them, nor should they have time whom I wish to see instructed for their salvation" (*LMG*, 2.10.23). There are hints here, at least, of a quite strong principle bearing on the relevance of Scripture to natural knowledge:

> *The Principle of Scriptural Limitation* (PSL): Since the primary concern of Scripture is with human salvation, we should not look to Scripture for knowledge of the natural world.

Augustine is admonishing his readers that the issue of salvation far outweighs the mere desire for natural knowledge. Conveying such knowledge was simply not part of what the Spirit of God who spoke through the writers intended. Does this mean that Scripture carries no weight at all with regard to the knowledge of nature? That would certainly seem to be the import of what he has to say about the question of the shape of the heavens. But elsewhere he sometimes explicitly appeals to Scripture in support of a claim about the natural world, even in one case where this claim runs counter to our commonsense view.

The Manichaeans were especially critical of the Genesis account of the placing of the waters both below and above the firmament, "and God called the firmament heaven" (Genesis 1:6–8). Surely the natural place of water was *below* the heavens, they argued. Here Augustine stands fast, however, insisting on the truth of the Scripture passage, quite literally interpreted. It is not enough, he remarks, to respond by saying that God could, by way of miracle, place waters wherever he wished (*LMG*, 2.1.2). The issue is about the *natural* place of water, and the Genesis text plainly says that water has a natural place both above and below the heavens. After some discussion, he relays an ingenious (if highly speculative) suggestion. The farthest planet, Saturn, has the longest path to run, and rapid motion causes heat. Yet Saturn is also said to be the coldest star. "Some of our scholars," he says, conclude that Saturn must be cooled by waters in the form of ice, far above the firmament. "But whatever the nature of that water and whatever the manner of its being there, we must not doubt that it exists in that place. *The authority of Scripture in this matter is greater than all human ingenuity*" (*LMG*, 2.5.9, emphasis mine).

Is it because the Genesis text is so plain that Augustine is adamant in maintaining the normal sense of the expression, "above the heavens (sky)"? There is almost a warrant here for a *Principle of Clear Sense* (PCS), which would say that if the sense of Scripture is clear and unambiguous, with no hint of accommodation, one should defend it at all costs, on the assumption, more or less symmetrical with PPD, that in such a case there would *have* to be some other way of construing the apparently conflicting claim of natural knowledge. Yet in the following passage he goes on to discuss a very similar text in Psalms 135:67: "(God) established the earth above the waters." It seems almost as plain as the earlier text, yet Augustine treats it quite differently. Here he gives the secular claim priority and allows himself to fall back on a figurative meaning. This Scripture passage should not, he warns, be used "against these people who engage in learned discussions about the weights of the elements. They are not bound by the authority of our Bible, and, ignorant of the sense of these words, they will more readily scorn our sacred books than disavow the knowledge they have *acquired by unassailable arguments or proved by the evidence of experience*"(*LMG*, 2.1.4, emphasis mine). Plain though the sense of the Scripture passage may be, PPD is invoked on the other side and is not to be gainsaid. For someone who might still insist on a literal interpretation of the Scripture passage, he has this to offer: Are there not "promontories that tower over the water" of the seas (*LMG*, 2.1.4)?

Augustine evidently cannot be counted on as a unqualified advocate of PSL. The Scriptures bear at least some relevance to natural knowledge for him; what PSL may amount to in that case may be no more than an admonition not to turn the Scriptures away from their main purpose by construing them as a cosmological text. To complicate matters further, there is at least a trace of another principle in his thinking that would be quite inconsistent with PSL. His frequent emphasis on the importance of *demonstration* in conflict issues of this sort might seem to imply that in the absence of demonstration on the side of sense or reason, the literal interpretation of the disputed passage should stand. In a passage quoted earlier he remarks that if the conflicting secular claim is false, "the truth is rather in what God reveals than in what groping men surmise." So the literal sense *would* constitute revelation on God's part in such a case and would carry authority accordingly. Surmise on the opposing side would carry no weight; only demonstration would, and in its absence (Augustine seems to imply) the Scripture text should be understood as conveying genuine knowledge of nature.

This would suggest something like the following:

The Principle of Priority of Scripture (PPS): Where there is an apparent conflict between a Scripture passage and an assertion about the natural world grounded on sense or reason, if that assertion falls short of proof, the Scripture passage should be taken in its normal literal sense to convey natural knowledge.

It should be emphasized that this is no more than a hint in the text. PPS would be inconsistent with PSL if the latter were to be understood strictly. But even if PPS were left aside entirely, PSL, understood strictly, would make PPD entirely redundant. There would be hardly any point in continually emphasizing the importance of *demonstrating* the counterclaim from sense or reason if the Scriptures were not relevant to natural knowledge in the first place.

I have emphasized the tensions between the two sets of principles here, PA/PSL on one side, PPD/PPS on the other, not to accuse Augustine of inconsistency in what were obviously only tentative strategies on his part, but because of the consequences of tensions of this sort when Augustine's texts later reappear from Galileo's pen.

Even the most casual reader of the *De Genesi* could hardly miss another principle, this time a second-order one, not a hermeneutic maxim guiding interpretation directly like the others above, one that contributes further to the tension within the implicit guidelines that Augustine is leaving to posterity. In the passage just quoted, he warns Christian readers of the Bible against advancing an interpretation that has not been adequately thought through lest it should lead non-Christians who know better to "scorn our sacred books." He returns to this theme over and over:

> In matters that are obscure and far beyond our vision, even in such as we may find treated in Holy Scripture, different interpretations are sometimes possible without prejudice to the faith we have received. In such a case we should not rush in headlong and so firmly take a stand on one side that, if further progress in the search for truth [diligentius discussa veritas] justly undermines this position, we too fall with it. That would be to battle not for the teaching of Holy Scripture but for our own, wishing its teaching to conform to ours, whereas we ought to wish ours to conform to that of Holy Scripture. (*LMG,* 1.18.37)

Such imprudent readers ought keep in mind two imperative reasons for caution. First, the matters dealt with in Scripture are far beyond our vision, and the text is, in consequence, often open to multiple interpretations. And from the side of natural knowledge, there is also a sobering possibility that further progress in the search for truth may establish a position that would undermine an incautious earlier claim to interpret Scripture in a contrary sense. Again: "We should always observe that restraint that is proper to a devout and serious person and on an obscure question entertain no rash belief. Otherwise, if the truth later appear [quod postea veritas patefecerit], we are likely to despise it because of our attachment to our error, even though this explanation may not be in any way opposed to the sacred writings" (*LMG,* 2.18.38).[12]

"If the truth later appear . . .": Augustine shows himself aware that knowledge progresses, so that prudence in interpreting difficult passages in Scripture is needful where the possibility of such advance in knowledge is real. Hence:

> *The Principle of Prudence* (PP): When trying to discern the meaning of a difficult scriptural passage, one should keep in mind that different interpretations of the text may be possible and that, in consequence, one should not rush into premature commitment to one of these, especially since further progress in the search for truth may later undermine this interpretation.

In his youth, Augustine turned away from the Christian community in part because its adherents in North Africa appeared naive and ill informed about the high culture of the day to his already highly educated taste. Now, once again a Christian, he is warning his fellow Christians against giving precisely this impression by proposing ill-founded interpretations of Scripture on issues in natural science where such interpretations could suffer easy refutation, thus bringing the Scriptures themselves into discredit:

> Usually, even a non-Christian knows something about the earth, the heavens, and the other elements of this world, about the motion and orbit of the stars and even their sizes and relative positions, about the predictable eclipses of the sun and moon, the cycles of the years and the seasons, about the kinds of animals, shrubs, stones, and so forth, and this knowledge he holds to as being certain from reason and experience. Now it is a disgraceful and dangerous thing for an infidel to hear a Christian, presumably giving the meaning of Holy Scripture, talking nonsense on these topics, and we should take all means to prevent such an embarrassing situation, in which people show up vast ignorance in a Christian and laugh it to scorn. The shame is not so much that an ignorant individual is derided, but that people outside the household of the faith think our sacred writers held such opinions, and, to the great loss of those for whose salvation we toil, the writers of our Scripture are criticized and rejected as unlearned men. If they find a Christian mistaken in a field which they themselves know well and hear him maintaining foolish opinions about our books, how are they going to believe those books in matters concerning the resurrection of the dead, the hope of eternal life, and the kingdom of heaven, when they think their pages are full of falsehoods on facts which they themselves have learnt from experience and the light of reason? (*LMG*, 1.19.41)[13]

Augustine speaks here with a degree of passion. This was a matter on which he evidently felt very strongly. He had encountered this sort of dogmatizing and had seen its consequences. When the Scriptures bear on issues where natural science (astronomy, the most developed natural science of his day, is his prime example) also claims competence, his urgent advice to Christian interpreters of Scripture is to go very cautiously.[14] At least, he says, be aware of the relevant knowledge of nature that is claimed to be "certain from reason and experience" (echoes here of PPD). And never lose sight of the harm that can be done to the Christian community by an imprudent handling of the sacred text.

The task of the exegete in Augustine's day was far less constrained than it would later become. The predominance of the allegorical mode of interpretation in the Alexandrine school, as well as the latitude allowed to "literal" interpretation, meant that the widest variety of meanings could be, and were, attributed to even the most straightforward-seeming text. The *De Genesi ad litteram,* besides, dealt with one of the most interpretatively difficult parts of the Bible, the account of the Creation. It is, after all, the only segment of the Old Testament "histories" for which there were no human witnesses. It treats of the creative action of a Being whose agency lies far outside the range of human comprehension. Accommodating such a narrative to the limitations of human ways of knowing inevitably means that the narrative will lend itself to a multiplicity of interpretations and will test exegetical norms to the utmost. Can the principles that Augustine formulated in response to this challenge be transferred from the majestic context of the Creation to that of straightforward remarks about the motion of the sun and the immobility of the earth? Galileo certainly hoped so.

Galileo: The Letter to Castelli

My narrative is going to shift now from the fifth to the seventeenth century, to 1613 A.D., to be precise. Copernicus's great work, the *De revolutionibus orbium coelestium,* was already seventy years old. But it had only been a few years before that the new telescopic evidence of the satellites of Jupiter, the ever-changing sunspots, and the phases of Venus had brought Copernican ideas of the earth's motion and the sun's rest to the broad public and had begun to give them a credibility among astronomers that they had heretofore lacked. Aristotelian philosophers were the most directly affected by the new discoveries: the evidence of Venus's phases was sufficient of itself to show that the Aristotelian system of concentric spheres was untenable. But it was not long before theologians, themselves Aristotelian in sympathy, also sounded the alarm, summoning (as Galileo put it) the "terrible weapon" of Scripture to their cause.[15]

Galileo, at the center of the growing storm, realized very quickly that the theological threat to the Copernican ideas had to be countered if his own proposed development of these ideas was to prosper. From his perspective he had really no other option. By now he was convinced of the merits of the heliocentric system, and he feared that the Church of which he was a loyal member risked making a terrible error unless someone could persuade its official representatives that the Copernican theses posed no challenge to Scripture after all. Never one to doubt his own powers of persuasion, even in an arena until that point entirely foreign to him, he turned his energies to the task.

His first try was in a letter to his former student Benedetto Castelli, a Benedictine who had succeeded Galileo at the University of Pisa and who had already encountered scriptural objections to the Copernican proposal at a meal in the Medici palace, with the dowager grand duchess, Christina of Lorraine, not only present but actively engaged. The dispute clearly worried Galileo. The Medici family were his patrons; were *they* to be persuaded by the theological opposition to the Copernican theses, he could face a very difficult choice. So in a short, hastily composed, letter to Castelli he set out "to examine some general questions about the use of Holy Scripture in disputes involving physical conclusions." His approach is a commonsense one. He quotes no theological authorities. His first point is that the Scriptures have to "accommodate the incapacity of ordinary people" (PA) and in so doing depart from the literal meaning of passages that would, for example, attribute hands and eyes to God. It follows, he says, that "in disputes about natural phenomena, [Scripture] should be reserved to the last place." Though both Scripture and nature derive ultimately from God, Scripture is necessarily open to multiple interpretations, whereas "nature is inexorable and immutable" and is in no way bound to accommodate human understanding.[16] Thus "[w]hatever sensory experience places before our eyes or necessary demonstrations prove to us concerning natural effects should not be called into question on account of Scriptural passages whose words appear to have a different meaning, since not every statement of the Scripture is bound to obligations as severely as is each effect of nature."[17]

This is PPD in a stronger form than Augustine gave it. It is obvious, he goes on, that two truths can never contradict one another (PC), so "[t]he task of wise interpreters is to strive to find the true meanings of Scriptural passages that would agree with those physical conclusions of which we are already certain and sure from clear sensory experience or from necessary demonstrations."[18] Even though Scripture is inspired, its interpreters are not. Thus:

> It would be prudent not to allow anyone to oblige Scriptural passages to have to maintain the truth of any physical conclusions whose contrary could *ever* be proved to us by the senses and demonstrative and necessary reasons. Who wants to fix a limit for the human mind? Who wants to assert that everything which is knowable in the world is already known? Because of this, it would be most advisable not to add anything beyond necessity to the articles concerning salvation and the definition of the Faith.[19]

Where Augustine, in counseling prudence, laid most stress on the potential danger to the Church that incautious interpreters of Scripture could cause, Galileo emphasizes two other motives for his version of PP, both of them also mentioned by Augustine: the undoubted fallibility of scriptural interpreters and the possibility that a claim to natural knowledge may prove true at a later time, even if at present it cannot be demonstrated. This latter was a far more pressing consideration for Galileo than it would have been for Augustine or for anyone in the later Aristotelian tradition. He had already seen at first hand how observational discoveries could alter the status of even the most venerable cosmological claims. The combination of PPD and this version of PP would imply that where natural knowledge is concerned, interpreters of Scripture should *always* hold back, whether the claim to natural knowledge is demonstrated or not. And Galileo adds one further argument in support of this far-reaching conclusion: "The authority of Holy Writ has merely the aim of persuading men of those articles and propositions which are necessary for their salvation and surpass all human reason, and so could not become credible through some other science or other means except the mouth of the Holy Spirit itself."[20]

This is PSL in the strongest possible form. The Scriptures are limited to doctrines that bear on human salvation; the sciences of nature lie outside their scope: "I do not think it necessary to believe that the same God who has furnished us with senses, language, and intellect would want to bypass their use and give us by other means the information we can obtain with them. This applies especially to those sciences about which one can read only very small phrases and scattered conclusions in the Scripture, as is particularly the case for astronomy."[21] Galileo leaves the reader in no doubt about his position. One should not expect to find natural knowledge (astronomical knowledge, in particular) in Scripture.

Galileo is confident at this point that he has made his case. Where knowledge of nature is concerned, "the one who supports the true side will be able to provide a thousand experiments and a thousand necessary demonstrations for his side, whereas the other person can have nothing but sophisms, paralogisms, and fallacies."[22] Those who call on the Scriptures in this context are implicitly conceding that they are unable to make their case by appropriately physical arguments. Galileo ends the letter with an ingenious ad hominem argument, which has puzzled some of his commentators who have not realized that he is arguing ad hominem. He starts: let us concede to our opponents that the words of the disputed text in Joshua about the sun's motion *are* to be taken literally. He then goes on to show that if one does this, the text can be shown to be incompatible with the Aristotelian world-system that these same opponents profess. To stop the apparent motion of the sun in the sky in the Aristotelian scheme, God would have to stop, not the sun's own proper motion, but the whole system of celestial spheres. So the Aristotelian *cannot* take the text literally.

Then Galileo cannot resist adding a further gloss that is a little *too* clever. His telescopic observations make it appear that the sun is rotating on its own axis. What if the sun's rotation is causally responsible for the motion of the planets? In that case, stopping the sun *would* have the desired effect of stilling the sun in the terrestrial sky. So Galileo's would be the system that in that case could abide by the literal meaning. Of course, this is incompatible with what he has just argued about the irrelevance of Scripture to matters physical. But I suspect he intended this postscript as an extension of the ad hominem argument: if you *insist* on literal interpretation here, he was saying to the Aristotelians, I will come out ahead. Moral: Better not insist! He assures Castelli that they have nothing to fear "as long as we are allowed to speak and to be heard by competent persons who are not excessively upset by their own emotions and interests."[23]

This is frank talk, not exactly likely to commend Galileo's case to a reader of more conservative theological sympathies. Interestingly, when a hostile critic later forwarded a copy of the letter to the Holy Office in Rome, the assessor appointed to evaluate it found no fault with its overall argument, or with the hermeneutic principles it advanced, or even with its rather dismissive tone where theological criticism of the Copernican system was concerned, but only with a couple of phrases that "sound bad," though he added that this might be just a matter of poor word choice.[24] What will have struck the reader by now is the similarity between Galileo's and Augustine's responses to the conflict issue. At this point, Galileo is reacting more or less intuitively, formulating what appear to him to be commonsense principles of interpretation and in each case offering some supportive argument. He proposes versions of PC, PA, PSL, PPD, PP, just as Augustine did.

Where a difference between them appears is with regard to the weight to be given to Scripture in the event that the claim to natural knowledge is *not* demonstrated. Augustine seems to allow priority to Scripture in such a case (PPS), at least if the meaning of the Scripture passage is plain and PA is not involved. And although, as we have seen, he appears at one point to sanction a version of PSL in the matter of the shape of the heavens, he himself has recourse to Genesis when discussing some general features of the physical world. Thus he would hardly have given PSL the scope that Galileo here does.

There is no reason to think that Galileo was aware of Augustine's discussion of the "conflict" issue at the time he wrote to Castelli in December 1613. The strong resemblance between their views seems due, rather, to the fact that here were two highly intelligent men reacting spontaneously to a very similar set of issues. And the difference between them might be traced to Augustine's quite natural emphasis, as a theologian, on the revealed character of Scripture and Galileo's equally natural conviction regarding the sufficiency of the human powers of sense and reason in coming to know the order of nature.

Foscarini to the Defense of Copernicanism

In the months that followed, Galileo was reminded over and over of the gathering opposition in Rome to the Copernican claims. A letter from a friend in Rome, Monsignor Piero Dini, let him know that the leading Roman theologian of the day, Cardinal Robert Bellarmine of the Society of Jesus, believed that the Copernican affair could immediately be settled by recalling that Copernicus himself made no claims regarding the *real* motions of earth and sun; mathematical astronomy in his eyes was no more than a practical device useful for prediction, calendar making, and the like. Galileo strenuously disagreed with this claim, pointing out to Dini that it misrepresented Copernicus (assuming too readily that the foreword appended to the *De revolutionibus* had indeed been Copernicus's own work) and that it also misrepresented the real intent of Copernican astronomy, which was to declare the "true structure" of the world.[25]

In the same month, however, an established Carmelite theologian and philosopher, Paolo Antonio Foscarini, published a short work in the form of a letter to the general of the Carmelite order whose aim was to defend the "clearly probable" Copernican system from theological attack. The exegetical principles on which he relies, PA, PSL, PP, and PPD, are the same as those we have already encountered in the *Letter to Castelli,* though there is no reason to suppose that Foscarini had seen Galileo's letter. Their close resemblance testifies to their being what one might call the commonsense, and less tradition-bound, response to apparent conflict between Scripture, literally taken, and the testimony of "sense or reason."

Foscarini emphasizes and argues in some detail for PA and PSL. Once theologians recognize that the language of Scripture must be that of the "ordinary people" for whom the Scriptures were intended and that it therefore must describe nature "according to the appearances and not according to the reality," the theological difficulties urged against the Copernican system will disappear. Besides, "the Scriptures have no other purpose than the attainment of salvation," so one should not expect to find in them deep knowledge of nature.[26] This combination of PA and PSL should, as we have already seen, ward off objections to Copernicanism from the side of Scripture without need of any further argument. But Foscarini weakens this straightforward point in two ways. If something is known to be contrary to the words of Scripture and thus to divine authority, he says, it should be abandoned even if it seems to have reason and sense on its side.[27] What he may mean here is that if the disputed issue is *known* to be a matter of faith, there must be a flaw on the opposed side of reason or sense. Or one might regard this, in the opening pages of the *Letter,* as a prudential bow to Church authority before the actual argument of the *Letter* is introduced.[28]

A more troublesome difficulty in interpreting Foscarini's message lies in the goal he evidently sets himself of accommodating Scripture to the Copernican world-system. This involves him in a lengthy (and, it must be admitted, somewhat contorted) attempt to show that the "stability" of the earth and the "motion" of the sun of which Scripture speaks can be interpreted in ways other than the more obvious everyday sense in order to make them harmonize with the Copernican insights, even harmonize with them in figurative ways more fruitfully than ever did the now "disintegrated" philosophy of Aristotle. What he seems to be suggesting here is that there is still a way to understand Scripture as conveying deep truths about nature, even in the disputed earth/sun passages.

This, on the face of it, seems to run counter to his emphatic "God's only intention [in Scripture] is to teach us the true road to eternal life."[29] And it does not easily mesh either with the elaborate (and persuasive) arguments he advances for holding that the wording of the earth/sun passages must be understood as accommodated to the language as well as to the cosmic situation of the hearers. But the tension here (which will recur in Galileo's later *Letter to the Grand Duchess* in a somewhat different form) is revealing: Does he really want to take the bold step of holding that the Scriptures carry no weight at all with regard to the knowledge of nature, and the concomitant that sense and reason carry final authority in that domain, even where demonstration of their case is lacking?[30]

Foscarini's *Letter* evoked a sharp response from an unnamed theologian (probably a consultor of the Holy Office, where his report was filed) who asserted that, among other things, the Copernican doctrine ran contrary to "the common explication of the fathers."[31] Foscarini took up the challenge and in a formal *Defense* turned to the fathers in his support.[32] Quoting a renowned theologian, Melchior Cano, a dominant figure in post-Reformation Catholic theology, he urges that in matters of philosophy the texts of the fathers ought to be accorded only as much weight as their own philosophic arguments carry. The fathers, after all, busy as they were with theological issues, did little more than "say hello at the borderline of philosophy."[33] Furthermore, here quoting Benito Pereira's authoritative *Commentary on Genesis,* the Scriptures are never to be interpreted in such a way as to set them in contradiction with what reason and sense can on their own account establish. Turning to Augustine's *De Genesi ad litteram,* he recalls the advice given there not to cling too tightly to an interpretation of Scripture with regard to nature that might later be shown to be false in terms of reason and sense, thus leading to mockery of the Scriptures.[34] Since "something new is always being added to the human sciences, one has to be particularly alert not to commit the Church prematurely to a position it may later regret" (PP).[35]

Foscarini sent a copy of both documents to Cardinal Bellarmine sometime in March/April 1615; from him they would have been transmitted to the Holy Office. The theologians of the Holy Office would thus have been made fully aware of Foscarini's arguments, including his appeal to Augustine, for almost a year before the decision was made to ban Copernicanism and with it Foscarini's *Letter.* His appeal to PA/PSL/PP was, in effect, set aside. True, his *Letter* strained Scripture to the extreme to accommodate the Copernican theses, in the sense of showing that the passages might be understood in a Copernican sense. This would not have helped. And his presentation of the exegetical principles themselves was nowhere near as effective as it would become in Galileo's hands. But the fact remains: the Roman theologians had before them in the *Letter to Castelli* and Foscarini's *Letter* and *Defense* what might seem a fairly strong case for not proceeding against Copernicanism. And they set it aside.

Composing the Letter to the Grand Duchess

No theologian himself, Galileo knew that he needed help if he were to supplement his argument with the authority of the fathers; this seemed to be the kind of evidence on which his critics most seemed to dwell. He probably began to solicit assistance from his many theologian friends in the course of 1614. In January 1615, Castelli wrote from Rome to say that a Barnabite priest of his acquaintance had promised to forward to Galileo some helpful references from Augustine and other fathers of the Church.[36] Galileo must have decided early on that Augustine would be the main witness for the defense. He would have been delighted to discover that every principle he had enunciated on his own in his earlier *Letter* found a precedent in the *De Genesi ad litteram,* a major work from the greatest of the early fathers. He calls on no less than fourteen passages from that work, interspersing them with pointed and effective commentary of his own. In addition, he refers to an impressive array of other theological authorities: from the earlier period, Tertullian, Jerome, Dionysius, Peter Lombard, Thomas Aquinas; closer to his own time, Diego de Zuñiga, Paul of Burgos, Alfonso Tostado, Benito Pereira.

How much help would he have had from Foscarini in assembling this list? It all depends on whether he had Foscarini's *Defense* at hand. He did have a copy of Foscarini's *Letter* sent to him by Federico Cesi in March.[37] But this would not have helped: there is not a single patristic reference in the entire work, an oversight that no doubt counted heavily against the *Letter* in Rome, and one that Foscarini consequently set out to remedy in the *Defense.* Did Galileo see this latter work, with its extensive patristic display? There are arguments on both sides, but there is no direct evidence.

In favor:[38] Foscarini cites the *De Genesi,* but it was probably common coin at this point. Foscarini and Galileo both refer to the fourth of the four "rules" for the interpretation of Scripture with which Pereira prefaces his *Commentary on Genesis,* meant to apply in cases of dispute about the literal sense.[39] They both quote the same paraphrase version of a passage from Augustine, taken evidently from Pereira.[40] And they both cite the same passages from two relatively obscure works of St. Jerome.[41] On the other side, however, though both cite Paul, bishop of Burgos, the passage cited by Foscarini is highly relevant to Galileo's argument (so one would have expected Galileo to include it if he was drawing on the *Defense*), whereas Galileo's own reference to Paul is on a relatively trivial issue. Furthermore, Galileo does not include a number of Foscarini's references, including two helpful ones to works of

Augustine other than the *De Genesi*. And he lists half a dozen authorities who do not appear in Foscarini's work.[42]

In the end, it is difficult to decide whether Galileo did have the Foscarini *Defense* available as guide, fortified with assistance from other quarters, or whether a common store of citations from the widest variety of sources, some of them quite obscure, was emerging, testifying to the diligent labor of unnamed theologians possibly dating back, in part at least, to sixteenth-century exegetic controversies. We do not know. What we do know is that Galileo made brilliant use of the theological witnesses he had available, most (or very possibly all) of which had been supplied to him. Above all, it was the witness of Augustine that counted, given Augustine's prestige among the theologians of the day. As already noted, except for his more radical version of PSL, there was nothing novel, strictly speaking, in the case Galileo was making: there was little there that could not find direct warrant in Augustine's text. This was above all what Galileo wanted to establish.

The *Letter* itself is nowhere mentioned in the Roman documents of 1615–16. In fact, the first reference to it in any remaining Roman source comes as late as Inchofer's report on the *Dialogo* in 1633, where Inchofer notes that "if I am not deceived [it has] passed through the hands of quite a few."[43] In a letter to Dini on February 16, 1615, Galileo mentions the "very long essay" he is composing but goes on: "I have not yet polished it so as to send you a copy."[44] Dini responds on March 7 that he has mentioned the essay to Bellarmine, who said he would "gladly" look at it but remarked, "[T]his is not something to jump into."[45] Almost certainly Bellarmine did not see it, prior to the Holy Office discussions in 1616 at least; had he done so, he would certainly have added it to the Holy Office file from 1616.

On June 20, Cesi wrote Galileo from Rome that until Foscarini finished the longer work that he was proposing (one that never did, in fact, make its appearance), "[t]he necessary caution will be to remain silent here, by not dealing any more with this [Copernican] opinion, and elsewhere also to treat it very little so as not to awaken in the meantime the passions of the most powerful Aristotelians."[46] By this time the *Letter* was probably in finished form, but Galileo, now warned, very likely decided (somewhat uncharacteristically!) that caution was the better part of valor and restricted circulation to a few trusted friends only. Though the *Letter* almost certainly played no direct part in the Holy Office discussion in 1616, its relevance to our understanding of how that discussion *might* have gone is considerable.

Galileo as Exegete

Now to the exegetical principles themselves that together constitute the case Galileo is making in the *Letter to the Grand Duchess*.[47] He shares with Augustine the presumption that genuine conflict between the two sources of truth is impossible (PC).

He lays particular stress on, and gives a persuasive justification for, the principle of accommodation (PA), going far beyond Augustine in the detail and variety of his arguments.[48] He counsels prudence (PP) on interpreters of Scripture, making explicit what was only a suggestion in Augustine: abstain from judgment regarding "physical conclusions whose contrary could *ever* be proved to us by the senses and demonstrative and necessary reasons."[49] And he formulates a much more explicit and far-reaching principle of limitation (PSL) than Augustine's, crystallizing it in an aphorism credited by him in a marginal note to Cardinal Baronio: "The intention of the Holy Spirit is to teach us how to go to heaven, and not how the heavens go."[50] The God who has given us senses, language, and intellect would surely not want to bypass these by revealing to us what we could have discovered on our own. So anything reachable on our part by sense or reason is not something we should turn to Scripture instead to learn. This is surely the voice of a natural philosopher! Besides, he goes on, astronomical matters are mentioned hardly at all in Scripture and only in passing. Had God wished to reveal truths about the natural world in Scripture, surely it would have been done in a more systematic and definitive way. "The Holy Spirit deliberately avoided teaching us such propositions, inasmuch as they are of no relevance to His intention, that is, to our salvation."[51] This is about as explicit as one could wish.

The combined implication of these three principles for the Copernican issue is clear. The Scriptures are simply irrelevant to deciding such matters as the motion of sun or earth (PSL). Further, even if PSL were to be left aside, the writers of Scripture are clearly accommodating themselves to our normal modes of speech, to what *appears* to us, when they speak of the sun as in motion or the earth as fixed (PA). Finally, even if both PSL and PA were to be set aside, ordinary prudence would counsel that on an issue where in the future a contrary demonstration could well be found, no dogmatic position should be taken now that at a later time could serve to discredit the Scriptures generally (PP). To the extent that the interpreting of Scripture in this particular context was governed by *this* set of principles, no real conflict could arise regarding the Copernican theses, since Scripture could have no bearing on them. It follows that the quality of the scientific argument in favor of Copernicanism would have been simply irrelevant. It would not have mattered in the least whether Galileo could demonstrate his Copernican claim on scientific grounds; theologians had no right to demand that he should. This is a powerful cumulative argument. And it would have carried particular weight with those who, like Foscarini, had some appreciation for the potential of the new sort of evidence being brought in support of the Copernican cosmology.

Interspersed in Galileo's discussion of these principles is a strong emphasis of a different sort: "the importance of necessary demonstrations in conclusions about natural phenomena."[52] Only demonstration or direct sensory evidence carries weight in natural philosophy. But the weight it carries there must be regarded as altogether compelling. He asks his theologian readers to examine very diligently the difference between debatable and demonstrative doctrines. Keeping firmly in mind the compelling power of necessary deductions, they should come to see more clearly that it is not within the power of practitioners of demonstrative sciences to change opinion at will, choosing now this, now that one; that there is a great difference between giving orders to a mathematician or a philosopher and giving them to a merchant or a lawyer, and that demonstrated conclusions about natural and celestial phenomena cannot be changed with the same ease as opinions about what is or is not legitimate in a contract.[53]

His Aristotelian conviction about the power of demonstration in natural philosophy shows through in this stark contrast between the findings of the demonstrative sciences (mathematics, philosophy) and what counts as knowledge in trade or law (he wisely leaves the status of theology out of the comparison). He has two points to make. The more general one: "The task of a wise interpreter is to strive to fathom the true meaning of the sacred texts; this will undoubtedly agree with those physical considerations of which we are already certain and sure through clear observations and necessary demonstrations." It is the demonstrated character of natural knowledge that helps the exegete, when sifting among the possible interpretations of a text, to avoid one that would clash with an established demonstration. He goes on to quote Pereira: "One must take diligent care to completely avoid holding . . . anything which contradicts the decisive observations and reasons of philosophy; since all truths always agree with one another, the truth of Holy Scripture cannot be contrary to the true reasons and observations of human doctrines."[54]

The more specific inference to be drawn here is that where the literal (in the sense of normal) reading of a scriptural text conflicts with a philosophical demonstration, a different interpretation of the text must be sought: this is the principle of priority of demonstration (PPD) that we already saw in Augustine. Taken by itself, PPD is consistent with the other three principles above: it simply affords a second possible response to a claim of conflict between Scripture and natural philosophy. If the latter has demonstration on its side, there will be no need to call on the further strategies of PA/PSL/PP.

But what if demonstration is lacking in cases of apparent conflict? Several passages in the *Letter* seem to suggest that in that event the literal interpretation should stand and, in context, carry weight as knowledge of nature (PPS). (These are two separate claims.) Galileo scholars have long debated whether the *Letter* ought to be so construed.[55] What makes this issue significant is that PPS is clearly inconsistent with PSL and risks tension also with PP. (It could be reconciled with PA provided that an exception from PPS could be allowed where there was clear evidence of accommodation.) What the difference reduces to is whether, in the absence of demonstration on the side of the philosophical/scientific claim, there is a presumption that the (conflicting) literal interpretation of the Scripture passage should be maintained and should be taken to convey proper knowledge of nature. According to PPS, yes; according to PSL, no.

A logical point first. If the disputed issue in natural philosophy cannot be demonstrated, the other set of principles, PSL/PA/PP, is sufficient *of itself* to exclude any definitive claim to natural knowledge on behalf of the challenged scriptural passage. This is a point Galileo could have made but did not. If his arguments for PSL/PA/PP are accepted, he does not need to produce a demonstration of Copernicanism. Instead, we find passages like the following:

> In the learned books of worldly authors are contained some propositions about nature that are truly demonstrated and others that are simply taught. In regard to the former, the task of wise theologians is to show that they are not contrary to Holy Scripture; as for the latter (which are taught but not demonstrated with necessity), if they contain anything contrary to the Holy Writ, then they must be considered indubitably false and must be demonstrated such by every possible means.[56]

The last part of this passage clearly implies that Scripture can contain "propositions about nature" that in the absence of a counterdemonstration must be held to be true. Might Galileo have had in mind here only doctrines that are part of the faith? This would convert the principle into what in Augustine appeared as PPF. But in context this seems a somewhat contrived interpretation.[57] Another passage runs: "Even in regard to those propositions which are not articles of faith, the authority of the same Holy Writ should have authority over any human writings, written not with a demonstrative method, but with pure narration or with probable reasons only. This principle should be considered appropriate and necessary inasmuch as divine wisdom surpasses all human judgment and speculation."[58] Does "written not with a demonstrative method" amount to "not demonstrated" or, rather, to "unscientific"?[59] Whichever interpretation one favors here, it would at least seem safe to infer that Galileo is conceding that the authority of Holy Writ extends to Scripture passages bearing on nature, literally interpreted, when on the conflicting side there are probable reasons or mere "unscientific" claims only. What animates this admission is clearly the theme Galileo has picked up from Augustine: divine wisdom of the sort found in revelation surpasses any (merely speculative?) human judgment. It is significant that this theme nowhere appears in Galileo's *Letter to Castelli*, composed prior to his discovery of the texts in the *De Genesi*.

Two other factors might have contributed to this weakening of PSL in the form he had argued for so vigorously. At the time he composed the *Letter* he was evidently optimistic about the chances of demonstrating the Copernican claims. He opens the *Letter* with an unqualified assertion: "I hold that the sun is located at the center of the revolutions of the heavenly orbs and does not change place, and that the earth rotates on itself and revolves around it."[60] If he could really make that case, he could rely on PPD alone to carry his argument.

Another disposing factor might have been the Aristotelian account of knowledge to which Galileo had been introduced in his early teaching career in Pisa and that he never seems to have seriously questioned. The phrase 'necessary demonstration,' which occurs over and over in the *Letter,* came naturally to him from his grounding in the *Posterior Analytics.* There is ample evidence in his writings that he had not developed any appreciation for the nuances of hypothetical reasoning such as one finds in, say, Kepler's *Apologia pro Tychone.*[61] There was really no secure place in his philosophy (any more than in that of the Aristotelians in Rome) for a well-supported theory that nevertheless fell short of actual demonstration. He might, therefore, be less disposed than he otherwise might have been to challenge claims for Scripture in the domain of natural knowledge where the rival philosophic/scientific claim was only "probable," even though his advocacy of PSL would have indicated otherwise.

Or would it? Here another issue of consistency arises. Many commentators have noted the apparent contradiction between PSL and Galileo's own practice, in both of the exegetic letters and elsewhere, of calling on Scripture himself in seeming support of the Copernican position. At first sight, this would appear to be a real, not just an apparent, contradiction. But is it? Those who argue that Galileo did propose Scripture as a source of astronomical knowledge rely mainly on the closing sections of the two letters where he treats of the miracle in Joshua of the sun's standing still. He argues that in the Ptolemaic system (if interpreted physically) this would entail an *acceleration* by a factor of 360 of the proper motion of the sun in order to give the appearance of the sun's standing still, whereas in the Copernican view the stilling of the earth's motion needed to bring about the same appearance could be achieved by halting the rotation of the sun (which he speculatively proposes as the cause of the earth's motion). Thus the Copernican could more easily retain the literal interpretation of Joshua than could the Ptolemaic.

As already noted, however, this argument is quite explicitly presented in the ad hominem form of a classical rhetorical strategy. It assumes, without conceding, a premise relied on by the opponent and shows that the contradictory of what the opponent seeks to establish will then, in fact, follow. The argument-form is completed by showing that one's own position *is* consistent with the opponent's premise. This technique was standard in the scholastic "disputations" that occupied so prominent a place in the system of education of the day, and Galileo makes it clear that this is the technique he is employing ("Let us then assume and concede to the opponent that the words of the sacred text should be taken precisely in their literal meanings.")[62] In no way does this commit Galileo to his opponent's premise.

What Galileo does allow, and indeed emphasize, is that philosophical/scientific knowledge can be used to clarify ambiguities in the scriptural texts—such ambiguities for example, as the command in Joshua that the sun should stand still "in the midst of the heavens." In this way, one can discover what the "literal" (in the sense of intended) meaning of the Scripture text may well be. But, of course, this is not to say that one could turn to the literal/normal reading of the text in the first place to support the Copernican position. Insofar as this way of reconciling the text with the Copernican view could be called "support," it would have to be understood as support of an altogether indirect sort that was quite consistent with PSL.

In a letter to Dini, written while the *Letter to the Grand Duchess* was still at a draft stage,[63] Galileo does indeed dally with the idea that Scripture provides a warrant of sorts for his own highly speculative theory of a "caloric spirit" that emanates from the sun and moves the cosmos as a whole. He emphasizes over and over the tentative character of his hypothesis, imploring Dini not to let others know of it. Significantly, it finds no place in the *Letter to the Grand Duchess*. Not too much weight should be placed on this venture of his. There is some reason to believe that he shared the common view of the time that the writers of Scripture did know deeper truths about nature, which is why he would be tempted by speculative trial balloons like the one he launches in the Dini letter. But this leaves PSL more or less intact. In his *Letter to Castelli* he had written that it was simply "disorderly" to call on Scripture "in disputes about natural phenomena that did not directly involve the faith."[64] On the substance of this warning, it seems doubtful that he ever changed his mind.

What we must remember in all this discussion of possible inconsistencies is that what we have in the two exegetic letters is an opportunistic collection of rhetorical strategies, not a formal axiomatic system. Can one really require complete consistency in such a context? Galileo was searching for arguments that would *work* with his readers. Whether the arguments would fit together as a single integrated whole was probably not of immediate concern to him. He could, for example, concede PPS to those who were disposed to emphasize the revealed character of the Scripture as a whole, but he could hope that his well-turned case for PP would deter them from committing themselves to a premature and potentially disastrous decision. The tension between the principles he sprinkles throughout the *Letter to the Grand Duchess* as ways to defuse the challenge to Copernicanism is worth the extended attention devoted to it here not so much because it implies a logical failure on Galileo's part but for what it tells us about the exegetic strategies potentially available at the time for dealing with the sort of crisis that was in the making in Rome.

It has sometimes been suggested that Galileo's supposed use of Scripture to bolster his Copernican claims was what brought down the wrath of the Holy Office on his head. There is no evidence of this in the record. We know the charges that Caccini alleged against him in the denunciation to the Holy Office that set off the inquiry. We know what Galileo was in the end enjoined to cease doing. In all of this, there is no hint of the charge that he was using Scripture to *support* Copernicanism; the charge was specifically that he was defending the latter, which was (it was decided) false on philosophic grounds and, more to the point, clearly contrary to Scripture. The further charge of his employing Scripture to make his own case for Copernicanism is nowhere mentioned.[65]

GALILEO'S THEOLOGICAL VENTURE FAILED in its immediate goals. It did not have to fail, but from the beginning its chances of success were small. Its great merit for us here is that it persuasively presents what lay within the limits of the theologically possible at that time in dealing with the Copernican controversy. It helps us to reconstruct some, at least, of the elements of the discussions that must (should?) have gone on among the consultors and cardinal-members of the Holy Office in February 1616, as well as to assess the outcome they arrived at. In chapter 6 of this volume I will turn to that broader story. The complexities we have encountered here in our efforts to trace the origins and the rhetorical strategies of Galileo's powerful brief for the Copernican defense are essential to an understanding of that larger story.

Notes

1. For an account of the complex of circumstances affecting the Holy Office decree of 1616, see chap. 6 of this book.

2. This essay takes off from an earlier piece, Ernan McMullin, "From Augustine to Galileo," *Modern Schoolman* 76 (1999): 169–94. It also draws in part on my more detailed study "Galileo on Science and Scripture," in *The Cambridge Companion to Galileo,* ed. Peter Machamer (Cambridge: Cambridge University Press, 1998), 271–347. It represents, however, a revision in some respects of both those earlier studies.

3. Augustine, *De Genesi ad litteram* (The literal meaning of Genesis) (hereafter cited parenthetically in the text by book, chapter, and section, as *LMG*), trans. John H. Taylor (New York: Newman Press, 1982), 8.2.5.

4. Augustine, *Retractationes,* 2.50 (text in Appendix I to the Taylor translation of *LMG*).

5. Roland Teske, introduction to *St. Augustine on Genesis,* a translation of Augustine's earlier two incomplete commentaries on *Genesis* (Washington, D.C.: Catholic University of America Press, 1991), 17–18.

6. See John J. O'Meara, "Augustine, Literal and Scientific: His Interpretation of *Genesis* on Creation," in *Understanding Augustine* (Dublin: Four Courts, 1997), 113. It is remarkable, as O'Meara points out, how very little attention has been paid to the Genesis commentaries of Augustine by contemporary exegetes. For Taylor's comment, see *LMG*, p. 10.

7. The labels and consequently the abbreviations I attach here to Augustine's exegetic principles are in some cases not the same as those I used earlier in McMullin, "Galileo on Science."

8. The translation here is my own.

9. The actual phrase is "something contrary to Scripture, that is [id est], contrary to the Catholic faith." Augustine has introduced a new consideration here, after all the talk of readings that are "contrary to Scripture." I take it that the second phrase, "contrary to the Catholic faith," where the issue of multiple interpretation should not arise, is the one to be emphasized in this context.

10. O'Meara draws attention to a variant reading here: "[W]e should either indicate a solution [showing that the conflict is only apparent] or believe without hesitation that it is false" ("Augustine, Literal and Scientific," 115).

11. This, as we shall see, was the only one of the passages cited here from Augustine that Galileo missed—significantly perhaps, as we shall see, since this text, above all the others, would have supported his argument that the movement of the sun and the immobility of the earth are only what appears "to the eyes of men on earth."

12. Translation of the Latin phrase above is mine.

13. This eloquent passage has recently been cited to some effect by theological critics of "creation science," an account of origins inspired by a literalist reading of Genesis that sets aside much of modern evolutionary and geological science.

14. O'Meara believes it likely that Augustine was acquainted with some of the manuals of astronomy of his day: "What is to be noted is the impression the exactitude of secular science made upon him: its certain findings had to be accepted." O'Meara, "Augustine, Literal and Scientific," 117.

15. See Galileo's *Letter to Castelli* in *Le opere di Galileo Galilei* (hereafter *OGG*), ed. Antonio Favaro (1890–1909; reprint, Florence: Giunti Barbèra, 1968), 5:285; translation in Maurice Finocchiaro, ed., *The Galileo Affair: A Documentary History* (hereafter *GA*) (Berkeley: University of California Press, 1989), 52.

16. Galileo, *Letter to Castelli*, *OGG*, 5:284; *GA*, 51.

17. *OGG*, 5:283; *GA*, 50.

18. *OGG*, 5:283; *GA*, 50; translation slightly modified.

19. *OGG*, 5:283–84; *GA*, 51 (emphasis mine).

20. *OGG*, 5:283–84; *GA*, 51.

21. *OGG*, 5:283–84; *GA*, 51.

22. *OGG*, 5:285; *GA*, 52. More than once in his writings, Galileo makes claims of this sort, as if controversy in natural science were a black-and-white affair where only the "true side" had valid arguments in its support.

23. *OGG*, 5:285; *GA*, 52.

24. For the text of the consultants' report, see Sergio Pagano and Antonio G. Luciani, eds., *I documenti del processo di Galileo Galilei* (Vatican City: Pontifical Academy of Sciences, 1984), 68–69; translation in *GA*, 135–36. Were the offending phrases in the original? Galileo scholars disagree. The majority have followed Favaro in supposing that they were deliberately added by the hostile person (the Dominican Niccolò Lorini is the most likely candidate) who sent a copy of the letter to the Holy Office. We also have a "correct" copy of the letter in which these phrases are missing; it was forwarded by Galileo to Piero Dini to be communicated to the Roman authorities, indicating that he suspected the first copy to have been adulterated (*OGG*, 5:291–94; *GA*, 55–58). Mauro Pesce argues, more plausibly to my mind, that the first copy *was*

correct and that Galileo, hearing that the letter was being scrutinized in Rome, decided to send an amended version omitting the offending phrases but leaving the substance of his argument untouched. He remarks to Dini that the original had been written "with a fast pen." Mauro Pesce, "Le redazioni originali della *Lettera Copernicana* di G. Galilei a B. Castelli," *Filologia e Critica* 17 (1992): 394–417; Annibale Fantoli, *Galileo: For Copernicanism and for the Church,* 2d ed., ed. and trans. George V. Coyne (Vatican City: Vatican Observatory Publications, 1996), 177.

25. Dini to Galileo, Mar. 7, 1615, *OGG,* 12:151–52; *GA,* 58; Galileo to Dini, Mar. 23, 1615, *OGG,* 5:299–300; *GA,* 60.

26. Paolo Antonio Foscarini, *Lettera sopra l'opinione de'Pittagorici e del Copernico,* translation in Richard J. Blackwell, *Galileo, Bellarmine, and the Bible* (hereafter *GBB*) (Notre Dame: University of Notre Dame Press, 1991), 223, 228, 232–33.

27. *GBB,* 220.

28. Blackwell concludes that there is an "unresolved tension" here, displaying "two critically different views of the relation between revelation and natural knowledge," but suggests that allowing primacy to demonstration on the side of reason or sense (PPD) is the "dominant view in the *Letter* generally" (*GBB,* 92–93).

29. *GBB,* 233. Perhaps one might say that although this would lie outside the *explicit* aim of Scripture, there could be truths about nature buried in Scripture all the same.

30. A further point alleged by some commentators is that Foscarini proposes Scripture as an independent support for Copernicanism; some suggest further that this may have been what, in particular, irked the Roman authorities who banned his book. In fact his *Letter* nowhere does this: his aim is clearly to remove a powerful objection rather than to make a positive case for Copernicus. What he wants to establish is that, among many possible interpretations, there is a way to interpret the disputed earth/sun passages that makes them consistent, at least, with the Copernican view. From this one cannot go on to infer that these passages can be used to support the Copernican theses directly. The ambiguities of interpretation forbid turning the inference around. But one can see how an unfriendly reader in 1615–16 might suppose that showing the Copernican earth/sun claims to be a *possible* reading of Scripture was, in effect, using Scripture to make the Copernican case.

31. For a translation, see *GBB,* Appendix VIIA, 253–54.

32. For a translation, and a note on the different versions of the *Defense,* see *GBB,* Appendix VIIB, 100.

33. *GBB,* 256. A nice turn of phrase!

34. *GBB,* 261. Foscarini may have taken this reference to Augustine from Pereira directly. The two passages he quotes are exactly those found in Benito Pereira's *Commentariorum et disputationum in Genesim, tomi quatuor* (Rome: Ferrari, 1591–95) 1.1.8, and in the Pereira paraphrase of Augustine, 1.21. Had he actually read the *De Genesi,* he surely would have made more extensive use of it.

35. There is an unsigned letter to Galileo, very probably from Foscarini, written apparently sometime later in 1615, where the writer lays out ambitious plans for a large work comparing the two world-systems and arguing for the Copernican one (*OGG,* 12:215–20). Scripture would be called on where it would lend itself to a possible Copernican interpretation. But on issues "which do not transcend natural limits and depend entirely on the senses," one should follow the testimony of "reasoning or factual evidence," even where this runs contrary to long-

standing traditions that depend on "the outward appearance of the words [of Scripture]" (216–17). See Irving Kelter, "Paolo Foscarini's *Letter to Galileo:* The Search for Proofs of the Earth's Motion," *Modern Schoolman* 70 (1992): 31–44.

36. *OGG*, 12:126–27; see Fantoli, *Galileo,* 247–48.

37. Cesi to Galileo, Mar. 7, 1615; *OGG*, 12:150.

38. Bruno Basile makes the case for a strong influence of the Foscarini documents on Galileo's writing in "Galileo e il teologo 'copernicano,' Paolo Antonio Foscarini," *Rivista di Letteratura Italiana* 1 (1983): 63–96.

39. *OGG*, 5:320; *GA,* 96. For Foscarini, *Defense,* see *GBB,* 259. Galileo quotes only from a single page of Pereira's work; he may well have been given a copy of that page alone.

40. *OGG*, 5:327; *GA,* 101. For Foscarini, *Defense,* see *GBB,* 259.

41. *OGG*, 5:333; *GA,* 107. For Foscarini, *Defense,* see *GBB,* 260.

42. A minor point: Galileo refers one of the passages cited from Jerome to the latter's commentary on Matthew 13; Foscarini makes it Matthew 4. Neither, as it happens, is correct.

43. *OGG*, 12:349; *GA,* 263. See Fantoli, *Galileo,* 253 n. 43.

44. *OGG*, 5:292; *GA,* 56.

45. *OGG*, 5:151; *GA,* 59.

46. *OGG*, 12:190; *GBB,* 109.

47. There is an abundant literature on these principles and a measure of disagreement as to how they should be defined and how exactly they relate to one another. See, for example, Fantoli, *Galileo,* 189–208; *GBB,* 75–85; William E. Carroll, "Galileo and the Interpretation of the Bible," *Science and Education* 8 (1999): 151–87; Mauro Pesce, "L'interpretazione della Bibbia nella lettera di Galileo a Cristina di Lorena e la sua ricezione: Storia di una difficoltà nel distinguere ciò che è religioso da ciò che non lo è," *Annali di Storia dell'Esegesi* 8 (1991): 55–104.

48. He could easily have been directed also to references to PA in medieval sources, notably in Thomas Aquinas, who frequently has recourse to the principle, but he is content with the strong authority of Augustine. See, for example, *Summa Theologia,* I, q. 98, a. 3; Nicole d'Oresme, *Le livre du ciel et du monde,* ed. A. D. Menut and A. J. Denomy (Madison: University of Wisconsin Press, 1968), 530.

49. Galileo, *Letter to the Grand Duchess, OGG*, 5:320; *GA,* 96 (emphasis mine).

50. *OGG*, 5:319; *GA,* 96.

51. *OGG*, 5:319; *GA,* 95.

52. *OGG*, 5:319; *GA,* 95.

53. *OGG*, 5:326; *GA,* 101.

54. *OGG*, 5:320; *GA,* 96.

55. Claiming an inconsistency of one form or another would be, for example, Jerome J. Langford, *Galileo, Science and the Church* (New York: Desclée, 1966), 72–74; *GBB,* 78–82; Michael Sharratt, *Galileo: Decisive Innovator* (Oxford: Blackwell, 1994), 123–26; and several of my own essays, most recently McMullin, "Galileo on Science." Denying inconsistency would be, for example, Fantoli, *Galileo,* 195–205; Maurice Finocchiaro, "The Methodological Background to Galileo's Trial," in *Reinterpreting Galileo,* ed. William Wallace (Washington, D.C.: Catholic University of America Press, 1986), 266.

56. *OGG*, 5:327; *GA,* 101–2.

57. See McMullin, "Galileo on Science," esp. n. 118, for more detail.

58. *OGG*, 5:317; *GA*, 94. Translation of the phrase "Scritte non con metodo dimostrativo" modified as suggested by Fantoli, *Galileo*, 250.

59. The latter is Fantoli's choice, the former mine. The principle that Fantoli sees as central to the *Letter* is the principle of the autonomy of scientific research (PASR), which would not be violated if his reading of the ambiguous phrase above were to be adopted (Fantoli, *Galileo*, 198–200). That Galileo was favoring a principle of that general sort seems right, although he does concede that it must yield on matters of faith (PPF). PASR and PSL are not equivalent on such issues, for example, as whether stars are animate, which Galileo (unlike Aristotle) sets outside the bounds of natural philosophy. He allows that "where human reason cannot reach and where consequently one cannot have a science but only opinion and faith, it is appropriate to conform absolutely to the literal meaning of Scripture" (*OGG*, 5:330; *GA*, 104). This would conform with PASR but could violate PSL, depending on some decisions about the exact scope of PSL which in turn would depend on the choice of arguments on which PSL was taken to rest.

60. *OGG*, 5:311; *GA*, 88.

61. See Ernan McMullin, "The Conception of Science in Galileo's Work," in *New Perspectives on Galileo*, ed. Robert Butts and Joseph Pitt (Dordrecht: D. Reidel, 1978), 209–27.

62. *OGG*, 5:285–86; *GA*, 52.

63. Galileo to Dini, Mar. 23, 1615; *OGG*, 5:297–305; *GA*, 60–67.

64. *OGG*, 5:285; *GA*, 52.

65. In a recent essay, Maurice Finocchiaro traces a fascinating tale of an apocryphal letter attributed to Galileo in the 1780s, aimed at showing that he was condemned for using Scripture to support his Copernican theses. This was then used to show that it was for his "bad theology" that Galileo was (rightly) condemned by the Church. And this claim kept surfacing over and over in the century that followed. Finocchiaro's own view (similar to that defended above) is that Galileo "preached and practiced the opposite principle, that Scripture should *not* be used to support physical propositions." See Maurice Finocchiaro, "Galileo as a 'Bad Theologian': A Formative Myth about Galileo's Trial," *Studies in the History and Philosophy of Science* 33 (2002): 753–91.

FIVE

THE DISPUTED INJUNCTION AND ITS ROLE IN GALILEO'S TRIAL

Annibale Fantoli

The 1616 Documents of the Holy Office Concerning Galileo

Galileo's announcement of his celestial discoveries in the *Sidereus nuncius* of March 1610 provoked a sort of chain reaction, first among Aristotelian philosophers and later among theologians. Even though the denunciations leveled against him by the Dominican friars Lorini and Caccini of the monastery of St. Mark in Florence did not result in a formal indictment by the Holy Office, the Roman authorities must have become increasingly concerned about the way he was advocating the Copernican view of the world and trying to show—in spite of being a simple layman—its compatibility with Scripture.

Their concern was further increased by the publication, at the beginning of 1615, of the *Letter . . . on the Pythagorean System of the World,* written by the Carmelite Antonio Foscarini. Coming this time from a theologian, such an attempt at reconciling Copernicanism with Scripture must have appeared to them utterly irresponsible. The much-commented-on answer to Foscarini by the Jesuit Cardinal Robert Bellarmine clearly illustrates the deep uneasiness of the Church authorities at this point.

Preoccupied with the likelihood of a rushed, negative decision on their part regarding the Copernican issue, Galileo decided toward the end of the same year, 1615, to go to Rome in order to do everything possible to prevent such an outcome, so disastrous in his eyes. Report of the heated discussions in which he immediately found himself involved with his adversaries was too disturbing for Pope Paul V and the cardinals of the Holy Office to ignore. On February 19, 1616, two propositions that summed up the main assertions of the Copernican system, taken almost verbatim from Caccini's deposition against Galileo, were submitted for "qualification" (assessment) on the part of the consultor-theologians of the Holy Office. Five days later, a general meeting of the consultors agreed on the following qualifications (censures):

1. Regarding the first proposition (The sun is the center of the world and hence immovable of local motion), "[I]t is foolish and absurd in philosophy and formally heretical, since it explicitly contradicts in many places the sense of Holy Scripture, according to the literal meaning of the words and according to the common interpretation and understanding of the Holy Fathers and doctors of theology."

2. Regarding the second proposition (The earth is not the center of the world, nor immovable, but moves according to the whole of itself, also with a diurnal motion), "[T]his proposition receives the same censure in philosophy and . . . in regard to theological truth it is at least erroneous in faith."[1]

On the following day, Thursday, February 25, a meeting of the Holy Office took place in the presence of the pope. As was customary, the meeting had three successive parts.[2] During the first one, the assessor, accompanied by the commissary, informed the pope and the cardinals about the censures approved by the consultors and other questions to be dealt with in connection with the Copernican issue. After that, both of them left the hall and the secret second part of the meeting started, in the presence of the pope and the cardinals alone. This explains why the only official document that is left about the meeting, published by Favaro, concerns solely the third part of it, which took place again in the presence of the assessor and the commissary. The necessity of informing those officials of the Holy Office about the decisions taken by the pope during the secret part of the session[3]—as stated in the document—becomes thus fully understandable:

The Most Illustrious Cardinal Millini notified the Reverend Lord Assessor and Lord Commissary of the Holy Office that, after the reporting of the judgment by the Father Theologians against the propositions of the mathematician Galileo, to the effect that the sun stands still at the center of the world and the earth moves even with a diurnal motion, His Holiness ordered the Most Illustrious Cardinal Bellarmine to call Galileo before himself and warn him to abandon these opinions; and if he should refuse to obey, the Father Commissary, in the presence of notary and witnesses, is to issue him an injunction to abstain completely from teaching or defending that doctrine and opinion or from discussing it; and further, if he should not acquiesce, he is to be imprisoned.[4]

Bellarmine thereupon carried out the task assigned to him, and Galileo acquiesced. This is shown by his declaration recorded at the beginning of the document dealing with the meeting of the Holy Office held on March 3: "The Most Illustrious Lord Cardinal Bellarmine having given the report that the mathematician Galileo Galilei had acquiesced when warned of the order of the Holy Congregation to abandon the opinion which he held till then, to the effect that the sun stands still at the center of the spheres but the earth is in motion."[5]

A further and more detailed confirmation of the actual summoning and of its content is given by the certificate Bellarmine wrote for Galileo on May 26 of the same year, intended as a denial of widespread rumors of an abjuration on Galileo's part of his Copernican convictions, imposed on him by the Holy Office:

We, Robert Cardinal Bellarmine, have heard that Signor Galileo Galilei is being slandered or alleged to have abjured in our hands and also to have been given salutary penances for this. Having been sought about the truth of the matter, we say that the above-mentioned Galileo has not abjured in our hands, or in the hands of others, here in Rome, or anywhere else that we know, any opinion or doctrine of his; nor has he received any penances, salutary or otherwise. He has only been notified of the declaration made by the Holy Father and published by the Sacred Congregation of the Index, whose content is that the doctrine attributed to Copernicus (that the earth moves around the sun and the sun stands at the center of the world without moving east to west) is contrary to Holy Scripture, and therefore cannot be defended or held. In witness whereof we have written and signed this with our own hands, on the 26th day of May 1616.[6]

Sixteen years later, however, when Pope Urban VIII was contemplating summoning Galileo to Rome in the wake of the publication of the *Dialogue,* a second document concerning Bellarmine's admonition was found in the archives of the Holy Office. Its content is as follows:

Friday, the 26th of the same month, at the palace, the usual residence of the said Most Illustrious Lord Cardinal Bellarmine, and in the chambers of His Most Illustrious Lordship, and in the presence of the Reverend Father Michelangelo Segizzi of Lodi, O.P., Commissary of the Holy Office, having summoned the above-mentioned Galileo before himself, the same Most Illustrious Lord Cardinal warned Galileo that the above-mentioned opinion was erroneous and that he should abandon it; and thereafter, indeed immediately, before me and witnesses, the Most Illustrious Lord Cardinal himself being also present still, the aforesaid Father Commissary, in the name of His Holiness the Pope and the whole Congregation of the Holy Office, ordered and enjoined the said Galileo, who was himself still present, to abandon completely the above-mentioned opinion that

the sun stands still at the center of the world and the earth moves, and henceforth not to hold, teach, or defend it in any way whatever, either orally or in
writing; otherwise the Holy Office would start proceedings against him. The
same Galileo acquiesced in the injunction and promised to obey.

Done in Rome, at the place mentioned above, in the presence, as witnesses,
of the Reverend Badino Nores of Nicosia, in the kingdom of Cyprus and Agostino Mongardo from the abbey of Rose in the diocese of Montepulciano, both
belonging to the household of the said Most Illustrious Lord Cardinal.[7]

The difference between this document and the two previous ones is obvious.
Bellarmine's reporting to the Holy Office is a matter-of-fact attestation that Galileo
was summoned, was subjected to an admonition, and acquiesced to it. No mention is
made of an intervention by the commissary, Segizzi. The same holds for Bellarmine's
later certificate to Galileo. Segizzi's intervention, on the contrary, is clearly stated
in the document discovered in 1632. No justification, however, is mentioned for such
an intervention. According to the pope's instructions that Cardinal Millini conveyed
to Segizzi, Segizzi was to intervene only if Galileo refused to acquiesce to Bellarmine's admonition. The document does not mention any such refusal. Moreover, the
words *successive ac incontinenti* ("thereafter, indeed immediately," according to
the Finocchiaro translation) are generally interpreted as affirming an intervention
that immediately followed Bellarmine's warning, apparently without Galileo's having had time to display his acquiescence.[8]

Past Attempts to Solve the Enigma of the Segizzi Injunction

These inconsistencies of the third document have been the object of widely different explanations. The most extreme one is that of a fraud, perpetrated in 1616 by Segizzi himself, or later by someone at the Holy Office, during the investigatory phase
of Galileo's trial in 1632. First advanced in the eighteenth century,[9] the fraud hypothesis was resurrected by Wohlwill in the second half of the nineteenth century.[10]
According to him, the second part of the document, in which Segizzi's intervention
is mentioned, was added at the time of Galileo's trial to make it possible to accuse
him of having disobeyed the admonition he had received and accepted in 1616. The
hypothesis of an addition, however, was rejected after a careful examination of the
Galileo files showed that the entire document was written by the same hand, which
appeared, moreover, to be that of the other documents of 1616.

Another hypothesis, first proposed by von Gebler and later revived by de Santillana,[11] suggests that the commissary, Segizzi, disillusioned by the moderate manner in which Bellarmine had delivered the admonition and by Galileo's prompt as-

sent, decided to omit an official report of what had taken place. Then, de Santillana speculates, "On going back to his office, he [Segizzi] told his assistant to arrange a more hopeful minute of the proceedings."[12] This "more hopeful minute" is the document as we know it, containing the Segizzi injunction, which, according to this reading, Segizzi never really gave to Galileo.

Other interpretations affirm, on the contrary, the authenticity of the document, even though they differ in the explanation of its content. I will limit myself to recalling here only the one proposed by Morpurgo-Tagliabue.[13] In his opinion, the document recording the Segizzi injunction is authentic: the very presence of inconsistencies with the pope's instructions conveyed by Millini is proof enough that it was not a forgery. According to this author, after Bellarmine's admonition, Galileo registered a measure of protest without going so far as to refuse to obey. In the light of this reaction on Galileo's part, Segizzi decided to proceed immediately to the formal injunction, without being able, however, to state in the document that Galileo had refused to obey. Morpurgo-Tagliabue concludes that the document thus displays a lack of proper procedure or even an abuse of initiative on the commissary's part. And he adds: "The very fact that the sentence of the Holy Office of 1633 quotes this document contained in the preliminary summary, without noticing or correcting its incongruity [with the papal instructions], and it uses it rather as the main charge against Galileo, leads us to believe that such procedural defects were not incompatible with the juridical practices of the time." What Morpurgo-Tagliabue finds really perplexing is the absence of the original (with the signatures of the notary and the witnesses) in the acts of Galileo's process, as would be expected in a document of such importance.[14]

In Favor of Authenticity on the Grounds of Textual Analysis

The absence of these signatures in the Segizzi document has often been considered an indication of its lack of juridical value. Given the role generally attributed to this document in the Galileo trial, such juridical deficiencies would also throw serious doubts on the validity of the trial verdict. Recent research, however, has shown that the absence of the signatures of the notary and the witnesses is normal in a document of the Holy Office registered (as is the present one) in the form of *imbreviatura* — that is, in a shortened form. Beretta writes:

> The *imbreviatura,* also called *"matrix, seu originale instrumenti"* [matrix, i.e., the original draft of the instrument], is distinct from the redaction in public form of a document by the notary, . . . which is called an "authentic instrument." Most of the documents to be found in a judicial file — the interrogations of the witnesses

and of the accused person, the decisions of the Tribunal concerning the conduct of the trial, copied in the trial files, and the prescriptions given to the accused— are written out in the form of *imbreviatura*. In all these instances, the authenticity of the document is guaranteed by its having been written by the notary.[15]

In turn, the authorship of the notary would be guaranteed by his signature on the lower part of the front folder cover of the file containing the trial documents. Unfortunately, in the case of the Galileo file, the signature is no longer visible.[16] We are, however, fairly sure—from the handwriting of the documents of 1616 included in the file—that the signature, now disappeared, was that of the notary of the time, Andrea Pettini. As Beretta himself affirms: "From the formal point of view, this document appears to be fully authentic. The writing seems to be that of the notary, Andrea Pettini, who recorded this document on the last pages of the Caccini denunciation, which had remained until then unused."[17]

Let us consider, next, the *content* of the document. From this point of view too I am strongly inclined to conclude, with Morpurgo-Tagliabue, that the document is authentic. Like him, I find myself persuaded by the very contrast between its content and the specific papal instructions that Segizzi had received personally from Cardinal Millini. If Segizzi, as de Santillana proposes, had inserted in the Galileo dossier a document containing an injunction that had never been delivered, he would surely have constructed it in accordance with those instructions. In particular, he would have made it clear that Galileo had refused to submit to Bellarmine's precept. Without some such statement, the words *successive ac incontinenti* are best interpreted as indicating a precipitate intervention, undertaken against instructions.

In addition, even the terms of the injunction, as quoted in the Segizzi document, do not correspond exactly to those of the instructions reported by Cardinal Millini. According to the latter, the commissary had to order Galileo, if he did not acquiesce, "to abstain completely from teaching or defending that doctrine and opinion or from discussing it [de ea tractare]." In the Segizzi document, however, instead of "to abstain completely from teaching" we find "to relinquish altogether" (the said opinion). And even more significantly, the prohibition even to *discuss* the theory is omitted.[18]

These discrepancies are out of keeping with the hypothesis that the Segizzi document is a forgery, inserted in the record either in 1616 or in 1632 to incriminate Galileo. The original language in which the injunction was to be delivered would have served this purpose much better; under its wording any sort of public discussion of the Copernican issue would have been enough to incriminate him.

These inconsistencies fit well with the hypothesis of a sudden and impulsive intervention of Segizzi after Bellarmine had administered the admonition and perhaps in reaction to the way it was administered (see below). On the contrary, they are difficult to understand if one accepts the forgery hypothesis. In this case, it would have been in Segizzi's own best interest to compile a document in strict accordance with the exact instructions he had received. The same applies, I think, to the hypothesis of a forgery perpetrated in 1632 by the notary or an unknown official of the Holy Office in order to make it possible to summon Galileo to Rome.

Charitable Admonition or Stern Injunction?

There is, however, an objection to the authenticity of the Segizzi injunction that must now be considered. According to Beretta,[19] the pope and the Holy Office had conceived Bellarmine's summoning of Galileo according to the format of a *denunciatio evangelica* (evangelical admonition). The first step, entrusted to Bellarmine, would have been that of a *caritativa monitio* (charitable admonition), which had to be secret. The second step, the injunction in a juridical form, would have been entrusted to Segizzi, in the presence of a notary and witnesses. If this was, in fact, the format followed, the presence of the commissary, as well as of the notary and of the witnesses, from the very beginning — as stated in the document — would have been illegitimate. And this would place in serious doubt the authenticity of the injunction itself as recorded.

In response,[20] one might compare this precept to that given Galileo sixteen years later, summoning him to Rome. According to the decision taken by Urban VIII on September 23, 1632 (see below), the Florentine inquisitor, Clemente Egidi, had to be instructed to give Galileo the precept to go to Rome, in the presence of witnesses who, in the event of Galileo's refusal, would register proof of this.[21] In the actual instructions sent on that same day, September 23, 1632, by Cardinal Antonio Barberini to the Florentine inquisitor, the precept to go to Rome had to be given in the presence of witnesses and of the notary but without telling Galileo why they were present. If Galileo assented, he had to sign a written attestation of his promise to go to Rome. The notary and the witnesses, after Galileo's departure, had to testify that he had written and signed the attestation. However, if Galileo were to refuse to obey, a formal precept to go to Rome had to be given to him "*in the presence of the notary and witnesses.*"[22] It appears possible, therefore, that even in the case of the Bellarmine precept the notary and witnesses (as well as the commissary) could have been present from the beginning, without Galileo's being aware of their identity and of the meaning of their presence.

In further confirmation of the propriety of their presence from the beginning, the document with the Segizzi injunction names two members of Bellarmine's household as witnesses. They could not have been so designated without his permission. Might this have happened in the second step of the precept? This seems to be excluded by the temporal and juridical meaning of the expression *successive ac incontinenti,* which implies an immediate transition and a juridical continuity between the first and the second step. According to Beretta, that formula (widely used in the records of the Inquisition trials) indicates that "the following act is a prolongation, without any interruption, of the preceding one, in the presence of the same persons, at the same moment and in the same place," and "[t]his expression replaces the repetition of the elements required for the validity of the document."[23]

It seems therefore that the assertion of the presence of the notary and witnesses from the very beginning does not constitute of itself a sufficient reason to deny the authenticity of the Segizzi injunction or its legality. And the inclusion of the names of the two members of Bellarmine's household as witnesses seems a further confirmation of that authenticity. How otherwise could Segizzi (let alone the supposed author of a forgery made in 1632) have known those names? Thus it seems possible to conclude that Bellarmine accepted the presence of the commissary and the notary from the beginning, on condition that they would remain unknown to Galileo, the format prescribed in the 1632 precept. After all, he would have been sure of Galileo's prompt submission to his admonition, which would make their intervention unnecessary.

The Segizzi Injunction and Bellarmine's Statements

A further and very important question remains to be dealt with. If the Segizzi injunction is authentic, why is there no mention of it in the statements about the precept made by Bellarmine to the Holy Office and later on to Galileo himself?

From Galileo's dispositions at the time of his trial, in 1633, and even from the sentence of condemnation (see below), there is reason to believe that Bellarmine dealt kindly with Galileo when admonishing him, on the pope's orders, in 1616. If so, the commissary might well have resented it. This could explain the rapidity of his intervention, taking advantage perhaps of some hesitation or questioning on Galileo's part. In turn, so precipitate an action by Segizzi would surely have displeased Bellarmine, since the first step entrusted to him would not yet have been completed by Galileo's submission or refusal to obey. Did he express his displeasure to the commissary? We do not know, but it is conceivable that he did.

One could ask further whether Bellarmine would have said anything to Galileo concerning Segizzi's intervention. Did he somehow reassure him, telling him not to be too concerned about the rushed way the commissary had acted? Or did he even go so far as to tell Galileo to ignore such an unjustified intervention, keeping in his mind only the precept he had received from him? Something of the kind could possibly be guessed from the assurance with which later on Galileo asked the cardinal for a certificate regarding what had actually happened, and perhaps also from the declarations he would later make on the subject of the injunction during the trial (see below).

We also do not know if Bellarmine ever considered that the commissary might have asked the notary to insert in the files of the Holy Office the document recording his intervention. He may well not have. Registered as it was in the form of *imbreviatura*, there was no need for the witnesses' signatures (which could not have been recorded without Bellarmine's knowledge). Segizzi and the notary knew their names, and that was sufficient for this kind of document, which could have been written after their return to the Holy Office. At any rate, Bellarmine knew that he had to report personally to the Holy Office about the accomplishment of the task of delivering the admonition. And he knew too that this report would be the authoritative one. Why, then, should he have been concerned about what Segizzi might do?

Let us recall now the report that Bellarmine actually gave to the meeting of the Holy Office on March 3, 1616. He informed the congregation that Galileo had acquiesced when warned of their order to abandon the Copernican opinion. He made no mention of the Segizzi injunction. On the supposition that the injunction had, in fact, been delivered, according to the interpretation of the events just proposed, the commissary's intervention would have been premature, against instructions, and consequently illegal. In the circumstances, Bellarmine would not have seen any reason to mention it. Possibly the cardinal, well known for his kindness, would not have wanted in any case to put the commissary in a difficult position before the congregation. At any rate, Galileo had been warned (legally, at least, by Bellarmine himself) and had certainly acquiesced. And this would have been sufficient for the report. Segizzi, who, as commissary of the Holy Office, would have been present at the meeting, would not have dared to object to the Bellarmine report. He knew that his action had been hasty and would, in consequence, have been grateful to Bellarmine for his silence about it.

The lack of any mention of a Segizzi injunction has been noted also in the certificate Bellarmine later gave to Galileo. It reads: "He has only been notified of the declaration." It should be noted, however, that the word 'only' refers to rumors that Galileo had abjured his Copernican opinion before Bellarmine. The cardinal denies that Galileo has abjured or received penances. He has only been warned. Thus 'only' cannot be taken to exclude an injunction by Segizzi. But again, for Bellarmine, that injunction would have been hasty and against instructions. Therefore, here again the cardinal would have omitted any mention of it.

It is, furthermore, worth noticing the existence of a discrepancy between the two declarations made by Bellarmine. According to the pope's instructions conveyed by Cardinal Millini, Bellarmine was to order Galileo to "abandon" the heliocentric doctrine. And this is what Bellarmine declared at the Holy Office meeting he had done. In the certificate, however, Galileo is said to have been told that such a doctrine "cannot be defended or held." Now, "not to hold" is more or less equivalent to "abandon." But "not to defend" belonged to the injunction to be given by Segizzi, again according to Millini's report. Furthermore, the way in which Bellarmine declares the task to have been achieved is impersonal: [Galileo] "had acquiesced when warned" and "he has only been notified." There is no mention of the person by whom the precept was given. At least in a certificate written by the person delivering the admonition, the addition of the specification "by us," after "notified," would have been very natural. Why did Bellarmine omit it?

It is perhaps not too speculative to see in such characteristics of the two documents a possible, although very indirect, acknowledgment of the Segizzi intervention. Once again, Bellarmine would not have recognized it as legitimate. That would be why he did not mention it. But if we are right, it did happen. And that is why, possibly, he preferred to use impersonal terms in his declarations.

In conclusion, the two documents do not seem to be in an irreconcilable contradiction with the one recording the Segizzi injunction. In other words, the absence of any mention of the Segizzi injunction in these other documents does not necessarily exclude the possibility of that injunction's having been given. The irreconcilable contradiction remains, of course, between the latter and the instructions recorded in the Millini report. Would this contradiction alone be sufficient to cast a doubt on the validity of Galileo's condemnation? I will come back to this later.

From all these considerations, it seems possible to conclude that the document discovered in the files of the Holy Office in 1632 is genuine, meaning that it was not forged in 1616 by Segizzi or any other official of the Holy Office or in 1632 by some unknown member of the same congregation.[24] Furthermore, the form of *imbreviatura* warrants its legal value, at least from the formal point of view.

The Role of the Injunction According to Galileo's Depositions at His Trial

Let us consider next whether the depositions made by Galileo during the trial yield any further reason to believe in the authenticity of the Segizzi document.

To better understand Galileo's line of self-defense during the interrogations, it seems worth noticing that he received well in advance indications about the charges that were being pressed against him. Most of them concerned the *Dialogue*. One, however, concerned a newly discovered document. On September 11, 1632, Ambassador Niccolini informed the secretary of the grand duke, Cioli, about the discovery in the archives of the Holy Office of a document saying that Galileo, "about twenty years [*sic*] before[,] . . . was called to Rome and prohibited from holding this opinion by the Lord Cardinal Bellarmine, in the name of the Pope and the Holy Office."[25] Given the close relationship between Cioli and Galileo, the latter would certainly have been made aware of this information and of what Niccolini's informant, the Master of the Sacred Palace, Riccardi, added: "[T]his alone is enough to ruin him utterly."

As we see, Riccardi gave an abridged summary of the content of the document, without any mention of the strict injunction by Segizzi. We know, however, from the records of Galileo's trial, that this document was certainly that recording the Segizzi injunction. At any rate, Cioli's information was sufficient for Galileo to recall what had happened on that black day for him, February 26, 1616. If the Segizzi injunction was indeed delivered, it is hard to believe that Galileo could have forgotten such a painful event. He might have forgotten, after sixteen years, the exact wording of the injunction, but surely not that it had taken place. Since, however, Riccardi's information mentioned only Bellarmine's admonition, and since Galileo knew nothing about the recording of the Segizzi injunction, he might have thought that the newly found document was one containing only the precept given to him by the Jesuit cardinal and that, consequently, he would be interrogated only about it at the trial.

He had, over the years, kept Bellarmine's certificate. Knowing from Riccardi's information that the discovered document would be used as a powerful weapon against him at the tribunal of the Holy Office, he must have prepared his defense very carefully—the more so since after his arrival in Rome he and Ambassador Niccolini were each reminded of the importance likely to be attached to the Bellarmine document in the forthcoming trial.[26]

In fact, the question of the precept he had received "by order of the Pope and the Holy Office" was at the center of the interrogation on April 12, 1633. To the question of how and by whom he had been notified about the decree of the Index of 1616, Galileo answered that he had been notified by Cardinal Bellarmine:

> In the month of February 1616, Lord Cardinal Bellarmine told me that since Copernicus's opinion, taken absolutely, was contrary to Holy Scripture, it could be neither held nor defended, but it could be taken and used *ex suppositione* (suppositionally).[27] In conformity with this I keep a certificate by Lord Cardinal Bellarmine himself, dated 26 May 1616, in which he says that Copernicus's opinion cannot be held or defended, being against Holy Scripture. I present a copy of this certificate, and here it is.[28]

The record of the interrogation states at this point that "the evidence was accepted and marked with the letter B."[29]

As we know, the certificate by Bellarmine makes no mention of the Segizzi injunction. However, the interrogator (Maculano) had in his hands the newly discovered document in which that injunction was clearly stated. The discrepancy between the two documents was obvious. What really happened on that February 26? This is why he asked "whether, when he was notified of the above-mentioned matters, there were others present, and who they were." Galileo's answer was: "When Lord Cardinal Bellarmine notified me of what I mentioned regarding Copernicus's opinion, there were some Dominican Fathers present, but I did not know them nor have I seen them since."[30]

To the crucial question "whether at that time, in the presence of those Fathers, he was given any injunction either by them or by someone else concerning the same matter, and if so what," Galileo answered:

> As I remember it, the affair took place in the following manner. One morning Lord Cardinal Bellarmine sent for me, and he told me a certain detail that I should like to speak to the ear of His Holiness before telling others,[31] but then at the end he told me that Copernicus's opinion could not be held or defended, being contrary to Holy Scripture. I do not recall whether those Dominican friars were there at first or came afterward; nor do I recall whether they were present when Cardinal Bellarmine told me that the same opinion could not be held. Finally, it may be that I was given an injunction not to hold or defend the said opinion, but I do not recall it since this is something of many years ago.[32]

As if to jog his memory, the interrogator noted at this point that "the said injunction, given to him then in the presence of witnesses, states that he cannot in any way whatever hold, defend, or teach the said opinion" and then asked whether he now remembered it and by whom he was ordered. Galileo answered:

> I do not recall that this injunction was given me any other way than orally by Lord Cardinal Bellarmine. I do remember that the injunction was that I could not hold or defend, and maybe even that I could not teach. I do not recall, further, that there was the phrase "in any way whatever," but maybe there was in fact. I did not think about it or keep it in mind, having received a few months thereafter Lord Bellarmine's certificate, dated 26 May, which I have presented and in which is explained the order given to me not to hold or defend the said opinion. Regarding the two other phrases in the said injunction now mentioned, namely "not to teach" and "in any way whatever," I do not retain them in my memory, I think because they are not contained in the said certificate, which I relied upon and kept as a reminder.[33]

After that, the interrogation shifted to the question of the concession of the imprimatur. Galileo was asked if, after the issuance of the injunction, he had obtained a special permission to write the *Dialogue*. His answer was: "After the above-mentioned injunction, I did not seek permission to write the above-mentioned book . . . because I do not think that by writing the book I was contradicting at all the injunction given me not to hold, defend or teach the said opinion, but rather that I was refuting it."[34]

If we consider now the second interrogation on April 30, following an unspeci-fied extrajudicial initiative on the part of Commissary Maculano, there is a reference to the words of the Segizzi injunction at the very beginning of Galileo's declaration: "For several days I have been thinking continuously and directly [better: only] about the interrogations I underwent the 16th [*sic*] of this month, and in particular about the question whether sixteen years ago I had been prohibited, by order of the Holy Office, from holding, defending, and teaching in any way whatever the opinion, then con-demned, of the earth's motion and the sun's stability."[35]

In the following declaration, however, Galileo omits any answer to this question, dealing instead with the matter of the "confession" already made orally to Maculano about the content of the *Dialogue*. The answer, however, is given in his written de-fense, delivered on May 10. The defense starts with the following words:

> In an earlier interrogation, I was asked whether I had informed the Most Reve-rend Father Master of the Sacred Palace about the private injunction issued upon me sixteen years ago by order of the Holy Office—"not to hold, defend, or teach in any way whatever" the opinion of the earth's motion, and sun's stability—and I answered: No. Since I was not asked the reason why I did not inform him, I did not have the opportunity to say anything else. Now it seems to me necessary to mention it, in order to prove the absolute purity of my mind, always averse to using simulation and deceit in any of my actions.[36]

It might seem strange that Galileo denies here having had the opportunity to explain in the first interrogation the reasons why he did not inform the Master of the Sacred Palace about the injunction he had received. We know that in the first interrogation he gave such an explanation, saying that he had not mentioned the in-junction because in the *Dialogue* he did not hold nor defend the Copernican opinion but, on the contrary, had intended to refute it. By now, however, he probably knew the answer given by the consultors of the Holy Office about the Copernican content of the *Dialogue*. It is conceivable that Maculano had informed him about it, on the occasion of the extrajudicial initiative, in order to encourage his confession. As a con-sequence, Galileo may have felt that the previous explanation was no longer credible and hence may have wanted to replace it with another.

After recalling the circumstances under which he had requested from Bellarmine the certificate whose original he was now attaching to his defense, Galileo added:

> Having the reminder of this authentic certificate, handwritten by the one who is-sued the order himself, I did not try later to recall or give any other thought to the words used to give me orally the said injunction, to the effect that one cannot defend or hold, etc.; thus, the two phrases besides "holding" and "defending"

which I hear are contained in the injunction given to me and recorded, that is, "teaching" and "in any way whatever," struck me as very new and unheard.[37]

Since those two phrases are not included in Bellarmine's certificate, Galileo continues, he should not be mistrusted when he affirms that he has lost any memory of them in the course of "fourteen or sixteen years." And he concludes this part of his defense by saying:

> Now, when those two phrases are removed and we retain only the other two mentioned in the attached certificate [namely 'holding' and 'defending'], there is no reason to doubt that the order contained in it is the same as the injunction issued by the decree of the Holy Congregation of the Index. From this I feel very reasonably excused for not notifying the Father Master of the Sacred Palace of the injunction given to me in private, the latter being the same as the one of the Congregation of the Index.[38]

Let us now consider what we can infer from these answers given by Galileo during the trial. In his first interrogation he admits the presence of "some Dominican Fathers," though at a later moment he does not recall whether they were there at the time of the Bellarmine precept or whether they came later on. Of course, admitting their presence does not necessarily imply that one of them delivered an injunction. It is, however, important to notice that Galileo himself confirms the fact of their presence and thus, we can safely infer, that of Segizzi.

But what about the injunction itself? There is reason to believe that Bellarmine dealt kindly when warning him, on the pope's orders, in 1616. In the first interrogation of the trial, Galileo recalled that Bellarmine had told him he could treat the Copernican issue "suppositionally." This went beyond (even though certainly not against) Bellarmine's instructions and could be interpreted as softening the blow. And during the same interrogation, Galileo also claimed that Bellarmine had told him "a certain detail" of a confidential sort, to be communicated at this later time only to the pope himself.[39] Again, this suggests something other than a stern rebuke and fits well with what is known about the gentle way the saintly cardinal went about his duties, even as an inquisitor. The sentence of Galileo's condemnation (see below) seems to confirm his disposition on this point, where it states that he was "gently admonished" by the cardinal.

Now, in the first interrogation, Galileo admits the *possibility* of having received a strict injunction in the terms suggested to him by the interrogator. And he attributes even that to Bellarmine. This attribution seems difficult, however, to reconcile with the indications above, that Bellarmine deliberately softened the manner in which the admonition was administered. As for not being able to recall the exact wording of the injunction, he invokes the long time elapsed since then, as well as Bellarmine's certificate containing only the words "not to hold or defend." Toward the end of the interrogation, however, when speaking about the imprimatur, he seems to admit to having received an injunction in the more rigorous form.

That admission becomes an even more plausible implication of the written defense that he submitted. At the beginning of the document, the injunction appears to be acknowledged *as a fact,* no longer as a mere possibility. Even later in the text, Galileo does not seem to question the authenticity of the injunction "given to me and recorded," even though he keeps invoking the lapse of memory concerning the two phrases not contained in Bellarmine's certificate and still attributes (but only once and *en passant*) the "order" to the cardinal alone. Why this apparent shift in his strategy?

To search for some possible explanation, it seems worth noticing that the written defense was prepared by Galileo after his return to the Tuscan embassy, following the conclusion of the extrajudicial initiative by Maculano. Galileo had had enough time and peace of mind to think carefully about the case building against him. He knew by then about the existence of a written document recording the full injunction, whose words Maculano had read during the first interrogation, adding that the injunction had been given in the presence of witnesses. Two different scenarios are here possible.

The first is the *false injunction scenario:* after Bellarmine's admonition, no injunction was actually given by Segizzi. In the absence of a written document, the easiest way for Galileo would have been simply to deny that an injunction had been given or to admit (as he did at first) the possibility that Bellarmine's admonition had been delivered to him in the form of an injunction. He had been, however, unexpectedly confronted with the existence of the written document read to him by Maculano, without any mention of its author. Galileo, of course, would never have thought it to be fraudulent. Thus he did not have any other alternative than to think it to be the record of Bellarmine's admonition, now seen as a full "injunction." Given the long time elapsed and the fact that in the certificate two phrases in the injunction were not mentioned, Galileo could have been in this case perfectly sincere in invoking his lack of recollection of them and in trying to justify himself with regard to the imprimatur. And this would explain quite well why at first he had admitted only the "possibility" of a full injunction and now he was admitting it as a fact. Furthermore, Galileo did not know anything about the instructions given to Bellarmine. Thus he was not aware that to ascribe the full injunction to him would imply that the cardinal himself had acted against his instructions, serving even the second part of the order, which should have been reserved to Segizzi.

The second scenario is the *authentic injunction scenario:* the injunction was given by Segizzi after Bellarmine's admonition. In this case, it is hard to believe that Galileo could have forgotten so solemn an event. He could have forgotten, quite under-standably, the exact phrasing of the injunction but not the fact of it, no doubt pain-ful to him. Neither could he have forgotten that it was a "Dominican Father" who had addressed it to him, in the name of the pope and of the congregation of the Holy Office. Why, then, not admit having received it from him? Two different but com-plementary explanations seem possible. First, admitting, after the Bellarmine ad-monition, the administration of an explicit injunction by a person in authority in the Holy Office would have made it much more difficult for Galileo to excuse him-self with regard to the question of the imprimatur. Second, as I have already sur-mised, Galileo had carefully prepared beforehand his line of defense, based on the existence of Bellarmine's certificate, as one can infer from his written defense. That is why in the first interrogation he initially spoke only of the ban on Copernicanism communicated by the Jesuit cardinal; there is no mention of an admonition of any kind directed to Galileo himself. After the question as to whether he had received an *injunction,* he continued to attribute that too, as a possibility, to Bellarmine. Thus, when Maculano finally read to him the words of that injunction from a written docu-ment, he had to continue to attribute them to Bellarmine (availing himself of the fact that the commissary had not mentioned the author of the injunction). Doing otherwise would have been equivalent to confessing that he had not told the truth previously. In this scenario also, Galileo would not have been aware of the problem arising from the contrast between a formal injunction given him by Bellarmine and the actual instructions Bellarmine (according to the Millini report) had received from the pope.

Which of these two scenarios is the correct one? The first scenario fits neatly with the discrepancies between the two declarations made by Bellarmine about the given precept and the document with the Segizzi injunction. However, the hypothe-sis of the latter as a fraudulent document runs up against serious difficulties. First of all, it presupposes a complete lack of integrity on the part of the commissary or some other later official of the Holy Office (not to mention Urban VIII himself). Such a grave breach of the rules in force at the Holy Office even at that time ought to be substantiated with much more convincing arguments than that of a discrepancy of documents, which seems, moreover, to be at least partially surmountable. Further-more, the textual analysis of those documents, together with the probable parallel between the instructions of 1616 and those of 1632, appears to offer some more posi-tive indications in favor of the authenticity of the injunction. As a consequence, the second scenario seems to stand a better chance than the first of being correct.

If this is so, should we conclude that Galileo lied about the author of the in-junction? One could answer that he simply tried to defend himself by making maxi-mum use of the fact of the Bellarmine certificate and availing himself of the cir-cumstance that Maculano had not mentioned the author of the injunction. One might even speculate (as already noted) that Bellarmine could have communicated to Galileo, in one way or another, his own disagreement with Segizzi's premature intervention, perhaps going so far as to tell Galileo to forget about it and to keep in mind only the admonition Bellarmine himself had given to him. If this was indeed what happened, Galileo could have been fully justified in his denial. After all, in this scenario, faithful to the cardinal's own suggestion, he did not have to recognize any other "order" than the one legitimately delivered to him.

The question of the authenticity of the injunction must, however, be distinguished from that of its legitimacy. To believe in that authenticity (as I do) is certainly not to acknowledge *the act of administering the injunction* to be legitimate. An evident (and, in this instance, insurmountable) contradiction exists between the wording of the document and the instructions the pope gave to Bellarmine. The latter seems himself to have been aware of this contradiction, if the interpretation of his declarations according to the second scenario is correct. Thus a further question arises about the role of this document in the Galileo trial: Did it play a significant role in bringing about his indictment and condemnation? If it did, this would inevitably call into question the legality of one of the most famous trials in Western history.

On the Role of the Segizzi Injunction in Galileo's Indictment

The discovery of the Segizzi injunction took place after the uproar caused by the publication of the *Dialogue* had already come to the ears of Urban VIII and he had entrusted the examination of the book to a Special Commission, about the middle of August.[40] Speaking to Ambassador Niccolini on September 4, 1632, the pope declared that the prohibition of the *Dialogue* "was the least ill which could be done to him [Galileo] and that he should take care not to be summoned by the Holy Office; that he has appointed a Commission of theologians and other persons versed in various sciences . . . who are weighing every minutia, word for word, since one is dealing with the most perverse subject one could ever come across."[41]

After five meetings, the commission concluded that "one could not avoid bringing the business to the attention of the Congregation."[42] Upon being informed of this answer, Urban VIII on September 15 sent one of his secretaries to Niccolini so that he would relay notice of that decision to the grand duke. The pope obviously considered the matter to be very serious; it is probable that, with that unusual step, he was preparing the grand duke for the further decision of summoning Galileo to Rome. This seems confirmed by his words to the ambassador three days later: "[T]his work of his [Galileo's] is indeed pernicious and the matter is more serious than His Highness thinks."[43] The pope made no mention of the discovery of the Segizzi injunction, even though that discovery had taken place before September 11.[44] Most probably he had not yet been informed about it. Otherwise he would hardly have omitted to mention such an aggravating circumstance to the ambassador.[45]

The decision to summon Galileo to Rome was taken, as already mentioned, during the meeting of the Holy Office on September 23, in the presence of Urban VIII. During that meeting, a report about the facts surrounding the imprimatur given to the *Dialogue* was read, as well as a summary of the charges moved against it as a result of the examination by the Special Commission.[46] In substance, those charges were based on the fact that Galileo had treated the Copernican theory not *ex hypothesi* but "by asserting absolutely the earth's motion and the sun's immobility, or by characterizing the supporting arguments as demonstrative and necessary, or by treating the negative side as impossible."[47] On that occasion notice was also given of the discovery of the document containing the Segizzi injunction: "[H]e [Galileo] has been deceitfully silent about the command laid upon him by the Holy Office, in the year 1616, which was as follows" (the quotation of the content of the document was restricted to Segizzi's words, but without mentioning his name). And the report concluded: "One must now deliberate on the way to proceed with regard to the person as well as to the book already printed." Urban's decision was to order Galileo to be summoned to Rome.

Was that decision motivated by the discovery of the injunction? Given the gravity of the matter concerning the content of the *Dialogue,* so much stressed by the pope in his talks with the ambassador Niccolini, it is hardly conceivable that, in the absence of that discovery, entrusting the question of the *Dialogue* to the Holy Office could have been limited to a new examination of its content without its author being summoned to Rome. In other words, one can surmise that the Galileo trial would have taken place anyhow. What the discovery of the injunction document did was offer Urban VIII a further reason to justify a decision he had probably taken from the very beginning.

On the Role of the Injunction in the Trial and Condemnation of Galileo

We know already that the existence of this document was at the center of the first interrogation of Galileo. And we have seen how Galileo tried to get rid of the aggravated charge against him, both on that occasion and in his later written defense. He used the Bellarmine certificate to explain why he had not mentioned the injunction while asking for the imprimatur. He also tried to dismiss the charge of having held and defended the Copernican doctrine, at first affirming that, far from having defended it, he had shown in his book that its reasonings were invalid and inconclusive. The basis of this unexpected assertion was evidently the dismissive terms 'chimeras' and 'dreams' that Salviati uses in the *Dialogue* to describe some of the most affirmative conclusions in favor of the Copernican thesis. Most of all, Galileo was trying to pass off as his own conclusion the argument of Urban VIII regarding divine omnipotence, inserted at the very end of the book. Hardly anyone would have been convinced.

Neither were the theologians convinced to whom a new examination of the *Dialogue* was entrusted. On the basis of the three terms found in Segizzi's injunction ("not to hold, teach, or defend"), the examination concluded that Galileo had taught and defended the Copernican opinion and that he was vehemently suspect of having held it, at least at the time of writing the *Dialogue.* He was thus found to have violated the prescriptions of the decree of the Index as well as the precept in the form in which it had been imposed upon him by the Segizzi injunction.

I cannot deal here with the debated question of the meaning and consequences of the later extrajudicial initiative of the commissary, Maculano, mentioned earlier in the essay. I remark only that the "confessions" made in Galileo's written defense appear not to have convinced anyone, any more than did his previous depositions.

Let us now consider the last phase of the Galileo trial. The question of the precept Galileo received at the time of his appearance before Bellarmine is raised once again by the process summary "Against Galileo Galilei," which purports to summarize the events of 1615–16, those surrounding the permission to print the *Dialogue,* and the content of the interrogations (including the defense presented by Galileo). Most probably composed, as was customary, by the assessor of the Holy Office (Pietro Paolo Febei), this document appears seriously biased against Galileo, with an often inaccurate or even distorted presentation of the facts.[48] It was submitted to the meeting of the Holy Office of June 16, for the *expeditio causae,* namely for the final decision to be taken by Urban VIII.

Concerning Bellarmine's admonition, the summary says: "[O]n 25 February 1616, His Holiness ordered the said Cardinal Bellarmine to summon Galileo and give him the injunction [better, 'precept,' *facesse precetto*] that he must abandon and not discuss in any way the above-mentioned opinion of the immobility of the Sun and the motion of the Earth."[49] This is clearly inaccurate. The pope's order, as we know, had foreseen two possible phases in the delivery of the precept. The compiler of the document must have known this, since he had available to him the complete dossier on Galileo, and must therefore have been aware that Bellarmine was instructed only to warn Galileo to abandon the Copernican opinion, while the injunction not to discuss it in any manner had to be given by the commissary, in the second possible phase of the procedure.

The following statement is still more inaccurate: "On the 26th the same Cardinal, in the presence of the Father Commissary of the Holy Office, notary and witnesses, gave him the said injunction, which he promised to obey. Its tenor is that he should abandon completely the said opinion, and indeed that he should not hold, teach, or defend it in any way whatever; otherwise the Holy Office would start proceedings against him."[50]

As one can see, the format of the admonition described here is substantially that of the strict injunction (to be given, if necessary, by Segizzi, according to the pope's instructions), but its administration is attributed not to the latter but to Bellarmine. Strangely enough, the author of the summary, without realizing it, is here making Bellarmine responsible for having acted against those instructions. During the interrogations and in his written defense, Galileo indeed always insisted that Bellarmine was the only person from whom he had received the admonition or even perhaps the full injunction. The compiler of the summary appears to have wanted to take advantage of this alternative possibility, which would eliminate the problem of the propriety of Segizzi's intervention (even though creating that of Bellarmine's!). Indeed, the commissary is now affirmed only to have been present, apparently without saying a word. But what about the Bellarmine certificate? Recalling later the content of the first interrogation, the summary cannot avoid mentioning its existence: "He [Galileo] admitted having been given an injunction, but he said that, based on this certificate in which the words 'to teach in any way whatever' do not appear, he did not remember them."[51] As one can see, a full confession of the whole precept is attributed here to Galileo, purporting to be based on his statements in the written defense. As a result, the force of Bellarmine's certificate is neatly neutralized. In fact, if the injunction in the fuller form had indeed been given by the Jesuit cardinal, with the full terms "confessed" by Galileo, the lack of those words in his certificate would be irrelevant.

We do not know if this summary was submitted, as was customary, to the cardinals and the consultors of the Holy Office on the meeting of the *feria quarta* (June 15), prior to the *expeditio causae,* that took place the following day in the presence of the pope. Was it accepted as it stood on both occasions, or on June 16 at least? Given the misrepresentations of the facts here and elsewhere in the summary, its acceptance would cast serious doubt on the validity of the pope's final decision. Indeed, the summaries of the processes usually carried considerable weight in the final decisions of the Inquisition trials. However, in Galileo's trial, it seems that Urban VIII's final decision was preceded by a discussion, with the participation of the cardinals and the consultors of the Holy Office. Some of the participants might have pointed out the inaccuracy of the summary, and the corrections would then have been entrusted to the person (Maculano?)[52] in charge of the redaction of the final sentence. In the absence of such a supposition, it is hard to explain the evident discrepancy, to be discussed in a moment, between the summary and the final sentence with respect to the quotation of the documents. How, otherwise, could the compiler of the sentence have corrected those quotations on his own initiative?[53]

Let us now consider the sentence itself. The text of the summary refers to the documents containing the pope's instructions to Bellarmine and the Segizzi injunction, without, however, quoting them. This allows the author to summarize their contents in an arbitrary way, with the aim of eliminating the contradiction between them. The author of the text of the sentence, on the other hand, quotes them correctly. After recalling the circumstances under which, on February 25, 1616, Bellarmine was ordered to summon Galileo, with the three stages foreseen by the instructions he had received, the sentence goes on:

> To execute this decision, the following day at the Palace of, and in the presence of, the above mentioned Most Illustrious Lord Cardinal Bellarmine, after being informed and warned in a friendly way by the same Lord Cardinal, you were given an injunction by the then Commissary of the Holy Office in the presence of a notary and witnesses to the effect that you must completely abandon the said false opinion, and that in the future you could neither hold, nor teach it in any way whatever, either orally or in writing; having promised to obey, you were dismissed.[54]

As it is evident from these words, the sentence, unlike the summary, carefully distinguishes between the first phase, the admonition by Bellarmine, and the following one, the injunction by the commissary. That the mere writing of the *Dialogue* broke the promise made by Galileo on that earlier occasion is dealt with immediately afterwards in the sentence:

> [T]he said book was diligently examined and found to violate explicitly the above-mentioned injunction given to you; for in the same book you have defended the same opinion already condemned and so declared to your face, although in the same book you try by means of various subterfuges to give the impression of leaving it undecided and labeled as probable; this is still a very serious error since there is no way an opinion declared and defined contrary to Divine Scripture may be probable.[55]

It is important to note that the sentence does not use here the simplest argument that could have been brought against the *Dialogue,* based on the actual instructions recorded in the Millini report. According to them, as we know, Segizzi should have issued to Galileo the injunction to abstain completely not only "from teaching or defending" the Copernican opinion but also "from discussing it." Thus the very fact of having written the *Dialogue* would have been sufficient to incriminate him. But in the document recording the Segizzi injunction, those last words are lacking. It appears, then, that given the discrepancy between the instructions and their execution according to that document (about whose authenticity Galileo's judges had no reason to doubt) they concluded that Galileo should be judged according to the order he had actually received. The main reason given by the sentence for the summoning of Galileo to the Holy Office was, in fact, an infringement of the prohibition to *defend* the heliocentric theory, a prohibition confirmed by the Bellarmine certificate itself. That theory had been "previously condemned," namely in the decree of the Congregation of the Index, and it had been declared to be so "to Galileo's face" by Bellarmine and by the Segizzi injunction. Galileo was thus not excused by ignorance.

As for the injunction, according to the sentence, Galileo had failed to mention its existence when requesting permission to publish the *Dialogue.* As we have seen, during the first interrogation, he had not denied the possibility that the injunction, with the last words "not to teach in any way whatever," might have been imposed on him by Bellarmine, and in his written defense he had seemingly admitted that injunction as a fact. He had, however, excused himself saying that he had forgotten, in the long intervening time, its exact formulation and that Bellarmine's later attestation had freed him from any worry about other details. The sentence mentions here the cardinal's attestation and correctly quotes its content. Commenting on Galileo's usage of that certificate in his defense, the sentence says: "However, the said certificate you produced in your defense aggravates your case further since, while it says that the said opinion is contrary to Holy Scripture, yet you dared to treat of it, defend it, and show it as probable; nor are you helped by the license you artfully and cunningly extorted since you did not mention the injunction you were under."[56] As one can see, the sentence here turns the key element of Galileo's defense against him as a confirmation of his delinquency. Far from excusing him, Bellarmine's certificate aggravates his responsibility for having dealt with the Copernican opinion as probable even though the cardinal had told him that it was contrary to Holy Scripture.

The other key point of Galileo's defense, namely the fact of the permission obtained to publish the *Dialogue,* is also dismissed. That permission was "cunningly extorted" because Galileo had not made known the injunction he had received. In his written defense, Galileo insisted, as we know, that since the Bellarmine certificate did not say anything more than the decree of the Index, known to everybody, he thought it was not necessary to mention it. But what about Segizzi's injunction? If its authenticity was assumed (and the sentence certainly did assume it), Galileo had received a special and very personal order by the Holy Office whose wording went much further than the decree of the Index. The imprimatur was therefore of no value whatsoever.

It seems clear, therefore, that the Segizzi injunction was relied on primarily to handle the thorny question of the existing imprimatur and to offer a way out to the Master of the Holy Palace, Father Riccardi, who had first granted it. It does not appear to have been considered, at least directly, as a further and different reason for Galileo's condemnation. This seems to be confirmed by the concluding wording of the sentence of condemnation:

We say, pronounce, sentence and declare that you, the above-mentioned Galileo, because of the things deduced in the trial and confessed by you as above, have rendered yourself according to the Holy Office vehemently suspected of heresy, namely of having held and believed a doctrine which is false and contrary to the Divine and Holy Scripture: that the sun is the center of the world and does not move from east to west, and the earth moves and is not the center of the world, and that one may hold and defend as probable an opinion after it has been declared and defined [to be] contrary to Holy Scripture. Consequently you have incurred all the censures and penalties imposed and promulgated by the sacred canons and all particular and general laws against such delinquents.[57]

Two comments are in order here. The first concerns Galileo's "confessions." What did Galileo confess? He confessed to being the author of the *Dialogue;* to having exaggerated in his book the arguments in favor of the Copernican opinion out of sheer vanity; and to having received a notification from Bellarmine that that opinion could not be held or defended. He further admitted in the first interrogation the *possibility* of having received from Bellarmine even a formal injunction containing the wording of the strict injunction, as this was "recalled to his memory" by the interrogator (without any mention of the person supposedly administering it, Segizzi). In his written defense, he seemingly admitted the injunction as a fact, though insisting on the difference between its words and those of the Bellarmine certificate. Evidently, the sentence follows here the assertion of the summary that Galileo made a full confession of the injunction. On the other hand, contrary to the summary and to Galileo's own statements, the sentence attributes the injunction, not to Bellarmine, but to Segizzi, the person who should have delivered it if it had been in accordance with the original instructions.

The second comment concerns the meaning of "vehemently suspect of heresy." The summary quoted among the antecedents of Galileo's trial the response given in 1616 by the qualifiers about the two main Copernican propositions. As we already know, they deemed the immobility of the sun to be heretical and the mobility of the earth to be at least an error in the faith. Taken together, the minimal theological "qualification" that they recommended to the cardinal-members of the Congregation of the Index was therefore that of an error in the faith. The cardinals, however, stopped short of accepting this recommendation. The decree of the Index states only that "the Pythagorean doctrine is false and altogether opposed to Holy Scripture." This rather vague formulation leaves open the possibility of different interpretations about the theological meaning of this "opposition." In order of decreasing severity, it could have been qualified as "heresy," "error in the faith," or "rashness."[58] And this last assessment seems to have been the one favored by Urban VIII in the years prior to the publication of Galileo's *Dialogue.* After that publication, however, or perhaps during the trial, he appears to have changed his opinion. In his declaration to Ambassador Niccolini three days after the decision taken against Galileo on June 16, the pope affirmed that there was "no way of avoiding prohibiting that opinion, since it is erroneous and contrary to Holy Scripture."[59] It seems, therefore, that the final decision was to consider the Copernican theory as erroneous in the faith. Even though less severe than the qualification of "heresy," this qualification implied nevertheless a "vehement suspicion of heresy" and therefore the necessity of eliminating that suspicion through abjuration. (An opinion qualified as "rash" had to be abandoned, but without the necessity to abjure.)

The text of Galileo's abjuration specifically mentions both the Segizzi injunction and the Bellarmine precept:

> However, whereas, after having been judicially instructed with an injunction by the Holy Office to abandon completely the false opinion that the sun is the center of the world and does not move and the earth is not the center of the world and moves, and not to hold, defend, or teach this false doctrine in any way whatever, orally or in writing; and after having been notified that this doctrine is contrary to Holy Scripture; I wrote and published a book in which I treat of this already condemned doctrine and adduce very effective reasons in its favor, without refuting them in any way; therefore I have been judged vehemently suspected of heresy, namely of having held and believed that the sun is the center of the world and motionless and the earth is not the center and moves.[60]

As is evident from these words, the Segizzi injunction is quoted before the Bellarmine admonition, contrary to the wording of the original papal instruction to Bellarmine, as well as the wording of the document recording the Segizzi injunction. The author of the abjuration formula may, perhaps, have wanted to emphasize the much stronger wording of the commissary's injunction, as against the "gentle" notification of Bellarmine. At any rate, even here no additional charge was laid against Galileo on the grounds of his merely having written the *Dialogue,* as it could have been. The vehement suspicion of heresy he was asked to eliminate through his abjuration arose from his having written a book in clear favor of the Copernican doctrine, even though that doctrine had been "already condemned."

Conclusion

Apparently the document that has been at the center of our attention did not have, by itself, a decisive influence on Galileo's condemnation. Even without its discovery, it seems plausible that the outcome of the trial would have been the same, based as it was on the content of the *Dialogue,* seen in the light of the (new) definition of the

Copernican opinion as erroneous in the faith. As we have seen, even before the discovery of the Segizzi injunction, the first analysis of Galileo's book resulted in the decision to entrust the question of the *Dialogue* to the Holy Office. Given Urban's strongly negative comments on the book, without the discovery of the Segizzi injunction Galileo's summons to Rome could possibly have been delayed but not avoided. In fact, during the inquiry, the document recording the papal instructions to Bellarmine as well as Bellarmine's report to the Holy Office about the execution of the admonition to Galileo would assuredly have been found among the documents of the Holy Office. And those findings alone would have been sufficient for summoning Galileo at a subsequent stage of the inquiry. As for Bellarmine's certificate, Galileo would surely have produced it during the interrogations. This certificate, as we know, clearly indicates that Galileo had been warned not to hold or defend the Copernican doctrine. Now, these two words 'hold' and 'defend' were at the center of the second analysis of the *Dialogue* during the course of the Galileo trial. Even without the two other terms added by the Segizzi injunction ("not to teach" and "in any way whatever"), they would have resulted in the same conclusion: Galileo was vehemently suspect of adhering to the Copernican opinion and consequently should be condemned and required to abjure.

The document reporting the Segizzi injunction appears thus to have been used chiefly to further emphasize that Galileo had contravened the decree of the Index and the Bellarmine injunction. Above all, it gave (together with that admonition) further proof to the judges that Galileo had acted "deceitfully" in asking for the imprimatur of his book. As such, it greatly helped to find a much-needed way to disarm the thorny issue of the concession of the imprimatur, allowing the Master of the Sacred Palace, Riccardi, and ultimately Urban VIII himself to save face.[61]

At the end of this inquiry about the "disputed injunction," we are left with the question of its legality. If the above analysis is correct, the hypothesis that the injunction document was a fraud is most probably excluded. Consequently, the gravest objection about the trial's legality does not seem sustainable. But the question remains of the contradiction between the injunction and the instructions given to Bellarmine. As we have seen, Galileo's judges seem to have been aware of it but to have implicitly decided in favor of the validity of the injunction. The question of its *legitimacy,* however, was left unanswered. Even if one concludes that the injunction document was not the determinant of Galileo's condemnation, such a serious flaw in juridical correctness, coupled with the no less serious misrepresentations present in the summary, some of which are repeated even in the sentence, can only leave us profoundly dissatisfied with the way Galileo's trial was carried on and concluded. To be sure, we cannot use our modern legal standards to judge a trial carried out in the epoch of absolutism, ecclesiastical as well as civil. Nevertheless, the juridical norms then in force at the Holy Office ought to have ensured fairer conduct of the trial.

Two further challenges might be raised to the legality of the trial. The first is whether Urban VIII was really unaware of the existence of Bellarmine's admonition to Galileo and, possibly, of the Segizzi injunction. He had, after all, several motives to claim ignorance of the admonition. What can we infer from the evidence at hand? As we have seen, being a cardinal member of the Index Congregation, Bellarmine had taken part, on March 1, 1616, in the decision about the decree to be published on the issue of the Copernican opinion versus Scripture. Among the cardinals attending the meeting, only he and Centini were also members of the Holy Office.[62] The meeting was held in Bellarmine's residence. We know also that it was once again Bellarmine who received from the pope the task of placing before the cardinals the problem as to what measures should be taken with respect to the works of Copernicus, de Zuñiga, and Foscarini. From the same document we can infer that the following discussion was long and probably quite lively: "after a *mature consideration* of the matter among the very Illustrious [cardinals], *finally* they decided . . ." (emphasis mine). The decision was approved later on by the pope and published as a decree of the Index on March 5. No mention is made in it of Galileo's book *On the Sunspots*. In fact, even though that book contains, in the "Third Letter to Welser," an affirmation of support for the Copernican theory, this appears in a marginal note and cannot, therefore, be taken as an open profession of Copernicanism. Moreover, and more important, the book contains no reference to Scripture.

It is hard to believe that *no* mention of Galileo was made during the meeting. Anyone there would have understood that one of the aims of the decree was to end Galileo's public advocacy of the Copernican theory. But the question is: Did Bellarmine mention that the Holy Office had decided to silence the famous mathematician? Given the very strict secrecy imposed on decisions of the Holy Office, it is difficult to suppose that Bellarmine or Centini would have spoken of the silencing of Galileo already ordered by the pope. It is much more probable that Bellarmine would have simply reassured the other cardinals regarding Galileo, stressing that the forthcoming decree of the Index would be adequate to solve the Galileo problem. Even less thinkable is that he could have said anything about the way his task had been carried out.

It seems, therefore, quite unlikely that Cardinal Barberini could have learned about the Bellarmine admonition on this occasion, and even less likely that he would have been told about the Segizzi injunction. It is less probable again that Galileo himself might have said anything about the whole affair to Bellarmine, at the time of his six audiences with the pope, now Urban VIII, in 1624 or, later, in 1630. This would be all the more unlikely because by then Galileo knew well that the pope was not open to any change with regard to the 1616 decision and was evidently cautious about allowing Galileo to proceed with his plans for a book dealing with Copernican astronomy. In conclusion, then, the hypothesis that Urban VIII pretended to be unaware of Galileo's appearance before Bellarmine in 1616 in order to circumvent the fact of the imprimatur given to the *Dialogue* and to furnish a new and powerful charge against Galileo does not appear to be sustainable.

One final possible challenge to the legality of the trial concerns the papal determination, at the conclusion of Galileo's trial, of the theological status of the opposition between the Copernican claims and Scripture. As already noted, Urban VIII determined on that occasion that holding such an opinion was an error in the faith. This justified Galileo's condemnation as vehemently suspect of heresy and his being required consequently to abjure. But Galileo's *Dialogue* was written *before* that definition, when the theologically less severe qualification of "rashness" was still possible; indeed, this seems to have been Urban's own view prior to 1632. Of course, the suspicion of holding a "rash" opinion was sufficient legally to bring Galileo to trial, all the more since he had also transgressed a precept intimated to him by Bellarmine in the name of the pope and of the Holy Office. A subsequent examination of the *Dialogue* would have shown that Galileo had defended the Copernican theory and was at least suspect of having held it at the time of writing the book. As a result, the book would have been prohibited and Galileo subjected to the penances provided for by the Holy Office jurisprudence. Since the *Dialogue* had provoked a public scandal, Galileo would have been obliged, moreover, to retract in public.[63] However, he would not have been required to abjure. "Rashness" did not involve a vehement suspicion of heresy, a charge that (together with formal heresy) needed to be disposed of through abjuration.[64]

Thus there seems to be a juridical problem about the legitimacy of Galileo's condemnation on the basis of a crime (vehement suspicion of heresy) that lacks an adequate basis, it would seem, in the Index decree, the sole doctrinal determination regarding Copernicanism at the time the *Dialogue* was composed. In defense of Urban VIII's determination, one could perhaps answer that the 1616 decree, in its vagueness, was open to and in need of, an authoritative interpretation and that this was, in fact, what the pope gave it in 1633. In that case, the basis for the charge against Galileo would not have changed, only clarified. Galileo's condemnation, then, would not have been illegal, on that basis at least.

Against such an interpretation, however, one could argue that the decision taken by the pope on June 16, 1633, was an act of the doctrinal magisterium, on the basis of which the theological status of Copernicanism at that point acquired a new, more negative, specification. If this was the case, a new and more radical questioning of the legitimacy of Galileo's condemnation would seem to be in order.

Notes

I am deeply indebted to Ernan McMullin for his very constructive criticism and for his many valuable suggestions, with regard both to the content and to the English style of this essay. I want to express here my sincere thanks to him. I have also greatly benefited from Francesco Beretta's excellent research work on the structure and functioning of the Roman Inquisition.

1. Galileo Galilei, *Opere di Galileo Galilei* (hereafter *OGG*), ed. Antonio Favaro (1890–1909; reprint, Florence: Giunti Barbèra, 1968), 19:321; Maurice E. Finocchiaro, *The Galileo Affair: A Documentary History* (hereafter *GA*) (Berkeley: University of California Press, 1989), 146.

2. The division in three parts of the meeting of *feria* V (Thursday), in the presence of the pope, is documented by several records on the functioning of the Holy Office in the first part of the seventeenth century. See Francesco Beretta, *Galilée devant le Tribunal de l'Inquisition* (Fribourg: Université de Fribourg, 1998), 71, and "Le procès de Galilée et les archives du Saint-Office: Aspects judiciaires et théologiques d'une condamnation célèbre," *Revue des Sciences Philosophiques et Théologiques* 83 (1999): 471 n. 108. The absence of any mention of these three stages of the meeting in the selection of documents of the Holy Office published by Favaro is due to the fact that those documents, as was customary, mention only the decisions taken, without any information about the way the meetings were held or about the discussions that took place during them.

3. The decision had probably been privately agreed upon by Paul V and Cardinal Bellarmine on the occasion of their meeting on the previous day, mentioned in a report by the Florentine ambassador, Guicciardini (*OGG*, 12:242). This would explain why the task of summoning Galileo (see below) was entrusted to Bellarmine. The decision taken on the occasion of the Feb. 25 meeting was registered in the judicial dossier of Galileo only, not in the volume of the *Decreta.* See Beretta, "Le procès de Galilée," 471, 475.

4. *OGG*, 19:321; *GA*, 147.

5. *OGG*, 19:278, *GA*, 148. The document goes on to register the decree of the Congregation of the Index concerning the Copernican writings, which was published two days later.

6. *OGG*, 19:348; *GA*, 153. I have changed Finocchiaro's translation of the Italian *ma solo* as "on the contrary" to "he has only." For the original text of Bellarmine's declaration, with corrections by his own hand, see Ugo Baldini and George V. Coyne, eds. and trans., *The Louvain Lectures (Lectiones Lovanienses) of Bellarmine and the Autograph Copy of His 1616 Declaration to Galileo,* Studi Galileiani 1:2 (Vatican City: Vatican Observatory Publications, 1984), 25–26.

7. *OGG*, 19:321–22; GA, 147–48.

8. There is by now a wide consensus on the translation of the words *successive ac incontinenti* along the lines indicated by Finocchiaro. For the juridical meaning of this expression, see Beretta, *Galilée devant le Tribunal,* 192, 194. I will return to his discussion on this issue later.

9. In his book *History of Galileo's Life and Work,* published in 1784, C. J. Jagemann proposed the fraud hypothesis in a notably different way than did later authors. Given the secrecy of the Holy Office documentation, Jagemann had nothing to go on except the text of the sentence of Galileo's condemnation, published by the Jesuit astronomer Riccioli in his *Almagestum novum.* Jagemann surmised that there had never been an injunction and that Riccioli had invented the passage in the sentence where such an injunction is mentioned. See Giorgio de Santillana, *The Crime of Galileo* (Chicago: University of Chicago Press, 1955), 314 n. 15.

10. See Emil Wohlwill, *Der Inquisitions-prozess des Galileo Galilei* (Berlin: Oppenheim, 1870), 5–15, and *Galilei und sein Kampf für die kopernikanische Lehre,* 2 vols. (1910–26; reprint, Wiesbaden: Martin Sändig, 1969), 1:626, 2:298–320.

11. See Carl von Gebler, *Galileo Galilei und die römische Kurie* (Stuttgart, 1876), translated by G. Sturge as *Galileo and the Roman Curia* (1879; reprint, Merrick, N.Y.: Richmond, 1977). See also de Santillana, *Crime of Galileo,* 266 ff.

12. De Santillana, *Crime of Galileo,* 266.

13. See Guido Morpurgo-Tagliabue, *I processi di Galileo e l'epistemologia* (1963; reprint, Rome: Armando, 1981), 18–20.

14. See ibid., 20, 20 n. 14. The hypothesis of Morpurgo-Tagliabue has been further developed, with a colorful, if speculative, elaboration of details, by Stillman Drake, *Galileo at Work: His Scientific Biography* (Chicago: University of Chicago Press, 1978), 253–54.

15. See Beretta, *Galilée devant le Tribunal,* 170. As for the "authentic instrument," the original document with the signatures of the notary and witnesses, it was inserted, not into the series of the *Decreta,* but into that of the so-called *Libri extensorum,* namely the registers of the acts written in a public form. Unfortunately this series of the *Libri diversorum* was almost completely lost as a result of the transport of the Holy Office archives to Paris under Napoleon. See chap. 7 of this book and Beretta's "L'archivio della Congregazione del Sant'Ufficio: Bilancio provvisorio della storia e natura dei fondi d'antico regime," in *L'Inquisitione romana: Metodologia delle fonti e storia istituzionale,* ed. Andrea Del Col and Giovanna Paolin (Trieste: Università di Trieste, 2000), 124. Thus the absence of an authentic instrument of the Segizzi injunction in the acts of Galileo's trial (if, indeed, it ever was compiled) is not necessarily something that should leave us "perplexed," as Morpurgo-Tagliabue concludes in the text already quoted.

16. See the plate of the front folder cover in Sergio M. Pagano and Antonio G. Luciani, eds., *I documenti del processo di Galileo Galilei* (Vatican City: Pontifical Academy of Sciences, 1984), 256. The original front cover appears heavily damaged all around the borders. In "Le procès de Galilée," 460, Beretta remarks that the left lower border gives the impression of having been torn. If the notary's signature was originally there and the tearing took place before the Galileo trial, adds Beretta, that alone would be sufficient to make the verdict against Galileo null from the juridical point of view. This, however, as Beretta himself acknowledges, is only a hypothesis. One might ask, furthermore, whether the signature would necessarily have been placed on the left side of the cover. If placed on the remaining lower right side, it could easily have disappeared because of the wear caused by the frequent handling of the cover. There are some faint black marks on that part of the cover page that could possibly be traces of a signature now worn away.

17. See Beretta, "Le procès de Galilée," 477. Despite the testimony of the handwriting, Beretta favors the hypothesis of a forgery perpetrated in 1632 within the Holy Office itself, with a view to securing Galileo's indictment. His reason: the discrepancies between the injunction document and the instructions communicated to Segizzi by Cardinal Millini.

18. The word *docere* (to teach), in the Segizzi injunction, is not equivalent to *tractare* (to discuss or deal with), in the instructions Millini conveyed to Segizzi. See the discussion of the meaning of *docere* contained in Inchofer's report to the Holy Office on the *Dialogue* (*OGG,* 19:350–51).

19. See Beretta, *Galilée devant le Tribunal,* 152 ff.

20. One could perhaps call into question, more radically, the likelihood of a *caritativa admonitio* on that occasion. As Beretta himself notices, "[T]he *caritativa admonitio* is not required by the inquisitorial jurisprudence" (*Galilée devant le Tribunal,* 152). See also Stefania Pastore, "A

Proposito di Matteo XVIII, 15. Correctio fraterna e Inquisizione nella Spagna del *Cinquecento,*" *Rivista Storica Italiana* 63 (2001): 323–68.

21. *OGG,* 19:279–80. The same decision is reported in a document with the title *Contra Galileum de Galileis (OGG,* 19:330). In it is specified that the precept has to be given "in the presence of a notary and witnesses, but without Galileo's knowledge."

22. *OGG,* 20:575 (emphasis in the original). For the actual document written by Galileo on October 1, 1632, and signed by four witnesses, see *OGG,* 19:331–32, 333. Other authors argue that supposing the presence of Segizzi and the notary would imply that the authorities (including Bellarmine) considered it, if not certain, at least very probable that Galileo would not accept Bellarmine's precept. See, for instance, Antonio Beltrán-Marí, *Galileo, ciencia y religión* (Barcelona: Paidos, 2001), 154. I cannot agree. From the juridical point of view, all the possibilities had to be considered, even the most unlikely ones. This is the evident meaning of the Millini instructions. The later documents of 1632 are the best confirmation of it.

23. See Berettta, *Galilée devant le Tribunal,* 475 n. 119

24. Beretta admits that the handwriting of the document appears to be that of the notary, Pettini, who wrote the other documents of the same period. The person who is supposed to have forged the document of 1632 would thus have to have been able to imitate that handwriting sufficiently well to elude later scrutiny. Beretta, however, quotes in a subsequent article some research that puts in doubt the similarity of the handwriting. See Francesco Beretta, "Le siège apostolique et l'affaire Galilée: Relectures romaines d'une condamnation célébre," *Roma Moderna e Contemporanea* 7 (1999): 455 n. 36. Apart from the unlikelihood of a forgery constructed in conflict with the instructions conveyed by Cardinal Millini, the question remains of how the forger could have known the names of Bellarmine's household members (Bellarmine died in 1621).

25. *OGG,* 14:389; *GA,* 233.

26. See the letter of Galileo to Geri Bocchineri, Feb. 25, 1633 (*OGG,* 15:50) and the two letters of Niccolini to Andrea Cioli, Feb. 27, 1633 (*OGG,* 15:55, 15:55–56). In the second of these letters, Niccolini quotes some remarks of Urban VIII to the effect that Galileo had dealt with the Copernican issue not hypothetically but assertively and conclusively and that "he had transgressed the order given to him in 1616 by Cardinal Bellarmine, by order of the Congregation of the Index [*sic*]." Niccolini would surely have informed Galileo about the pope's remarks.

27. The Latin expression *ex suppositione* had a different meaning for Bellarmine than it did for Galileo. For the cardinal it meant that the Copernican theory could be used as a purely mathematical hypothesis for astronomical calculations and thus for "saving the phenomena." For Galileo, it meant that the Copernican theory could be used as a physical hypothesis, which might later on be shown to represent the real constitution of the world. Galileo relied on the latent ambiguity of this expression to justify the writing of the *Dialogue.*

28. *OGG,* 19:339; *GA,* 259.

29. The documents accepted as juridical evidence by the Holy Office were customarily marked with the letters A, B, C, D, etc. See, for instance, the text in Beretta, *Galilée devant le Tribunal,* 192. For the course of the Galileo process, see *OGG,* 19:326, lines 73–80. In the present instance there is no indication of what the document corresponding to A might have been.

30. *OGG,* 19:339; *GA,* 259.

31. According to Francesco Buonamici (*OGG,* 15:111), Cardinal Maffeo Barberini and Cardinal Bonifacio Caetani were successful in their opposition to the intention of Paul V to declare

the Copernican theory contrary to the faith. Urban VIII himself told Tommaso Campanella, in 1630, that "if it had been left to us, that decree [of the Congregation of the Index] would not have been passed" (*OGG,* 14:88). According to some autobiographical notes dictated by Urban VIII himself (Vatican Library, cod. Barb. Lat., 4901, fol. 40r–v), the future pope and Caetani were able to prevent the complete prohibition of Copernicus's *De revolutionibus.* Even Bellarmine— "after consultation with the Jesuit geometers," he notes—strongly approved of their action. Quoted in M. D'Addio, *Considerazioni sui processi a Galileo* (Rome: Herder, 1985), 97 n. 94, and Francesco Beretta, "Urbain VIII Barberini protagoniste de la condamnation de Galilée," in *Largo campo di filosofare: Eurosymposium Galileo 2001,* ed. José Montesinos and Carlos Solís (La Orotava: Fundacion Canaria Orotava de Historia de la Ciencia, 2001), 557. Bellarmine might have said something about Cardinal Barberini's action to Galileo before pronouncing the admonition in order to make it less painful to Galileo.

32. *OGG,* 19:339; *GA,* 259.

33. *OGG,* 19:340; *GA,* 260.

34. *OGG,* 19:340; *GA,* 260.

35. *OGG,* 19:342; *GA,* 277.

36. *OGG,* 19:345; *GA,* 279.

37. *OGG,* 19:346; *GA,* 280.

38. *OGG,* 19:357; *GA,* 281.

39. For its possible meaning, see above, n. 31.

40. *OGG,* 14:372. Some doubts have been advanced about the actual existence and working of the "Special Commission." See Francesco Beretta, "*Magno Domino & Omnibus Christianae, Catholicaeque Philosophiae amantibus. D. D.:* Le *Tractatus syllepticus* du jésuite Melchior Inchofer, censeur de Galilée," *Freiburger Zeitschrift für Philosophie und Theologie* 48 (2001): 10–11. According to him, the examination of the *Dialogue* was probably entrusted from the very beginning to the Holy Office. Urban VIII, however, wanting to show a particular regard for the Grand Duke of Tuscany for political reasons, spoke to the ambassador, Niccolini, of the establishment of a commission, which, however, never really came into existence. According still to Beretta, the real intention of Urban VIII was probably to obtain the consent of the Grand Duke to the summoning of his "personal mathematician" so that the process against him could be instituted in Rome under the pope's personal control. This interpretation of the documents, if accepted, would further support my own conclusions (see below).

41. *OGG,* 14:383; *GA,* 230.

42. See the letter of Francesco Barberini to the Florentine Nuncio of Sept. 25, 1632; *OGG,* 14:398; *GA,* 222.

43. *OGG,* 14:392; *GA,* 236.

44. See *OGG,* 14:389.

45. Speaking to the ambassador, Urban VIII had affirmed that Galileo was still his friend. It is hardly conceivable that he would have used that expression if he already knew about the document reporting the Segizzi injunction. In fact, it appears that the report given to the pope on its discovery may have given him the final proof that he had been betrayed by Galileo. From that moment on, he apparently ceased to consider Galileo as a friend.

46. *OGG,* 19:324–27. The report was written by Riccardi and Oreggi under orders from Urban VIII. See the information given about it by Oreggi himself in the very short report written as a member of the second commission that analyzed the *Dialogue* in April 1633 (*OGG,*

19:348). The original form of the report seems to be that contained among the documents of the trial (*OGG*, 19:325–27). After a detailed exposition of the facts concerning the imprimatur for permitting the printing of the *Dialogue*, the report enumerated *come corpo di delitto* (as material evidence) eight charges against the book. They were followed by the surprisingly benign statement that "all of these things could be corrected, if it is decided that the book to which such favor should be shown is of any value" (*OGG*, 19:327; translation by de Santillana, *Crime of Galileo*, 211). At the very end, the Segizzi injunction was quoted in the exact form, but without mentioning the commissary's name and without any comment. These circumstances seem to indicate that Riccardi, while presumably trying desperately to escape blame for the imprimatur disaster, still wanted to help Galileo as far as he could. This report is preceded by a summary of its contents (*OGG*, 19:324–25), composed by the assessor of the Holy Office, Alessandro Boccabella (see Beretta, "*Magno Domino*," 311 n. 52). In it, the Segizzi injunction is quoted in full (again without mentioning the commissary's name) and is preceded by the severe assessment already quoted in the text above. The summary continues: "Now it is necessary to decide on the way to proceed both as to the person and the book already printed." That the author of this shortened version of the report was neither Riccardi nor Oreggi is confirmed by the fact that the name of Father Raffaello Visconti, correctly written in the more extended report, in the more concise one is erroneously transcribed as "Raffaele Visconte."

47. *OGG*, 19:326; *GA*, 221.

48. For an analysis of the inaccuracies and distortions that mar this document, see Annibale Fantoli, *Galileo: For Copernicanism and for the Church*, 2d ed., ed. and trans. George V. Coyne (Vatican City: Vatican Observatory Publications, 1996), 437–39. For the authorship of the document, see Beretta, *Galilée devant le Tribunal*, 16.

49. *OGG*, 19:294; *GA*, 282.

50. *OGG*, 19:294; *GA*, 282.

51. *OGG*, 19:295; *GA*, 284.

52. According to Beretta, the final sentence (*sententia diffinitiva*) of a criminal process of the Inquisition was written by the notary, on the basis of the *decretum diffinitivum*, namely, the final decision taken by the pope or by the cardinals of the Inquisition. The commissary and the assessor, who had followed the course of the process and had formulated the propositions that constituted the matter of the crime, probably collaborated in the preparation of the final sentence (Beretta, *Galilée devant le Tribunal*, 221). In Galileo's case, however, the final sentence, still according to Beretta, was probably written by the commissary himself. See Beretta, "Urban VIII Barberini," 567.

53. Beretta, *Galilée devant le Tribunal*, 277, argues that the discrepancy between the text of the summary and that of the sentence of condemnation constitutes a different reason to impugn the juridical validity of the process. One might respond, however, that it is the correctness of a sentence that ensures the juridical validity of a process, not its reliance on previous documentation that might not be correct. It can moreover be observed that the summary was compiled in preparation for a decision by the pope. In spite of its weight, the summary was not a document the pope and the cardinals necessarily had to accept as it was.

54. *OGG*, 19:403–4; *GA*, 288–89.

55. *OGG*, 19:404; *GA*, 289.

56. *OGG*, 19:405; *GA*, 290.

57. *OGG,* 19:405–6; *GA,* 291.

58. On the different theological censures, see Beretta, *Galilée devant le Tribunal,* 93–97.

59. *OGG,* 19:160.

60. *OGG,* 19:406; *GA,* 292.

61. After the uproar caused by the publication of the *Dialogue* containing Riccardi's imprimatur (and that of the Florentine inquisitor), Urban VIII strongly denied having been informed about the permission to print and even more strongly denied that he had himself personally given the permission, accusing the secretary of the briefs to the princes, Ciampoli, of having falsely pretended to Riccardi that this was the case. (See Fantoli, *Galileo,* 399, 469, 486.) In any case, the pope's high esteem for and friendly attitude toward Galileo were so well known to everybody that the natural assumption on their part would have been that Urban VIII was, in fact, the person ultimately responsible for allowing the publication of the *Dialogue.*

62. We know the names of those attending from a recently published document. See Walter Brandmüller and Egon Johannes Greipl, eds., *Copernico, Galileo, e la chiesa: Fine della controversia (1820),* Atti del Sant'Ufficio (Florence: Leo S. Olschki, 1992), 145–46. It is surprising that these authors put the date of Mar. 21 as that of the document describing the meeting of the congregation that took place, instead, on Mar. 1. The error is all the more evident since the decree of the Index, which this meeting was to prepare, followed on Mar. 5. I have personally checked the original and found that the date is "Die pa. [prima] Martii." Another no less conspicuous error is that giving the name of the Master of the Sacred Palace, also present at the meeting, as Niccolò Riccardi. (145 n. 2). Riccardi became Master of the Sacred Palace only in 1629.

63. See Beretta, *Galilée devant le Tribunal,* 204.

64. See Eliseo Masini, *Sacro Arsenale overo prattica dell' Officio della santa Inquisitione* (Genoa, 1621), 163 f., quoted by Beretta, *Galilée devant le Tribunal,* 204.

SIX

THE CHURCH'S BAN ON COPERNICANISM, 1616

Ernan McMullin

Two events stand out in the tangled story of the Church's dealings with Galileo. First was the issuing of a decree by the Congregation of the Index in 1616 suspending Copernicus's *De revolutionibus orbium coelestium* (1543) on the grounds that its postulation of the earth's motion and the sun's rest, if taken literally, would be "contrary to Scripture," since it contradicted a number of passages in the Old Testament where the sun's motion or the earth's stability was affirmed. Galileo was spared any mention in the decree, though his widely circulated *Letters on Sunspots* (1613) had, in fact, endorsed the Copernican system. The Roman authorities obviously did not want a public confrontation with the most celebrated writer in Europe on matters planetary, someone who had, besides, many friends and admirers among those authorities themselves. Nor was there, strictly speaking, a need for one. Up to that point the Copernican position had not been condemned by the Church; indeed, two reputable theologians, de Zuñiga and Foscarini, had argued in print that it was compatible with Scripture. Galileo could not, then, be accused of having a "heretical intention."[1] But he would have to be warned that the situation had now changed drastically. His active advocacy, more than any other person's, had brought the Copernican challenge to a head.[2] So he was called on to appear before Cardinal Bellarmine and warned to abandon the condemned "opinions."

The second event was the famous trial in 1633 where Galileo was sentenced on "vehement suspicion of heresy" subsequent to the publication in 1632 of his *Dialogue on Two Chief World-Systems*. The "heresy" in question was, first, that of "having held and believed" the Copernican theses, and, second, that of maintaining the probability of a doctrine that had in 1616 been authoritatively declared to be "contrary to Scripture." The original decree had not used the term 'heresy,' leaving open which of three possible "qualifications"—rash ("temerarious"), erroneous in matter of faith, or formally heretical—would fit the case. That uncertainty persisted until (more or less!) resolved by the texts of the sentence and abjuration in 1633. These took a harder line than Urban VIII himself is known to have favored at an earlier stage. The relatively full documentary record of the trial (the Holy Office was careful about its record keeping) raises many intriguing questions. These will be the subject of other essays in this collection.

But there is a prior question, one that this essay will treat at some length. From the sequence of events outlined above, it is clear that the Index decree of 1616 was the foundation for what came after. What came after did not have to happen— again, this will be left to others to spell out—but it was the decree that made the trial possible, that plausibly could be made to underwrite charges sufficient of themselves to render a guilty verdict credible (though not inevitable, again a topic for others).

The question then is: What could have led the Roman decision makers of 1616 to set their Church on a collision course with an astronomical claim backed by the most talked-of astronomer of the day? Assuming their intelligence and their good faith (assumptions, admittedly, that some writers on the Galileo case have questioned), what could have seemed important enough, assured enough, to lead them to run the risk they did of declaring on behalf of the Church that a doctrine to which many natural philosophers might well turn was inconsistent with Christian faith?

Many answers have been advanced to this question over the years, some clearly partisan, some clearly relevant though incomplete. In the first part of this essay, some of the most widely favored of those answers will come up for assessment. In the second part, a case will be made for one answer, in particular, though one that allows some of the others considerable relevance. And this answer will, finally, allow a highly tentative approach to the first of the sensitive questions implicit in the initiative Pope John Paul II proposed in 1979, leading to the establishment in 1981 of the Vatican's Galileo Commission: Who, if anyone, was at fault in this first stage of the Galileo affair?

It will be helpful first to lay out in the barest outline the events of those fateful weeks in early 1616 around which so much controversy has swirled since the Galileo file from the archives of the Holy Office made its (highly circuitous!) way to publication more than a century ago.

1616: The Index Decree

On February 19, 1616, the Holy Office instructed a committee of eleven theological "qualifiers" to advise on the theological status of (to "qualify") two propositions drawn from the work of Copernicus.[3] What had brought to a head this question about a book that had, after all, been in circulation for over seventy years were the telescopic discoveries made by Galileo over a short two years, 1609–11, and his subsequent energetic advocacy of the claim that these discoveries decisively favored a realist heliocentric cosmology that had all along (he asserted) been the proper reading of the Copernican work. The two propositions were:

1. The sun is in the center of the world and is altogether immovable in respect to local motion.
2. The earth is not the center of the world nor is it immovable, but it moves as a whole and also with a daily motion.[4]

The propositions belonged in the first place to natural philosophy, but none of the qualifiers was known for his expertise in that area, though all of them would have had a formation in Aristotle's natural philosophy prior to their work in theology. Most were Dominicans, including the vicar-general of the Dominican order, the commissary general (or head official) of the Holy Office, and the Master of the Sacred Palace, official censor for works published in Rome. The ranking member was the exiled Peter Lombard, archbishop of Armagh and primate of all Ireland, who had lectured on Aristotle in Louvain and had played a major role in the earlier theological controversy, *De auxiliis,* pitting Jesuits against Dominicans. In Roman terms, the committee carried impressive weight.

Four days later, the committee met to consider its response, and on the following day, February 24, the members agreed on the status of the two propositions. The first, denying the sun's motion, was declared to be "foolish and absurd in philosophy, and formally heretical since it explicitly contradicts the sense of Holy Scripture in many places, according to the literal meaning of the words and according to the common interpretation and understanding of the Holy Fathers and the doctors of theology." And the second proposition was adjudged "the same in philosophy, and in regard to theological truth . . . at least erroneous in faith."[5] The difference between the two censures was presumably due to the more explicit support in Scripture for the sun's motion, particularly in the by then famous text in Joshua 10, where the Lord answers Joshua's prayer that the sun's motion might be stilled in order that the daylight might be extended and the rout of his enemies completed.

The wording of the qualifiers' verdict is important. First, the Copernican propositions are evaluated both in (natural) philosophy and in theology, the two evaluations being understood to be linked, the first as preliminary to the second. The Copernican theses are adjudged to be not just false but "foolish and absurd," suggesting that the decision was motivated by an appeal to common sense over and above a call on the Aristotelian arguments for geocentrism. Further, the authority of the literal interpretation of the relevant Scripture passages is presented as the primary motive for the theological condemnation. And this is buttressed by a reference to tradition in the form of the writings of the Church fathers and of later theologians. From these indications, one can infer fairly safely the lines that the committee discussions followed.

On the same day, the pope met the cardinals of Rome (not just those who were members of the Holy Office) in consistory. According to a report forwarded a week later to Florence by Piero Guicciardini, the Tuscan ambassador to the Vatican, the pope was irritated by the intervention there of the young Cardinal Orsini on behalf of Galileo and summoned to him Cardinal Bellarmine, his principal theological adviser.[6] He learnt, quite possibly from Bellarmine, of the judgment arrived at by the qualifiers earlier that day.[7] According to Guicciardini, the two thereupon agreed that the Copernican propositions were "erroneous and heretical." Whether or not this was, in fact, the exact wording agreed on, the weekly executive committee meeting of the cardinals of the Holy Office on the following day, February 25, marked the decisive moment in the events of 1616. Its outcome was an agreement that the pope should instruct Bellarmine to call Galileo to appear before him and to warn him to abandon the condemned Copernican claims.[8] If he should refuse to obey, the commissary who served the role of prosecutor in the Holy Office was to issue Galileo with a personal injunction enjoining him "to abstain completely from teaching or defending this doctrine or even from discussing it. And if he should still refuse, he was to be imprisoned."[9] The much-disputed issue of whether Galileo, was, in fact, served with an injunction and if so, under what circumstances, is discussed in chapter 5 of this book.

A laconic minute from the files of the Holy Office tells us that Cardinal Millini, secretary of the Holy Office, informed his two major subordinates, the assessor and the commissary, of the action taken by the pope.[10] The occasion was apparently that of the same meeting of the Holy Office. The meeting had presumably terminated since neither the assessor nor the commissary were members of the executive and so would not have attended the meeting itself. They thus had to be told officially of the qualifiers' negative judgment and of the pope's order. Though the responsibility for the decision rested with the Holy Office as an executive body, it seems fair to say that the matter may have been virtually decided by the pope on the day before with the advice of Cardinal Bellarmine.

A few days later, on March 1, the cardinal members of the Congregation of the Index met at Bellarmine's home to decide on how this decision would find expression in the *Index of Prohibited Books,* legacy of the Council of Trent. Bellarmine was in charge of the discussion, which was, apparently, a lively one.[11] According to a diary entry written a long time after by Gianfranco Buonamici, two of the cardinals present at the Index meeting, Maffeo Barberini (later to become pope) and Bonifazio Caetani (who would be charged with drawing up the corrections to be made in the work of Copernicus), were able to secure agreement on a weaker censure than that recommended by the qualifiers, to which the pope (who was not present) assented.[12] Be that as it may, the Index decree substituted for the assessment of formal heresy the lesser but still grave charge "contrary to Scripture." Copernicus's book was not banned entirely, in recognition of its immense utility in mathematical astronomy (and the unlikelihood in consequence of its being surrendered by those who owned it!). It was to be "suspended until corrected." (It never was, in fact, withdrawn; the congregation satisfied itself with the distribution in 1620 of a list of ten corrections that were to be inserted in the existing copies.) Diego de Zuñiga's *Commentary on Job* (1584) was also suspended until corrected.[13] On the other hand, the treatise in which the theologian Paolo Antonio Foscarini had attempted to use Scripture to support the Copernican alternative was banned entirely. The pope approved the congregation's decision and suggested that the censures on the Copernican works should be merged with other censures in the formal Index decree (as indeed they were), presumably in order to avoid drawing undue attention to the Copernican decision.

The content of the decree was announced and approved at the next meeting of the Holy Office, under whose name it would be issued. The pope, who was present at the meeting, authorized the publication of the decision. At this point, the die was cast. The damning qualification "contrary to Scripture" had been attached to the Copernican propositions, with the concurrence of the pope. The status of the decree was both disciplinary and doctrinal: disciplinary since its purpose was to remove theologically objectionable books from circulation and to issue warnings about books that might remain in circulation, but also (quite unusually for an Index decree) doctrinal since the theological motive for the action was made explicit. How much doctrinal weight it should be accorded was left unclear. That unclarity would effectively be ended by the interpretation of the 1616 decree adopted by Galileo's judges in 1633. But that is a topic for others.

An Attack on Aristotle's Philosophy?

Now to return to the lead question of this essay—How did the 1616 decree come about?—and to some favored answers that fall short if presented as all-explaining, though each contributes to an understanding of the larger context of that complicated affair. Perhaps the commonest response to the question has been to argue that what was primarily at stake was Aristotle's natural philosophy, the philosophy that had served the Church's theologians well over several centuries. That philosophy was fundamentally threatened by the new Copernican cosmology. On detail after detail — the basic account of natural motion, the incorruptibility of the heavens, the centrality of the earth — Galileo's discoveries and their theoretical embodiment in the Copernican argument called Aristotle's system into serious question.

The first reaction in Florence did, indeed, come from Aristotelian philosophers whom Galileo derisively dismissed as the "Pigeon League" after their most visible spokesman, Ludovico delle Colombe. It was they and not theologians who first took up the cudgels against the "Galileists," a point that Stillman Drake (who had no more use for Aristotelian philosophers than did Galileo himself) liked to emphasize. But the theologians of Florence, once engaged, were quick to agree with the philosophers in asserting that the tie between Aristotle's philosophy and the Church's theology gave one reason to challenge the Copernican theses. In his denunciation of the "Galileists" to the Holy Office in February 1615, the Florentine Dominican Niccolò Lorini charged that "they trampled underfoot all of Aristotle's philosophy, which is so useful to scholastic theology."[14] Bellarmine would later warn Foscarini and Galileo that their Copernican ambitions were "likely to irritate all scholastic philosophers,"[15] among whom, of course, the Index qualifiers would assuredly have counted themselves.

Claudio Acquaviva, the general of the Society of Jesus, instructed Jesuit teachers in 1611 to maintain "solid and uniform doctrine" in the face of the dissensions of the times, and this was specifically to include Aristotle's philosophy, which had long before been made the teaching norm for Jesuit colleges by Ignatius Loyola, the founder of the Society.[16] It had not always been so; rather than the norm, Aristotle's philosophy had been perceived as a threat by the theologians of the thirteenth century on its first appearance in the West. But in the interim, and in large part due to the labors of Thomas Aquinas, it had come to seem to many an indispensable support for Christian theology, a position that had been emphatically confirmed by the Council of Trent. Most of the qualifiers in 1616 were Dominicans; their fidelity to Aquinas and his Aristotelian worldview was by tradition unswerving. These men would certainly react negatively to any challenge to the natural philosophy that was so central to the entire Aristotelian edifice. Was this, then, what propelled them to their decision?

In the "warfare" scenario that writers like J. W. Draper and A. D. White popularized in the nineteenth century and that still finds echoes in popular writings on the scientific worldview and its history that have proliferated in recent years, the Galileo episode has often been presented as a struggle between the adherents of a fossilized natural philosophy and the protagonists of a new way of science that would transform the world. Familiar dichotomies flow easily from the pen at this point: tradition versus innovation, authority versus individual initiative, dogma versus empirical hypothesis. It is attractive in this perspective to associate theology with outmoded science and thus to set it down as a stubborn barrier to scientific progress. In this simplistic version of history, what animated Galileo's opponents above all was the defense of ancient science, by then become dogma, against the intrusion of modernity. Here, then, is one answer to the question we are examining: what was really going on in 1616 was the defense of an ancient outmoded philosophy of nature against its upstart scientific rival.

What should one make of this diagnosis? Clearly it has some validity. But how much? Aristotle's natural philosophy was under attack from the Copernicans, and those who issued the Copernican ban were for the most part Aristotelian in conviction. The qualifiers drew attention, indeed, to their negative evaluation of the Copernican propositions from the perspective of philosophy—primarily Aristotelian philosophy, one would assume. Did this serve as a premise for their theological judgment? Should it have? In the *Letter to Castelli,* which the qualifiers had before them, Galileo responded to this latter question that it should not. The disputed passages in Scripture were simply not relevant to the Copernican issue in the first place: the language of these passages was accommodated to the intended audience and hence not to be taken literally, and in any event astronomical truth lay outside the purposes for which Scripture was intended.[17] But Bellarmine and the qualifiers evidently had set both those arguments aside. The only condition under which a relaxation of the literal meaning would be permitted was, apparently, that the opposing propositions from natural philosophy should be strictly demonstrated.

And this would be difficult, even at best, given the severity of the criteria of demonstration as these were understood in the Aristotelian tradition. Were this exegetical principle to rule, it would not, strictly speaking, be necessary to introduce a particular natural philosophy, whether Aristotelian or other, into the discussion in the first place. It would be sufficient (see the section "Non-Copernican Alternatives?" below) to argue that demonstration was impossible in natural philosophy (Urban) or that "mathematical" astronomy of the Copernican type could not serve as ground for demonstrations about the real (Bellarmine). One could then claim, a priori, that the Copernican case could not, even in principle, reach the level of demonstration and hence that the literal interpretation of the earth/sun passages in Scripture would have to stand. But, of course, the warrant for retaining the literal interpretation could be made all the more emphatic by turning to Aristotelian natural philosophy in order to argue that the Copernican theses were not only not demonstrated but demonstrably false. This last is the strategy that the qualifiers' report to the Holy Office strongly suggests. In that case, Aristotle's natural philosophy would have served in their eyes as a crucial part of the warrant for the theological censure.

But the wording of the qualifiers' verdict, labeling the Copernican propositions "foolish and absurd," could also convey a simple dismissal of the Copernican case on commonsense grounds. One might recall here Bellarmine's appeal to common sense when closing his case against the earth's motion in his letter to Foscarini: of course, the earth was at rest![18] There would not be any need, in this case, to appeal to the specifics of a particular natural philosophy in order to assert the falsity of the Copernican claims. In short, we shall never know for certain the precise role played by Aristotle's natural philosophy in the qualifiers' two days of discussion and in the briefer discussions at the Congregation of the Index. But it seems safe to say that underlying the assurance that the discussants showed in regard to the falsity of the Copernican claims was, for most of them, the solid rock of the Aristotelian worldview.

But this does not answer the question of prime concern to us here: Did the defense of Aristotle's natural philosophy *motivate* the Copernican ban? Were the Roman theologians making use of scriptural warrant primarily in order to defeat the challenge to Aristotle, as the "Pigeon League" in Florence had done? On balance, it would seem that the answer here would have to be negative. First, as we shall see later, the perceived threat was to theological, not philosophical, beliefs. But apart from that, it does not seem as though the Roman theologians saw Copernicanism as a real threat to their own natural philosophy. As far as their own beliefs about the natural world were concerned, the Copernican propositions were simply absurd. The reference to "philosophy" in the qualifiers' verdict, besides, did not necessarily signify a specific commitment to Aristotle.

And such a commitment would have been unlikely on the part of one influential member of the prosecution: Cardinal Bellarmine. As we shall see in more detail later, unlike his Jesuit confrères, he took his inspiration in natural philosophy from a very different source than Aristotle and was expressly critical of key elements in Aristotle's cosmology. Defense of Aristotle, one can be fairly sure, was very far from his mind when he and the pope got together for their assessment of how to respond to the Copernican challenge, prior to the formal decision of the Holy Office.

For Want of a Demonstration?

One response to the question "Why did the Roman theologians ban the Copernican propositions in 1616?" is: because the Copernicans, in the person of their main protagonist, Galileo, could not produce a demonstration of these propositions. In the absence of such a demonstration, to assert the truth of these propositions would run contrary to the literal meaning of the relevant biblical texts and hence could properly be designated as "contrary to Scripture." Indeed, unless such a demonstration could be produced, the propositions would have to be deemed false.

This construal has proved popular with those who are concerned to explain why the Church took several centuries to remove Galileo's *Dialogue* from the *Index of*

Prohibited Books. The Church was quite properly waiting, so the story goes, until the level of proof for the once-banned propositions had finally reached the point of demonstration, and then at last it became licit to interpret the earth/sun passages in Scripture in a way other than the literal—exactly, indeed, along the lines Galileo had proposed two centuries before.

This apologia may be found in the report described as conveying the findings of the Galileo Commission, presented to the Pontifical Academy of Sciences in 1992. Galileo, the report states, "had not succeeded in proving irrefutably the double motion of the earth. . . . More than 150 years still had to pass before the optical and mechanical proofs for the motion of the earth were discovered. . . . In 1741, in the face of the optical proof of the fact that the earth revolves around the sun, Benedict XIV had the Holy Office grant an *imprimatur* to the first edition of the complete works of Galileo."[19]

This, to say the least, is less than candid. What Benedict XIV permitted was the publication of Galileo's works (not including, significantly, the *Letter to Grand Duchess*) but with the addition of a new preface stating that the motion of the earth might not be admitted to be anything more than a "pure mathematical hypothesis"; with Galileo's marginal summaries altered, when necessary, to the "hypothetical" mode; and with the inclusion of the text of the sentence on Galileo and of his abjuration. It would seem that the "optical proof" of the earth's motion had not accomplished much after all! The original unaltered edition of the *Dialogue* remained on the *Index* until the edition of 1835, when it was deleted without comment. It is hardly accurate, therefore, to explain the two-century delay by invoking the want of a demonstration of the earth's motion. Something else was obviously at work. But that is a topic for discussion elsewhere in this volume.

What is relevant here, however, is the original suggestion that the lack of a demonstration explains, perhaps even justifies, the Index decision. It certainly does explain it in the minimal sense already sketched: had there been a demonstration that the theologians would have admitted *as* a demonstration (and the Aristotelian norm of demonstration, as already noted, was very exacting if enforced), the legitimacy of interpreting the Scripture passages in a nonliteral way would have had to be conceded. But this does not explain why the Roman theologians adopted this severely literalist stance in the first place: why, for example, they were unmoved by the accommodation argument, which would seem to have had a strong sanction in the earlier Church tradition. We shall return to this question later.

Since the employment of the principle of accommodation and the principle of scriptural limitation advanced by Galileo to warrant setting Scripture aside as an authority in matters astronomical was finally recognized as valid by the Church itself,[20] it follows that the rejection by Bellarmine and the qualifiers of the application of these principles constituted an objective error on their part, as well as on the part of Paul V and the members of the Holy Office who ratified the qualifiers' condemnation of the Copernican theses on the grounds that they were "contrary to Scripture." The lack of a Copernican demonstration cannot, therefore, be said to justify in today's theological terms the decision on the part of the Congregation of the Index to ban Copernicanism. In the eyes of those who made the decision, however, it evidently did justify it in terms of *their* exegetical principles. But they were wrong in terms of a later exegetical perspective, though (as we shall see) there were reasons for their perspective in terms of their day. And this means that the protracted demand for a demonstration over the long years that followed was also in objective terms a mistake. The embargo on the *Dialogue* continued long after the rest of the world took the motion of the earth to be proved,[21] so that even this justification of the embargo — that the Church remained faithful to the exegetical principles followed by the Index theologians — does not quite convince.

Non-Copernican Alternatives?

For want of a demonstration? Some, at least, of the theologians of 1616 must have been aware of Augustine's warning against pronouncing a definitive negative verdict on a proposition about nature that, though it might not be demonstrated now, could conceivably be demonstrated at a later time. In such a case, "the truth may later appear," Augustine said, and it may not be the "truth" to which the theologians have unwisely committed themselves.[22] So the present lack of a demonstration is by no means sufficient to warrant an unqualified claim that a particular proposition about nature is contrary to Scripture, let alone heretical. And let there be no mistake, the judgment of the qualifiers in 1616 and the language of the decree supported by it *were* couched in definitive terms; it was not proposed as something "reformable," to use a term favored by some recent theologians. The decree did not say that in the absence of a demonstration, maintaining the Copernican theses would be risky ("temerarious"). It described the theses as "contrary to Scripture," period, just as the qualifiers had "qualified" the heliocentric claim as "formally heretical." What permitted the theologians to rule out a future demonstration of that claim so confidently? In particular, should not the shock of the Galilean discoveries, even if these had been only imperfectly grasped, have alerted the theologians to the possibility of more to come, of a "truth that might later appear"?

There were at least three ways in which the prospect of such an outcome could be excluded, or so it seemed, at least, to their proponents, even apart from a conviction about the unshakable rightness of the Aristotelian cosmology. Each of the three ways had its own defenders: many philosophers liked the instrumentalist strategy; some theologians, most notably Urban, propounded the voluntarist one; while the astronomically inclined could appeal to the Tychonic alternative. It will not be necessary to lay these out in detail, since they are touched on elsewhere in this volume. But these alternatives played a crucial role in dealing with the challenge to geocentrism offered by Galileo's "new astronomy," and dealing with it, furthermore, in such a way that a later demonstration of the Copernican world-system could seem to be ruled out in principle.

Saving the Phenomena

Astronomy developed along two different lines in the early period of Greek dominance.[23] Unlike their Babylonian predecessors, those who turned their attention to the skies in the Greek world of the fourth century B.C. were interested above all in giving a *causal* account of why the planets followed the irregular motions they did. Again unlike the Babylonians, they developed geometrical techniques, relying on the circle as the basic element in their construction. Eudoxus produced an ingenious geometrical model employing combinations of circles that could easily be converted into the equators of concentric (but not coaxial) carrier spheres; in this way, he could (only very approximately) describe, and in that sense explain, the striking "loops" or retrograde motions that characterized the planetary orbits. Aristotle developed this model further, estimating that a total of fifty-five spheres would be needed, their motions to be explained causally by a combination of mechanical and teleological agencies.

In contrast, those who were concerned with astronomy as a way to describe and predict observed planetary motions diverged more and more as time went on from their more philosophically minded contemporaries. *Their* goal was to construct mathematical formalisms that would get the observed positions right; interpretation in terms of causal agency was secondary. As these formalisms increased in complexity, interpretation of them in causal terms became ever more difficult. By Ptolemy's day, c. 100 A.D., the separation between the two approaches to the study of the celestial bodies had widened in a way that forced an awkward question: Which of the two astronomies, the "physical" or the "mathematical," tells us how the planets are really moving? It seemed that both should, and Averroes spoke for many when he lamented the obvious contradiction between the two sorts of construction. They clearly could not both reveal the real motions. The debate would go on right through the Middle Ages.

Its legacy in Copernicus's day was a recognized division between "physical" and "mathematical" astronomy and a tendency to solve the troublesome contradiction between them by assuming that physical astronomy, because of its causal coherence, took priority when it came to revealing the real motions. Mathematical astronomy was simply a complex, though indispensable, technique for "saving the phenomena" of the planetary motions; it made no ontological commitment as to what was really in motion and exactly how it moved. Apollonius had early showed that eccentrics and epicycles, though involving combinations of different physical motions, could converge, under certain conditions, to describe exactly the same motion. Saving the phenomena was clearly not a sufficient condition, therefore, for making stronger ontological claims about the real orbits followed by the planets in space. (Of course, an increasingly awkward question for those "physical" astronomers who still defended the intuitively persuasive concentric spheres of the Aristotelian tradition was why they did such a poor job of saving the phenomena!)

The philosophers of Galileo's day were the inheritors of this distinction. In their eyes, an astronomical system that employed a high degree of mathematical complexity in the service of accurately saving the phenomena could not also be trusted as an ontological guide. True, there had been innumerable attempts (the last major one being that of the Jesuit astronomer, Christopher Clavius) to blend the two astronomies and somehow find a causal interpretation of the Ptolemaic equants and epicycles. But most philosophers, and all Aristotelian philosophers, by Galileo's day would have been taught to question, as a matter of principle, any claim on the part of "mathematical" astronomy to disclose real motion.

As far as they were concerned, Copernicus's work was obviously in the tradition of Ptolemaic astronomy. Had not the preface of the work assured the reader that the book was (as Bellarmine would put it in his letter to Foscarini) to be understood as "speaking suppositionally, not absolutely"—that is, as saving the appearances but making no claim about real motion or rest? Cardinal Millini, relaying official news of Galileo's summons, described the condemned Copernican theses as "the propositions of the mathematician Galileo."[24] Galileo had gone to some lengths to have himself appointed as "philosopher," and not just as "mathematician," to the grand duke, and one can now see one good reason why. But as far as official Rome was concerned, he was still a "mathematician," someone whose constructions could never, in principle, lay claim to reality. Had they but known it, the ancient split between the "physical" and the "mathematical" in astronomy had already begun to close, thanks in large part to the efforts of the "mathematician" whose "physical" claims they dismissed.

The Voluntarist Objection

The second strategy for ensuring the definitive character of the Copernican condemnation has often been confused in the Galileo literature with the first, but they are really quite different. When giving Galileo leave to proceed with the writing of his book on the Copernican system, Urban VIII expressed a reservation that should govern any claim for that system that the Church would tolerate. It was not simply to present the system as a mathematical device, the reservation that Bellarmine would, in Urban's place, have been likely to insist on. Rather, it was to keep in mind that an omnipotent Creator was not to be confined by the causal reasonings of a merely human science. Such a Creator could always, if he so chose, bring about any given physical effect "in many ways, some of them outside our human ken," the description Galileo put in the mouth of Simplicio in the perfunctory "medicine of the end" that closed the *Dialogo*. De Santillana dismisses that argument as nothing more than "theological weasel words,"[25] but in fact it had an impeccable theological/philosophical pedigree and would make frequent appearance in the natural philosophy of the later seventeenth century.[26]

Its origins are highly relevant to an understanding of the role it played in the Copernican discussion. One of the most contentious features of Aristotle's "natural works," as they gained in popularity in the thirteenth-century West, was their ideal of demonstration in natural philosophy. A proper science, in Aristotle's terms, could claim to demonstrate its conclusions, to present them not just as true but as necessarily true. To grasp the essence of water, for example, was to know how exactly it *had* to behave in any given situation. The challenge this presented to Christian notions of divine omnipotence and miracle was early grasped. The story of the ensuing debate, involving a condemnation by the archbishop of Paris in 1277 of several of the suspect features of Aristotelian natural philosophy, including its claims to express the necessities of natural action, is well known.

In the century that followed, a complex set of reactions to that philosophy took shape. One of those reactions was a new stress on the primacy of the divine will (hence the label 'voluntarism'). In the broader nominalist philosophy of that century, the Aristotelian ideal of demonstration was a constant target. A distinction was drawn between God's *potentia absoluta,* which knew no limits save self-contradiction, and God's *potentia ordinata,* which expressed God's free choice to allow nature to act in regular patterns accessible to the human senses and reason. Nicholas d'Autrecourt, a disciple of the philosopher William of Ockham, who was the leading figure in this nominalist repudiation of Aristotle, rejected as impious the claims to necessity implicit in Aristotelian natural philosophy and even argued that experience could not show that physical objects acted on one another at all. The only real efficient cause might be God; all that experience could show was regularity of recurrence among phenomena. Nicholas's work was condemned in 1346 by the Roman authorities as being too radical. But the voluntarist suspicion that animated many theologians' opposition to Aristotelian claims of demonstration in natural philosophy was to continue.

This was undoubtedly what Urban VIII had in mind in his discussions with Galileo in 1624. He had been one of those who counseled caution in 1616 regarding the censure appropriate to the Copernican theses. What may well have inspired him to believe that the grave assessment of formal heresy on the part of the qualifiers was unnecessary is strongly suggested by his remarks to Cardinal Zollern (as reported by Galileo) in 1624: the Church had not in 1616 condemned the Copernican doctrine as heretical, he said, only as temerarious: "[I]t was not to be feared that anyone would ever be able to demonstrate it as necessarily true."[27] His more strictly Aristotelian colleagues in the Congregation of the Index might not have had the same assurance that claims to demonstration on behalf of any cosmology, Copernican or otherwise, could be ruled out so easily a priori.

But matters changed in the late 1620s. Galileo realized all along that saving the phenomena of the planetary motions could never serve as a sufficient criterion to warrant the Copernican claim to decide what was really moving. So he had sought causal arguments instead, the method that "physical" astronomy had always advocated. The explanation of the seas' tidal motions by postulating as cause the double motions of the earth seemed to him to fill the bill perfectly. But, of course, this was exactly the argument pattern from observed phenomena to postulated causes, not themselves observed *as* causes, that was suspect from the voluntarist perspective if demonstration were claimed as the outcome. The affinity between this restriction on the certainty of causal inference from effect to sufficient cause and that consequent on "underdetermination" in the philosophy of science of today has often been noted. The scope and the warrant of the two are, of course, quite different. Anything short of a claim to demonstration was acceptable from the voluntarist perspective. Here the voluntarist restriction on claims of demonstration differed sharply from the instrumentalist one; this may explain why Urban in 1624 permitted Galileo to proceed with his plans for the *Dialogue*. Arguments in favor of the earth's motion would be allowable (not true if the instrumentalist restriction were to be what Urban had in mind) just so long as demonstration (or even, perhaps, a high degree of likelihood) was not being asserted.

This may help to explain the course of events later when the Roman censor, Riccardi, was struggling with the decision whether to allow the *Dialogue* to be printed. The pope was clearly aware that Galileo was using the argument from the tides (which the instrumentalist restriction would have disallowed). And Riccardi knew quite well where the pope's reservations with regard to the Copernican case lay. They permitted "physical" argument in support of that case up to a point. But just how far could the argument go? No wonder Riccardi was so torn. But to pursue this part of the story further would lead us away from 1616, our main focus here.

The relevance of the voluntarist restriction on demonstration to the events of 1616 is indirect. It would not, perhaps, have occurred to the stricter Aristotelians of the Holy Office or to the Index committee. But it might just possibly have influenced Barberini (and Caetani?) to regard the Copernican threat as less serious than did their colleagues. After all, if demonstration was required for the literal sense of Scripture to be set aside, and if demonstration could be ruled out a priori on theological/ philosophical grounds, why worry? But the confident tone of the Copernican arguments propounded later in the *Dialogue* and the clumsy placement there of Urban's prize argument in the mouth of Simplicio instead of that of Salviati would later lead Urban to change his mind. The voluntarist strategy, unlike the first one above, did not exclude serious argument in favor of Copernicanism over its cosmological rivals. But it did not, alas, decide how serious it could be allowed to become.

The Tychonic Alternative

The third strategy to deflect the force of the Copernican argument was the Tychonic one. It is unlikely that any of the Roman theologians involved in the 1616 decision were supporters of Tycho's cosmology. The arguments for abandoning the earth as center of the planetary revolutions would have lain well outside their professional interests and would in any event have been resisted by most of them on standard Aristotelian grounds. But they were well aware that Galileo's discoveries posed a threat to their assurance in that regard. So it seems possible that some of them, at least, would have consulted the views of those in Rome whose profession *was* astronomy.

The Jesuit natural philosophers of the Collegio Romano were aware of the significance of Galileo's discoveries, the phases of Venus and the satellites of Jupiter notable among them. As early as 1612, Christoforo Borro, described as a "Doctor of the Mathematical Sciences" at the Collegio, completed a lengthy manuscript, *De astrologia universa tractatus,* defending the merits of the Tychonic system over its Ptolemaic and Copernican rivals, preferring it over the Copernican on strictly scriptural grounds.[28] He did not refer to the Galilean discoveries, only then coming to be known. The Jesuit astronomers were evidently taking Tycho seriously even before the Galilean evidence came into play, principally because of his advocacy of the fluid-heavens cosmology instead of the problematic solid-spheres cosmology of the Aristotelian tradition. The Galilean evidence undermined the Ptolemaic-Aristotelian cosmology in short order, as the astronomers of the Collegio would have appreciated. But the campaign on theological grounds against the Copernican system launched by Jesuit exegetes twenty years before Galileo pointed his telescope to the moon[29] had brought to the notice of the Jesuit astronomers the availability of the Tychonic alternative. It saved the phenomena of the planetary motions more or less as well as did the Copernican system; in that respect the two were seen to be equivalent. And it had the twin merits in Roman eyes of conforming to the literal sense of the Scriptures as well as to the commonsense geocentrism of Aristotelian physics.

It seems likely, then, that the availability of the Tychonic alternative played a modest role, at least, in the assurance with which Rome issued its ban on the Copernican propositions, foreseeing no danger in consequence that the evidence from astronomy could call that ban into question at a later time. If the astronomers of the Collegio Romano were consulted unofficially by those in whose hands the decision rested, and it seems likely that they might have been, they could have responded that all of the evidence from planetary motions that told for the Copernican cosmology could be handled equally well by the Tychonic alternative. Whether other sorts of evidence might not tip the balance in the Copernican direction was another matter; it remained for Galileo to plan the construction of his *Dialogue* around that conviction. But for someone who was impressed in advance by the weight of the scriptural authority and who was told that there was a viable cosmological alternative to the Copernican one, the choice would have been made easy. Such, for example, was Christopher Scheiner, perhaps the most accomplished Jesuit astronomer of his generation. The availability of the Tychonic alternative was decisive for him; it is interesting to speculate what he and many Jesuit astronomers after him would have done after 1616 without it.

The Center of the World?

One construal of the motivation behind the decree of 1616 that finds favor in some quarters today comes from long after the fact. It is that the proposed shift of the cosmic center from earth to sun effectively displaced humans from their exalted place at the center of the universe and thus had to be resisted by a Church that saw human beings as the center of God's creation, as the privileged beings around whom the rest of the world circled. One of the best-known expressions of this ingenious speculation is that of the aged cardinal in Bertolt Brecht's play *The Life of Galileo*, who rages on about how Galileo, that "enemy of mankind," has degraded the earth and those who inhabit it by transferring it from the center of the universe to its far outskirts. "The earth is the center of all things," he fumes, and human beings are "God's greatest effort, the center of creation."[30] Associating Copernicus with Darwin and Freud, those other challengers to man's centrality, became indeed a commonplace of twentieth-century histories of modern Western culture.

But this will not do. It may well be what an enlightened modern would say *should* have been the Church's reaction to this displacement of human beings from the center of the Creation they had occupied, unchallenged, until then. But in fact there is hardly any reference to this consideration in the abundant criticisms of Copernicanism from the theologians of the immediate post-1633 period. It seems very unlikely that it played a major role in the qualifiers' discussions; they had plenty of other reservations of more immediate consequence in mind. And, of course, of itself it would not have warranted the censure found in the decree.

What is more, the center was not, in fact, regarded by the theologians of that day as a particularly favorable location.[31] The abode of the blessed was at the circumference, and Bellarmine was not alone in situating hell at the center of the universe— that is, at the center of the earth. In the Aristotelian view of the matter, the earth was the locus of change, of corruption, by contrast with the serenity of the celestial regions. It was true, of course, that in the Christian vision human beings, made in the image of God, were central to the work of Creation, for on them alone was bestowed the ability, at once fatal and ennobling, to choose freely. But to go from this sort of "centrality" to the literal sort of centrality that these modern interpreters of 1616 have in mind is an inference that the theologians of 1616 would have been far less inclined to make than would the speculative interpreters of today.

Overzealous Advocacy?

One further reading of the Galileo story that has elicited strong support all the way from Johannes Kepler in Galileo's own day down to Arthur Koestler in ours is that Galileo brought on the 1616 decision by his own intemperate advocacy of Copernican cosmology and by his unfortunate habit of making enemies of all those who disagreed with him in natural philosophy generally. If anyone was to blame for the 1616 debacle, these critics would say, it was Galileo himself. This construal has been popular, needless to say, with those who defend the Church's decision, but by no means with them only. It deserves careful consideration.

These critics point to the scathing contempt that Galileo poured on the Aristotelian philosophers, the "Pigeon League"; these were the men who, in his view, had drawn the Church into unnecessary combat in a vain attempt to salvage their own doomed cause. They were hypocrites; the religious zeal that they affected was simulated. Those who raised the hue and cry against him in Florence were uneducated, quite unable "to follow even the simplest and easiest of arguments."[32] He deplored "their wickedness and ignorance."[33] Was it any wonder that Galileo should eventually be denounced to the Holy Office by people who knew themselves to be the target of this level of invective? They might claim religious zeal as their motive (as they did), but one can reasonably guess that this was not their only motive.

And his scorn was not restricted to his Florentine opponents. Most astonishingly, there are evidences of it even in the document that he wrote as an *apologia* for the Copernican cause, the *Letter to the Grand Duchess Christina*. And its targets were the very people the *Letter* was supposed to persuade. He chided "some theologians whom I regard as men of profound learning" for "claiming the right to force others by the authority of Scripture to follow the opinions they think most in accordance with its statements, and at the same time, they believe that they are not obliged to answer observations and reasons to the contrary."[34] Though theology might well be regarded by them as queen of the sciences with regard to the preeminence of the topics it treated, he argued, it certainly did not deserve that title with regard to lesser topics such as those treated by land surveyors or accountants. Practitioners of those fields (he did not mention astronomy explicitly, but he did not need to) would rightly turn to mathematics for their principles, not to theology. Theologians, in short, ought not "arrogate to themselves the authority to issue decrees in professions they neither exercise nor study."

But these same theologians could quite understandably reverse that charge. And this brings up another way in which Galileo could not but antagonize in advance his intended audience among the Roman theologians. They obviously could respond to his challenge by asking what right he, a mere "mathematician" in their eyes, had to advance interpretations of biblical texts, assuming competence in a field that *he* likewise had never "exercised nor studied." The habit of mind encouraged by the traditional belief in theology as queen of the sciences would almost inevitably allow advantage to a theological over a natural-philosophical judgment on any disputed issue where the natural philosopher did not have a cast-iron, generally admitted, case.

In the wake of the Council of Trent, there was a new insistence on the exclusive right of qualified theologians to hold forth on matters theological. In March 1615, Ciampoli wrote Galileo from Rome to say that Bellarmine had remarked with regard to the growing Copernican debate that the discussion of scriptural interpretation was "reserved to professors of theology who are approved by the public authority"— that is, by the Church.[35] So there was a second reason why Galileo's intervention would provoke a hostile reaction in Rome, even apart from the content of the actual claim being debated. This latter reason Galileo had no control over; the former, of course, was his own responsibility. In interaction with one another, the two factors would surely have influenced, to some degree at least, the judgment of those responsible for the Index decree.

The news from Rome became more and more ominous as 1615 wore on. Galileo decided that he should travel to Rome and present the Copernican case in person, believing, as he wrote, that he could "more easily persuade by the tongue than by the pen."[36] The Tuscan ambassador, hearing of the plan and well aware of Galileo's proclivity for causing trouble, strongly advised the Florentine authorities of the extreme unwisdom of the visit. It was no time for new ideas in Rome, he wrote, nor was it the place, at that particular moment, to debate astronomical issues.[37] But Galileo was not to be deterred and on his arrival began an active campaign among his many Roman contacts. Antonio Querengo describes the whirlwind of activities in which he immediately engaged, fifteen or twenty guests at a time, now in one house, now in another, demolishing his opponents' arguments in such a way "as to make them look ridiculous."[38]

One of those he won over was evidently the young Cardinal Alessandro Orsini, whom he persuaded to present the Copernican case directly to the pope, as we have already seen. Writing directly to Cosimo II, Guicciardini reported that Orsini's effort backfired: "the Pope cut him short and told him he would refer the business to the Holy Office."[39] The "business" had, of course, been secretly referred to the Holy Office months before, and indeed the panel of qualifiers had already communicated its verdict on the very day that Orsini approached the pope. What the pope may have had in mind (assuming Guicciardini's report to be accurate) was the decision he was to convey on that same day to have Bellarmine call in Galileo and admonish him to abandon his Copernican views. Did Orsini's well-meaning intervention influence that decision?

This is a question about Paul V as much as it is about Galileo. In the same report, Guicciardini made it clear that it was the combination of a pope intolerant of controversy and a Florentine philosopher who reveled in it that he regarded as very dangerous for all concerned. Galileo was still in Rome buttonholing whoever would listen, "all afire about his own opinions . . . showing little self-restraint and disregarding caution. . . . [I]t is impossible for those around him to escape from his hands." But what the shrewd ambassador had to say about Paul V is even more to the point: "A Pope of this sort who abhors the humanities and [Galileo's] kind of mind cannot stand these novelties and these subtleties. And everyone here tries to accommodate his mind and nature to that of the ruler. Furthermore, even those who do understand something and are curious try, if they are wise, to appear the opposite in order not to fall under suspicion."[40]

This was the same pope who early in his papacy put an end to the long-drawn-out and often acrimonious debate between the Dominicans and the Jesuits on the topic of grace and free will (*De auxiliis*) by ordering each side to cease and desist and by refraining from issuing the apostolic decision ex cathedra that both sides sought, a decision that could have deeply divided the Catholic world, no matter on which side of the controversy it came down.[41] The Copernican controversy, with its potential for dividing theologians and its appeal to astronomical subtleties, would have seemed to him something to be nipped in the bud, if at all possible, before it became really divisive. He would have relied on Bellarmine's advice in the matter, but his own instinct could very well have been to cut off discussion; only a ban would accomplish that. The matter was already before the Holy Office, but here was Galileo setting ecclesiastical Rome in an uproar as though he, a layman, had official standing in the affair.

Is the moral to be drawn from all this (as some have urged) that Galileo should be held largely responsible for the Index action of 1616, with its disastrous aftermath? As it stands, the question is too general: it has to be broken down into at least three more specific questions. First: Did Galileo by his sometimes provocative behavior, and also because of his "outsider" status, contribute significantly to bringing matters to a head in February 1616? To which the answer is: very likely yes. Second: Would the Holy Office have moved against Copernicanism anyway, even apart from Galileo's passionate pursuit of the Copernican cause? To which the answer is: probably yes. Third: Does Galileo's personal role in prosecuting the Copernican case in Rome help to explain why the two Roman congregations arrived at the verdict they did? To which the answer is quite simply: no.

Taking these in order: first, the evidence sketched above seems persuasive. Galileo's antagonizing of his Florentine critics, his whirlwind campaign in Rome, and his attempt to influence the pope almost certainly prejudiced the Copernican cause in the eyes of many of those who counted. Above all, the fact that this pressure was coming from someone who was not himself a theologian and therefore had no title to speak on theological issues as far as Rome was concerned would have antagonized those responsible for the Index decision even further, particularly the Dominicans who constituted a majority of the qualifiers' panel. That his intervention would have negatively affected the manner in which the Copernican case came to be understood and the abrupt way in which it was terminated seems, then, fairly likely.

How much, in consequence, might he be said to have been to blame? Here it is important to separate the two different sources of the antagonism he occasioned. He was undoubtedly to blame for his dismissive way with opponents. But he should not be blamed for entering the theological lists in the first place. The tactics of his opponents left him with no other option. Were he to stay within the bounds of natural philosophy, there was a real chance that the Copernican theses could be prematurely condemned before he could produce the demonstration that he was convinced was within reach. Furthermore, as a professed Catholic he could not simply stand by and allow the disaster for the Church to occur that a wrong decision would mean. How much he was driven by selfless concern for the Church's welfare, and how much by motives of a more secular sort, we shall never know. But it does not really affect the issue at hand. Either way he could be excused for doing his best to avert the catastrophe, and this necessarily meant tackling the exegetical issues raised by his opponents' literalist reading of the disputed Scripture passages.

What would further have encouraged him to venture on dangerous ground was that their way of reading those particular passages was open to commonsense objection. One did not have to be a trained theologian to see the force of the appeal to accommodation or the unlikelihood of the claim that Scripture was intended to adjudicate on technical astronomical issues. One was not challenging the authority of the fathers by proposing that that authority should not be involved on a matter that the fathers themselves had every reason in their day to take for granted.

In short, then, if he stayed out of the fray, the battle could well be lost. As he was the leading protagonist of the Copernican cause, the responsibility was his. If he did engage the theologians directly, he ran the risk (as he must have known) of being dismissed by them as an outsider. But if his arguments were no more than common sense, why not at least try? And then, of course, he discovered (probably to his aston-ishment) that he had Augustine on his side. What better title than that?

The second question: Would something like this have been likely to happen any-way? Counterfactuals regarding complex historical issues of this sort are, of course, no better than educated guesses. But the best guess would seem to be that even apart from the furor caused by Galileo's handling of the affair, the Holy Office would probably have had to act at some point anyway. Galileo's astronomical discoveries had called the Aristotelian geocentric cosmology into question for natural philoso-phers, a challenge that was bound to become more insistent. The earlier negative reaction of Catholic exegetes to de Zuñiga's brief Copernican venture was a foretaste of what was bound to come when the challenge posed by the Copernican theses was more widely perceived.[42]

The intense reaction to Foscarini's strongly pro-Copernican treatise in March 1615 may be particularly significant. Here was a respected theologian, a member of the guild, challenging the literalist consensus, independently of Galileo's efforts. Ciampoli wrote to Galileo to predict that this controversial work ran "a great risk of being condemned by the Holy Office."[43] Would Bellarmine have allowed the Fos-carini treatise to stand unchallenged, once the issue *was* raised at the level of the Holy Office? For reasons that will become clearer in a moment, it does not seem so. To this question, then, the answer is an appropriately tentative yes.

The third question: Does Galileo's personal involvement in the Copernican de-bate help to explain how the Roman theologians arrived at their negative assessment of the Copernican propositions? Was it a significant factor in that assessment? We can never really know, of course, but we can, at least, say that the Holy Office's de-cision can be explained in a more direct way without calling on personal antagonism toward Galileo as a major factor. It is to that explanation, finally, that we now turn.

The Authority of Scripture

What *was* at issue in the decision to ban the Copernican propositions? Were there not ample precedents in the theological tradition for a more moderate, more cautious response? What would have led these to be overruled? The most plausible general answer would have to point to the effect at that time of the Reformation controversies on any issue involving the interpretation of disputed passages in Scripture. Issues of this sort were at the root of the divisions that had torn Western Christendom apart. Each side hurled proof-texts at the other; establishing the proper meaning of those texts gave rise to endless controversy. Even more divisive was the preliminary issue of where the authority lay to validate one interpretation of a text over another. The Reformers' rule of *sola Scriptura* and their insistence on the accessibility of Scripture to all the faithful generally favored a heavily literalist approach to interpretation. And this was further strengthened by the widely shared belief that the Scriptures had been dictated directly to the human agents.

Catholic exegetes on the whole were less inclined to the dictation view, but their own account of inspiration still sought to ensure that Scripture could be understood as in a real sense the Word of God.[44] And for them, the emphasis on tradition as deserving veneration equal to that given Scripture meant that there would be an additional barrier to any attempt to depart from the traditional. The injunctions of the Council of Trent, which had been summoned to meet the Reformers' challenge, would have been fresh in the minds of the Roman theologians who were called on to decide on the merits of the Copernican case. Their decision would undoubtedly have been influenced by the legacy of the council.[45]

The second decree of the council may be cited in support of this construal:

> Furthermore, to control petulant spirits, the Council decrees that in matters of faith and morals pertaining to the display of Christian doctrine, no one relying on his own judgment and distorting the Sacred Scriptures according to his own conceptions, shall dare to interpret them contrary to that sense which Holy Mother Church (to whom it belongs to judge of their true sense and meaning) has held and does hold, or even contrary to the unanimous agreement of the Fathers, even though such interpretations were not at any time to be published. Those who do otherwise shall be identified by their Ordinaries and punished in accordance with the penalties prescribed by the law.[46]

At the conclusion of the council in 1564, the wording of an oath was approved in the form of a profession of faith to which future priests and all Church officials would be required to swear. It runs in part: "I also accept Sacred Scripture in the sense in which it has been held, and is held, by Holy Mother Church, to whom it belongs to judge the true sense and interpretation of the Sacred Scripture, nor will I interpret it or accept it in any way other than in accordance with the unanimous agreement of the Fathers."[47]

This wording would have been familiar to theologians generally in Galileo's day. The two elements in the oath reflect the council's major concerns: first, to emphasize the sole authority of the Church as interpreter of Scripture against the claims of the Reformers regarding the decisive role of the individual believer; and second, to underline the authority of tradition, in the form of assent to the agreement of the fathers, in response again to the Reformers' challenge, this time to the separate authority of tradition.

This appeal to the authority of the fathers, to their consensus on a literal reading of the earth/sun passages in Scripture, is already much in evidence in the original denunciations of Galileo to the Holy Office by Lorini and Caccini. In his deposition Caccini reports that he reminded his audience in Florence that "no one is allowed to interpret Holy Scripture in a way contrary to the sense on which all the Holy Fathers agree, since this was prohibited both by the Lateran Council under Leo X and the Council of Trent."[48] Galileo had his own way of countering this appeal to the consensus of the fathers. But one can see that in the Tridentine atmosphere of the day in Rome, this argument would carry a lot of weight. It was a deeply conservative argument, calling on one of the two sources of theological authority to interdict any change in the interpretation of the other. It did not require one to examine the earth/sun passages themselves, now for the first time under serious scrutiny because of the Copernican developments, and ask on exegetical grounds how plausible the traditional literalist reading of these passages was.

The combined emphasis on the primacy of the literal meaning in interpreting Scripture and the authority of patristic consensus in arriving at that meaning is reflected, as already discussed, in the Index decree itself. These were exactly the grounds given for the condemnation. And they bear the immediate mark of Trent and of the half-century of debate that had intervened between the council and the fateful month in 1616.

What about the precedent set by an earlier council, Lateran V (1513–21)? It had been concerned with a partly philosophical issue, the immortality of the human soul, which Aristotelians of the day in the tradition of Averroes were accused of denying. The council issued a bull, *Apostolici regiminis* (1513), in response, condemning the thesis that the human soul was mortal.[49] It did so on strictly theological grounds, making no commitment as to whether the Church's position, that the soul was immortal, could also be philosophically demonstrated. Indeed, the leading Dominican theologian of the day, Cardinal Cajetan, in several of his last works denied that it could be, maintaining that it could be known only as part of Christian faith.[50] The principle implicit in the council's action was that theology, as explication of the faith, took precedence over philosophy. If there were a conflict, it would have to be the case that the philosophers' arguments were, in some way, faulty. And in the light of this, the council requested Catholic philosophers to show that those arguments were, in fact, flawed.

The issue in 1616 was fundamentally different. True, a philosophic thesis was involved in both cases, in the capacious sense of the term 'philosophy' current at that time. True, a leading philosopher was involved in both cases, Cremonini in the first and Galileo in the other. But beyond that, the theologians' case against Copernicanism proceeded quite differently. The sun's motion and the earth's rest had, of themselves, no major theological significance. Had they not, as it happened, been mentioned in a handful of passages in the Old Testament, the issue would scarcely have arisen in the first place. The issue was primarily an exegetical one. Should the disputed passages be understood as being accommodated to the capacity of the hearers, as the defenders of Copernicus suggested? That this was the key question was clearly grasped in Rome well before the Copernican issue came before the Holy Office for formal decision.

In July 1612, when Galileo first encountered the recourse to Scripture as a defense rampart thrown up by the Aristotelian philosophers in Florence, he wrote to Cardinal Carlo Conti, prefect of the Holy Office, to ask him for an official view on whether Scripture favored Aristotle's principles regarding the constitution of the world. Conti responded that Scripture certainly did not favor such Aristotelian doctrines as the incorruptibility of the heavens.[51] Where the stability of the earth, however, was concerned, the Copernican claim for the double motion of the earth might be acceptable if one took the scriptural references to the stability of the earth to be merely "conforming to the language of the common people." But, he went on, this mode of interpretation (i.e., accommodation) should not be invoked except for "great necessity."

Was it, then, necessary? Not if it could be shown, in philosophic terms, that the Copernican thesis was false. That was why, in the decree itself, unusually, a philosophic claim to this effect preceded the theological one. So far different from Lateran V's asserting precedence of theology over philosophy, in 1616 theology was actually relying on philosophy to make its own case. The theologians of the Holy Office in 1616 would hardly have called on the precedent of Lateran V in the circumstances. Had the Copernican position been defended by a substantial number of philosophers (as the Averroist one was in 1513) so that its falsity in philosophic terms could not have been taken for granted, as it was in 1616, the Copernican issue would have been regarded quite differently. Perhaps in those circumstances the appeal to the traditional principle of accommodation would have overcome the literalist exegetical presupposition that the theologians of the day evidently brought to the discussion.

And so to return to our main point: given the guidelines set down by Trent and the siege mentality that prevailed in the Rome of the Counter-Reformation, one would be tempted to say that the Index decision in 1616, once the machinery of the Holy Office had been set in motion, was, if not inevitable, at least very likely. But this brings to mind a tantalizing counterfactual. It seems fair to conclude that Galileo was the victim of extraordinarily bad luck in the timing of the Copernican debate. Suppose that his discoveries had been made a century earlier—as they could have been—and that an earlier Copernicus had written his book before Luther and Calvin took to the lists, as could easily have happened. Instead of a Cardinal Bellarmine, a man of his time, there might have been a Cardinal Nicholas of Cusa, likewise a man of his very different time. Would the Church in Rome have responded in the same way? This "what-if" is best left to the imagination of the reader.

All of this reinforces the single conclusion that by far the most significant factor in explaining how the Index decision went the way it did was the theological climate of that particular time in Rome. In the papal address in 1992 closing the work of the Galileo Commission, the theologians involved (by implication, the qualifiers) are gently chided for not scrutinizing more closely the criteria of scriptural interpretation they were employing. "Most of them did not know how to do so."[52] Yet one should not blame the theologian-consultors of 1616 too much in this case. Were they to have been queried later about their decision, they might have responded that they were following the norms laid down for them only a few years before at Trent.

Yet one still wonders. Conti's response to Galileo in 1612 suggests that the accommodation option would, at least, have been taken into account. Could it just possibly have gained the day? A further circumstance is worth noting. When Lorini earlier forwarded a copy of the *Letter to Castelli* to Rome, complaining about Galileo's forays into Scripture, the *Letter* was submitted by the Holy Office to a consultor, whose identity is unknown to us. And this consultor, in contrast to those of the later panel, found "nothing to question" in Galileo's argument for the irrelevance of the earth/sun passages in Scripture to the Copernican issue.[53] Much had happened, of course, in Rome in the intervening year. Still, the mere fact that a consultor, officially so designated by the Holy Office, had allowed the argument of the *Letter* to stand invites reflection. Is it conceivable after all, then, that the qualifiers a year later might have agreed with this earlier evaluation, might have been swayed by the appeal to accommodation, for example, despite the references to Trent by Galileo's accusers? Might there be a further factor to take into account here to explain why they did not? One possibility here, a factor that *may* have played a significant role in the 1616 verdict, is the intellectual influence of Cardinal Bellarmine, the preeminent Roman theologian of his day, a man greatly respected for his piety and his dedication to the welfare of his Church in those difficult times.

Bellarmine, Cosmologist

As a young man, Bellarmine had taught astronomy in several Jesuit colleges as part of the required curriculum in natural philosophy. It is fortunate that a manuscript record remains of his course in astronomy at the University of Louvain in 1570–72.[54] What leaps out from these lectures is the fact that, unlike other Jesuit teachers of his day, Bellarmine turned to the Bible and to patristic commentaries on the Bible for his cosmology rather than to Aristotle. In fact, he was constantly critical of Aristotle's cosmology and of the scholastic versions of that cosmology, including that of Aquinas. Scholastic cosmology was too remote, in his view, from ordinary experience, and thus from the Hebrew cosmology enshrined in the books of the Old Testament, notably in Genesis. Since the fathers were for the most part unaware of Aristotle's cosmology and drew their accounts of the cosmos almost entirely from the Bible, it is not surprising that this unquestioning turn to the fathers, prompted no doubt in part by the mandate of Trent, would tend to shift the authority of tradition away from the sophisticated constructions of the Greek astronomical tradition, whether those of Aristotle or those of Ptolemy.

Bellarmine's response to Aristotle's fundamental dichotomy between celestial and terrestrial substance was to deny it flatly. Citing in his support numerous biblical texts and the authority of dozens of the Church fathers, he declared that the heavenly bodies and even the heavens themselves were constituted by a familiar element, fire, not by a mysterious quintessence. They were corruptible: Did not the Bible say over and over that they would perish on the last day? The fiery heavenly bodies were not transported by spheres of any kind; each moved with its own distinctive motion, "like the birds of the air and the fish of the water."[55] As for "such complex and extraordinary structures as epicycles and eccentrics," these "figments" were among a number of alternatives debated by astronomers. In such a case, the theologian was free to choose among the alternatives "the one which corresponds best to the Sacred Scriptures," which in his view was to have each heavenly body pursue its own admittedly irregular path.

If, however, one could show "in an evident way" that these bodies were not, after all, autonomous in their motions, a different way of interpreting Scripture would have to be found, since the true meaning of Scripture could not be in contradiction with any other truth, philosophical or astronomical (what I have called elsewhere the principle of priority of demonstration).[56] But Bellarmine obviously believed that such "evident" proofs regarding the nature and motions of the heavens were few and far between in natural philosophy, so he turned to Scripture and the fathers on issue after issue: taking, for example, the moon to be the largest of the heavenly bodies after the sun, setting waters both above and below the "firmament," and taking the firmament itself to have been formed on the first day by the rarefaction of the first-created water.

It must be emphasized that Bellarmine's way of relating the Bible to cosmology was not the standard one among the Catholic theologians of his day, most especially not among the Jesuit theologians, whose adherence to the Aristotle whom Bellarmine had so emphatically set aside as an authority in cosmology was more or less firm. When it is remembered that the Jesuits of Galileo's time were under orders from their general to *defend* the philosophy of Aristotle, one can appreciate how idiosyncratic, in certain respects at least, the intellectual influence of Bellarmine was likely to have been in the discussions surrounding the Copernican theses, taken as realistic claim rather than as mathematical device, the latter being the alternative Bellarmine insisted on.

The matter was otherwise among the Reform theologians. There Aristotle tended to be regarded as a threat to Christian theology rather than as a foundation for it. And the emphasis on the *sola Scriptura* principle favored Genesis as an authority on matters cosmological. Best known among the proponents of a "Mosaic physics" was Johann Comenius, whose *Physicae ad lumen divinum reformatae synopsis* appeared in 1633, the very year of Galileo's trial.[57] His motto was to "fetch all things from sense, reason, and Scripture," with Scripture being the corrective where human sense and reason might fail. The naturalism of Aristotle's philosophy was above all what had to be guarded against. The frequent references to nature in the Old Testament, taken in their literal sense as revealed by God, would then be an obvious source of cosmological wisdom. This sort of emphasis on Scripture as the first authority when constructing a physics was never favored, however, by more than a minority of Protestant theologians. And among their Catholic counterparts it was hardly to be found.

Bellarmine might not have gone so far as to describe his cosmology as "Mosaic." But long years after his Louvain lectures he reminded Foscarini that Solomon, who had written that "the sun also ariseth and goeth down" (Ecclesiastes 1:5), "not only spoke inspired by God, but was a man above all others wise and learned in the human sciences and in the knowledge of created things. He received all this wisdom from God; therefore it is not likely that he was affirming something contrary to truth already demonstrated or capable of being demonstrated."[58]

This last phrase is interesting. It shows that Bellarmine was aware that he had to block off the objection that Galileo had already so trenchantly raised in his *Letter to Castelli*. And among the arguments he marshaled against the Copernican propositions in the *Letter,* the one he chose to refute the possibility of their later demonstration was the appeal to Solomon's God-given insight into "the nature of created things." That for him was clearly decisive. The famous quip from Cardinal Baronio that Galileo quoted in his *Letter to the Grand Duchess*—"The Scriptures teach us how to go to heaven, not how the heavens go!"[59]—would have had a chilly reception from that other cardinal, whose motto in this context might, on the contrary, have been "The Bible teaches us not only how to go to heaven but also how the heavens go"!

What chance, further, would Galileo's carefully crafted argument against reliance on the consensus of the fathers regarding geocentrism have? One should not look to the testimony of the fathers, Galileo concluded, regarding an issue they had no reason to see as problematic. The fact that the patristic commentators took the biblical texts describing the motion of the sun or the stability of the earth in a literal sense, he urged, ought to carry no weight as theological testimony. The fathers had no reason in their day to ask the Copernican question: Was the language of Scripture in this context that of the appearances simply or that of reality? One can see from Bellarmine's stunning assembly of texts early in his career from a wide array of the fathers as a primary way to teach astronomy that he would be entirely unsympathetic to this move. The habitual literalism of the fathers in their use of the Bible as a source of cosmological knowledge he never questioned.

Bellarmine's Role in the Index Decision

Bellarmine served as a consultor and later as one of the judges at the trial of Giordano Bruno that led to the execution of Bruno on the charge of heresy in 1600. Much has been made of the "long shadow" of Bruno in explaining the course of events in the later rejection of Copernicanism by the theologians of the Holy Office in 1616.[60] The role played by Bellarmine on both occasions has been one of the threads thought to link the two episodes, the other principal one being that one of the charges brought against Bruno (though by no means one of the weightier ones in theological terms) was his invocation of a Copernican astronomy we now realize he barely understood.[61] Though the Bruno-Galileo connection is tenuous in the absence of any direct evidence, dependent largely on assumed likelihood, still the Bruno precedent must undoubtedly have been in people's minds in 1616, only sixteen short years after Bruno's horrific death. And the fact that the Copernican heliocentric doctrine was part of the eclectic mix of ideas that Bruno's ill-fated attempt to retrieve a lost pre-Mosaic wisdom offered would surely have been in the mind of at least one person directly involved once again in 1616. That person was, of course, Robert Bellarmine.

When Galileo came to Rome in March 1611 in the wake of the triumphant reception of his astronomical discoveries, Bellarmine asked some of his Jesuit colleagues, including the venerable Christoph Clavius, to assess the veracity of Galileo's claims, showing himself to be aware of just what these claims were.[62] The Jesuit astronomers assured Bellarmine that Galileo's assertions were indeed reliable, though Clavius had some doubts about Galileo's claim that the surface features of the moon showed it to be similar to the earth. This means that Bellarmine would almost surely have become aware of the devastating implications for Aristotelian cosmology of the phases of Venus and of Jupiter's satellites; he might even have believed that his own very different cosmological beliefs might escape these implications and indeed even be confirmed by one of them (the mutability of the heavens).

But while Galileo was still in Rome, an inquiry was noted in the Holy Office files as to whether he was involved in any way in the trial of his colleague Cesare Cremonini, an Aristotelian whose views had incurred the Inquisition's suspicion. This was the first time, so far as we know, that Galileo had come to the notice of the Holy Office, and Bellarmine was one of those present when the matter was discussed. Guicciardini wrote back to Tuscany that Bellarmine had remarked to him that if Galileo had stayed much longer, "they" (presumably the Roman authorities) would assuredly have begun an investigation of his views.[63]

More ominously, a letter soon after from Galileo's friend Prince Federico Cesi warned him to conduct himself with great caution: "As for the theory of Copernicus, Bellarmine himself . . . has told me that he considers it heretical, and that the motion of the earth is, beyond any doubt, contrary to Scripture. So that you can see how things stand. I have always wondered whether he would not, when he finds it convenient, bring Copernicus up in the Congregation of the Index and have him prohibited. Nor is there any need to say more."[64]

Westfall notes that this warning from Cesi antedated the Lorini-Caccini attack on Galileo in Florence and the transfer of that attack to Rome. If Cesi was right (of course, it is possible that he exaggerated), there is some reason to believe that as early as 1614 Bellarmine was leaning toward a ban on "the theory of Copernicus"—that is, on the Copernican theory if interpreted in a realistic manner, not necessarily on the book itself.[65] In response to an agitated letter from Galileo, his Roman friend Monsignor Piero Dini wrote in March 1615 to say that he had talked with Bellarmine about the growing storm regarding Copernicanism. Bellarmine's response was that he did not think Copernicus's book would be prohibited as long as it was made clear that its constructions were meant simply to save the appearances as epicycles did, useful devices but not something to be believed.[66] There was no reason, therefore, to make a fuss, he went on, or to condemn the Copernican opinions if understood in this way. But, of course, Galileo, not surprisingly, reacted negatively to this way out: the Copernican constructions were not just practical devices, they were directed to "the true constitution of the world."[67]

A letter from Ciampoli brought further disquieting news: Bellarmine said that there would be no problem regarding Copernicus as long as one did not engage in discussion of Scripture: "It is difficult to admit statements about Scripture, however ingenious, when they disagree so much with the common opinion of the Fathers of the Church."[68] Bellarmine was evidently still leaning on the fact that the fathers, whose commentaries on Scripture he had read so diligently all those years before, had treated the disputed earth/sun passages as literal statements, without further comment.

With the appearance of Foscarini's book at just this time, we have seen that the theological skies darkened appreciably. And then came the most significant evidence of Bellarmine's own assessment of the troubled situation, a document, incidentally, that has occasioned more discussion than any other (save perhaps one) in the entire Galileo saga. This was Bellarmine's response in April 1615 to Foscarini's book and to Foscarini's more careful later elaboration of his arguments in a formal *Defense.*[69] The response was directed, significantly, to Galileo as well as to Foscarini, indicating that the two were linked in Bellarmine's mind, not a favorable omen for Galileo's own more cautious defense of the Copernican theses.

The letter opened with a clear warning, courteously disguised. As long as the Copernican theses were presented as mere mathematical devices whose purpose was only to save the appearances, there would be no trouble. But of course Bellarmine knew perfectly well that neither Galileo nor Foscarini was restricting his claims for the Copernican system in this way, the only way that Bellarmine himself was willing to conceive the status of mathematical astronomy. His warning was made plain: if they were to go further, it would be a very dangerous thing "likely not only to irritate all scholastic philosophers and theologians, but also harm the Holy Faith by rendering Holy Scripture false." This was a flat and unconditional declaration, announced almost a year before the assessors rendered their verdict in 1616. Bellarmine appears to have made up his mind: accepting the Copernican claims about earth and sun ran contrary to Scripture and thus could not be tolerated.

Then came the familiar appeal to the consensus of the fathers: no prudent person could go against such a consensus. But now a new note was struck, one that would doom one of Galileo's main lines of defense. It might *seem* as though the sun's motion and the earth's rest were not matters of faith, he wrote. But they were because of the speaker—that is, because the text of the Bible as a whole had God as its primary author. Thus every passage with a clear literal intent (and Bellarmine always assumed that the earth/sun passages displayed such an intent) had the same status: it was a matter of faith. To challenge it would be, implicitly, to challenge the divine authorship of Scripture, and that was *explicitly* a matter of faith: it would be as "heretical to say that Abraham did not have two children" as to say that "Christ was not born of a virgin."

This was how Bellarmine managed to construe the decree of the Council of Trent as extending to the earth/sun passages at the center of the Copernican debate. The decree, as we have seen, explicitly restricted its scope to matters of faith or morals. The phrase was admittedly ambiguous, but Bellarmine was undoubtedly stretching it in order to have its scope decided not just by the content of what was said but by the mere fact that the entire text was God's revelation. And maintaining *this* claim would, Bellarmine believed, be a matter of faith. This extreme form of biblical literalism was not peculiar to Bellarmine, of course.[70] It is best understood as the fruit of the bitter years of controversy between the Reform and the Counter-Reform, controversy in which Bellarmine himself had played a leading role. One can easily see how a theologian like Bellarmine who had been wielding proof-texts as weapons in defense of his Church would have been likely to adopt so conservative a stance.

Next in the letter came a much disputed passage: "I say that if there were a true demonstration that the sun is at the center of the world and the earth in the third heaven, and that the sun does not circle the earth but the earth the sun, then one would have to proceed with great care in explaining the Scriptures that appear contrary, and say rather that we do not understand them than that what is demonstrated is false. But I will not believe that there is such a demonstration until it is shown me." Some have read this as a testimonial to Bellarmine's open-mindedness, and they contrast his attitude favorably in that regard with that of his antagonist in the

Copernican debate. After all, they say, Galileo had not produced a demonstration, and here was Bellarmine allowing that if he indeed could do so, Bellarmine would simply concede that we did not understand the apparently conflicting Scripture passages.[71] (It is worth noting that the surprising fallback position Bellarmine here described was not that of understanding the passages in the accommodated sense that Foscarini and Galileo both argued for so strongly, the alternative that had a persuasive precedent in earlier theological traditions.) Was he being open-minded? Did he think that a demonstration might conceivably be found?

It seems altogether unlikely that he did. Nor was his concession an evidence of open-mindedness with regard to this issue; it was evidence only of the innate courtesy for which Bellarmine was famous. He went on in the remainder of the letter to list several reasons why such a proof would not be forthcoming. Mathematical astronomy, the genre to which he thought Copernicus's constructions to belong, was inherently incapable of producing such a proof; the best it could do was to save the appearances. He believed (as almost everyone else had earlier done) that this was Copernicus's own view, as the foreword to the *De revolutionibus* seemed to assert. This had been Bellarmine's view when teaching astronomy long before in Louvain, and indeed, as we have seen, it was a view with a long history among natural philosophers. He had not changed his mind in the years since. This objection left no room for the mathematical astronomer to produce a genuine demonstration of the earth's motion. Bellarmine to all appearances seems to have entirely overlooked the possibility that a "physical" (as against a purely "mathematical") treatment of the phenomena might yield something approaching demonstration, the hope that animated Galileo's argument from the tidal motions.

To the claim that the biblical language regarding the earth's stability might simply be accommodated to the appearances, just as someone on a moving ship might describe the shore as moving, Bellarmine's surprisingly simplistic answer was that the person on the boat could find out whether shore or boat was in motion, whereas the person on earth had no need even to ask whether the earth was moving since he immediately experienced that the earth was, in fact, at rest. This begged the question, of course, but more to the point, it left no room open for a later demonstration of the opposite. And he added two other considerations: the consensus of the fathers and (as we have seen) the wisdom of Solomon, whom he took to be the author of the passage in Psalms mentioning the sun's motion, each of these, he said, rendering a later reversal altogether unlikely. It certainly does not sound as though he was, in fact, open to the possibility of a later demonstration. Any proof on the Copernican side alleged to be demonstrative would, as far as he was concerned, have to be shown to be only apparently so.

What reinforces this reading is the outcome of the deliberations in Rome in 1616 that ended with the ban on Copernicanism. One of the principles that both

Galileo and Foscarini had urged in their discussions of how apparent conflict between Scripture and the products of sense or reason could be resolved was a principle of prudence: one should not commit the Church to a position that it might later have to abandon. Even if the Copernican theses could not now be demonstrated, if there was a chance that they later might be, then it would be imperative not to commit the Holy Office, the highest doctrinal authority in the Church, to a position that might later prove incorrect. If Bellarmine, solicitous for the reputation of the Church as he was, had believed that there was the slightest possibility that the Copernican ordering of sun and earth might later prove correct, he would never have allowed the decree of 1616 to go through.

To summarize, then, Bellarmine had early made his misgivings plain about the new way of reading Copernicus in the light of Galileo's telescopic observations. The carefully worked-out cosmology of his early teaching years had relied to an altogether unusual extent on the text of Scripture as its source. He would be likely to react much more negatively than most, then, to Galileo's not only turning that cosmology upside down but, even more provocatively, rejecting entirely the category of evidence on which it was based. There could be no more direct a challenge than that.

The lines of argument on which Galileo had most relied in his attempt to ward off Scripture-based attack would crumble for anyone who shared Bellarmine's approach to astronomy. First, the claim that Scriptures were not intended to teach cosmology would not get far with someone who thought that that was just where one should look for one's evidence. Second, the claim that the authors of Scripture would have accommodated their language to the appearances when describing such things as the motion or lack of it on the part of sun and earth would not have found favor with someone whose own cosmology relied at every step on the language of Scripture not being accommodated in that way. Third, the warning against premature commitment of the Church to a position that later it might have to allow to be false could readily be dismissed by someone who believed that the Copernican "opinion," as he called it, could, in principle, never be demonstrated. He was wrong, and Galileo was right, as it happened, on all three scores.

It seems reasonable to conclude, then, that Bellarmine may bear a considerable share of the responsibility for the decision to characterize the heliocentric world-system as "altogether contrary to Scripture," thus leaving the way open for Galileo's judges in 1633 to interpret this as grounds for suspicion of heresy. At the very least, as the congregation's dominant theologian, Bellarmine would have been in a position in 1616 to prevent what proved to be a disastrous move. But if this analysis is correct, his likely responsibility goes further than that. He had quite possibly decided on the theological unacceptability of the Copernican theses long before, and he would have been impelled to this in part by a degree of biblical literalism with regard to cosmology that the others involved in the 1616 decision may not have shared.

His authority was such that even if the qualifiers had leaned toward a different estimate of the Copernican issue (unlikely in the case of the Dominican qualifiers), they might have hesitated to oppose what they must have known in advance to be his view and also, of course, the decision the pope had on his own very likely already arrived at. One could, of course, object that Bellarmine and the Dominicans had been on opposite sides in the protracted and acrimonious *De auxiliis* controversy, so that the Dominican theologians would hardly have been disposed in advance to follow his lead. But all this, of course, is no more than speculation. We will never know for sure.

Westfall is more emphatic than I in assigning the major responsibility to Bellarmine in the genesis of the Index decision. But he concludes his essay "Bellarmine and Galileo" by warning the reader against a facile demonizing of Bellarmine in consequence:

> It was not ignorance and narrow-mindedness that condemned Copernicanism. Cardinal Bellarmine represented the finest flower of Catholic learning. . . . Far from being ignorant, Bellarmine was the captive, as all of us are captives, of his lifetime's experience, in his case the defense of his Church and of the worldview his experience fostered. The tragedy of his Church lay in the fact that he saw the rise of modern science on the analogy of Protestantism, and failed to recognize that it was instead a fundamental reshaping of the intellectual landscape within which Christianity, Catholic and Protestant alike, would have henceforth to proceed.[72]

Westfall might have added that, given that lifetime's experience, there was no way in which Bellarmine could have anticipated what lay ahead.

Summing Up

When he proposed a formal inquiry in 1979 into the Church's dealings with Galileo, Pope John Paul spoke of "an honest recognition of wrongs, on whatever side they occur."[73] It is easy enough to conclude that those responsible for the decree of 1616 made an objective error: Copernicanism is not—and never was—contrary to Scripture. But "wrongs"? That term suggests blame besides. Should we also conclude that those same people were to blame, that they should, all things considered, have acted differently? That is a far more difficult question to answer. In complex historical contexts like this, as Westfall warns, one has to be wary of the deceptive clarities of hindsight.

One possible approach to the question would be to recall at this point the defense brief that Galileo laid out in his *Letter to the Grand Duchess*.[74] It can be regarded, in both its strengths and its weaknesses, as about the best case that might have been made for the Copernican cause at that point.[75] One can imagine that, had the procedures of the Holy Office been different, had those whose position was impugned been allowed to speak in their defense, this or something like it would have been the counterposition that the Holy Office would have had to consider—and that, in one way or another, perhaps they did consider.

Was it novel? Some commentators have emphasized its novelty, seeing in its strong separation between science and Scripture a key contribution to modernity, to the profound changes that would altogether transform the intellectual climate of Western culture over the next couple of centuries.[76] Galileo himself surely did not see it as so dramatically novel. Indeed, his overriding aim in the *Letter to the Grand Duchess* was to show that his position was not novel at all, that it harked back to principles that found a clear echo in the work of the greatest of the early Church theologians.

How would his argument have struck the theologians of the Holy Office in 1616? Of the exegetic principles that he proposed, the only one they would have questioned was the principle of scriptural limitation, which denied the relevance of Scripture to those cosmological issues that were already within the bounds of human sense and reason to determine. There was a long tradition in the Church of turning to the Bible for knowledge of the most general features of the natural world: if, indeed, it was the revealed word of God, would one not expect it to carry that sort of weight? Augustine himself, though he warned against treating Scripture as a resource for deciding on abstract issues in cosmology, in practice did assume that the writers of Scripture enjoyed a knowledge of nature beyond the ordinary, conveyed to them by divine revelation. So the precedent he set on this issue, despite Galileo's best efforts to present him as an advocate of Galileo's own separation of astronomy from Scripture, was at best mixed.

Two major developments between Augustine's day and Galileo's bear directly on this issue. Both we have already noted. First was the advent of Aristotle's cosmology in the West in the thirteenth century and the impact of its apparent completeness on the theology of the time. The strongly negative reaction to it of many theologians was prompted, in part, by the apparent devaluation of Scripture as a source of natural knowledge when confronted with Aristotle's *Physics*. In the Aristotelian tradition of theology that found its major patron in Aquinas, there was an accepted precedent for invoking the principle of accommodation when divergences appeared between the cosmology of the Bible and that of Aristotle.

On the other hand, the impact of the Reformation had the opposite effect. The literalism in scriptural interpretation that it fostered, among Protestants and Catholics alike, reaffirmed the Bible as a plausible resource for authoritative general knowledge of God's creation. We have already seen this in the case of Bellarmine, who saw the Psalms as the work of Solomon, "a man above all otherwise and learned in the human sciences." The impact of Trent would have further accentuated the literalist exegetical implications of the council's dominant theme: the decisive role of "the unanimous agreement of the Fathers." In short, then, denying the relevance of Scripture to cosmology, as Galileo's most distinctive exegetical principle did, would have found little support in the Rome of the early seventeenth century. Among Aristotelians, perhaps, there might have been some sympathy for its application to specific astronomical issues, but in general the leaning would have been in the direction that Bellarmine so strongly favored.

Without this principle, how would the others have fared among the Roman theologians? In essence, all of them would (or, at the very least, should) have been allowed some weight. But this is where the prior conviction on the theologians' part of the falsity in philosophic terms of the Copernican position would have played a crucial role. Given this, it would probably have seemed to them unnecessary to call on the principle of accommodation in their exegetical approach to the disputed passages, plausible though this would seem to us to have been. The geocentric language of the Bible was, after all, the language of the cosmology they took for granted both on philosophical and on commonsense grounds. Why call on accommodation if there was no difference to reconcile? Still, from the perspective of a later day, the evident plausibility of accommodation in the event that the Copernican challenge later turned out to be justified ought, in the light of Augustine's stern warning about the need for prudence in such cases, to have raised a doubt as to the real need for theological intervention in the issue in the first instance.[77]

There were among the consultors and the cardinal members of the Holy Office none, so far as we know, who were conversant with the new astronomy and its potential, particularly its potential to produce new *physical* proofs of the earth's motion. This last was, after all, the key to Galileo's entire effort. This group was simply not qualified to make a decision that, in effect, denied the possibility that such a proof might be found. Should they, as some have said, have realized that a new sort of science was in the process of being born, one that might possibly challenge confident declarations like "foolish and absurd in philosophy," on which they were so fatefully relying? Hardly. There was scarcely a whisper of this as early as 1616. Even had they been proficient in astronomy, they could not have guessed how profound a change was in the making. But a proficiency in physical astronomy might have warned them, even in terms of traditional science, that they should, at the very least, hold back.

Had there been any hesitation in their minds along these lines, however, there would have been counterarguments to allay any possible worry they might have had about including a highly unusual declaration of doctrine ("contrary to Scripture") in what would ordinarily be no more than a list of prohibited publications. As we have seen, they could have called on one or other of several considerations at this point to assure themselves that the Copernican position in any event could never be demonstrated and that in the absence of such a demonstration the literal interpretation (given the prior presupposition in its favor in this case) could safely stand. They could have appealed to the Tychonic alternative, as indeed Jesuit philosophers and theologians would, after 1616, routinely do. Or, like Urban, they could have recalled the voluntarist exclusion, on theological grounds, of the possibility of demonstration in such a case. Still, one wants to ask: Why go beyond a simple ban on a list of publications?

Once again, we come back to a single overriding consideration that almost surely animated the discussions in Rome at that time: a fear that Scripture itself and the Church's unique authority to determine its interpretation were under attack. How much blame for overreaction should we lay on those responsible for a decision involving the pope, cardinals, and consultors alike? Should we suppose that if they had had their exegetical principles straight, all would have been well? Should we suppose that in the intellectual climate of the day, they *could* have got them straight — "straight," that is, in ours (or Galileo's) terms? Your call . . .

THIS ANALYSIS OF THE intellectual issues involved in the 1616 decision presupposes, of course, that the decision was made on the merits of the case as these were perceived by the qualifiers and the members of the Holy Office. But, of course, influences of a more personal sort were actively at work also: deference to an autocratic pope who had very probably made his own preferences clear in advance; active dislike of a brash outsider who did not pay theologians the respect they were accustomed to receive; angry reaction to the perceived threat to Aristotelian philosophy; the inclination of busy people to delegate decisions to others, especially if these others were perceived as leading authorities in the matter.

Untangling the knot of factors that go into the making of a complex decision is difficult even when one is dealing with a single contemporary public figure. When the event is at a distance of almost four centuries and involves several dozen people about whom we only have generalities to rely on, untangling the knot will, at best, tell us only how it could have happened. But perhaps this is answer enough to the question from which this essay began: How could the Roman theologians have given their assent to a verdict that to later generations would seem so clearly wrong? We have seen how they could — and (perhaps) why they did.

Notes

In composing this essay, I relied heavily on Annibale Fantoli's magisterial work *Galileo: For Copernicanism and for the Church,* 2d ed., ed. and trans. George V. Coyne (Vatican City: Vatican Observatory Publications, 1996), and on Richard J. Blackwell's extremely useful compilation of documents and commentary in his *Galileo, Bellarmine and the Bible* (hereafter *GBB*) (Notre Dame: University of Notre Dame Press, 1991). Maurice A. Finocchiaro's *The Galileo Affair: A Documentary History* (hereafter *GA*) (Berkeley: University of California Press, 1989), is invaluable for the translations it provides of many of the key documents. I should acknowledge also how much I have benefited from the advice of Annibale Fantoli and Francesco Beretta on some of the more arcane details of the Galileo story.

1. See Francesco Beretta, *Galilée devant le Tribunal de l'Inquisition* (Fribourg: Université de Fribourg, 1998), 272.

2. In the Inquisition minutes for Feb. 25, 1616, the condemned propositions are described as "the propositions of the mathematician, Galileo." Galileo Galilei, *Opere di Galileo Galilei* (hereafter *OGG*), ed. Antonio Favaro (1890–1909; reprint, Florence: Giunti Barbèra, 1968), 11:321.

3. The Holy Office employed a number of "qualifiers" who would advise the cardinal members (whose vote determined the decisions of the Holy Office) on technical theological issues. Among the broader group of consultors to the Holy Office, there were Masters in Theology from among whom panels such as this one would primarily be constituted. Their task was to "qualify," or determine the theological status of, propositions the Holy Office was considering as possibly meriting censure.

4. *OGG*, 19:320. The cumbersome (though accurate) wording is assumed to have been drawn from Tommaso Caccini's denunciation of Galileo to the Holy Office the previous March that had set the judicial process in motion.

5. *OGG*, 19:321; *GA*, 146.

6. Guicciardini to Curzio Picchena, Mar. 4, 1616; *OGG*, 12:242. The ambassador was, of course, dependent on hearsay for this sort of information.

7. Mentioned in the Millini instruction (below) on the following day.

8. The exact sequence of events is not clear at this point due to gaps in the documentation. This reconstruction is due to Annibale Fantoli, who draws on the account given by Francesco Beretta of the normal routines of the Holy Office in his *Galilée devant le Tribunal*. See chap. 5 of this book.

9. Wording from the Millini instruction.

10. Minutes of the Holy Office recording the Millini instruction, Feb. 25. *OGG*, 19:321; *GA*, 147.

11. Some details of this meeting are known from documents recently discovered in the archives of the Holy Office and published in Walter Brandmuller and Egon Johannes Greipl, eds., *Copernico, Galilei e la chiesa: Fine della controversia (1820)* (Florence: Leo S. Olschki, 1992), 145–51; see Fantoli, *Galileo*, 261–63.

12. *OGG*, 15:11; Fantoli, *Galileo*, 262–63.

13. De Zuñiga's commentary was the first work by a Catholic exegete to have defended the Copernican position in interpreting a biblical text, in this case Job 9:6, which speaks of God "moving the earth from its place." De Zuñiga argued that this text is more easily understood in a Copernican sense, that references to the motion of the sun can also be interpreted in that sense, and (showing some knowledge of astronomy) that in any event Copernicus had "demonstrated the causes" of the planetary phenomena much better than Ptolemy had. See *GBB*, 185–86, for this text. This brief passage in de Zuñiga's book had already excited vigorous

criticism from numerous other Catholic exegetes, beginning with de Pineda in 1597. See chap. 2 of this book. The debate about the theological status of Copernicanism had already begun before Galileo brought that debate to a new level of intensity.

14. *OGG*, 19:298; *GA*, 135.

15. Bellarmine to Foscarini, Apr. 12, 1615; *OGG*, 12:171; *GA*, 67.

16. *GBB*, 140–41.

17. See chap. 4 of this book for further discussion of these exegetical principles.

18. Bellarmine to Foscarini, Apr. 12, 1615; *OGG*, 12:172; *GA*, 68–69.

19. Cardinal Paul Poupard, "Galileo: Report on Papal Commission Findings," *Origins* 22 (1992): 374–75.

20. In the first papal encyclical of modern times to deal with exegetical issues, *Providentissimus Deus* (1893). In recognizing them, Pope Leo XIII actually quotes some of the same passages in Augustine that Galileo drew on, but rather pointedly without mentioning Galileo. "The Holy Spirit did not intend to teach men . . . the essential nature of things bearing on the visible universe, things in no way profitable unto salvation." The writers "did not seek to penetrate the secrets of nature but rather dealt with things in more or less figurative language." We are not required to uphold the views of the fathers where they comment on physical matters, "for it may be . . . that they have sometimes expressed the ideas of their own times." Leo XIII, *Providentissimus Deus: The Study of Holy Scripture,* in *The Papal Encyclicals, 1878-1903,* ed. Claudia Carlen (Raleigh, N.C.: McGrath, 1981), 334–35.

21. In a volume edited by Cardinal Paul Poupard and issued on behalf of the Galileo Commission in 1983, Bernard Vinaty makes short work of this attempt to justify the long delay by citing Galileo's lack of demonstration. He contends that Galileo himself proved the earth's motion to all intents and purposes in the first place. Thus "it is erroneous to maintain that the decisive proof of Copernicanism came only with the first observation of the annual parallax of a star by the astronomer Friedrich Bessel." Bernard Vinaty, "Galileo and Copernicus," in *Galileo Galilei, 350 anni di storia, 1633-1983,* ed. Paul Poupard (Casale Monferrato: Piemme, 1984), 42.

22. Augustine, *De Genesi ad litteram* (The Literal Meaning of Genesis), trans. J. H. Taylor (New York: Newman Press, 1982), 2:18.

23. For a fuller discussion, see Ernan McMullin, "The Goals of Natural Science," *Proceedings of the American Philosophical Association* 58 (1984): 37–64.

24. *OGG*, 19:321; *GA*, 147.

25. Giorgio de Santillana, *The Crime of Galileo* (Chicago: University of Chicago Press, 1955), 182.

26. See Margaret J. Osler, *Divine Will and the Mechanical Philosophy: Gassendi and Descartes on Contingency and Necessity in the Created World* (Cambridge: Cambridge University Press, 1994).

27. *OGG*, 13:182.

28. See James Lattis, *Between Copernicus and Galileo: Christoph Clavius and the Collapse of Ptolemaic Cosmology* (Chicago: University of Chicago Press, 1994), 205–11.

29. See chap. 2 of this book.

30. Bertolt Brecht, *Galileo,* adaptation by Charles Laughton (New York: Grove, Weidenfeld, 1966), 72–73.

31. See Dennis R. Danielson, "The Great Copernican Cliché," *American Journal of Physics* 69 (2001): 1029–35.

32. Galileo to Dini, May 1615; *OGG,* 12:184. Arthur Koestler comments, with an abundance of detail, on the "contemptuous arrogance" of passages such as these in *The Sleepwalkers* (London: Hutchinson, 1959), 450.

33. Galileo to Dini, Feb. 16, 1615; *OGG,* 5:294; *GA,* 57.

34. *Letter to the Grand Duchess Christina, OGG,* 5:323–24; *GA,* 99.

35. Ciampoli to Galileo, Mar. 21, 1615; *OGG,* 12:160.

36. Galileo to Dini, May 1615; *OGG,* 12:184.

37. Guicciardini to Picchena, Dec. 5, 1615; *OGG,* 12:207.

38. Querengo to d'Este, Jan. 20, 1616; *OGG,* 12:226–27.

39. Guicciardini to Cosimo II, Mar. 4, 1616; *OGG,* 12:242; Fantoli, *Galileo,* 217–18.

40. *OGG,* 12:242–43.

41. For details of this controversy and a speculative account of its possible impact on the Galileo affair, see Rivka Feldhay, *Galileo and the Church: Political Inquisition or Critical Dialogue?* (Cambridge: Cambridge University Press, 1995).

42. See chap. 2 of this book.

43. Ciampoli to Galileo, Mar. 21, 1616; *OGG,* 12:160.

44. See F. J. Crehan, S.J., "The Bible in the Roman Catholic Church from Trent to the Present Day," in *The Cambridge History of the Bible: The West from the Reformation to the Present Day,* ed. S. L. Greenslade (Cambridge: Cambridge University Press, 1963), 199.

45. This has been persuasively argued by several recent authors, especially Olaf Pedersen in his *Galileo and the Council of Trent,* Studi Galileiani 1:1 (Vatican City: Vatican Observatory Publications, 1991), and by Richard Blackwell in *GBB,* chap. 1.

46. The relevant decrees of the Council of Trent appear in translation as Appendix I in *GBB;* see 183.

47. *GBB,* 14.

48. *OGG,* 12:308; *GA,* 137.

49. M. Daniel Price, "The Origins of Lateran V's *Apostolici Regiminis,*" *Acta Historiae Conciliorum* 17 (1985): 464–72.

50. In his *Commentary on Matthew,* chap. 22 (1527), and his *Commentary on Ecclesiastes,* chap. 3 (1534).

51. *OGG,* 11:355.

52. John Paul II, "Lessons of the Galileo Case," *Origins* 22 (1992): 372.

53. His only complaint was with the wording in three passages that "sound bad," though they could also be taken in a "benign sense" (*OGG,* 19:305; *GA,* 135–36). As we now know, these three passages appear in the copy Lorini sent to Rome but not in the "true" copy that Galileo later forwarded to Dini in Rome for distribution to the appropriate recipients, suggesting that the Lorini copy might have been tampered with. These passages may, of course, have been deliberately added by Lorini or someone else (somewhat risky if the original could be produced in rebuttal), or more likely, as Pesce has recently argued, Galileo took the opportunity to excise them in the "true" copy he later forwarded, since, as he noted in the covering letter to Dini (Galileo to Dini, Feb. 16, 1615; *OGG,* 5:292; *GBB,* 203), the original letter had been written in haste. Mauro Pesce, "Le redazioni originali della Lettera 'copernicana' di G. Galilei a B. Castelli," *Filologia e Critica* 17 (1992): 394–417. In support of this latter reading is the fact that when the archbishop of Pisa (on secret orders from the Holy Office) requested the original letter from

Castelli (*OGG*, 19:276), Galileo (who had the original in his keeping) would not allow Castelli to hand it over but insisted that he should only read the letter aloud to the archbishop. Sending the original to Rome would lead to its being compared to the "true" copy he had earlier sent. Were he to have modified this letter before sending it, this could have led to damaging consequences (Fantoli, *Galileo,* 253 n. 44). Whichever of these two readings one adopts does not affect the main point here: that the consultor found no fault with the argument of the letter overall.

54. Baldini and Coyne have published excerpts from this course; see Ugo Baldini and George V. Coyne, eds. and trans., *The Louvain Lectures (Lectiones Lovanienses) of Bellarmine and the Autograph Copy of His 1616 Declaration to Galileo,* Studi Galileiani 1:2 (Vatican City: Vatican Observatory Publications, 1984).

55. Baldini and Coyne, *Louvain Lectures,* 20.

56. See chap. 4 of this book.

57. See Ann Blair, "Mosaic Physics and the Search for a Pious Natural Philosophy in the Late Renaissance," *Isis* 91 (2000): 32–58.

58. *OGG,* 12:162; *GA,* 68.

59. *OGG,* 5:319; *GA,* 96. Probably heard when Baronio visited Padua in 1598; Fantoli, *Galileo,* 248.

60. See Edward A. Gosselin and Lawrence S. Lerner, "Galileo and the Long Shadow of Bruno," *Archives Internationales d'Histoire des Sciences* 25 (1975): 223–46. Koyré goes so far as to claim that Bruno's condemnation was "the occult but real cause of the condemnation of both Copernicus and Galileo." Alexandre Koyré, *Galileo Studies* (Atlantic Highlands, N.J.: Humanities Press, 1978), 136.

61. Bruno's discussion of the Copernican system in *The Ash Wednesday Supper,* ed. and trans. E. A. Gosselin and L. S. Lerner (Hamden, Conn.: Archon, 1977), suggests that his grasp of it extended no farther than to its helicocentric character. See Ernan McMullin, "Bruno and Copernicus," *Isis* 78 (1987): 55–74.

62. *OGG,* 11:87–88. Fantoli notes that the first of the five questions Bellarmine proposed to his Jesuit colleagues concerned the multitude of the fixed stars, and he wonders whether this might have been prompted by a memory of the charges against Bruno (*Galileo,* 129).

63. Guicciardini to Picchena, Dec. 5, 1615; *OGG,* 12:207.

64. Cesi to Galileo, Jan. 12, 1615; *OGG,* 12:129; Richard S. Westfall, *Essays on the Trial of Galileo* (Vatican City: Vatican Observatory Publications, 1989), 13.

65. Westfall, *Essays,* 13.

66. Dini to Galileo, Mar. 7, 1615; *OGG,* 12:151. For the text, see *GBB,* 207–8.

67. Galileo to Dini, Mar. 23, 1615; *OGG,* 5:298. For the text, see *GBB,* 209.

68. Ciampoli to Galileo, Mar. 21, 1615; *OGG,* 12:160.

69. Bellarmine to Foscarini, Apr. 12, 1615; *OGG,* 12:161–62; *GA,* 67–69.

70. Nor would it die with him. The status of *obiter dicta* in the Bible (like Abraham's having two sons) would give rise to a great deal of controversy later among Catholic theologians. Henry Holden, an English Catholic theologian later in the seventeenth century excluded such *obiter dicta* from the scope of divine inspiration and thus from authoritative status, but his view was strongly criticized. Cardinal Newman espoused a similar view with regard to *obiter dicta* two centuries later, again giving rise to controversy among theologians. See Crehan, "The Bible," 225.

71. Rivka Feldhay is one of those who defends this benign interpretation of Bellarmine's remark about demonstration. She infers from it, indeed, that his "advice to Galileo and Foscarini was not meant to bury the discussion of Copernicanism but to enable its continuation." Rivka Feldhay, "Recent Narratives on Galileo and the Church; or: The Three Dogmas of the Counter-Reformation," in *Galileo in Context,* ed. Jürgen Renn (Cambridge: Cambridge University Press, 2001), 235.

72. Westfall, *Essays,* 23.

73. John Paul II, "Faith, Science, and the Search for Truth," *Origins* 9 (1979): 391.

74. See chap. 4 of this book.

75. Prescinding from its occasionally provocative rhetoric, which was almost bound to further antagonize an already suspicious theological readership.

76. See, for example, Mauro Pesce, "L'interpretazione della Bibbia nella Lettera di Galileo a Cristina di Lorena e la sua ricezione: Storia di una difficoltà nel distinguere ciò che è religioso da ciò non lo è," *Annali di Storia dell'Esegesi* 4 (1987): 239–86; see also Giorgio Stabile, "Linguaggio della natura e linguaggio della scrittura in Galilei: Dalla 'Istoria' sulle macchie solari alle lettere copernicane," *Nuncius* 9 (1994): 37–64.

77. As it should have done for the Jesuit exegetes, critics of Copernicanism, a generation earlier. See chap. 2 of this book.

SEVEN

THE DOCUMENTS OF GALILEO'S TRIAL

Recent Hypotheses and Historical Criticism

Francesco Beretta

Any reconstruction of the Galileo affair and, more generally, any analysis of the history of the relationship of the Tuscan philosopher to the Church, must logically be based upon the study of the documents of the trial. The most important of these legal documents are to be found in a collection entitled the "Vatican File on Galileo" (VF), which is kept in the Vatican secret archive (ASV).[1] This volume has been reproduced in many editions since the middle of the nineteenth century.[2] The one prepared in 1907 by Antonio Favaro, professor of mathematics and of the history of science at the University of Padua, takes precedence because of both its quality and its inclusion in the reference publication of Galileo's *Opere.*[3] Following the opening of the Vatican archive ordered by Pope Leo XIII in 1880, Favaro was able to consult the VF freely. Even more exceptionally, especially at that particular time, he was given access to the archive of the Holy Office. Thus he published a good number of tribunal decrees relating to Galileo's trial.[4]

Recent Hypotheses

The last decades of the twentieth century were marked by three events of great significance for the issues surrounding the documents of the trial of Galileo. Within the context of the work of the Galileo Commission instituted by Pope John Paul II, Sergio M. Pagano produced, in collaboration with Antonio G. Luciani, a new edition of the VF.[5] In the introduction, an entirely new hypothesis concerning the precious volume's origin was set forth. The hypothesis was based on an examination of the documents in the archives of the Congregations of the Holy Office and of the Index, to which the edition's authors enjoyed access although these were still closed at the time to other researchers.

According to the traditional hypothesis, set forth by Favaro and generally followed by historical experts on Galileo's trial, the VF contains the documents that were collected in connection with the condemnation of the philosopher in 1633. Other documents may have existed, but if so, from the beginning, they were never included in the file.[6] According to the novel explanation of the VF's contents proposed in the new Vatican edition, the volume does not constitute the documentation of the trial; rather, it is to be considered as a collection of documents excerpted from the original judicial file. This collection had been compiled for transmission to the Congregation of the Index and was to be inserted into the series of *Censurae librorum* of that congregation. The original documentation of Galileo's trial retained in the archive of the Holy Office in the seventeenth century would then have been lost during the transport of the papal archives to France, ordered by Napoleon I in 1810.[7] It is clear that if this hypothesis, which met a favorable reception,[8] had been confirmed, it would have represented a key historiographical turning point. We shall see below, however, that the hypothesis lacks any real foundation because of a misunderstanding on the part of the authors of the Vatican edition of the nature of the series of the *Censurae librorum.*

A second event was the appearance of a number of debatable interpretations of the Galileo affair based on controversial readings of the VF file. Most discussed was Pietro Redondi's *Galileo Heretic* (1983), which was translated into many languages and which included a formerly unpublished document from the Congregation of the Index, the famed "G3" concerning the "atomism" of Galileo. According to Redondi, the "official sentence" and the legal documents on which it was based were fabricated so as to cover the steps being taken to allow Galileo to escape being condemned for the "atomism of the *Dialogo*" and, consequently, for the "eucharistic heresy" of which "the official philosopher of the Pope" had been accused.[9] If the Vatican edition in 1984 refuted Redondi's attribution of the new document "G3" to the Jesuit Orazio Grassi,[10] it gave some support to the incomplete or haphazard state of the trial documentation alleged by Redondi, who in an addendum to the French edition of his work commented that the hypothesis of the Vatican edition concerning the VF's nature could be accepted on the grounds of "logical justification." It was not possible, of course, at that time to verify it directly, as the archive of the Holy Office was still closed.[11]

Italo Mereu had already attempted in 1979 to prove that Galileo had been tortured. His analysis was based on a double presupposition concerning the documents of the trial. Like Redondi, he held that the VF documents were incomplete as well as falsified and thus practically useless. Further, he claimed that the record of the sentence and the abjuration bearing Galileo's own signature are the only known authentic documents we possess from the trial. The analysis of the sentence in the light of the Inquisition's known procedures would, according to Mereu, lead to the conclusion that Galileo was indeed tortured.[12] But, in reality, the originals of the sentence and of Galileo's abjuration are unknown, although numerous copies still exist of these documents that, by the decree of Pope Urban VIII, were disseminated throughout the whole of Catholic Europe in order to inform the learned public of Galileo's condemnation. On the other hand, the authentic record from the session where Galileo was cross-examined about his intentions, in which the threat of torture was indeed mentioned, shows that the philosopher was not ultimately subjected to any such torment.[13]

The absence of the originals of the sentence and of the abjuration of Galileo itself undermines Mereu's argument, which is exclusively based on the authenticity of these two documents. To try to get around this, in 1992 Gino Ditadi fabricated a new document, supposedly the original abjuration of Galileo, which he claimed to be preserved in the National Library in Florence. To that end, he placed a facsimile of the handwritten signature of Galileo from one of the trial depositions at the bottom of the text of the abjuration, while adapting the formulation of the last sentence and adding the note: "Handwritten signature of Galileo on his abjuration. National Library of Florence."[14] Good luck to those who would set themselves to hunting down this "never-before-published" autograph of Galileo!

These examples highlight the decisive importance of the question of the nature of the VF, as well as that of the documentation of the trial more generally. This crucial problem could not be settled until the archive of the Congregation for the Doctrine of the Faith (ACDF), which contains the documentary collections of the former Congregations of the Holy Office and of the Index, was opened to all researchers. This opening, officially celebrated in 1998, constituted the third very significant, even in some respects decisive, event with regard to the issues surrounding the documents of Galileo's trial.[15] It enabled the recovery and publication of certain new and until then unknown documents (one of which concerns Galileo's atomism), but it failed to bring to light any sensational new knowledge. However, the study of the preserved documents and the reconstruction of the history of these collections settle—definitively, in my opinion—the question of the nature of the VF, confirming that it is indeed composed of the original documents that led Urban VIII to pronounce the verdict requiring Galileo's abjuration on June 6, 1633. The VF documents, then, represent the legal basis of Galileo's condemnation and are of the utmost importance for the reconstruction and proper interpretation of his trial.

I shall begin by providing some essential facts concerning the history of the archives of the Congregations of both the Holy Office and the Index. Then I will point out the implications of this study for the critical discussion of the nature of the VF and the identification of the documents that served as the basis for Galileo's condemnation. Finally, I will present the principal documents preserved in the ACDF that have been published in the last few years.

The Archives of the Congregations of the Holy Office and of the Index

After the headquarters of the Roman Holy Office—the Congregation of the Inquisition—was transferred to the palace located near St. Peter's Basilica in 1566, the documents produced by the tribunal were kept in the chancellery. In 1593, the cardinals of this congregation decided to create an archive for these documents.[16] The accumulation of new files continued until the end of the eighteenth century. The most quantitatively significant collection consisted of criminal records, collected either in volumes or in numbered bundles: these numbered more than 4,400 by the end of the eighteenth century.[17] Proceedings relating to certain notorious trials, such as that of Cardinal Morone or of Pietro Carnesecchi, were preserved separately from the other criminal records. In the chancellery of the tribunal, besides documents relating to trials still in process, were some volumes dealing with "doctrinal matters and jurisdiction," grouping together files of general importance that were kept outside the archive to be used as reference works when similar cases were being considered.[18] In effect, great importance was attached to jurisprudence in the workings of the Roman Tribunal of the Inquisition, especially in the decisions of the Sovereign Pontiff, the tribunal's president.

Beginning in the 1760s and over the next three decades, a significant transformation of the archive of the Holy Office took place, aiming to facilitate access to the tribunal's jurisprudence. An overhaul of part of the old collections had been planned ever since the canonical visitation of the archive in 1735. After underlining the importance of the jurisprudence of the Congregation of the Holy Office, the author of a document dealing with this need, probably the assessor Raffaele Girolami, pointed out the necessity of reorganizing and taking inventory of the archive's contents in order to locate more easily the documents that could illuminate the tribunal's decisions since its foundation.[19] Following this principle, Giuseppe Maria Lugani, a Dominican who was appointed as doctrinal archivist in December 1762,[20] grouped together a new series of documents, singling out those with the most important doctrinal and jurisdictional implications.

These new volumes of materials bearing on doctrine and jurisdiction, still recognizable today by their uniform bindings in white parchment,[21] were created by selecting, from the vast collection of judicial files, documents that chronicled cases of particular importance. The selections made clearly indicate the concern for jurisprudence that characterized these new collections. In general, the archivist Lugani limited himself to removing from the judicial files (preserved in the large collection of the criminal records) the originals of the censures written by consulting theologians, as well as other documents that would help to explain the judgments arrived at by the tribunal court. The relevant decree, taken from the register of the *Decreta,* was then copied on the cover of the new folder, which also indicated the archival volume in which the full judicial file could be found.[22]

Furthermore, some collections already in existence were reorganized, or even in some cases completely transformed. Such was the case with the series concerning the censure of books, *Censurae librorum,* compiled by Lugani using for the most part the files that had previously contained some volumes from the tribunal's chancellery.[23] The series of the *Censurae librorum* thus belongs to the collection of the Congregation of the Holy Office, and not to that of the Congregation of the Index, as the Vatican edition of the VF asserts.[24] This series did not exist in its current form until the last decades of the eighteenth century.

This significant transformation of the archive of the Holy Office, carried out in the second half of the eighteenth century, created a marked distinction between the *criminal collection,* consisting of judicial files dealing with suits conducted from the mid–sixteenth until the end of the eighteenth centuries, and the *jurisprudential collection,* grouping together the essential elements of the doctrinal decisions and the jurisdiction of the Holy Office. Lacking any other internal documents concerning the state of the archive after this important change, we turn to a summary inventory of the collections of the congregation as these could be found in 1813 in the archives of the empire in Paris. Compiled by Parisian archivists following the seizure of the archive of the Holy See and its transfer to France decreed by Napoleon I, the inventory recorded the state of the principal collections making up the archive of the Holy Office by the end of the eighteenth century: 4,000 volumes of judicial files and roughly 1,000 volumes of *Decreta,* sentences, and correspondence of the congregation, as well as almost 450 volumes of petitions, pardons, exemptions, and concessions of inquisitorial powers. In addition to these older collections were the 1,600-odd volumes of the newly assembled doctrinal and jurisdictional series (Appendix I).[25]

Concerning the part of the archives that made the return trip to Rome between 1815 and 1817,[26] it can be said in summary that the jurisprudential collection, as it had been compiled at the end of the eighteenth century by the doctrinal archivist Lugani, was recovered, while the criminal records, which is to say almost the entirety of the judicial files, were destroyed. The financial difficulties encountered by Father Marino Marini and Count Giulio Ginnasi, who had been sent to Paris to recover the archives of the Roman Curia, led them to sell a considerable portion of the records to paper manufacturers. The selection was carried out following instructions received from Rome. These indicate that the Congregation of the Holy Office was extremely anxious to recover the records that dealt with doctrinal and jurisdictional matters and that in contrast the fate of the vast collection of trial documents was left at the discretion of the pontifical representatives.[27] This was the source of Ginnasi's and Marini's decision to put the files up for sale in order to finance the return of the rest of the archives. Along with the four thousand volumes of criminal records, almost the entirety of the registers of correspondence was lost, as well as the volumes containing the sentences and abjurations.[28]

Now to the archive of the Congregation of the Index. One should point out first of all that the administrative workings of this congregation were fundamentally different than those of the Holy Office. The Congregation of the Inquisition was a criminal tribunal that conferred on its chancellery a particularly important function, one carried out by a dozen officials: the commissary and his assistant, the assessor and his secretary, the public prosecutor, a notary and his four deputies, and an archivist. On the other hand, the administrative functioning of the Congregation of the Index, like that of other congregations, was carried out solely by its secretary, in this case a Dominican priest, who was assisted by another friar.[29] This situation explains, for one thing, the much less imposing dimensions of the archive of the Index, and for another, their unsystematic and incomplete character, even at the time they were first assembled, for their maintenance depended to a great extent upon the effectiveness and the individual capabilities of the secretaries who succeeded one another.

Before the French occupation of Rome, the records of the archive of the Index were preserved in the convent of Minerva, the residence of the master-general of the Dominican order, which also housed the secretary of the congregation. At the time of the transporting of the pontifical archives to France ordered by Napoleon I, the documents of the Index were combined with those of the Holy Office,[30] but once they were returned to Rome, apparently without having suffered any major losses, they were returned to the secretary of the congregation. After Rome was taken by Italian troops in 1870, the headquarters of the Congregation of the Index and its archive was moved to the palace of the Vatican chancellery. It was not until 1917, when the Congregation of the Index was disbanded and its role in the censure of books was handed over to the Congregation of the Holy Office, that the archive of the Index was transferred to the custody of the Holy Office.[31]

Galileo's Judicial File: External Clues

The preceding history of the archives allows us now to approach the question of the nature of the VF. First of all, the convergence of both internal and external considerations leads to a particularly confident affirmation that the actual judicial file of the

Galileo case may be identified with the VF, comprising therefore the documents that served as the legal basis for the condemnation of the philosopher pronounced by the pope on June 16, 1633. The VF also contains numerous letters from nuncios and inquisitors concerning the publication throughout the Catholic world of the sentence and the abjuration of Galileo, ordered by Urban VIII that same day.

Here, then, first are the external elements at our disposal, notably those that have become available with the opening of the archive by the Congregation of the Doctrine of the Faith. Thanks to some new documents, we now know that until the middle of the eighteenth century the judicial file of Galileo's trial was not kept among the records of the censures of books preserved in the chancellery,[32] and certainly not in the series of *Censurae librorum,* which, as we have seen, did not at that time exist yet in its later form, the one produced by the doctrinal archivist Lugani. Instead, Galileo's judicial file was preserved in volume 1181 of the criminal collection. There are several lines of evidence to support this claim.

The first comes to us from a guide to circulars of the Congregation of the Holy Office, most likely written in 1717.[33] Among the letters mentioned by this guide, there is one of July 2, 1633, that transmits to the nuncios and inquisitors a copy of the sentence and the abjuration of Galileo. A notation in the margin indicates that Galileo's judicial file was, at that time, located in volume 1181 of the collection of criminal records.[34] A second piece of evidence may be found in the documentation concerning the erection of a monument to the memory of Galileo. On June 8, 1734, the inquisitor in Florence wrote to the congregation to determine whether he had to grant permission for a monument to Galileo to be placed in the Church of Santa Croce. On June 16, the cardinal inquisitors decided to give permission to proceed with the construction of the monument. Following this decree, the notary added, "Vol. Proc. 1181."[35] We thus have here two specific indications that, until the middle of the eighteenth century, Galileo's judicial file was located in volume 1181 of the collection of criminal records.

Was this volume, then, included in the sale of this collection, with the four thousand others, in Paris in 1816? It might have seemed so, but some other documents housed in the archive of the Holy Office shed light on a new aspect of the history of Galileo's judicial file that marks it off from the others. A note concerning the reordering of different judicial files indicates that on December 18, 1755, the secretary to the assessor removed the records of Galileo's trial from volume 1181 of the collection of criminal records (Appendix II).[36] What could have been the reason for such a removal, unsuspected until now? We do not have direct evidence for such a reason, but doubtless there is a connection between the removal and the steps taken in 1757 to delete from the *Index* the general proscription of Copernican works.[37] It was probably under orders from Benedict XIV himself, then, that Galileo's judicial file was removed from the archive of the Roman Inquisition, and the file must have been kept, for some time, in the pope's own library. In support of this, the table of contents of a volume that itself no longer exists has been preserved, listing together various files relating to the Holy Office that were placed at the disposition of the Sovereign Pontiff.[38] The table of contents mentions, fourth on the list, the judicial file of the Galileo case.[39]

After the death of Benedict XIV in 1758, this volume in the papal library must have been returned to the Congregation of the Holy Office, for it is at that location that the author of an anonymous note, dating probably after 1781, was able to view the responses of the nuncios and inquisitors to the circular of July 2, 1633 (Appendix III).[40] However, Galileo's judicial file does not appear to have been replaced in volume 1181 with the records of the other trials, since the list drafted by the Holy Office archivists in Rome, indicating which files were to be brought back from Paris, referred to the Galileo file as one of the more sensational trial records among those that were kept separately from the numbered series of criminal records.[41] But the archivists seem not to have been aware that Galileo's judicial file had been taken from the archive of the Holy Office in 1810, to be sent by special courier to Napoleon's Ministry of Cults, with a few other documents considered by the French to be very important.[42] Kept in Paris, apart from the rest of the archive of the congregation, the file was not returned to Rome until 1834, after having passed through Vienna with the personal papers of the exiled Duc de Blacas. On May 8, 1850, Pope Pius IX handed it over to the Vatican archive. After undergoing restoration in 1923, the file was classified under its current heading in 1926: ASV, Misc., Arm. X, 204.[43]

Galileo's Judicial File: Internal Clues

This identification of the file now in the Vatican archive (VF) needs further justification. And this leads us to the second part of our inquiry, namely an investigation of the clues contained in the VF itself. The question facing us is simply this: Can Galileo's judicial file, which until 1755 was included in volume 1181 of the collection of criminal records, be legitimately identified with the VF on Galileo? Let us first point to certain characteristics of the VF that are related to some external clues of Galileo's judicial file that we have reconstructed above. The notation "Vol. 1181," written at the top of both the first and last pages of the VF (fols. 1 and 228 v°), appears to be in the same handwriting as is the 1755 note attesting to the removal of the file from volume 1181 of the criminal records.[44] The notation "Ex archivo S. Officii" does not appear to be in the same handwriting, but it could have been added at around the same time or, if not, at the time when the file was sent to Paris in 1810. Volume 1181, which to all appearances was destroyed in Paris, must also have contained files relating to other trials, as the original pagination of the VF (336–561), according to the archive's system of notation, would indicate. Volumes in the archive of the Holy Office could easily contain pages numbering in the thousands.[45]

In the VF itself, aside from the two notations that appear on the first and last pages, there are only two places where a number indicating a volume in the series of criminal records can be found: "in vol. 1178" (VF, fol. 223v°) and "in vol. 1181" (VF, fol. 222v°). These two notations, which seem indeed to have been written in the same hand, most probably that of the archivist, can be found on the back of two letters received by the Congregation of the Holy Office in 1638. This would lead one to believe that at that time the VF was already kept in the archive of the congregation. This was not yet the case in 1634, as the documents from that time do not bear any indication as to the volume number in the collection of criminal records in which they were to be filed. Volume 1178 might have been where the documents produced in 1615–16 were kept before 1632. In any case, by 1638 the archivist's notation "vol. 1178" proved inexact, for the document in question had been inserted in volume 1181 along with the other documents belonging to the VF. Otherwise, we would not have it today.

To settle definitively the questions surrounding the status of the VF, one must first analyze its formal characteristics in comparison with those of the other judicial files prepared by the officers of the Roman Holy Office at that time and then see whether we can determine the moment at which Galileo's judicial file was presented to the Sovereign Pontiff for him to pronounce his verdict. The analysis of the numbering inscribed on the VF and of its manner of assembly—which I shall here limit to a provision of the conclusions[46]—leads to the conclusion that the VF contains, on folios 7 to 116 in the modern numbering, inserted after the volume's restoration in 1926, a judicial file written between 1615 and May 1633 in the context of a trial instituted against Galileo. It includes the documents commonly found in judicial files: denunciations, witnesses' accounts, censures written by consultors, depositions of the defendant, and writings presented in his defense. The documents are grouped together in two large fascicles (fols. 18–51 and 78–116) that correspond to the two phases of the trial of Galileo, those of 1615–16 and 1632–33. The documents contained in the VF on folios 7 to 116 have been given a working numbering of 1 to 103,[47] a practical pagination that contains no lacunae, utilized in a *summarium,* an outline of the essential elements of the trial (VF, fols. 2–5).

Galileo's judicial file seems, then, to have undergone preparations, following a standard procedure, to ready it for submission to the pope for judgment. Taking into account the common practices of the Roman Tribunal of the Inquisition,[48] if we analyze the provisions of the decree pronounced by Urban VIII 16 June 1633, setting forth the verdict of Galileo's trial,[49] we notice that its elements correspond exactly to the contents of the VF. Analysis of Galileo's depositions (VF, fols. 78–87) shows that his situation in May 1633, after the presentation of his defense, was that of an accused person who had confessed to having written a book defending a doctrine

that had been proscribed by the Holy See in 1616 but who denied having had heretical intentions, persisting in his refusal to admit that he had himself subscribed to
the Copernican doctrine. The reports submitted by the two consultors, Melchior Inchofer and Zacharia Pasqualigo, are both included in the records; their conclusions
are likely to have been read before the tribunal following the presentation of the *summarium.* They agreed in concluding that Galileo was strongly suspect of having assented to the doctrine of Copernicanism. The items contained in the file—including
the censure issued by the consultors to the Holy Office on February 24, 1616, and the
decree of the Index of March 5, 1616—taken together would thus allow the judge to
conclude that Galileo had rendered himself strongly suspect of heresy, which corresponds in fact to the verdict pronounced by the pope on June 16, 1633.[50]

In conclusion, if one considers in their entirety all the elements, internal and external, that have just been presented and takes into consideration the style of the
Roman Holy Office in the first half of the seventeenth century, there can be no doubt
that the VF contains the actual documents that led Urban VIII, on June 16, 1633, to
pronounce the verdict of condemnation on Galileo. In other words, we can identify
the VF with Galileo's judicial file. On June 16, 1633, and then again two weeks later,[51]
the pope ordered that the content of the sentence and of the abjuration of Galileo
be made known to philosophers and mathematicians throughout the Catholic world.
The numerous responses of nuncios and inquisitors to the circular of the congregation of July 2, 1633, which forwarded the copies of the sentence and abjuration, were
placed within the judicial file after the trial records (VF, fols. 120–212).

Between 1634 and 1638, the VF was stored in the Holy Office archive, in volume
1181 of the criminal records. Documents were added to the file in 1638 and again in
1734. It should be noted in this regard that the VF does not at all have the appearance
of one of the numerous new files assembled by the doctrinal archivist Lugani in the
second half of the eighteenth century. Rather, it is a complete judicial file, as is clear
from the numbering at the bottoms of its pages. This is further confirmed by the fact
that in December 1755, and therefore before the reorganization of the archive, the VF
was removed from volume 1181 of the collection of criminal records and from that
point forward went its own way as it traveled from the library of Benedict XIV back
to the palace of the Holy Office, then to Paris and to Vienna, ending up in the Vatican archive under the identification "ASV, Misc., Arm. X, 204."

The VF, containing Galileo's judicial file, represents, therefore, the greater part
of the documents of the trial, especially those that served as the basis for the condemnation of the philosopher and his subsequent abjuration of heliocentrism, decreed by Pope Urban VIII on June 16, 1633. There is no reason to suspect the existence
of other so far undiscovered collections of documents relating to the trial. Imagin-
ing that the documentation of the trial has been falsified, as Mereu and Redondi have
in order to justify their own interpretations of the famous case, would imply that Ga-

lileo's depositions and the papal decrees alike were counterfeits, as well as implying the same of numerous other documents in the file presented in authentic form by the Holy Office notaries. Falsification on such a grand scale is quite simply unimaginable to any historian possessing even minimal knowledge of the functioning of the Roman Holy Office during the period in question. On the other hand, falsification cannot be excluded a priori in the case of single documents, especially the record of the injunction said to have been delivered to Galileo on February 26, 1616, a much-debated issue.[52] Also, the manner in which Commissary Maculano later directed the course of Galileo's trial, placing all responsibility upon Galileo in the affair of the imprimatur granted the *Dialogo*, raises important procedural issues but implies no falsification of the judicial records.[53]

Older and Newer Documents Concerning the Trial

To have at one's disposal the entire corpus of the legal documentation of Galileo's trial, one must add to those contained in the VF several other documents, some of which have been published for the first time only in recent years. First of these are the decrees of the tribunal—including the one of June 16, 1633, mentioned above—recorded by notaries in the annual volumes of the *Decreta*. The greater part of these were published by Favaro and reedited in the Vatican edition.[54] It should be noted, however, that the new documents published along with the decrees relating to the trial are not themselves originals but rather copies of these same minutes dating from the eighteenth century (Appendix III).[55] In the context of a project under the direction of Ugo Baldini, the goal of which is an edition of all the documents preserved in the ACDF that concern "the encounters between the Church and science,"[56] the entirety of the surviving collections has been analyzed. This has led to the recovery of certain new documents, two previously unknown decrees from 1634 and 1636, as well as the files of the Holy Office dealing with Antonio Favaro's consultation of the archives early in the twentieth century.[57]

The next items are the records of the sentence of condemnation and of Galileo's abjuration, compiled in Italian by the commissary and the notary of the Holy Office on the basis of the papal verdict of June 16, 1633. The originals of these documents, dated June 22, 1633, and bearing the autograph signatures of the cardinal inquisitors, for the first, and of Galileo, for the second, must be regarded as lost. They must have been kept in the volume belonging to the series *Sententiae urbis* containing the sentences and abjurations for the year 1633, which was most likely destroyed in Paris along with the other volumes of the collection of criminal records.[58] Favaro published in volume 19 of the *Opere* the copies of these documents housed in the archive of the Inquisition in Modena.[59] But, from the legal perspective, the most important among all the extant copies is the one found among the trial documents contained in the records of the Florence Inquisition, which are preserved in the diocesan archives of that city and were published by Canon Michele Cioni in 1908.[60] These documents are indispensable for the completion of the corpus of the legal records of Galileo's trial.[61]

If a sentence was pronounced in Rome, the Congregation of the Holy Office usually sent a copy of it to the inquisitorial tribunal in the place of residence of the condemned so that it could be published there as well if necessary. In Galileo's case, the inquisitor in Florence moved quickly to publish the sentence and Galileo's abjuration on July 12, 1633, in the presence of consultors of the Florentine Holy Office and of mathematics professors from that region.[62] But, as we have seen, by Urban VIII's order the copies of Galileo's sentence and abjuration were spread all over Europe, having been sent to all nuncios and inquisitors. Many of these copies have been preserved, and most often they are accompanied by a copy of the circular letter dated July 2, 1633.[63] As Michel-Pierre Lerner has pointed out, their diffusion throughout Italy and across Europe is eminently worthy of further study.[64]

Among the documents recently discovered in the archive of the Roman Holy Office, one particularly worthy of mention is the April 22, 1633, letter from Commissary Vincenzo Maculano to Cardinal Francesco Barberini.[65] This important document bears witness to the decisive role played by Maculano in Galileo's trial and, in particular, in taking it in the direction in which he did. In effect, it appears from this letter, as well as from the formulation of the sentence against Galileo—the doctrinal section of which was most probably written by Maculano himself—that the commissary considered heliocentrism to have already been outlawed in 1616 as contrary to Holy Scripture, which in itself could have justified a verdict demanding abjuration on the suspicion of heresy, avoiding a discussion in 1633 concerning the theological status of Copernicanism.[66]

Other documents, including reading permits requested for the *Dialogo*, excerpts from internal registers, archival notes, and so forth were also discovered and published.[67] To these records belonging to the Congregation of the Holy Office must be added some other documents kept in the archive of the Congregation of the Index. First in importance are those concerning the preparation and application of the Index decree of March 5, 1616. These comprise the minutes of the meeting of the congregation on March 1, 1616, the text of the circulars sent to all the nuncios and inquisitors accompanying the printed decree,[68] the documents relating to the placing of Kepler's *Epitome* on the *Index,* in 1619, and the details of the preparation of the instruction correcting the *De revolutionibus* of Copernicus, published in 1620.[69]

In the archive of the Congregation of the Index a new document was also found immediately preceding in the same volume the famous document "G3" published by Redondi. It consists of a report that has been attributed to Melchior Inchofer criticizing on theological grounds the implications of Galileo's atomist philosophy. It goes on to recommend that the matter be referred to the Congregation of the Holy Office.[70] Can one establish a tie between these two documents—the "G3" and the recently discovered one—warning of the challenge to eucharistic doctrine posed by the atomist philosophy of Galileo and his trial in 1632–33? In spite of the undeniable interest they could have for reconstructing the intellectual environment of the reception of Galileo's thought in Rome, the answer can only be in the negative, at this stage in our knowledge at least. These documents belong to the archive of the Congregation of the Index (not to that of the Holy Office, as Redondi supposes),[71] and they are not even included in the table of contents of the volume in which they are located.[72] With no indication of either author or date, they would be useless in the context of an Inquisition trial. In addition, their actual dating is conjectural and uncertain. Above all, no trace has been found of any actions taken by the Congregation of the Holy Office then or later with regard to the atomist doctrine of Galileo.

But one could suggest that this fact might constitute in itself an indication that in 1632–33 an attempt was made to erase all traces of Galileo's "eucharistic heresy" in order to save him from the stake. It seems to me, however, that the perception of atomism as doctrinally pernicious has been greatly exaggerated.[73] This results from an incomplete understanding of the theological criteria employed by the Tribunal of the Inquisition in the seventeenth century, according to which a proposition is not to be considered as heretical unless it is manifestly and univocally shown to be opposed to the faith or unless it is defined as such by the Church Councils or by the Holy See.[74] The opposition between heliocentrism and Christian faith was much easier to prove by way of a literal reading of the Bible—the absolute truthfulness of Holy Writ being considered at that time an article of faith[75]—than the opposition between the atomist theory and the eucharistic dogma, which called for a considerably greater level of conceptual mediation. This would explain why, in spite of different measures taken by the Roman Holy Office in the second half of the seventeenth century against the spread of atomism, we know of no *abjuration* for "eucharistic heresy." Further, even if the accusation of "eucharistic heresy" were to have been sustained against Galileo (which has not yet been established), he could quite simply and in good faith have abjured, as he did with heliocentrism.

If, hypothetically, he had been tried for defending "atomism," Galileo could have quite easily have extricated himself from the affair on the level of doctrine, incurring consequences less weighty than those he met with in 1633. In fact, he could very well have been pardoned, as a layperson, for not having mastered the criteria that led theologians to perceive an opposition between atomist philosophy and the doctrine of the Eucharist. That alone, given the normal mode of proceeding of the Roman Holy Office, would probably have saved Galileo from even having to abjure.[76] On the other hand, the Holy See, through the Index decree of March 5, 1616, had publicly declared that the Copernican doctrine was "altogether contrary to the

Holy Scripture,"[77] something that had never happened in the case of atomism. By publishing the *Dialogo,* Galileo thus became guilty of having upheld "as probable an opinion after it has been declared and defined contrary to Holy Scripture,"[78] according to the trial sentence, and consequently was made to abjure.[79]

In addition to the documents mentioned thus far, the ACDF possesses files relating to the challenge faced by the Holy See due to the progressive confirmation of heliocentrism as time went on and the gradual softening of its condemnation until the works of Galileo and Copernicus were finally dropped from the Index in 1835.[80] These files consist of documents dealing with the denunciations of books and individuals maintaining the truth of the new world-system in the second half of the seventeenth and first half of the eighteenth centuries.[81] Next comes the abortive attempt to revise the condemnation of Copernican works during the general revision of the *Index* in 1757.[82] Then there are records of the internal discussions in the Holy Office during the controversy surrounding the publication of the treatise on optics and astronomy of Canon Settele in 1820 – 22.[83] Finally, one can trace the vicissitudes of Paschini's biography of Galileo, as well as the abortive attempts to reopen Galileo's trial that were opposed by the Holy Office.[84] These different files would be indispensable for anyone who would undertake to reconstruct the complex history of the reception of the condemnation of heliocentrism and its revocation.

Conclusion

This brief (though, I hope, inclusive) review of the documentation relating to Galileo's trial allows us to make two points in conclusion. First, the results of the research conducted during the past few years in the ACDF, particularly the systematic review of the records conducted by the team led by Ugo Baldini, do not suggest that any revolutionary new discoveries will be forthcoming.[85] This conclusion becomes all the more persuasive when the improved understanding of the functioning of the Roman Holy Office and of the style in which it conducted its trials is taken into account, enabled by the opening of the ACDF. This permits an entirely rethought interpretation of long-familiar judicial documents, one that is better supported in historical terms.

Second, our review makes it abundantly clear that the documents relating to Galileo's trial are dispersed throughout many different collections and have been published in editions of widely varying quality: the VF, the *Decreta,* the documents of the Florence Inquisition, the copies of the sentence and of the abjuration, the documents of the Congregation of the Index, and so on. It seemed opportune, therefore, to envision an edition that would draw together all of these disparate sources. This project is now underway under the direction of Michel Lerner and myself. Our goal is a single volume, accompanied by critical apparatus and commentary, that will contain the entirety of the corpus of the judicial documents bearing on the trial of Galileo.

Appendix I. Summary Totals of the Documents of the Holy Office and of the Index Transported to Paris, as of January 1, 1813 (Total Numbers of Volumes in Square Brackets)

L. Congregation of the Holy Office

1. Trials between 1540 and 1771 (L 1–4158) [4,158]
2. Sentences, *intra* and *extra urbem*, 1497–1771 (L 4159–4630) [472]
3. Petitions and indulgences, 1600–1804 (L 4631–4944) [314]
4. Dispensations and faculties (L 4945–5075) [131]
5. Decrees or general decisions concerning dogma and discipline, 1548–1771 (L 5076–5280) [205]
6. *Diversorum dubia diversa:* consultations and opinions on dogmatic and canonical questions, 1590–1793 (L 5281–5411) [131]
7. Jansenism, Bull *Unigenitus,* Immaculate Conception, Chinese liturgy, et cetera; theological controversies (L 5412–5542) [131]
8. Minutes of letters; outgoing and incoming correspondence of the Holy Office from 1554 to 1804 (L 5543–5900) [358]
9. Collections of acts and documents of the Holy Office in alphabetical order by the names of cities, provinces, and kingdoms (L 5901–6324) [424]
10. Collection of acts and documents of the Holy Office in alphabetical order by subject: baptism, Eucharist, Judaism, quietism (L 6325–6683) [359]
11. Jurisprudence, procedures, officers, and internal administration of the Holy Office (L 6684–7093) [410]
12. Censure of books by the Holy Office (L 7094–7215) [122]
13. Congregation of the Index: catalogues of permitted and forbidden books; registers of the Congregation of the Index; its letters; permissions granted for the reading of condemned books (L 7216–7499) [284]

Source: Transcribed by Henry Bordier, *Les archives de la France* (Paris: Dumoulin, 1855), 400.

Note: After these 7,499 items were numbered, some 400 additional files and registers were found in various other locations in the Vatican archive. These documents are to be included in the preceding series and will bring the number of items it contains to roughly 7,900.

Appendix II. Note in Archive of the Holy Office on Removal of Records of Galileo's Trial from Volume 1181 (December 18, 1755)

Source: ACDF, SO, *Extravagantia,* V, 2 (detail). Unidentified author (see n. 36).

Appendix III. Eighteenth-Century Copy of the June 16, 1633 Decree (Extract)

Source: ACDF, SO, *Extravagantia,* V, 1, n. 2 (detail). Upper handwriting: Domenico Cavazzi, after 1766. Rider: unidentified author (see n. 40).

Notes

Text translated by Rayanne K. Truesdell and Ernan McMullin. This study was completed under the auspices of a research project concerning the documents of Galileo's trial, financed by the Swiss National Science Foundation and undertaken in collaboration with Michel-Pierre Lerner, director of research at the Centre nationale de la recherche scientifique.

1. ASV, Misc., Arm. X, 204.

2. Sergio M. Pagano and Antonio G. Luciani, eds., *I documenti del processo di Galileo Galilei* (Vatican City: Pontifical Academy of Sciences, 1984), 26–35. See also Maurice A. Finocchiaro, *The Galileo Affair: A Documentary History* (hereafter *GA*) (Berkeley: University of California Press, 1989), 40–41.

3. Galileo Galilei, *Opere di Galileo Galilei* (hereafter *OGG*), ed. Antonio Favaro (1890–1909; reprint, Florence: Giunti Barbèra, 1968), 19:272–421; separately published as Antonio Favaro, *Galileo e l'Inquisizione: Documenti del processo galileiano esistenti nell'Archivio del S. Uffizio e nell'Archivio segreto vaticano* (Florence: Giunti Barbèra, 1907; reprint, with foreword by Luigi Firpo, Florence: Giunti Barbèra, 1983).

4. Pagano and Luciani, *I documenti,* 32–43; Ugo Baldini and Lean Spruitt, "Nuovi documenti galileiani degli archivi del Sant'Ufficio e dell'Indice, " *Rivista di Storia della Filosofia* 56 (2001): 662–72.

5. Pagano and Luciani, *I documenti.*

6. Favaro, *Galileo e l'Inquisizione,* 8–9; *OGG,* 19:274.

7. Pagano and Luciani, *I documenti,* 7–9.

8. Vincenzo Ferrone and Massimo Firpo, "Galileo tra inquisitori e microstorici," *Rivista Storica Italiana* 97 (1985): 185; and, more recently, Giovanni Romeo, *L'Inquisizione nell'Italia moderna* (Rome: Laterza, 2002), 88.

9. Pietro Redondi, *Galileo eretico* (Turin: Einaudi, 1983), translated by Raymond Rosenthal as *Galileo Heretic* (Princeton: Princeton University Press, 1987), esp. chap. 8, "Theater of Shadows."

10. Pagano and Luciani, *I documenti,* 43–48.

11. Pietro Redondi, *Galilée hérétique* (Paris: Gallimard, 1985), 426–27.

12. Italo Mereu, *Storia dell'intolleranza in Europa. Sospettare e punire: Il sospetto e l'Inquisizione romana nell'epoca di Galilei* (Milan: Mondadori, 1979), 375, 413.

13. Pagano and Luciani, *I documenti,* 154–55; *GA,* 286–87.

14. Gino Ditadi, ed., *Tommaso Campanella, Apologia di Galileo: Tutte le lettere a Galileo Galilei e altri documenti* (Este: Isonomia, 1992), 266.

15. *L'apertura degli archivi del Sant'Uffizio romano* (Rome: Accademia nazionale dei Lincei, 1998); Olivier Poncet, "L'ouverture des archives du Saint-Office et de l'Index: Échos d'une journée de présentation," *Revue d'Histoire de l'Eglise de France* 84 (1998): 97–103; Herman H. Schwedt, "Das Archiv der römischen Inquisition und des Index," *Römische Quartalschrift* 93 (1998): 267–80.

16. For the following, see Francesco Beretta, "L'archivio della Congregazione del Sant'Ufficio: Bilancio provvisorio della storia e natura dei fondi d'antico regime," in *L'Inquisizione romana: Metodologia delle fonti e storia istituzionale,* ed. Andrea Del Col and Giovanna Paolin (Trieste: Edizioni Università di Trieste, 2000), 119–44; Alejandro Cifres, "Das Archiv des Sanctum Officium: alte und neue Ordnungsformen," in *Inquisition, Index, Zensur: Wissenskulturen der Neuzeit im Widerstreit,* ed. Hubert Wolf (Paderborn: Ferdinand Schöningh, 2001), 45–69.

17. In the index of the volume ACDF, SO, St. st. M 5 m, documentation can be found that relates to a case from Bologna, 1783, that was taken from a volume of the criminal records, numbered 4419.

18. The chancellery files, collected in numbered volumes, dealt with different questions of doctrine or of jurisdiction: "materiae doctrinales et jurisdictionales," ACDF, SO, St. st. LL 5 a, visitation 1735, original, fol. 17. At the end of the seventeenth century, just over two hundred such volumes existed, treating questions ranging from the censure of books, to theological controversies, to conflicts of jurisdiction among different seats of the Inquisition. The contents of these volumes can be reconstructed using the collection of indexes gathered in the volume ACDF, SO, St. st. P 1 a, fols. 1 ff./22 ff./138 ff./168 ff.

19. ACDF, SO, St. st. LL 5 c, page inserted after a letter dated Sept. 6, 1635. See also ACDF, SO, St. st. LL 5 a, the original account of the 1735 visit, fols. 16–19.

20. ACDF, SO, *Privilegia,* 1760–64, fol. 453v. For the identification of Lugani's handwriting, see Beretta, "L'archivio," 56–57.

21. "Le prime due classi [materie dottrinali e giurisdizionali] erano tutte raccolte in volumi legati in carta pecora bianca, co' loro rispettivi titoli nell'esterno di ogni volume." Pagano and Luciani, *I documenti,* 13.

22. By way of example, one may review the complete and indexed series of censures of propositions found in ACDF, SO, St. st. O 1 b to O 1 o.

23. Materials concerning the first half of the seventeenth century were to be found in volumes 53 and 54 of the chancellery files, ACDF, SO, St. st. P 1 a, fol. 179r°v°. For example, let us take the case of the file containing the documents relating to the Holy Office's decree of Jan. 24, 1647, in which Innocent X condemns the claim of equality between the apostles Peter and Paul. In an index of the chancellery volumes, this file is mentioned to be among those contained in vol. 53: "Liber de Primatu S. Pauli et eius Censura. Vol. 53," ibid., fol. 179. Currently, the file can be found in the volume of the ACDF, SO, *Censurae librorum* 1641–48, fasc. 14, and the documents it contains have been published by Adriano Garuti, *S. Pietro unico titolare del primato: A proposito del decreto del S. Uffizio del 24 gennaio 1647* (Bologna: Edizioni francescane, 1993), 191–301.

24. "La serie *Censurae librorum* dell'Indice," Pagano and Luciani, *I documenti,* 7. See also n. 25, below.

25. Henri Bordier, *Les archives de la France* (Paris: Dumoulin, 1855), 400. The labels that can still be seen today, attached to the spines of the volumes of the *Censurae librorum* series, indicate that these were transported to Paris and that they were organized into a series that Napoleon's archivists called "Censures de livres par le Saint Office" and assigned the numbers L 7094 through 7215. For example, the first volume (ACDF, SO, *Censurae librorum,* 1570–1606) is labeled L 7095. The listing drafted by the Holy Office archivists in Rome and sent to Paris in 1815 mentions the *Censurae librorum* as among the volumes of doctrinal and jurisdictional materials. Pagano and Luciani, *I documenti,* 13.

26. Remigius Ritzler, "Die Verschleppung der päpstlichen Archive nach Paris unter Napoleon I. und deren Rückführung nach Rom in den Jahren 1815 bis 1817," *Römische historische Mitteilungen* 6/7 (1962–63/1963–64): 144–90; John Tedeschi, *The Prosecution of Heresy: Collected Studies on the Inquisition in Early Modern Italy* (Binghamton, N.Y.: Medieval and Renaissance Texts and Studies, 1991), 23–25; Pagano and Luciani, *I documenti,* 10–22.

27. Pagano and Luciani, *I documenti,* 14. See also Ritzler, "Die Verschleppung," 166.

28. Thirty-six volumes of judicial files and eighteen volumes of sentences, most likely a portion of those sold by Ginnasi, by 1854 had found their way, after having passed through dif-

ferent hands, to the Library of Trinity College in Dublin, where they are currently housed ; see John Tedeschi, "Die Inquisitionsakten im Trinity-College, Dublin," in Wolf, *Inquisition*, 71–87.

29. Francesco Beretta, *Galilée devant le Tribunal de l'Inquisition* (Fribourg: Université de Fribourg, 1998), 74–75.

30. See Appendix I, n. 13.

31. Alejandro Cifres, "L'archivio storico della Congregazione per la Dottrina della Fede," in *L'apertura degli archivi del Sant'Uffizio romano* (Rome: Accademia Nazionale dei Lincei, 1998), 82.

32. No mention is made of Galileo or of his book in the index of items preserved in the chancellery, ACDF, SO, St. st. P 1 a, fols. 168r–189.

33. ACDF, SO, St. st. N 4 b. The guide includes summaries of the contents of circular letters of the congregation from 1578 until 1761, but the handwriting changes in 1717, which leads one to believe that the first draft dates from that year and that the later parts were added afterwards.

34. Here is a transcription of the entire text relating to Galileo:

"1633—2 luglio [at left, below the date:] Galileo Galilei per aver composto un libro, trattando sopra la materia del libro di Niccolò Copernico intitolato De Revolutionibus orbium coelestium. Processus volumen 1181 [at right, the body of the text:] Alli Nunzij, et Inquisitori <Probitione> Sopra la sospensione del trattato di Niccolò Copernico de Revolutionibus orbium coelestium, e sopra la proibizione del libro di Galileo Galilei da Fiorenza, trattando sopra la stessa materia, perloche il detto Galileo si è reso vehememente sospetto d'eresia, e condannato in carcere." ACDF, SO, St. st. N 4 b, pages not numbered.

35. ACDF, SO, *Decreta,* 1734, fol. 164. See also Pagano and Luciani, *I documenti,* 241. For more on the erection of the monument to Galileo, see Francesco Beretta, "Le siège apostolique et l'affaire Galilée: Relectures romaines d'une condamnation célèbre," *Roma Moderna e Contemporanea* 7 (1990): 435, and Paolo Galluzzi, "The Sepulchers of Galileo: The 'Living' Remains of a Hero of Science," in *The Cambridge Companion to Galileo,* ed. Peter Machamer (Cambridge: Cambridge University Press, 1998), 417–47.

36. "A di 18. Dicembre 1755. il Signor Zanabetti Segretario di Monsignor Illustrissimo Assessore levò dal Vol. 1181 = il Processo contro Galileo Galilei," ACDF, SO, *Extravagantia,* V, 2 (formerly a loose page in ACDF, St. st. E 5 l). This note makes reference to Giuseppe Maria Lugani as the assistant commissary and must therefore date from before December 1762, the date of Lugani's nomination as doctrinal archivist of the congregation. See n. 20, above.

37. See Beretta, "Le siège apostolique," 439–42.

38. "S. O. Scripta et Monumenta Varia. Sacrae Inquisitionis Tribunal eiusque Praxim, Causas, et Resolutiones spectantia prout versa pagina Index exhibit," ADCF, SO, St. st. P 1 a, fol. 190.

39. "Galileo Galilei. Processo contro il medesimo. S. O. n° 4°," ibid, fol. 191.

40. Pagano and Luciani, *I documenti,* 230 (doc. 17). This text—just like the two others belonging to the same series (see below, n. 55)—consists of a copy of the decree of June 16, 1633, prepared by Domenico Cavazzi, with addenda and commentary in different handwriting. Cavazzi was named as substitute notary of the Holy Office in 1766 and as its archivist in 1781, ACDF, SO, *Privilegia,* 1781–83, fols. 133/151v°. For an example of Cavazzi's signature, see ACDF, SO, *De sacramento poenitentiae dubia,* 1625–1770, fol. 437v°.

41. See the documents published in Pagano and Luciani, *I documenti,* 14, and Ritzler, "Die Verschleppung," 166. See also n. 25, above.

42. Marino Marini, "Memorie storiche," in *Regestum Clementis Papae V,* ed. Cura et Studio Monachorum Ordinis S. Benedicti (Rome, 1885), ccxxix. It is perhaps at this point that someone wrote on the folder containing the VF (fol. 1), "Ex archivo S. Officij."

43. Pagano and Luciani, *I documenti,* 24–26.

44. See Appendix II (see n. 36, above) and the first photograph in Pagano and Luciani, *I documenti,* following 256.

45. See Beretta, "L'archivio," 38.

46. For a more detailed analysis, see Francesco Beretta, "Le procès de Galilée et les archives du Saint-Office: Aspects judiciaires et théologiques d'une condamnation célèbre," *Revue des Sciences Philosophiques et Théologiques* 83 (1999): 455–57.

47. For an explanation of the distinction between the working numbering and the archival numbering, see Beretta, "L'archivio," 36, 38. For a chronological table of the pagination of the VF, see Beretta, "Le procès de Galilée," 487–89.

48. For more on the "style" of the Roman Holy Office, see Beretta, *Galilée devant le Tribunal,* 30–49, and "Giordano Bruno e l'Inquistione romana: Considerazioni sul processo," *Bruniana e Campanelliana* 7 (2001): 20–23.

49. Pagano and Luciani, *I documenti,* 229. Unfortunately, this very important document was not translated by Finocchiaro in *GA,* although it is implicitly mentioned on 38.

50. For a more detailed analysis, see Beretta, "Le procès de Galilée," 458–59, as well as chap. 9 of this book for the doctrinal issues involved.

51. Decree of June 30, 1633, Pagano and Luciani, *I documenti,* 231.

52. For a synthesis of this debate, see Antonio Beltrán Marí, *Galileo, ciencia y religión* (Barcelona: Paidós, 2001), 129–70. See also chap. 5 of this book.

53. For some perspectives on the subject, see Francesco Beretta, "Urbain VIII Barberini protagoniste de la condamnation de Galilée," in *Largo campo di filosofare: Eurosymposium Galileo 2001,* ed. José Montesinos and Carlos Solís (La Orotava: Fundacion Canaria Orotava de Historia de la Ciencia, 2001), 549–73, and "Un nuovo documento sul processo di Galileo Galilei: La lettera di Vincenzo Maculano del 22 aprile 1633 al cardinale Francesco Barberini," *Nuncius* 16 (2001): 629–41.

54. Pagano and Luciani, *I documenti,* 219–42.

55. These three documents are currently preserved in the ACDF, SO, *Extravagantia,* V, 1, nn. 1–3, and have been published in Pagano and Luciani, *I documenti,* 222–23 (doc. 6), 230 (doc. 17), and 242–43 (doc. 38), respectively. See also ibid., 42; *GA,* 344 n. 38; Annibale Fantoli,*Galileo: For Copernicanism and for the Church,* 2d ed., ed. and trans. George V. Coyne (Vatican City: Vatican Observatory Publications, 1996), 221; Baldini and Spruit, "Nuovi documenti," 684–86. They are copies produced by Domenico Cavazzi, with additions in another's handwriting; see above, n. 40.

56. Ugo Baldini, "Intervento," in *L'apertura,* 141–53. See also Ugo Baldini, "Le Congregazioni romane dell'Inquisizione e dell'Indice e le scienze dal 1542 al 1615," in *L'Inquisizione e gli storici: Un cantiere aperto* (Rome: Accademia Nazionale dei Lincei, 2000), 329–64, and "Die römischen Kongregationen der Inquisition und des Index und der naturwissenschaftliche Fortschritt im 16. bis 18. Jahrhundert: Anmerkungen zur Chronologie und zur Logik ihres Verhältnisses," in Wolf, *Inquisition,* 229–78.

57. Baldini and Spruit, "Nuovi documenti," 662–72, 689–91.

58. The sentences pronounced by the Roman Tribunal were collected into annual volumes, entitled "Liber sententiarum et abiurationum." See Trinity College Dublin (TCD) 1238, TCD 1239, etc. In 1745, 163 volumes of sentences pronounced in Rome, spanning the period between 1546 and 1739, were located in the archives of the Holy Office, ACDF, SO, St. st. P 1 a, fol. 119. Only two volumes of these appear to remain in ACDF keeping, those of the years 1682 and 1686, SO, St. st. M 6 g/h.

59. *OGG,* 19:402–7.

60. Florence, Archivio Arcivescovile, Miscellanea S. Uffizio, Busta 1. Michele Cioni, *I documenti galileiani del S. Uffizio di Firenze* (1908; reprint, Florence Pagnini, 1966), 30–38. For a new edition of these texts, see Francesco Beretta, "Rilettura di un documento celebre: redazione e diffusione della sentenza e abiura di Galileo," *Galilaeana* 1 (2004).

61. These documents have been reproduced by Favaro in *OGG,* 20:568–86.

62. Cioni, *I documenti,* 38. See also the letter from Mario Guiducci to Galileo of Aug. 27, 1633, *OGG,* 15:241.

63. Pagano and Luciani, *I documenti,* 244. The ACDF has had access to the archives of the Inquisition at Siena (Cifres, "L'archivio"), but the editors of the Vatican edition have unfortunately declined to publish the copy of Galileo's sentence and abjuration conserved there.

64. Michel-Pierre Lerner, "Pour une édition critique de la sentence et de l'abjuration de Galilée," *Revue des Sciences Philosophiques et Théologiques* 82 (1998): 607–29. See also Lerner, "La réception de la condamnation de Galilée en France au xviie siècle," in Montesinos and Solís, *Largo campo di filosofare,* 513–47.

65. Published in Beretta, "Urbain VIII Barberini," 571, and in Baldini and Spruit, "Nuovi documenti," 682–84.

66. See Beretta, "Un nuovo documento," 637–38. Regarding the doctrinal issues raised by the abjuration of heliocentrism imposed on Galileo, see chap. 9 of this book.

67. Baldini and Spruit, "Nuovi documenti," 684–89, 691–99.

68. Ibid., 674–77.

69. Pierre-Noël Mayaud, *La condamnation des livres coperniciens et sa révocation à la lumière de documents inédits des Congrégations de l'Index et de l'Inquisition,* Miscellanea Historicae Pontificiae 64 (Rome: Gregorian University, 1997). A copy of these documents made in the early nineteenth century had already been published in Walter Brandmüller and Egon Johannes Greipl, eds., *Copernico, Galileo, e la chiesa: Fine della controversia (1820),* Gli Atti del Sant'Ufficio (Florence: Leo S. Olschki, 1992).

70. The text and a translation of this report will be found in an appendix to chap. 8 of this book. See also Baldini and Spruit, "Nuovi documenti," 677–82; Thomas Cerbu, "Melchior Inchofer, 'un homme fin & rusé,'" in Montesinos and Solís, *Largo campo di filosofare,* 608–9; Rafael Martinez, "Il manoscritto ACDF, Index, Protocolli, vol. EE, fol. 291rv," *Acta Philosophica* 10 (2001): 234–35. For more on the attribution of the text to Inchofer, see Cerbu, "Melchior Inchofer," 594, and Martinez, "Il manoscritto," 227.

71. Redondi, *Galileo Heretic,* in particular chap. 5, "The Holy Office's Secrecy."

72. On this subject, see the treatment of Baldini and Spruit, "Nuovi documenti," 682.

73. For a critical discussion of Redondi's argument, see Ferrone and Firpo, "Galileo tra inquisitori"; for a discussion of the doctrinal issues, see Lucas F. Mateo-Seco, "Galileo e l'Eucaristia: La questione teologica dell'ACDF *Index, Protocolli,* EE, fol. 291 r-v," *Acta Philosophica* 10 (2001): 243–56, esp. 254–55.

74. See Beretta, *Galilée devant le Tribunal,* 94–108.

75. See chap. 9 of this book.

76. Beretta, *Galilée devant le Tribunal,* 155–56, 239–40.

77. *GA,* 149.

78. *GA,* 291.

79. Regarding the doctrinal issues raised by the abjuration of heliocentrism imposed on Galileo, see chap. 9 of this book.

80. Mayaud, *La condamnation,* 271–74.

81. See Beretta, "Le siège apostolique," 432 ff.

82. Mayaud, *La condamnation,* 189–212, and Ugo Baldini, *Saggi sulla cultura della Compagnia di Gesù (secoli XVI-XVIII)* (Padua: CLEUP, 2000), 281–347.

83. Brandmüller and Greipl, *Copernico, Galilei.* See Beretta, "Le siège apostolique," 443 ff.

84. Fantoli, *Galileo,* 503–6, and the related notes, 523–31.

85. See Baldini and Spruit, *Nuove documenti,* 661–62.

—————

EIGHT

NEW LIGHT ON
THE GALILEO AFFAIR?

Mariano Artigas, Rafael Martínez, and William R. Shea

A new document that may bear on Galileo's trial was discovered by Mariano Arti-gas in December 1999 in the archives of the Holy Office, which are housed in the palace of the Holy Office next to Saint Peter's Square in Rome. Rafael Martínez tran-scribed the document and carried out the extensive research in Italian archives that led to the identification of the author. This, in its turn, suggested a relationship be-tween the document and the work of the Special Commission appointed by Pope Urban VIII in August 1632 to help him decide whether Galileo should be summoned before the Holy Office in Rome.

The Congregation of the Roman Inquisition, generally known as the Congre-gation of the Holy Office, was instituted by Pope Paul III in 1542 to defend the Roman Catholic Church from heresy, which at the time meant the Protestant Reformation. When the congregation was transformed by Pope Paul VI in 1965, it was renamed the Congregation for the Doctrine of the Faith. The Holy Office worked closely with the Congregation of the Index of Forbidden Books that was created in 1571, and it published an *Index* (or list of forbidden books) covering the period from 1559 until 1917, when the congregation was merged with the Holy Office. Both congregations played a central role in the Galileo affair. Our story deals with years 1610–33, at a time when Rome was engaged in the so-called Counter-Reformation and stressed aspects of the Catholic doctrine that helped to counteract the effects of Protestantism. Two are particularly relevant to the Galileo affair. The first is an emphasis on reading the Scriptures in accordance with tradition, as represented mainly by the holy fathers and the doctors of the Church. The second is the affirmation of the real presence of Jesus Christ in the Eucharist, which was explained by the concept of transubstantiation. The second aspect has a direct bearing on the new document.

In this chapter we describe the new document (named by Artigas "EE 291" for reasons given below), discuss its authorship, and draw some consequences for our knowledge of the Galileo affair.[1] The Latin original and an English translation of the document are given in Appendices I and II. We shall begin by examining G3, another document discovered in 1982, because the new document is a direct sequel to G3.

Redondi's Reinterpretation of the Trial of Galileo

The volumes that contain the records (*Protocolli*) of the Congregation of the Index are numbered with capital letters A, B, C . . . AA (or A²), BB (or B²), and so on. The new document discovered by Artigas was bound in volume EE (or E²), the same one in which Pietro Redondi in 1982 found another, until then unknown, three-page document, which is usually identified by the code "G3" that appears at the top of the first page (nobody knows what "G3" stands for).

G3 is a denunciation of the atomism that Galileo defended in his book *Il saggiatore* (The assayer) of 1623,[2] a work in which he argues that sensible qualities do not have an objective status but merely result from the way atoms impinge on our sense organs. Colors, tastes, smells, or tactile properties exist, as such, in the persons who experience them, not in the objects themselves. The anonymous author of G3 believed that this interpretation of sensible properties was at variance with the doctrine of the Eucharist called transubstantiation, the word used to indicate that after the consecration at the Mass there was no longer the substance of bread and wine but the body and blood of Jesus Christ. According to this doctrine, what remained of the bread and wine were only the so-called *accidental* properties (color, odor, general appearance), which were miraculously sustained by divine power. No miracle would be needed if those properties were pure names.

On the basis of G3, Redondi proposed a reinterpretation of the Galileo affair in which Pope Urban VIII, a former friend and admirer of Galileo, manipulated the proceedings in such a way that Galileo had to face "only" the accusation of Copernicanism and not the more serious accusation contained in G3.[3] Few people followed this interpretation, but the new document calls for a reexamination of G3.

Galileo's Copernican Campaign

Galileo created a sensation when he used the newly invented telescope to look at the heavens in the autumn of 1609. He published his spectacular observations in 1610, and in 1611 he went to Rome, where he was given a hero's welcome by the Jesuits of the Roman College. The discoveries for which he was hailed include the rocky surface of the Moon, the existence of new stars, the nature of the Milky Way, the satellites of Jupiter, and the phases of Venus.

Galileo was a Copernican by that time, but he presented his views in a cautious and courteous way. His discoveries threatened the traditional view that the earth was at rest at the center of the universe, but they did not constitute a definitive proof of the Copernican system. Some Aristotelian professors first, and afterwards a couple of friars, felt that Galileo's heliocentrism was at variance with a literal reading of the Scriptures, and they denounced him to the Holy Office in Rome. In 1615 Galileo decided to take a stronger stand and went to Rome to argue the case for the motion of the earth. The outcome was not a happy one. Copernicus's *De revolutionibus* was banned by the Congregation of the Index on March 5, 1616, and Galileo was told in private, but nonetheless officially, that he was not to teach Copernicanism in any way. He complied, albeit reluctantly.

In 1623 Cardinal Maffeo Barberini, a Florentine who had praised Galileo's achievements, was elected pope under the name of Urban VIII. Galileo had recently helped his nephew, Francesco Barberini, obtain his doctorate at the University of Pisa, and the cardinal had written to express his appreciation. The postscript to his letter, which is in his own hand, leaves no doubt about his feelings. "I am much in your debt," he writes, "for your abiding goodwill towards myself and the members of my family, and I look forward to the opportunity of reciprocating. I assure you that you will find me more than willing to be of service in consideration of your great merit and the gratitude that I owe you."[4] Events moved rapidly; less than two months after writing this letter, Maffeo Barberini had become Urban VIII and was about to appoint his nephew, then only twenty-seven years old, to the College of Cardinals. Francesco became the pope's right hand.

Two close friends of Galileo, Giovanni Ciampoli and Virginio Cesarini, were also named to important posts. Cesarini was appointed lord chamberlain, and Ciampoli secret chamberlain and secretary for the correspondence with princes. Under these favorable auspices Galileo thought the moment had come to renew his campaign for Copernicanism, and in 1624 he set off for Rome, where he had the rare privilege of being received by the pope six times in six weeks. Although the 1616 decree of the Index against Copernicus's *De revolutionibus* was not suspended, Galileo felt that he could now argue for the motion of the earth as long as he avoided declaring that it was the only system that fitted the astronomical observations.

Here lurked the danger of serious misunderstanding. Maffeo Barberini, while he was a cardinal, had counseled Galileo to treat Copernicanism as a "hypothesis," not as a confirmed truth. But the term 'hypothesis' could mean two very different things. On the one hand, mathematical astronomers were assumed to deal only with "hypotheses"—that is, accounts of the observed motions of the stars and planets that were mere instruments for calculation and prediction, making no further claim on truth, a view that is often called instrumentalism. On the other hand, a "hypothesis" could also be understood as a theory that was not yet proved but was open to eventual confirmation. This was a realist position. Galileo thought that Copernicanism was true and presented it as a hypothesis in the latter sense—as a provisional idea that was potentially physically true—and he discussed the pros and cons, leaving the issue undecided. This did not correspond to the instrumentalist view of Copernicanism held by Maffeo Barberini and others. They thought that Copernicus's system was a purely instrumental device, and Maffeo Barberini was convinced that it could never be proved. This ambiguity pervaded the whole Galileo affair.

The Dispute with Orazio Grassi

Unfortunately, Galileo had embarked around that time on a drawn-out dispute with the Jesuit Father Orazio Grassi, something that did not help his relationship with the Jesuits. He took Grassi to task in his book *The Assayer,* a witty and devastating work that was wildly acclaimed, not so much by scientists as by writers and men of letters.

The Assayer was a part of a long dispute between Galileo and Grassi. Three comets had appeared in 1618, and Grassi had discussed them in a lecture at the Roman College in Rome.[5] Galileo replied in a *Discourse on the Comets*[6] that was delivered by Mario Guiducci, his disciple and close friend. Galileo probably embarked on this dispute because he felt that Grassi's ideas might be used to support Tycho Brahe's geocentrism against Copernicus's heliocentrism. Grassi replied with his *Balance,*[7] published under the pen name of Lothario Sarsi. Writing under a pseudonym was not unusual among Jesuits when they discussed nontheological subjects, as they did not wish to involve their religious order. Galileo's friends urged him to retort, which he did in his *The Assayer* in 1623. It is in this work that we find the celebrated passage in which Galileo pokes fun at the Jesuit for thinking

> that philosophy is a book of fiction created by one man, like the *Iliad* or the *Orlando Furioso,* books in which the least important thing is whether what is written is true. Sig. Sarsi [Grassi's nom de plume], this is not the way matters stand. Philosophy is written in that great book that ever lies before our eyes—I mean the universe—but we cannot understand it if we do not first learn the language and grasp the symbols in which it is written. It is written in mathematical language, and the symbols are triangles, circles and other geometrical figures, without whose help it is humanly impossible to comprehend a single word, and without which one wanders in vain in a dark labyrinth.[8]

Urban VIII, who liked to have someone read to him at mealtimes, listened to a number of choice passages as soon as *The Assayer* was published in October 1623, and the one we have just quoted was probably included. In any event, the pope was so pleased that he took the book home to read it at leisure.

The Assayer *Denounced*

Not everyone in Rome was as enthusiastic as the pope, and Galileo suspected that his enemies (a broad category) were plotting against him. When he returned to Florence in June 1624, he heard rumors that his theory of sensible qualities was being criticized, and he asked Mario Guiducci, who was in Rome, to investigate. On June 21, 1624, Guiducci reported as follows:

> I hear from all sides rumors of the war with which Grassi is threatening us, to the point that I am tempted to believe that he has his reply ready. On the other hand, I cannot see where he can attack us, since Count Virginio Malvezzi is virtually certain that he cannot gain a foothold against your position about the nature of heat, taste, smell, and so on. The count says that you must have written about that in order to give rise to a debate for which you must be armed to the teeth.[9]

Over the next months, Guiducci kept his ears open, but the rumor died out. On April 18, 1625, however, he had a new bit of gossip to pass on. It was provided by Federico Cesi, the founder of the Lyncean Academy, and concerned "a pious person" who had asked the Holy Office to ban *The Assayer* because it argued for the motion of the earth. The pope's nephew, Cardinal Francesco Barberini, had agreed to look into the matter and had entrusted Father Giovanni Guevara with the task of examining the work. Guevara saw no reason to condemn the "doctrine concerning motion" that was found in the book, and the Holy Office let the matter drop. But Galileo did not argue for the motion of the earth in *The Assayer,* and this incident puzzled historians until Pietro Redondi discovered G3, which sheds light on the problem. The "doctrine concerning motion" in G3 refers, not to the motion of the earth, but to that of atoms, precisely what is at issue in *The Assayer.* The information that Guiducci had passed on to Galileo was not only secondhand, it was distorted. He, or his informant, had misunderstood 'motion' as referring to the earth when it was about atoms. Galileo discusses in *The Assayer* not how planets move but how atoms cause heat, and it is in this context that he explains away the reality of sensible qualities:

> As soon as I think of a material object or a corporeal substance, I immediately feel the need to conceive that it is bounded and has this or that shape, that it

is big or small in relation to others, that it is in this or that place at a given time, that it moves or stays still, that it touches or does not touch another body, and that it is one, few, or many. I cannot separate it from these conditions by any stretch of my imagination. But my mind feels no compulsion to understand as necessary accompaniments that it should be white or red, bitter or sweet, noisy or silent, of sweet or of foul odor. Indeed, without the senses to guide us, reason or imagination alone would perhaps never arrive at such qualities. I think that tastes, odors, colors, and the like are no more than mere names so far as pertains to the subject wherein they seem to reside and that they only exist in the body that perceives them. Thus, if all living creatures were removed, all these qualities would also be removed and annihilated.[10]

Some people, such as the author of G3, may in good faith have considered this passage as incompatible with the permanence of real accidents in the Eucharist, but the Holy Office saw no grounds to proceed against Galileo. The Church had for centuries used the concept of transubstantiation when formulating the doctrine of the Eucharist, but without giving the word a technical meaning. The Church declared that the bread and wine were transformed into the body and blood of Jesus Christ while the appearances of wine and bread remained. It is noteworthy that in the definitions of the Council of Trent, the word 'accident' was not used. Instead, the council spoke of 'species'—that is, appearances—and usually of "the species of bread" or "the species of wine" in the singular. Although the concept of substance was borrowed from Aristotelian philosophy, the council did not intend to enter into a philosophical discussion, and this was explicitly noted. The appearances of bread and wine after the consecration were the same, whatever scientific or philosophical explanation was offered for the reality of sensible qualities. Cardinal Francesco Barberini's adviser, Father Guevara, was quite correct in saying that Galileo's theory about the motion of atoms did not contradict the doctrine of the Church. If the accusation had concerned the motion of the earth, Guevara would surely have pointed out that this matter was not raised in *The Assayer.* The denunciation contained in G3 lay dormant in the archives for several centuries until Redondi discovered it and used it to reinterpret the Galileo affair. We shall return to it after examining the new document discovered by Mariano Artigas.

EE 291

On December 9, 1999, Artigas happened to be working in the archives of the Index, searching for documents related to the Church's stance on the theory of evolution. As he was also preparing a book on Galileo with William Shea, it occurred to him that it might be useful to look up G3. He asked for volume EE, in which Redondi's document occupies sheets 292 (recto and verso) and 293 (recto). When he was given the volume he remembered that Redondi had commented that he was not allowed to look at more than that document. The archives had not yet been opened to the public and access was restricted. Seventeen years later, however, the archives had become fully accessible to scholars, and Artigas was allowed to examine the volume at leisure.

The document just before G3 turned out to be another anonymous and undated document that dealt with the same subject. It filled sheet 291 recto and half of sheet 291 verso. This is why Artigas called it EE 291.[11] Whereas Redondi's G3 is in Italian, EE 291 is in Latin. Galileo is not mentioned by name, but the text begins with "I saw the discourse of the Lyncean," an unmistakable reference to Galileo, who had been admitted to the Lyncean Academy in 1611 and was fond of putting *Linceo* on the frontispiece of his books, as he did in the case of *The Assayer,* the work considered in G3. That EE 291 comes just before G3 confirms that the discussion of the presumed incompatibility of Galileo's interpretation of sensible qualities with the doctrine of the Eucharist is related to what he wrote in *The Assayer.* Artigas immediately realized that he had found an unknown and unpublished document and suspected that it might be relevant to the Galileo affair.

EE 291 is written with less care than G3 and has a number of handwritten corrections. This would seem to indicate that the author of EE 291 was familiar with the Congregation of the Index and had been asked to write an internal report on whether to proceed with the accusation made in G3. EE 291 consists of an introductory paragraph, eight numbered sections, and a conclusion. The author is critical of Galileo's views on atomism and concludes that the Holy Office could proceed with a formal inquiry.

Artigas communicated his discovery to Shea, and both found it difficult to interpret EE 291 without first determining the author and the date of composition. This is when they turned to Rafael Martínez and asked him to join the team.

The Author of EE 291

Rafael Martínez undertook a systematic study of the volume in which EE 291 appears, and he came across two documents in the same handwriting signed by Melchior Inchofer, a Jesuit. The son of an official of the Imperial Army, Inchofer was born in Köszeg in Hungary around 1585 and died in Milan on September 28, 1648. He came to Rome to study at the German Hungarian College in 1605, and he entered the Society of Jesus as a novice on March 26, 1607. He spent the rest of his life mainly in Italy except for a brief period in Graz in Austria.[12]

Inchofer was probably a member of the Preparatory Commission appointed by Urban VIII to examine Galileo's *Dialogue on the Two Chief World-Systems* in the summer of 1632.[13] The next year he was asked, along with Agostino Oregio and Zaccaria Pasqualigo, to assess the work for the Holy Office and determine whether Galileo had disobeyed the injunction not to write on Copernicanism that he had received in 1616. They concurred that Galileo had contravened the order, but Inchofer was particularly damning in his report and, in the very same year, he published in Rome a book entitled *Tractatus syllepticus* against the motion of the earth.[14]

Two other documents in Inchofer's handwriting that were identified by Martínez in the Casanatense, another Roman library, strengthen our claim that Inchofer is the author of EE 291. The slight differences in the handwriting of the two other documents by Inchofer in volume EE can be explained by special circumstances. For instance, in one case, he states that he is compelled to stop writing because his hand is unsteady.

Artigas, Martínez, and Shea drafted an article in 2000, but they had not published it when they heard in January 2001 that two other scholars acting independently had also seen the document. The Italian historian Ugo Baldini, who had been asked by the Vatican authorities to head a systematic search for papers on science and religion in the archives of the Holy Office prior to the nineteenth century, came across many documents with his colleagues but only a few connected with Galileo. Those concerning Galileo refer to minor points except for EE 291, which would seem to be the only genuinely important document related to Galileo to have been uncovered to date. Baldini and his team have published these new texts with some explanatory notes.[15] A second scholar, Thomas Cerbu, of the University of Georgia, also found EE 291 and published a paper on Inchofer, in which EE 291 is reproduced with some comments.[16] The fact that EE 291 has been found independently three times in a short period of time proves that free access to the Vatican archives has already produced excellent results.

We agree with Cerbu on the authorship of EE 291, and we can take as established that EE 291 was written by Inchofer. This, in its turn, permits us to establish, also in agreement with Cerbu, when EE 291 was written.

The Date of EE 291

Inchofer's personal circumstances provide a reliable clue toward establishing when EE 291 was written. In 1617 he was sent to Messina to teach mathematics, philosophy, and theology. He was a prolific writer, very interested in historical controversies. In 1629 he published a work supporting the authenticity of a letter supposedly written by the Virgin Mary to the people of Messina, which had been declared apocryphal by the Holy Office. This caused some difficulties with the Congregation of the Index, and Inchofer went to Rome to defend himself. He did this so well that he was allowed not only to print a revised publication of the book but even to remain in Rome. He became a confidant of the Dominican Niccolò Riccardi, the Master of the Apostolic Palace, one of the main offices in the Vatican Curia. Riccardi could authorize the publication of books, and he had close ties to the Holy Office and the Congregation of the Index.

Inchofer's collaboration with Riccardi could not have begun before he had been cleared of the charges against him. A positive report on his behalf was presented by Riccardi on April 23, 1630, and this was approved by the Holy Office. In December 1630 Riccardi notified the Holy Office that the corrections to Inchofer's book had been made, and the cardinals approved the publication of the revised edition. Shortly thereafter Inchofer began to be consulted by the Congregation of the Index, except for the period when he returned to Sicily between 1634 and 1636. In 1640, he was officially appointed a consultor, a title he retained until his death.

From these circumstances we can infer that the end of 1630 or the beginning of 1631 is the absolute lower limit for the initial collaboration of Inchofer with Riccardi and the Congregation of the Index. It is likely that he was consulted, not immediately after having been cleared, but sometime in 1631 or early in 1632. EE 291 could not have been written later than 1642, the year of Galileo's death, because the criticism of the "Lyncean" is directed against a living person. The suggestion, at the end of the document, that the matter should be examined more closely would make no sense if Galileo were already dead. Since there is no reference to Galileo's condemnation on June 22, 1633 (which the author would have mentioned had the document been written after the trial), we can surmise that EE 291 was written before that date. Moreover, Inchofer's conclusion that the denunciation provided grounds for examining the matter at the Holy Office would suggest that EE 291 was written before the decision, on September 23, 1632, to summon Galileo to the Holy Office, although the document might perhaps have been written when the trial was being prepared, in that case before April 12, 1633.

We can conclude, therefore, that the document was written sometime in 1631 or 1632 but in any case not later than April 12, 1633. This is consistent with the evidence provided by the similarity between the handwriting of EE 291 and that found in the documents we know to be in Inchofer's own hand and prior to 1634.[17] It is also consistent with Inchofer's being a member of a Preparatory Commission appointed in the summer of 1632 to consider whether Galileo should be called before the Holy Office. But before developing this line of argument we must raise a few questions concerning G3.

The Date and Authorship of G3

To ascertain why Inchofer wrote EE 291, we must first ask about the date of G3. Redondi conjectured that it was written after the publication of *The Assayer* in 1623 and before Father Grassi answered it in his *Ratio ponderum* of 1626. It was around this time that Galileo heard the ugly rumor that his theory of "motion" had been denounced. We cannot exclude the possibility that G3 was written some years *after* the publication of *The Assayer*. There have been cases of such delayed attacks in more recent times. For example, at the end of the nineteenth century, a book on evolution by the Dominican Marie-Dalmace Leroy was denounced to the Index several years after it was published. There was no particular rule governing the arrival of denunciations at the Congregation of the Index or the Holy Office. Nevertheless, it seems more reasonable to assume that G3 was produced in 1624, shortly after *The Assayer* appeared. This date agrees with what we know about the circumstances, above all the uneasiness manifested by Galileo when he returned to Florence in June 1624 and the denunciation mentioned by Mario Guiducci in his letter to Galileo of April 18, 1625.[18] The only detail that does not fit so well is Guiducci's reference to the motion of the earth as the cause of the denunciation, but as we have seen, this was surely a mistake, because there is no mention of the motion of the earth in *The Assayer*. That the person who informed Cesi had difficulties in grasping that the real issue was the motion of atoms is quite understandable, and Cesi himself, or Guiducci for that matter, could have missed the point. The second time Guiducci refers to the denunciation in his letter, he speaks only of "motion," not "the motion of the earth." Once this matter is clarified, the denunciation reported by Cesi and transmitted by Guiducci fits perfectly well with Galileo's worries: a theory concerning sensible qualities was a subject he had treated in *The Assayer*.

Our conclusion is that G3 was written and sent to the Congregation of the Index or the Holy Office in 1624. As Guiducci says in his letter, the cardinal, who declared that he would examine the matter, asked Father Guevara to read the book and report on it. Now, Father Guevara shortly thereafter went off to France with the Cardinal Legate, who was no other than Cardinal Francesco Barberini. Everything falls into place if we assume that the cardinal who took matters in hand was Francesco Barberini, the nephew of the pope and friend of Galileo. He had a genuine interest in the issue. When Father Guevara reported that Galileo's views on qualities did not oppose the doctrine of the Church, G3 was placed in the archive and lay dormant until it was discovered in 1632 or 1633.

But who wrote G3? It is difficult to identify the author because the neat copy of G3 in the archives is almost certainly the work of a copyist. Redondi initially conjectured that the author was none other than Father Orazio Grassi, but Sergio Pagano has now shown this to be most unlikely.[19] Several persons in Rome disliked Galileo on personal or doctrinal grounds, but none of those we have studied qualify as the author of G3. One possibility is Francesco Ingoli (1578–1649), with whom Galileo had clashed in Rome in 1616. Ingoli was largely responsible for carrying out the revisions to Copernicus's *De revolutionibus* that the Index had requested, and he had his share in the prohibition of Kepler's *Epitome astronomiae Copernicanae*. Several of his manuscript notes are in the archives of the Congregation for the Evangelization of the Peoples (formerly the Propaganda Fidei), of which he was the first secretary, and Rafael Martínez was able to determine that he did not write G3. Martínez also examined the work of several copyists who worked at the Propaganda Fidei at the time, but their handwriting does not match that of G3.

Sergio Pagano has drawn attention to what might be another clue: the watermark of G3. It is an ecclesiastical coat of arms, probably that of Cardinal Tiberio Muti, the bishop of Viterbo between 1611 and 1636.[20] Martínez found several variants of this watermark in documents in the diocesan archive of Viterbo. The Mutis were a noble Roman family, and Galileo was acquainted with Cardinal Tiberio Muti, his brother Giacomo, and his nephew Carlo. When Galileo came to Rome in 1611, he carried a letter of recommendation to Tiberio Muti from Antonio de' Medici.[21] He saw Tiberio again in 1616,[22] but he was closer to Carlo Muti, who became a member of the Lyncean Academy, and with whom he corresponded until Carlo's death in 1621.[23] Cardinal Tiberio Muti was a member of the Congregation of the Index, whose meetings he attended at least until 1633.[24]

It is most unlikely that Cardinal Muti was involved in drafting G3 because his handwriting is different (of course, G3 could be the work of a copyist, as already noted) but much more because of the tone of the document. It is just not what we would expect from a cardinal who belonged to the Congregation of the Index. Several persons in the entourage of the cardinal could have had access to paper with his watermark, but thus far we are in the dark about who this may have been.[25]

G3, EE 291, and the Galileo Affair

The evidence we have examined strongly suggests that G3 was written in 1624. It was placed in the archive, and then discovered in 1632, in relation to the early stage of Galileo's trial. The author of G3 mentions that he experienced "doctrinal scruples" after reading *The Assayer*, a statement that would have been welcomed by those who wanted to see Galileo taken down a peg or two after the publication of his *Dialogue on the Two Chief World-Systems*. Galileo's trial was preceded by several months of inquiry, and in August 1632 Rome tried to halt the sale of the *Dialogue*. At that time the pope appointed a Commission of Inquiry that probably numbered Inchofer among its members.

We know that the commission met in August and September 1632, but we do not know its mandate, how it went about its task, or what reports were produced. One thing is clear: the commission recommended that Galileo be called before the Holy Office. We also have another item of important information: a document describing a very damaging injunction directed to Galileo in 1616 was discovered in the archives of the Holy Office. On September 11, 1632, the Tuscan ambassador in Rome, Francesco Niccolini, wrote to Andrea Cioli, the Tuscan secretary of state, that Father Riccardi, the Master of the Apostolic Palace, mentioned that his Jesuit confidant (surely Inchofer) was a member of the commission. Riccardi also added that the injunction of 1616 had been found in the Holy Office. On February 26, 1616, Cardinal Bellarmine, acting on orders of the pope, had intimated to Galileo to abandon Copernicanism. This had been recorded in the archives, and now it came to light.

Once he had been made aware of the content of the *Dialogue* in 1632, Pope Urban VIII took the whole affair in hand. The archives were searched for anything concerning Galileo's antecedents, in all likelihood on the pope's instructions, for Urban VIII remembered that the Holy Office had dealt with Galileo in 1616. As a cardinal member of the Index but not of the Holy Office, Urban VIII did not have direct access in 1616 to the proceedings of the Holy Office, which were kept secret. This is why, in an interview with Galileo's friend Piero Dini in April 1615, he had declared that nothing was brewing against Galileo in Rome, although a friar by the name of Lorini had already denounced him to the Roman authorities, and another friar, Tommaso Caccini, had made a statement against him before the Holy Office.[26] More specifically, Urban VIII did not know about the order issued by Pope Paul V, transmitted to Galileo by Cardinal Bellarmine on February 26, 1616. Now, two documents (not just one) in the Holy Office recorded this event. The authenticity of the first document, which contains a very explicit description of an admonition by Bellarmine and the imposition of an injunction on Galileo by the commissary of the Holy Office, has been queried, but the second document is not controversial and is found in the proceedings of the Holy Office, where the subject matter and the decisions of every meeting were recorded.[27] This document clearly says that Bellarmine, acting on the orders of the Holy Office, formally warned Galileo that he should abandon the Copernican opinion and that Galileo acquiesced.[28]

When the documents of the Holy Office came to light, Urban VIII would have realized to his surprise that his much-admired friend Galileo had told him nothing about this admonition. But this is what one should expect in normal circumstances. In 1616 the Holy Office was anxious to protect Galileo's reputation, and there was no reason why Galileo should have told anybody about the precept. Galileo had even obtained a certificate from Cardinal Bellarmine, who was a man who respected confidentiality. But secrecy was so strict at the Vatican that Bellarmine could not refer in his own writings to the procedures of the Holy Office or explain in detail the orders received from the pope. Nonetheless, Galileo should have mentioned that he had received such an admonition when he brought the manuscript of his *Dialogue* to Rome in 1630 to have it approved for publication. The discovery of the record of the admonition turned against him, and it became the focus of the trial. Galileo's only defense was to claim that he did not argue for Copernicanism in the *Dialogue*. The three experts who read the work soon realized that he argued as persuasively as he could for the motion of the earth, and they told the pope.

G3 was probably discovered when the archives were searched for information about Galileo. The accusation contained in G3 was not about Copernicanism, and a report about its relevance was necessary. Inchofer was the right person to prepare such a report; he knew some science and was a member of the Preparatory Commission. He thought that the accusation contained in G3 was justified and that the matter deserved to be more fully investigated by the Holy Office.

The violation of the 1616 admonition regarding Copernicanism was sufficient to call Galileo before the Holy Office. It was directly related to the *Dialogue* and provided juridical grounds for a trial. EE 291 and G3 were not needed. One can imagine that both documents were carefully saved, with an eye to the later development of the affair. They were not forgotten. After all, the trial might not work out quite so easily.

Galileo did not arrive in Rome until February 13, 1633. To his surprise, he had to wait a long time before he was summoned to the Holy Office. On February 26 Ambassador Niccolini asked the pope for a rapid trial, but Urban VIII told him that he did not know how long the trial would last because the case was still being investigated.[29] Since the pope was the head of the Holy Office, it is clear that the matter was taken very seriously. It was only on April 12, two months after his arrival in Rome, that Galileo appeared before the Holy Office to make his deposition. We can assume that all relevant documents were examined in the meantime, including G3 and EE 291. We know the outcome. The trial focused on the *Dialogue,* and there could be no doubt that Galileo had disobeyed the admonition of 1616. From a legal point of view it seemed that the accusation could be entertained. Philosophical opinions about sensible qualities seemed irrelevant, and G3 and EE 291 were returned to the archive, where they remained unnoticed until now.

There is always the possibility that G3 was not deposited in the Vatican archives but remained with Cardinal Francesco Barberini, who remembered it in 1632 and had it reexamined by Inchofer. Cerbu suggests that EE 291 was "a strictly personal memorandum, drafted in conjunction with the meetings of the special commission. . . . The two pieces [G3 and EE 291] may well have remained in his [Inchofer's] possession for several years after he drafted his opinion, and been deposited with the Index in connection with his [Inchofer's] later duties as consultant here."[30] It seems difficult to admit, however, that a member of the Preparatory Commission, such as Inchofer, could keep G3 for himself unless Cardinal Barberini handed it over to him. But in this case it would still be difficult to understand why Inchofer should have deposited G3 and EE 291 in the archives some years later.

The Meaning of EE 291

Historians lament two lacunae in our knowledge of how preparations for the trial of Galileo were carried out. The first concerns the discussions that took place prior to his being summoned to Rome (August–September 1632), the second the preparation of the trial after he had arrived in Rome (February–March 1633). We know very little of the first and almost nothing at all of the second. Presumably, most of the discussion would have focused on the contents of the *Dialogue,* whose publication had brought matters to a head. But EE 291 may very well hint at an additional charge against Galileo that might have influenced Galileo's accusers during those crucial months.

We are not told in the official documents who first accused Galileo and whether anyone approached the pope personally.[31] Neither do we know if the *Dialogue* was examined alone or whether other writings of his were taken into consideration. We do know, however, that the situation was very tense in Rome in 1632, when the papacy was deeply involved in the consequences of the Thirty Years' War. In a consistory, the pro-Spanish Cardinal Borgia accused the pope of favoring the Protestants on the grounds that his support of France served the interests of Sweden, an ally of France. The pope would not have wanted to appear weak on doctrinal matters and would thus have felt obliged to act firmly. Galileo's *Dialogue* could only too easily be represented as a source of doctrinal error, and his adversaries suggested that it might even be thought an affront to the papacy. The three-dauphin logo on the frontispiece of the book was said to convey an implicit criticism of the nepotism of the pope, who had given important jobs to three members of his family. A more serious accusation was that the pope's argument about the undecidability of scientific theories had been placed at the end of the book in the mouth of Simplicio, the Aristotelian pedant who had made himself ridiculous earlier in the book. Seen in this light, G3 could be used to accuse Galileo of deviating from Catholic doctrine in fields other than the motion of the earth. Although G3 and EE 291 were not mentioned at the trial, they could have played an important role during the period when evidence was being marshaled against him.

Galileo later regarded the Jesuits as the source of his misfortunes. Might Inchofer have been one of those who (hypothetically) denounced Galileo in July 1632? According to Thomas Cerbu, "Inchofer's troubles with his fellow Jesuits, starting with his two writings against heliocentrism, the *Tractatus* and the *Vindiciae,* and continuing to the very end of his life, make it difficult to count him among the Jesuits reputed in 1632 to be persecuting Galileo."[32] In 1632, however, Inchofer's troubles with the members of his order were not so great, and in his 1633 report on the *Dialogue* he went out of his way to claim that "Galileo's main purpose was to fight Father Christopher Scheiner [a Jesuit], who had very recently written against the Copernicans."[33] This would suggest that in 1633 Inchofer placed himself on Scheiner's side.

Conclusion

Other scenarios are possible. Although we think it extremely likely that Inchofer wrote EE 291 between 1631 and September 1632, and that G3 was very probably written around 1624, we cannot exclude the possibility that G3 was written in 1632, shortly before EE 291. But this would not affect our suggestion that G3 and EE 291 may have influenced discussions during the work of the Preparatory Commission in the summer of 1632, or when the trial was being prepared in 1633, or perhaps at both times. Perhaps we shall one day know who wrote G3 and when it was presented to the Index or the Holy Office. Other documents may surface, and new light may be shed on the circumstances that led to Galileo's trial. We do not believe, however, that the well-known facts about the Galileo affair will be challenged. What was at stake was Galileo's failure to comply with a formal warning not to defend the claim that the earth moved. The background theological issues were the authority of Scripture in scientific questions and the relevance of geocentrism to Christian doctrine generally. Many Catholics, some of them high-ranking members of the Church, were aware of these problems and felt that they could be faced. As we learn more about the circumstances of the trial, we are strengthened in our conviction that Galileo's condemnation was not inevitable.

Appendix I. The Original Latin Document EE 291

[fol. 291r] Vidi discursum Lyncei et agnovi philosophiam esse eius hominis qui nunquam non verae philosophiae imposuit, sive errore, sive ignorantia, semper temerarie.

Errat in primis negando qualitates primas et secundas etiam in iis corporibus quae agunt in materiam externam, velut cum negat calorem inesse igni qui in nos agit calefaciendo.

2. Errat dicendo non posse conceptu separari a substantiis corporeis accidentia modificantia, velut quantitatem et quae ad quantitatem consequuntur. Quae opinio est absolute contra fidem, exemplo Eucharistiae, ubi quantitas non solum realiter distinguitur a sua substantia, sed etiam separata existit.

3. Errat cum dicit saporem, odorem, colorem, esse pura nomina, et quasi denominationes extrinsecas a corporibus sentientibus, quibus sublatis ipsa quoque huiusmodi accidentia tolli et annihilari, praesertim si sint distincta a primis veris et realibus accidentibus. Ex quo errore duo alii consequuntur: 1. Corpora eandem quantitatem et figuram habentia habere eosdem sapores, odores etc. 2. Corpora amittentia odorem et saporem, amittere etiam quantitatem et figuram a quibus sapor, odor etc. non distinguuntur in phantasia Lyncei.

4. Errat quod sensationes in corpore animalis vocet actiones, cum patitur ab obiecto extrinseco, velut cum titillatur a penna aut alio corpore. Sed hoc condonandum ruditati Philosophi.

5. Errat cum eandem velit esse rationem odoris et saporis, ac titillationis causatae ab agentibus extrinsecis; haec enim sentitur in passo iuxta dispositionem corporis organici, ad cuiusmodi sensationem per accidens se habet hoc vel illud agens in individuo: at sapores et odores etc. oriuntur ex qualitatibus obiectorum, ratione mixtionis hoc vel illo modo temperatae; ad quod viceversa per accidens se habet hoc vel illud organum sensationis in individuo, unde iuxta varias dispositiones, unus altero plus vel minus sentit.

6. Errat cum dicit, ferrum v.g. candens tantum calefaceret animalia sensu praedita; nam quodvis corpus appositum igni, dummodo sit mixtum et non quintae alicuius essentiae recipit calorem.[34] Idem dico si iuxta ponatur quodvis aliud corpus cuivis agenti per species sensibiles, a quo recipit easdem qualitates.

[fol. 291v] 7. Recte deducitur ex opinione huius authoris, non manere accidentia in Eucharistia sine substantia panis. Patet, agunt enim in organum sensationis resolutione minimarum partium, quae cum sint heterogeneae a quantitate, alioqui[n] non afficerent nisi sensum tactus, erunt substantiae, non nisi ex substantia panis, quae enim alia potest assignari, proinde habetur intentum. Idemque sequitur non minus evidenter in ea sententia quae ponit partes substantiae entitativas, distinctas a quantitate dimensiva, nec distinctas realiter a substantia.

8. Recte etiam deducitur non manere alia accidentia in Eucharistia nisi quantitatem, figuram etc. nam sapor odor, sunt pura vocabula si non habeatur relatio ad sensum, in opinione scilicet erronea Lyncei; proinde absolute non sunt distincta accidentia a quantitate figura etc.

Si auctor per partes minimas intelligat species sensibiles, habebit patronos quosdam ex philosophia Aboriginum, sed plura cogetur asserere absurda nec salva in fide. Interim sufficiant ista ex quibus ulterior inquisitio fieri potest coram S. Officio.

Source: Archives of the Congregation for the Doctrine of the Faith, *Index, Protocolli,* vol. EE, fol. 291r (new 301r–v).

Note: The original punctuation, which is not always consistent, has been normalized. Other details have also been normalized, for instance, by substituting "ij" by "ii" or writing full words instead of abbreviations.

Appendix II. English Translation of EE 291

1. I saw the discourse of the Lyncean, which I recognize as the philosophy of someone who does not adhere to the true philosophy. Whether this be through error or ignorance, it is always rash.

He errs in the first place, in denying primary and secondary qualities even in bodies that act on external matter, as when he denies that heat inheres in the fire that acts on us to warm us.[35]

2. He errs when he says that it is not possible to conceptually separate corporeal substances from the accidental properties that modify them, such as quantity and those that follow quantity. Such an opinion is absolutely contrary to faith, for instance in the case of the Eucharist, where quantity is not only really distinguished from substance but, moreover, exists separately.

3. He errs when he says that taste, smell, and color are pure names, or like extrinsic denominations taken from bodies that can have sensations, so that if these bodies were destroyed the accidental properties would also be removed and annihilated, especially since they are said to be distinct from the primary, true, and real accidents. From this error two others follow: 1. Bodies that have the same quantity and the same shape will have the same taste, smell, etc. 2. Bodies that lose their smell and taste will also lose their quantity and their shape, which, in the Lyncean's imagination, are not distinguished from taste, odor, etc.

4. He errs in calling *actions* the sensations of a living body that is acted upon by some external object, for instance when it is tickled by a feather or some other body. But this can be excused by the philosopher's lack of sophistication.[36]

5. He errs when he claims that the cause of smell and taste is the same as that of tickling that is caused by external agents, since someone feels tickling according to the disposition of his organic body, so that such a sensation is accidentally related to whatever acts on the individual. But tastes and smells, etc., proceed from the properties of objects and result from the way they are mixed. Likewise the organ of sensation in a given individual is accidentally disposed in this or that way so that one person feels more or less than another one according to these different dispositions.

6. He errs when he says, for example, that a heated iron can only warm sentient beings, for any object, placed before a fire, will receive heat as long as it is a "mixed" body and is not composed of some fifth essence.[37] And I say that the same happens whenever a body, placed next to a substance that acts by sensible qualities, receives the same qualities as that substance.

7. It immediately follows from the opinion of this author that in the Eucharist the accidental properties do not remain without the substance of the bread. This is evident, for the accidental properties are said to act on the organ of sensation by being divided into very small particles which, since they are not the same as quantity (otherwise they would only act on the sense of touch) must be parts of the substance. And this can only be the substance of bread, for what else could it be? This clinches the argument. The same follows no less clearly from the statement that posits that the parts of the substance are distinct from dimensional quantity but not really distinct from the substance.

8. It also follows immediately that in the Eucharist no other accidental properties remain other than quantity, figure, etc., because taste and smell are mere words if they are not related to the senses, as the Lyncean erroneously believes. Therefore the accidental properties are absolutely not distinct from quantity, shape, etc.

If the author considers the smallest particles to be sensible species, he will find some support among ancient philosophers,[38] but he will have to affirm many things they are absurd and contrary to the faith. So much for now, which is enough for this matter to be further investigated by the Holy Office.

Notes

1. We have published several studies on the scientific, philosophical, and theological aspects of the document in *Acta Philosophica,* the periodical of the Faculty of Philosophy of the Pontifical University of the Holy Cross in Rome: Mariano Artigas, "Un nuovo documento sul caso Galileo: EE 291," *Acta Philosophica* 10 (2001): 199–214; Rafael Martínez, "Il manoscrito ACDF, *Index, Protocolli,* vol. EE, f. 291 r-v," *Acta Philosophica* 10 (2001): 215–42; Lucas F. Mateo-Seco, "Galileo e l'Eucaristia: La questione teologica dell'ACDF, *Index, Protocolli,* EE, f. 291 r-v," *Acta Philosophica* 10 (2001): 243–56; William R. Shea, "Galileo e l'atomismo," *Acta Philosophica* 10 (2001): 257–72. An earlier version of the present essay appears in *Religious Values and the Rise of Science in Europe,* edited by John Brooke and Ekmeleddin Ihsanoglu (Istanbul: Center for Islamic History, Art, and Culture, 2005).

2. Galileo Galilei, *Opere di Galileo Galilei* (hereafter *OGG*), ed. Antonio Favaro (1890–1909; reprint, Florence, Giunti Barbèra, 1968), 6:197–372.

3. Pietro Redondi, *Galileo eretico* (Turin: Einaudi, 1983), translated by Raymond Rosenthal as *Galileo Heretic* (Princeton: Princeton University Press, 1987).

4. Maffeo Barberini to Galileo, June 24, 1623, in *OGG,* 13:119.

5. *De tribus cometis anni MDCXVII Disputatio astronomica* (1619), in *OGG,* 6:19–35.

6. *Discorso delle comete di Mario Guiducci* (1619), in *OGG,* 6:39–105.

7. *Libra astronomica ac philosophica* (1619), in *OGG,* 6:111–80.

8. *OGG,* 6:232.

9. Mario Guiducci to Galileo, June 21, 1624, in *OGG,* 13:186.

10. *OGG,* 6:347–48.

11. There is a pencil pagination, apparently more recent, where sheets 291, 292, and 293 are indicated as 301, 302, and 303. We prefer the older pagination that Redondi used in his book. The new document EE 291 occupies 291 recto–verso (301 in the pencil pagination), and G3 292 recto–verso and 293 recto (302 and 303 in the pencil pagination).

12. See L. Szilas, "Inchofer," in *Dictionnaire d'histoire et de géographie ecclésiastiques,* (Paris: Letouzey et Ané, 1995), vol. 25, cols. 979–80; L. Lukács, ed., *Catalogi personarum et officiorum provinciae Austriae S.I.,* Monumenta Historica Societatis Iesu 125 (Roma: Institutum Historicum S.I., 1982), vol. 2; D. Dümmerth, "Les combats et la tragédie du Père Melchior Inchofer S.J. à Rome (1641–1648)," *Annales Universitatis Scientiarum Budapestinensis, Sectio Historica* 17 (1976): 81–112.

13. Francesco Niccolini to Andrea Cioli, Sept. 11, 1632, in *OGG,* 14:389.

14. William R. Shea, "Melchior Inchofer's *Tractatus Syllepticus:* A Consultor of the Holy Office Answers Galileo," in *Novità celesti e crisi del sapere,* ed. Paolo Galluzzi (Florence: Giunti Barbèra, 1983), 283–92; Francesco Beretta, "*Magno Domino & Omnibus Christianae, Catholicaeque Philosophiae amantibus. D. D.:* Le *Tractatus syllepticus* du jésuite Melchior Inchofer, censeur de Galilée," *Freiburger Zeitschrift für Philosophie und Theologie* 48 (2001): 301–25.

15. Ugo Baldini and Leen Spruit, "Nuovi documenti galileiani degli archivi del Sant'Ufficio e dell'Indice," *Rivista di Storia della Filosofia* 56 (2001): 661–99.

16. Thomas Cerbu, "Melchior Inchofer, 'un homme fin & rusé,'" in *Largo campo di filosofare: Eurosymposium Galileo 2001,* ed. José Montesinos and Carlos Solís (La Orotava: Fundación Canaria Orotava de Historia de la Ciencia, 2001), 587–611.

17. It is very similar especially to EE fol. 125r–v, which seems to date from 1630, and to FF fol. 521r–v, from the first half of 1634.

18. Mario Guiducci to Galileo, in *OGG,* 13:265.

19. See Sergio M. Pagano and Antonio G. Luciani, eds., *I documenti del processo di Galileo Galilei* (Vatican City: Pontifical Academy of Sciences, 1984), 43–48.

20. Patritium Gauchat, *Hierarchia catholica medii et recentioria aevi* (Münster, 1935), 12. There is another possibility, namely, that the coat of arms was that of one of the Cardinals Gondi, who in the sixteenth and seventeenth centuries occupied the see of Paris: Pietro (1533–1616), since 1595 ambassador in Rome; his nephew Enrico (1572–1622); or Giovanni Francesco (1584–1654), who succeeded his brother.

21. Tiberio Muti to Antonio de' Medici, Apr. 9, 1611, in *OGG,* 11:87. There is an error in the Favaro edition, where the letter is signed "Il Car. Muti." In 1611, Tiberio Muti was not yet a cardinal but was a member of the chapter of Saint Peter. Instead of "Car." (Cardinal) one should read "Can." (Canon).

22. See *OGG,* 12:240–41, 411–12.

23. See *OGG,* 20:491. Carlo Muti was born in 1591.

24. The last meeting he attended was on Sept. 19, 1633 (see the archive of the Congregation for the Doctrine of the Faith, *Index, Diari,* 4:68).

25. We sometimes find variants of watermarks in writings apparently unrelated to the original. For instance, there are different versions of the watermark with Muti's coat of arms in the manuscript of Th. Ameyden, *Elogia Summorum Pontificum et S.R.E. Cardinalium suo aevo defunctorum* (Bibl. Casanatense, ms. 1336). This is explained by the friendship between Muti and Ameyden, who had access to his writing paper.

26. Piero Dini to Galileo, Apr. 18, 1615, in *OGG,* 12:173.

27. See chap. 5 of this book.

28. Pagano and Luciani, *I documenti,* 223 (doc. 7). There we find also another document on the same subject, found by Pagano in the "Stanza Storica" in the archives (doc. 6, pp. 222–23), but we do not know whether it is an original or a later copy.

29. Francesco Niccolini to Andrea Cioli, Feb. 26, 1633, in *OGG,* 15:56.

30. Cerbu, "Melchior Inchofer," 598.

31. It seems to be agreed that the volume containing the trial documents is complete. But, of course, this still leaves much in shadow. In many instances when the Holy Office or the Index Congregations proceeded against a book, the case was initiated by a denunciation in the form of a letter or a deposition, as was the case in 1616, when Lorini and Caccini took the

initiative. It seems unlikely that Urban VIII would have read the *Dialogue* and initiated proceedings on his own. Who, then, denounced Galileo?

The content of the denunciation would have made a difference, perhaps even a considerable difference. Did it perhaps mention the logo on the frontispiece of the *Dialogue* that evidently worried Riccardi so much until he discovered that it was simply the printer's mark? Or did it point to the unfortunate placing of Urban's argument in Simplicio's mouth, presenting this as a deliberate affront? It is obvious, furthermore, that over the long two months of delay in preparing the trial all sorts of other issues could have been raised that do not make their appearance in the formal documents of the trial process itself.

32. Cerbu, "Melchior Inchofer," 598.

33. Pagano and Luciani, *I documenti,* 143.

34. After *calorem,* and before *cuivis agenti,* the author had written *iuxta positum igni, aut,* now canceled. Between the lines, the same hand has added the corrected text: *Idem dico si iuxta ponatur aliud corpus.*

35. The words 'primary and secondary qualities' (literally, "first and second qualities") that are used in the document are not found in *The Assayer,* where Galileo uses 'first accidents' when he refers to objective qualities. The terminology of primary and secondary qualities was developed by John Locke in his *Essay Concerning Human Understanding,* where he describes the *primary qualities* of bodies as "utterly inseparable from the body, in what state soever it be . . . viz. solidity, extension, figure, motion or rest, and number." John Locke, *An Essay Concerning Human Understanding,* ed. A. Campbell Fraser (Oxford: Oxford University Press, 1894), bk. 2, chap. 8, para. 9, in vol. 1, pp. 169–70. This is close to what Galileo writes in *The Assayer:* "I say that upon conceiving of a material or corporeal substance, I immediately feel the need to conceive simultaneously that it is bounded and has this or that shape, that it is big or small with respect to others, that it is in this place or that at any given time; that it moves or stays still; that it does or does not touch another body; and that it is one, few, or many. I cannot separate it from these conditions by any stretch of my imagination" (*OGG,* 6:347). *Secondary qualities* of bodies for Locke are "such qualities which in truth are nothing in the objects themselves but powers to produce various sensations in us by their primary qualities, i.e. by the bulk, figure, texture, and motion of their insensible parts, as colors, sounds, tastes, &c." Locke, *Essay,* para. 10, in vol. 1, p. 170. Galileo says much the same in *The Assayer:* "I think that tastes, odours, colours, and so on are no more than mere names so far as pertains to the subject wherein they seem to reside, and that they have their habitation only in the sensorium. Thus, if the living creature [l'animale] were removed, all these qualities would be removed and annihilated. Yet since we have given them particular names that differ from the names of the other first and real attributes [primi e reali accidenti], we like to believe that they are also truly and really different from them" (*OGG,* 6:348).

36. The author is interpreting Galileo in the light of his own Aristotelian philosophy. Galileo does not refer to "sensations" as "actions." This is an error of interpretation. What Galileo actually says in *The Assayer* is the following: "I believe I can explain my idea better by means of some examples. I move my hand first over a marble statue and then over a living man. Now as to the action derived from my hand, this is the same with respect to both subjects so far as the hand is concerned; it consists of the primary phenomena of motion and touch, which we have not designated by any other names. But the animate body, which receives these

operations, feels diverse sensations according to the various parts that are touched. Being touched on the soles of the feet, for example, or upon the knee or under the armpit, it feels in addition to the general sense of touch another sensation upon which we have conferred a special name, calling it *tickling;* this sensation belongs entirely to us and not to the hand in any way. It seems to me that anyone would seriously err who might wish to say that the hand had within itself, in addition to the properties of moving and touching, another faculty different from these, that of tickling—as if the tickling were an attribute that resided in the hand. A piece of paper or a feather drawn lightly over any part of our bodies performs what are inherently quite the same operations of moving and touching; by touching the eye, the nose, or the upper lip it excites in us an almost intolerable titillation while in other regions it is scarcely felt. Now this titillation belongs entirely to us and not to the feather; if the animate and sensitive body were removed, it would remain no more than a mere name. And I believe that many qualities that we come to attribute to natural bodies, such as tastes, odors, colors, and other things, may be of similar and no more solid existence" (*OGG,* 6:348).

37. In other words, a sublunary body and not a celestial one of the kind Aristotle considered to be composed of a "fifth" kind of matter. It is interesting that in the passage of *The Assayer* being considered (*OGG,* 6:348, line 36, to 6:350, line 21) Galileo applies the theory of the four elements to his own purposes: the different sensations are produced by the particles of fire (odor), earth (touch), water (taste), and air (sound).

38. The censor writes, "the philosophy of the Aborigines," which is probably intended as a reference to the pre-Socratic philosophers.

———

NINE

GALILEO, URBAN VIII, AND THE PROSECUTION OF NATURAL PHILOSOPHERS

Francesco Beretta

Minerva Defeats the Giants: The Prosecution of Rebellious Philosophers

A visitor to the Barberini palace, ascending the main staircase, crossing the vestibule and entering the central salon, finds himself right in front of one of the most striking features of the great fresco by Pietro da Cortona. The mythical figure of Minerva, brandishing shield and lance, appears, overthrowing the giants (figure 9.1). The program of this immense fresco that covers the ceiling of the salon, a masterpiece of Roman baroque, celebrates the divinely ordained election of the Barberini family, chosen by Providence for the supreme rule of the Church, and Minerva's combat with the giants has a special place in the celebration. The importance of this particular theme appears from the situation of this part of the fresco, placed so as ideally to meet the visitor's eye on entering, as well as from the decision to simplify the composition by making the action converge around a single movement. In contrast, the other lateral vaults of the fresco each show three groups of figures.[1]

The scene of Minerva's combat reproduces, in the form of a mythological allegory, the image of the Archangel Michael's struggle with Satan, with figures whose massive bodies recall Michelangelo's Last Judgment in the Sistine Chapel. Minerva's triumph over the giants represents the victory of the Church in its struggle against

Figure 9.1.   Pietro da Cortona, *The Vault of Minerva*. Detail of *Divine Providence*, fresco, Palazzo Barberini, Rome. Photograph courtesy of John Beldon Scott.

heresy. The significant place that this scene takes in the program of the ceiling is intended to emphasize the defense of the true faith as an important feature of Pope Urban VIII Barberini's pontificate.[2]

Now if one pauses to observe this part of the fresco, one suddenly notices, in a very particular position, just beside Minerva's shield, the figure of an aged man with a white beard, almost bald and with a long nose, his shoulder bare above a floating robe. The position of this singular figure, together with his features, so different from those of the other giants, leads us to wonder if there is not here an allusion to a particular figure—a discreet allusion, no doubt, but one that cannot be ignored once it has been noticed. Who could it be? Neither the program of the fresco, as described by the court poet Francesco Bracciolini, nor any of the accounts of the period seem to provide a clue to identifying this figure.[3]

Figure 9.2.   Raphael, *The School of Athens,* fresco, Stanza della Segnatura, Vatican. Scala/
Art Resource, New York.

From an iconographic point of view the mysterious aged man may be compared
to an important figure in a fresco by Raphael, usually called *The School of Athens,* that
is in the Stanza della Segnatura in the Vatican Palace (figure 9.2). Sitting on the steps,
in a central position in relation to the composition, Raphael's aged figure represents—
according to Vasari and other interpreters—Diogenes the Cynic and possibly the
physician Fabio Calvo, "a true Pythagorean man of wisdom," a learned contemporary
who led a very modest life.[4] In Pietro da Cortona's fresco, the similar figure would
thus represent the rebellious philosopher, defeated with other heretics by Minerva,
as well as by the Church embodied in the person of the pope.

It is not improbable that Urban VIII himself proposed inserting the striking
figure of the aged man. He personally supervised the painting of Pietro da Cortona's
fresco in the Barberini palace and occasionally crossed the gardens that then separated the family palace from the Apostolic Palace of the Quirinal to see how the work
of the painters was progressing.[5] Furthermore, from the middle of the 1620s, the
Roman Tribunal of the Inquisition undertook, under the leadership of the pope, an intense struggle against the philosophers supporting the doctrines of radical Aristotelianism, especially that of the mortality of the human soul, as taught at Padua by the
celebrated Cesare Cremonini.

Urban VIII was, when cardinal, prefect of the Tribunal of the Signature of Justice, over which he later presided as pope, so he must have been familiar with Ra-

Figure 9.3.   Galileo Galilei: *Dialogo . . . sopra i due massimi sistemi del mondo* (Florence, 1632), detail of frontispiece.

phael's fresco. As we learn from a letter written by Celio Calcagnini to Jakob Ziegler around 1519—published with other letters in an edition of Calcagnini's works found in the Barberini library[6]—Raphael welcomed the Pythagorean Calvo in his home and treated him as a father.[7] Thus Urban VIII probably knew who the persons were whose features had been reproduced by Raphael in the figures of the *School of Athens,* particularly Diogenes–Calvo.[8]

The use of this figure to represent the rebellious philosopher in Cortona's fresco suggests that the supporters of Aristotelianism were not the only philosophers aimed at. The historian of Galileo's trial cannot avoid making an iconographic comparison with the frontispiece of the *Dialogue Concerning the Two Chief World-Systems,* in which Galileo seems to be depicted on the right in the personage of Copernicus (figure 9.3).[9] Much more significant is the comparison with the engraved portrait of Galileo in the *Saggiatore,* reproduced by the publisher from the *Letters on Sunspots.*[10] The left ear, and especially the long nose, recall the features of the aged man in Pietro da Cortona's fresco (figure 9.4). If our hypothesis is correct, there would be a surprising iconographic blending of two "Pythagorean" philosophers, Raphael's Diogenes—with the features of Fabio Calvo—and Galileo as he was represented in his principal works.

The blending could only be allusive, suggesting an identification to the visitor who had a copy of the *Saggiatore* but not imposing it explicitly, which would have been considered as an improper attack ad hominem.[11] But this allusive blending would have struck in all its topicality any visitor who was initiated in the symbolism of Minerva's vault. The sentencing of Galileo to abjure heliocentrism in June 1633—at the moment when Pietro da Cortona began to paint the ceiling of the central salon—had shown the determination with which Urban VIII opposed anything that

 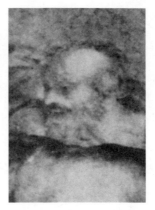 

Figure 9.4.   Left: Raphael, Diogenes' head (reversed), detail of *The School of Athens.* Center: Pietro da Cortona, Old man's head, detail of *The Vault of Minerva.* Right: Galileo Galilei, from *Istoria e dimostrazioni intorno alle macchie solari* (1613).

might call into question the faith of the Church, even in the domain of natural philosophy. At that time, it was known that Celio Calcagnini, who had written about Raphael's friendship with the Pythagorean Fabio Calvo, had suggested that the phenomenon of the tides could be explained by the motion of the earth.[12] And Galileo did the same in the last part of his *Dialogue,* which led to his trial.

One should not be surprised to find both Cremonini and Galileo suggested by the features of the rebellious philosopher. Although they supported very different understandings of natural philosophy, from the perspective of the Roman Inquisition they both deserved to be prosecuted. The scholastic conception of the subordination of natural philosophy to theology held by the members of the Holy Office, and by Pope Urban VIII himself, justified the inquisitorial intervention against Cremonini's Aristotelianism as well as Galileo's heliocentrism.

I shall thus proceed in three stages. First, I shall outline the essential points of the reaction of the Roman Inquisition to the teachings of Cremonini, paying particular attention to the conception it reveals of Christian philosophy—that is to say, of a natural philosophy in accordance with faith. Then I shall show how this same conception led to the proscription of heliocentrism in 1616 and was vigorously restated by Pope Urban VIII, through the works of his theological counselor, Agostino Oreggi, in the early 1630s. Finally, I shall show that the scholastic conception of the relations between theology and natural philosophy was utilized by the Jesuit Melchior Inchofer in his *Tractatus syllepticus* with a view to furnishing a doctrinal legitimation for the sentencing of Galileo in 1633. This will help us to grasp the meaning of the striking figure of the philosopher inserted in the scene of the combat between Minerva and the giants in Pietro da Cortona's fresco.

Cremonini and the Mortality of the Human Soul

The legal basis of the Roman Inquisition's intervention in the field of natural philosophy can be found in the decree *Apostolici regiminis,* promulgated in 1513 by the Fifth Lateran Council. This decree condemned as heretics those who, on a strictly philosophical plane, affirmed the mortality of the human soul. To this pointed condemnation was added the solemn formulation of a general principle. For the decree of 1513 rejected the existence of a "double truth," one philosophical and the other theological: any proposition that went against the truth as revealed through faith was defined as false and unsustainable, even from a strictly philosophical point of view. In this way the council not only affirmed the oneness of truth but, in accordance with the principles of scholastic criteriology,[13] further declared philosophy to be subordinate to theology. In other words, a hierarchy of disciplines was officially established to legitimate the prosecution of those who supported such propositions, together with their punishment as heretics.[14]

To these doctrinal considerations the decree of 1513 added several practical provisions. On the one hand, the council required university professors to teach Christian truth on such matters as the immortality of the human soul and the temporal origin of the world, points on which it was known that ancient philosophers had defended doctrines contrary to the Christian faith: "[Professors should] apply themselves to the full extent of their energies to refuting and disposing of the philosophers' opposing arguments, since all the solutions [i.e., refutations] are available."[15] In the teaching of philosophy it was thus necessary, according to the council, not only to teach Christian truth but also to refute arguments of the philosophers that were opposed to faith.[16] On the other hand, since Christian faith was absolutely necessary for knowing truth, the council decreed that to avoid any chance of error, the study of theology or of canon law should be made part of a complete university training in philosophy.

If we now turn to the reception and application of the 1513 decree in Italy at the beginning of the seventeenth century, right in the middle of the Counter-Reformation, we find that the efforts of the theologians and of the Inquisition to apply these provisions aroused strong resistance on the part of the professors of natural philosophy.[17] The situation had become very tense, especially at the University of Padua, the flower of the Venetian Republic, which jealously defended its freedom. Some professors of the university, among them the celebrated Cesare Cremonini, claimed a complete freedom of teaching in the field of natural philosophy. Aristotelianism at Padua, oriented to the teaching of medicine, was characterized by the avoidance of metaphysical problems and by careful following of Aristotle's thought as interpreted in the light of his Arab or Greek commentators. Such an approach, while remaining strictly on a philosophical plane, led to the denial of the immortality of the soul, a position considered by the Paduan philosophers to be closest to Aristotle's thought.

Theologians could not but have misgivings regarding the intellectual and institutional freedom claimed by the philosophers, which represented a threat to the traditional hierarchy of disciplines. In the teaching given outside the universities, or in the advantage taken of the chairs of theology progressively created in the Italian Faculties of Arts throughout the sixteenth century, the theologians defended the principle that a basic agreement must be maintained between philosophy and revealed truth. At the beginning of the sixteenth century, at the time of the Council of Lateran V, some of them, the Scotists and the famous Dominican Cajetan, had been reluctant to allow that natural reason, of itself, could prove the immortality of the human soul. But by the late sixteenth century, the theologians, especially the Jesuits, tried not only to prove the immortality of the soul by exclusively rational arguments but also to show that this doctrine corresponded to the thought, or at least to the principles, of Aristotle.[18]

The struggle of the Jesuits against claims to freedom in the teaching of philosophy was one of their principal efforts. This struggle, which they sought to carry forward especially in the field of education, was expressed paradigmatically in Antonio Possevino's *Bibliotheca selecta,* published in 1593 and reprinted several times.[19] Regarding philosophy, Possevino recognized the outstanding value of Aristotle's thought, far superior to that of the other philosophers of antiquity. But at the same time he insisted on the need to correct its errors in the light of faith. The weakness of philosophical thought resulted from the darkening of the human intellect as a consequence of original sin. Only with the aid of the light of revelation could the content of true philosophy be soundly laid down.

These considerations found support in the doctrine of the Lateran Council's decree, to which Possevino explicitly referred. Christian doctrine must provide the basis for all Christian and true philosophy: "Christiana, et vera Philosophia." The philosophers must thus subordinate their discipline to theology on pain of being accused not only of heresy but even of atheism. Indeed, to prefer the opinions of the philosophers to revealed doctrine meant not only calling into question one or another of the articles of Christian faith, which amounted to heresy, but denying the absolute value of divine revelation itself.[20]

The philosophical section of Possevino's *Bibliotheca selecta* thus represented an important theoretical restatement of the scholastic hierarchy of the disciplines, but its practical implementation was entrusted to the Inquisition. This explains the difficulties with the Roman Holy Office that Cesare Cremonini encountered from the start of his teaching at Padua in 1591 and that were to last until his death in 1631. His case became even more significant because Cremonini, from the beginning of his teaching in Padua, undertook publicly to defend the university against attempts by the Jesuits to create an institution of higher education in competition with the university.[21]

In Cremonini's courses, and especially his commentaries on Aristotle's *Treatise on the Soul,* he sought as the principal aim of his teaching to reproduce Aristotle's doctrine as faithfully as possible. According to him, he sought to teach, not what was true in an absolute sense, but only what Aristotle maintained, and he referred his audience back to the works of the theologians to seek out a refutation of the philosophers' arguments in favor of the mortality of the human soul. According to Cremonini, "solutions"—that is, refutations of those of Aristotle's arguments that were opposed to Christian faith—did exist, but it was up to theologians, and not to philosophers, to provide such refutations.[22]

Out of the numerous denunciations of, and accusations against, Cremonini during the long inquiry that continued for more than thirty years, two points should be noted. First, Cremonini was accused of teaching the doctrine of the mortality of the human soul as true and not just as Aristotle's doctrine. The attitude of the theologians and of the Inquisition was characterized by the fear of seeing anti-Christian doctrines spread among Cremonini's students, especially among students of medicine. Indeed, there are indications in the archives of the Holy Office in Rome of formal abjurations imposed on some of Cremonini's students who admitted to having believed the doctrine of the mortality of the human soul.[23]

Second, the Tribunal of the Inquisition put pressure on Cremonini to follow Christian doctrine in his teaching and to abandon the pagan commentators.[24] Faced with the theologians, in particular the Jesuits, who asserted that it was possible to interpret Aristotle as favoring the immortality of the soul, Cremonini defended himself, relying on the support of the Venetian Republic, in maintaining the interpretation of Aristotle in favor of the unity of the Agent Intellect and the mortality of the individual soul. He was thus asked to refute on his own account the arguments proposed in favor of such doctrines, following the provisions of the Fifth Lateran Council. The documents produced by the Holy Office, in the course of the different stages of the trial, show that the decree of 1513 was considered to be the basis for legal action by the Inquisition in the domain of natural philosophy.[25]

The crisis became particularly acute following the publication of Cremonini's *Disputatio de coelo* in 1613, and Pope Paul V intervened personally in 1614 to require Cremonini, through the intermediary of the inquisitor of Padua, to correct his book in conformity with the decree of Lateran V by providing a "solution"—that is, a refutation of Aristotle's pernicious doctrine so as to show that philosophy and faith were not in contradiction. If Cremonini did not agree, steps would have to be taken against him on suspicion of heresy and atheism.[26] But Cremonini, protected by Venice, managed, by various subterfuges, to avoid having to accede to this command. His book was finally banned in June 1623.

When Cardinal Maffeo Barberini became pope in August 1623, and thus president of the Supreme Tribunal of the Inquisition in Rome, he inherited this situation. In the face of new denunciations, a circular letter was addressed by order of the pope in June 1625 to all the inquisitors of Italy, requesting them to seek out in their archives all the files relating to Cremonini's students and to those who had maintained the mortality of the human soul.[27] In 1626, the Franciscan Filippo Fabri, a professor of theology at the University of Padua who had been in 1614 one of the executors of the measures taken by the Holy Office against Cremonini, was appointed counselor to the Roman Inquisition.[28] The Franciscan theologian did not take up the post but published the following year a treatise *Against Impious Atheists,* dedicated to the cardinal nephew of the pope, Francesco Barberini. Among other topics, he argued for the immortality of the human soul by rational arguments and attempted to refute the arguments of the philosophers against it.[29]

In 1631, it was the turn of the theological counselor to Urban VIII, Agostino Oreggi, to publish a treatise in which he presented what he claimed to be the true doctrine of Aristotle on the subject of the immortality of the human soul. This work is very important, not only because it was the pope's personal theologian who adopted on his own account a Christian interpretation of Aristotle's thought, but because he attributed the initiative to Urban VIII himself. This he did discreetly by introducing into the treatise an account of an interview he claimed to have had with Maffeo Barberini in Bologna when the latter was still a cardinal. Oreggi claimed that it was the cardinal himself who had, twenty years previously, given him the idea of undertaking a careful reading of Aristotle's text in the original Greek. He further claimed that the future pope had added that if Aristotle had really maintained the mortality of the human soul, the teaching of his doctrine should be banned in the schools, for it was pernicious and contrary to revealed truth.[30] The publication of this interview in 1631 in the papal theological counselor's treatise clearly showed Urban VIII's attitude regarding the necessity of submitting natural philosophy to the control of theology, not excluding the possibility of having recourse to censure and coercion.

The appearance of Oreggi's work coincided with the death of Cremonini himself. But the Roman Tribunal of the Inquisition continued to receive alarming accounts concerning the spread of the doctrine of the mortality of the soul, not only in the academies, among the elite classes and the physicians, but also in the popular classes in society.[31] Not having been able to arrest Cremonini himself—protected by the Venetian Republic until his death—the Roman Inquisition tried in 1631–32 to establish proof of Cremonini's heterodox beliefs by having the manuscripts left by the deceased secretly inspected. This strategy, which the pope entrusted to his counselor Oreggi, does not seem to have produced any result, not least because of the vigilance of the Venetian authorities. But it is important to note the judgment expressed by the theologian-counselors of the Roman Holy Office on July 16, 1632: "Cremonini's books contain erroneous propositions, and even ones that are formally heretical, which do not come from Aristotle's texts, but which he seeks to prove on their own account. Furthermore, in seeking to prove these errors, he provides demonstrations which, according to him, cannot be solved [i.e., refuted]."[32] This judgment, which in a few words summarizes the problem posed by Cremonini's teaching, is very important, for the following year the Roman Holy Office formulated the crime of Galileo in practically the same terms. The attitude of the inquisitorial authorities regarding natural philosophers described above makes it possible, in the following sections, to situate the sentencing of Galileo in its intellectual context and to understand the verdict pronounced by Urban VIII on the Tuscan philosopher on June 16, 1633.

Indeed, in the text of his abjuration, drawn up by the officials of the Holy Office on the basis of the papal verdict,[33] Galileo admitted the accusation of being vehemently suspect of heresy, for "after it had been notified to me that the said doctrine is contrary to Holy Scripture [I] wrote and gave to be printed a book [*the Dialogue*] in which I treat of this same doctrine, previously condemned, and bring forward in its favor *fully efficacious reasons* without advancing any *solution* [i.e., refutation]."[34] The doctrine imputed to Galileo being that of heliocentrism, this essential passage in his abjuration, as formulated by the tribunal, poses two fundamental questions. First, when and how was the doctrine of the earth's motion round the sun condemned? Second, was heliocentrism to be considered as a doctrine contrary to the Christian faith, so that the arguments in its favor required a refutation, just as in the case of the mortality of the human soul?

The Proscription of Heliocentrism in 1616

To answer the first question we must go back to March 20, 1615, when the Dominican Tommaso Caccini denounced Galileo to the Roman Inquisition, accusing him of supporting the doctrine of Copernicus. Caccini judged heliocentrism to be opposed to Christian faith because it contradicted the literal interpretation of a number of passages in Scripture as well as the exegetic consensus of the Church fathers. One classic passage of this kind appears in Joshua describing the miracle of the sun's being stopped in its motion by God in order to give the Israelites more time to rout their enemies in battle (Joshua 10:12–13).[35]

Caccini's denunciation was preceded by the tribunal's processing of other relevant information submitted by Caccini's fellow Dominican Niccolò Lorini, who in February 1615 forwarded to the cardinal inquisitor, Paolo Emilio Sfondrati, a copy of the celebrated letter that Galileo had sent to his disciple Benedetto Castelli in December 1613. Lorini too believed that the Copernican view was entirely contrary to the Bible, and he reprimanded Galileo for presenting an interpretation of Scripture opposed to that of the Church fathers as well as for having asserted that on cosmological issues exegetes could be mistaken.[36]

In his letter to Castelli, Galileo affirmed the absolute truth of the Bible, but at the same time he applied the principle of accommodation to scriptural assertions relevant to natural philosophy. In this domain, which did not directly concern salvation, itself the ultimate concern of Scripture, the writers of Scripture, inspired by the Holy Spirit, accommodated their language to the limited knowledge of the people and left to philosophers the task of seeking the true design of the universe. According to Galileo, therefore, it was wrong to use scriptural arguments in cosmological discussions that did not directly concern the faith, for in that domain, philosophical research should come before the work of exegesis.[37]

Two irreducibly opposed conceptions came here into collision. On one side was the view of the Dominicans Caccini and Lorini, shared widely by theologians of the day, that accorded primacy, even in the domain of cosmology, to a literal interpretation of Scripture in accordance with the exegetical consensus of Catholic theologians.[38] On the other side was that of Galileo, who after the discoveries he had made with the astronomical telescope was convinced of the reality of the heliocentric world-system and sought to propose a new interpretation of the relevant cosmological passages in the Bible in order to deprive the defenders of geocentrism of the scriptural weapon they had brought against him. In his letter to Castelli, Galileo therefore proposed a novel exegesis of the miracle in Joshua, exploiting his discovery of the sun's rotation in order to show that heliocentrism was reconcilable even with a literal reading of the scriptural passage.[39]

To understand the fundamental opposition between these two conceptions, one must refer to the criteriology developed by scholastic theology.[40] It should be emphasized that the issue is not primarily concerned with hermeneutics—that is, the principles of biblical exegesis—but with criteriology—that is, inquiry about the validity of knowledge, establishing criteria by which truth can be distinguished from error.[41] With regard to the relation between theology and natural philosophy, scholastic criteriology established a hierarchy of disciplines grounded on a twofold argument. First, it affirmed the absolute truth of the Bible: because of divine inspiration, the content of the Bible as a whole pertained to the faith, so its truth was directly guaranteed by the veracity of God. Second, since the tenets of theology were founded upon the absolute truth of divine revelation, the human disciplines—which were themselves products of weak and limited intellects—were subordinated to theology.[42]

The position of Thomas Aquinas with regard to criteriology can serve as a guide here, despite the fact that his exegetic principles were rather broad in matters of cosmology. Aquinas considered the entirety of the content of Scripture to belong to the faith, even though certain items of the faith did not directly concern salvation: "Incidentally or secondarily related to the object of faith are all the contents of Scripture handed down by God, e.g. that Abraham had two sons."[43] The truth of Scripture was assured by God, the First Truth and the author of Scripture. It was therefore absolute.[44] Furthermore, for Aquinas theology was a science "which takes on faith its principles revealed by God."[45] Because theology was founded upon divine truth—the criterion—and notably on biblical revelation, its degree of certitude was greater than that of the disciplines founded upon human knowledge.[46] According to this hierarchy of disciplines, theology was thus authorized to pass judgment on other sciences, "for whatsoever is encountered in the other sciences which is incompatible with its truth should be completely condemned as false."[47]

In spite of the clarity of the principles of Aquinas's criteriology, their application to hermeneutics—that is, to biblical exegesis—is not an easy task, for the complex problem is to discern the precise meaning of any given passage of Holy Scripture.[48] In his commentary on the Creation story, Aquinas set forth the principles that were to guide the interpreter: on the one hand, the truth of Scripture had to be held inviolable (criteriology), but on the other hand, since there were different interpretations of the Genesis narrative, no particular interpretation should be maintained that was already known on other grounds to be false (hermeneutics).[49] If a "theory can be shown to be false by solid arguments, it should not be maintained that this is the sense of the scriptural text." In such a case it should be recalled that "Moses was speaking to ignorant people" and "presented to them only things that are immediately obvious to the senses."[50] Just as Galileo had done in his letter to Castelli, Aquinas applied here the principle of accommodation and sought a literal explanation of the biblical text in conformity with the cosmological principles to which he was committed.

However, this hermeneutical flexibility, as expressed in the exegesis of passages whose interpretation was controversial among the Church fathers, should not lead us to forget that for Aquinas—who approached the problem from the perspective of a theologian and not that of a philosopher—the goal was to uncover the exact meaning of a biblical passage, the revealed and absolute truthful sense, and to show its fundamental accordance with the results of a sound exercise of the faculties of human reason. In the case of biblical passages whose interpretation had been already decided by the Church or had not, at least, been a source of disagreement among the fathers, such as that of the creation of the body of the first man, natural philosophy was called upon to show that it was in fundamental agreement with the orthodox interpretation of the biblical text.[51]

One whole section of Aquinas's writings, most notably the *Summa contra Gentiles,* was thus devoted to the refutation of philosophical arguments that were opposed to the faith. To Aquinas, a proposition that contradicted the faith was necessarily false and thus impossible to prove:[52] "For since faith rests on unfailing truth, and the contrary of truth cannot really be demonstrated, it is clear that alleged proofs against faith are not demonstrations, but arguments that can be refuted [*solubilia argumenta*]."[53]

Because of a commitment to scholastic criteriology, and to the basic principle of the hierarchy of disciplines, formulated by Aquinas in the same terms as the later decree of Lateran V,[54] the bounds on the latitude allowed in biblical hermeneutics were clearly defined. Thus denying the historicity of biblical narratives, which would imply that Scripture contained false propositions, would bring with it a charge of heresy.[55]

It was in the intellectual context of this scholastic criteriology, at the time of the so-called Second Scholasticism, that the Copernican issue came to be debated at the beginning of the seventeenth century.[56] From the perspective of the Dominicans Lorini and Caccini, who denounced Galileo to the Roman Holy Office, what was at stake was not only a question of biblical exegesis but the fundamental principle of the hierarchy of disciplines. In his *Letter to Christina,* Galileo gave an eloquent account of this attitude: "Some theologians of profound learning and of the holiest lifestyle add that whenever in the subordinate science there is a conclusion which is certain on the strength of demonstrations and observations, and which is repugnant to some other conclusion found in Scripture, the practitioners of that science must themselves undo [*sciogliere*] their own demonstrations and disclose the fallacies of their own observations."[57] But Galileo could not accept this basic principle of scholastic criteriology, and in the *Letter to Christina,* which discussed issues belonging as much to biblical hermeneutics as to criteriology, he repeatedly affirmed the autonomy of the human knowledge of nature from theology and the necessity for exegetes to adapt their interpretation of the Bible to the new discoveries in astronomy.[58]

Galileo was joined in his battle for Copernicanism by the Carmelite Paolo Antonio Foscarini, who at just the time of Caccini's denunciation of Galileo, in early 1615, published a work that gave immediate rise to public debate in Rome. His publication took the form of a lengthy letter addressed to the general of his order. A reputable theologian and the provincial of Calabria, protected by the cardinal inquisitor, Giangarsia Millini, who had called him to Rome to preach a course of Lenten sermons, Foscarini also busied himself in showing that Copernicanism was not in contradiction with the Bible.[59]

In his *Lettera,* and in a Latin piece addressed personally to the cardinal inquisitor, Robert Bellarmine, Foscarini argued that the new astronomical discoveries were giving support to the heliocentric world-system.[60] In his view, it was time to abandon the traditional interpretation of Scripture in the domain of astronomy and to adopt an exegesis founded on the principle of accommodation. The aim of Scripture was to lead men to salvation, and in doing so it had to accommodate itself to human ways of thinking. Unlike Caccini and Lorini, Foscarini held that the exegete was not constrained by the consensus of the fathers of the Church in his interpretation of biblical texts relating to cosmology. According to him, the Council of Trent had explicitly limited its reference to the authority of the fathers to the area of the faith and morals: "Hence it is not rash to depart from the common interpretation of the Fathers in matters not pertaining to the faith, especially if this occurs because of a pressing and persuasive reason."[61]

Foscarini's intervention, as a reputable theologian far better qualified than Galileo to weigh in on this question, provoked a celebrated response from Bellarmine (April 12, 1615) in which the cardinal inquisitor firmly rejected the suggestion offered by the Carmelite theologian. In his response to Foscarini, Bellarmine relied on scholastic criteriology to reject the hermeneutic solution proposed by Foscarini and Galileo. According to Bellarmine, affirming the truth of the Copernican cosmology would not only "irritate all scholastic philosophers and theologians, but also harm the Holy Faith by rendering Holy Scripture false."[62] Indeed, he continued, the Church fathers and doctors were unanimous with regard to the geocentric interpretation of Scripture.

In opposition to Foscarini, Bellarmine asserted that the scriptural passages in question pertained to faith because they were to be considered as "a matter of faith as regards the speaker," which meant God, the author of Scripture. "And so it would be heretical to say that Abraham did not have two sons."[63] The Jesuit cardinal drew here on the same example as that used by Thomas Aquinas in his discussion of the objects of faith in order to assert that biblical cosmology was itself an item of faith, albeit indirectly. Therefore, according to Bellarmine, the hermeneutical principle of the unanimous interpretation of the fathers, which had been enacted by the Council of Trent, had to be applied to biblical passages relating to cosmology, which meant that the Copernican doctrine was to be considered virtually heretical.[64] In other words, the cardinal inquisitor used scholastic criteriology to legitimate a hermeneutical choice.

However, in the third part of his response to Foscarini, Bellarmine acknowledged, as a careful theologian, that a major problem would arise if a real proof of the earth's movement were one day to be given. This section of his letter shows that such a proof would call into question the whole criteriology of the cardinal inquisitor, according to which heliocentrism, to the extent that it was opposed to biblical truth, was indemonstrable. For how could one admit that Solomon, who spoke of the sun's motion in Ecclesiastes and who benefited not only from divine inspiration but also from the deep wisdom granted him by God himself, "was affirming something that was contrary to truth already demonstrated or capable of being demonstrated?" In response to Foscarini, Bellarmine mentioned the principle of accommodation, but according to him, because of his criteriology, there was no valid reason "to abandon the Holy Scriptures as interpreted by the Holy Fathers."[65]

The theologian-consultors of the Roman Holy Office, in February 1616, gave their support to a position still more radical. In November 1615, the deposition of a witness favorable to Galileo had confirmed the latter's adherence to the Copernican doctrine.[66] The Tribunal of the Inquisition therefore had to determine the theological status of that doctrine. On February 24, 1616, the two propositions that defined heliocentrism in Caccini's original denunciation were submitted to the theologian-consultors of the Holy Office for their judgment. In their opinion, the propositions were, first of all, false and absurd according to natural philosophy. From a theological point of view, the first proposition, stating the immobility of the sun, was deemed "formally heretical since it explicitly contradicts in many places the sense of Holy Scripture, according to the literal meaning of the words and according to the common interpretation of the Holy Fathers." The second proposition, affirming the earth's motion, was judged to be "erroneous in the matter of faith."[67] The difference between the two theological censures was due to the less obvious opposition between the second proposition and the letter of Scripture.[68]

Behind this double censure lay scholastic criteriology, which allowed the geocentrism of Scripture to be considered as an object of faith and therefore allowed the application of the censure of formal heresy to heliocentrism. To pronounce such a censure the theologian-consultors of the Holy Office relied on this criteriology, although they did not mention it explicitly; for the theologian-consultors, five of whom were Dominicans, it went without saying, since it represented the foundation of their conception of a hierarchy of disciplines, subordinating philosophy to theology. They relied on it, just as Bellarmine had in 1615, to handle the hermeneutical problem posed by Galileo and Foscarini. In other words, the theologian-consultors of the Holy Office used scholastic criteriology, implicitly but effectively, to legitimate the application of the hermeneutics of the Council of Trent, which asserted the primacy of the literal meaning, according to the interpretation commonly given by the Church fathers, of cosmological passages of Scripture, disallowing the application to them of the principle of accommodation. It should be noted that, according to this criteriology, heliocentrism was to be considered false not primarily on philosophical grounds but because of its opposition to faith.

Supporting an entirely opposed position, Galileo was trying at the same time to prevent the condemnation of the Copernican worldview. Having learnt of his denunciation, he had come to Rome in December 1615. In particular, he was trying his best to provide a physical proof of the heliocentric system, which he attempted to do by invoking the movement of the earth as an explanation of the phenomenon of the tides, in the hope of overcoming the resistance of the numerous proponents of the traditional cosmology.[69]

Because of the increasingly public character of the controversy on heliocentrism, and especially because of the authoritative intervention of Foscarini, a theologian of renown, an effective papal doctrinal declaration was considered to be necessary, in accordance with the usual functioning of the Roman Tribunal of the Inquisition, of which the pope was the president.[70] Cardinal Bellarmine's certificate, dated May 26,

1616, and delivered to Galileo, gives us the key to the proper interpretation of what happened in February–March 1616: "The above-mentioned Galileo has not abjured in our hands. . . . On the contrary, he has only been notified of the *declaration made by the Holy Father* and *published* by the Sacred Congregation of the Index, whose content is that the doctrine attributed to Copernicus . . . is *contrary to Holy Scripture* and therefore cannot be defended or held."[71]

It was most probably during the meeting of the Congregation of the Inquisition on February 25, 1616, that Paul V declared the Copernican doctrine to be contrary to Scripture.[72] This decision was communicated personally to Galileo by Cardinal Bellarmine. By acquiescing, the philosopher allowed the tribunal to suspend the trial that had been set in motion against him because of the denunciation by Caccini.[73]

The pontifical doctrinal declaration was then published, even if not explicitly as such, in a decree of the Congregation of the Index, which was prepared in the congregation's meeting of March 1.[74] The Index decree was presented to Paul V in the meeting of the Congregation of the Inquisition of March 3 and was approved by the pope.[75] It was promulgated under the date of March 5, 1616, in the form of a printed bill posted up in Rome and sent to all nuncios and inquisitors.[76] According to the Index decree, the heliocentric doctrine, that of the "Pythagoreans" taught by Copernicus and Foscarini, was "false and entirely contrary to Scripture." Upon this basis, which expressed the papal doctrinal declaration, the Carmelite theologian's book was proscribed definitively, as it affirmed the compatibility between heliocentric doctrine and Holy Scripture, while Copernicus's treatise, *De revolutionibus orbium coelestium,* was suspended until it would be corrected.[77]

The indications for the correction were published in 1620, in a document signed by the secretary of the Congregation of the Index. They are based on the interpretation of the heliocentric world-system as a hypothesis in the instrumental sense of the term customary among the specialists in astronomy of that time. What that amounted to was that the Copernican world-system was false from the point of view of natural philosophy but that it "saved the appearances"—that is, it accurately described the observed motions of the heavenly bodies.[78] The correction of Copernicus's treatise, therefore, entailed transforming all the passages in which he had affirmed the reality of the heliocentric world-system to make them say no more than that this system simply saved the appearances.[79]

The pontifical declaration published in the Index decree of March 5, 1616, was intended to settle the public controversy going on in Florence and in Rome. It decided it in favor of the view, shared by Caccini, Lorini and Bellarmine, that affirmed the primacy of Scripture and of its traditional interpretation over the new theories of the astronomers. Our reconstruction of the origins of the decree's wording shows that the Index decree doubtless declares the Copernican doctrine to be false from the perspective of traditional cosmology. But, much more important, it does so because heliocentrism, being contrary to Scripture, simply *cannot* be true. This conviction of the theologians, founded on scholastic criteriology, was ratified by the pope, but— and this should be emphasized—with a degree of restraint, indicated by the fact that the censure of formal heresy, applied *in camera* by the theologian-consultors of the Holy Office, on February 24, 1616, was not proclaimed in the decree published on March 5. This may have been because of the influence of Cardinal Bellarmine, who had adopted, as we has seen, a more careful position than the consultors.

In a letter of March 6, 1616, Galileo commented on this doctrinal decision and indicated that, despite attempts by Caccini to have the Copernican doctrine condemned as heresy, the Church—that is to say, the papal *magisterium* exercised through the Congregations of the Inquisition and the Index—had only determined that this doctrine was "contrary to Scripture." Consequently, only books attempting to reconcile Copernicanism with the biblical text would be proscribed.[80] This was a minimalist interpretation on Galileo's part, since the decree in reality had forbidden all books affirming the truth of the heliocentric world-system.[81] But it points to an essential fact: the pontifical declaration of 1616 did not explicitly indicate whether the cosmology of the Bible was to be considered to be a matter of faith.

We have seen above the decisive importance of this criterion: if the geocentrism of the Bible were to be regarded as belonging to the faith, albeit indirectly, then heliocentrism, which had been declared to be entirely contrary to Scripture, would merit the censure of heresy. If it were not to be so regarded, one could say that heliocentrism was opposed to an exegetic consensus but not to faith. This would mean that it could be categorized as "rash" but not as heretical. In his commentary on the Index decree published in 1631, Libert Froidmont, a Belgian theologian, hesitated between the censure for heresy and the censure for temerity but declared that he would not dare to call heliocentrism heresy as long as the pope himself had not himself explicitly done so.[82]

The Condemnation of Galileo in 1633

Froidmont's view seems to have been shared by Urban VIII, a member of the Congregation of the Index in 1616, who was elected pope in 1623. Galileo heard in 1624 that according to the new pope, with whom he was on good terms, the Copernican doctrine had been condemned as rash and not as heretical. Thus the condemnation of 1616 did not seem to be irrevocable, though according to the pope there was no need to fear that someone might prove it to be true.[83] To understand these significant words of Urban VIII, it is helpful to refer to a treatise published in 1629 by Agostino Oreggi in which the pope's theological counselor gave an account of an interview that he claimed had taken place between Galileo and the-then Cardinal Barberini some years previously. There is a striking parallel between this interview and the one about the mortality of the human soul published by Oreggi in 1631, discussed above.

According to Barberini at that time (Oreggi wrote), it was not possible to assert the truth of a particular system of the world if it could not be proved that all the other conceivable systems contained in themselves contradictions, for this claim would constitute a limit imposed on God's omnipotence and on divine knowledge.[84] The context in Oreggi's treatise of this famous interview indicates that the basic problem was that of the existence of apparently contradictory philosophical and theological truths. According to Oreggi, if philosophical assertions contradicted revelation, if objections appeared that seemed insoluble to human reason (difficultates solvere minus apti essemus), one could still rely on the argument of divine omnipotence.[85] This meant acknowledging that God could produce the cosmology described in Scripture in numerous ways other than that conceived by the philosophers, ways that exceeded in their perfection those of which we could ever have knowledge.

Oreggi had expounded this same conception in his 1631 book dealing with the Aristotelian doctrine of the soul, referred to above, which was included in a larger treatise on the Creation published by him in 1632. In that treatise Oreggi repeatedly asserted that the truth of Scripture had to be given priority over the opinions of scholars.[86] Outside the domain of revealed truth, knowledge of the cosmos might be left to natural philosophers and to mathematicians, but they had to avoid maintaining as true any opinions that ran contrary to Scripture.[87] Several hints in these works suggest that Oreggi was expounding principles shared by Urban VIII himself.

The sense of the provisions handed down by the pope to Niccolò Riccardi, who as Master of the Sacred Palace was the official censor of Rome, is now clearly apparent. The first condition to be observed to grant permission to Galileo to print his new work, the *Dialogue Concerning the Two Chief World-Systems,* was that the motion of the earth must never be asserted; only its "hypothetical" nature could be conceded. Further, any interpretation of the Bible was to be avoided.[88] Above all, Galileo was to insert in the conclusion to his book the argument of divine omnipotence, which had been suggested to him by the pope and which was intended to undercut any potentially realist implications of the arguments developed in the work.[89]

Galileo did not, in fact, present the heliocentric hypothesis in the *Dialogue* in the instrumental sense indicated by the 1620 document of the Index Congregation. Rather, he presented it as a physical hypothesis, allowing him to propose a natural explanation of the phenomenon of the tides. The ambiguity in the notion of hypothesis, having at the same time both an instrumental and a realist meaning, enabled him to introduce a physical argument in favor of the movement of the earth while claiming that he was respecting the provisions of the Index.[90] Doing this was risky because the realist implication of the demonstrative method used by Galileo was quite evident.[91] Furthermore, convinced that human reason had received from God the capacity to discover the true structure of the universe, Galileo took over the argument suggested by Urban VIII and used it in the *Dialogue* in a subtle but definite way to suggest the legitimacy, even in a theological sense, of the realist hypothesis of the motion of the earth.[92]

When the book arrived in Rome in the summer of 1632, Urban VIII, of course, reacted violently. Not only did the book maintain, in a scarcely disguised manner, that the earth truly moved, but the argument offered by the pope had been turned back on him.[93] On September 23, 1632, Urban VIII decreed the opening of a trial by the Inquisition. Without entering here into the details of this cause célèbre,[94] let us note the main point of the expert testimony sent to the tribunal by the Jesuit Melchior Inchofer in April 1633 to prove that Galileo believed heliocentrism to be really true.

Inchofer carefully analyzed the strategy adopted by Galileo in playing upon the double meaning, instrumental and realist, of the notion of hypothesis. According to him, Galileo claimed in the title of the *Dialogue,* as well as in the work's preface, that he sought to limit himself to setting out the arguments in favor of the two systems of the world, Ptolemaic and Copernican, without committing himself in favor of one or the other. In reality he had adopted the hypothesis of the motion of the earth as a physical principle, not merely an instrumental one, and he had attempted, through an argument overtly demonstrative in form, to prove the reality of heliocentrism. If Galileo had really sought to proceed hypothetically, he would have had to bring forward also a refutation of the arguments advanced in favor of the motion of the earth (iis deinde solutis).[95]

The last feature of Inchofer's argument, which follows the same line as that applied by the Holy Office in the case of Cremonini, was taken up in the text of Galileo's abjuration. This says, as we have seen, that he had "brought forward in favor [of heliocentrism] fully efficacious reasons without advancing any solution." The expert testimony of Zaccaria Pasqualigo, in the report on the *Dialogo* that he handed over to the Holy Office, fully agreed with Inchofer on this point, underlining the implicitly demonstrative character of Galileo's strategy.[96]

These expert testimonies allowed Urban VIII to pronounce on June 16, 1633, the verdict stating that Galileo had to abjure on the grounds that he was vehemently suspect of heresy.[97] Following the practice of the Roman Tribunal of the Inquisition at that time, the sentence and the abjuration of Galileo were then drafted, on the basis of the papal verdict, most probably by the notary of the Holy Office, under the supervision of the commissary. They were then signed and promulgated by the cardinal inquisitors on June 22, 1633. In the same meeting of the Congregation of the Inquisition, Galileo abjured heliocentrism and signed the text of his abjuration drafted by the commissary.[98]

The pope's verdict raises the problem of the doctrinal legitimacy of the abjuration inflicted on Galileo. The sentence of condemnation insists that heliocentrism had been declared contrary to Scripture by the Apostolic See in 1616.[99] However, we have seen that the doctrinal value of this condemnation had not been precisely defined by Pope Paul V, since no theological censure was explicitly mentioned in the decree issued by the Index Congregation. Urban VIII himself seems to have asserted in 1624, as we have seen, that the Copernican doctrine was to be considered rash rather than heretical. In accordance with the Roman Inquisition's custom, however, only doctrines opposed to the faith needed to be abjured, not those defined just as rash.[100] Therefore, the condemnation of Galileo to abjure heliocentrism represents a more rigorous interpretation of the decree of 1616. This appears also from the interview given by Urban VIII to the Tuscan ambassador on June 19, 1633, during which the pope announced not only the condemnation of Galileo but also that of heliocentrism itself, a doctrine "contrary to Scripture as dictated by God," both decreed by himself on June 16.[101]

The task of providing a doctrinal justification of Galileo's abjuration was entrusted to Inchofer, who, during the summer of 1633, published his *Tractatus syllepticus,* a brief treatise bringing together theological arguments arguing that the geocentrism of Holy Scripture was a matter of faith.[102] The engraving on the title page of Inchofer's treatise makes obvious the link between this book and the condemnation of Galileo, as decreed by Urban VIII (figure 9.5). For the engraving shows three bees holding up the earth, which are to be identified with the three bees of the Barberini coat of arms. They are placed in a triangle representing the Trinity and are surmounted by the motto *His fixa quiescit,* which can be translated as "[The earth] lies fixed, sustained by these [the bees]." In the iconographic context of papal Rome at the beginning of the 1630s,[103] the meaning of the engraving stands out clearly: it hints at Pope Urban VIII ruling the world in the name of divine wisdom and even guaranteeing the cosmological stability of the earth.

The twelfth chapter of Inchofer's treatise contains obvious allusions to the case of Galileo's *Dialogue:* although the philosopher is not mentioned explicitly, the line of argument is similar to the one developed in the expert testimony earlier provided by the Jesuit to the Holy Office. In his treatise, Inchofer emphasized the risks one runs in applying to heliocentrism the principles of a scholastic dispute, allowing one to put forward arguments in favor of theses opposed to the faith, even if such a proceeding was common in the case of other topics of natural philosophy, such as the mortality of the human soul.[104]

The twelfth chapter of the treatise also contains a reference to the provisions of the Fifth Lateran Council, stating that in the teaching of philosophy the doctrine of Christian truth must be affirmed and that a "solution" (a refutation) must be provided for theses that are opposed to the faith (solutisque argumentis contrariis).[105] According to Inchofer, this principle also applied to astronomers, so heliocentrism was likewise to be included in the general condemnation of philosophical statements contrary to the faith, as formulated by the council.[106]

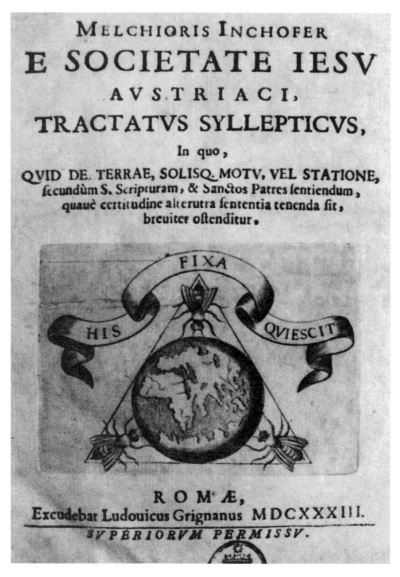

Figure 9.5.   Melchior Inchofer. From his *Tractatus syllepticus* (Rome, 1633), frontispiece. Courtesy of the Biblioteca Casanatense, Rome.

Thus the decree of 1513, applied to the case of heliocentrism, furnished, according to Inchofer, a doctrinal justification for the sentencing of Galileo. It was for having adduced very effective reasons in favor of the motion of the earth without also providing a refutation of them, that Galileo, according to the wording of his abjuration, had become vehemently suspect of believing in heliocentrism, a doctrine contrary to the Christian faith. From the same perspective as that of the Possevino's *Bib-*

liotheca selecta,[107] the treatise of the Jesuit Inchofer was dedicated to "God and all those who love the Christian and Catholic philosophy"[108]—that is, a philosophy subordinated to the control of theology.

At the same time, the Lateran V decree's disciplinary provisions concerning the teaching of philosophy probably inspired the order given by Urban VIII on June 16, 1633, and repeated two weeks later, to have the sentencing of Galileo made known to all teachers of mathematics and philosophy. It was to be made known, in particular, to all those in the main Italian university centers of Bologna and Padua, to ensure that they would "avoid committing so grave a fault, running the risk in consequence of being punished in the same manner."[109] Thus copies of the sentence, together with Galileo's abjuration, were sent out to the whole of Catholic Europe, resulting, for example, in Descartes's suspension of the publication of his treatise on cosmology, *Le monde.*

Conclusion

We now have the necessary background to grasp the significance of the striking figure of the philosopher inserted, probably at Urban VIII's own request, in Pietro da Cortona's fresco. In the center of the ceiling, Divine Providence sends Immortality to crown the coat of arms of the Barberini, the three bees. In the lateral vaults of the fresco, allegorical figures illustrate, in the form of a vast program inspired by the values of the Counter-Reformation, the different virtues of the papacy in its ruling of the Church, spiritually and temporally. In one of the lateral vaults, Science, aided by Piety, ascends to heaven, an allegorical representation of the essential principle that determines the relationship between philosophy and theology: faith must give its support to reason in seeking truth.[110]

Beside this scene, just opposite the salon entrance, Minerva's triumph over the giants illustrates the same values in another way (figure 9.1). As president of the Tribunal of the Inquisition, Urban VIII had put himself at the head of the struggle against rebellious philosophers, whether the Aristotelians of Padua, such as Cremonini, or the astronomers supporting heliocentrism, such as Galileo. In doing so, the pope was reaffirming, in conformity with the principles of the Fifth Lateran Council, the hierarchy of disciplines, the superiority of Christian doctrine over human knowledge, and with it that of the theologians over the natural philosophers.

The comparison between Raphael's *School of Athens* and Pietro da Cortona's fresco celebrating the "Glory of the House of Barberini" shows how much the climate of opinion had changed from one century to another. The classic harmony of Raphael's fresco, expressing the climate of the Renaissance, with its fascination for the models of pagan antiquity, had given place to the dynamic composition of the baroque, the expression of the Church's new commitment under the impetus of the

Counter-Reformation. The positive character of Diogenes the Cynic, possibly immortalizing Raphael's Pythagorean friend Fabio Calvo, had metamorphosed, through Pietro da Cortona's brushwork, into a negative figure, stigmatizing in this way the rebellious philosophers. Minerva, watching from a distance in Raphael's fresco (figure 9.2), had now aroused herself, brandishing her arms, to defeat the enemies of the Church, including the striking figure of the old man at whom her spear was directed. And it should be recalled that it was precisely in the Dominican Convent of Santa Maria sopra Minerva, on June 22, 1633, that Galileo, in carrying out Urban VIII's verdict, pronounced his abjuration of heliocentrism.

Notes

Translated by W. G. L. Randles, revised by Ernan McMullin. An earlier version of this essay appeared as "Urbain VIII Barberini protagoniste de la condamnation de Galilée" in *Largo campo di filosofare,* edited by J. Montesinos and C. Solís (La Orotava: Fundacion Canaria Orotava de Historia de la Ciencia, 2001), 549–73. I wish to thank the Swiss National Science Foundation for support of research related to this chapter.

1. Jörg Martin Merz, *Pietro da Cortona: Der Aufstieg zum führenden Maler im barocken Rom* (Tübingen: Ernst Wasmuth, 1991), 247.

2. John Beldon Scott, *Images of Nepotism: The Painted Ceilings of Palazzo Barberini* (Princeton: Princeton University Press, 1991), 139; Merz, *Pietro da Cortona,* 247.

3. Merz, *Pietro da Cortona,* 248; Maurizio Fagiolo dell'Arco, *Pietro da Cortona e i "Cortoneschi": Bilancio di un centenario e qualche novità* (Rome: Bulzoni, 1998), 49.

4. Wolfgang von Lohneysen, *Raffael unter den Philosophen—Philosophen über Raffael: Denkbild und Sprache der Interpretation* (Berlin: Duncker & Humbolt, 1992), 163.

5. Merz, *Pietro da Cortona,* 240.

6. Vatican Library, Barberini O. IV.16.

7. Celio Calcagnini, *Opera aliquot* (Basileae: Hier. Frobenium et Nic. Episcopium, 1544), 101.

8. This interpretation of Raphael's figure is attested to in the seventeenth century; see Père & Fils Richardson, *Traité de la peinture et de la sculpture divisé en trois tomes* (1728; reprint, Geneva: Minkoff, 1972), 247. For Calcagnini's letter about Raphael and Calvo, see 276–77.

9. W. B. Ashworth, Jr., "Divine Reflections and Profane Refractions: Images of a Scientific Impasse in Seventeenth-Century Italy," in *Gianlorenzo Bernini: New Aspects of His Art and Thought,* ed. I. Lavin (University Park: Pennsylvania State University Press, 1985), 187; Isabelle Pantin, "Une Ecole d'Athènes des astronomes? La représentation de l'astronome antique dans les frontispices de la Renaissance," in *Images de l'antiquité dans la littérature française: Le texte et son illustration,* ed. E. Baumgartner and L. Harf-Lancner (Paris: Presses de l'École normale supérieure, 1993), 95.

10. Galileo Galilei, *Opere di Galileo Galilei* (hereafter *OGG*), ed. Antonio Favaro (1890–1909; reprint, Florence: Giunti Barbèra, 1968), 5:89, 6:204. See also Antonio Favaro, "Studi e ricerche per una iconografia galileiana," *Atti del Reale Istituto Veneto di Scienze, Lettere ed Arti* 72 (1912–13): 1002.

11. For the same reason, Inchofer included clear allusions to the case of Galileo in his *Tractatus syllepticus,* published in 1633, without mentioning explicitly the philosopher; see Melchior Inchofer, *Tractatus syllepticus, in quo, quid de terrae, solisq. motu, vel statione, secundum S. Scripturam, et Sanctos Patres sentiendum, quave certitudine alterutra sententia tenenda sit, breviter ostenditur* (Rome: Grignanus, 1633), 49–59.

12. Calcagnini, *Opera aliquot,* 392. See Père & Fils Richardson, *Traité de la peinture,* 248; Galileo Galilei, *Dialogo sopra i due massimi sistemi del mondo tolemaico e copernicano,* ed. O. Besomi and M. Helbing (Padua: Antenore, 1998), 2:831–34; Michel-Pierre Lerner, *Le monde des sphères,* vol. 2, *La fin du cosmos classique* (Paris: Les Belles Lettres, 1997), 88–91.

13. See below, "The Proscription of Heliocentrism in 1616."

14. Norman P. Tanner, ed., *Decrees of the Ecumenical Councils* (Washington, D.C.: Georgetown University Press, 1990), 1:605–6. See also Daniel Price, "The Origins of Lateran V's *Apostolici Regiminis," Annuarium Historiae Conciliorum* 17 (1985): 464–72; John Monfasani, "Aristotelians, Platonists, and the Missing Ockhamists: Philosophical Liberty in Pre-Reformation Italy," *Renaissance Quarterly* 46 (1993): 247–76.

15. "[C]um omnia solubilia existant." Tanner, *Decrees,* 1:606.

16. See Thomas Aquinas, *Summa theologiae* (hereafter *ST*), IA, q.1, a.8, c, Blackfriars ed., ed. Thomas Gilby (New York: McGraw-Hill, 1964–).

17. For the following, see Ugo Baldini, "Die Philosophie an den Universitäten," in *Die Philosophie des 17. Jahrhunderts,* vol. 1, *Allgemeine Themen: Iberische Halbinsel. Italien,* ed. J.-P. Schobinger (Basel: Schwabe, 1998), 642–45; Paul F. Grendler, *The Universities of the Italian Renaissance* (Baltimore: Johns Hopkins University Press, 2002), 281–97; Antonino Poppi, *Introduzione all'aristotelismo padovano* (Padua: Antenore, 1991).

18. This was also the position of Thomas Aquinas. See his *Contra gentes,* II, 78–79, with the presentation and refutation of the opposite arguments, *rationes solvere,* in the following sections, 80–81.

19. See Antonino Poppi, "La difficile integrazione dell'aristotelismo padovano nella teologia tridentina: Iacopo Zabarella e Antonio Possevino," in *Aristotelica et lulliana magistro doctissimo Charles H. Lohr septuagesimum annum feliciter agenti dedicata,* ed. F. Dominguez et al. (The Hague: M. Nijhoff, 1995), 245–58; Luigi Balsamo, "How to Doctor a Bibliography: Antonio Possevino's Practice," in *Church, Censorship and Culture in Early Modern Italy,* ed. G. Fragnito (Cambridge: Cambridge University Press, 2001), 51–56.

20. Antonio Possevino, *Bibliotheca selecta de ratione studiorum, ad disciplinas, et ad salutem omnium gentium procurandam* (Coloniae Agrippinae: apud Ioannem Gymnicum, 1607), 2:12–45.

21. Heinrich Kuhn, *Venetischer Aristotelismus im Ende der aristotelischen Welt: Aspekte der Welt und des Denkens des Cesare Cremonini (1550-1631)* (Frankfurt am Main: Peter Lang, 1996), 94–134.

22. Cesare Cremonini, *In Aristotelis primum librum de anima commentaria,* Vatican Library, Vat. lat. 12601, 1v°–2r°. See also Leen Spruit, "Cremonini nelle carte del Sant'Uffizio Romano," in *Cesare Cremonini: Aspetti del pensiero e scritti,* ed. E. Riondato and A. Poppi (Padua: Academia Galileiana, 2000), 1:201; Antonino Poppi, *Cremonini, Galilei e gli inquisitori del Santo a Padova* (Padua: Centro Studi Antoniani, 1993), 89 n. 5, 105.

23. Spruit, "Cremonini," 198.

24. Poppi, *Cremonini,* 60–61.

25. Ibid., 92, 95, 102.

26. Xavier-Marie Le Bachelet, *Auctarium Bellarminianum* (Paris: Beauchesne, 1913), 685 n. 1. See also Spruit, "Cremonini," 197–99.

27. Michele Cioni, *I documenti galileiani del S. Uffizio di Firenze* (1908; reprint, Florence: Giampiero Pagnini, 1996), 21, doc. 13.

28. Archives of the Congregation for the Doctrine of the Faith (ACDF), SO, *Decreta,* 1626, 175r°v°.

29. Filippo Fabri, *Adversus impios atheos disputationes quatuor philosophicae* (Venice: Cinammi, 1627), 265 ff.

30. Agostino Oreggi, *Aristotelis vera de rationalis animae immortalitate sententia accurate explicata* (Rome: Camera Apostolica, 1631), 35–36; Luca Bianchi, "Agostino Oreggi, qualificatore del *Dialogo,* e i limiti della conoscenza scientifica," in *Largo campo di filosofare: Eurosymposium Galileo 2001,* ed. José Montesinos and Carlos Solís (La Orotava: Fundacion Canaria Orotava de Historia de la Ciencia, 2001), 578–79.

31. ACDF, SO, *Decreta,* 1631, 146v°.

32. "[A]tque in erroribus probandis ait, se demonstrationes afferre, quae solvi nequeant." ACDF, SO, St. st. O 1 a, no. 16, 104r°.

33. About the author of Galileo's sentence and abjuration, see Francesco Beretta, "Rilettura di un documento celebre: Redazione e diffusione della sentenza e abiura di Galileo," in the new journal from the Istituto e Museo di Storia della Scienza in Florence: *Galilaeana* 1 (2004) 91–115.

34. "[A]pporto *ragioni con molta efficacia* a favor di essa senza apportar alcuna *soluzione.*" Cioni, *I documenti,* 37–38 (emphasis mine). The translation by Finocchiaro gives the following interpretation of the crucial words: "I treat of this already condemned doctrine and adduce very effective reasons in its favor, without refuting them in any way," Maurice A. Finocchiaro, *The Galileo Affair: A Documentary History* (hereafter *GA*) (Berkeley: University of California Press, 1989), 292.

35. *GA,* 137–38. About heliocentrism considered as heretical, see chap. 1 of this book.

36. *GA,* 134–35.

37. *GA,* 50–52. See also Mauro Pesce, "Le redazioni originali della Lettera 'Copernicana' di G. Galilei a B. Castelli," *Filologia e Critica* 17 (1992): 394–417.

38. Corrado Dollo, "Le ragioni del geocentrismo nel Collegio Romano (1562–1612)," in *La diffusione del copernicanismo in Italia, 1543-1610,* ed. Massimi Bucciantini and Maurizio Torrini (Florence: Leo S. Olschki, 1997), 102–29, and chap. 2 of this book.

39. *GA,* 52–54.

40. Marie-Dominique Chenu, *La théologie comme science au XIIIe siècle* (Paris: Vrin, 1969); Albert Lang, *Die theologische Prinzipienlehre der mittelaltlicher Scholastik* (Freiburg im Br.: Herder, 1964).

41. *New Catholic Encyclopedia,* 2d. ed. (Washington, D.C.: Catholic University of America Press, 2003), 4:366.

42. Ugo Baldini, *Legem impone subactis: Studi su filosofia e scienza dei gesuiti in Italia, 1540-1632* (Rome: Bulzoni, 1992), 19–22; Francesco Beretta, *Galilée devant le Tribunal de l'Inquisition* (Fri-

bourg: Université de Fribourg, 1998), 100–104, and "Une deuxième abjuration de Galilée ou l'inaltérable hiérarchie des disciplines," *Bruniana e Campanelliana* 9 (2003): 11–21.

43. *ST,* IIa IIae, q.2, a.5, c., Blackfriars ed., ed. Thomas Gilby (New York: McGraw-Hill, 1964–74), vol. 31, p. 81. All further volume and page citations for quotations are from the Blackfriars translation.

44. *ST,* Ia, q.1 a.10. IIa IIae, q.1, a.1 and a.4. See also Eugène Mangenot, "Inspiration de l'Ecriture," *Dictionnaire de théologie catholique* (Paris: Letouzey et Ané, 1922), 7:2219–21.

45. *ST,* Ia, q.1, a.2 c. and ad. 2, vol. 1, p. 11.

46. *ST,* Ia, q.1, a.5.

47. *ST,* Ia, q.1, a.6, ad 2m, vol. 1, p. 23. See also Mark Jordan, "Theology and Philosophy," in *The Cambridge Companion to Aquinas,* ed. N. Kretzmann and E. Stump (Cambridge: Cambridge University Press, 1993), 235–36.

48. Gilbert Dahan, *L'exègese chrétienne de la Bible en Occident médiévale, XIIe-XIVe siècle* (Paris: Cerf, 1999), 38–56.

49. *ST,* Ia, q.68, a.1, c.

50. *ST,* Ia, q.68, a.3, c., vol. 10.

51. *ST,* Ia, q.91, vol. 10, p. 224.

52. Aquinas, *Contra gentes,* I, 7. See above, n. 18.

53. *ST,* Ia, q.1, a.8, c, vol. 1, p. 31.

54. See Tanner, *Decrees,* 1:606.

55. ST, Ia, q.32, a.4. See also IIa IIae, q.11, a.2, c., and Mangenot, "Inspiration," 2182.

56. See Beretta, "Une deuxième abjuration," 22–32.

57. *GA,* 99.

58. *GA,* 87–118. See also Galileo Galilei, *Lettera a Cristina di Lorena sull'uso della Bibbia nelle argumentazioni scientifiche,* ed. Franco Motta and Mauro Pesce (Genoa: Marietti, 2000); Ernan McMullin, "Galileo on Science and Scripture," in *The Cambridge Companion to Galileo,* ed. Peter Machamer (Cambridge: Cambridge University Press, 1998), 302–24, and chap. 4 of this book.

59. Emmanuele Boaga, "Annotazioni e documenti sulla vita e sulla opere di Paolo Antonio Foscarini teologo 'copernicano' (ca. 1562–1616)," *Carmelus* 37 (1990): 187–89.

60. For a translation of Foscarini's *Letter,* see Richard J. Blackwell, *Galileo, Bellarmine and the Bible* (hereafter *GBB*) (Notre Dame: University of Notre Dame Press, 1991), 221–23.

61. Translation of the Latin *Defense* in *GBB,* 234–35; on the Council of Trent's decree, *GBB,* 5–14.

62. *GA,* 67.

63. *GA,* 68.

64. See Cesi's letter to Galileo, Jan. 12, 1615: Bellarmine holds the Copernican doctrine "to be heretical, and the movement of earth doubtless contrary to Scripture." *OGG,* 12:129.

65. *GA,* 68.

66. Sergio M. Pagano and Antonio G. Luciani, eds., *I documenti del processo di Galileo Galilei* (Vatican City: Pontifical Academy of Sciences, 1984), 96 ff.

67. *GA,* 146.

68. For more regarding theological censures, see Bruno Neveu, *L'erreur et son juge* (Naples: Bibliopolis, 1993), 239–382, and Beretta, *Galileo devant le Tribunal,* 93–97.

69. *OGG,* 5:377–95.

70. See Beretta, *Galilée devant le Tribunal,* chap. 3, esp. 128–39, and "Le procès de Galilée et les archives du Saint-Office: Aspects judiciaires et théologiques d'une condamnation célèbre," *Revue des Sciences Philosophiques et Théologiques* 83 (1999): 451–54.

71. "[L]a dichiarazione fatta da Nostro Signore e publicata dalla Sacra Congregazione dell'Indice." Cardinal Bellarmine's certificate, in Pagano and Luciani, *I documenti,* 138; *GA,* 153.

72. See Beretta, "Le procès," 470–73, and "L'affaire Galilée et l'impasse apologétique: Réponse à une censure," *Gregorianum* 84 (2003): 175–79.

73. Decree of Mar. 3, 1616, *GA,* 148.

74. The recently discovered minutes are published in Pierre-Noel Mayaud, *La condamnation des livres coperniciens et sa revocation à la lumière des documents inédits des Congrégations de l'Index et de l'Inquisition* (Rome: Gregorian University Press, 1997), 37–40.

75. Decree of Mar. 3, 1616, *GA,* 148.

76. *GA,* 148–49. The text of the circulars sent to all the nuncios and inquisitors, forwarding to them the printed decree, is in Ugo Baldini and Leen Spruit, "Nuovi documenti galileiani degli archivi del Sant'Ufficio e dell'Indice," *Rivista di Storia della Filosofia* 56 (2001): 674–77.

77. See Pagano and Luciani, *I documenti,* 103.

78. Regarding astronomical "hypotheses," see Michel-Pierre Lerner, *Tre saggi sulla cosmologia alla fine del Cinquecento* (Naples: Bibliopolis, 1992).

79. The documents relating to this correction have been published by Massimo Bucciantini, *Contro Galileo: Alle origini dell'Affaire* (Florence: Leo S. Olschki, 1995), 207–12, and by Mayaud, *La condamnation,* 69–72, 77–79.

80. *OGG,* 12:244.

81. The titles of the works proscribed by the decree of Mar. 5, 1616, were to be added to the list of books forbidden by the earlier Index of Pope Clement VIII (1596). The new list was published in Rome in 1619. This list also included a special entry explaining the general ban on works propounding the movement of the earth and the immobility of the sun: "Libri omnes docentes mobilitatem terrae, et immobilitatem Solis." *Edictum librorum qui post Indicem fel. Rec. Clementis VIII: Prohibiti sunt . . . ubique publicandum* (Rome: Camera Apostolica, 1619), xxvii.

82. Libert Froidmont, *Anti-Aristarchus sive orbis-terrae immobilis liber unicus . . .* (Antwerp: Ex officina Plantiniana Balthasaris Moreti, 1631), 29. See Isabelle Pantin, "Libert Froidmont et Galilée: L'impossible dialogue," in Montesinos and Solís, *Largo campo di filosofare,* 615–35.

83. For more details about the following, see Francesco Beretta, "Urbain VIII Barberini protagoniste de la condamnation de Galilée," in Montesinos and Solís, *Largo campo di filosofare,* 558–64.

84. Agostino Oreggi, *De Deo uno: Tractatus primus* (Rome: Camera Apostolica, 1629), 193–95. See also Galilei, *Dialogo,* 2:899–902.

85. Oreggi, *De Deo uno,* 184 (emphasis mine).

86. Agostino Oreggi, *De opere sex dierum* (Rome: Vatican Press, 1632), 3 and passim.

87. Oreggi, *De opere sex Dierum,* 15–16. See Bianchi, "Agostino Oreggi," 584.

88. *GA,* 212.

89. *GA,* 213, 354 n. 57.

90. Galilei, *Dialogo,* 2:392–94.

91. *OGG,* 14:282–83.

92. "Salv. But do you not believe that the terrestrial globe could be made movable super-naturally, *by God's absolute power? . . .* That is the way I feel about it, and saying that the *natural cause* of the tides is the motion of the earth does not exclude this operation from being miraculous." Galileo Galilei, *Dialogue Concerning the Two Chief World Systems: Ptolemaic and Copernican,* trans. Stillman Drake (New York: Modern Library, 2001), 489–90 (emphasis mine).

93. Luca Bianchi, "Galileo fra Aristotele, Clavio e Scheiner: La nuova edizione del *Dialogo* e il problema delle fonti galileiane," *Rivista di Storia della Filosofia* 54 (1999): 224–27.

94. See Beretta, "Le procès de Galilée," 479–83.

95. Pagano and Luciani, *I documenti,* 144–45. *GA,* 266–67, esp. sections 3–5.

96. *GA,* 275.

97. Pagano and Luciani, *I documenti,* 229.

98. Beretta, *Galilée devant le Tribunal,* 221, and "Rilettura."

99. *GA,* 288–91.

100. See Beretta, "L'affaire Galilée," 180 ff.

101. *OGG,* 15:160, line 13.

102. For more details, see Francesco Beretta, "*Magno Domino & Omnibus Christianae, Catholicaeque Philosophiae amantibus. D. D.:* Le *Tractatus syllepticus* du jésuite Melchior Inchofer, censeur de Galilée," *Freiburger Zeitschrift für Philosophie und Theologie* 48 (2001): 301–27.

103. Sebastian Schütze, "*Urbano inalza Pietro, e Pietro Urbano:* Beobachtungen zu Idee und Gestalt der Ausstattung von Neu-St. Peter unter Urban VIII," *Römisches Jahrbuch der Bibliotheca hertziana* 29 (1994): 213–87; Scott, *Images of Nepotism.*

104. Inchofer, *Tractatus syllepticus,* 49–59.

105. Ibid., 58.

106. In the table of contents, "Doctrina de motu Terrae et Statione Solis implicite prohibita a Leone X" refers to *Tractatus syllepticus,* 57, where the doctrine of the 1513 decree is applied to the case of heliocentrism.

107. Possevino, *Bibliotheca selecta,* 2:12–45.

108. Here the full text of the printed dedication: "Magno Domino, Qui fecit illum (Solem) et in sermonibus eius festinavit iter (Ecclesiastici 43), Qui fundavit Terram super stabilitatem suam (Psal. 103), et Omnibus Christianae, Catholicaeque Philosophiae amantibus. D. D."

109. Pagano and Luciani, *I documenti,* 244; see 231, doc. 20.

110. Merz, *Pietro da Cortona,* 246.

PART THREE

THE AFTERMATH

TEN

———

GALILEO'S RELAPSE

On the Publication of the Letter to
the Grand Duchess Christina (1636)

Stéphane Garcia

Among the numerous questions raised by the problematic relationship of Galileo
to the Church, one has never been the object of an in-depth analysis: that of the fidelity of the Italian thinker to the oath he took, on his knees, on June 22, 1633: "I
will never again say or assert, orally or in writing, anything which might cause a suspicion [of heresy] about me." He was not to relapse into heliocentric heresy, knowing that otherwise he could incur the ultimate punishment for the relapsed faithful,
burning.[1]

Approached from an essentially polemical angle, this question attracted the attention of several writers in the nineteenth century, following the publication of
the first collections of Galileo's letters, such as Giambattista Venturi's *Memorie e lettere inedite* (1821) and Eugenio Alberi's *Commercio epistolare di Galileo Galilei* (1859).
During this period, the first historiographically oriented versions of the Galileo affair appeared, with Venturi, Alberi, and other authors such as Karl von Gebler (1876)
maintaining that Galileo had perjured himself.[2] In the aftermath of his trial, the condemned was said to have entrusted to some foreign friends the production of a Latin
version of his *Dialogo sopra i due massimi sistemi del mondo,* which appeared in the Protestant city of Strasbourg in 1635 under the title *Systema cosmicum.*[3]

Still, their explanations rested more on conjecture than on rigorous and documented reasoning, as Antonio Favaro set himself to proving in his introduction to

the *Dialogo* in volume 7 of the *Opere*.[4] And indeed, it is now established that the initiative that led to the translation of the *Dialogo* into Latin did not come from Galileo. Relying on Favaro's conclusion, the "Galilean" camp could then express the further conviction conveyed to good effect by Canon Michele Cioni in 1908: "We know that Galileo, although he continued, to the great benefit of science and civilization, to philosophize until his death, could never be accused of having transgressed the orders he had received, doing great honor to his religious faith and his personal dignity."[5] This conclusion, along the same lines that the thinker's "ultimo discepolo," Vincenzo Viviani (1622–1703), defended all his life, thus perpetuated the image of Galileo as a good son of the Church that has permeated the apologetic literature ever since the seventeenth century.

However, this version does not stand up to a scrupulous examination of the available sources concerning the *princeps* edition of the *Letter to the Grand Duchess Christina* (Strasbourg, 1636), which was to have been published originally as an appendix to the *Systema cosmicum*.[6] I will show in this article that there are strong indications that Galileo did indeed compromise himself and thus violated the oath he had taken. Beyond the necessity of recovering once and for all the definitive time line of events, an analysis of the genesis of a work that appeared in 1636 leads to a compromise conclusion: even while breaking his word, Galileo paradoxically felt himself to be working in the service of the Church.[7]

To understand the circumstances surrounding the printing of Galileo's famous epistolary treatise, completed in 1615, it is advisable to briefly recall beforehand the circumstances that led to the appearance of the *Systema cosmicum*. And this for a simple reason: the two principal promoters of the Strasbourg editions, Elie Diodati and Matthias Bernegger, hoped to combine in one volume the Latin translations of the *Dialogo* and the *Letter to the Grand Duchess Christina*.

The Parisian lawyer Elie Diodati (1576–1661) was the one who launched the project in the summer of 1633. His motivation for undertaking it resulted from the combination of three elements. First, friendship: friends by correspondence since 1620, Galileo and Diodati further strengthened their ties in October of 1626, when the latter decided, while traveling in Italy, to pay a visit to the philosopher and mathematician of the Grand Duke of Tuscany.[8] Second, the role Diodati was to play in the intellectual movements of his time: he facilitated by various means communication between natural philosophers to the greater benefit of science, which, as an avid reader of Francis Bacon, he passionately desired. Anything hindering the free pursuit of the truth in matters of natural philosophy was unacceptable in his eyes. Third, opportunity: there was an opportunity, much like others he had seized in previous cases, to play his contacts off one another at the center of the international intellectual community, the Respublica Literaria, to ensure the diffusion of a forbidden literature.[9]

One of his friends, the history professor Matthias Bernegger (1582–1640) from Strasbourg, appeared to him to be the fitting person to carry out the translation of the voluminous *Dialogo*. This mathematics enthusiast, himself in correspondence with Johannes Kepler between 1613 and 1630, had already shown proof of his abilities in 1613 by translating into Latin—of his own accord, and indeed without asking the author's permission—Galileo's *Operations of the Geometric and Military Compass*.[10] Bernegger agreed to undertake the lengthy and difficult task and managed to convince the powerful Dutch publishing house Elzevier to fund the printing of the work by the young Strasbourg printer David Hautt (1603–87). The volume was ready in time for the Frankfurt Fair, in March 1635.

This volume contains, however, more than just a translation of the *Dialogo*—a translation remarkable, be it said, for its precision. It also includes two important appendices concerning the debate over the compatibility of the theory of the earth's movement with Scripture. The first piece, entitled *Perioche ex introductione in Martem Iohannis Kepleri Mathematici Caesarei,* is an excerpt from the introduction of Kepler's *New Astronomy* (1609) in which the author explains in a few pages his conception of the relationship between science and the sacred texts. The second is the Latin translation, by Diodati himself, of the famous *Letter* of the Carmelite Paolo Antonio Foscarini (1580–1616), which was published in Naples in 1615 and was directly responsible for the censure by the Congregation of the Holy Office of the heliocentric theory, pronounced in the following year.[11]

This edition would have been considered exactly right to achieve its purposes if the *Letter to the Grand Duchess Christina* could also have been included, as both promoters had hoped. But Elie Diodati's delay in communicating the text to his friend in Strasbourg did not permit this. The *Letter* thus appeared in a separate publication in 1636, translated into Latin (with the Italian text facing), and with a preface by Diodati under the pseudonym of "Robertus Robertinus."[12] But from where did the Parisian lawyer procure this key work, now regarded as one of the foundational texts in defining the epistemic status of natural science? And why did he wait until November 1634 to reveal its existence to Bernegger?

Until now, historians have put their faith in Diodati's account, or at least in the details furnished by "Robertinus" in the preface to the 1636 edition. According to this account, Diodati brought back a copy of the precious document from a voyage to Italy in 1619 or 1620.[13] Few of the facts, however, lend credence to this version of events. For one, Diodati's supposed journey to Italy is not otherwise attested to; it seems doubtful that it ever occurred.[14] Also, considering the role of organizer that he saw himself as playing at the center of the "Republic of Letters," it would have been uncharacteristic of him never to have made known to any of his friends or correspondents that he was in possession of Galileo's *Letter*. One of his correspondents, Nicolas Fabri de Peiresc of Provence (1582–1637), who himself maintained close ties with numerous Italian intellectuals, did not even learn of the letter's existence until December 1633.[15] But above all, it is entirely implausible that this text, had it been in Diodati's hands for fifteen years, would not have occupied a prominent place from the beginning in the appendices of the *Systema cosmicum.* One of Diodati's first reactions was to take advantage of the publication of the Latin version of the *Dialogo,* as we have seen, to add as appendices two highly relevant documents supporting the compatibility of heliocentrism with Scripture, one of them by then unavailable in print, Foscarini's *Letter,* a copy of which he had procured earlier from Peiresc.[16]

The most believable hypothesis, corroborated by the fact that there was suddenly an opportunity to replace Foscarini's *Letter* with the much better *Letter to Christina* at the beginning of 1635,[17] is that Diodati, familiar as he was with Galileo's writings, did not himself become acquainted with the *Letter* before November 1634. In a letter to Diodati of January 15, 1633, written just before his departure to Rome, Galileo had alluded to the *Letter to Christina* and had even declared his intention of forwarding him a copy when times would become less turbulent, but subsequent events did not, apparently, afford him such leisure.[18] The evidence thus leads one to believe that, in effect, the "Robertinus" version of how Diodati had come by the *Letter to Christina* is but a story fabricated by Diodati himself, whose only objective was to conceal the name of the person at the origin of the publication: Galileo himself.

In his letter of May 16, 1634, Diodati asked Galileo if he wished to take advantage of the forthcoming publication of the *Systema cosmicum* to quietly compose a new piece, whether to complete the demonstrations set forth in the text or to respond to the attacks of the Aristotelians, who had had ample time to sharpen their weapons since the publication of the *Dialogo* in February 1632.[19] Galileo did not follow up these suggestions in his response of July 25: though he certainly would have liked to publish the comments with which he had filled the margins of his copies of books written by adversaries of Copernicanism, he preferred to devote himself to the completion of his other great work, the treatise on mechanics that appeared in Leyden in 1638 under the title of *Discorsi e dimostrazioni matematiche, intorno a due nuove scienze.* This, at least, is what can be gleaned from a reading of the letter so far as it has come down to us; the text we have is unfortunately incomplete.[20] One cannot exclude the possibility that Galileo might have transmitted other information in this letter, or even in a separate note.

The packet containing Galileo's letter was dispatched from Florence in late July. But it took its time in reaching Galileo's merchant cousin in Lyon, Roberto Galilei, who served as a reliable intermediary between the two friends. Diodati, who returned to Paris in October 1634 after a few months' stay in his hometown of Geneva, passed through Lyon on his way home, where Roberto gave him a further letter from Galileo in Florence dated September 23; the July 25 letter, it appears, had not yet arrived. The second letter of September 23, lost today, apparently made known to Diodati something of the content of the first; he was clearly worried, in consequence, over what had become of the packet.[21] Was he worried only because it contained lenses for astronomical telescopes, destined for the French astronomer, Pierre Gassendi, a mutual friend? When Diodati finally received the packet in early November, he had the lenses delivered to their intended recipient[22] and sent off a letter from Galileo to Matthias Bernegger in Strasbourg, thanking him for his work on the translation.[23] On December 4, Bernegger replied to Diodati:

> Your letter and Galileo's have filled me with great pleasure. . . . I hope, or rather I have firm confidence, that it [the *Systema cosmicum*] will be out for the Spring Fair, as long as the appendices for which you are hoping are not too long in coming. I beg you to hasten to send me both the poem from Pisa and that piece of Galileo's, regarding which you have certainly made my mouth water and which you have undertaken to add. I will make sure that both the one and the other are printed in an irreproachable manner.[24]

It is difficult to see only coincidence between the fact that Diodati passed on a letter of Galileo's to Bernegger and that he revealed to him at the same time his intention to attach two supplementary texts to the Latin edition being prepared in Strasbourg. One of these two pieces, whose delay caused as much anxiety in Lyon as it did in Florence, was evidently a copy of the *Letter to Christina,* intended for publication.[25] As for the *carmen Pisanum* mentioned by Bernegger, it never reached Diodati. And the matter of the poem affords another substantial clue to support the thesis that Galileo did, indeed, send the *Letter* himself. It is known, from the pen of Vincenzo Viviani who received from Diodati in 1655 the entire correspondence that Galileo had sent to Paris, that it was Galileo himself who had indicated to Diodati his intention of sending him a poem by Niccolò Aggiunti, mathematics professor in Pisa ("the poem from Pisa"), though he never became able to do it.[26]

After receiving the manuscript at the beginning of November 1634, Diodati, probably preoccupied by other affairs, delayed in sending his translation back to Bernegger. Four months went by before the translation reached Strasbourg in March 1635, too late to appear with the *Systema cosmicum.*[27] Since the *Letter to Christina* would now have to be published separately, it became necessary to write a preface for this new text. In late August, Bernegger, expecting to complete this task himself as he had done in his just published translation of the *Dialogo,* consulted Diodati regarding the arguments he should develop there.[28] But Diodati took it upon himself to do it, not surprisingly under the pseudonym of "Robertinus," the man whom Bernegger, in his own preface to the *Systema cosmicum* (March 1635), had already involved as the supposed messenger of the *Letter to Christina.* Robert Roberthin (1600–1648) was not a fictitious person: the German poet, living in Danzig, was a friend of Bernegger's but had nothing to do with either Galileo or the publication of the *Letter to Christina.*[29]

This shows that the date of January 6, 1635, heading the printed version of the preface to the *Letter to Christina,* signed "Robertinus," could not have been accurate; it had evidently been set back by several months, indeed by almost a year, for it was not until December 20, 1635, that Bernegger finally acknowledged receipt of the preface from Diodati![30] Bernegger himself modified the date to make the timing more plausible. He had told his readers in the preface of the earlier *Systema cosmicum* that Roberthin had sent him a new piece, which, having arrived too late for publication, would appear in a separate edition. "Roberthin's" letter, prefacing the *Letter to Christina,* by this logic would have to have been composed some weeks at least before this, the minimum time necessary for it to pass from Danzig through warring Germany to reach Strasbourg.

Why, then, did Bernegger have to wait until the end of 1635 to receive the preface? The answer to this question can be found in the National Library in Florence, which owns a manuscript version of "Roberthin's" letter-preface in the handwriting of the letter's real author, Diodati.[31] The importance of this manuscript is twofold. First, it represents a version prior to the one printed in 1636, as it differs in certain respects from the latter, principally in matters of style. Second, the letter, already signed "Robertus Robertinus" but without mention of the date, bears the inscription *Pref.^{ne}* (preface), in Galileo's distinctive handwriting, on the reverse.[32]

If Diodati sent what he had composed to Galileo, it must have been in order to ask his advice about it. He could not have sent it merely to inform him, for three reasons. First, because if this had been the case, he would surely have waited and sent the printed version, which was soon to be released. Second, because the handwritten version is not completely identical to the printed one: if he had been simply sending Galileo a copy by way of information, he would have sent it in the definitive format that he was preparing to send to Bernegger. Third, because the content was in itself too sensitive and personal for Diodati—who was always careful to protect Galileo's interests—to act without first consulting his friend. The fact that Bernegger did not receive the preface until December allowed Diodati, to all appearances, the window of time necessary to consult the principal person involved, the author and originator of the *Letter to the Grand Duchess Christina.*[33]

If this collection of clues indeed gives good grounds to believe that it was Galileo who originated the 1636 edition of his *Letter,* it would not be surprising that evidence of it would have been deliberately concealed by the affair's protagonists. Diodati, for his part, displayed the utmost discretion regarding the intentions of Galileo, as is proven by the copy of Galileo's letter dated July 25, 1634, kept at Carpentras among Peiresc's papers: a passage missing from the copy sent by Diodati to Peiresc could be reinserted by the editors of the *Opere,* thanks to the notes Viviani took on the original that Diodati sent him in 1655. The content of this excised passage was hardly trivial: in it, Galileo announced to his correspondent that he planned to publish one day, under a pseudonym, a collection containing the numerous annotations that he had made in the margins of his adversaries' books. This was a piece of information that, quite obviously, was not to be divulged and that Diodati voluntarily omitted from the copy of Galileo's letter that he sent to Peiresc.[34]

This concern for discretion is all the more relevant to questions pertaining to the edition of the *Letter to the Grand Duchess Christina,* for which no answers are forthcoming in the known correspondence between Galileo and Diodati. Prudent in even the most minor details, the Parisian lawyer signed his letters to his Tuscan correspondent with a pseudonym, without indicating the recipient's name.[35] Furthermore, he strongly urged Bernegger not to mention his name in the preface to the *Systema cosmicum,* which was why Bernegger had called upon "Roberthin" to explain how he could have the *Letter to Christina* in his possession. It was absolutely necessary to avoid linking Diodati to the *Letter to Christina* so that Galileo should not be suspected of connivance.[36] One can understand, then, his displeasure upon reading Bernegger's printed response to the letter-preface of "Roberthin";[37] he shared his unhappiness with Peiresc in a letter of March 6, 1637: "Mr. Bernegger, specifically against my wishes, has without any reason and also without care for the author, who must not be suspected of being involved, named me in his epistle responding to the preface."[38]

Finally, one last hint. Viviani's desire to preserve the memory of his master free from all reproach led him to set forth, in his *Historical Account of the Life of Galileo* (composed in large part in 1654, published in 1717), an "official" version of the genesis of the Latin edition of the *Dialogo,* one that takes its own liberties with the facts:

> It was impossible to prevent this work, the System of the World, from arriving in the countries beyond the Alps, and for this reason it was soon translated into Latin and published in Germany by the below-named Matthias Bernegger. . . . When he became aware of these translations and of these new publications of his writings, Signor Galileo was greatly mortified by them, realizing as he did the impossibility of succeeding in suppressing these writings and all those others that he knew to be dispersed in manuscript form throughout Italy and abroad.[39]

It is not surprising, then, that the direct proofs we would like to have regarding the transmission of the *Letter to Christina* to Paris failed to make it through the filters of discretion and of prudence imposed by those most directly involved, even after Galileo's death.

Turning to a different topic, should we be surprised that Galileo would decide to send, to Strasbourg via Paris, a manuscript more than twenty years old, given the risks that this involved for him? The *Letter to Christina* possesses a certain quality, conveyed by the name *Apologeticus* or *Apologia* that Bernegger gave it in his correspondence as well as in his preface to the *Systema cosmicum*. It is a combative text, written in the tense context of the mid–1610s, at the very time a complaint was being lodged with the Holy Office against Galileo and the theories he supported. The first pages of the *Letter to Christina* recall, in effect, the "vain discourses" of the philosophy professors who had challenged him in defense of the opinions they taught, in total disregard of the evidence furnished by the proofs he had given them; they recall above all the personal attacks to which the professors had resorted in order to bring him down to earth. Galileo was already presenting in this work his "justification to the whole world."[40]

This text, the manuscript circulation of which in the year of its writing (1615) has certainly been overestimated, was thus resurrected for use at this opportune moment. Friends of Galileo, hopeful of its apologetic value, had the *Letter* shown in high places, to the Master of the Sacred Palace, Niccolò Riccardi, in September 1632, when they learned the news of the investigative commission set up by the Holy Office, and later to Cardinal Antonio Barberini in 1636, as a testimonial that might alleviate the hardship of the prisoner of Arcetri.[41] In the meantime, the author himself seized the first available opportunity to make the *Letter* known, an opportunity that would also have seemed to him especially attractive. The publication of the *Systema cosmicum* would carry his apology outside the microcosm of Rome to the European stage, as a just response to the enormous publicity given his condemnation by the ecclesiastical authorities.

Diodati and Bernegger may well have considered this apologetic work to be capable of standing on its own. But its appearance as a separate publication offered Diodati the opportunity to shore it up further by writing, in the guise of an introduction, the first public defense of the man condemned in 1633. Testimony to Galileo's extreme satisfaction at this initiative appeared in a missive sent to Bernegger on July 15, 1636,[42] as well as the desire he expressed to have a number of copies of the work immediately imported to Italy, "to the confusion" of his "calumnious enemies"![43]

The Parisian lawyer's defense of Galileo, which he had sent to his "client" before its publication, conveys faithfully Galileo's own interpretation of the events of 1633. If one rereads the two letters Diodati received from Galileo dated March 7 and July 25, 1634, as well as those written to Peiresc on February 21 and March 16, 1635, of which Diodati had obtained copies from Galileo himself,[44] and if one then adds to these the first few pages of the *Letter to Christina* itself, one can follow in these sources, sometimes word for word, the essentials of the arguments that Diodati set forth in his preface. Thus in the aftermath of his condemnation Galileo had found a providential forum that allowed him to take a devastating revenge on his judges and his censors.

Without going into detail here regarding Diodati's preface, it should be emphasized that, rather than running the risk of venturing into the controversy on his own account, he preferred to restrict himself closely to the arguments that Galileo himself had provided in his various letters. In none of those did Galileo enter into the details of the trial. He returned again and again, however, to two themes: his innocence and the relentlessness of his rabid adversaries.[45] He shared with his Parisian friend, in his letter of July 25, 1634, a personal conviction: "You see that it is not for this or that opinion that I was and am attacked, but because I incur the disfavor of the Jesuits."[46]

Diodati was quick to pick up on this message, and indeed he structured his preface around this theme of hidden machinations. Although he preferred not to name the Jesuits explicitly in order to keep the Strasbourg editions free of any suspicion of having confessional designs, the Jesuits found themselves in fact implicitly implicated, since they were regarded as the principal guardians of orthodoxy within the large reactionary faction composed, according to Diodati, of the dogmatic defenders of the philosophy of the schools.

The most severe blow that Galileo had suffered, the author of the preface emphasized, was to be pronounced "extremely harmful, and stained by the most horrible heresies and impieties against the Church and the Catholic Faith."[47] Such slanders were what affected him the most deeply, as he wrote to Peiresc on February 21, 1635: "Many might have been able to behave and speak in a much more learned manner, but no one, not even among the Holy Fathers, would have been able to do so with more piety or with a greater zeal for the Holy Church, or ultimately with a holier intention than mine. . . . In reading all my works, nobody will find even the smallest shadow of anything straying from piety and reverence towards the Holy Church."[48]

Before his arrival in Rome in January 1633, in response to the summons of the Holy Office, Galileo had already called on these same arguments in a letter to Cardinal Francesco Barberini on October 13, 1632:

> I am more than sure to have made so perfectly clear and evident my sincerity of soul and my very pure, very zealous, and very holy affection for the Holy Church, its Head and its ministers, that no one, except for those whose minds have been affected by their passions, could fail to recognize that I have conducted myself in a way so pious and Catholic that not even one of the Fathers bearing the title of "saint" could have displayed a greater piety.[49]

If the reconstruction above of the events surrounding the publication of the *Letter to Christina* in 1636 could raise a doubt as to the sincerity of lines like these penned by Galileo, nevertheless recourse to a broader context would lead one to understand that the Italian savant never stopped thinking of himself as a faithful ally of the Catholic Church.[50] Against the backdrop of rivalry between *germanitas* and *romanitas,* he always strove to draw the doctrine of the Canon Copernicus into the embrace of the Roman Church, much though one might have perceived it to be the province of heretics only. More than this, in that context of orthodoxies that kept hardening, his concern was to challenge a Protestant monopoly on the *libertas philoso-phandi* so necessary to the advancement of the sciences.

There is a double paradox, then, about what happened in those days following the 1633 condemnation. Not only did Galileo disobey the ecclesiastical authorities, all the while proclaiming his unfailing loyalty to the Church, but he appealed to the devotion of his Protestant admirers in order once again to attempt to convert Rome to heliocentrism. This attitude was certainly the product of blindness as much as of sincerity. The Italian philosopher was still convinced that it was not the whole Church but a faction at its center that had provoked his condemnation. What he did not understand—or did not care to understand—was that the institution as a whole was committed by the exercise of authority on the part of Pope Urban VIII and that the time had passed for the debating of ideas.[51]

Notes

Translation by Rayanne K. Truesdell and Ernan McMullin.

1. This is evident from the decree pronounced by Urban VIII on June 16, 1633; see Galileo Galilei, *Opere di Galileo Galilei* (hereafter *OGG*), ed. Antonio Favaro (1890–1909; reprint, Florence: Giunti Barbèra, 1968), 19:283. On the question of the doctrinal significance of Galileo's condemnation, see Francesco Beretta, "Le procès de Galilée et les archives du Saint-Office: Aspects judiciaires et théologiques d'une condamnation célèbre," *Revue des Sciences Philosophiques et Théologiques* 83 (1999): 441–90, esp. 483.

2. Antonio Favaro, "Mattia Bernegger," in *Amici e corrispondenti di Galileo,* ed. Paolo Galluzzi (Florence: Salimbeni, 1983), 3:1358–59.

3. *Systema cosmicum, authore Galilaeo Galilaei Lynceo, Academiae Pisanae mathematico extraordinario, Serenissimi Magni-Ducis Hetruriae philosopho et mathematico primario: In quo quatuor dialogis, de duobus maximis mundi systematibus, Ptolemaico & Copernicano, utriusque rationibus philosophicis ac naturalibus indefinite propositis, disseritur. Ex Italica lingua Latine conversum. Accessit appendix gemina, qua SS. Scripturae dicta cum terrae mobilitate conciliantur* (Augustae Treboc ([Strasbourg]: Impensis Elzeviriorum, Davidis Hautti, 1635).

4. Based most notably on the research of Emil Wohlwill, "Galilei betreffende Handschriften der Hamburger Stadtbibliothek," *Jahrbuch der Hamburgischen Wissenschaftlichen Anstalten* 12 (1894): 149–223.

5. Michele Cioni, *I documenti galileiani del S. Uffizio di Firenze* (1908; reprint, Florence: Pagnini, 1996), 38 n. 3.

6. *Nov-antiqua sanctissimorum patrum et probatorum theologorum doctrina de Sacrae Scripturae testimoniis, in conclusionibus mere naturalibus, quae sensata experientia et necessariis demonstrationibus evinci possunt, temere non usurpandis: in gratiam Serenissimae Christinae Lotharingae, Magnae-Ducis Hetruriae, privatim ante complures annos Italico idiomate conscripta a Galilaeo Galiaeo,*

nobili florentino, primario serenitatis eius philosopho et mathematico: nunc vero iuris publici facta, cum Latina versione italico textui simul adiuncta (Augustae Treboc ([Strasbourg]: Impensis Elseviriorum, Typis Davidis Hautti, 1636). For convenience's sake, this work will henceforth be referred to by the commonly used title *Letter to the Grand Duchess Christina.*

7. The conclusions presented here were the subject of an earlier article, Stéphane Garcia, "L'édition strasbourgeoise du *Systema cosmicum* (1635–1636), dernier combat copernicien de Galilée," *Bulletin de la Société de l'Histoire du Protestantisme Français* 146 (2000): 307–34.

8. Leone Allaci, *Apes urbanae, sive de viris illustribus, qui ab anno MDCXXX per totum MDCXXXII Romae adfuerunt, ac typis aliquid evulgarunt, Romae, exc. L. Grignanus* (1633; reprint, with introd. by Michel-Pierre Lerner, Lecce: Conte, 1999), 119.

9. See Stéphane Garcia, "Elie Diodati–Galilée: La rencontre de deux logiques," in *Largo campo di filosofare: Eurosymposium Galileo 2001,* ed. José Montesinos and Carlos Solís (La Orotava: Fundacion Canaria Orotava de Historia de la Ciencia, 2001), 883–92. See also Stéphane Garcia, *Galiléi-Elie Diodati: Naissance d'un réseau scientifique dans l'Europe du XVIIe siècle* (Geneva: Georg, 2004).

10. Claus Bünger, *Matthias Bernegger, ein Bild aus dem geistigen Leben Straßburgs zur Zeit des dreissigjährigen Krieges* (Strasbourg: Trübner, 1893).

11. Original title: *Lettera del R. P. M. Paolo Antonio Foscarini, Carmelitano, sopra l'opinione de' Pittagorici e del Copernico della mobilità della Terra e stabilità del Sole e del nuovo pittagorico sistema del mondo, nella quale si accordano ed appaciano i luoghi della Sacra Scrittura e le proposizioni teologiche che giammai possano addursi contro tale opinione. Al Reverendissimo P. M Sebastiano Fantone, Generale dell' Ordine Carmelitano* (Naples: Lazaro Scoriggio, 1615). Title of the Latin edition: *Epistola R. P. M. Pauli Antonii Foscarini Carmelitani, circa Pythagoricum et Copernici opinionem de mobilitate Terrae et stabilitatis Solis: et de novo systemate seu constitutione mundi: In qua Sacrae Scripturae autoritates et theologicae propositiones, communiter adversus hanc opinionem adducate conciliantur. Ad Reverendissimum P. M. Sebastianum Fantonum, Generalem Ordinis Carmelitani. Ex Italica in Latinam linguam perspicue et fideliter nunc conversa. Iuxta editonem Neapoli typis excusam Apud Lazarum Scorrigium anno 1615 cum approbatione theologorum.* The text appears on pages 465–95 of the *Systema cosmicum.*

12. The Robertus Robertinus preface, which is presented in the form of a letter addressed to Bernegger, Jan. 6, 1635, is reproduced in *OGG,* 16:194–95. It is followed by a brief response from Bernegger (*OGG,* 16:389–90).

13. "I carefully kept this discourse among the precious things I brought back . . . fifteen years ago from my journey, in Italy" (*OGG,* 16:194–95). The letter is dated Jan. 6, 1635.

14. He is known to have been in Paris in August 1620, from where he sent Galileo a letter, the contents of which indicate clearly that the two men had never met (*OGG,* 14:48).

15. *OGG,* 15:363.

16. *OGG,* 16:433.

17. Diodati, in a letter now lost, had therefore suggested to Bernegger that it would be better to replace Foscarini's *Letter* by the *Letter to Christina,* which he judged to be markedly better. Why else wait until the beginning of 1635 to recommend this editorial decision, if not because Diodati had only just discovered the contents of the *Letter to Christina?* "I eagerly await your advice, and all the more eagerly wait for Galileo's promised appendix, to be attached in the place of the Foscarini piece" (Bernegger to Diodati, Feb. 2–12, 1635, *OGG,* 16:212)

18. *OGG,* 15:25.

19. "Thus it seemed to me advisable to let you know, your lordship, and have you consider whether, with such an opportunity offering and given also the fact of the Latin translation, it would seem to you opportune to introduce a memoir of some sort, by way of amplification or clarification, or as a refutation of [Jean-Baptiste] Morin or [Libert] Froidmont, which, if done under another name and with the necessary care and precaution, should entail no untoward consequence" (*OGG,* 16:96).

20. See the clarification offered by Favaro that heads letter no. 2970 (*OGG,* 16:115) and below, n. 34.

21. In his letters, Roberto Galilei distinguishes the letter (*lettera,* like that of Sept. 23) from the *piego,* which signifies a package like that of July 25. R. Galilei to Galileo, Oct. 16, 1634: "E ancora lui [Diodati] è in pensiero del piegho, havendoli fatto vedere in quello consisteva" (*OGG,* 16:142). Galileo himself seems to have been particularly preoccupied by the delay ("S. S.ᵃ ne era in pena e travaglio," Oct. 30, *OGG,* 16:146).

22. Diodati to Gassendi, Nov. 10, 1634 (*OGG,* 16:153): "Peu de jours après mon arrivée, j'ay receu le pacquet de M. Galilei, qui estoit demeuré par chemin avec les cristaux du telescope qu'il vous envoye." ("A few days after my arrival, I received Mr. Galilei's package, which shared its journey with these telescope lenses that he sends you.")

23. This letter of Galileo's, dated July 16, 1634, was in fact written in April 1634 by Niccolò Aggiunti at the request of Galileo, who was still stricken by the death of his daughter Virginia (Favaro, "Mattia Bernegger," 1363–64). The marginal annotation in the manuscript in the National Library of Florence ("1634. Lettre de M.ʳ Galilei à M.ʳ Bernecker du 16 Aoust," Ms Gal. 87, fol. 82v), in handwriting not identified by Favaro, is actually in Diodati's hand. The error in the date is corrected just beside it by Viviani (see the explanation of this letter, *OGG,* 16:111).

24. "Ingenti me voluptate perfuderunt et tuae et vero Galilaicae litterae. . . . Spero, vel confido potius, mercatu verno proditurum, nisi tamen accessoria illa, quorum spem feci, remorentur longius. Oro festines mittere et carmen illum Pisanum et maxime, de qua salivam certe movisti mihi, Galilaei scriptum, quod addendum suscepisti. Curabo, utrumque imprimatur emendatissime" (*OGG,* 16:168).

25. It is also noteworthy that on Oct. 14, 1634, Fulgenzio Micanzio, a longtime friend of Galileo's, acknowledged receipt of a copy of the *Letter to the Grand Duchess,* of whose existence he had not previously been aware (*OGG,* 16:140–41). This was undoubtedly not a coincidence: Galileo had evidently decided to circulate this apologetics text among his most loyal supporters.

26. Viviani to Diodati, Feb. 23, 1656: "Reading the letters has excited my curiosity and has prompted the desire to know, your Excellency, whether your Excellency has received a copy of Signor Niccolò Aggiunti's poem, which Signor Galileo in a letter of his says that he wishes to send you." Diodati's response, June 24, 1656: "Signor Niccolò Aggiunti's poem has indeed not reached me, but Signor Galileo in his letter of December 18 [1635; see *OGG,* 16:361], wrote me that the Grand Duke had all of his [Aggiunti's] writings called in with a view to their publication; even though this has not been done, it is nevertheless plausible that they should have been retained." Paolo Galluzzi and Maurizio Torrini, eds., *Le opere dei discepoli di Galileo Galilei* (Florence: Giunti Barbèra, 1975–84), 306, 351.

27. Bernegger to Diodati, Mar. 14, 1635 (*OGG,* 16:233).

28. To Diodati, Aug. 31, 1635: "In the preface of the Apologetic (which will be printed once the other pages are done), I will try to offer praises to the author more than I have done in the *Systema* itself. I would like very much to know from you whether, briefly summarized, which praises I could write, not because they are unknown to me but because they are better known to you" (*OGG,* 16:307).

29. The idea of calling upon "Robertinus" to play a role was Bernegger's: he presented it to Diodati on May 4, 1635 (*OGG,* 16:263).

30. *OGG,* 16:366.

31. Ms Gal. 316, fol. 296r–297v.

32. Ibid., fol. 297v. The editors of Galileo's *Opere* in their reproduction of the preface to the *Letter to the Grand Duchess,* indicate the existence of this manuscript version and themselves positively identify Galileo's handwriting (*OGG,* 16:194).

33. Between the months of June and November 1635, the period that interests us here, Diodati and Galileo exchanged twelve letters, of which only four were recopied (and then only partially) by Viviani and printed in the *Opere.* The others were lost.

34. The copy in the Carpentras Library (ms. 1810 fols. 23–25r) is not in Diodati's handwriting but in that of one of Peiresc's secretaries. Rather than a copyist's error (which is Favaro's hypothesis, in *Miscellanea Galileiana inedita: Studi e ricerche* [Venice: Antonelli, 1887], 163), it is more likely that the omission from the text is due to an intervention from the person most directly responsible, Diodati himself.

35. R. Galilei to Galileo, Mar. 19, 1635 (*OGG,* 16:238): "[The letter] which Signor Diodati has entrusted to me I enclose here in the same state in which he sent it to me, without any title and under a false name."

36. Their relationship had been public knowledge since they were named by Allaci in 1633. See Allaci, *Apes urbanae,* 119.

37. Reproduced in *OGG,* 16:389–90.

38. *OGG,* 17:41.

39. "Racconto istorico della vita del Sig. Galileo Galilei . . . ," in *OGG,* 19:618.

40. "[G]iustificazione appresso l'universale." *Lettera a Cristina sull'uso della Bibbia nelle argumentazioni scientifiche,* ed. Franco Motta (Genoa: Marietti, 2000), 92.

41. Magalotti to Guiducci, Rome, Sept. 4, 1632, with Castelli's agreement (*OGG,* 14:380); Castelli to Galileo, Aug. 9, 1636 (*OGG,* 16:461): "At the moment, I am having the letter to the most Serene [Grand Duchess] copied for the use of Cardinal Antonio. Who knows?"

42. "I just recently received the frontispiece, with the two letters [that of Robertinus as well as Bernegger's short response], which I like very much" (*OGG,* 16:451).

43. While in Micanzio (and thus in direct contact with Louis Elzevier in Venice), June 28 and July 12, 1636 (*OGG,* 16:445, 449).

44. Galluzzi and Torrini, *Le opere dei discepoli,* 350–51.

45. To Diodati, Mar. 7, 1634 (*OGG,* 16:59): "The infamy abounds on traitors and those who are firmly fixed in ignorance of the highest degree, the mother of malignity, of envy, of rage, of anger, and of all those other vices and sins that are wicked and ugly"; again to Diodati, July 25, 1634 (*OGG,* 16:116): "the mad rage of my most powerful persecutors"; to Peiresc, Feb. 21, 1635 (*OGG,* 16:215–16): "I do not hope for any pardon and that because I have not committed any crime. . . . Toward someone who is condemned even though innocent, it is

appropriate to maintain the rigor [of the law] in order to make it seem as though one had acted justly."

46. *OGG,* 16:117.

47. "Nocentissimum et atrocissimis haeresibus impietatibusque contra Catholicam Ecclesiam ac Fidem inquinatum."

48. *OGG,* 16:215–16. In his preface, Diodati wrote of his friend: "a nullo, etiam eorum qui sanctimoniae celebritate claruerunt, quicquam religiosius in hoc argumento dici potuerit." He also noted his "opera in quibus nihil quicquam Catolicae fidei et debitate erga Ecclesiam observantiae adversum reperire est."

49. *OGG,* 15:408.

50. See Isabelle Pantin, "New Philosophy and Old Prejudices: Aspects of the Reception of Copernicanism in a Divided Europe," *Studies in History and Philosophy of Science* 30:2 (1999): 237–62, and "'Dissiper les ténèbres qui restent encore à percer': Galilée, l'Eglise conquérante et la république des philosophes," in *Révolution scientifique et libertinage,* ed. A. Mothu (Turnhout: Brepols, 2000), 11–34.

51. Francesco Beretta, "Urbain VIII Barberini protagoniste de la condamnation de Galilée," in Montesinos and Solís, *Largo campo di filosofare,* 549–73.

ELEVEN

CENSORSHIP OF ASTRONOMY IN ITALY AFTER GALILEO

John L. Heilbron

In 1820, Giuseppe Settele, a professor at the University of Rome, submitted a book on optics and astronomy to the Master of the Sacred Palace (the pope's official theologian and overseer/censor of the Roman press) for a license to print. The censor, Filippo Anfossi, refused permission because Settele taught the heliocentric system openly in defiance of the decrees issued at the time of the condemnation of Galileo. Anfossi interpreted the old finding that Copernican theory was false and contrary to Scripture, and the Inquisition's charge that, in teaching it, Galileo had made himself "vehemently suspected of heresy," as establishing heliocentrism as heretical. With the help of colleagues who wanted to see the long outdated legacy of the punishment of Galileo set aside, Settele protested to the pope, Pius VII. Pius referred the matter to the Congregation of the Index, which granted the license, and to the Holy Office, which corrected the censor: the old inquisitors had not meant that heliocentrism was contrary to faith, only that it was contrary to the "traditional reading of Scripture." Consequently, it resolved, without saying so publicly, that "[n]othing is opposed to defending Copernicus's opinion about the motion of the earth in the manner in which it customarily is now held by Catholic authors."[1]

The customary manner of talking and writing about astronomy by Catholic authors in Italy in 1820 did not differ from the customary manner in Britain, France, or Germany. That had been the case for some time. Although Galileo's *Dialogue* remained on the *Index* until 1835 (the first published revision of the *Index* after the

Settele affair), Italians had easy access to the banned work in several editions printed during the eighteenth century with the permission of the censors. The earliest of them appeared in 1744, in Galileo's *Opere,* with a preface by its editor, Giuseppe Toaldo, later a professor at the University of Padua, on the hypothetical character of astronomical systems and a dissertation by a theologian, Agostino Calmet, on the impossibility of knowing how things are. "It seems that God, being jealous, as it were, of the beauty and magnificence of his work, has reserved to himself the perfect understanding of its structure, and the secrets of its motions."[2] Apart from removal of a few postils (marginal indications of page content) in which Galileo had slipped into treating the Copernican theory as truth, the *Dialogue* issued unscathed from the press of the Seminario of Pisa with the approval of officials of the system that continued to prohibit it. The implication that Copernican theory could be held and taught as the most useful of all the necessarily hypothetical systems of the world merely recognized the manner of teaching astronomy that by then—1744—had been customary in Italy for a long time.

The policy of tolerating violations of the law when enforcement would do more harm than good, and annulling the law when violation has become the ordinary practice, is often employed in church and state. A good administrator, like a good judge, knows when to be implacable and when to be lenient. Church officials who connived at ways to elude the force of the decrees against Copernicanism deserve notice and credit. Historians have ignored them because in not doing their jobs—that is, in not attempting to enforce a ridiculous and injurious ruling—they made no noise and because the imputed immobility of the Church over the two hundred years or so between the condemnation and reprieve of the *Dialogue* makes too good and simple a story to ruin with facts. The Roman Catholic Church itself does not claim the wise inaction of its censors as a contribution to science in Italy. The Galileo Commission created at the instigation of Pope John Paul II missed an opportunity to blunt criticism of the Church by noticing officials who found a practical way out of the predicament into which Urban VIII and his Holy Office had plunged it.[3]

In what follows I define various customary manners of handling Copernican astronomy in Italy between Galileo's defeat and Settele's victory and assign periods to their dominance. Although circumstances differed from place to place and fluctuated in the same place over time, a fourfold division may give an adequate preliminary orientation: (1) from the condemnation of heliocentrism as false in philosophy and contrary to Scripture to the elimination of the philosophical objection to the earth's motion (1633–70); (2) from the blanket condemnation of heliocentrism to its allowance if expressly designated as hypothetical (1670–1710); (3) from the requirement of explicit fictionalism to pro forma professions of it (1710–60); and (4) from nods toward fictionalism to nonchalant realism (1760–1820).

The Hunt for Heresy (1633-70)

In the Heavens

Urban VIII and the Holy Office went out of their way to frighten Copernicans. They ordered that copies of Galileo's sentence and abjuration be sent to all nuncios and inquisitors for further distribution to Catholic mathematicians and philosophers. Potential offenders living in Florence had the additional treat of hearing the sentence and recantation read to them at the local office of the Inquisition, as if they had been so many Galileos standing before the cardinals of the Holy Office. Some fifty of them attended.[4]

The circulated sentence contained not only the punishment but also the grounds for it, namely that Galileo had intentionally disobeyed an injunction given to him by Robert Bellarmine not to hold or teach the Copernican system. The decision of the Inquisition as conveyed by Bellarmine to Galileo in 1616 and by Galileo's judges to the rest of the world in 1633 ran as follows:

> That the sun is the center of the world and motionless is a proposition which is philosophically absurd and false, and formally heretical, for being explicitly contrary to Holy Scripture;

> That the earth is neither the center of the world nor motionless but moves even with diurnal motion is philosophically equally absurd and false, and theologically at least erroneous in the faith.[5]

Despite this warning and the prohibition of all Copernican books by the Congregation of the Index (the sentence continued), Galileo had persisted and at last had published his *Dialogue on the Two Chief World-Systems* without intimating to the censors that he had been enjoined from writing it. The book contained arguments in favor of the "pernicious [Copernican] doctrine" strong enough to convince credulous readers. Consequently, the Supreme and Universal Inquisition found Galileo "vehemently suspected of heresy, namely, of having held and believed a doctrine which is false and contrary to the Divine and Holy Scripture: that the sun is the center of the world and does not move from east to west, and that the earth moves and is not the center of the world, and that one may hold and defend as probable an opinion after it has been declared and defined contrary to Holy Scripture."[6]

"Vehement suspicion of heresy" (the middle degree, between light and violent suspicion), a term of inquisitorial art, was raised by such behavior as hindering the work of the Inquisition; favoring, defending, advising, or receiving heretics; and denying openly well-known tenets of the faith. A serious crime that had nothing to do with faith might also raise a vehement suspicion, "for a Catholic fears God." "Also a person can be properly suspected in faith who asserts new and singular opinions in moral matters and supports them tenaciously against common and received opinions: whence the way to heresy is very easy."[7] Galileo certainly had obstructed holy work by promulgating the strongest arguments he could devise in favor of a condemned doctrine he had been ordered to abandon; he had been obstructive and disobedient, and so confessed.

For canonical purgation *ex vehementi,* the confessed criminal knelt before the Gospels, foreswore all heresies whatsoever (the abjuration), and accepted whatever punishment the Inquisition thought fit to impose. Moderate inquisitorial opinion considered canonical penance a very serious affair and recommended that only those "whose good reputation is absolutely necessary to Christians, like bishops, priests, and preachers," should be subjected to it.[8] Galileo may have undergone an unusual procedure for a layman. Not only did he have to submit to purgation *ex vehementi,* he also received the stiffest punishment, perpetual imprisonment, usually reserved for "such as are with difficulty brought to repentance, or who have for a long while denied the truth during the trial, or who have perjured themselves." In practice the Inquisition usually commuted the imprisonment after three years and in the harshest cases after eight.[9] All this happened to Galileo, from the humiliating recantation to "formal imprisonment in this Holy Office at our pleasure." The pope soon commuted the formal detention into perpetual house arrest at Galileo's small villa outside Florence; but there was to be no reprieve.[10]

Although the inquisitors of 1633 did not know it, Galileo had progressed from light to vehement suspicion just as their manuals anticipated. He first came to the attention of the Inquisition in 1604 when he was a professor in Padua. A former assistant of his, inspired by a Jesuit orator and urged on by his confessor, appeared "spontaneously" before the Tribunal of the Inquisition in Venice to "discharge his conscience" of indications of a heretical bent he had observed in his employer. They were casting horoscopes for clients and interpreting the predictions literally; visiting his mistress over the objections of his mother; not going to church; reading the doubtful letters (eventually prohibited) of the libertine writer Aretino; and frequenting the company of Cesare Cremonini, a Paduan professor of philosophy accused of denying the immortality of the soul. Under pressure from the overseers of the University of Padua, the tribunal decided that missing Mass, living in sin, befriending a likely heretic, and practicing astrology (a standard activity of mathematicians) more literally than the Church permitted did not raise more than a light suspicion of heresy and quashed the proceedings. Fortunately for Galileo, a bureaucrat archived the documents so well that they did not surface again until 1992.[11]

The sentence against Galileo does not state explicitly that belief in the sun-centered universe is a heresy. The Holy Office judged Copernicanism to be "contrary to Scripture," which is not ipso facto heretical in the sense of contrary to faith; to proceed from "opposed to the literal meaning of Scripture" to "heretical" required at a minimum express approbation by a pope. Francesco Beretta argues that the actions of Paul V and Urban VIII met this test and, consequently, that in 1633 belief in a heliostatic universe was, or was made, a heresy; and the view of Master Anfossi of the Settele affair shows that as late as 1820 at least one high official of the Church interpreted the condemnation of the Copernican system as a finding of heresy.[12] Much informed opinion of the seventeenth century, however, held that the sun's motion had not been declared Catholic dogma. On this interpretation, which eventually won out, Galileo's offense that raised vehement suspicion was not belief in a formally declared heresy but disobedience to an order. To muddy the water further, inquisitors sometimes applied 'heresy' loosely to rebellious, licentious, or impious talk or acts that, in their experience, revealed a propensity for it.[13] In this loose and informal sense Galileo may have been a heretic to the Inquisition.

Another source of confusion about the theological status of the resting sun was a misfit between the crime specified in Galileo's sentence, which can be understood as disobedience, and the offenses mentioned in his abjuration, which cannot. The abjuration reads:

> I, Galileo . . . have been judged vehemently suspected of heresy, namely of having held and believed that the sun is in the center of the world and motionless and the earth is not in the center and moves. Therefore, desiring to remove from the minds of Your Eminences and every faithful Christian this vehement suspicion, rightly conceived against me. . . . I abjure, curse, and detest the above-mentioned errors and heresies, and in general every other error, heresy, and sect contrary to the Holy Church.[14]

The first heresy in this standard formula of recantation *de violenti* may refer to disobedience, as in the sentence of condemnation; but the "above-mentioned heresies" that rank with all the other heresies contrary to the Holy Church appear to include the Copernican system.[15]

Since the sentence and abjuration could be interpreted either as a disciplinary action against Galileo personally or as a formal condemnation of Copernicanism as a heresy, Urban's nuncios and inquisitors faced a pretty puzzle in hermeneutics. In replying to Rome (as the pope had ordered) on their methods of warning mathematicians, several nuncios characterized the abjuration as a consequence of Galileo's violation of an injunction placed by the Holy Office expressly on him. Did it apply to others? What was the relation between a finding *contra scripturam* and the declaration of a heresy? "A proposition can be heretical . . . if it is contrary to Scripture." Who was to decide? "In ambiguous questions of faith, the pope or a general council."[16] Had Urban VIII proclaimed Copernicanism a heresy? The nuncio to Venice did not think so. He referred to the Inquisition's interpretation of the passages of Holy Writ apparently opposed to Copernican geometry as an "opinion."[17]

In the short run, Urban's persecution had the effect he desired. Catholic mathematicians and philosophers living in Italy and inclined to the new astronomy kept their opinions to themselves. Galileo's disciples seldom if ever mentioned Copernicus or Kepler in their correspondence during the 1640s.[18] Eventually, however, the persecution backfired by reinforcing the perception that Galileo had suffered not for his ideas but for his disobedience to the Holy Office and his betrayal of Urban. For so Urban saw it. He had regarded Galileo as an ornament of his court. A long notice of Galileo's accomplishments, sweetened by snippets from verses in his honor written by Urban before he became pope, was scheduled for publication in the *Apes urbanae,* a *Who's Who* of men prominent in Rome between 1630 and 1633, when the scandal over the *Dialogue* erupted.[19] The editors cut the notice and removed the honey from it. That made it clear to all the other bees that Galileo had done something unpardonable to the beekeeper. The nature of the affront also was widely known.

Urban had set great store on the argument that, since God in his wisdom and power could do anything noncontradictory he pleased, he did not have to make the world to Copernicus's specifications. Urban's personal theologian, Agostino Oreggi, had published this clinching argument in 1629 together with the news that when still a cardinal Urban had discussed its bearing on the provability of heliocentrism with his learned and pious friend Galileo. On the understanding that Galileo shared or at least would respect this view and would handle competing world-systems as mere hypotheses, Urban had approved the granting of the imprimatur for the *Dialogue* by the Master of the Sacred Palace. He imposed the condition that Galileo should change the title of the book and introduce the argument from divine omnipotence against any claim of astronomy to truth.

Galileo changed the title and added the argument. He used it to make room for the Copernican system (God could have chosen it) and put its formal pronouncement in the mouth of Simplicio, the Aristotelian butt of the book. When to these insults was added Galileo's duplicity as revealed by the discovery of the (problematic)[20] injunction of 1616, Urban's cup of wrath spilled over.[21] The public humiliation and perpetual imprisonment further advertised the personal enmity in the affair. Contemporaries consequently had a wide choice for the crime or crimes of Galileo: lèse-majesté against his patron the pope; persistent disregard of the order given him by the Holy Office in 1616; inquisitorial or behavioral "heresy"; pertinacious defense of a doctrine declared contrary to Scripture by the Holy Office in decisions approved by two popes; and outright heresy.[22]

Among Atoms
From first and fundamental principles Descartes had deduced that our sun sits in the middle of a vast vortex that sweeps the planets, including the earth, in their courses.

Further, the vast vortex and the planets, and everything on the planets, and all the other solar systems required by Descartes's reasoning, were made out of the same stuff, a "matter" differentiated only verbally from space and deprived of all qualities save shape, size, and motion. Descartes had in hand a treatise on these propositions, provisionally entitled *Le monde,* when he read, in November 1633, five months after Galileo's trial, the sentence and abjuration as published in Liège in September by the papal nuncio to Cologne. "Which so astonished me," Descartes wrote to the communication center of French philosophy, the monastic cell of Father Marin Mersenne in Paris, "that I am almost resolved to burn all my papers or at least not to let anyone see them. . . . If Copernican theory is false so are all the foundations of my philosophy." Descartes shelved *Le monde,* although, living in Holland, he was well beyond the reach of Rome. He preferred a quiet life, he told Mersenne, and "for nothing in the world [!]" would he publish the slightest word against the Church.[23] He hoped eventually to win his former teachers, the Jesuits, to his opinions and to see his philosophy replace Aristotle's in their schools.

On further thought Descartes glimpsed some hope in the confusion over "heresy" in the sentence and abjuration. The Inquisition's opinion about the resting sun had not been ratified by a pope or a council, so, in his view, it could not be a matter of faith. "It might turn out as it did for [belief in] the antipodes, which once was condemned in almost the same way, and my *Monde* might see the light in our time." Still, Descartes would not jump incontinently through this loophole. "I'm not so fond of my own ideas to want to use such exceptions to maintain them."[24] A decade later, in the year of Urban's death, *Le monde* appeared, upgraded to *Principia philosophiae.* Descartes had looked deeply into the matter of motion during the interval and discovered that he could "deny the motion of the earth with greater care than Copernicus [took] and more truth than Tycho." Descartes observed that the planets floated, that is, rested, in the vortex, while the sun, by not participating in the whirlpool, rotated relative to it.[25] By giving Descartes time and cause for these reflections, the Inquisition made an important contribution to the theory of relativity.

A few French clerics during the 1640s espoused Copernican ideas more or less openly by taking advantage of the loophole that Descartes had disdained. A leading example is Pierre Gassendi, who, in his *Institutio astronomica* of 1647, justified including the Copernican as well as the Ptolemaic and Tychonic "hypotheses" on the quibble that the Holy Office had silenced only Galileo. No doubt, Gassendi added, should the Church properly proscribe heliocentrism in general, Copernicans would be happy to recognize and renounce their error. Gassendi's often reprinted *Institutio* was the most important early source of Copernicus's ideas in France.[26] Mersenne publicized Galileo's results, blamed his trouble on his disobedience, favored heliocentrism, recommended the Tychonic system, and offered planetary distances according to the Copernican hypothesis.[27] Even in Italy during the 1630s and 1640s some bold souls taught heliocentrism hypothetically, protected by the arguments that the prohibition applied only to Galileo or, if more general, then only to physics, not to astronomy.[28]

Descartes's *Principia* attracted heresy hunters. The Jesuits prohibited his philosophy on their general principle that novelties should not be taught in their schools until generally accepted elsewhere—that is, until they were no longer novel.[29] Thus, concerning the anti-Aristotelian proposition that the heavens were fluid and corruptible, the Society's pedagogical police (*revisori*) wrote in 1649, long after Jesuit astronomers had accepted celestial change in novas and sunspots and free motion of planets in Tycho's world-system, "[T]his doctrine, since it is now common, can be permitted although at another time it had been prohibited in the Society, since it was not yet common."[30] At the same time (1651), the Society issued a new syllabus that prohibited, among many other still dangerous novelties, the atomic theory and the motion of the earth.[31]

In 1663, with the help of the Society, Descartes's *Monde,* in the form of the *Principia,* and several other Cartesian texts, reached the *Index of Prohibited Books.* Action followed a complaint by the theological faculty of the University of Louvain against their colleagues in arts and medicine, who entertained Descartes's ideas. The papal nuncio, alarmed not so much by the penetration of the new doctrine as by the prospect of disorder in the university, informed the professor of theology at the Jesuits' normal school, the Collegio Romano, whence the news traveled to the Vatican. The expert assigned by the Holy Office to read the *Principia* found worthy of censure the theses that

- "prime matter, material substantial forms, and accidental qualities do not exist"
- "material substance consists in the actual extension of a thing . . . nor is there anything else"
- "the earth moves with a circular motion and is one of the planets, and the sun stands fixed and unmoved"
- "the universe of corporeal substances has no bounds and ends in no place, and all possible worlds in fact exist."[32]

Four volumes of Descartes's work were duly indexed "until corrected," but since the obnoxious propositions touched the foundation of his system, the corrections never appeared.

The first pair of Descartes's errors was more grievous than the second. He left no room for real accidents like color, taste, and smell capable of existence outside the mind of their perceivers. But the physics of transubstantiation as confirmed by the Council of Trent preserved the real accidents (and thus the taste and appearance) of the bread and wine while the priest transformed their substance into the body and blood of Christ. Descartes destroyed the meanings of the terms in which theologians were wont to make mystery less mysterious.[33]

The threat of materialism to transubstantiation had been discerned earlier by enemies of Galileo, who had tried to interest the Holy Office in the occasional atomism of Galileo's anti-Jesuitical tract *Il saggiatore* (1624). They pointed to the distinction he drew between primary qualities truly existing in bodies (size, position, number) and secondary qualities like "taste, odor, colors and so on . . . [which] reside only in the consciousness" and to his elucidation of heat, light, and other secondaries in terms of atoms or corpuscles. An anonymous whistle-blower pointed out to the Holy Office that Galileo's theory made "greatly difficult the existence of the accidents of the bread and wine which in the Most Holy Sacrament are separated from their substance."[34] Redondi's ascription of this denunciation to the Jesuit butt of the *Saggiatore,* Oratio Grassi, is now generally doubted, but a second anonymous accusation to the same effect, recently discovered in the same file in the archives of the former Holy Office, points to the Society. The accuser was Melchior Inchofer, S.J., who also advised Galileo's judges during the trial.

The discoverer of the first document, Pietro Redondi, imagined that had charges been brought against Galileo for teaching an atomistic materialism subversive of the mystery of the Eucharist, he would have suffered a dreadful fate, but that owing to his friendship with Pope Urban he was allowed to plead guilty to the lesser offense of disobeying the old order against teaching Copernicanism.[35] The discoverer of the second document, Mariano Artigas, observed that it probably was an in-house evaluation of the first one and that it played no significant role in the trial.[36] Apparently the Holy Office judged, perhaps with the help of friends of Galileo and enemies of the Jesuits, that the atomism of the *Saggiatore,* which makes no reference to the Eucharist or any other theological business, gave them no plausible basis for action. The accusations went to a clerk, who archived them.[37] Nonetheless, they were revived from time to time, especially during the campaign against Descartes, who could be the more easily compromised by showing that a person vehemently suspected of heresy had shared his world-system.[38]

These few episodes in the hunt for heresy in atomistic and Cartesian physics illustrate wider aspects in the functioning of the censorship. For one, as with Descartes and his *Monde,* it encouraged self-censorship. For another, pressing home an accusation usually required assiduity, a champion, and luck. Descartes's *Principia* did not become the subject of an inquisitorial proceeding until trouble at an important Catholic university caused a worried nuncio to report the problem to a Jesuit theologian, who informed the pope, and the pope, Alexander VII, thinking that Cartesianism might give support to Jansenism, referred the business to the Holy Office. Action followed swiftly. Third, the machinery of censorship could be put in train to settle grudges or indulge jealousies. Those who accused Galileo of teaching an atomism subversive of the Eucharist very probably were motivated at least as much by ill will toward him as by concern for the faith. Higher-ups stopped the process because they knew it would not succeed, or because they recognized it as a vendetta, or because they favored Galileo. With different people in authority, the attack might have succeeded and the menace to the eucharistic mystery been added to the other derogatory evidence in Galileo's file.

Around the New Almagest

In 1651, Giovambattista Riccioli, S.J., published a most valuable compendium of the astronomy of his day, an *Almagestum novum*, or updating, as he saw it, of Ptolemy's ancient masterpiece. Riccioli made space for a detailed coverage of Copernican writers by clearly declaring the status of the muddled references to heresies in Galileo's sentence and abjuration:

> The Sacred Congregation of Cardinals [the Holy Office], considered apart from the pope, does not make doctrine into matters of faith even if it so defines them, or the contrary doctrines, heretical. Since no conclusion on this issue has yet been made by a pope, or by a council directed or approved by a pope, it is not a matter of faith that the sun moves and the earth stands still, on the strength of the decree of the congregation; but only at the most by force of the Holy Scripture on those to whom it is morally evident that this is God's revelation. However, all Catholics are obliged by prudence and obedience to accept what the congregation decreed, or at least to teach nothing contrary to it.[39]

Riccioli professed the greatest admiration for Copernicus and also for Copernican theory, taken hypothetically. "The deeper one digs into the Copernican hypothesis, the more ingenuity and precious subtlety one may unearth." Unfortunately, sometimes Copernicus wrote as if he believed in the truth of the great structure he was building. "Would that he had kept himself within the limits of his hypothesis!"[40] The same went for Galileo, "a mathematician of immense power wonderfully skilled in astronomy; he would have been greater still if he had put forward the opinion of Copernicus as a mere hypothesis."[41]

Under the shield of hypothesis, Riccioli discussed sympathetically all the chief astronomies—not just the Ptolemaic and Copernican, to which Galileo limited his world-systems, but also Kepler's and Tycho's. As typical among the Jesuits, he favored the Tychonic system or, rather, his modification of it, which left Jupiter and Saturn circling the earth. But he was by no means a fellow traveler of the modern astronomers he praised. He believed that he owed it to his superiors and to himself to seize the opportunities his studies had given him to destroy the realist interpretation of heliocentrism. He assembled 126 arguments philosophical, mathematical, and theological, 49 *pro* and 77 *contra* Copernicus. He judged the physical arguments against the sun's rest to be equivocal, those against the earth's motion determinative: weights fall to the base of a tower, birds and clouds are not blown back by a steady wind from the east, cannonballs carry as far east as west, and so forth.[42] Here Scripture, interpreted in the manner of the Holy Office, confirmed the deductions of reason.

Despite his heroic work compiling tables, sifting numbers, and annihilating Copernicans, Riccioli had a tough time sailing his *Novum almagestum* through the straits of the Jesuit censorship. The *revisori* worried that as a theologian not fully prepared in astronomy Riccioli might make mistakes that would embarrass the Society. They demanded that he send them his own contributions (beyond mere compilation) to the book. His reassuring response: he did not write about his own inventions, and he did not denigrate older astronomers. Changing tack, one of the censors wanted to know what Riccioli could add to the works of such masters as Tycho and Kepler, who had had much better support than he, and also what sorts of instruments he had and how he used them. "Once these matters are resolved, I do not doubt that the work will redound greatly to the honor and esteem of the Society."[43] Thus, with patience, by midcentury Jesuits could do, and publish, up-to-date astronomy even though their censorship could be more rigorous than the Roman. As one of them wrote in irritation at the slowness of Jesuit censors in clearing some philosophical books, including Athanasius Kircher's *Mundus subterraneus,* "[C]ertain minds are so stupefied by new things, or rather [these are Jesuits!] old truth recently discovered, that by deluded love of their own trivia they are totally unable to recognize anything seemingly in disagreement with their little ideas."[44]

Clearing the Jesuit censorship did not in itself procure a license, as Riccioli had to learn the hard way, twice. As a theologian he ventured into the difficult question of the Immaculate Conception of the Virgin Mary. After some changes in the text, the society's censors approved it. The Roman censor did not, however, and added to Riccioli's anxiety and chagrin by refusing to return the manuscript. Finally, in 1657, Pope Alexander VII, who had an interest in astronomy and was alerted to Riccioli's plight by the astronomer Gian Domenico Cassini, ordered the tenacious censor to send back the offending work. Here reputation in science helped free a priest from an embarrassment over an error in theology.[45] Riccioli's fellow Jesuit Honoré Fabri enjoyed a similar but grander rescue, from the jail of the Inquisition, where he was sent to ponder the errors of the doctrine of probabilism he had defended; Cardinal Leopold de' Medici, who had been impressed with Fabri's contributions to the short-lived, Galilean-inspired, Medici-funded Accademia del Cimento, intervened to procure his release.[46]

Riccioli's second hard lesson came over papal infallibility, which he undertook to maintain against the opinion of the Dominicans. His manuscript on the subject cleared the Society but not the inquisitor of Bologna; Riccioli appealed to the pope, who referred the case to the Holy Office, where it fell victim to Dominican opposition. Riccioli's friends found a way around the Dominicans, and the Holy Office licensed the printing. Subsequent quarreling between Riccioli, who had added some unapproved front matter, and his printer, and among the inquisitors of Bologna and Rome, reopened the case. This time the Dominican side won. The book, which by then had been printed, was prohibited.[47] Riccioli, defender of papal infallibility and champion of the Holy Office against Copernican astronomy, suffered almost as much grief from the Inquisition as did Galileo.

Riccioli's sufferings may account in part for his inflation, in the *Apologia* he published in the same year as his unfortunate defense of papal infallibility, of Galileo's crime from disobedience to heresy. A further cause was a counterattack by Galileo's disciples, who had been too demoralized in 1651 to respond to Riccioli's physical arguments against a moving earth. When he repeated his attack on Galilean kinematics in his *Astronomia reformata* (1665), however, he awakened several Galileans willing to correct him.[48] In the *Apologia* (1669), he admitted that all the physical and mathematical arguments he had adduced did not bear on the truth of world-systems. In the end, there was only the decree of the Holy Office: "That the sun is revolved by diurnal and annual motion, and that the earth is at rest I firmly hold, infallibly believe, and openly confess, not because of mathematical reasons, but solely at the command of the faith, by the authority of Scripture, and by the intimation [*nutu*] of the Roman See, whose rules, laid down at the dictation of the spirit of truth, may I, as everyone should, uphold as law."[49]

There remained only to make geocentrism an article of faith. Riccioli now saw that the cardinals who had sentenced Galileo had intended to condemn Copernicanism as heretical because it contradicted the literal meaning of Scripture. The only reason to withhold the horrible name of heresy was the possibility that further discoveries would require reinterpretation of the texts. But that, Riccioli inferred from the necessarily nondemonstrative character of astronomy, would never happen. "I say therefore that both the most eminent cardinals and the theologian qualificators of the Sacred Congregation of the Inquisition, taking it for certain that the contrary could never be demonstrated, proclaimed their censure as absolute, and not only provisional, or for this moment in time."[50] Riccioli thus elevated the fictionalist epistemology, in which the vicissitudes of his career had confirmed him, into a principle as effective as Urban VIII's argument from divine omnipotence.

The choice of 1670 as the date of the evisceration of the physical objections against the Copernican system has more to recommend it than Riccioli's admission that only Scripture furnished a definitive argument. The old physical arguments had by then been answered, and the new ones could scarcely command wide assent. For example, by attributing a finite width to the fixed stars, Pietro Cavina, the author of *Congetture fisico-astronomiche* (1669), deduced that in paling from a first- to a second-magnitude star a supernova would lose some 2,552,569,939 earth masses. That was absurd: "[T]he annual motion of the sun is inadmissible." As for the diurnal motion, modern physics would not allow it. "The principles of natural bodies are restricted to two, that is MATTER and MOTION," the one passive, the other active; "and the sun has the glory of all this action." Hence it does the moving and the earth rests to receive its life-giving rays. "For I have never seen it happen that a statue revolves around the sculptor, but always the sculptor around the statue."[51] Q.E.D.

"Physical" arguments became a source of ridicule. Giuseppe Ferrone, S.J., a teacher of mathematics and Galilean sympathizer, taught the heliocentric system in a *Dialogo fisico astronomico contra il sistema copernico* (1680). Ferrone's characters pretend to discuss astronomy rhetorically, that is, by treating at length a fable (Copernicanism) more interesting and exciting than true history (geocentrism). After an effective defense of Copernicus against all objections, the more insistent Copernican annihilates his own astronomy with a historical-physical argument "that I have not read in any author." The Bible tells us that the Lord reassured Hezekiah of his deliverance from mortal illness by causing the sun's shadow to "back up ten steps where it had advanced down the stairway of Ahaz" (2 Kings 20:11). The trick, though not easy, could be done harmlessly on the geocentric system by making the sun retrograde; whereas Copernicans would have the Lord suddenly reverse the spin of the earth, causing "all the towers and campanili and houses to fall in ruins, and an immense loss of life of men and animals, just as when a ferry trying to land strikes the bank, rebounds, and knocks all the passengers to the ground."[52]

Philosophical Fig Leaves

It was Riccioli of the *Almagest*, not of the *Apologia*, who represented the drift of his and wider Catholic society. His influential fellow Jesuits Athansius Kircher and Honoré Fabri, both stationed in Rome, set the agenda. Writing in 1660 about a new astronomy book, Kircher found nothing deserving censure, "not a shadow of an error against orthodox faith." By presenting the competing systems as suppositions, the author made the Copernican useful to the Republic of Letters without challenging the Church's right and proper rejection of it as rash and contrary to Scripture.[53] In 1661 Fabri, writing under the name of the telescope maker Eustachio Divini, interpreted the condemnations of 1633 as merely provisional, enacted to meet the surprise and challenge set by Galileo in a way that would not upset and confuse the faithful. It was expected, he said, that after careful and prudent review and the evaluation of subsequent progress in astronomy, the authorities would relax or remove their strictures.[54] Following up on an opinion Riccioli had slipped into his *Almagest,* Fabri insisted that Scripture must be interpreted literally only as long as no absurdity resulted. Should it become absurd, the Church, which understood the true character of science, would know what to do: "the Church will not hesitate to declare that those passages are to be understood in a figurative and nonliteral sense."[55]

In Jesuit Pedagogy

By the 1660s, Copernican ideas had passed the test of time. The Jesuits urgently needed to incorporate them into their textbooks to maintain their place as schoolmasters to Catholic Europe.[56] The general of the Society of Jesus commissioned André Tacquet, who taught in the society's conservative Belgian province, to write a course of mathematics for classroom use.[57] Tacquet's *Opera mathematica,* published posthumously in 1669, devoted 350 pages to mathematics. Just under two-thirds of them concerned sun, moon, and stars and so had no need of the heliocentric hypothesis. "Both in the common, and true, opinion and in the Copernican . . . the earth is apparently [quoad sensum] at rest in the center of the firmament."[58] In the last third, which dealt with the planets, Tacquet insisted on bringing in the simpler heliocentric hypothesis. Many great astronomers favored it, and so too might Tacquet's students if they took it in a poetical sense, as in Vergil's verse *Provehimur portu, terraque urbesque recedunt* (We set out from port, and the land and cities recede). Could it be taken as true? "For my part, since I see no arguments adduced on either side that are anything more than probable, I am not going to worry about them." However, where logic, mathematics, and astronomy could not decide, Scripture spoke plainly. Tacquet allowed that the words of the Bible had to be taken literally unless (here he followed Riccioli and Fabri) they conflicted with a clearer part of Scripture, or were reinterpreted by the Church, or were decisively confronted "by the very light of nature." The response of the Copernicans, that Scripture expressed popular notions in the manner of Vergil's verse, could not alter its plain meaning. Hence their remedy had not been applied.[59]

Claude-François-Milliet Deschales, S.J., spent most of his life teaching mathematics at the great Jesuit College in Lyon. His pedagogical writings followed the style of Tacquet's. His full course, first published in 1674 in three unwieldy volumes, reappeared in 1690, edited by a disciple, who increased the compass to four volumes by adding a history of mathematics and a refutation of Descartes.[60] Whoever made it to Deschales's third volume would learn that "Copernicus explains [the retrogradations of the planets] more simply than all the other systems so that, if his hypothesis were not contrary to Scripture, it could be called *divina prorsus,* utterly divine."[61] However, Deschales explained, the physical truth of heliocentrism, whether it could be proved or not, did not interest astronomy. That was a job for philosophy.

Deschales's students could easily take home the lesson that the Copernican was the best hypothesis but could not be held as true—which, however, did not bother astronomers, who blushed to hear speculations about the truth of things.

The approach to Copernicus and heliocentrism worked out by the Jesuits during the 1660s and 1670s was not peculiar to them. One preeminent example, *Philosophia vetus et nova ad usum scholae acommodata* (1678), by the Oratorian Jean-Baptiste Duhamel, can stand for many. Duhamel has a particular authority because he served as the secretary of the Paris Academy of Science while he adapted his views about astronomy to the level of the students at the Oratorian Collège de Bourgogne. Since Duhamel had made a niche for himself in the republic of letters by balancing, harmonizing, compromising, and trimming ancient and modern opinions on controversial subjects, he was a perfect expositor of a liberal-conservative, geo-heliocentric, Ricciolian-Copernican astronomy. As he explained in his *Astronomia physica* (1660), "A philosopher is not too enthusiastic an admirer of antiquity nor does he condemn completely the discoveries of the moderns."[62]

Philosophia vetus et nova delivered astronomy as a part of physics. First came the Ptolemiac system, which would have offered great simplicity and facility "if it agreed with the phenomena." Then there was Copernicus's hypothesis, "which almost all contemporary astronomers follow." These propositions might appear to settle the matter. That was not, however, the method of Duhamel. He reviewed the various arguments, arrived at the usual impasse, and jumped to the usual safety net: "No argument demonstrates the stability or the motion of the earth, still it is safer to defend its quiescence than its mobility."[63] But then it was no less safe, and more in keeping with the nature of the subject, to defend nothing at all: "[W]hether the Copernican system is true or false is not for an astronomer to say; for he draws conclusions hypothetically, not absolutely. It is enough for him if he can explain the celestial motions in any way at all; the physicist investigates their causes."[64] Duhamel's even-handed formulations had a strong appeal around 1680, and the book enjoyed several editions. The Jesuits used it in their missions in Asia and translated it into the Tartar language for the benefit of the Emperor of China, that he might thereby learn the diverse opinions of the mandarins of Europe.[65]

Leibniz, who noticed everything, kept track of the development of the astronomical apologetics of the Jesuits. He noticed Fabri's apparent willingness to reinterpret Scripture in favor of heliocentrism. But there was no need to be so violent. Had Joshua been a Copernican, his address to the sun would have been the same. "Otherwise, he would have shocked the people as well as common sense." To patch up the dispute over the world-systems, the Roman Church had only to allow people to hold the Copernican hypothesis as truth and the Copernicans had only to acknowledge that Scripture could not have spoken more appropriately.[66] Each party would retain authority within its domain. In 1689 Leibniz set off for Italy to arrange a marriage between the daughter of his employer, the Elector of Hanover, and the Duke of Modena.[67] He managed the marriage and brought the Church to the brink, he thought, of accepting his hermeneutics. At the very heart of Catholic assertiveness, in the Congregatio de Propaganda Fidei established by Urban VIII, Leibniz found "the light of enlightenment."[68] Antonio Baldigiani, S.J., professor of mathematics at the Roman college and an advisor to the Congregation of the Index, seemed to fall in with his plans.[69] "If there are more like [him] in ability and authority, I would hope that the old liberty can be regained, whose loss much restricts the lively minds of the Italians."[70]

With this encouragement, Leibniz composed an essay on the relativity of motion that outdid Descartes. Which, if any, of several bodies in relative motion truly rested? No one could say. The analyst chose one or another as stationary as best suited his purpose of making motions intelligible: "the truth of an hypothesis is nothing but its intelligibility." The apparent motion of the sun and stars was more intelligible on the geocentric than on the heliocentric hypothesis; Copernicus did better with planetary motions than Ptolemy. Joshua spoke correctly when commanding the sun to stand still; but had he been talking about Mars instead of the sun, he would have spoken badly.[71] No doubt Leibniz's solution had an appeal for subtle minds sick of the obsolescent controversy. But the higher reaches of the Roman hierarchy, though no longer intransigent about world-systems, were not yet prepared to bury the legacy of Urban VIII.

Four years before Leibniz set forth for Italy, the Master of the Sacred Palace reported to the Congregation of the Inquisition that he had exercised his authority on a certain *Tabula cosmica systematis Copernici* then recently published. He had ordered that "erroneous hypothesis" be added to the *Tabula*'s engraved title and that the text be enriched with the words "Since the Church has declared that the Holy Scripture expressly teaches the contrary, this system cannot be defended in any way." The cardinals praised his "prudence and diligence." The censor's formulation went beyond that of the cardinals of 1633 in insinuating that the Bible taught geocentrism.[72] Did the censor's act and formulation represent a hardening of position? Or did they amount to condoning an ineradicable evil, the equivalent of requiring a notice on cigarette packets that declares a danger while allowing the risk?

Thrust Aside in Naples

Leibniz missed his mark owing in part to a change in the variable Roman intellectual climate during the reign of Innocent XII, who became pope in 1691. Innocent was devout, charitable, economical, and literal. He believed in discipline. There were always zealots around the curia eager to charge savants with going beyond the bounds of licensed expression. In January 1693, Baldigiani warned that "all of Rome is in arms against the mathematicians and physico-mathematicians, extraordinary meetings are held by the cardinals of the Holy Office, and with the pope, and there is talk of a general prohibition against all writers on modern physics, they are making very long lists of them, and at the top Galileo, Gassendi, and Descartes as most pernicious to the republic of letters and the candor of religion."[73]

The trouble centered in Naples, where Descartes's philosophy and other materialisms had been cultivated since the middle of the century by a band of doctors and lawyers. Their intellectual leader, Tommaso Cornelio, died in 1685. Plans for a large funeral fired up the conservative reaction: it was rumored that the late philosopher had thought his soul was mortal but that the devil knew better and had carried it off. The religious authorities hesitated, and only with the help of Cardinal Baldigiani did Cornelio's friends succeed in burying him with the pomp they planned.[74] The clerical authorities had responded to the materialism to which, they believed, Cornelio's teaching, the banned books of Descartes, and an unlicensed, unpublished translation of Lucretius by Alessandro Marchetti had given rise. The vice-regent (Naples then belonged to Spain), who made common cause with the professional classes against the old-fashioned clerical and educational establishments, had not cared to clamp down. Nor had the local inquisitor, even after a young lawyer denounced three of his colleagues for rejecting God, the immortality of the soul, the sacraments, and the pope and for believing that men composed solely of atoms existed before Adam.[75]

A new inquisitor, assigned to persecute the offenders, over-reached, fought with the professional classes and the aristocratic families, and set Rome and Madrid at loggerheads. He was recalled. A third inquisitor dispatched from Rome jailed a few doctors and lawyers, including the most prominent among those originally accused, Giacinto de Cristaforo. The influential people yelled the louder. Rome and Madrid did not have the unity or the stomach to persist. The pope and the viceroy agreed to withdraw the offensive inquisitor, and the intellectual professionals, apart from the jailed Cristaforo, went back to their obnoxious ways.[76] The teaching of the new philosophy, with which the battle began, turned out to be the smallest of the stakes. Cartesianism made its way as a rallying cry against conservatism, not as a world-system; and against the revolutionary power of materialism the question whether the sun moved or not sank to appropriate insignificance.

A similarly instructive episode took place almost simultaneously with the Neapolitan troubles at the Catholic University of Louvain. There the papal nuncio stifled a fight between the faculty and a professor of mathematics, Martin van Velden, who wanted to dispute the thesis that "the Copernican system of the motion of the planets is indubitable: and with good reason the earth is considered a planet." The faculty had expelled van Velden, who sued for reinstatement; the noise attracted the attention of the Estates of Brabant, with which the Church contested jurisdiction over the university. The nuncio appreciated that the problem was not to make Van Velden comply with the sentence against Galileo but to force him back on his colleagues before the Estates could intervene. The nuncio succeeded and van Velden resumed where he had left off, unabashedly teaching the Copernican system as the truth.[77]

The parties to the mischief in Naples also learned something. On emerging from his jail, Cristaforo declared that only mathematics could lead to certainty; he became an excellent applied mathematician and assisted the Holy Roman Empire with its water problems in Italy.[78] The Inquisition turned its cheek from the provocations of another Neapolitan lawyer, Lorenzo Ciccarelli, who had a hobby of publishing proscribed or doubtful books: Jacques Rohault's Cartesian *Physique* as annotated by the Newtonian Samuel Clarke ("Cologne," 1713), Marchetti's *Lucretius* ("London," 1717), and Galileo's *Dialogue* ("Florence," 1710). Ciccarelli had the protection of the Neapolitan savants who had returned to their Descartes after the trials of the 1690s and of Newtonianizing philosophers in Rome, like Celestino Galiani, who used their contacts in the censorship system to ensure that the reprints did not "fall into the hands of some rogue zealot."[79] The Vatican, faced with the aftermath of the War of the Spanish Succession and the serious religious-political Jansenist controversy in France, had neither the resources nor the will to impose the prohibition against Galileo's by then harmless treatise. The inclusion of the sentence and abjuration in Ciccarelli's edition no doubt helped the authorities to rationalize neglect of their duty.[80]

Fitted Elsewhere

By 1700, any book or article teaching or using Copernican theory could pass the censorship—if duly self-censored. An innocent example is a calendar of 1703 that used Copernican values for the length of the tropical year. The self-censorship: "What the true value is, let Saint Peter bless it; for my part I will make use of Longomontanus's value of the mean motion based on the observations of Copernicus."[81] Also, by the same time, Descartes no longer appeared to be a serious danger. Even the Jesuits relaxed their proscriptions. Although the fifteenth congregation of the Society, held in 1706, prohibited the teaching of thirty propositions in Descartes's physics alone, the last of these "prohibitions" undid the others by allowing the "defense of the Cartesian system as an hypothesis." The sixteenth congregation reduced the thirty prohibited propositions to a more economical ten.[82]

Four examples will indicate the sorts of successful self-censorship practiced around 1700. The first involved Eustachio Manfredi, professor of mathematics and astronomy at the University of Bologna. The pressure felt by astronomers and philosophers in the intellectual center of the Papal States to act in accordance with the condemnation of Galileo may be gauged from a draft statute of 1702 for what became the Accademia delle Scienze of Bologna. The statute required the academicians to swear "never to fight with Copernicans, but to convince them with physical reasons, and in general to promise as much for astronomy as for any physical principle in experimental philosophy, viz., to bring everything into conformity with the Holy Roman Church."[83] Although this excessive self-censorship did not survive into the definitive statute, it lived on in Manfredi, who, as will appear, made such full and frequent use of the ointment of hypothesis that the head of the Congregation of the Index told him that he took the matter too seriously.

In contrast to Manfredi, who wrote technical astronomical books, Vincenzo Coronelli issued popular texts on astronomy, geography, and hydrography to help instruct purchasers of the celestial and terrestrial globes he made in his workshop in Venice. Coronelli protected himself by describing the Ptolemaic, Copernican, Tychonic, and Cartesian world-systems together with their advantages and defects. He devoted more space to the Copernican than to the others combined. He held it for certain that Mercury and Venus orbited the sun and that recent observations ruled out the Ptolemaic system. As for the Copernican, the major astronomers had accepted it, and Galileo had confirmed it, but "he became suspect to the Inquisition during the pontificate of Urban VIII, was imprisoned, and forced to retract." At this point Coronelli inserted an inspired euphemism. "Since the thought of a moving earth did not content [!] most astronomers and philosophers, many abandoned Copernicus for the opinion of Tycho." Descartes found a middle way: "[T]he earth is a part of the whole [solar vortex]; the vortex moves, but we cannot say that the earth does [relative to it]." As for practical applications, Coronelli in effect used Copernicus for the planets but smudged the results. To obtain the distance of Saturn, 14,373 t.r. (terrestrial radii), "from the earth," he silently invoked Copernicus's model, which he assimilated to Tycho's by assigning Saturn twenty-nine years "to go around the sun and the earth." In a similar confusion, Coronelli placed Mars 1,212 t.r. from the earth and observed, in flagrant contradiction, that Mars approached the earth much more closely at opposition that at conjunction.[84] Here self-censorship ended in incoherence.

Another dodge was to write poetry. In this form, even Manfredi hazarded support for modern ideas.[85] Tommaso Ceva, S.J., a mathematician and Latin poet at the Jesuit college in Milan, sang against Cartesianism and for something even newer, Newton's system of gravity. Taking gravity to be innate to bodies, Ceva proved the existence of God and, orbiting back along a vicious circle, demonstrated gravity from God's existence. Ceva's *Philosophia nova-antiqua* (1704), written in the style of Lucretius, accepted Galileo's treatment of motion and attacked his cosmology; insisted on Aristotelian hylomorphism but rejected most of Aristotle's philosophy; described the Copernican system and explained Protestants' preference for it as opposition to the pope; in short, presented a mix of new and old pleasing to those who liked their physics dressed up as literature. The poem became an important text in Jesuit schools, which required five editions and one translation between 1704 and 1732.[86]

A Sicilian poet, a devout self-taught doctor named Tommaso Campailla, under-took the reverse task, to defend and versify Descartes. *L'Adamo, ovvero il mondo creato* (1709) began with God's making the world à la Descartes. Most of its matter dis-posed itself in vortices: "Del residuo formò sferica mole / In centro al nostro cielo; ed ecco il sole" (From the rest a spherical mass formed / In the center of our heaven, and that was the sun). The sun was the center around which the planets moved. On the third of them life appeared, and one Adam, who spontaneously reasoned thus: "io penso dunque; io son." Like Descartes, Adam perceived that he could depend on ideas as clear and distinct as that of his existence; and, unlike Descartes, he had the archangel Raphael as his private tutor. Raphael explained the law of inertia, Des-cartes's odd rules about collisions, and the doctrine of relativity that allowed philoso-phers to feign that the moving earth rested.[87] Adam then learned about vacua (there could be none), the vortices, and the constitution of plants and animals, all accord-ing to "l'immortale Renato e de la Carte" and Raphael his agent. But the fundamen-tal legislation of the physical universe was found in the Bible. "Entro quei sacri libri eccelsamente / La divina sua legge è registrata / . . . / Sol basta dir, che quanto in lor si uniò / Lo detterà lo spirito di Deo."[88]

Adamo proved a best-seller. Italians praised its author, "a great philosopher," "acute," "eminent," "a wonderfully penetrating mind filled with all of ancient and modern philosophy." The Royal Society of London, amazed to find "so great a light of science in a remote corner of Sicily," sent Campailla a copy of its president's *Prin-cipia,* in the hope, perhaps, of a versified Newton.[89] Campailla practiced freedom of thought, "as do all the true philosophers of the modern age, approving only those doc-trines demonstrated either by [divine] Wisdom or by the most probable reasons."[90] A pity, therefore, some readers judged, that Campailla stuck so close to Descartes. "I [the great polymath Ludovico Muratori] have to laugh that in the epilogue he [Campailla] says plainly that the earth does not move, when he bravely holds the system of Messer Copernicus."[91] Muratori wrote in 1732, Campailla in 1709. Laughing was easier later.

In 1744 a new Cartesian poet appeared in the form of Benedict Stay, S.J., whose *Philosophiae . . . versibus traditae libri vi* made a great hit in Rome as poetry. By then, however, as Stay learned from his cousin and confrère, the great natural philoso-pher Roger Boscovich, all modern thinkers were abandoning Descartes for Newton. Stay thereupon began a Newtonian poem, completed in 1752 in 24,000 lines. It took forty years and three volumes to print. The delay was occasioned not by the censors but by Boscovich, who prepared many lengthy notes and short epistemological dis-quisitions that made Stay's didactic poem a carrier of the latest in Newtonian natu-ral philosophy. A significant example concerned the analysis of measurements rela-tive to the shape of the earth, a subject that demonstrated the superiority of Newton's physics to Descartes's and of Copernicus's system to Tycho's.[92]

Retreat of the Index

According to the standard history of eighteenth-century Italian literature, "the moderns" began to make important gains in their liberty of thought during the 1720s and prevailed during the 1730s and 1740s. Emblematic of their triumph were the deposit of Galileo's remains in a magnificent tomb in Santa Croce in 1737 and the republication of his *Dialogue,* with the permission of the censors, in 1744. Emblematic of the process was the continuing interest in Campailla's *L'Adamo,* which remained popular until Italians lost interest in Descartes's natural philosophy toward the middle of the century. Newton and also Locke made up the advanced party for the rehabilitation of Galileo and the retreat of the Inquisition from the field of astronomy.[93] The advance and retreat did not take place without a few pitched battles. But it went more smoothly than the Church's rough treatment of Galileo might have led people to expect.

The reformers combated the old way of thinking but not the old institutions. "There came an equilibrium of thought difficult to find in other countries." "Fortunately, religious sentiment was never entirely spent in Italy and existed together with an aversion to the Church; these, along with the moderation characteristic of Italian minds [!], prevented sensationalism [Locke's philosophy] from degenerating into materialism." There were no Holbachs or La Mettries in Italy.[94] It is not necessary to credit Italians with a national talent for moderation to concede that they might harbor a true religious sentiment along with a strong anticlericalism. They knew how to live with inconsistencies. Sincere professions of faith could lie behind the cynical phrases with which astronomers complied with the decrees against Copernicus.

Turning Points

In 1718 an edition of Galileo's *Opere* was published with license in Florence. Despite the advocacy of several well-placed clerics, it did not include the *Dialogue.* Still, the outcome was mixed. On the one hand, no *Dialogue,* "no shaft of light in the closed and hegemonic culture of ecclesiastic power"; on the other hand, access to much of Galileo and, in the editorial preface to the *Opere,* praise of the *libertas philosophandi.*[95] But people remained cautious. "There are those who think that the motion of the earth need no longer be held as a simple hypothesis, but as a certainty. But with us [in Rome] their reasons can have no weight, since the decree of the Inquisition alone fully suffices to remove every doubt from our minds." Thus Celestino Galiani, an avid student of Newtonian physics and a cleric with close ties to the Curia, sarcastically put the case for self-censorship in 1714.[96] Textbook writers continued to practice the dodge of their predecessors.

Galileo's successor several times removed in the chair of mathematics at the University of Pisa, Angelo Marchetti, hid his views behind a presentation of the competing systems of Ptolemy, "Pythagoras," and Tycho and left it to his students to decide which of them seemed "more like the truth, and more in conformance with the sacred dogmas of our Catholic faith." He gave some clues: the Ptolemaic-Aristotelian system was wrong; Copernicus's, dedicated to a pope and confirmed by the discoveries of the "great Galileo," was "truly easy, simple, and most suitable for application to all the appearances." But "[i]t is suspect to us other Catholics because it does not conform well with Divine Scripture, and opposes the . . . sentence against Galileo." Catholic astronomers therefore embraced Tycho's system, "even though, at first glance, it does not appear as simple or coherent." How could it? The Copernican system, "according to its upholders," was the "simplest, best ordered, and in fullest agreement with astronomical observations." But

> [i]t is opposed by many passages of Holy Scripture, to which, as the safest rule of the truth, to avoid error, every human discourse ought to submit with humility; and, moreover, it has been condemned by the Sacred Congregation of Cardinals. For my part I say in full compliance with and reverence for the passages in Scripture and the decree of the cardinals that I do not intend to approve the Copernican theory; but in everything and for everything, I defer to those competent to judge the matter, contenting myself with having explained it in the form in which its inventors proposed and approved it.[97]

A perfect dissimulation.

Jacopo Francesco Riccati, a noble mathematician educated in Padua, was not a professor and could say more directly what Marchetti may have had in mind. Also, he wrote a decade or so later and did not publish his views. Nonetheless, they have a familiar look. There exist three systems. Observations like Venus's phases rule out Ptolemy, as does his maze of circles, "which force nature so to speak to behave incoherently, at the whim of the astronomer." Kepler's third law, which applies generally around the heavens, does not work for the sun and moon in Tycho's system, which is a hodge-podge of the others. That leaves Copernicus. "I do not hold the Copernican structure as a mere hypothesis, for a double reason: because it explains the phenomena more fully, and because the others do not have the consistency of rules necessary to build a system." That seems unequivocal. "But if by chance I have asserted something badly, since I do not deny my weakness, and have been warned about it by the supreme authority of the Church, which has greater weight with me than any human reason; now and for the time being I retract everything that may have flowed imprudently from my pen, and I wish to make known that my errors are purely of the intellect, and never of obstinate will."[98] Many of these prudent phrases replied directly, in advance, to standard inquisitorial questions and procedures.

The Inquisition might have been in touch with Riccati over his attempts to explain the physics of Noah's flood by Copernican theory. Nothing could be easier:

God had only to speed up and slow down the diurnal rotation, creating an effect similar to those in Galileo's deadly serious theory of the tides and Ferrone's tongue-in-cheek model of the miracle on Ahaz's stairs. Riccati had been concerned with God's pluvial problem for almost twenty years when, in 1737, he described his solution to Giovanni Poleni, professor of mathematics at the University of Pavia, and warned that "for the nonce, it must be considered as unsaid in Italy." The occasion for the communication was another exercise in rotations, a calculation of the oscillation of a pendulum "on the theory of the moving earth." Riccati later accepted the results of the French expeditions to measure a meridian in Lapland and Peru as a full demonstration of Newton's physics and the diurnal rotation.[99]

A final example of the self-censorship of men of the generation of Marchetti (born 1674) and Ricatti (born 1676) is the dedication of a book by Manfredi (born 1674) to the cardinal president of the Congregation of the Index, Giovantonio Davia. The book concerned the delicate subject of stellar parallax. Manfredi did not hide that should the evidence for parallax prove conclusive it would be an unanswerable demonstration of Copernican truth. Although he cagily and correctly found that existing observations were not decisive, he more than hinted that he expected that conclusive positive evidence would be found using his methods. After a short delay the censor approved the manuscript, and the book appeared from the Inquisition's printer with a dedication to Davia. When they discussed the dedication, Manfredi proposed to put in the usual ritual censure of heliocentrism, which the censor had recommended. Davia did not want it. His reason: the ritual might "make an article of faith of what certainly is not one." He materialized his viewpoint in a Copernican armillary, which he gave to the Bologna Academy; its members, as timid as Manfredi, commissioned two others, a Ptolemaic and a Tychonic, to flank Davia's unwelcome gift and to demonstrate that they did not claim to know the true system of the world.[100]

This caution may not have been misplaced. While procuring a license for his piece on parallax, Manfredi was following up James Bradley's discovery of the aberration of starlight, which he confirmed and explained on Copernican principles. He wrote a lengthy report for the first volume of the Bologna Academy's *Commentarii*. The academy's secretary, Francesco Maria Zanotti, planned a historical preface to review the articles that followed. He wrote a friend, the pope's physician Antonio Leprotti, about his problems. "I am very much afraid that the censors will require that . . . where I say what Copernicus thought, I must immediately add that I detest his system as a heresy." And what to say about Davia's gift? "I would not want them to oblige me to say that both His Eminence and I regard the machine as a jeu d'esprit, knowing as we do that it is contrary to the faith. You see very well how these [ridiculous] protestations would be received by Catholics, especially learned ones, in the first book published by this academy of sciences, which supposes that it contains the flower of the literature of Bologna."[101] Eventually the censor approved the volume, including Manfredi's dissertation, which characterized the assumption of a moving earth as a "principle" in Bradley's unreflective usage and a "hypothesis" ("nothing prohibits us from making them") in the correct interpretation made by the Church.[102]

Manfredi exercised the same caution (or practiced the same epistemology) in his lectures on astronomy. In their posthumously published form, they set the goal of astronomy as the discovery of precise laws confirmed by observation; hypotheses about the structure and nature of the heavens were at best instruments for seeking regularities, and, if taken too literally, as by the Cartesians with their vortices and Newton with his gravity, they stymied the hunt. Astronomers did not have to believe in a world-system to write about astronomy. The division of Manfredi's posthumous *Istituzioni astronomiche* (1749) conveyed this wisdom. The book began with a Ptolemaic-elliptic description of the sun, moon, and stars in 225 pages; went on to a Copernican-elliptic account of the motions of the planets in 160 pages; and ended with 15 pages of directions for translating Copernicus into the languages of Ptolemy and Tycho.

Manfredi tried in vain to instil his sense of caution and propriety in his student Francesco Algarotti, who spent much of his time beyond the Alps and entertained an extravagant admiration for English philosophy. When he sought in Rome a license for his *Newtonianismo per le dame,* he ran into what Manfredi described as "the sort of hatefulness that cannot be regarded lightly by people who live in Italy."[103] Manfredi and Davia intervened, but the Congregation of the Index, alarmed by Algarotti's association of Newtonian physics with Lockean philosophy, which it had condemned three years earlier, could not let the ladies have their Newton so contaminated. Even Algarotti's supporters had trouble tolerating his enthusiasm for foreign thought. According to Zanotti, "That devil of an Algarotti appears like an aurora borealis that lasts but briefly and smells a lot of the North; he is so full of France and England that he seems a barbarian." After much negotiation the business was composed. The prohibition, which did not prevent publication, softened to *donec corrigatur.* To "correct" for the Italian market, Algarotti dropped his ardent praise of the transalpine and his irrelevant psychologizing, changed the title of his book, and saw the new edition, of 1746, approved with the inclusion of a "Notice from the Printer" rehearsing the usual disclaimer. A newer edition, of 1750, came through without the epistemology of the printer, although, of course, it was thoroughly heliocentric. The original edition remained on the *Index.*[104]

Astronomers younger than Manfredi or better insulated than he from the influence of Rome could write more assertively and less sincerely. Thus Poleni of Padua (born 1683) opened his book on celestial vortices, published in 1712, with the perfunctory disclaimer, "Dear reader, I want you to know that I hold the Copernican system to be completely false and, with due veneration, accept the decree by which, most fairly, the system was condemned." Poleni then went about his business, discussing gravity and a spinning earth, without further qualification. As for the younger generation, we already know the compromise achieved by Algarotti. Two other examples are the French Minim monks François Jacquier and Thomas Le Seur, who taught in Rome and dissimulated as follows in their important commentary on Newton's *Principia:* "In this third book, Newton assumes the hypothesis of the moving earth. The author's propositions can be explained in no other way. . . . Hence we are forced to play another person's part. Otherwise, we openly declare that we comply with the popes' decrees against the earth's motion."[105] The then reigning pope secured a professorship at the Sapientia for Jacquier and ordered the evisceration of the decrees.[106]

A Pope in the Van

Like his great friend Davia, Prospero Lambertini had favored the Bologna Academy of Sciences, to which he gave instruments more useful and less compromising than Davia's Copernican armillary. He continued to promote science in Bologna and Rome after his accession to the papacy in 1740 as Benedict XIV. He understood perfectly how powerful parties, particularly the Jesuits, with whom he was often at war ("docility is not their character"), manipulated the censorship system. And he knew that recent developments in science, particularly the discovery of stellar aberration, made the Church's insistence on lip service to earth-centered astronomy agonizingly anachronistic and ridiculous. As Riccati had written, echoing Manfredi, "I do not now seek to determine whether [Bradley's] demonstration is conclusive; but I affirm that since the observations correspond so perfectly to his hypothesis, it should not be abandoned lightly."[107] Bradley confirmed Newton, who by 1740 was making a conquest of the peninsula. Newton had sent copies of the *Principia* in 1713 to Manfredi, Galiani, and a few others; the book had never been prohibited, but self-censorship and perhaps also fascination with Descartes had kept Italians from publishing popular accounts of the Newtonian world-system until the 1730s.[108] Then Newtonian ideas quickly gained currency. Campailla did them the honor of refuting them, in prose, in some *Opuscoli filosofici* (1737); Jacquier and Le Seur eased access to them with their three-volume commentary (1739–42); and the success of Newton's physics added to the overwhelming astronomical evidence to deprive the dodge of hypothesis or the refuge in Tycho of any plausibility.

In 1741 the inquisitor of Padua, Paolo Antonio Ambrogi, forwarded to Rome a request from the printers of the Padua Seminary to publish all of Galileo's works. To reduce the damage that might thus be done to unfortified minds, they promised to print the sentence and abjuration together with the *Dialogue,* as in the edition of 1710, and to remove or correct passages in which Galileo appeared to embrace Copernicanism in the condemned way (*per modum thesis*) rather than by the approved *per modum hypothesis.* They would use as their text Galileo's own copy of the *Dialogue,* with his handwritten corrections and additions, once owned by a cardinal and deposited by him in the Padua Seminary. The response from Rome must have astonished the printers and their academic editor, Toaldo. The quick answer, from a group of consultants perhaps given authority to act during the cardinal-censors' summer recess by Benedict, was "Go ahead."

Apparently emboldened by this easy conquest, the printers proposed to neutralize the realistic passages of the *Dialogue* by a single declaration, in the style of Galileo's original taunting preface, that Copernicanism could be held comfortably as a hypothesis but had to be detested as a thesis. Ambrogio took alarm; Rome ordered the printers to stick to their promise to include the sentence and abjuration; they agreed, and the fourth volume of Galileo's works received an imprimatur.[109] Galileo would have been amused by the results. Toaldo had argued, successfully, that the speeches of the participants in the *Dialogue* should be considered their views and should not be changed; only the running marginal commentary, which might be construed as a resolution of the discussion, needed to be rendered faithfully *per modum hypothesis*. Thirteen postils were dropped and forty others decontaminated by inserting "supposed" before "motion of the earth."[110]

Two other features of the book deserve notice. One is the ritualized pledge of allegiance: "As far as the principal question of the motion of the earth is concerned, we too conform to the retraction and declaration of the author, stating in the most solemn manner that it cannot and must not be admitted except as a pure mathematical hypothesis for the easier explanation of certain phenomena."[111] The second feature was Calmet's long dissertation on the cosmological ideas of the ancient Hebrews. How it got there no one knows. Perhaps, as has been suggested, Ambrogi proposed it as a counterweight to Galileo's accommodationist arguments. If so, he missed his mark. Although Calmet gave a long and literal account of biblical cosmology, he ended with the accommodationist twist that the geocentric view represented the world, not necessarily as it was, but in a manner accessible to the limited knowledge of an ancient tribe. Apparently neither Ambrogi nor any of the staff in Rome nor any of the cardinal censors noticed that the learned Calmet supported Galileo's theology.[112] Altogether, the Roman side of the business showed signs of haste and indifference. Benedict kept in touch with the proceedings and probably was neither surprised nor disappointed at the show of incompetence. "Our court is not very prolific of great men these days."[113]

Another revealing episode that matured during Benedict's pontificate centered on Enrico Noris, a one-time censor friendly to astronomy and a cardinal exemplary for his talent and erudition.[114] The Jesuits attacked his books for their Augustinian accounts of the efficacy of grace and the freedom of the will. Three separate committees of theologians, stacked by the popes, exonerated him. Each victory brought Noris preferment: from qualificator to consultor in the Congregation of the Index, then overseer of the Vatican Library, and, in 1695, cardinal.[115] While Noris climbed the ecclesiastical ladder, Jansenism, with its Augustinian theology, gained strength in France as a political movement. Despite the issuance of the famous bull *Unigenitus,* which anathematized 101 Jansenist propositions, Jansenism gained ground, and the Jesuits, alarmed at the progress of their adversaries, countered at random.[116] They revived the old charges against Noris and managed in 1748 to persuade the grand inquisitor of Spain to ban his books.[117]

The general of the Augustinian order appealed to Benedict, and Benedict reprimanded the Spanish inquisitor. He pointed out that Noris's books had been cleared on several occasions but that even if there had been no previous examination and they did contain condemnable propositions, they would not have to be prohibited on that ground alone. That was because, according to the pope, the Church should not ban books when the prohibition would do more harm than good. Furthermore, he admonished, the censorship process must not be invoked to resolve conflicts in the schools. Thomists, Augustinians, and Jesuits could all say what they pleased about predestination, grace, and free will, since the popes had not condemned their opinions. "In a word, bishops and inquisitors should not notice the arguments that the doctors throw at one another in their mortal combat."[118]

The pope said much more to the inquisitor: "It will not have escaped your erudition that Church history offers examples of prudent economy, in which, to curb scandal and avoid present dangers, our elders thought to draw back from the rigor of the law." Benedict gave the example of the polymath Muratori. "How often in his books are things deserving of censure found! How much of this material have I not encountered myself in reading them! How many have been pointed out to me by rivals and denouncers!" Muratori sailed close to Jansenism; taught a political philosophy opposed to the interests of the Holy See; and praised Galileo, Gassendi, and Descartes, all of whom had been indexed, as models for "extracting truth from the deep mine of mind and things." But Benedict was not going to do anything about it, "instructed by the examples of my predecessors, who for the love of peace and concord ceased from proscribing what merited proscription when, manifestly, they thought more evil than good would come from it."[119] The exploitation of a system established to protect the faithful in the interest of small-minded politics irritated the pope. "I cannot hear a word about the affair without getting angry."[120]

The affair of the Spanish inquisitor followed immediately on an attempt by several French bishops to co-opt the censorship system against another Augustinian, a teacher of ecclesiastical history in Rome named Berti. Benedict refused to buckle under the pressure from France. "It is a very unhappy thing to condemn even one book without the author's being able to defend it, even a book denounced by an eminent churchman, for this condemnation is an indelible mark on both the author and those who approved the book." The bishops complained again: Berti had dared to answer their censure in print. Benedict: "Since the accusation was printed, you should not be surprised that the response should be." And finally, against a mighty church-man: "We conclude that the archbishop of Vienna [formerly a bishop in France] was the attacker; [carried away] by his zeal and in the name of his doctrine he thought that he could publicly name scholars and gentlemen as heretics and ignoramuses." Under Benedict's protection, Berti left Rome unscathed for a prestigious professor-ship in Pisa.[121]

Benedict institutionalized his insights into the censorship system in a bull, *Sollicita et provida,* issued in July 1753. It condemned castigating books through "public and unfair quarrels," "as if we conducted the business rashly and perfunctorily." Benedict insisted that consultors be experts in the material entrusted to them; that they read books all the way through and deliver their opinions in writing, with exact references to offending passages; that a second reader (consultor) be engaged should the first reader of a book by a Catholic author recommend prohibition; and that a third reader be consulted if the first two disagreed. If the Catholic author was a per-son of excellent character and distinguished reputation, every effort should be made to persuade him to remove the erroneous parts; and, if that could not be achieved, the weakest stricture available should be invoked. In general, the censor should show charity, consult widely, give the benefit of the doubt: "let the censors and consultors keep these and similar rules . . . always in mind; so that in this very serious sort of judgment, they may be able to consult their own consciences, the reputation of the authors, the good of the Church, and the advantage of the faithful."[122]

On October 3, 1753, Benedict wrote to his friend Cardinal Tencin that he had had the revision of the censorship of books in mind since the second year of his pontificate—that is, since 1742. "At last I have been able to correct the abuses that have crept into it."[123] However, the fair play imposed by the bull of July 1753 related only to current and future proceedings; a full correction would require the removal of books already on the *Index* but no longer if ever harmful. Knowing Benedict's ongoing concern to inject charity and objectivity into the activities of the Congregation of the Index, the congregation's secretary, Agostino Ricchini, wrote Benedict early in 1754 suggesting a revision of the *Index librorum prohibitorum.* Among the books the secre-tary nominated for reprieve were works of Copernicus, Galileo, and Descartes. The pope approved the initiative on February 12; the congregation fixed criteria for revi-sion in the spring; and the staff work, which would take three years, began.[124]

Opinions differ over whether Benedict or Ricchini deserves credit for the ini-tiative. The problem probably lacks significance as well as a solution, since in large hierarchical bureaucracies programs previously agreed on verbally are often put as a formal proposal from a lower to a higher official.[125] In any case, a spur to action, if not, as has been suggested, the original stimulus, was the arrival in Rome of the volume of the *Encyclopédie* containing the article on Copernicus by Jean d'Alembert. The article urged the "enlightened pope who leads the church today, a friend of the sciences and a scholar himself," to remove strictures that could only injure the Catholic cause. Since everyone sufficiently instructed agreed that the world had the form that Copernicus specified, further proscription of heliocentrism on the ground that it conflicted with Scripture would accomplish precisely what the old inquisitors feared, the subversion of belief in Scripture.[126]

Removing the Copernican books from the *Index* presented difficulties. For one, the decision taken by the Holy Office in 1616 and immediately endorsed by Pope Paul V distinguished three grades of Copernican offenses. They decreed that Copernicus's masterpiece and a certain commentary on Job be forbidden until corrected; that a booklet by a Carmelite, Paolo Antonio Foscarini, that supplied the hermeneutics to square heliocentrism with Scripture, be condemned utterly; "and that all books which teach the same be likewise prohibited, according to whether with the present decree it [the congregation] prohibits, condemns, or suspends them, respectively."[127] The printed *Index* had accommodated these various possibilities by listing the specially mentioned works, to which Galileo's *Dialogue* was soon added, alphabetically by author, with the status (correctible or not) of each; and by placing the general policy, "and all other books," with other blanket condemnations. How much of this was to be deleted? In April 1757 the cardinal prefect of the Congregation of the Index, A. A. Galli, reported to his colleagues that, "the matter having been discussed with the Holy Father, the decree prohibiting all books teaching the immobility of the sun and the mobility of the earth will be omitted." Whether or not Benedict meant to include the specially mentioned works as well does not appear. He signed off on a partial manuscript of the new *Index* and never saw it in print. It appeared in 1758 after his death.[128]

There is good reason to think that, although he may well have wished to remove the special Copernican works, and Descartes's as well, Benedict did not think the effort worth the risk. The removal would have required the agreement of the Holy Office. To reprieve Foscarini would amount to accepting his hermeneutical principles, to which the Church did not yet subscribe. To reprieve Galileo would be to rescind a decision in which a pope had taken the leading part. As the French astronomer J. J. Lalande learned from Cardinal Galli, changing a solemn sentence of the Holy Office was a "complex undertaking." Neither Benedict nor his successor Clement XIII, who did not oppose further reforms, had the time or energy for the fight.[129] By removing the general and leaving the specific prohibitions, the Church did nothing to clarify the status of heliocentrism. Many Italian theologians and natural philosophers believed that the *Index* of 1758 changed nothing except, perhaps, the likelihood of harassment, and they continued to exercise their habitual caution.[130] Most astronomers and mathematicians, however, inferred that they could express themselves freely, at least in their technical work. They did so without incident.

Once it had recognized the difficulties of implementing the original proposal of dropping the censure against individual Copernican works, the Congregation of the Index commissioned a report from one of its frequent advisors, a professor of mathematics at the Roman College, Pietro Lazzari, on the merits and demerits of removing the general prohibition. Lazzari showed the congregation that in practice the prohibition did not restrict access to Copernican materials in Italy and exposed the Roman hierarchy to ridicule abroad. "I say first of all that the opinion of a moving earth is today the common opinion in all the principal academies, including Italy's, and among the most famous philosophers and mathematicians." Lazzari pointed to d'Alembert's claim that the Copernican system was generally and openly accepted in France and England; to various foreign works, like Chamber's *Dictionary,* which taught heliocentrism and circulated freely in Italy in Italian; to Jacquier and Le Seur's edition, made in Rome, of Newton's *Principia;* to Wolff, Keill, and Mme du Châtelet; and to an essay on the diurnal motion of the earth, published in 1756 with more than the usual quantum of ecclesiastical permissions.

This essay, the work of a Barnabite professor of mathematics at Pisa, Paulo Frisi, was particularly striking for not having recourse to the balm of hypothesis. The first words of the preface invoked "phenomena in astronomy, mechanics, and physics refined everywhere during the eighteenth century and widely studied by distinguished men" as confirmation of the "most elegant and most celebrated opinion of the great Galileo."[131] Among the phenomena were the aberration of light and the nutation of the earth. "All this can be explained easily and wonderfully in this system. . . . Is this not a kind of certainty and demonstration? . . . On the contrary, in the system of the immobile earth either these things cannot be explained (and no one has yet managed an explanation) or to explain them intricate and arbitrary hypotheses, which are implausible when judged by the light of reason, must be adopted."

Lazzari came to two alternatives: either let the opportunity slip and do nothing, or remove the general proscription silently, along with others slated for suppression. "There is no middle way. Replacing the ban with the moderate position that prohibits [heliocentrism] as a thesis but not as an hypothesis does no good, and the same or greater damage as [doing nothing]; for it will seem a frivolous subterfuge, which our enemies will deride, since they know perfectly well that no one thinks or writes that way anymore."[132]

Retreat of the Inquisition

Two Long Falls

The relaxation effected by Benedict stimulated Italian mathematicians to seek a clinching argument for the motion of the earth. Giambattista Guglielmini of Bologna responded. While holding the sinecure of mathematical tutor to the nephews of the cardinal papal secretary of state, Guglielmini developed the old idea of proving the diurnal motion by measuring the distance east of the vertical at which a weight dropped from a high tower would strike the ground. He asked his cardinal for permission to drop balls from the dome of Saint Peter's into the saint's sepulcher at the base of the Bernini altar. That would be a perfect place to exonerate Galileo. The cardinal agreed.[133]

As Guglielmini pondered why no one, not even, apparently, the all-knowing Newton, had tried this simple experiment, his cardinal lost his place. Guglielmini took his experiment home, to the Torre degli Asinelli in Bologna. There he found out why no one had succeeded earlier. The calculations had to be developed to account for air friction and the experiment had to be managed without giving the balls any lateral displacement or spin on their release. Competing mathematicians pointed out that Guglielmini's elementary theory did not take into account that the direction of the vertical changed as the rock fell, that the deflection had a component to the south, that the Alps and the tower exerted gravitational forces, and so on. Guglielmini solved his main problem, releasing the balls, by burning rather than cutting the strings that suspended them. The result, published in 1792, could be interpreted as agreeing with the theory, more or less.[134]

Another significant fall was that of the Jesuits. The suppression of the Society in 1773 removed some of the last opposition to doing without the magic tetragrammaton 'hypo' that transformed a banned thesis into permissible discourse. Remaining true to the position they had taken since the middle of the seventeenth century, the Jesuits did not regard the elimination of the general proscription against Copernican books as permission to treat heliocentrism *per modum thesis.* Two examples indicate the continuity. In 1768 the professor of mathematics at the Roman College ended a dissertation on stellar parallax, which he interpreted from a Copernican viewpoint (how else?), with the veiled affirmation, "[T]hat is the way things behave assuming the motion of the earth; if the earth is at rest, it is necessary to reason differently." No doubt. The leading Jesuit natural philosopher of the eighteenth century, Roger Boscovich, added a note of even greater profundity to a reprinting in 1785 of an earlier essay of his on comets: "[T]he immobility of the earth, which is a unique case among infinitely many equally possible ones, would be infinitely improbable; but this improbability would vanish immediately [we would never consider an immobile earth?] if the Author of Nature himself had not declared to men, in his revelation, that he chose this case."

In this conservatism the Jesuits did not depart from the ungenerous interpretation of the relaxation of 1758 allowed or encouraged by the Congregation of the Index itself. Thus an account of comets versified on the "Copernican hypothesis," which came out in Rome in 1777 with the imprimatur of the congregation's secretary

Ricchini, hewed to the old line with exemplary clarity: "[A]lthough in accordance with the decrees of the Sacred Congregation of 1616 . . .we cannot in any way uphold the system of a moving earth as an absolute thesis . . . , however, it is permitted according to the same congregation to adopt it as a hypothesis abundantly able to represent the phenomena."[135]

One Slow Rise

As the star of Ignatius declined, that of Galileo rose. He had not enjoyed the scientific reputation of a Descartes or a Newton, not only because of the Church's effort to demean him, but also because he did not leave a systematic treatise like his successors' respective *Principia.* His immediate disciples had neither the freedom nor the foundation to do much more than perform disparate and inconclusive experiments, as recorded in the *Saggi* of the Accademia del Cimento. In this way historians have accounted for the surprisingly few references to Galileo's ideas in the philosophical literature from 1650 to 1750. For example, Campailla's lengthy *L'Adamo* mentioned Galileo only once, in a bibliography set to rhyme. Even poetical bibliographers have trouble with classification. Campailla decided to put Galileo among the stargazers, not the thinkers, along with his arch-rival Christoph Scheiner, S.J. "But where do I put you, great Galileo / Searcher of the stars fixed and mobile / Which vainly try to elude your lynx eyes / In the celestial abyss? / And where you, Scheiner . . . ?"[136]

A revolution began in France in 1758 in Jean Etienne Montucla's pioneering *Histoire des mathématiques,* perhaps the first book to set out the scientific revolution in the modern manner.[137] Galileo appeared as a revolutionary hero. The process accelerated in Italy when the redoubtable Frisi, informed by Montucla and inspired by admiration of Galileo and dislike of the Jesuits, presented an éloge of the revived hero in the avant-garde periodical *Il caffè* in 1768. The immediate occasion was the two hundredth anniversary of Galileo's birth. An enlarged version of the *Elogio,* enriched by documents concerning Galileo's trial found in the Florentine archives by Angelo Fabroni, came out in 1775.[138] There we read that Galileo saw far further than his co-agitator in the "general revolution," Francis Bacon; whereas Bacon rejected the system of Copernicus, Galileo recognized the "first phenomena disclosed by the telescope . . . as so many proofs of it." Frisi explained the appearance of Saturn's rings and Venus's phases as consequences of heliocentrism taken as a fact and Jupiter's satellites as a demonstration that the earth's possession of a moon did not make it unique. As for Galileo's troubles with the Church, they had no objective basis. In 1616 Galileo had wished only to obtain the *libertas philosophandi,* "a great objective"; in his *Dialogue,* though perhaps he allowed the Copernican party to prevail (as Frisi certainly did in his summary of the book), he did not resolve the matter; why then the persecution and prosecution? The Jesuits, Clavius, Bellarmine, Scheiner, and their brethren were behind it all.[139]

Frisi shouted his éloge from the safety of Milan, then ruled by Vienna through Count Carlo di Firmian, a promoter of modern philosophy and applied mathematics. Frisi's outspokenness had brought him some trouble earlier elsewhere. Educated by the Barnabites, whom he joined in 1743 at the age of fifteen, he began teaching philosophy at his order's college in Lodi in 1750. The following year he published a "mathematical disquisition," with license, in Milan, that opened with the news that Newton's gravity could not be doubted. It accounted for the motion of the moon around the earth, the planets and the comets around the sun, the fall of bodies, and the beat of pendulums, "which is indeed a very strong proof of the truth of this theory." So Frisi assumed that the earth spun on its axis and revolved around the sun, rejected all the usual arguments against Copernican theory, and added that stellar aberration "perfectly fit with the motion of the earth."

He thought that he had protected himself sufficiently by this perfunctory prefatory notice: "The hypothesis of the moving earth is assumed in the second chapter, as necessary for deriving its shape and size from a physical cause. The author wants it known that he assumes it in the manner permitted by the sacred congregation and the popes, and that he openly declares his compliance with their broad decrees in the matter." The notice did not satisfy Frisi's superiors, who ordered him to stop teaching and start preaching. Soon, however, powerful patrons helped him obtain the professorship of mathematics at the University of Pisa, by then, with all of Tuscany, no longer the archduchy of the Medici, who had died out, but of the Duke of Lorraine. Frisi returned to his brazen Copernicanism in the prize-winning text that the Jesuit consultor to the Index, Lazzari, mentioned as an example of the standard treatment of Copernican and Newtonian ideas in Italy in 1756.[140]

Brought to Milan in 1764, Frisi became an éminence grise of the Austrian reformers, advisor on scientific studies at the University of Pavia and the higher schools of Milan, and, to strengthen his hand, royal censor of books on mathematics and natural science. His last texts do not show the slightest deference to the rigamarole of hypothesis and scarcely stop to argue the merits of heliocentrism over other world-systems. "Copernicus and Galileo fully demonstrated the failings of the old astronomy; the first explained the order and motion of the heavenly bodies, the second confirmed the system through the telescope. . . . This is the constitution of the planetary system: the primary planets Mercury, Venus, Earth, Mars, Jupiter, and Saturn, and all the comets, describe elliptical orbits around the sun at a focus." Aberration is the "most certain indicator" of the annual motion.[141] All these discoveries and theories traced their origin to the persecuted master. "We owe the beginnings of the universal theory of motion to Galileo."[142]

According to a contemporary, Frisi was the grand marshal of Italian mathematicians.[143] The author of a poem inspired by the founding of the Brera Observatory in Milan should be counted among his followers. "First I should say that around the immobile sun / As if around their Lord, describing circles / So go the wandering stars." The poem came out with a license provided by the apparatus that Frisi oversaw.[144] Italian astronomers dealt with Copernican and Newtonian details just as their transalpine colleagues did: Giorgio Fontana worried whether the diurnal motion would affect aberration; Anton-Mario Lorgna improved the derivation of the earth's shape from a spinning molten spheroid; and Giuseppe Piazzi devoted himself to refining "the elliptical elements of the earth's orbit."[145]

A similar emboldening may be found in Spain, in successive editions of Jorge Juan's *Observaciones astronómicas y physicas hechas . . . en los reynos del Perú* (Madrid, 1748, 1774). In the first, Juan's report of the expedition that confirmed Newton's prediction of the shape of the earth, was couched in Newtonian theory protected by the non sequitur "although the hypothesis is false." The second edition, published a quarter of a century later, contained a defense of Copernicanism as the true system of the world, a necessary consequence of Newtonian physics, by then, according to Juan, accepted throughout Europe.[146]

Perhaps more instructive than these technical works are the discourses aimed at a broad audience that Antonio Cagnoli prefaced to his annual almanac from 1788 to 1796; models of popularization, collected and reissued in several editions, they guided many beginners in astronomy for forty years. The first discourse began: "The planets can be divided into three classes: primary planets, secondary planets, and comets. . . . Each planet of the first class, according to the Copernican system now adopted by all astronomers, orbits the sun."[147] Cagnoli started as a diplomat and switched to full-time study of astronomy at the age of thirty-seven in Paris under the guidance of Lalande. Returned to Italy, he set up a private observatory in his hometown, Verona, whence he issued his *Almanac* and its associated discourses.[148]

As a good pedagogue, Cagnoli (or his editor) could not ignore questions important to many of their readers. Why, although Galileo was still barred and Copernicus could be read only if expurgated, did astronomers all believe in the truth of heliocentrism? And, then, what crime had Galileo committed? As to the first question, "They [Copernican astronomers] do not go around begging the explanation of the phenomena from fantastic causes, capriciously invented, nor from that miserable 'we cannot know what nature can do.' They do nothing more than compare the phenomena with the few and very simple laws of their system. So far no astronomical phenomenon has contradicted it." As to the second question, Galileo was a good Christian and badly treated. He committed no crime. "So profoundly did he contemplate nature that he did not disdain to read in it, and often to infer from it, the 'infinitely infinite wisdom of the Creator.'"[149]

A generation after Cagnoli had ridiculed the traditional dissimulation ("we cannot know what nature can do"), Master Anfossi refused to license Giuseppe Settele's open teaching of heliocentrism. In this incoherence, Settele appealed Anfossi's ruling to Pius VII. He had every reason to expect a favorable outcome. Over a decade earlier, in 1806, the pope had accepted the dedication of a booklet in which the head of the Vatican Observatory, Giuseppe Calendrelli, announced the long-sought demonstration of the earth's motion through detection of the parallax of the stars. The fact that Calendrelli was mistaken only adds to the significance of the pope's recognition of his right to declare his proof.[150]

After Napoleon's fall, Pius joined other restored heads of state on a backward march toward the ancien regime. One sector gravely needing his attention was higher education. Napoleon had closed the smaller universities in the Papal States and starved the Sapienza in Rome. Pius appointed a commission of aged cardinals to revitalize the education of the young. The commission began as conservatively as even Anfossi could have desired. It proposed to require all professors to publish their courses in versions approved by the Roman censors. A leading power on the commission was the secretary of the Holy Office, Giulio Maria della Somaglia. He and many of his cardinal colleagues wanted to use the educational system to inculcate traditional Christian values. Nonetheless he and they favored Settele. Their reasoning may be captured in della Somaglia's argument against the method for choosing professors proposed by a retrograde member of the commission. "In this cultured and sensitive age, can we really require a *viva voce* examination of candidates for professorships in the form of syllogisms without exposing ourselves to the derision of the learned?"[151] The fear of ridicule at being out of step with accepted learning in cultured Europe moderated the zeal of the pope's advisors in intellectual matters.

Pius VII's earliest memorialists did not mention the Settele affair in the two thousand pages they devoted to his life and works.[152] Apparently they did not regard it as noteworthy. Cardinal Wiseman, in his recollections of Rome during the time of Pius VII, listed Settele among those "well versed in the sciences," but without any other distinguishing marks. For later historians, however, the affair is significant, and Anfossi deserves their thanks for having created it. His intervention forced the Holy Office and the Congregation of the Index to make formal decisions where, in conformity with the practice of generations of responsible censors, they might otherwise have proceeded by winks and nods. In the sincerity of his conviction and the narrowness of his reasoning, Anfossi serves as an example of what Galiani called "rogue zealots" who would do their duty, whatever the damage thereby done to the institution they strove to protect.

The ambiguities concerning the nature of Galileo's crime and the extent of the application of his sentence gave authors and censors scope for creative mutual adjustments. The spectrum of authorial adjustments ran from extreme self-censorship, such as Descartes's temporary suppression of *Le monde,* through writing in the hypothetical mode as practiced by the Jesuits and the hypersensitive Manfredi, to the brazen realist formulation of Frisi. The spectrum of censorial adjustments ran from the playful permissiveness of a Davia to the rigidity of an Anfossi. The progress of astronomy, the realization that the Church had no important stake in proscribing heliocentrism, and the recognition that persistence in proscription exposed the Roman hierarchy to well-merited ridicule from the rest of the Western world favored the Davias.

The primary result of the inquiry undertaken here is that the proportion and influence of the Anfossis in the censorship system had been in decline for several generations before the principled stand of the real Anfossi forced the Church's internal machinery to invalidate his conception of Copernican cosmology as a heresy. The machinery worked silently, according to its nature; perhaps the only noise it made audible at a distance was the dropping of Galileo's *Dialogue* from the *Index of Prohibited Books*. That occurred in 1835, fifteen years after the Holy Office took up Settele's case. The machinery moved glacially, guardedly, grudgingly; *eppure si muove!*

Notes

It is a pleasure to thank Ernan McMullin for his useful suggestions and incomparable vigilance.

1. Mario d'Addio, *Considerazioni sui processi a Galileo* (Rome: Herder, 1985), 117–19; Walter Brandmüller and Egon Johannes Greipl, eds., *Copernico, Galileo, e la chiesa: Fine della controversia (1820)* (Florence: Leo S. Olschki, 1992), 183–484; and Paolo Maffei, *Giuseppe Settele, il suo diario e la questione galileiana* (Foligno: dell'Arquata, 1987), reprint the documents in the case.

2. Annibale Fantoli, *Galileo: For Copernicanism and for the Church*, 2d ed., ed. and trans. George V. Coyne (Vatican City: Vatican Observatory Publications, 1996), 471–72, 492–93; Agostino Calmet, "Dissertatione sopra il sistema del mondo degli antichi ebrei," in Galileo Galilei, *Opere*, 4 vols. (Padua: Stamperia del Seminario, 1744), 4:1–2; "A chi legge," Galilei, *Opere*, 4:a.2r.

3. Cf. the judicious remarks of John L. Russell, "Catholic Astronomers and the Copernican System after the Condemnation of Galileo," *Annals of Science* 46 (1989): 365–86.

4. Enrico Genovesi, *Processi contro Galileo* (Milan: Ceschina, 1966), 283, 331–32; Sergio M. Pagano and Antonio G. Luciani, eds., *I documenti del processo di Galileo Galilei* (Vatican City: Pontifical Academy of Sciences, 1984), 158–205.

5. Maurice E. Finocchiaro, *The Galileo Affair: A Documentary History* (hereafter *GA*) (Berkeley: University of California Press, 1989), 291, 288 (text of June 22, 1633); Pagano and Luciani, *Il documenti*, 101–3.

6. *GA*, 290–91. More than half the known extant copies of the sentence have 'earth' for 'world' in the condemned opinion, "the sun is the center of the world," perhaps by a scribal slip for "earth's orbit." The historical actors do not seem to have made use of the discrepancy. John L. Russell, "What Was the Crime of Galileo?" *Annals of Science* 52 (1995): 404–9; Michel-Pierre Lerner, "Pour une édition critique de la sentence et de l'abjuration de Galilée," *Revue des Sciences Philosophiques et Théologiques* 82 (1998): 612–21.

7. Jacobo de Simancas, *De catholicis institutionibus liber, ad praecavendas et extirpendas haereses admodum necessarius,* 3d ed. (Rome: In aedibus populi Romani, 1575), 415–17 (titulus 50, §§ 23, 30, 31). Bishop Diego Simancas, one-time tutor to Charles V, was an authoritative and moderate inquisitor.

8. Simancas, *De catholicis institutionibus liber,* 438 (t. 56, § 31). Simancas disagreed with his colleagues who favored torture for the vehemently suspected (t. 56, §17, pp. 434–35). Cf. Francesco Beretta, *Galilée devant le Tribunal de l'Inquisition* (Fribourg: Université de Fribourg, 1998), 214–17.

9. Philippus van Limboch, *The History of the Inquisition . . . Abridged* (London: Simpkin and Marshall, 1816), 315–16, 437–38 (quotations).

10. *GA,* 291.

11. Antonino Poppi, *Cremonini, Galilei e gli inquisitori del santo a Padova* (Padua: Centro Studi Antonini, 1993), 9–14, 51–55; Nicholas Kollerstrom, "Galileo's Astrology," in *Largo campo di filosofare: Eurosymposium Galileo 2001,* ed. José Montesinos and Carlos Solís (La Orotava: Fundacion Canaria Orotava de Historia de la Ciencia, 2001), 422–23.

12. Beretta, *Galilée devant le Tribunal,* 98–99, 104–13, 270–71, 276–78.

13. Léon Garzend, *L'Inquisition et l'hérésie: Distinction de l'hérésie théologique de l'hérésie inquisitoriale* (Paris: Desclée, 1912), 6–7, 14–23, 56–57, 106–12, 429–73, 501–16. Beretta, *Galilée devant le Tribunal,* rejects Garzend's concept of "inquisitorial heresy"; Bruno Neveu and Pierre-Noël Mayaud, "L'affaire Galilée et la tentation inflationiste," *Gregorianum* 82 (2002): 288, 308–9, defend Garzend and attack Beretta for claiming that the trial of 1633 judged Galileo to be a heretic; Beretta defends himself ably in "L'affaire Galilée et l'impasse apologétique: Réponse à une censure," *Gregorianum* 84 (2003): 163–92.

14. *GA,* 292.

15. Francesco Beretta, "Urbain VIII Barberini protagoniste de la condamnation de Galilée," in Montesinos and Solís, *Largo campo di filosofare,* 567; Christopher Scheiner, S.J., to Athanasius Kircher, S.J., July 16, 1633, reporting Galileo's recantation, "ut vocant, de vehementi," cited in Lerner, "Pour une édition critique," 516 n.

16. Simancas, *De catholicis institutionibus liber,* 424 (t. 53, § 5), 426–27 (t. 54, § 20).

17. Genovesi, *Processi contro Galileo,* 287–95.

18. Franco Motta, "I criptocopernicani: Una lettura del rapporto fra censura e coscienza intelletuale nell'Italia della controriforma," in Montesinos and Solís, *Largo campo di filosofare,* 696.

19. Thomas Cerbu, "Melchior Inchofer, 'un homme fin & rusé,'" in Montesinos and Solís, *Largo campo di filosofare,* 595–99, 607.

20. See chap. 5 of this book.

21. Beretta, "Urbain VIII," 559, 563–66; Mario Biagioli, *Galileo, Courtier: The Practice of Science in an Age of Absolutism* (Chicago: University of Chicago Press, 1993), 329–52.

22. Cf. Vincenzo Ferrone, "Galileo, Newton e la libertas philosophandi nelle prima metà del xviii secolo in Italia," *Rivista Storica Italiana* 93 (1981): 158–59; Beretta, "Urbain VIII," 569–70; Maurizio Torrini, *Dopo Galileo: Una polemica scientifica (1684-1711)* (Florence: Leo S. Olschki, 1979), 12–14; John L. Heilbron, *The Sun in the Church: Cathedrals as Solar Observatories* (Cambridge, Mass.: Harvard University Press, 1999), 203; Alfredo Dinis, "Giovanni Battista Riccioli and the Science of His Time," in *Jesuit Science and the Republic of Letters,* ed. Mordecai Feingold (Cambridge: MIT Press, 2003), 207. The other pope, Paul V, had approved the finding of 1616.

23. Michel-Pierre Lerner, "La réception de la condamnation de Galilée en France au xviie siècle," in Montesinos and Solís, *Largo campo di filosofare,* 517–19; Descartes to Mersenne, Nov. 1633, in Anne Bitbol-Hespériès, "Introduction," in René Descartes, *Le monde, l'homme* (Paris: Seuil, 1996), xxxiii–xxxiv.

24. Descartes to Mersenne, Feb. and Apr. 1634, in Bitbol-Hespériès, "Introduction," xxxiv–xxxv.

25. René Descartes, *Principes de la philosophie,* in *Oeuvres de Descartes,* ed. Charles Adam and Paul Tannery (1647; Paris: Vrin, 1964), 9:109 (pt. 3, §19).

26. Pierre Gassendi, *Institutio astronomica: Juxta hypotheses tam veterum quam recentiorum,* 2d ed. (London: Cornelius Bee, 1653), 143; Maurice Thirion, "Influence de Gassendi sur les premiers textes français traitant de Copernic," in *Avant, avec, après Copernic: La représentation de l'univers et ses conséquences epistémologiques,* ed. Centre international de synthèse (Paris: Blanchard, 1975), 258–59.

27. Robert Lenoble, *Mersenne ou la naissance du mécanisme,* 2d ed. (Paris: Vrin, 1971), 392–410; William L. Hine, "Mersenne and Copernicanism," *Isis* 64 (1973): 25–26, 30–31.

28. D'Addio, *Considerazioni,* 113; Walter Brandmüller, "Commento," in Brandmüller and Greipl, *Copernico, Galileo,* 26; Russell, "Catholic Astronomers," 370–71, referring to Ismail Bouilliau, *Astronomia philosophica* (1645), and the Latin translation of the *Dialogue,* printed in Lyon with license in 1641.

29. G. M. Pachtler, *Ratio studiorum et institutiones scholasticae societatis Jesu,* 4 vols. (Berlin: A. Hofmann, 1887–94), 3:121–27; Gaston Sortais, *Le cartésianisme chez les jésuites français au xviie et xviiie siècle* (Paris: Beauchesne, 1929), 20.

30. Ivana Gambaro, *Astronomia e techniche di ricerca nelle lettere di G. B. Riccioli ad A. Kircher* (Genoa: Università, Centro di Studio sulla Storia della Tecnica, 1989), 15.

31. Alfredo Dinis, "Was Riccioli a Secret Copernican?" in *Giambattista Riccioli e il merito scientifico dei gesuiti nell'età barocca,* ed. Maria Teresa Borgato (Florence: Leo S. Olschki, 2002), 53, 71.

32. Jean Robert Armogathe and Vincent Carraud, "La première condamnation des *Oeuvres de Descartes,* d'après des documents inédits aux Archives du Saint-Office," *Nouvelles de la République des Lettres* 2 (2001): 104–10.

33. The relevant text is session 13, canon 2. Cf. Marcus Hellyer, "Jesuit Physics in 18th Century Germany: Some Important Continuities," in *The Jesuits: Cultures, Sciences, and the Arts, 1540-1773,* ed. John W. O'Malley et al. (Toronto: University of Toronto Press, 1999), 545–47.

34. Galileo Galilei, "Assayer," in Stillman Drake, *Discoveries and Opinions of Galileo* (New York: Doubleday, 1957), 274; Pietro Redondi, *Galileo Heretic* (Princeton: Princeton University Press, 1987), 334.

35. Redondi, *Galileo Heretic,* chaps. 6–8.

36. See chap. 8 of this book.

37. Mariano Artigas, "Un nuovo documento sul caso Galileo: EE 291," *Acta Philosophica* 10 (2001): 210–13; Rafael Martínez, "Il manoscrito ACDF, *Index, Protocolli,* vol. EE, f. 291 r–v," *Acta Philosophica* 10 (2001): 217–18, 226–31.

38. Torrino, *Dopo Galileo,* 19–25.

39. G. B. Riccioli, *Almagestum novum,* 2 pts. (Frankfurt: Beyer, 1651), pt. 1, chap. 2, 52.

40. Ibid., pt. 1, chap.2, quotations on 309, 304, 309; cf. Dorothy Stimson, *The Gradual Acceptance of the Copernican Theory of the Universe* (New York: Baker and Taylor, 1917), 82, 83.

41. Riccioli, *Almagestum novum*, pt. 1, chap. 1, xxxiv.

42. Ibid., pt. 1, chap. 1, xix (quotations), pt. 1, chap. 2, 478.

43. Correspondence of 1646, in Gambaro, *Astronomia*, 40–41, 70–71; cf. Dinis, "Was Riccioli a Secret Copernican?" 56–58.

44. G. A. Kinner to A. Kircher, Dec. 17, 1661, in "Correspondence of Athanasias Kircher," Gregorian University Library, Rome, VIII, 13.

45. G. D. Cassini, *Mémoires pour servir à l'histoire des sciences,* ed. J. D. Cassini (Paris: Bleuet, 1810), 271–72; Cesare Preti, "Riccioli e l'Inquisitione," in Borgato, *Giambattista Riccioli,* 218–22.

46. John L. Heilbron, *Electricity in the Seventeenth and Eighteenth Centuries: A Study in Early Modern Physics* (Berkeley: University of California Press, 1979), 110, 113–14.

47. Preti, "Riccioli," 222–30.

48. G. B. Riccioli, *Astronomiae reformatae tomi duo,* 2 vols. (Bologna: Benati, 1665), 1:86; Heilbron, *Sun in the Church,* 182.

49. G. B. Riccioli, *Apologia* (Venice: Salerni and Cagnolini, 1669), 4, translation slightly modified from Stimson, *Gradual Acceptance,* 83–84.

50. Riccioli, *Apologia,* 104.

51. Pietro Cavina, *Congetture fisico-astronomiche della natura dell'universo sopra alcune osservazioni celesti nelle fisse havute in Faenza* (Faenza: Zarafagli, 1669), 35, 43–44 (quotation).

52. Maurizio Torrini, "Giuseppe Feroni, gesuita e galileano," *Physis* 15:4 (1973): 412–13.

53. A. Kircher, memo of July 4, 1660, Kircher Papers, IX, 102.

54. Eustachio Divini, *Pro sua annotatione in systema saturnium Christiani Hugenii adversus eiusdem assertionem* (Rome: Dragondelli, 1661), 46–48. Fabri was understood to be the author of Divini's books; Christiaan Huygens, *Brevis assertio systematis saturnii sui* (The Hague: Vlacq, 1660), 25.

55. Divini, *Pro sua annotatione,* 49. The statement was deemed sufficiently authoritative for republication, in English, in *Philosophical Transactions* 1 (1665), 74–75; Russell, "Catholic Astronomers," 278–79.

56 Cf. Ugo Baldini, *Saggi sulla cultura della Compagnia di Gesù (secoli xvi-xviii)* (Padua: CLEUP, 2000), 218–19.

57. Henri Bosmans, "Tacquet, André," in *Biographie nationale* (Brussels: Académie royale des sciences, 1926–29), vol. 24, cols. 441–43, 450–51, and "Le jésuite mathématicien anversois André Tacquet (1616–1660)," *De Gulden Passer/Le Compas d'Or* 3 (1925): 65, 83–84.

58. André Tacquet, *Astronomiae libri octo,* in *Opera mathematica,* 3 vols. (Louvain: apud I. Mersium, 1669), 12.

59. Ibid., 330–31.

60. M. Michaud, ed., *Biographie universelle ancienne et moderne* (Paris: C. Desplaces, 1854–65), 7:440; Claude François Milliet Deschales, *Cursus seu mundus mathematicus,* 4 vols. (1674; reprint, Lyon: Anisson, Poisuel, and Rigaud, 1690), 3:636 (quotation).

61. Deschales, *Cursus,* 1: preface, and 3:287 (quotation), 486.

62. Jean Baptiste Duhamel, *Astronomia physica* (Paris: Lamy, 1660), "Praefatio"; *Biographie universelle* (1855), 11:464–65.

63. Jean Baptiste Duhamel, *Philosophia vetus et nova,* 2 vols., rev. ed. (Nuremberg: Zieger, 1682), 356–58.

64. Ibid., 365.

65. Michaud, *Biographie universelle,* 11:464–65.

66. Text of 1689, in Domenico Bartolomeo Meli, "Leibniz on the Censorship of the Copernican System," *Studia Leibniziana* 20 (1988): 21–24.

67. Kurt Müller and Gisela Krönert, *Leben und Werk von G. W. Leibniz: Eine Chronik* (Frankfurt am Main: Klostermann, 1969), 99, 101.

68. Quotations from, respectively, Leibniz to Antonio Magliabecchi, Oct. 20/30, 1689, in Meli, "Leibniz," 28; and to M. Thévenot, Sept. 3, 1691, in Gottfried Wilhelm Leibniz, *Sämtliche Schriften und Briefe,* vol. 2, *Philosophischer Briefwechsel,* ed. Preussischen Akademie der Wissenschaften (Darmstadt: Otto Reichl, 1926), 352–53; Müller and Krönert, *Leben und Werk,* 95–96, 98.

69. Leibniz to Ciampini, Sept. 14/24, 1690, in Leibniz, *Sämtliche Schriften,* 248–49; Müller and Krönert, *Leben und Werk,* 97.

70. Leibniz to Magliabecchi, Oct. 20/30, 1699, in Antonio Magliabecchi, *Clarorum germanorum ad Magliabechium nonullosque alios epistolae* (Florence: Typ. ad Insigne Apollonis, 1746), 93.

71. Quotations from Leibniz to Huygens, Sept. 4/14, 1694, and from Leibniz's paper, are from the translation in Gottfried Wilhelm Leibniz, *Philosophical Essays,* ed. Roger Ariew and Daniel Garber (Indianapolis: Hackett, 1989), 91–92, 309.

72. Pierre-Noël Mayaud, *La condamnation de livres coperniciens et sa révocation à la lumière des documents inédits des Congrégations de l'Index et de l'Inquisition* (Rome: Università Gregoriana, 1997), 110–11.

73. Baldigiani to Viviani, Jan. 25, 1693, in Torrini, *Dopo Galileo,* 28; W. E. Knowles Middleton, "Science in Rome, 1675–1700, and the Accademia Fisicomatematica of Giovanni Giustino Ciampini," *British Journal for the History of Science* 8 (1975): 138–54, 154.

74. Maurizio Torrini, "La discussione sullo statuto delle scienze tra la fine del '600 e l'inizio del '700," in *Galileo e Napoli,* ed. Fabrizio Lomonaco and Maurizio Torrini (Naples: Guida Editori, 1987), 359, 364–73.

75. Luciano Osbat, *L'Inquisizione a Napoli: Il processo agli ateistici, 1688-1697* (Rome: Storia e Letteratura, 1974), 15–25, 29, 43–53, 63–64; Gabriel Maugain, *Etude sur l'évolution intellectuelle d'Italia de 1657 à 1750 environ* (Paris: Hachette, 1909), 136–42.

76. Osbat, *L'Inquisizione,* 101–22, 172–76, 247–52; Maugain, *Etude,* 153–61, 244–32; Pasquale Lopez, *Riforma cattolica e vita religiosa e culturale a Napoli dalla fine del cinquecento ai primi anni del settecento* (Naples: Mezzogiorno, 1964), 149, 158–64, 176–77, 182–97.

77. Georges Monchamp, *Galilée et la Belgique* (Saint-Trond: Moreau-Schouberechts, 1892), 187, 191–210, 215–19, 230–34, 263–96, 320–24, 329–30.

78. Torrini, "La discussione," 357–58.

79. Vincenzo Ferrone, *The Intellectual Roots of the Italian Enlightenment: Newtonian Science, Religion, and Politics in the Early Eighteenth Century,* trans. Sue Brotherton (Atlantic Highlands, N.J.: Humanities Press, 1995), 34–35 (quotation, from Celestino Galiani to Giovanni Bottara, Aug. 25, 1714); Ferrone, "Galileo, Newton," 163–66, 51–53, 186–87.

80. Mayaud, *La condamnation,* 113–18; Motta, "I criptocopernicani," 634–36, 705 (quotation), 713.

81. Alderano Desiderio, *Tavole de' cycli solari, e lettere domenicali* (Rome: Charcas, 1703), 19.

82. Heilbron, *Sun in the Church,* 212–16.

83. Quoted in Marta Cavazza, *Settecento inquieto: Alle origini dell'Istituto delle scienze di Bologna* (Bologna: Il Mulino, 1990), 215.

84. Vincenzo Coronelli, *Epitome cosmografica* (1693; reprint, Venice: n.p., 1696), quoting from 27, 301, 32, 196–97.

85. Cavazza, *Settecento,* 240, referring to Manfredi's *Il paradiso* (1698).

86. Tommaso Ceva, *Philosophia antiqua-nova* (1704; Milan: Bellagatta, 1718), fol. A.3v, 9, 28–30, 48, 68, 88.

87. Tomaso Campailla, *L'Adamo, ovvero il mondo creato* (Catania: Bisagni, 1709), 7 (quotation), 17 (quotation), 19–23, 27–28; Alberto M. Ghisalberti, ed., *Dizionario biografico degli Italiani* (Rome: Istituto della Enciclopedia Italiana, 1960–2003), 17:324–28.

88. Tomaso Campailla, *L'Adamo ovvero Il mondo creato,* ed. Secondo Senesio (Siracuse: Pulejo, 1783), 56 (verse 55), 65 (verses 173–74): "Within these most holy books / the divine law is registered / . . . / It need only be said that what is in them / the spirit of God dictated."

89. Appreciations, including a letter of Feb. 25, 1718, from George Berkeley, who discovered Campailla for England during a visit to Sicily, in Campailla, *L'Adamo* (1783), xxxvii, xliv–xlvi.

90. Giacomo de Mazava, in Campailla, *L'Adamo* (1783), "Al lettore."

91. Muratori, letter of July 9, 1732, in A. Schiavo-Lena, *Lettere inedite di L. A. Muratori, Francesco de Aguirre e Andrea Lucchesi* (Catania: Gianotta, 1907), 6.

92. Russell, "Catholic Astronomers," 388–89; Germano Paoli, *Ruggiero Giuseppe Boscovich nella scienza e nella storia del '700* (Rome: Accademia Nazionale delle Scienze Detta dei Quaranta, 1988), 27, 72; Richard William Farebrother, "Boscovich's Method for Correcting Discordant Observations," in *R. J. Boscovich: Vita e attività scientifica,* ed. Piers Bursill-Hall (Rome: Istituto della Enciclopedia Italiana, 1993), 255–61.

93. Giulio Natali, *Il settecento,* 2 vols. (Milan: Vallardi, 1929), 1:204–5, 191–95. The Holy Office approved the monument but insisted on reviewing the inscription; see Pagano and Luciani, *Il documenti,* 216.

94. Quotes from, respectively, Michele Federico Sciacca, "Introduzione," in Francesco Maria Zanotti, *Scritti filosofici* (Milan: Bocca, 1943), 6, and Natali, *Il settecento,* 1:198.

95. Ferrone, "Galileo, Newton," 159–61.

96. Ferrone, *Roots,* 8, 18, 38–39 (quotations).

97. Angelo Marchetti, *Breve introduzione alla cosmografia,* 2d ed. (Pistoia: Bracali, 1738), "A chi legge," 101, 95, respectively.

98. Jacopo Riccati, *Opere,* 3 vols. (Lucca: Giusti, 1761–64), 1:173–74, 294, texts from the 1730s and 1740s.

99. Riccati to Poleni, 1737, in *Jacopo Riccati-Giovanni Poleni carteggio (1715-1742),* ed. Maria Laura Soppelsa (Florence: Leo S. Olschki, 1997), 220, 223; see also Soppelsa's commentary, 40–41.

100. Enrica Baida et al., *Museo della Specola* (Bologna: Università di Bologna, 1995), 63–65, 147.

101. Letter of 1729, quoted by Ettore Bortolotti, *La storia della matematica nell'Università di Bologna* (Bologna: Zanichelli, 1947), 157.

102. Eustachio Manfredi, "De novissimis circa fixorum siderum errores observationibus," *Commentarii* (Accademia delle Scienze, Bologna) 1 (1748): 619 (quotation), 628–31, 639.

103. Manfredi to Algarotti, Feb. 19, 1737, in Cavazza, *Il settecento,* 245.

104. Mauro de Zan, "La messa all'Indice del 'Newtonianismo per le dame' di Francesco Algarotti," in *Scienza e letteratura: Cultura italiana del settecento,* ed. Renzo Cremante and Walter Tega (Bologna: Il Mulino, 1984), 140–46, 147 n. (Zanotti to A. Leprotti, Feb. 6, 1737, quotation).

105. Giovanni Poleni, *De vorticibus coelestibus dialogus* (Padua, 1712), "Praefatio," quoted by Ferrone, *Roots,* 292 n. 4; Newton, *Principia,* ed. T. Le Seur and F. Jacquier (Geneva, 1739–42), quoted by Franz Heinrich Reusch, *Der Index der verbotenen Bücher,* 3 vols. in 2 (Bonn: Weber, 1883–85), 2:399.

106. Benedict XIV, *Correspondance,* ed. E. de Heeckeren, 2 vols. (Paris: Plon-Nourrit, 1912), 1:305 (Feb. 17, 1747): "[Jacquier] est un vrai et savant religieux, d'une probité à toute épreuve." Cf. 1:56 (May 17, 1743) regarding Le Seur.

107. Riccati, *Opere,* 3:205–8 (text of the 1730s?).

108. Paolo Casini, "Les débuts du Newtonianisme en Italie, 1700–1740," *Dix-Huitième Siècle* 10 (1978): 87–91.

109. Mayaud, *La condamnation,* 130–39.

110. Marco Restiglian, "Nota su Giuseppe Toaldo e l'edizione toaldina del Dialogo di Galileo," *Studia Patavina* 29 (1982): 723–24; Fantoli, *Galileo,* 471–72, 492–93; Mayaud, *La condamnation,* 153–54.

111. Toaldo, in Galilei, *Opere,* fol a.2r.

112. Mayaud, *La condamnation,* 141–45, 152–53.

113. Ibid., 133, 156–57, 161; Benedict XIV to Cardinal Tencin, Dec. 29, 1742, in Benedict XIV, *Correspondance,* 1:20 (quotation), in general reference to the Curia and its protégés.

114. Paolo Simoncelli, "Inquisizione romana e Riforma in Italia," *Rivista Storica Italiana* 100 (1998): 72–73.

115. Ludwig von Pastor, *The History of the Popes from the Close of the Middle Ages,* trans. E. Graf, 40 vols. (London: Hodges and Kegan Paul, 1891–1953), 32:576, 621; Reusch, *Der Index,* 2:672–76; Marta Pieroni Francini, "Da Clemente XI a Benedetto XIV: Il caso Davia (1734–1750)," *Rivista di Storia della Chiesa in Italia* 37 (1983): 444–54.

116. Louis Cognet, "Ecclesiastical Life in France," in *History of the Church,* vol. 6, *The Church in the Age of Absolutism and the Enlightenment,* ed. Herbert Jedin (London: Burns and Oates, 1981), 53–57, 381–404.

117. Francini, "Da Clemente XI," 454–62.

118. Benedict XIV, *Bref au Grand Inquisiteur d'Espagne* (n.p., July 31, 1748), 3–5, 8–11 (quotation); and Benedict XIV, *Opera omnia,* 17 vols. (Prati: Typ. Aldina, 1839–47), 14:96–98; Reusch, *Der Index,* 2:832–34.

119. Benedict XIV, *Bref,* 5–6.

120. Benedict to Tencin, May 14, 1749, in Benedict XIV, *Correspondance,* 1:484.

121. Benedict XIV, *Correspondance,* 1:216, and quotations from 281–82 (Nov. 16, 1746), 313, 316 (Mar. 22 and Apr. 4, 1747).

122. Benedict XIV, *Opera,* 17:2:109 (quotation), 12, 114 (quotation); Reusch, *Der Index,* 2:5–6; Josef Hilgers, *Der Index der verbotenen Bücher, in seiner neuen Fassung dargelegt und rechtlich-historisch gewürdigt* (Frieburg/Br.: Herder, 1904), 60–61.

123. Benedict XIV, *Correspondance,* 2:294–95; Mayaud, *La condamnation,* 179.

124. Baldini, *Saggi,* 304–5.

125. The authorities most familiar with the archives differ with Mayaud, *La condamnation,* 175–78, championing Benedict, and Baldini, *Saggi,* 305 n., who found Ricchini's proposal, championing Ricchini.

126. Mayaud, *La condamnation,* 175, 176 (quotation), 78.

127. *GA,* 149.

128. Mayaud, *La condamnation,* 188, 190, 197 (quotation), 199, 204–11.

129. Brandmüller, "Commento," 35–37; Baldini, *Saggi,* 334–38, 340–41.

130. Examples in Baldini, *Saggi,* 388–89 n.

131. Ibid., 305–6, 323; Lazzari, quoted in Baldini, *Saggi,* 313 (quotation), 314–16; Paolo Frisi, *De motu diurno terrae disputatio* (Pisa: Giovanelli, 1756), praefatio.

132. Lazzari, quoted in Baldini, *Saggi,* 322–23, 328.

133. Maria Teresa Borgato, "La prova fisica della rotazione della terra e l'esperimento di Guglielmini," in *Copernico e la questione copernicana in Italia dal xvi al xix secolo,* ed. Luigi Pepe (Florence: Leo S. Olschki, 1996), 211–14.

134. Borgato, "La prova fisica," 28–33, 239, 247–50, 255–60.

135. Examples from Mayaud, *La condamnation,* 213–15.

136. Campailla, quoted in Torrini, *Dopo Galileo,* 10–12; Casini, in Paolo Frisi, *Elogi: Galilei [1775], Newton [1778], d'Alembert [1786],* ed. Paolo Casini (Rome: Theoria, 1985), 9–10.

137. Noel M. Swerdlow, "Montucla's Legacy: The History of the Exact Sciences," *Journal of the History of Ideas* 54 (1993): 301–4; H. Floris Cohen, *The Scientific Revolution: A Historiographical Inquiry* (Chicago: University of Chicago Press, 1994), 23–24, 530 n. 12.

138. Casini, in Frisi, *Elogi,* 11–13.

139. Frisi, *Elogi,* 25 (quotation), 58 (quotation), 59, 64–69. Cf. Gianni Michele, "L'idea di Galileo nella cultura italiana dal xvi al xix secolo," in *Galileo: La sensata esperienza,* ed. Paolo Galluzzi (Florence: A. Pizzi, 1982), 172–77.

140. Casini, in Frisi, *Elogi,* 19–20; Paolo Frisi, *Disquisitio mathematica in caussam physicam figurae, et magnitudinis telluris nostrae* (Milan: Regia Curia, 1751), 10–14, 16 (first quotation), f. b.4v (second quotation).

141. Casini, in Frisi, *Elogi,* 20; quotations from Paolo Frisi, *Opera,* 3 vols. (Milan: Galeati, 1782–85), 3:5–6, 23, 25.

142. Paolo Frisi, *Cosmographiae physicae et mathematicae, pars prior [et altera],* 2 vols. (Milan: Marelli, 1774–75), 1:1.

143. Natali, *Il settecento,* 1:230.

144. Gaspare Luigi Cassola, *Dell'astronomia libri sei* (Milan: Galeazzi, 1774), 102–3.

145. Fontana in Charles Bossut, *Saggio sulla storia generale delle matematiche . . . con riflessioni ed aggiunte di Gregorio Fontana,* 4 vols. (Milan: Nobile and Giegler, 1802–3), 4:299–300; Anton-Maria Lorgna, *Principi di geografia astronomico-geometrica* (Verona: Ramanzini, 1789), 41–58; Francesco Carlini, *Espositione d'un nuovo metodo di costruire le tavole astronomiche applicato alle tavole del sole* (Milan: Reale Stamperia, 1810), viii, referring to the work of Piazzi, Delambre, and Zach. Cf. Mayaud, *La condamnation,* 218–20.

146. Victor Navarro Brotóns, "Tradition and Scientific Change in Early Modern Spain: The Role of the Jesuits," in Feingold, *Jesuit Science,* 360–61, 383–84 n.

147. Antonio Cagnoli, *Notizie astronomiche, adatte all'uso commune,* 2 vols. (Reggio: Fiaccadori, 1827), 1:v, 1–2 (quotation; text of 1799); cf. Mayaud, *La condamnation,* 227–28.

148. Cagnoli, *Notizie,* 1:xx–xvi; Natali, *Il settecento,* 1:227–28; Paola Govoni, *Un pubblico per la scienza: La divulgazione scientifica nell'Italia in formazione* (Rome: Carocci, 2002), 65–68.

149. Cagnoli, *Notizie,* 1:23 (text of 1799), 68 n.

150. Brandmüller, "Commento," 163, 176–77.

151. François Gasnault, "La réglementation des universités pontificales au xixe siècle. I. Réformes et restaurations," Ecole française de Rome, *Mélanges: Moyen age—Temps modernes* 96:1 (1984): 185–86; Brandmüller, "Commento," 51–52.

152. Artaud de Montor, A. F., *Storia di Pio VII,* 2 vols. (Naples: Manfredi, 1840); Erasmo Pistolesi and Giuseppe di Novaes, *Vita del sommo pontifice Pio VII,* 4 vols. (Rome: Bourliè, 1824–30); H. E. Cardinal Wiseman, *Recollections of the Last Four Popes and of Rome in Their Time,* rev. ed. (London: Hurst and Blackett, n.d.), 105.

TWELVE

GALILEO'S "REHABILITATION"

Elbow-Room in Theology

Michael Sharratt

Like many people, I found Pope John Paul's address of October 31, 1992, on the Galileo case fascinating. Although the occasion was frequently referred to in the press as the rehabilitation of Galileo, it is noticeable that neither the pope nor Cardinal Poupard used that word in his address. Hence the quotation marks in my title.[1] In any case, Galileo did not need rehabilitating. If 'rehabilitation' is at all applicable in this context, then it applies to the authorities of the Roman Catholic Church and its theologians. In addressing the Galileo case Pope John Paul is endeavoring to remove an obstacle to understanding between faith and science. He is convinced that there can be useful dialogue between faith and science and that such dialogue is of vital importance to both. I shall return to this theme toward the end of this chapter.

Later in this chapter I shall comment on aspects of the Galileo case and of Pope John Paul's address, and I shall go on to discuss the relations of science and theology, but initially I wish to concentrate on two points. First, I take something that will always be a live issue in Christian theology, namely the interplay of intellectual freedom and faith. This is a topic that can interest Christians of all denominations—and others too, for that matter—but as an amateur theologian I shall confine myself to what I know something of, namely Roman Catholic theology. Second, I bring in another personal interest, to indicate how the Galileo case affected one particular Roman Catholic seminary. I hope that these two topics will throw some fresh light on the Galileo case and its lasting relevance. First, then, I turn to intellectual freedom, hinted at by the "elbow-room" of my title.

John Henry Newman and Elbow-Room

'Elbow-room' is a pet phrase of John Henry Newman. He may seem an unlikely guide to the Galileo case. It is easy to pick out from his Catholic publications incidental passages on Galileo that do little more than echo moralizing apologetics based on an inadequate understanding of what was actually at stake in the Galileo affair. But in his private notes and letters he is more interesting. He recognized earlier than most that Catholicism's claims to truth depend on acknowledging that doctrine develops. And he was a skilful practitioner of the theological art of interpreting doctrinal definitions.² Pope John Paul has shown himself more than willing to apologize for mistakes made by the Church. He too clearly recognizes that doctrine has developed, and he is happy, in his address, to give Galileo credit for an important contribution to the Church's developed understanding of Scripture in relation to science (§ 5). The pope also expects theologians to be alert to scientific advances to see whether there are reasons for taking them into account in their reflection or for introducing changes in their teaching (§ 8). The changes theologians introduce into their teaching constitute one source of the development of Catholic doctrine, as was evident at the Second Vatican Council. That is where elbow-room comes in. One might even say, "No development without elbow-room." So Newman is no ill-chosen companion for anyone reflecting on the Galileo case.

The Second Vatican Council is sometimes called "Newman's Council" because it implicitly and sometimes explicitly developed Catholic teaching. Given that the bulk of the documents prepared before the council were jettisoned and replaced by very different ones, it seems reasonable to say that there was more elbow-room at the council than there had been immediately before—I mean more elbow-room not only for the bishops who were responsible for adopting the documents but for the theologians who played such a large part in advising them. The clearest instance is the declaration on religious freedom that was explicitly presented to the bishops as a development. It is not surprising that this was one of the most controverted documents in the discussions of the council. As the pope has reminded us, development is not always linear (§ 14).

I shall quote passages from Newman's letters, where he is often very unbuttoned, but I start with a published remark: "Great minds need elbow room, not indeed in the domain of faith, but of thought. And so indeed do lesser minds, and all minds." Later in the same paragraph, talking about loyal Catholics, expert in their own line, he says: "Yet, if you insist that in their speculations, researches, or conclusions in their particular science, it is not enough that they should submit to the Church generally, and acknowledge its dogmas, but that they must get up all that divines have said or the multitude believed on religious matters, you simply crush and stamp out the flame within them, and they can do nothing at all."³

That sentence would have pleased Galileo, because he trespassed on theological ground only when others invoked theological arguments to interfere with his work as a scientist. But in that passage Newman is not talking about elbow-room in *theology*. For that we have to look to Newman's letters, reminding ourselves not only that Newman was wedded to what he called the dogmatic principle but also that he made it a rule "not to take any public step or to commit myself to any public act, in opposition to legitimate authority."[4] He was a loyal, conservative Catholic. He could, nevertheless, be very sharp in his criticism of those in authority. I introduce such criticisms because, like the Galileo case, they help Catholics, and perhaps others, to appreciate how difficult it is to exercise authority in doctrinal matters in a way that will retain the trust of theologians. I start with something that did not involve doctrine.

When Newman met with repeated frustration in his endeavors to found a Catholic University in Dublin, he considered the source of his troubles to be Archbishop Cullen of Dublin, a man, according to Newman, writing in 1860, "without trust in anyone—I wonder he does not cook his own dinners."[5]

At that time English and Welsh Catholics, even after the restoration of their hierarchy in 1850, were still accountable to the Congregation of Propaganda—the department concerned with spreading the Catholic faith. Newman in 1863 was scathing about how the system worked:

> I suppose, in the middle ages, which had a manliness and boldness of which there is now so great a lack, a question was first debated in a University; then in one University against another; or by one order of friars against another; then perhaps it came before a theological faculty; then it went to the metropolitan, and so by various stages and after many examinations and judgments, it came before the Holy See. But now what do Bishops do? All courts are superseded, because the whole English-speaking Catholic population all over the world is under Propaganda, an arbitrary, military power. . . . And who *is* Propaganda? One sharp man of business, who works day and night, and dispatches his work quick off, to the East and West, a high dignitary, perhaps an Archbishop, but after all little more than a clerk, or (according to his name) a Secretary, with two or three clerks under him.[6]

A couple of months later, he again harks back to the healthy days of the medieval schools and draws the moral:

> Truth is wrought out by many minds, working together freely. As far as I can make out, this has ever been the rule of the Church until now, when the first French Revolution having destroyed the schools of Europe, a sort of centralization has

been established at headquarters—and the individual thinker in France, England, or Germany is brought into immediate collision with the most sacred authorities of the Divine Polity.[7]

Then a cri de coeur: "This country is under Propaganda and Propaganda is too shallow to have the wish to use such as me. It is rather afraid of such. . . . It does not understand an intellectual movement. It likes quick results—scalps from beaten foes by the hundred."[8] In this letter Newman is reflecting on his reluctant and unsuccessful attempt to edit a periodical called *The Rambler* without falling foul of authority; that attempt was so unsuccessful that he was actually delated to Rome and thereafter was under a cloud.[9] It is in this context that elbow-room is mentioned: "All those questions of the day which make so much noise now, Faith and Reason, Inspiration etc. etc. would have been, according to my ability, worked out or fairly opened. Of course I required elbow room—but this was *impossible.*" Newman asked: "*Now,* [he means, in contrast to healthier times] if I as a private priest, put anything into print, *Propaganda* answers me at once. How can I fight with such a chain on my arm? It is like the Persians driven on to fight *under the lash.*"[10]

We are reminded of Galileo's fears in 1615. In Newman's terminology, Galileo wanted the issue of heliocentrism to be "fairly opened." Newman himself had not got over the fact that authority had intervened to take the editorship of *The Rambler* from him: "[I]t has been the same shock to my nerves that a pat from a lion would be."[11]

What Newman habitually resisted was "the narrowing of the terms of Catholicity."[12] That was why he was insistent that the school of theologians had an essential part to play in the interpretation of the Church's authoritative definitions and rulings of one kind or another. It is well known that both before and after the First Vatican Council he resisted the efforts of those we may call "maximizers," meaning those who, like Ward or Manning, seemed to extend the range of papal infallibility beyond what Newman thought credible.[13] We can understand how in 1879 Newman was glad to accept a cardinal's hat from Leo XIII. As he wrote to his friend from Anglican days, Pusey: "Here have I for thirty years been told by men of all colors in belief that I am not a good Catholic. . . . When after this period of penance, and this long trial of patience and resignation, say, would you not yourself in such a case feel it a call of God not to refuse so great a mercy as a thorough wiping away for ever of this stigma such as the offer of a Cardinal's Hat involves . . . ?"[14]

So Newman saw this honor from Leo XIII as his rehabilitation as a Catholic theologian. Already some of his remarks may resonate with thoughts prompted by what Pope John Paul calls Galileo's sufferings, especially since no such consolation was extended to Galileo. I am not suggesting that Newman's criticisms of Propaganda can be transferred to the Congregation of the Doctrine of the Faith in our time. But the issue of elbow-room will always be with us and I shall return to it.

A Seminary and the Galileo Case

The college in which I lecture in philosophy, Ushaw College, Durham, in England, is a direct descendant of the English College at Douai in France. Douai College was founded in 1568 in what was then the Spanish Netherlands. Its principal purpose was to train Catholic priests for work in England and Wales. In those troubled times more than 120 of those men were executed as traitors in their own homeland, so it is good to record that as successors of Douai we work daily in partnership with Anglicans and Methodists in offering undergraduate and postgraduate qualifications validated by the University of Durham. That is surely a development. Douai College too was affiliated to a university, the newly founded University of Douai, though for most of its history, until it was forced to close, the college gave its own lectures, while contributing fully to the public disputations that were such an important part of the teaching year in a town with many colleges.

On September 7, 1633, an Englishman called Matthew Kellison wrote an official reply to a letter sent to him a few days earlier by the papal nuncio at Brussels. Kellison reported that, in accordance with the nuncio's instructions, he had informed the chancellor and the professors of the University of Douai that the treatise of Nicholas Copernicus and the book of a certain Galilei had been condemned by the Sacred Congregations. Kellison observed that, so far from assenting to this fanatical opinion about the earth being in orbit, they thought it should always be exploded and hissed out of class. Kellison then remarked that in his own English College at Douai that paradox had never been approved and never would be. They had always been against it and always would be.[15]

Kellison was the president of the English College at Douai. He is remembered by those who care for these things not only as a respectable theologian in his own right but also as a man whose able and lengthy presidency entitles him to be treated as the second founder of his college. His letter reminds us of the notable effort made by the Inquisition in 1633 to ensure that the condemnation of Galileo should serve as an effective warning to philosophers and mathematicians in all the places and institutions where its authority was acknowledged.[16] One can understand Kellison's eagerness to emphasize the loyal orthodoxy of his university and college, but his emphatic use of 'always' was a hostage to fortune. His letter, like many others published by Favaro, is also needlessly rhetorical: why call Galileo's opinion "fanatical"? As Newman habitually insisted, moderation of language is an insufficiently esteemed virtue. This is important not just for people like Kellison but also for anyone exercising authority in the Church. Bellarmine understood this when he provided Galileo with the carefully phrased certificate in 1616. Pope John Paul reminded Bellarmine's own university of Bellarmine's attempts to avoid useless tensions and dangerous inflexibility in the relations between faith and science.[17] As

Newman saw, exaggerated language can be an unnecessary narrowing of the terms of catholicity.

Catholic scholars find their embarrassment deepened by the contrast between the concerted official strategy in 1633 to make the disciplining of Galileo reinforce the 1616 ruling on what was permissible doctrine for all Catholics and the recondite way in which the ruling was eventually withdrawn, simply by omitting from the *Index* of 1758 the general clause banning all books that advocated heliocentrism, while leaving the specifically banned works of Copernicus and Galileo still listed. It is, however, worth remarking that not every Catholic waited until 1758 before espousing heliocentrism. The teaching of philosophy and theology in my own College at Douai was competent enough but not likely to set Europe alight. So it is interesting to note when the college eventually accepted heliocentrism.

Alban Butler, better known for his often reprinted *Lives of the Saints,* presided over a philosophical disputation almost a century after Galileo's death in February 1741. He is often credited with having introduced Newtonianism into the college's philosophy course, but he makes it clear that, though Copernicus's hypothesis is most ingenious and finds great favor with astronomers, it has not been proved: "Indeed, because of the authority of Scripture, a wise decree has laid down that it may not be held as a thesis. In physics too it is not without difficulties."[18]

But William Wilkinson presided over a disputation of July 1758 where he seems quite comfortable with Newtonianism. The course started in 1757, as is shown by the full manuscript version of the course—a "dictate"—taken down by a student.[19] It is highly unlikely that Wilkinson had advance notice that the Congregation of the Index was about to omit the general prohibition of all books advocating heliocentrism. He had, moreover, been teaching philosophy since 1752, so evidence may turn up that he was teaching substantially the same course from the beginning. In any case, I have discovered a disputation poster from 1755 showing that Robert Banister, who in later life was proud to be an arch-conservative, taught a course that was a competent introduction to the work of a man he calls "the most sagacious Newton."[20] No worries about mere hypotheses there; no sign there of any concern about a wise decree of 1616. It seems that quite ordinary teachers simply decided for themselves that the ruling of 1616 was obsolete. In recent decades there has been frequent talk about how to avoid another Galileo case. Attention should also be given to how mistakes made by Church authority actually come to be corrected and whether this process is sometimes unnecessarily protracted and just left to risky ventures of private enterprise.

Elbow-Room in 1616

I now touch on whether the original Galileo case could have been avoided. Here I am not referring to his condemnation. I am asking: Could the Congregations of the Inquisition and the Index have acted differently in 1616? I should also mention that I am not adverting to what used to be a traditional strand of Catholic apologetics, the strand that reduces to saying that Galileo brought all his troubles on himself by trespassing on theological grounds and by making exaggerated claims about the evidence for Copernicanism; that is more or less what Newman says in several passages. What I find interesting is that when a version of Galileo's *Letter to Castelli* was sent for examination, the consultor found little wrong with it beyond the fact that it contained certain unhappy expressions that could be interpreted *in malam partem*—unfavorably.[21] It is true that this opinion had no authority beyond that of an approved consultor. But the version of the *Letter to Castelli* that he was examining contained the core of what Galileo required to allow him to continue his work without theological interference.[22] One might say: it claimed elbow-room in science for Galileo precisely by pointing out to theologians that they had more elbow-room in theology than they realized. It is not that the expert consultor was endorsing Galileo's opinion, with all its implications. But he was allowing that it was an opinion compatible with Catholic orthodoxy. He used sober language. It was not he who narrowed the terms of Catholicity. So it is not an anachronism to say that there was nothing *inevitable* about the condemnation of Copernicanism in 1616.

Nor is it an anachronism to say that people were aware of the problem of elbow-room in philosophy (including what we call science) and theology. The decades-long discussion within the Society of Jesus concerning what became the *Ratio Studiorum* was grappling with the problem of maintaining fidelity to Catholic tradition in its many educational institutions. We can sympathize with the difficulties facing the Society on many topics, including the new astronomy. Pope John Paul reflected that "the pastoral judgement which the Copernican theory required was difficult to make." He went on to say, in a general way, "that the pastor ought to show a genuine boldness, avoiding the double trap of a hesitant attitude and of hasty judgement" (§ 7). But it so happens that in the crucial half-dozen years from 1610 the general of the Jesuits, Claudio Acquaviva, laid most emphasis on caution. That is why in February 1613 we find the peaceable Jesuit Grienberger concluding a letter to Galileo with best wishes and the remark: "Do not be surprised that I do not mention your work: I do not have the same freedom as you do."[23] Grienberger and his fellow-Jesuits were, of course, more than entitled to assess Galileo's writings critically and to look for him to prove his case. But Acquaviva's policy for the Society tended to confine them to the role of traditionalist critics of novelties, whereas hitherto they had been at least cautiously open to new discoveries, as they had shown in the academic honors the Roman College paid to Galileo in 1611. To use Pope John Paul's phrase, they had, in fact, been considering whether there were reasons for introducing changes in their teaching, changes that could affect what their colleagues would teach in theology. Acquaviva's hesitant attitude and the hasty judgment of the Congregation of the Index left Jesuit astronomers and theologians with no adequate elbow-room.

Bellarmine, as I have noticed, was certainly concerned to avoid useless tensions between faith and science. That was the whole purpose of his letter to Foscarini in 1615. When he wrote that letter, he clearly thought he was allowing more than sufficient elbow-room for Galileo to get on with his science. All that Galileo and Foscarini needed, he thought, was to accept the customary interpretation of the astronomer's role, which had it that astronomical hypotheses were mere calculating devices that did not involve any question of truth or falsity. If that had been good enough for Copernicus, surely it should satisfy Galileo.[24] Before long, however, Bellarmine learned that Copernicus had *not* been satisfied with such an instrumentalist or fictionalist approach, so he was not being inconsistent when he was party to the official intervention of 1616 that he conveyed personally to Galileo. The elbow-room officially allowed to Galileo, as far as Galileo knew, was the same as that left for all Catholics. Heliocentric hypotheses could be freely used as calculating devices, but that was all. One could not say that the earth really was a planet. This was confirmed by the corrections to Copernicus's book that the Congregation of the Index issued in 1620.

The Ambiguity of 'Hypothesis'

Now it is true that 'hypothesis' is a slippery notion. But it is unfortunate that Pope John Paul in his address commented on it in a way that could easily mislead: "In the first place, like most of his adversaries, Galileo made no distinction between the scientific approach to natural phenomena and a reflection on nature, of the philosophical order, which that approach generally calls for. That is why he rejected the suggestion made to him to present the Copernican system as a hypothesis, inasmuch as it had not been confirmed by irrefutable truth" (§ 5).[25]

My impression is that Galileo and his adversaries did reflect philosophically on the implications of what they were doing. It would be more helpful to say that Galileo's forays into the epistemology of science enabled him to see the shortcomings of an instrumentalist account of the findings of astronomy. In fact, one of the publications of Pope John Paul's own commission provides a detailed explanation of why Galileo was right not to be content with the instrumentalist suggestion.[26] Galileo's adversaries too can be given some credit for philosophical reflection, so long as we acknowledge that such reflection is never a guarantee of satisfactory results or even of consensus. Galileo found many useful things in what we may call the philosophy of science of Benedict Pereira: that did not commit him to accepting Pereira's Aristotelian rejection of the claim that the stars move through the heavens like fish in water, a point on which Bellarmine too felt free to disagree with Aristotelians.

But the fact that Bellarmine's highly selective instrumentalism was less than satisfying does not mean that Galileo himself had arrived at a satisfactory epistemology of science. He wanted to be able to say that heliocentrism did more than fit the facts—"save the appearances," in the customary phrase—but despite occasional boasting, what he could produce fell short of conclusive proof. Ernan McMullin points out that Galileo did not manage to find an appropriate category to describe the epistemic status of the Copernican hypothesis: "Perhaps it was because he was so heavily influenced by the traditional Aristotelian emphasis on demonstration that he did not develop in response to Bellarmine the notions of likelihood or probability that he so badly needed. It was all or nothing—and in the intellectual climate of Rome in 1615, the latter was a more likely verdict on Copernicanism."[27]

That is well worth saying. But it is worth adding (as McMullin does) that, in occasional jottings, Galileo did show that he was trying to find a way of justifying heliocentrism that would show it was more probable than its rivals.[28] In his *Dialogue* he went to great lengths to make it look as though he was conforming to the ruling of 1616 while in fact insinuating that there were so many weaknesses in geocentrism that heliocentrism was much more probable. Before publication, Riccardi, the official Roman censor, told the Florentine inquisitor that in the book Galileo "discourses probably" about the Copernican system.[29] In fact, of course, the decree of the Congregation of the Index did not leave room for any such attempt to show that heliocentrism was probable; the mere fact that in his *Dialogo* of 1632 Galileo had occasionally let slip the word 'probable' would have been enough to get him into serious trouble, even if the controversial personal injunction had never figured in his trial.[30] It is a great pity that Pope John Paul's address elides the crucial distinction between hypotheses as mere calculating devices and hypotheses as conjectures that could eventually be shown to be true. Cardinal Poupard's presentation (§ 2) of the same issue is, one has to say, garbled.

Galileo was, of course, not the only one to be heavily influenced by the Aristotelian emphasis on demonstration. Bellarmine shared his presuppositions. That, taken with Bellarmine's view of hypotheses in astronomy as mere calculating devices, is enough to undermine the claim made by Cardinal Poupard and endorsed in Pope John Paul's address (§ 9) that Bellarmine "had seen what was truly at stake in the debate." Like Galileo, Bellarmine had seen important elements; neither had grasped all that was needed for a satisfactory understanding. It is also worth recalling that the scientific case put forward by Galileo was not actually examined by the consultors of the Inquisition in 1616. They simply took the awkward summary provided by Caccini's delation and promptly concluded that heliocentrism was scientifically absurd.

One thing that Galileo did see more clearly than Bellarmine is of lasting significance. He realized that in Catholic theology it cannot be sufficient to appeal, without further ado, to the constant tradition of the fathers of the Church and of theologians.[31] Such an appeal is conclusive only if it can be shown that the fathers (and theologians) did more than simply take for granted what is now coming into serious question for the first time. If we are looking for lessons for the Church from the Galileo case, this is one, and one that is not confined to possible conflicts between faith and science. Quite generally, a new idea may be so novel (as heliocentrism was in 1616) that it has never been adequately discussed. The tradition of the Church may often enough give sufficient pointers to show that the novelty cannot be reconciled with the Church's faith. But it needs to be shown in each case that the tradition has a better basis than long-standing unquestioned assumptions.

Certainly it was difficult for theologians to adjust to the major shift in thinking that Galileo was calling for. Pope John Paul adverts to this: "Thus the new science, with its methods and the freedom of research which they implied, obliged theologians to examine their own criteria of scriptural interpretation. Most of them did not know how to do so" (§ 5).

As others have pointed out, completeness would require that one include among the theologians, as Cardinal Poupard does, Galileo's judges. The cardinal may have intended 'judges' to include the cardinals of the Holy Office and Pope Urban VIII. It would have been healthier if the role of both Paul V and Urban had been explicitly acknowledged. It also occurs to me that if theologians had been given time to reflect—given elbow-room—then they might well have reexamined their principles of interpretation. It seems hard to offload the blame onto "most theologians" of the time—Bellarmine seems to be presented as an honorable exception—when theologians barely had a chance to tackle the problem before the intervention of 1616.

So far I have been offering criticisms of details in the addresses made by Pope John Paul and Cardinal Poupard in 1992. I think these criticisms matter and need to be taken into account in any attempt to summarize the lessons to be learned from the Galileo case. But despite the shortcomings I have mentioned, both addresses do something important. They show a genuine attempt to remove an obstacle to dialogue, and they speak of Galileo in a generous spirit. Naturally it is not difficult to record admiration for Galileo's achievements as a scientist, and it is surely allowable on such an occasion to say, as the pope did, that "he practically invented the experimental method" (§ 12). The addresses give high praise to Galileo's excursion into theology in his *Letter to the Grand Duchess Christina* and do not carp at the known weaknesses of that brilliant essay. This generous tone is significant. My impression is that most theologians do not give Galileo credit for his remarkable piece of amateur theology. He certainly gets such credit from the pope and Cardinal Poupard. This forthright praise was needed. It was remarked with some forcefulness in a speech at the Second Vatican Council that the Catholic Church had never made any sort of amends to Galileo.[32] That speech led to a coded reference to a work on Galileo by Pio Paschini, *Vita e opere di Galileo Galilei,* in a footnote to the *Constitution on the Church in the Modern World.*[33] But for the specialist in Galileo studies there is something ambiguous about referring, without comment, to that work, which had itself suffered from its treatment by Church officials.[34] For the general public such a coy hint had the whiff of

Kremlinology rather than the transparent open-handedness of the document to which it was a footnote. So I want to emphasize that, though the addresses of both Pope John Paul and of Cardinal Poupard could easily have been improved and improved by making fuller use of the work of the pope's own commission, still those missed opportunities should not obscure the fact that the pope is fully committed to furthering the dialogue between faith and science and wishes to encourage theologians to enter into that dialogue wholeheartedly.

Science and Theology

Naturally such dialogue is not likely to be easy. It demands a certain competence that most theologians can reasonably disclaim. Even a theologian as committed to dialogue as Karl Rahner said in his last address a few weeks before his death: "Yet, as a theologian, every time I open a book on modern science, I become quite panic-stricken. Most of what is written in these books is quite foreign to me. Moreover, I am more than likely not capable of understanding their content. Hence, as a theologian, I feel somewhat compromised faced with this reality. Then the pale abstraction and hollowness of my own theological concepts hits me with a shock."[35]

Rahner, as you might expect, managed to draw consolation from this human limitation, so the rest of us need not be too discouraged. In any case, it is clear that scholarly study of the relations between religion and science generally, and of the Galileo case in particular, have greatly benefited from the contributions of people, including Roman Catholics, who are committed believers in God. Such contributions have often included philosophy of science. I seize on this because Pope John Paul frequently emphasizes the importance of philosophy and has devoted a whole encyclical, *Faith and Reason,* to themes relevant to our discussion. He expects theologians to take philosophy seriously throughout their work, so his exhortations to them in the address we are considering can be taken to include not just current developments in science but their philosophical implications or presuppositions. It seems to me likely that a good proportion of any dialogue between faith and science is likely to use history and philosophy of science as a potential meeting ground, even though—or perhaps because—left to themselves, working scientists may feel no need to attend to the history of their discipline or to philosophical issues. In this context I want to touch on some typical contributions of Pope John Paul to the dialogue between faith and science.

In a speech to those who were commemorating the 350th anniversary of what Pope John Paul called Galileo's "great work," the *Dialogo,* the pope remarks that the Galileo affair has helped the Church to a more mature and more accurate understanding of its own authority. He also says, as roundly as one could wish: "One thus perceives more clearly that divine revelation, of which the Church is the guarantor and witness, does not of itself involve any particular scientific theory, and the assistance of the Holy Spirit in no way lends itself to guaranteeing the explanations that we would wish to maintain of the physical constitution of reality."[36]

That is a reassurance, if one were needed, that what is usually called creationism, or any other position based merely on a literalistic reading of Scripture, does not now form part of the agenda of Catholic theologians in dialogue with scientists. Time and again the pope also insists on the autonomy of science. In the address to the Pontifical Academy that we are revisiting, he also quietly moves beyond the preoccupation with conclusive proof that Bellarmine and Galileo shared:

> What is important in a scientific or philosophic theory is above all that it should be true or, at least, seriously and solidly grounded. And *the purpose of your Academy* is precisely *to discern and to make known,* in the present state of science and within its proper limits, *what can be regarded as an acquired truth* or at least as enjoying such a degree of probability that it would be imprudent and unreasonable to reject it. In this way unnecessary conflicts can be avoided. (§ 13)

Any fuller treatment of the task of theologians would have to recognize that it is not just science that has come to see its acquired truths as falling short of the sort of certainty that Galileo and Bellarmine aspired to. Something similar has changed the face of Catholic theology in the past fifty years. I do not mean that Catholic theologians consider themselves free to jettison defined dogmas of the Church or to dilute other important parts of Catholic teaching. But even in the area where a theologian is expert, he or she will have a lively sense that doctrine has developed, that even dogmas have a history, that there is development within the New Testament itself, and that the growth of historical consciousness can sometimes make earlier confidence about what is theologically certain seem naive. It is, after all, the historical-critical method as much as the development of science itself that enables Pope John Paul to say, "In fact, the Bible does not concern itself with the details of the physical world, the understanding of which is the competence of human experience and reasoning." That goes beyond Bellarmine but not beyond Galileo. Both Bellarmine and Galileo, however, would concur with the pope's next sentence: "There exist two realms of knowledge, one which has its source in Revelation and one which reason can discover by its own power. To the latter belong especially the experimental sciences and philosophy" (§ 12).

The pope does not see these two realms of knowledge as being in opposition to each other. But they do have points of contact (§ 12). Their interests can overlap. So he recognizes that there is no guarantee that they will never come into conflict (§ 4). Revisiting the Galileo case is meant to help all parties to avoid unnecessary conflict and to use dialogue to find an acceptable way through whatever remaining controversial issues seem to have the partners to the dialogue at cross-purposes. Such a dialogue will require both science and faith to be aware of the limits of their own competencies (§ 4).

What is clear from the encyclical *Faith and Reason* is that, in the terms of the Galileo affair, the pope sees himself as a realist in science, as Galileo was. (So was Bellarmine, except when it came to astronomy.) I do not mean that the pope proscribes instrumentalism for Catholic philosophers of science. I mean simply that he himself is a realist. I personally find this position congenial, but that is not my point. My point is that to defend realism in philosophy of science is not easy, but it is a valuable contribution to the very diversified debate of the past few decades. Next, it is plain that the pope is hostile to relativism. He clearly considers that some forms of relativism in their implications are incompatible with the requirements of a Catholic understanding of truth. In other words, some forms of relativism would so undermine Catholic teaching that they cannot be accepted by a Catholic. But the point here is not to take refuge in Catholic dogma. It is rather to appeal to the implications of the search for truth shared by all human beings. It voices a confidence that the truth can be discovered. No doubt this rejection of relativism is highly controversial. No doubt it has to be argued for. But it is a very significant contribution to the dialogue between faith and science and, as it happens, one that many scientists who are innocent of philosophy seem to find congenial.

Elbow-Room in the Church

It is natural, of course, to ask how the doctrinal authority that the Catholic Church claims relates to demands that the autonomy of science, philosophy, and theology should be respected. Those who exercise or acknowledge that authority are well aware that this is a massive topic, not to be disposed of in the concluding paragraphs of a single paper, especially in a paper written by someone who is not a theologian. Nor need we assume that all the important issues involved can best be handled by extrapolation from the Galileo affair. But in the context of this volume it is worth saying that things have come a long way since the Florentine ambassador asked Urban VIII whether Galileo could not be told what was objectionable in his *Dialogue*. The answer was: "The Inquisition doesn't work like that."[37] It is noticeable that the Congregation of the Doctrine of the Faith acknowledged in its important document "The Ecclesial Vocation of the Theologian" that its own procedures might need improvement.[38] Those procedures were in fact revised in 1997. They are accessible on the Vatican's Web site. I take it that if they need further revision that can happen as part of the routine life of the Church. But I said I would take Newman as a guide, and I offer as a possible topic for discussion a long unpublished passage by Newman in which many of the themes dear to his heart are evident. The alternative phrasings in angled brackets are Newman's:

> If I find that scientific inquiries are running counter to <against> certain theological opinions, it is not expedient to refuse to examine whether those opinions are well founded, merely because those inquiries have not attained a triumphant success <reached their issue>. The history of Galileo is the proof of it. Are we not at a disadvantage as regards that history? and why? why, except because our theologians, instead of cautiously examining what Scripture, that is, the Written Word of God really said, thought it better to put down with a high hand the astronomical views which were opposed to its popular interpretation?

Newman concedes that it might not have been prudent in the 1630s to allow the free publication of Galileo's treatises but then says, "[T]hat does not show that it was justifiable to pronounce that they were against the faith and to enforce their abjuration."

So far, Newman seems to be merely anticipating the address of Pope John Paul. But he continues:

> I am not certain that I might <may> not go further, and advocate the full liberty to teach the motion of the earth, as a philosophical truth, not only now, but even three centuries ago. The Father Commissary said it was a scandal to the whole of Italy; that is, I suppose, an offence, a shock, a perplexity. This might be, but there was a class, and even is a class, whose claims to consideration are too little regarded now, and were passed over then. I mean the educated class; to them the prohibition would be a real scandal in the true meaning of the word, an occasion of their falling. Men who have sharpened their intellects by exercise and study anticipate the conclusions of the many by some centuries. If the tone of public opinion in 1822 called for a withdrawal of the prohibition to treat of the earth's motion, the condition of the able and educated called for it in Galileo's age; and it is as clear to me that their spiritual state ought to be consulted for, as it is difficult to say why in fact it so often is not. They are to be tenderly regarded for their own sake; they are to be respected and conciliated for the sake of their influence upon other classes. I cannot help feeling, that, in high circles, the Church is sometimes looked upon as made up of the hierarchy and of the poor, and that the educated portion, men and women, are viewed as a difficulty, an incumbrance, as the seat and source of heresy; as almost aliens to the Catholic body, whom it would be a great gain, if possible, to annihilate. For all these reasons I cannot agree with those who would have us stand by what is probably

or possibly erroneous, as if it were dogma, till it is acknowledged on all hands, by the force of demonstration, to be actually such.[39]

Notes

1. I refer to the pope's address (and Cardinal Poupard's) on Oct. 31, 1992. See John Paul II, "Lessons of the Galileo Case," *Origins* 22 (1992): 370–74, and Paul Poupard, "Galileo: Report on the Papal Commission Findings," *Origins* 22 (1992): 374–75. In the original French, both are in *Acta Apostolicae Sedis* 85 (1993): 764–72.

2. I refer to what are called "theological notes"—that is, terms used to grade theological propositions on a descending scale from "dogma of the faith" to "probable" or "pious" opinions. See Sixtus Cartechini, *De valore notarum theologicarum et de criteriis ad eas dignoscendas* (Rome: Gregorian University, 1951). More useful are Francis Sullivan, *Magisterium: Teaching Authority in the Catholic Church* (Dublin: Gill and Macmillan, 1983), and *Creative Fidelity: Weighing and Interpreting Documents of the Magisterium* (Dublin: Gill and Macmillan, 1996); and Ladislas Örsy, *The Church: Learning and Teaching: Magisterium, Assent, Dissent, Academic Freedom* (Dublin: Dominican Publications, 1987).

3. John Henry Newman, *The Idea of a University Defined and Illustrated: I. In Nine Discourses Delivered to the Catholics of the University of Dublin; I.* [sic] *In Occasional Lectures and Essays Addressed to the Members of the Catholic University* (London: Longmans, 1897), 476. For instances of Newman's adopting an unfavorable view of Galileo's trespassing on theological grounds, see 219–20 and 472.

4. All references to Newman's letters are to *The Letters and Diaries of John Henry Newman* (hereafter *LD*), ed. Charles Stephen Dessain et al. (London: Thomas Nelson, 1961–72; Oxford: Clarendon Press, 1973–). This letter is to J. J. Ignaz von Döllinger, June 25, 1859, *LD*, 19:159.

5. Newman to Robert Ornsby, July 1, 1860, *LD*, 19:379.

6. Newman to William Monsell, Jan. 13, 1863, *LD*, 20:391.

7. Newman to Robert Ornsby, Mar. 26, 1863, *LD*, 20:425–26.

8. Newman to Emily Bowles, May 19, 1863, *LD*, 20:447.

9. For background to this episode and a reprint of the article that got Newman into trouble, see Newman, *On Consulting the Faithful in Matters of Doctrine*, ed. and introd. John Coulson (London: Geoffrey Chapman, 1961).

10. Newman was willing allow to Protestants elbow-room in the interpretation of the 39 Articles: see his letter to W. J. O'Neill Daunt, June 17, 1863, *LD*, 20:475–76. Newman even worked into his *Apologia* the phrase "fighting, as the Persian soldiers, under the lash," but—in contrast to what he says in letters—gives the impression that this was not likely to be the condition of a Catholic theologian. See his *Apologia pro Vita Sua, Being a History of His Religious Opinions* (London: Longmans, 1900), 266–67. In the original edition, published by Longman and Green (London, 1864), the phrase comes in the "General Answer to Mr. Kingsley," 410.

11. Newman to Mrs. T. W. Allies, Jan. 20, 1864, *LD*, 21:23. In a letter of Feb. 12, 1864, to her husband, he again mentions the "lash" and "elbow-room": see *LD*, 21:48–49. Elbow-room is also mentioned as late as Feb. 19, 1885, in a letter to Anne Mozley: see *LD*, 31:31.

12. Newman to James Laird Patterson, Apr. 25, 1867, *LD,* 23:189–90.

13. Newman resented being called a "minimizer," but the fact that his interpretation of the definition of papal infallibility coincided with that of the secretary general of Vatican I (who had the approval of Pius IX) "clearly proves to us that a moderation of doctrine, dictated by charity, is not inconsistent with soundness in the faith." See his *Letter Addressed to His Grace the Duke of Norfolk on Occasion of Mr. Gladstone's Recent Expostulation* (London: B. M. Pickering, 1875), 112.

14. Newman to E. B. Pusey, Mar. 2, 1879, *LD, 29:55.*

15. Galileo Galilei, *Opere di Galileo Galilei* (hereafter *OGG*), ed. Antonio Favaro (1890–1909; reprint, Florence: Giunti Barbèra, 1968), 11:392–93.

16. See the letters in *OGG,* 19:363–93.

17. John Paul II, "Ad academicas auctoritates, professores et alumnos Pontificiae Universitatis Gregorianae," Dec. 15, 1979, *Acta Apostolicae Sedis* 71 (1979): 1538–49; see 1541.

18. Michael Sharratt, "Alban Butler: Newtonian in Part," *Downside Review* 96:323 (Apr. 1978): 108. The catalogue of the library of the University of Glasgow lists lecture notes on this course of 1740–41. I owe this reference to my brother, Dr. Peter Sharratt. I have not yet had the opportunity to study the manuscript.

19. Michael Sharratt, "Copernicanism at Douai," *Durham University Journal,* n.s. 36:1 (Dec. 1974): 41–48.

20. Michael Sharratt, "Natural Philosophy at Douai, Crook Hall and Ushaw," in *Lingard Remembered,* ed. Peter Phillips (London: Catholic Record Society, 2004), 9–22.

21. *OGG,* 19:305.

22. See *OGG,* 5:281–88, for Galileo's letter to Castelli.

23. *OGG,* 11:480.

24. Bellarmine's letter to Foscarini is in *OGG,* 12:171–72.

25. Cardinal Poupard's speech has often been commented on for its misleading presentation of Bellarmine's thought. See, for instance, Michael Sharratt, *Galileo: Decisive Innovator* (1994; Cambridge: Cambridge University Press, 1996), 215; Annibale Fantoli, *Galileo and the Catholic Church: A Critique of the "Closure" of the Galileo Commission's Work,* Studi Galileiani 6:1 (Vatican City: Vatican Observatory Publications, 2003); and chap. 13 of this book.

26. See Józef M. Zycinski, *The Idea of Unification in Galileo's Eipistemology,* Studi Galileani 1:4 (Vatican City: Vatican Observatory Publications, 1988), 8–10.

27. Ernan McMullin, "Galileo on Science and Scripture," in *The Cambridge Companion to Galileo,* ed. Peter Machamer (Cambridge: Cambridge University Press, 1998), 287.

28. See, for example, *OGG,* 5:368–69.

29. *OGG,* 19:327.

30. See *OGG,* 7:139, 144, 149, 368.

31. See the passage in the *Letter to the Grand Duchess Christina, OGG,* 5:335–36.

32. "In this, the fourth centenary of the birth of this most worthy man, many scientists throughout the world are celebrating his memory, but right up to today no reparation has been made for that wretched, unjust condemnation. In the world of today *acts* are more important than words. The rehabilitation of Galileo carried out by the Church, humbly and properly, would be an eloquent action." *Acta Synodalia Sacrosancti Concilii Oecumenici Vaticani II,* vol. 3, pt. 6 (Vatican City: Polyglot Press, 1975), 268. The speaker was Bishop Arthur Elchinger, coadjutor of Strasbourg.

33. See *The Documents of Vatican II,* ed. Walter M. Abbott (New York: Herder, 1966). par. 36, p. 234.

34. See Fantoli, *Galileo,* 503–6.

35. Karl Rahner, "Experiences of a Catholic Theologian," trans. Declan Marmion and Gesa Thiessen, *Theological Studies* 61:1 (Mar. 2000): 12; from an address given at a conference held on Feb. 11–12, 1984, and published in German in *Vor dem Geheimnis Gottes den Menschen verstehen: Karl Rahner zum 80. Geburtstag,* ed. Karl Lehmann (Munich: Schnell and Steiner, 1984).

36. John Paul II, "A Papal Address on the Church and Science," May 9, 1983, *Origins* 13:3 (1983): 51.

37. See *OGG,* 14:384.

38. Congregation of the Doctrine of the Faith, "Introduction on the Ecclesial Vocation of the Theologian," July 5, 1990, *Origins* 20 (1990): 118–26. The Latin original is in *Acta Apostolicae Sedis* 89 (1997): 830–35.

39. *The Theological Papers of John Henry Newman on Biblical Inspiration and on Infallibility,* selected, ed., and introd. J. Derek Holmes (Oxford: Clarendon Press, 1979), 34–43.

THIRTEEN

THE CHURCH'S MOST RECENT ATTEMPT TO DISPEL THE GALILEO MYTH

George V. Coyne, S.J.

On October 31, 1992, John Paul II, in an address to the Pontifical Academy of Sciences,[1] said that one of the lessons of the Galileo affair is that we now have a more correct understanding of the authority that is proper to the Church and that "[f]rom the Galileo affair one can draw a lesson that remains valid in relation to similar situations that occur today and that may occur in the future."[2] Just 350 years before, Pope Urban VIII had declared that Galileo had made himself guilty of an "opinion very false and very erroneous and which had given scandal to the whole Christian world."[3] The contrast between these two official Church judgments on Galileo separated by a 350-year period is enormous. The question is: What does it bode for the next 350 years? So the import of my paper is not just academic; it attempts to present a judgment on the past and on the present with a view to the future.

In that same speech John Paul II, as he had done on previous occasions, describes the Galileo affair as a "myth":

> From the beginning of the Age of Enlightenment down to our own day, the Galileo case has been a sort of myth, in which the image fabricated out of the events was quite far removed from reality. In this perspective, the Galileo case was the symbol of the Church's supposed rejection of scientific progress, or of

dogmatic obscurantism opposed to the free search for truth. This myth has played a considerable cultural role. It has helped to anchor a number of scientists of good faith in the idea that there was an incompatibility between the spirit of science and its rules of research on one hand and the Christian faith on the other.[4]

A myth it may be. Or it may be a genuine historical case of a continuing and real contrast between an intrinsic ecclesial structure of authority and the freedom to search for the truth in whatever human endeavor, in this case in the natural sciences.

There is an ample history of the Church's attempts to remedy the Galileo "myth."[5] While making passing reference to these, I will limit myself to addressing directly the most recent and, as best I know, latest attempt. I will seek to evaluate how well it has succeeded and what it bodes for the future. I am referring to the so-called Galileo Commission constituted on behalf of John Paul II by a letter of the cardinal secretary of state of July 3, 1981, to the members of the commission.[6] On October 31, 1992, John Paul II, in a solemn audience before the Pontifical Academy of Sciences, brought to a close the work of the commission. The pope's address was preceded by that of Cardinal Paul Poupard,[7] who had been invited by the cardinal secretary of state by letter of May 4, 1990, to coordinate the final stages of the work of the commission. An analysis of these two addresses reveals some inadequacies. I would first like to discuss those inadequacies and then try to trace their origins in a history of the commission's workings and the circumstances that surrounded them.

In the discourse prepared for the pope, the Galileo affair is described as a "tragic mutual incomprehension,"[8] and the incomprehension is specified by what can be identified as the following four principal conclusions of the two discourses: (1) Galileo did not understand that, at that time, Copernicanism was only "hypothetical" and that he did not have scientific proofs for it—thus he betrayed the very methods of modern science of which he was a founder; (2) "theologians" were not able, at that time, to correctly understand Scripture; (3) Cardinal Robert Bellarmine understood what was "really at stake"; (4) when scientific proofs for Copernicanism became known, the Church hastened to accept Copernicanism and to admit implicitly that it had erred in condemning it. I will discuss each of these four conclusions in turn.

The Methodology of Science and the Meaning of 'Hypothesis'

According to the papal discourse, the "incomprehension" on Galileo's part was that he did not understand the difference between science and philosophy. He would not accept Copernicanism as hypothetical and thus did not understand science, even though he was one of the founders of it. This accusation against Galileo is suspect on two accounts: (1) a mistaken attribution to Galileo of the failure to distinguish between the notions of science and philosophy—Galileo never denied that there could be considerations beyond scientific ones; (2) the ambiguous notion of "hypothesis." It is wrong, therefore, to imply that Galileo was not faithful to the experimental method of which he was a founder.

In the papal discourse we read: "[L]ike most of his adversaries, Galileo made no distinction between the scientific approach to natural phenomena and a reflection on nature, of the philosophical order, which that approach generally calls for. That is why he rejected the suggestion made to him to present the Copernican system as an hypothesis, inasmuch as it had not been confirmed by irrefutable proof. Such, therefore, was an exigency of the experimental method of which he was the inspired founder."[9] Much could be said about this characterization of the scientific method and Galileo's use of it. I limit myself to discussing the ambiguity involved in the use of the word 'hypothesis.' There are two distinctly different uses of the word in this context: a purely mathematical expedient to predict celestial events or an attempt to understand the true nature of the heavens. This important difference in meaning must be seen against the history of the word's use from antiquity through medieval Christianity to the time of Copernicus through to Galileo. The best historical example of this is, of course, the case of Osiander. In his attempt to save Copernicus, Osiander, unbeknownst to the author and contrary to the latter's intent, wrote his famous preface to advise the reader that the *De revolutionibus* was intended, in the tradition of medieval astronomy, only in the former sense, as a mathematical expedient. There is no doubt that Galileo understood his own investigations to be an attempt to understand the true nature of things. It is well known that he preferred to be known as a philosopher of nature rather than as a mathematician. It can be debated as to whether Galileo himself was ever convinced that he had irrefutable proofs for Copernicanism (involved in that debate would be the very meaning of "proof" for him and for us), but it cannot be denied that he sought evidence to show that Copernicanism was really true and not just a mathematical expedient. Galileo rejected the claim that Copernicanism was a hypothesis in the former sense. He sought to find experimental verification of it in the latter sense. He can certainly not be accused of betraying the very method "of which he was the inspired founder."

The final report given by Cardinal Poupard (hereafter referred to as "the final report") asserts that Galileo did not have proof for the earth's motion, and it cites Galileo's erroneous use of the argument from the tides. However, up until 1616, when the earth's motion was declared by the Congregation of the Index to be "false and altogether contrary to Scripture," Galileo had not yet propagated publicly his argument from the tides. But it did not matter; neither in 1616 nor in 1633 was any science discussed. It was principally for scriptural considerations and also thanks to philosophical convictions that Copernicanism was condemned. Galileo's telescopic observations of the phases of Venus, of the satellites of Jupiter, of the sequential motions of spots on the sun, and so on were completely ignored. Although not proofs, they were certainly persuasive indications of Copernicanism, and they clearly challenged Aristotelian natural philosophy. Scholars debate as to what degree of likelihood Galileo's arguments for Copernicanism up until 1616 conferred on his final arguments in the *Dialogue*. But there is no doubt that the arguments available from his telescopic observations merited a hearing. But in 1616 the Congregation of the Index did not listen to scientific arguments.

The Church's Incomprehension

As to the Church's "incomprehension," the papal address exclusively faults theologians: "The problem posed by theologians of that age was, therefore, that of the compatibility between heliocentrism and Scripture. Thus, the new science, with its methods and the freedom of research which they implied, obliged theologians to examine their own criteria of Scriptural interpretation. Most of them did not know how to do so."[10] These words echo those of the final report: "Certain theologians, Galileo's contemporaries, being heirs of a unitarian concept of the world universally accepted until the dawn of the 17th century, failed to grasp the profound, non-literal meaning of the Scriptures when they describe the physical structure of the created universe. This led them unduly to transpose a question of factual observation into the realm of faith."[11] And:

> It is in that historical and cultural framework, far removed from our own times, that Galileo's judges, incapable of dissociating faith from an age-old cosmology, believed, quite wrongly, that the adoption of the Copernican revolution, in fact not yet definitively proven, was such as to undermine Catholic tradition, and that it was their duty to forbid its being taught. This subjective error of judgment, so clear to us today, led them to a disciplinary measure from which Galileo "had much to suffer."[12]

The incomprehension of "theologians," it is said, was due to the fact that, although the new science, and the freedom of research that the methods of the new science supposed, should have obliged theologians to reexamine their criteria for interpreting Scripture, "most of them" did not know how to do this.

The point, however, is that the majority of theologians of that epoch did not even know of the existence of a new science, did not know its methods, and did not feel obliged to respect the freedom of scientific research. Galileo and others of his time (Kepler, Castelli, Campanella, etc.) were ahead of their time in proposing freedom of research. (Galileo wrote of it in the *Letter to Castelli* and in the *Letter to Christina.*) It took a long time, with the development of modern science, before this became an accepted principle. It would have carried no weight, therefore, with the theologians of Galileo's day, during either the events of 1616 or those of 1632–33.

The papal address also claims that the error of the theologians was due to their failure to "recognize the distinction between Sacred Scripture and its interpretation."[13] This cannot be correct. Since the time of Augustine, this distinction was well established, and it was taught in all the schools of exegesis at the time of Galileo. In fact, in 1616 the qualifiers/consultors of the Holy Office knew this distinction and used it in formulating their philosophical-theological opinion on Copernicanism. Their opinion did not ignore the distinction, but their exegetical principle was flawed in that they required a demonstration of Copernicanism before one could abandon the literal interpretation of the scriptural text.

The "theologians" in both discourses are unidentified and unidentifiable. There is no mention of the Congregation of the Holy Office (the Roman Inquisition), or of the Congregation of the Index, nor of an admonition given to Galileo by Cardinal Bellarmine in 1616, acting on orders from the Pope, nor of the abjuration required of him in 1633 by official organs of the Church. Nor is mention made of Paul V or Urban VIII, the ones ultimately responsible for the activities of those official institutions.

Bellarmine Saw What Was at Stake

When the papal discourse refers to "most" theologians, the implication is that a minority knew how to interpret Scripture, among whom, of course, was Cardinal Bellarmine. The discourse proceeds to accept the erroneous interpretation of Bellarmine's role that was proposed in the final report.

The papal discourse, echoing the final report, describes Bellarmine, in contrast to "most" theologians, as the one "who had seen what was truly at stake in the debate [since he] personally felt that, in the face of possible scientific proofs that the earth orbited around the sun, one should 'interpret with great circumspection' every biblical passage which seems to affirm that the earth is immobile and 'say that we do not understand rather than affirm that what has been demonstrated is false.'"[14] Following the final report, the papal discourse then offers an interpretation of Bellarmine's *Letter to Foscarini* in which two conclusions are derived that appear to make Bellarmine both the most open-minded of theologians and a scholar respectful of science. One must, according to this interpretation of Bellarmine, be circumspect in interpreting scriptural statements about natural phenomena in the face of possible scientific proofs contrary to the interpretation. If such proofs are forthcoming, one must reinterpret Scripture. Note that the epistemic priority is given here to Scripture. Since Galileo had no irrefutable proofs of Copernicanism, the current interpretation of Scripture by theologians, including Bellarmine, should remain but always be subject to reinterpretation. Is this a correct presentation of Bellarmine's position?

The final report interprets Bellarmine as saying, "As long as there are no proofs for the movement of the Earth about the Sun, it is necessary to be cautious in interpreting Scripture."[15] What Bellarmine actually says is, "Should proofs be had, then we must go back and reinterpret Scripture." The difference is: Bellarmine did not say, "Theologians should be cautious *now* in interpreting Scripture in expectation that proofs for Copernicanism might appear" but rather "If a proof *were* to appear, then *on that day in the future* theologians would have to be cautious in interpreting Scripture."

This interpretation of Bellarmine's position, in both the final report and the papal address, is based on a partial and selective reading of the *Letter to Foscarini*. In the passage immediately preceding the one just cited, Bellarmine had taken a very restrictive position by stating: "Nor can one answer that this [geocentrism] is not a matter of faith, since if it is not a matter of faith 'as regards the topic,' it is a matter of faith 'as regards the speaker'; and so it would be heretical to say that Abraham did not have two children and Jacob twelve, as well as to say that Christ was not born of a virgin, because both are said by the Holy Spirit through the mouth of the prophets and the apostles."[16] Clearly if geocentrism is a matter of faith "as regards the speaker," then openness to scientific results and circumspection in interpreting Scripture are simply ploys. They lead nowhere. Furthermore, Bellarmine cites Scripture itself in the person of Solomon to show that proofs for Copernicanism are very unlikely. And still more, at the end of the *Letter to Foscarini* Bellarmine appears to exclude any possibility of a proof by stating that our senses clearly show us that the sun moves and that the earth stands still, just as someone on a ship "sees clearly" that it is the ship that is moving and not the shoreline. Both discourses cite Bellarmine's statement: "I say that if there were a true demonstration [of Copernicanism] then one would have to proceed with great care in explaining the Scriptures that appear contrary and say rather that we do not understand them, rather than that what is demonstrated is false."[17] What they do not cite is the next sentence of Bellarmine: "But I will not believe that there is such a demonstration until it is shown me." From the concluding sentences of the letter it is clear that Bellarmine was convinced that there could be no such demonstration. A further indication of this conviction on Bellarmine's part is that he supported the decree of the Congregation of the Index aimed at excluding any reconciliation of Copernicanism with Scripture. If he truly believed that there might be a demonstration of Copernicanism, would he not have recommended waiting and not taking a stand, a position embraced at that time, it appears, by Cardinals Barberini and Caetani?[18] And why did he agree to deliver the admonition to Galileo in 1616? This admonition prohibited Galileo from pursuing his research with regard to Copernicanism. Galileo was forbidden to seek precisely those scientific demonstrations that, according to Bellarmine, would have driven theologians back to reinterpret Scripture.

The Church Corrected Its Error

The judgment rendered in the final report that "the sentence of 1633 was not irreformable"[19] is accepted in the papal address. In both discourses there is an attempt to establish that a reformation actually started as soon as the scientific evidence for Copernicanism began to appear. It is claimed that the reform was completed with the imprimatur granted under Pope Pius VII to the book of Canon Settele entitled *Elements of Optics and Astronomy* (1822), in which Copernicanism was presented as a thesis and no longer as a mere hypothesis.[20] There are a number of inaccuracies of historical fact and interpretation in these judgments.

The imprimatur of 1822 did not refer to Galileo or to the sentence of 1633. It referred to the teaching of Copernicanism. And if it is claimed that the imprimatur implicitly reformed the sentence of 1633, why was that not made explicit? As a matter of fact, the works of Copernicus and Galileo remained on the *Index* until 1835, more than a decade after the Settele affair. And since the sentence of 1633 refers explicitly to Galileo's failure to observe the decree of 1616, why was that decree not also reformed? Of course, if the tactical maneuver of the commissary of the Holy Office, Olivieri, for granting the imprimatur to Settele's book were to be accepted, then the decree of 1616 and the sentence of 1633 would have been fully justified.[21] At the recommendation of the cardinals of the Holy Office, in order to resolve the issue and to "safeguard the good name of the Holy See," Olivieri devised the following formula. Copernicus was not correct, since he employed circular orbits and epicycles. The Church was, therefore, justified on scientific grounds to condemn Copernicanism in 1616 and 1633. Obviously, there was no need to revoke a decree that rejected what was incorrect at the time of the decree! It appears, from the diaries of Settele, that Olivieri himself had some doubts about his argumentation. Considering all of these circumstances, the resolution of the Settele affair can hardly be considered a definitive reform of the sentence of 1633.

But antecedent to this purported definitive reform are several intermediate reform movements that the final report addresses. Referring to the discoveries of aberration and parallax, it states that "[t]he facts were unavoidably clear, and they soon showed the relative character of the sentence passed in 1633. This sentence was not irreformable. In 1741 . . . Benedict XIV had the Holy Office grant an *imprimatur* to the first edition of the complete works of Galileo,"[22] and "This implicit reform of the 1633 sentence became explicit in the decree of the Sacred Congregation of the Index which removed from the 1757 edition of the *Catalogue of Forbidden Books* works favoring the heliocentric theory."[23] To what extent were the activities of 1741 and 1757 reform decisions? The imprimatur of Benedict XIV was granted under the condition that the stipulations of the Padua inquisitor, who had requested the imprimatur, be observed. The result was that the publication in 1744 of the "complete works" had to exclude the *Letter to Christina* and the *Letter to Castelli.* Furthermore, the *Dialogue* had to be printed in volume 4, accompanied by the 1633 sentence and the text of Galileo's abjuration, and it had to contain a preface emphasizing its "hypothetical" character.

In 1757 after the cardinal prefect of the Congregation of the Index had spoken about the matter with Pope Benedict XIV, a decision was taken at a meeting of the consultors (not the cardinal members) to omit the general prohibition of Copernican books in the new *Index of Forbidden Books,* to be published in 1758. What was to be admitted and prohibited? In the 1619 edition of the *Index of Forbidden Books,* the first after the 1616 decree, and in subsequent editions there were two categories of prohibitions of Copernican works: *nominatim* (specific works) and general. The edition of 1758 excluded *only* the general. Included still were Copernicus's *De revolutionibus,* Galileo's *Dialogue,* and Kepler's *Epitome.*

The Roots of the Inadequacies

The inadequacies discussed above in the discourses that closed the workings of the Galileo Commission would, almost unanimously, be regarded as such by the community of historians and philosophers of science. In fact, I am indebted to that community, to which I cannot claim to belong, for all that I have discussed thus far.[24] As a first attempt at tracing the origins of those inadequacies, it is obvious that one must examine the workings of the commission itself. I shall now do that by discussing the constitution of the commission, the membership, the chronology of the activities, including the meetings, and the official publications and by evaluating the overall activities of the commission.

A critical problem with doing all of this is that, to my knowledge, there is no centralized commission archive. Minutes of each of the commission meetings are available, but much, probably critical, correspondence among the commission members and between the commission and the Vatican Secretariat of State is scattered among the Pontifical Academy of Sciences (Father di Rovasenda was chancellor of the academy at that time and secretary of the commission), the Pontifical Council of Culture and its predecessor councils[25] (Cardinal Poupard was head of the commission's section on culture and was appointed to close the commission's work), and various section heads. Thus far, I have been able to consult only some parts of the archives. Those researches and my personal participation as a member of the commission are the sources for the following.

Constitution of the Commission

On November 10, 1979, John Paul II, near the end of the first year of his pontificate, gave an address to the Pontifical Academy of Sciences on the occasion of the commemoration of the birth of Albert Einstein.[26] In section 6 the pope expressed the "hope that theologians, scholars and historians . . . might examine more deeply the Galileo case." That wish became reality when, on July 3, 1981, a letter of Cardinal Agostino Casaroli, secretary of state, constituted the "Galileo Commission" in the name of the pope, announcing Cardinal Gabriel-Marie Garrone as president with Father Enrico di Rovasenda as his assistant and inviting six persons to accept positions on the commission: Archbishop Carlo Maria Martini for the exegetical section; Archbishop Paul Poupard for the section on culture; Prof. Carlos Chagas and Father George Coyne for the section on scientific and epistemological questions; Monsignor Michele Maccarrone and Father Edmond Lamalle for historical and juridical questions. (Names and titles of persons and the titles of the sections are as given in the letter of Cardinal Casaroli.) The letter requested that "the work be carried out without delays and that it lead to concrete results." There was no public announcement of the constitution of the commission. The existence of the commission only became known when its first publications appeared.[27]

The first meeting of the commission was held at the Pontifical Academy of Sciences on October 9, 1981. Seven meetings of the commission were held, the last on November 22, 1983. On May 4, 1990, a letter of Cardinal Casaroli, then secretary of state, to Cardinal Poupard, then president of the Executive Council of the Pontifical Commission for Culture, invited Poupard to coordinate the final stages of the commission's work. On October 31, 1992, at the biennial meeting of the Pontifical Academy of Sciences, Cardinal Poupard presented in the final report what were described as "the results of the interdisciplinary inquiry" with which the commission had been entrusted, and the pope gave the closing address, the two discourses already discussed above.

Members of the Commission

As best I can judge from the archival material available to me, only those named in the letter of Cardinal Casaroli that founded the commission were official members. In addition, each section had collaborators whose identity can be obtained from the list of publications, from the list of those named as collaborators of the sections on culture and on exegesis, and from the editorial board of Studi Galileiani, a series published by the Vatican Observatory.[28] It is of some interest to consider each official commission member in turn.

Cardinal Gabriel-Marie Garrone, president of the commission, was made a cardinal in 1967. He had been archbishop of Toulouse, France, and he was very much involved at the Second Vatican Council in the formulation of the document *Gaudium et spes*, which treated of the Church in the modern world.[29] He served as prefect of the Congregation for Catholic Education. He suffered ill health from the mid-1980s and died on January 15, 1994. It can be surmised that the long interval between the last meeting of the commission, November 22, 1983, and the conclusion of the work of the commission on July 13, 1990, as announced by a letter of Cardinal Poupard to the commission members in which he states that "various reasons" had contributed to the commission's inactivity, was due in no small part to the personal circumstances of Cardinal Garrone's health.

Cardinal Carlo Maria Martini was named archbishop of Milan on December 29, 1979, the month after John Paul II's Einstein address in which the pope called for a reconsideration of the Galileo affair. He was made cardinal on February 2, 1983. Because of his pastoral responsibilities, he participated only in the first meeting of the commission. He was an eminent biblical scholar and had been rector of the Pontifical Biblical Institute and then the Pontifical Gregorian University.

Cardinal Paul Poupard was named pro-president of the Secretariat for Non-Believers in 1980 (in 1988 this became the Pontifical Council for Dialogue with Non-Believers). In 1982 the Pontifical Council for Culture was established and Poupard was named president of its Executive Council. In 1993 the two councils were united into one, the Pontifical Council of Culture, and Poupard became pro-president. He was made cardinal on May 25, 1985. In addition to chairing the commission's section on culture, he was called upon, as described in the previous section, to coordinate the conclusion of the commission's work.

Father Enrico di Rovasenda, O.P., was chancellor of the Pontifical Academy of Sciences from 1974 to 1986 and was appointed as assistant to the commission's president. He served as secretary of the commission and recorded the minutes of the meetings up until the last one in 1983.

Professor Carlos Chagas, a biophysicist, was president of the Pontifical Academy of Sciences from 1972 to 1988. He died on February 16, 2000.

Father George Coyne, an astrophysicist, has been director of the Vatican Observatory since 1978.

Monsignor Michele Maccarrone, a Church historian, was president of the Pontifical Committee for Research in History (Pontificio Comitato di Scienze Storiche).[30] He was a disciple of Monsignor Pio Paschini and promoted the publication of Paschini's much-contested book *Vita e Opere di Galileo Galilei* (The life and works of Galileo Galilei).[31] He died on May 4, 1993.

Father Edmond Lamalle, S.J., a historian, was archivist for the Curia of the Society of Jesus in Rome. At the request of the president of the Pontifical Academy of

Sciences, Georges Lemaître, he prepared Paschini's book for publication, introducing numerous revisions on his own account, thus adding new complications to the controversy.[32] He participated in no public commission activities, and it appears that he was replaced by Professor Mario d'Addio, but I know of no documentation to support that conclusion. Lamalle died on December 8, 1989.

Professor Mario d'Addio, philosopher and professor at the University of Rome "La Sapienza," participated in the second meeting of the commission on December 11, 1981. He was not named as a member of the commission but may have been a substitute for Father Lamalle, as I have just mentioned.

What conclusions might be drawn from these brief sketches of the commission members? It appears that most members were selected by reason of their office: prefect of the Congregation for Catholic Education, pro-president of the Pontifical Council of Culture, president of the Pontifical Academy of Sciences, chancellor of the same academy, director of the Vatican Observatory, president of the Pontifical Committee for Research in History. There was no philosopher of science or historian of science among the members, nor was there a section dedicated to those disciplines. (Some of the collaborators in the publications of the commission were historians and/or philosophers of science.)[33] Furthermore, several key members for reasons of health or other pressing responsibilities were not able to take an active role in the commission's work. Had Cardinal Martini, for instance, been able to take a more active role in the commission's work, the inadequacies in the interpretation of the role that scriptural exegesis played in the Galileo affair and especially the role of Robert Bellarmine could have been avoided.

Chronology of the Activities of the Commission

On October 9, 1981, the first meeting of the commission was held at the Pontifical Academy of Sciences. At that meeting Father di Rovasenda informed those present that in February 1981 the Holy Father had requested from him a proposal as to the Galileo affair and that on March 11, 1981, he had replied with the suggestion of a commission, with Cardinal Garrone as president and with four sections. At the subsequent meeting on December 11, 1981, Cardinal Garrone was absent due to hospitalization. Archbishop (at that time) Poupard presided. Professor Mario d'Addio participated and presented a note concerning the lack of unanimity in the sentence condemning Galileo. The commission invited Cardinal Garrone as president to request of the Holy Father that he open the archives of the one-time Congregations of the Holy Office and of the Index. At the meeting of June 17, 1982, Cardinal Garrone reported that by letter of January 9, 1982, he had requested of the Holy Father that those archives be opened. At the meeting of October 8, 1982, it was suggested that an audience be requested with the Holy Father to report on what had been done and to ask for further directives. To my knowledge no such audience occurred. At the meeting of May 9, 1983, Cardinal Garrone referred to a discourse of the pope of that same day[34] in which His Holiness recognized the work of the commission. Cardinal Garrone suggested that all of the works of the commission be published together in a volume(s) with a preface by him and introductions by the various section presidents. To my knowledge, this publication never appeared. At the meeting of November 22, 1983, there was further discussion of the request to open the archives of the one-time Congregations of the Holy Office and of the Index.

On May 4, 1990, Cardinal Casaroli, as already noted, wrote to Cardinal Poupard inviting him, as a result of a previous discussion of Cardinal Poupard with the substitute of the secretary of state of which the Holy Father had been informed, to coordinate the final stages of the commission's work. On May 22, 1990, Cardinal Poupard wrote to the members of the commission recalling that the commission had met seven times and stating that seven years had gone by during which for "various reasons" communications between the members of the commission had discontinued. He referred to the letter of May 4, 1990, sent to him by Cardinal Casaroli, and, in order to proceed to conclude the commission's work, he asked for reports of the various sections. On July 13, 1990, Cardinal Poupard sent a letter to the members of the commission thanking them for their responses and declaring concluded the work of the commission.[35] To the same effect a letter of the same date was sent to the cardinal secretary of state.[36]

What conclusions might we draw from this summary chronology of the commission's activities? There are three periods of apparent inactivity that are difficult to understand. About twenty months passed between the call of November 10, 1979, the "first" call, and the constitution of the commission by the letter of Cardinal Casaroli of July 3, 1981, the "second" call. Why this long interval? During this interval journalistic speculations ripened: a "retrial," a "rehabilitation," even a "canonization." Who initiated this "second" call? The letter of Cardinal Casaroli gives only general hints when it says that the pope was responding to "expectations . . . expressed both in studies and in letters sent to the Holy See and to one or other of its qualified offices and in articles published in scientific journals and information releases." To what extent were parties involved in the "first" call also involved in the "second"? It would be interesting to know whether such insistent pressure existed.[37]

The interval between the last meeting of the commission on November 22, 1983, and the closing of the commission's work with the discourses of Cardinal Poupard and of the pope on October 31, 1992, also requires explanation. There was no unified commission activity during that period. In his letter of May 22, 1990, Cardinal Poupard attributes the lull to "various reasons." Other than the health conditions of Cardinal

Garrone, the commission president, mentioned above, no indication is given of what the "various reasons" were. Finally, about twenty-eight months passed between Cardinal Poupard's letter of July 13, 1990, declaring the work of the commission closed and his final report of October 31, 1992, in which he presents, as he says, "the results of the interdisciplinary enquiry which you [the pope] asked the commission to undertake."[38] The last two publications listed in the Appendix occur during this interval, and, as we shall see, they appear to have had a significant role to play in the final report.

The commission requested several times, as already noted, that the archives of the one-time Congregations of the Holy Office and of the Index be opened, but without success at that time. As a result, however, of the insistence of the commission, the Pontifical Academy of Sciences in the immediate postcommission years initiated a project, *The Catholic Church and Science,* to publish all documents concerning the Catholic Church and science contained in the archives of the previous Congregations of the Holy Office and of the Index.[39] I have no further knowledge of the progress of this project.

Except at the seven meetings of the commission over a three-year period, there was little or no exchange between the four sections of the commission. Apparently the only list of the publications officially sponsored by the commission, including those in preparation at the time of the closure of the commission, are those referred to in the final report of October 31, 1992. (See the Appendix for a list of these publications in chronological order.) The commission as a whole never accepted or rejected any of the publications so referred to, and the last two publications in chronological order appeared after the letter of Cardinal Poupard of July 13, 1990, in which he declared the work of the commission to be concluded.

Evaluation of the Activities of the Galileo Commission

What are we to make of the four points on which the final report and the papal discourse following it are subject to criticism? I suggest that two summary statements can be made: (1) there appears to have been a retreat within the Church from the posture taken in 1979 to that which concluded the work of the Galileo Commission in 1992; (2) history continues to show that the differences between authority in the Church and authority in science are persistent.

In his discourse of November 10, 1979, John Paul II said that "Galileo had much to suffer . . . from the men and agencies of the Church."[40] In his discourse and in the final report of October 31, 1992, the whole Galileo affair is summed up as a "tragic mutual incomprehension" from which a "myth" has endured according to which the Galileo controversy has become a symbol of what some think to be an inevitable conflict between science and faith. Both Galileo and "some theologians" were uncomprehending: Galileo because he did not respect the very scientific method of which he was one of the principal founders, the need to prove hypotheses by sound scientific evidence; "some theologians" because they did not know how to interpret Scripture. The discourse of 1979 seems to imply that Galileo need not have suffered and that the official Church held some responsibility for his sufferings. In the discourses of 1992 the implication is that Galileo's suffering was inescapable ("tragic" in the sense of the classical Greek tragedies) because of the "mutual incomprehension," inevitable if we consider those times. In the end it appears that no one was responsible for Galileo's sufferings. They had to be; they were "tragic"; they were driven in an inevitable way by the circumstances of that historical period, by an incomprehension of which Galileo himself could be accused.

From what I have presented above, the picture given in the discourses of October 31, 1992, does not stand up to historical scrutiny. What happened between 1979 and 1992? Why was the pope's wish for the work of the commission not fulfilled, namely, the desire that he expressed in his 1979 discourse and that Cardinal Casaroli repeated in his letter constituting the commission, that by "a frank recognition of wrongs from whatever side they come, [it might] dispel the mistrust that still opposes, in many minds, a fruitful concord between science and faith"?

What made the "mutual incomprehension" "tragic" and therefore provided the basis for the "myth" of Galileo? The most reasonable response, it appears, is that the "incomprehension" should be attributed to the official organs of the Church and in the end to Pope Paul V and Pope Urban VIII. This would have been more in keeping with the pope's 1979 statement that Galileo had suffered at the hands of institutions of the Church. And it could have arisen consistently with the pope's pastoral concerns in the Galileo case.[41]

The pope alludes explicitly to these concerns. At that time the geocentric universe seemed to be part of the teaching of Scripture. So pastoral concerns made it difficult to accept Copernicanism. He says: "Let us say, in a general way, that the pastor ought to show a genuine boldness, avoiding the double trap of a hesitant attitude and of hasty judgment, both of which can cause considerable harm." However, he draws no conclusion from this. What conclusions might be drawn? First, the Church's position with respect to Galileo was surely not "hesitant." Was it hasty? The pope makes an ambiguous admission that it was when he says, in comparing the Galileo case to the one that arose later concerning biblical exegesis, that "certain persons" rejected well-founded conclusions from history in their preoccupation to defend the faith.[42] "That," the pope admits, "was a hasty and unhappy decision." But note that the protagonists of this hasty conclusion are "certain persons," not theologians, not institutions of the Church, certainly not popes! In fact, it was the Pontifical Biblical Commission that drew the hasty conclusion in the exegesis case, and it was the Congregation of the Index, the Congregation of the Holy Office, and Paul V who enacted a hasty decree in 1616 and the Congregation of the Holy Office and Urban VIII who proclaimed a hasty condemnation of Galileo in 1633.

This reluctance to place responsibility where it truly belongs is repeated in the papal discourse of October 31, 1992, with regard to the condemnation of Galileo. The claims made in the final report that the sentence of 1633 was not irreformable and that as the debate evolved it was concluded with the imprimatur granted to the work of Settele are accepted verbatim. The verdict passed on Copernicanism at that time would, of course, today be regarded as erroneous, in that sense showing that it was "reformable." But, so far as we can conclude from the circumstances of the condemnation, Pope Urban VIII and the cardinals of the Holy Office did not themselves think it to be "reformable." Furthermore, if it was reformable, why has the condemnation of 1633 or, for that matter, the decree of the Congregation of the Index in 1616 never been explicitly "reformed"?

Myths are founded in concrete happenings. In the Galileo case the historical facts are that further research into the Copernican system was forbidden by the decree of 1616 and then condemned in 1633 by official organs of the Church with the approbation of the reigning pontiffs. This, and not a "tragic mutual incomprehension," is at the source of the "myth" of Galileo. Galileo was a renowned world scientist. The publication of his *Sidereus Nuncius* (The starry messenger) established his role as a pioneer of modern science. He had tilted the Copernican-Ptolemaic controversy decisively against the long-held Ptolemaic system. Observational evidence was increasingly challenging Aristotelian natural philosophy, which was the foundation of geocentrism. Even if Copernicanism in the end were proven wrong, the scientific evidence had to be pursued. A renowned scientist, such as Galileo, in those circumstances should have been allowed to continue his research. He was forbidden to do so by official declarations of the Church. There lies the tragedy. Until that tragedy is faced with the rigor of historical scholarship, the "myth" is almost certain to remain.

Neither the final report nor the papal discourse appears to reflect the majority of the conclusions enunciated in the official publications of the commission.[43] There are strong indications, from a textual comparison of the two documents of 1992 with the commission's publications, that the views of some collaborators, not commission members, weighed disproportionately in the formulations of these documents. And, judging from an overall view of the commission's publications, their opinions are minority ones on many important issues. At any rate, the conclusions stated in the final report and repeated in the papal discourse were never submitted, as best I know, for comment to the members of the commission. For those two reasons (they appear to reflect a minority opinion and they were not approved), these two documents cannot justifiably be considered to be conclusions of the commission's work.

The Future

Could the Galileo affair, interpreted with historical accuracy, provide an opportunity to understand the relationship of contemporary scientific culture and inherited religious culture? In the Catholic tradition there is what Blackwell calls a "logic of centralized authority" required by the fact that revelation is derived from Scripture and tradition, which are officially interpreted only by the Church.[44] In contrast, authority in science is essentially derived from empirical evidence, which is the ultimate criterion of the veracity of scientific theory. In the trial of 1616 Blackwell sees the defendant to be a scientific idea and the authority that condemned that idea to be derived from the decree of the Council of Trent on the interpretation of Scripture. What would have been the consequences if, instead of exercising its authority in this case, the Church had suspended judgment? But, having already exercised that authority over a scientific idea, the Church then applied that authority in the admonition given by Bellarmine to Galileo in 1616. That admonition would go on later to play a key role in the condemnation of Galileo in 1633 as "vehemently suspect" of heresy.[45]

There is a clear distinction here between authority exercised over the intellectual content of a scientific idea and that exercised over a person in the enforcement of the former. Thus, as Blackwell so clearly puts it, the abjuration forced on Galileo in 1633 "was intended to bend—or break—his will rather than his reason." Could this contrast between the two authorities result in other conflicts? In the third part of the same discourse whereby he received the final report, John Paul II says: "And the purpose of your Academy [the Pontifical Academy of Sciences] is precisely to discern and to make known, in the present state of science and within its proper limits, what can be regarded as an acquired truth or at least as enjoying such a *degree of probability that it would be imprudent and unreasonable to reject it*. In this way unnecessary conflicts can be avoided."[46] Would that the Congregation of the Index in 1616 had displayed a similar kind of caution regarding Copernicanism! Would that the wisdom expressed by John Paul II might guide the Church's action in times to come!

Appendix. List of publications of the Galileo Commission in chronological order as derived from the final report by Cardinal Poupard of October 31, 1992:

1982   Brandmüller, Walter. *Galilei und die Kirche oder das Recht auf Irrtum.* Regensburg: Pustet.

1983   Pedersen, Olaf. *Galileo and the Council of Trent.* Studi Galileiani 1:1. Vatican City: Vatican Observatory Publications.

1983   Poupard, Paul, ed. *Galileo Galilei, 350 ans d'histoire, 1633–1983.* Paris: Descleé.

1984   Baldini, Ugo, and George V. Coyne, eds. and trans. *The Louvain Lectures (Lectiones Lovanienses) of Bellarmine and the Autograph Copy of His 1616 Declaration to Galileo*. Studi Galileiani 1:2. Vatican City: Vatican Observatory Publications.

1984   Pagano, Sergio M., and Antonio G. Luciani, eds. *I documenti del processo di Galileo Galilei*. Scripta Varia 53. Vatican City: Pontifical Academy of Sciences.

1985   Coyne, George V., Michael Heller, and Józef Zycinski, eds. *The Galileo Affair: A Meeting of Faith and Science*. Studi Galileiani 1:3. Vatican City: Vatican Observatory Publications.

1985   d'Addio, Mario. *Considerazioni sui processi a Galileo*. Quaderni della Rivista della Chiesa in Italia 8. Rome: Herder.

1986   Fabris, Rinaldo. *Galileo Galilei e gli orientamenti esegetici del suo tempo*. Scripta Varia 62. Vatican City: Pontifical Academy of Sciences.

1987   Brandmüller, Walter. *Galileo y la iglesia*. Madrid: Rialp.

1988   Zycinski, Józef M. *The Idea of Unification in Galileo's Epistemology*. Studi Galileiani 1:4. Vatican City: Vatican Observatory Publications.

1989   Westfall, Richard S. *Essays on the Trial of Galileo*. Studi Galileiani 1:5. Vatican City: Vatican Observatory Publications.

1992   Brandmüller, Walter. *Galileo e la chiesa ossia il diritto ad errare*. Vatican City: Libreria Editrice Vaticana.

1992   Brandmüller, Walter, and Egon J. Greipli, eds. *Copernico, Galileo, e la chiesa: Fine della controversia (1820)*. Atti del Sant'Ufficio. Florence: Leo S. Olschki.

Notes

1. John Paul II, "Lessons of the Galileo Case," *Origins* 22 (1992): 370–74, English translation; original in *Discorsi dei Papi alla Pontificia Accademia delle Scienze (1936-1993)* (Vatican City: Pontifical Academy of Sciences, 1994), 271 ff. The occasion of the discourse was the audience usually granted at the conclusion of the biennial plenary session of the Pontifical Academy of Sciences. The topic of the plenary session was the emergence of complexity in mathematics, physics, chemistry, and biology, and the first part of the discourse is dedicated to that theme. The last part speaks to the role of the academy in the development of human culture. The central and most substantial part of the discourse, however, is dedicated exclusively to responding to the final report of the Galileo Commission's work, which had been given by Cardinal Poupard immediately preceding the papal address.

2. John Paul II, "Lessons," sec. 11, para. 1.

3. See Annibale Fantoli, *Galileo: For Copernicanism and for the Church*, 2d ed., ed. and trans. George V. Coyne (Vatican City: Vatican Observatory Publications, 1996), 447.

4. John Paul II, "Lessons," sec. 10, para. 1.

5. See, for example, Fantoli, *Galileo*, 487 ff.

6. (The composition of the Commission will be discussed below.)

7. Paul Poupard, "Galileo: Report on Papal Commission Findings," *Origins* 22 (1992): 374–75, English translation; original in *Après Galilée* (Paris: Desclée de Brouwer, 1994), 96–97.

8. John Paul II, "Lessons," sec. 10, para. 1.

9. Ibid., sec. 5, para. 2.

10. Ibid., sec. 5, paras. 3 and 4.

11. Poupard, "Galileo," sec. 5, para. 1. The use of the word 'profound' here is a bit puzzling. A description of the heavens from the way they appear to human observers is hardly profound.

12. Ibid., sec. 5, para. 2.

13. John Paul II, "Lessons," sec. 9, para. 1.

14. Ibid., sec. 9, para. 2.

15. Poupard, "Galileo," sec. 2, para. 3.

16. Maurice E. Finocchiaro, *The Galileo Affair: A Documentary History* (hereafter *GA*) (Berkeley: University of California Press, 1989), 68.

17. *GA,* 68.

18. See Fantoli, *Galileo,* 262–63 n. 79.

19. Poupard, "Galileo," sec. 3, para. 2.

20. Paolo Maffei, *Giuseppe Settele, il suo diario e la questione galileiana* (Foligno: dell'Arquata, 1987), shows that, although the imprimatur to Settele's book was a de facto recognition of Copernicanism, it did not refer at all to the Galileo affair. He furthermore shows that Settele had hoped that his case would bring the Church to reconsider that affair.

21. This is essentially the thesis of Walter Brandmüller, *Galilei und die Kirche oder das Recht auf Irrtum* (Regensburg: Pustet, 1982), and Walter Brandmüller and Egon J. Greipl, eds., *Copernico, Galileo, e la chiesa: Fine della controversia (1820),* Atti del Sant'Ufficio (Florence: Leo S. Olschki, 1992). In fact, the latter work is referred to in a footnote in the final report to support this thesis.

22. Poupard, "Galileo," sec. 3, para. 2.

23. Ibid., sec. 4, par. 1.

24. A meeting was held in September 1998 at the Vatican Observatory at Castel Gandolfo (Rome) to discuss the results of the Galileo Commission. The participants were Ugo Baldini, Richard Blackwell, Annibale Fantoli, Paolo Maffei, Ernan McMullin, and Michael Segre. I am indebted to all of them but especially to Annibale Fantoli for much of what I have presented thus far. See especially Annibale Fantoli, *Galileo and the Catholic Church: A Critique of the "Closure" of the Galileo Commission's Work,* Studi Galileiani 4:1 (Vatican City: Vatican Observatory Publications, 2002), translation of "Galileo e la chiesa cattolica: Considerazioni critiche sulla 'chiusura' della questione galileiana," in *Largo campo di filosofare: Eurosymposium Galileo 2001,* ed. José Montesinos and Carlos Solís (La Orotava: Fundacion Canaria Orotava de Historia de la Ciencia, 2001), 733–50.

25. See Melchor Sánchez de Toca Alameda, "Un doble aniversario: XX aniversario de la creación de la Comisión de Estudio del Caso Galileo y X de su clausura," *Ecclesia* 16:2 (2002): 142 n. 4, for a summary of the history leading to the creation of the current Pontifical Council of Culture.

26. John Paul II, "Faith, Science, and the Search for Truth," *Origins* 9 (1979): 384–92, sec. 6, para. 2.

27. At the meeting of the commission on June 17, 1982, it was decided that all publications of the commission would carry the title "Studi Galileiani," and at the meeting of Oct. 8, 1982,

it was further specified that the title would be "Studi Galileiani—Research Promoted by the Study Group Instituted by His Holiness John Paul II."

28. See the Appendix for the list of publications. Sánchez de Toca Alameda, "Un doble aniversario," gives lists of the collaborators for the section on culture (154) and for the section on exegesis (156). The editorial board of Studi Galileiani consisted of Juan Casanovas, S.J. (Vatican Observatory), George Coyne, S.J. (Vatican Observatory), Jerzy Dobrzycki (Polish Academy of Sciences), Michael Hoskin (Cambridge University, U. K.), Francisco Gomes Magalhães (Federal University of Minas Gerais, Brazil), Ernan McMullin (University of Notre Dame), and Olaf Pedersen (University of Aarhus, Denmark).

29. In this regard, see Fantoli, *Galileo,* 503–6, for a history of the role of the Galileo affair in discussions at the Second Vatican Council concerning the relationship of the Church to science.

30. This committee represents the Holy See on the International Committee for Historical Research (Comité international des sciences historiques). It is also a subcommission of the Holy See to the International Commission for Comparative Church History (Commission internationale d'histoire ecclésiastique comparée). It has nothing to do with the history of science as such, despite the temptation to think so from the French and Italian expressions. It is a research institute in Church history, not the history of science.

31. See Fantoli, *Galileo,* 503 ff, for a thorough discussion of the travails of this publication and the contribution it made to nourishing the myth of Galileo.

32. See ibid., 526–28.

33. See note 28.

34. John Paul II, "A Papal Address on the Church and Science: Commemoration of the 350th Anniversary of the Publication of the *Dialogue on the Two Chief World Systems,*" *Origins* 13 (1983): 50–52.

35. Due to the dispersal of the commission files, it is difficult to know in what these reports consisted. For the section on epistemological and scientific questions the publications up to that date sponsored by that section of the commission were submitted with a letter of Coyne to Poupard of June 19, 1990, with the notice that other publications of the section were pending. See the publications in chronological order in the Appendix (those with the attribution "Studi Galileiani" represent the contributions of this section). The pending publications appeared only after Oct. 31, 1992, when the final report was presented. Poupard replied to Coyne in the letter referred to of July 13, 1990, in which he expressed thanks for the "exhaustive response."

36. Sánchez de Toca Alameda, "Un doble aniversario," 158 n. 34.

37. In 1964 at the Second Vatican Council in the course of the commission meetings leading up to the formulation of the document on the Church in the modern world (*Gaudium et spes*), several cultural and scientific associations (Pax Romana, Union des scientifiques français) and many individual scientists urged that there be a "solemn rehabilitation of Galileo." The efforts were in vain. See Fantoli, *Galileo,* 528–31.

38. Poupard, "Galileo," sec. 5, para. 3. It does not appear that the papal audience at which the pope received the report was scheduled specifically for that purpose. See note 1.

39. At the Council Meeting of the Pontifical Academy of Sciences, on Jan. 26, 1998, this report was presented:

About 2500 codices kept in the archives of the current Congregation of the Doctrine of the Faith and derived from the previous Congregation of the Inquisition and Congregation of the Index had been examined and all the documents concerning the Catholic Church and Science had been catalogued. On this subject there are from 4000 to 4500 documents which deserve publication. The length of each document varies from a few lines up to 15 pages. In order to publish all documents four volumes will be necessary. The languages used in the documents are Latin and Italian. Some documents on the Galileo trial were so far unknown. Also some new documents on Giordano Bruno and Tommaso Campanella have been found. After copying and transcribing the text, the four volumes will be published. The first volume will contain the 16th century materials; the 2nd volume the Galileo process; the 3rd volume the 17th century and the 4th volume the 18th century.

40. John Paul II, "Faith, Science," sec. 6, para. 2.

41. John Paul II, "Lessons," sec. 7.

42. Ibid., sec. 8.

43. As I have mentioned above in the section on the chronology of the activities of the commission, the last two publications appeared after the commission's activities had been officially terminated.

44. Richard J. Blackwell, "Could There Be Another Galileo Case?" in *The Cambridge Companion to Galileo,* ed. Peter Machamer (Cambridge: Cambridge University Press, 1998), 348–66.

45. See chap. 5 of this book.

46. John Paul II, "Lessons," sec. 13, para. 2 (emphasis mine).

SELECTED BIBLIOGRAPHY

Compiled by Ryan MacPherson and Ernan McMullin

Allaci, Leone. *Apes urbanae, sive de viris illustribus, qui ab anno MDCXXX per totum MDCXXXII Romae adfuerunt, ac typis aliquid evulgarunt, Romae, exc. L. Grignanus.* 1633. Reprint, with an introduction by Michel-Pierre Lerner, Lecce: Conte, 1999.

Amerio, R. "Galileo e Campanella: La tentazione del pensiero nella filosofia della riforma cattolica." In *Nel terzo centenario della morte di Galileo Galilei,* edited by Università Cattolica de Sacro Cuore, 299–325. Milan: Vita e Pensiero, 1942.

Artigas, Mariano. "Un nuovo documento sul caso Galileo: EE 291." *Acta Philosophica* 10 (2001): 199–214.

Augustine. *De Genesi ad litteram* (The literal meaning of Genesis). Translated by J. H. Taylor. New York: Newman Press, 1982.

Baldini, Ugo. "L'astronomia del cardinale Bellarmino." In *Novità celesti e crisi del sapere,* edited by Paolo Galluzzi, 293–305. Florence: Giunti Barbèra, 1984.

———. "Additamenta Galileana I. Galileo, la nuova astronomia e la critica dell'aristotelismo nel dialogo epistolare tra Giuseppe Biancani e i Revisori romani della Compagnia di Gesù." *Annali dell'Istituto e Museo di Storia della Scienza di Firenze* 9:2 (1984): 13–43.

———. *Legem impone subactis: Studi su filosofia e scienza dei gesuiti in Italia, 1540-1632.* Rome: Bulzoni, 1992.

———. "Die Philosophie an den Universitäten." In *Die Philosophie des 17. Jahrhunderts,* vol. 1, *Allgemeine Themen: Iberische Halbinsel. Italien,* edited by J.-P. Schobinger, 621–68. Basel: Schwabe, 1998.

———. "Intervento." In *L'apertura degli archivi del Sant'Uffizio romano,* 141–53. Rome: Accademia Nazionale dei Lincei, 1998.

———. *Saggi sulla cultura della Compagnia di Gesù (secoli XVI-XVIII).* Padua: CLEUP, 2000.

———. "Die römischen Kongregationen der Inquisition und des Index und der naturwissenschaftliche Fortschritt im 16. bis 18. Jahrhundert: Anmerkungen zur Chronologie und zur Logik ihres Verhältnisses." In *Inquisition, Index, Zensur: Wissenkulturen Neuzeit im Widerstreit,* edited by Hubert Wolf, 229–78. Paderborn: Ferdinand Schöningh, 2001.

Baldini, Ugo, and George V. Coyne, eds. and trans. *The Louvain Lectures (Lectiones Lovanienses) of Bellarmine and the Autograph Copy of His 1616 Declaration to Galileo.* Studi Galileiani 1:2. Vatican City: Vatican Observatory Publications, 1984.

Baldini, Ugo, and Leen Spruit. "Nuovi documenti galileiani degli archivi del Sant'Ufficio e dell'Indice." *Rivista di Storia della Filosofia* 56 (2001): 661–99.

Banfi, Antonio. *Vita di Galileo Galilei.* Milan: Feltrinelli, 1962.

Barone, Francesco. "Diego de Zuñiga e Galileo Galilei: Astronomia eliostatica ed esegesi biblica." *Critica Storica* 19 (1982): 319–35.

Basile, Bruno. "Galileo e il teologo 'copernicano,' Paolo Antonio Foscarini." *Rivista di Letteratura Italiana* 1 (1983): 63–96.

Battistini, Andrea. *Galileo e i gesuiti: Miti letterari e retorica della scienza.* Milan: Vita e Pensiero, 2000.

Beltrán Marí, Antonio. *Galileo, ciencia y religión.* Barcelona: Paidós, 2001.

———. "Tratos extrajudiciales, determinismo procesal y poder." In *Largo campo de filosofare: Eurosymposium Galileo 2001,* edited by José Montesinos and Carlos Solis, 463–89. La Orotava: Fundacion Canaria Orotava de Historia de la Ciencia, 2001.

Beretta, Francesco. *Galilée devant le Tribunal de l'Inquisition.* Fribourg: Université de Fribourg, 1998.

———. "Le siège apostolique et l'affaire Galilée: Relectures romaines d'une condamnation célèbre." *Roma Moderna e Contemporanea* 7 (1999): 421–61.

———. "Le procès de Galilée et les archives du Saint-Office: Aspects judiciaires et théologiques d'une condamnation célèbre." *Revue des Sciences Philosophiques et Théologiques* 83 (1999): 441–90.

———. "L'archivio della Congregazione del Sant'Ufficio: Bilancio provvisorio della storia e natura dei fondi d'antico regime." In *L'Inquisizione romana: Metodologia delle fonti e storia istituzionale,* edited by Andrea Del Col and Giovanna Paolin, 119–44. Trieste: Università di Trieste, 2000. Also published in *Rivista di Storia e Letteratura Religiosa* 37 (2001): 29–58.

———. "Urbain VIII Barberini protagoniste de la condamnation de Galilée." In *Largo campo di filosofare: Eurosymposium Galileo 2001,* edited by José Montesinos and Carlos Solis, 549–73. La Orotava: Fundacion Canaria Orotava de Historia de la Ciencia, 2001.

———. "*Magno Domino & Omnibus Christianae, Catholicaeque Philosophiae amantibus. D. D.:* Le *Tractatus syllepticus* du jésuite Melchior Inchofer, censeur de Galilée." *Freiburger Zeitschrift für Philosophie und Theologie* 48 (2001): 301–27.

———. "Giordano Bruno e l'Inquisizione romana: Considerazioni sul processo." *Bruniana e Campanelliana* 7 (2001): 15–49.

———. "Un nuovo documento sul processo di Galileo Galilei: La lettera di Vincenzo Maculano del 22 aprile 1633 al cardinale Francesco Barberini." *Nuncius* 16 (2001): 629–41.

———. "L'affaire Galilée et l'impasse apologétique: Réponse à une censure." *Gregorianum* 84 (2003): 169–92.

———. "Une deuxième abjuration de Galilée ou l'inalterable hiérarchie des disciplines." *Bruniana e Campanelliana* 9 (2003): 9–43.

———. "Rilettura di un documento celebre: Redazione e diffusione della sentenza e abiura di Galileo." *Galilaeana* 1 (2004): 91–115.

Berti, D. "Antecedenti al processo galileano e della condanna della dottrina copernicana." *Atti della Reale Accademia dei Lincei (Rome),* 3d ser., 10 (1883): 72–78.

Bertolla, Pietro. "Le vicende del Galileo di Paschini." In *Atti del Convegno di Studio su Pio Paschini nel Centenario della Nascità: 1878-1978,* edited by Giuseppe Fornasir, 172–208. Udine: Pubblicazioni della Deputazione di Storia Patria del Friuli, 1980.

Biagioli, Mario. *Galileo, Courtier: The Practice of Science in an Age of Absolutism.* Chicago: University of Chicago Press, 1993.

Bianchi, Luca. "Galileo fra Aristotele, Clavio e Scheiner: La nuova edizione del Dialogo e il problema delle fonti galileiane." *Rivista di Storia della Filosofia* 54 (1999): 189–227.

———. "Interventi divini, miracoli e ipotesi soprannaturali nel *Dialogo* di Galileo." In *Potentia Dei: L'onnipotenza nel pensiero dei secoli XVI e XVII*, edited by G. Canziani, M. A. Granada, and Y. C. Zarka. Milan: Franco Angeli, 2000.

———. "Agostino Oreggi, qualificatore del *Dialogo*, e i limiti della conoscenza scientifica." In *Largo campo di filosofare: Eurosymposium Galileo 2001*, edited by José Montesinos and Carlos Solís, 575–84. La Orotava: Fundacion Canaria Orotava de Historia de la Ciencia, 2001.

Blackwell, Richard J. *Galileo, Bellarmine, and the Bible.* Notre Dame: University of Notre Dame Press, 1991.

———. "Could There Be Another Galileo Case?" In *The Cambridge Companion to Galileo*, edited by Peter Machamer, 348–66. Cambridge: Cambridge University Press, 1998.

Blair, Ann. "Mosaic Physics and the Search for a Pious Natural Philosophy in the Late Renaissance." *Isis* 91 (2000): 32–58.

Blanchet, Léon. *Campanella.* Paris, 1920. Reprint, New York: Franklin, 1971.

Boaga, Emanuele. "Annotazioni e documenti sulla vita e sulle opere di Paolo Antonio Foscarini teologo 'copernicano' (ca. 1562–1616)." *Carmelus* 37 (1990): 172–216.

Bonansea, Bernardino M. "Campanella's Defense of Galileo." In *Reinterpreting Galileo*, edited by William A. Wallace, 205–39. Washington, D.C.: Catholic University of America Press, 1986.

Booth, Sarah E., and Albert van Helden. "The Virgin and the Telescope: The Moons of Cigoli and Galileo." In *Galileo in Context*, edited by Jürgen Renn, 193–216. Cambridge: Cambridge University Press, 2001.

Borgato, Maria Teresa, ed. *Giambattista Riccioli e il merito scientifico dei gesuiti nell'età barocca.* Florence: Leo S. Olschki, 2002.

Brandmüller, Walter. *Galilei und die Kirche oder das Recht auf Irrtum.* Regensburg: Pustet, 1982. Translated into Spanish as *Galileo y la iglesia* (Madrid: Rialp, 1987). Translated into Italian as *Galileo e la chiesa ossia il diritto ad errare* (Vatican City: Libreria Editrice Vaticana, 1992).

———. "Commento." In *Copernico, Galileo, e la chiesa: Fine della controversia (1820)*, edited by Walter Brandmüller and Egon Johannes Greipl, 15–130. Florence: Leo S. Olschki, 1992.

Brandmüller, Walter, and Egon Johannes Greipl, eds. *Copernico, Galileo, e la chiesa: Fine della controversia (1820).* Atti del Sant'Ufficio. Florence: Leo S. Olschki, 1992.

Brecht, Bertolt. *Galileo.* Adaptation by Charles Laughton. New York: Grove, Weidenfeld, 1966.

Brodrick, James, S.J. *The Life and Work of Blessed Robert Francis Cardinal Bellarmine, S.J., 1542–1621.* London: Burns Oates and Washbourne, 1928.

Bruno, Giordano. *The Ash Wednesday Supper.* Edited and translated by E. A. Gosselin and L. S. Lerner. Hamden, Conn.: Archon, 1977.

Bucciantini, Massimo. *Contro Galileo: Alle origini dell'affaire.* Florence: Leo S. Olschki, 1995.

———. "Novità celesti e la teologia." In *Largo campo di filosofare: Eurosymposium Galileo 2001*, edited by José Montesinos and Carlos Solís, 795–808. La Orotava: Fundacion Canaria Orotava de Historia de la Ciencia, 2001.

Bucciantini, Massimo, and Maurizio Torrini. *La diffusione del copernicanesimo in Italia 1543-1610.* Florence: Leo S. Olschki, 1997.

Bünger, Claus. *Matthias Bernegger, ein Bild aus dem geistigen Leben Straßburgs zur Zeit des dreissigjährigen Krieges.* Strasbourg: Trübner, 1893.

Burstyn, Harold L. "Galileo's Attempt to Prove That the Earth Moves." *Isis* 53 (1962): 161-85.

Campanella, Tommaso. *Apologia per Galileo.* Edited by S. Femiano. Milan: Marzorati, 1971.

———. *A Defense of Galileo, the Mathematician from Florence.* Translated with introduction and notes by Richard J. Blackwell. Notre Dame: University of Notre Dame Press, 1994.

———. *Apologia pro Galileo/Apologie de Galilée.* Latin text with French translation and notes by Michel-Pierre Lerner. Paris: Les Belles Lettres, 2001.

Carolino, L. M. "Philosophical Teaching and Mathematical Arguments: Jesuit Philosophers versus Jesuit Mathematicians on the Controversy of Comets in Portugal (1577–1650)." *History of Universities* 16 (2000): 65–95.

Caroti, S. "Un sostenitore napoletano della mobilità della terra: Il padre Paolo Antonio Foscarini." In *Galileo e Napoli,* edited by Fabrizio Lomonaco and Maurizio Torrini, 81–121. Naples: Guida Editori, 1987.

Carroll, William E. "Galileo, Science, and the Bible." *Acta Philosophica* 6 (1997): 5–37.

———. "Galileo and the Interpretation of the Bible." *Science and Education* 8 (1999): 151–87.

———. "Galileo and Biblical Exegesis." In *Largo campo di filosofare: Eurosymposium Galileo 2001,* edited by José Montesinos and Carlos Solís, 677–91. La Orotava: Fundacion Canaria Orotava de Historia de la Ciencia, 2001.

Carugo, Adriano, and Alistair C. Crombie. "The Jesuits and Galileo's Ideas of Science and of Nature." *Annali dell'Istituto e Museo di Storia della Scienza di Firenze* 8:2 (1983): 3–46.

Centre international de synthèse, ed. *Avant, avec, après Copernic: La représentation de l'univers et ses conséquences epistémologiques.* Paris: Blanchard, 1975.

Cerbu, Thomas. "'Melchior Inchofer, 'un homme fin & rusé.'" In *Largo campo di filosofare: Eurosymposium Galileo 2001,* edited by José Montesinos and Carlos Solís, 587–611. La Orotava: Fundacion Canaria Orotava de Historia de la Ciencia, 2001.

Cerbu, Thomas, and Michel-Pierre Lerner. "La disgrâce de Galilée dans les Apes urbanae: Sur la fabrique du texte de Leone Allacci." *Nuncius* 15:2 (2000): 589–609.

Cifres, Alejandro. "L'archivio storico della Congregazione per la Dottrina della Fede." In *L'apertura degli archivi del Sant'Uffizio romano,* 73–84. Rome: Accademia Nazionale dei Lincei, 1998.

———. "Das Archiv des Sanctum Officium: Alte und neue Ordnungsformen." In *Inquisition, Index, Zensur: Wissenkulturen Neuzeit im Widerstreit,* edited by Hubert Wolf, 45–69. Paderborn: Ferdinand Schöningh, 2001.

Cioni, Michele. *I documenti galileiani del S. Uffizio di Firenze.* Florence: Libreria Editrice Fiorentina, 1908. Reprint, Florence: Pagnini, 1996.

Copernicus, Nicholas. *De revolutionibus orbium coelestium libri VI.* Nuremberg, 1543. Translated by A. M. Duncan as *On the Revolutions of the Heavenly Spheres* (New York: Barnes and Noble, 1976).

———. *Briefe, Texte und Uebersetzung.* Edited by Andreas Kühne. Vol. 6, pt. 1 of *Nicolaus Copernicus Gesamtausgabe,* edited by Heribert M. Nobis. Documenta Copernicana. Berlin: Akademie, 1994.

Costabel, Pierre. "Galileo, ieri e oggi." In *Galileo Galilei, 350 anni di storia, 1633-1983,* edited by Paul Poupard, 196–209. Casale Monferrato: Piemme, 1984.

Coyne, George V., and Ugo Baldini. "The Young Bellarmine's Thoughts on World Systems." In *The Galileo Affair: A Meeting of Faith and Science,* edited by George V. Coyne, Michael Heller, and Józef Zycinski, 103–10. Vatican City: Vatican Observatory Publications, 1984.

Coyne, George V., Michael Heller, and Józef Zycinski, eds. *The Galileo Affair: A Meeting of Faith and Science.* Studi Galileiani 1:3. Vatican City: Vatican Observatory Publications, 1984.

Crehan, F. J. "The Bible in the Roman Catholic Church from Trent to the Present Day." In *The Cambridge History of the Bible: The West from the Reformation to the Present Day,* edited by S. L. Greenslade, 3:199–237. Cambridge: Cambridge University Press, 1963.

Crombie, Alistair C. "The Sources of Galileo's Early Natural Philosophy." In *Reason, Experiment, and Mysticism in the Scientific Revolution,* edited by Maria L. Righini-Bonelli and William R. Shea. New York: Science History Publications, 1975.

D'Addio, Mario. *Considerazioni sui processi a Galileo.* Rome: Herder, 1985.

———. *Il caso Galilei: Processo, scienza, verità.* Rome: Studium, 1993.

Danielson, Dennis R. "The Great Copernican Cliché." *American Journal of Physics* 69 (2001): 1029–35.

de Santillana, Giorgio. *The Crime of Galileo.* Chicago: University of Chicago Press, 1955.

Dear, Peter. *Mersenne and the Learning of the Schools.* Ithaca: Cornell University Press, 1988.

della Terza, Dante. "Galileo, Man of Letters." In *Galileo Reppraised,* edited by Carlo Golino, 1–22. Berkeley: University of California Press, 1966.

Dinis, Alfredo. "Was Riccioli a Secret Copernican?" In *Giambattista Riccioli e il merito scientifico dei gesuiti nell'età barocca,* edited by Maria Teresa Borgato, 49–77. Florence: Leo S. Olschki, 2002.

Ditadi, Gino, ed. *Tommaso Campanella, Apologia di Galileo: Tutte le lettere a Galileo Galilei e altri documenti.* Este: Isonomia, 1992.

Dollo, Corrado. "Le ragioni del geocentrismo nel Collegio Romano (1562–1612)." In *La diffusione del copernicanesimo in Italia, 1543-1610,* edited by Massimo Bucciantini and Maurizio Torrini, 99–167. Florence: Leo S. Olschki, 1997.

d'Oresme, Nicole. *Le livre du ciel et du monde.* Edited by A. D. Menut and A. J. Denomy. Madison: University of Wisconsin Press, 1968.

Drake, Stillman. *Discoveries and Opinions of Galileo.* New York: Doubleday, 1957.

———. *Dialogue Concerning the Two Chief World Systems.* Berkeley: University of California Press, 1967.

———. *Galileo at Work: His Scientific Biography.* Chicago: University of Chicago Press, 1978.

———. "Reexamining Galileo's Dialogue." In *Reinterpreting Galileo,* edited by William A. Wallace, 155–75. Washington, D.C.: Catholic University of America Press, 1986.

———. "Galileo's Steps to Full Copernicanism and Back." *Studies in the History and Philosophy of Science* 18 (1987): 93–105.

Ernst, Germana. *Religione, ragione e natura: Ricerche su Tommaso Campanella e il tardo Rinascimento.* Milan: Franco Angeli, 1991.

Fabri, Filippo. *Adversus impios atheos disputationes quatuor philosophicae.* Venice: Cinammi, 1627.

Fabris, Rinaldo. *Galileo Galilei e gli orientamenti esegetici del suo tempo.* Vatican City: Pontifical Academy of Sciences, 1986.

Fantoli, Annibale. Galileo: *Per il copernicanesimo e per la chiesa.* Vatican City: Vatican Observatory Publications, 1993. Translated with revisions by George V. Coyne as *Galileo: For Copernicanism and for the Church* (Vatican City: Vatican Observatory Publications, 2d ed., 1996, 3d ed., 2003).

———. *Galileo and the Catholic Church: A Critique of the "Closure" of the Galileo Commission's Work.* Studi Galileiani 4:1. Vatican City: Vatican Observatory Publications; Notre Dame: University of Notre Dame Press, 2002. Originally published as "Galileo e la chiesa cattolica: Considerazioni critiche sulla 'chiusura' della questione galileiana," in *Largo campo di filosofare: Eurosymposium Galileo 2001,* edited by José Montesinos and Carlos Solís, 733–50 (La Orotava: Fundacion Canaria Orotava de Historia de la Ciencia, 2001).

Favaro, Antonio. *Miscellanea galileiana inedita: Studi e ricerche.* Venice: Antonelli, 1887.

———. *Galileo e l'Inquisizione: Documenti del processo galileiano esistenti nell'archivio del S. Uffizio e nell'archivio segreto vaticano.* Florence: Giunti Barbèra, 1907. Reprint, with foreword by Luigi Firpo, Florence: Giunti Barbèra, 1983.

———. "Studi e ricerche per una iconografia galileiana." *Atti del Reale Istituto Veneto di Scienze, Lettere ed Arti* 72 (1912–13): 995–1051.

———. *Galileo e lo studio di Padova.* 2 vols. Padua: Antenore, 1966.

———. "Mattia Bernegger." In *Amici e corrispondenti di Galileo,* edited by Paolo Galluzzi, 3:1349–73. Florence: Salimbeni, 1983.

Feingold, Mordecai, ed. *Jesuit Science and the Republic of Letters.* Cambridge, Mass.: MIT Press, 2003.

Feldhay, Rivkha. *Galileo and the Church: Political Inquisition or Critical Dialogue?* Cambridge: Cambridge University Press, 1995.

———. "The Use and Abuse of Mathematical Entities: Galileo and the Jesuits Revisited." In *The Cambridge Companion to Galileo,* edited by Peter Machamer, 80–145. Cambridge: Cambridge University Press, 1998.

———. "The Cultural Field of Jesuit Science." In *The Jesuits: Cultures, Sciences, and the Arts, 1540-1773,* edited by John W. O'Malley, S.J., Gauvin Alexander Bailey, Steven J. Harris, and T. Frank Kennedy, 107–30. Toronto: University of Toronto Press, 1999.

———. "Recent Narratives on Galileo and the Church; or: The Three Dogmas of the Counter-Reformation." In *Galileo in Context,* edited by Jürgen Renn, 219–37. Cambridge: Cambridge University Press, 2001.

Feldhay, Rivkha, and M. Heyd. "The Discourse of Pious Science." *Science in Context* 3 (1989): 109–42.

Ferrone, Vincenzo. "Galileo, Newton e la libertas philosophandi nelle prima metà del xviii secolo in Italia." *Rivista Storica Italiana* 93 (1981): 143–85.

Ferrone, Vincenzo, and Massimo Firpo. "Galileo tra inquisitori e microstorici." *Rivista Storica Italiana* 97 (1985): 177–238.

Festa, Egidio. *L'erreur de Galilée.* Paris: Austral, 1995.

Finocchiaro, Maurice A. "The Methodological Background to Galileo's Trial." In *Reinterpreting Galileo,* edited by William A. Wallace, 241–72. Washington, D.C.: Catholic University of America Press, 1986.

———. *The Galileo Affair: A Documentary History.* Berkeley: University of California Press, 1989.

———. "Galileo as a 'Bad Theologian': A Formative Myth about Galileo's Trial." *Studies in the History and Philosophy of Science* 33 (2002): 753–91.

Fornasir, Giuseppe, ed. *Atti del Convegno di Studio su Pio Paschini nel Centenario della Nascità: 1878-1978.* Udine: Pubblicazioni della Deputazione di Storia Patria del Friuli, 1980.

Frajese, Vittorio. "Venezia e la chiesa durante i decenni galileiani." In *Galileo Galilei e la cultura veneziana,* edited by the Istituto Veneto di Scienze, Lettere ed Arti, 87–122. Venice: Istituto Veneto di Scienze, Lettere ed Arti, 1995.

Galilei, Galileo. *Opere di Galileo Galilei.* Edited by Antonio Favaro. 1890–1909. Reprint, Florence: Giunti Barbèra, 1968.

———. *Dialogo sopra i due massimi sistemi del mondo tolemaico e copernicano.* Edited by O. Besomi and M. Helbing. Padua: Antenore, 1998.

———. *Lettera a Cristina di Lorena sull'uso della Bibbia nelle argumentazioni scientifiche.* Edited by Franco Motta. Genoa: Marietti, 2000.

———. *Dialogue Concerning the Two Chief World Systems: Ptolemaic and Copernican.* Translated by Stillman Drake. New York: Modern Library, 2001.

Galluzzi, Paolo, ed. *Galileo: La sensate esperienza.* Florence: A. Pizzi, 1982.

———, ed. *Novità celesti e crisi di sapere.* Florence: Giunti Barbèra, 1984.

Galluzzi, Paolo, and Maurizio Torrini, eds. *Le opere dei discepoli di Galileo Galilei.* Florence: Giunti Barbera, 1975–84.

Garcia, Stéphane. "L'édition strasbourgeoise du *Systema cosmicum* (1635–1636), dernier combat copernicien de Galilée." *Bulletin de la Société de l'Histoire du Protestantisme Français* 146 (2000): 307–34.

———. "Elie Diodati—Galilée: La rencontre de deux logiques." In *Largo campo di filosofare: Eurosymposium Galileo 2001,* edited by José Montesinos and Carlos Solís, 883–92. La Orotava: Fundacion Canaria Orotava de Historia de la Ciencia, 2001.

Garin, Eugenio. "A proposito di Copernico." *Rivista di Storia della Filosofia* 26 (1971): 79–96.

Garuti, Adriano. S. *Pietro unico titolare del primato: A proposito del decreto del S. Uffizio del 24 gennaio 1647.* Bologna: Edizioni Francescane, 1993.

Garzend, Léon. *L'Inquisition et l'hérésie: Distinction de l'hérésie théologique de l'hérésie inquisitoriale.* Paris: Desclée, 1912.

Genovesi, Enrico. *Processi contro Galileo.* Milan: Ceschina, 1966.

Geymonat, Ludovico. *Galileo Galilei: A Biography and Inquiry into His Philosophy of Science.* Translated by Stillman Drake. New York: McGraw-Hill, 1965.

Giacchi, Orio. "Considerazioni giuridiche sui due processi contro Galileo." In *Nel terzo centenario della morte di Galileo Galilei,* edited by Università Cattolica del Sacro Cuore, 383–406. Milan: Vita e Pensiero, 1942.

Gingerich, Owen. "The Censorship of Copernicus' *De revolutionibus.*" *Annali dell' Istituto e Museo di Storia della Scienza di Firenze* 6 (1981): 45–61.

Golino, Carlo, ed. *Galileo Reappraised.* Berkeley: University of California Press, 1966.

Gosselin, Edward A., and Lawrence S. Lerner. "Galileo and the Long Shadow of Bruno." *Archives Internationales d'Histoire des Sciences* 25 (1975): 223–46.

Grant, Edward. "In Defense of the Earth's Centrality and Immobility: Scholastic Reaction to Copernicanism in the Seventeenth Century." *Transactions of the American Philosophical Society* 74 (1984): 1–65.

————. *Planets, Stars, and Orbs: The Medieval Cosmos, 1200-1687.* Cambridge: Cambridge University Press, 1994.

Grisar, Hartmann, S.J. *Galileistudien: Historische-theologische Untersuchungen über die Urtheile der Römischen Congregationen im Galilei-process.* Regensburg: Pustet, 1882.

Harris, Steven J. "Transposing the Merton Thesis: Apostolic Spirituality and the Establishment of the Jesuit Scientific Tradition." *Science in Context* 3 (1989): 29–65.

Headley, John. *Tommaso Campanella and the Transformation of the World.* Princeton: Princeton University Press, 1997.

Heilbron, John L. *The Sun in the Church: Cathedrals as Solar Observatories.* Cambridge, Mass.: Harvard University Press, 1999.

Hine, William L. "Mersenne and Copernicanism." *Isis* 64 (1973): 18–32.

Hooykaas, Reyer, ed. and trans. *G. J. Rheticus' Treatise on Holy Scripture and the Motion of the Earth.* Amsterdam: North Holland, 1984.

Howell, Kenneth J. *God's Two Books: Copernican Cosmology and Biblical Interpretation in Early Modern Science.* Notre Dame: University of Notre Dame Press, 2002.

Inchofer, Melchior. *Tractatus syllepticus, in quo, quid de terrae, solisq. motu, vel statione, secundum S. Scripturam, et Sanctos Patres sentiendum, quave certitudine alterutra sententia tenenda sit, breviter ostenditur.* Rome: Grignanus, 1633.

John Paul II. "Faith, Science, and the Search for Truth." Einstein Centenary, Pontifical Academy of Sciences. *Origins* 9 (1979): 389–92.

————. "A Papal Address on the Church and Science: Commemoration of the 350th Anniversary of the Publication of the *Dialogue on the Two Chief World Systems.*" *Origins* 13 (1983): 50–52.

————. "Lessons of the Galileo Case." Pontifical Academy of Sciences. *Origins* 22 (1992): 370–74.

Kelter, Irving A. "Paolo Foscarini's *Letter to Galileo:* The Search for Proofs of the Earth's Motion." *Modern Schoolman* 70 (1992): 31–44.

————. "The Refusal to Accommodate: Jesuit Exegetes and the Copernican System." *Sixteenth-Century Journal* 26 (1995): 273–83.

————. "A Catholic Theologian Responds to Copernicanism: The Theological *Judicium* of Paolo Foscarini's *Lettera.*" *Renaissance and Reformation* 21 (1997): 59–70.

Kepler, Johannes. *Apologia pro Tychone contra Ursum.* In *The Birth of History and Philosophy of Science: Kepler's "A Defence of Tycho against Ursus" with Essays on Its Provenance and Significance,* edited by Nicholas Jardine. Cambridge: Cambridge University Press, 1984.

————. *Gesammelte Werke.* Edited by M. Caspar and F. Hammer. Munich: Beck, 1937–93.

Koestler, Arthur. *The Sleepwalkers.* London: Hutchinson, 1959.

Kollerstrom, Nicholas. "Galileo's Astrology." In *Largo campo di filosofare: Eurosymposium Galileo 2001,* edited by José Montesinos and Carlos Solís, 421–31. La Orotava: Fundacion Canaria Orotava de Historia de la Ciencia, 2001.

Koyré, Alexandre. *Galileo Studies.* Atlantic Highlands, N.J.: Humanities Press, 1978.

Kuhn, Heinrich. *Venetischer Aristotelismus im Ende der aristotelischen Welt: Aspekte der Welt und des Denkens des Cesare Cremonini (1550-1631).* Frankfurt am Main: Peter Lang, 1996.

Langford, Jerome J. *Galileo, Science, and the Church.* New York: Desclée, 1966. 3d ed., Ann Arbor: University of Michigan Press, 1992.

L'apertura degli archivi del Sant'Uffizio romano. Rome: Accademia Nazionale dei Lincei, 1998.

Lattis, James M. *Between Copernicus and Galileo: Christoph Clavius and the Collapse of Ptolemaic Cosmology.* Chicago: University of Chicago Press, 1994.

Leo XIII. "Providentissimus Deus: The Study of Holy Scripture." In *The Papal Encyclicals, 1878-1903,* edited by Claudia Carlen, 326–39. Raleigh, N.C.: McGrath, 1981.

Lerner, Michel-Pierre. "L'Achille des coperniciens." *Bibliothèque d'Humanisme et Renaissance* 42 (1980): 313–27.

———. *Tre saggi sulla cosmologia alla fine del Cinquecento.* Naples: Bibliopolis, 1992.

———. "L'entrée de Tycho Brahe chez les jésuites ou le chant du cygne de Clavius." In *Les jésuites à la Renaissance: Système éducatif et production de savoir,* edited by Luce Giard, 145–85. Paris: Presses Universitaires de France, 1995.

———. *Le monde des spheres.* Vol. 1. *Genèse et triomphe d'une representation cosmique* (1996). Vol. 2. *La fin du cosmos classique* (1997). Paris: Les Belles Lettres.

———. "Pour une édition critique de la sentence et de l'abjuration de Galilée." *Revue des Sciences Philosophiques et Théologiques* 82 (1998): 607–29.

———. "'L'hérésie' héliocentrique: Du soupçon à la condamnation." In *Sciences et religions de Copernic à Galilée (1540-1610),* 69–91. Rome: École français de Rome, 1999.

———. "Le moine, le cardinal et le savant: À propos de l'*Apologia pro Galileo* de Tommaso Campanella." *Les Cahiers de l'Humanisme* 2 (2001): 71–94.

———. "Vérité des philosophes et vérité des théologiens selon Tommaso Campanella, O.P." *Freiburger Zeitschrift für Philosophie und Theologie* 48 (2001): 281–300.

———. "La réception de la condamnation de Galilée en France au xviie siècle." In *Largo campo di filosofare: Eurosymposium Galileo 2001,* edited by José Montesinos and Carlos Solís, 513–47. La Orotava: Fundacion Canaria Orotava de Historia de la Ciencia, 2001.

———. "Aux origines de la polémique anticopernicienne I. L'*Opusculum quartum* [1547–1548] de Gio. Maria Tolosani O.P." *Revue des Sciences Philosophiques et Théologiques* 86 (2002): 681–721.

———. "Tycho Brahe Censured." In *Tycho Brahe and Prague: Crossroads of European Science,* edited by John R. Christianson, Alena Hadravova, Petr Hadrava, and Martin Sole, 95–101. Frankfurt am Main: Deutsch, 2002.

———. "Copernic suspendu et corrigé: Sur deux decrets de la Congregation romaine de l'Index (1616–1620)." *Galilaeana: Journal of Galilean Studies* 1 (2004): 21–89.

Lindberg, David C., and Ronald L. Numbers, eds. *God and Nature: Historical Essays on the Encounters between Christianity and Science.* Berkeley: University of California Press, 1986.

Litt, A. *Les corps célestes dans la philosophie de S. Thomas d'Aquin.* Louvain: Publications Universitaires, 1963.

Lomonaco, Fabrizio, and Maurizio Torrini, eds. *Galileo e Napoli.* Naples: Guida Editori, 1987.

Maccarrone, Michele. "Mons. Paschini e la Roma ecclesiastica." In *Atti del Convegno di Studio su Pio Paschini nel Centenario della Nascità: 1878-1978,* edited by Giuseppe Fornasir, 49–93. Udine: Pubblicazioni della Deputazione di Storia Patria del Friuli, 1980.

Machamer, Peter, ed. *The Cambridge Companion to Galileo.* Cambridge: Cambridge University Press, 1998.

Maffei, Paolo. "Il sistema copernicano dopo Galileo e l'ultimo conflitto per la sua affermazione." *Giornale di Astronomia* 1 (1975): 5–12.

———. *Giuseppe Settele, il suo diario e la questione galileiana.* Foligno: dell'Arquata, 1987.

Mangenot, Eugène. "Inspiration de l'Ecriture." In *Dictionnaire de théologie catholique,* 7:2068–2266. Paris: Letouzey et Ané, 1922.

Martínez, Rafael. "Il manoscrito ACDF, Index, Protocolli, vol. EE, f. 291 r-v." *Acta Philosophica* 10 (2001): 215–42.

Martínez, Rafael, M. Artigas, L. F. Mateo-Seco, and W. Shea. "Un inedito sul caso Galilei." *Acta Philosophica* 10 (2001): 197–272.

Martini, Carlo M. "Gli esegeti al tempo di Galileo." In *Nel quarto centenario della nascità di Galileo Galilei,* ed. Università Cattolica de Sacro Cuore, 115–24. Milan: Vita e Pensiero, 1966.

Mateo-Seco, Lucas F. "Galileo e l'Eucaristia: La questione teologica dell'ACDF Index, Protocolli, EE, f. 291 r–v." *Acta Philosophica* 10 (2001): 243–56.

Mayaud, Pierre-Noël, S.J. "Les 'Fuit Congregatio Sancti Officii in . . . coram . . .' de 1611 à 1642: 32 ans de vie de la Congrégation du Saint Office." *Archivium Historiae Pontificiae* 30 (1992): 231–89.

———. "Une nouvelle affaire Galilée?" *Revue d'Histoire des Sciences* 45 (1992): 161–230.

———. "Deux textes au coeur du conflit: Entre l'Astronomie Nouvelle et l'Ecriture Sainte: La lettre de Bellarmin à Foscarini et la lettre de Galilée à Christine de Lorraine." In *Après Galilée,* edited by Paul Poupard, 19–91. Paris: Desclée de Brouwer, 1994.

———. *La condamnation des livres coperniciens et sa révocation à la lumière des documents inédits des Congrégations de l'Index et de l'Inquisition.* Miscellanea Historicae Pontificiae 64. Rome: Editrice Pontificia Università Gregoriana, 1997.

McColley, Grant. "A Facsimile of Salusbury's Translation of Didacus à Stunica's Commentary upon Job." *Annals of Science* 2 (1937): 179–82.

McMullin, Ernan. "The Conception of Science in Galileo's Work." In *New Perspectives on Galileo,* edited by Robert Butts and Joseph Pitt, 209–57. Dordrecht: D. Reidel, 1978.

———. "Bruno and Copernicus." *Isis* 78 (1987): 55–74.

———. "Galileo on Science and Scripture." In *The Cambridge Companion to Galileo,* edited by Peter Machamer, 271–347. Cambridge: Cambridge University Press, 1998.

———. "From Augustine to Galileo," *Modern Schoolman* 76 (1999): 169–94.

———, ed. *Galileo, Man of Science.* New York: Basic Books, 1967.

Meli, Domenico Bartolomeo. "Leibniz on the Censorship of the Copernican System." *Studia Leibniziana* 20 (1988): 19–42.

Mereu, Italo. *Storia dell'intolleranza in Europa. Sospettare e punire: Il sospetto e l'Inquisizione romana nell'epoca di Galilei.* Milan: Mondadori, 1979.

Monchamp, Georges. *Galilée et la Belgique.* Saint-Trond: Moreau-Schouberechts, 1892.

Monfasani, John. "Aristotelians, Platonists, and the Missing Ockhamists: Philosophical Liberty in Pre-Reformation Italy." *Renaissance Quarterly* 46 (1993): 247–76.

Montesinos, José, and Carlos Solís, eds. *Largo campo di filosofare: Eurosymposium Galileo 2001.* La Orotava: Fundacion Canaria Orotava de Historia de la Ciencia, 2001.

Morpurgo-Tagliabue, Guido. *I processi di Galileo e l'epistemologia.* Milan: Edizione di Comunità, 1963. Reprint, Rome: Armando, 1981.

Moss, Jean Dietz. *Novelties in the Heavens: Rhetoric and Science in the Copernican Controversy.* Chicago: University of Chicago Press, 1993

Motta, Franco. "I criptocopernicani: Una lettura del rapporto fra censura e coscienza intelletuale nell'Italia della controriforma." In *Largo campo di filosofare: Eurosymposium Galileo 2001,* edited by José Montesinos and Carlos Solís, 693–718. La Orotava: Fundacion Canaria Orotava de Historia de la Ciencia, 2001.

Navarro Brotóns, Victor. "The Reception of Copernicus in Sixteenth-Century Spain: The Case of Diego de Zúñiga." *Isis* 86 (1995): 52–78.

Neveu, Bruno. *L'erreur et son juge.* Naples: Bibliopolis, 1993.

Neveu, Bruno, and Pierre-Noël Mayaud. "L'affaire Galilée et la tentation inflationiste." *Gregorianum* 82 (2002): 287–311.

Nonis, Pietro. "L'ultima opera di Paschini, Galilei." In *Atti del Convegno di Studio su Pio Paschini nel Centenario della Nascità: 1878-1978,* edited by Giuseppe Fornasir, 158–72. Udine: Pubblicazioni della Deputazione di Storia Patria del Friuli, 1980.

———, ed. "Galileo Galilei e Padova: Libertà di indagine e principio di autorità." Special issue, *Studia Patavina* 29(3) (1982).

O'Meara, John J. "Augustine, Literal and Scientific: His Interpretation of Genesis on Creation." In *Understanding Augustine,* 109–19. Dublin: Four Courts, 1997.

Oreggi, Agostino. *De Deo uno: Tractatus primus.* Rome: Camera Apostolica, 1629.

———. *Aristotelis vera de rationalis animae immortalitate sententia accurate explicata.* Rome: Camera Apostolica, 1631.

———. *De opere sex dierum.* Rome: Vatican Press, 1632.

Osler, Margaret J. *Divine Will and the Mechanical Philosophy: Gassendi and Descartes on Contingency and Necessity in the Created World.* Cambridge: Cambridge University Press, 1994.

Pagano, Sergio M., and Antonio G. Luciani, eds. *I documenti del processo di Galileo Galilei.* Vatican City: Pontifical Academy of Sciences, 1984.

Palisca, Claude. *Humanism in Italian Renaissance Musical Thought.* New Haven: Yale University Press, 1985.

Pantin, Isabelle. "New Philosophy and Old Prejudices: Aspects of the Reception of Copernicanism in a Divided Europe." *Studies in History and Philosophy of Science* 30:2 (1999): 237–62.

———. "'Dissiper les ténèbres qui restent encore à percer': Galilée, l'Eglise conquérante et la république des philosophes." In *Révolution scientifique et libertinage,* edited by A. Mothu, 11–34. Turnhout: Brepols, 2000.

Pardo Tomás, José. *Ciencia y censura: La Inquisicíon Española y los libros científicos en los siglos XVI y XVII.* Madrid: Consejo Superior de Investigaciones Cientìficas, 1991.

Paschini, Pio. *Vita et opere di Galileo Galilei.* Rome: Herder, 1965.

Pastor, Ludwig von. *The History of the Popes from the Close of the Middle Ages.* Translated by E. Graf. 40 vols. London: Hodges and Kegan Paul, 1891–1953.

Pastore, Stefania. "A proposito di Mateo XVIII, 15: Correctio fraterna e Inquisizione nella Spagna del *Cinquecento.*" *Rivista Storica Italiana* 113 (2001): 323–68.

Pastore Stocchi, Manlio. "Il periodo veneto di Galileo Galilei." In *Storia della cultura veneta,* edited by Girolamo Arnaldi and Manlio Pastore Stocchi, 6 vols., 5:37–66. Vicenza: Neri Pozza, 1984.

Pedersen, Olaf. *Galileo and the Council of Trent.* Studi Galileiani 1:1. Vatican City: Vatican Observatory Publications, 1983.

Pepe, Luigi, ed. *Copernico e la questione copernicana in Italia dal xvi al xix secolo.* Florence: Leo S. Olschki, 1996.

Pereira, Benito. *Commentariorum et disputationum in Genesim, tomi quatuor.* Rome: Ferrari, 1591–95.

Pesce, Mauro. "L'interpretazione della Bibbia nella Lettera di Galileo a Cristina di Lorena e la sua ricezione: Storia di una difficoltà nel distinguere ciò che è religioso da ciò che non lo è." *Annali di Storia dell'Esegesi* 4 (1987): 239–86.

———. "Momenti della ricezioni dell'ermeneutica biblica galileiana e della Lettera a Christina nel XVII secolo." *Annali di Storia dell'Esegesi* 8 (1991): 55–104.

———. "Le redazioni originali della Lettera copernicana di G. Galilei a B. Castelli." *Filologia e Critica* 17 (1992): 394–417.

———. "Gli ingegni senza limiti e il pericolo per la fede." In *Largo campo di filosofare: Eurosymposium Galileo 2001,* edited by José Montesinos and Carlos Solís, 637–59. La Orotava: Fundacion Canaria Orotava de Historia de la Ciencia, 2001.

Poncet, Olivier. "L'ouverture des archives du Saint-Office et de l'Index : Échos d'une journée de présentation." *Revue d'Histoire de l'Eglise de France* 84 (1998): 97–103.

Poppi, Antonino. *Introduzione all'aristotelismo padovano.* Padua: Antenore, 1991.

———. *Cremonini, Galilei e gli inquisitori del Santo a Padova.* Padua: Centro Studi Antoniani, 1993.

———. "La difficile integrazione dell'aristotelismo padovano nella teologia tridentina: Iacopo Zabarella e Antonio Possevino." In *Aristotelica et lulliana magistro doctissimo Charles H. Lohr septuagesimum annum feliciter agenti dedicata,* edited by F. Dominguez, R. Imbach, T. Pindl, and P. Walter, 245–58. The Hague: M. Nijhoff, 1995.

Possevino, Antonio. *Bibliotheca selecta de ratione studiorum, ad disciplinas, et ad salutem omnium gentium procurandam.* Cologne, 1607.

Poupard, Paul. "Galileo: Report on Papal Commission Findings." *Origins* 22 (1992): 374–75. French original in Paul Poupard, *Après Galilée* (Paris: Desclée de Brouwer, 1994), 93–97.

———, ed. *Galileo Galilei, 350 ans d'histoire, 1633-1983.* Paris: Descleé, 1983. Translated into Italian as *Galileo Galilei, 350 anni di storia, 1633-1983* (Casale Monferrato: Piemme, 1984). Translated into English by I. Campbell as *Galileo Galilei: Toward a Resolution of 350 Years of Debate, 1633-1983* (Pittsburgh: Duquesne University Press, 1987).

———, ed. *Après Galilée.* Paris: Desclée de Brouwer, 1994.

Preti, Cesare. "Riccioli e l'Inquisizione." In *Giambattista Riccioli e il merito scientifico dei gesuiti nell'età barocca,* edited by Maria Teresa Borgato, 213–49. Florence: Leo S. Olschki, 2002.

Price, M. Daniel. "The Origins of Lateran V's *Apostolici Regiminis.*" *Annuarium Historiae Conciliorum* 17 (1985): 464–72.

Randles, W. G. L. *The Unmaking of the Medieval Christian Cosmos, 1500-1760: From Solid Heavens to Boundless Æther.* Brookfield, Vt.: Ashgate, 1999.

Redondi, Pietro. *Galileo eretico.* Turin: Einaudi, 1983. Translated by Raymond Rosenthal as *Galileo Heretic* (Princeton: Princeton University Press, 1987).

———. "From Galileo to Augustine." In *The Cambridge Companion to Galileo,* edited by Peter Machamer, 175–210. Cambridge: Cambridge University Press, 1998.

Reinhard, W. "Il Concilio di Trento e le scienze naturali: La controversia fra Bellarmino e Galilei come paradigma." In *Il Concilio di Trento e il moderno,* edited by P. Prodi and W. Reinhard, 485–501. Bologna: Il Mulino, 1996.

Renn, Jürgen. *Galileo in Context.* Cambridge: Cambridge University Press, 2001.

Restiglian, Marco. "Nota su Giuseppe Toaldo e l'edizione toaldina del *Dialogo* di Galileo." *Studia Patavina* 29 (1982): 723–27.

Rheticus, Goerg Joachim. *Narratio prima.* Edited with French translation and commentary by H. Hugonnard-Roche and J.-P. Verdet, with the collaboration of M.-P. Lerner and A. Segonds. Studia Copernicana 20. Wrozlaw: Ossolineum, 1982.

Riccioli, Giovanni Battista. *Almagestum novum.* 2 parts. Frankfurt: Beyer, 1651.

———. *Astronomiae reformatae tomi duo.* 2 vols. Bologna: Benati, 1665.

———. *Apologia.* Venice: Salerni and Cagnolini, 1669.

Righini-Bonelli, Maria L., and William R. Shea, eds. *Reason, Experiment, and Mysticism in the Scientific Revolution.* New York: Science History Publications, 1975.

Ritzler, Remigius. "Die Verschleppung der päpstlichen Archive nach Paris unter Napoleon I. und deren Rückführung nach Rom in den Jahren 1815 bis 1817." *Römische historische Mitteilungen* 6/7 (1962–63/1963–64): 144–90.

Romeo, Giovanni. *L'Inquisizione nell'Italia moderna.* Rome: Laterza, 2002.

Rosen, Edward. "Was Copernicus's *Revolutions* Approved by the Pope?" *Journal of the History of Ideas* 36 (1975): 531–42.

———. "Kepler and the Lutheran Attitude towards Copernicanism in the Context of the Struggle between Science and Religion." In *Kepler: Four Hundred Years,* edited by A. Beer and P. Beer, 317–38. Vistas in Astronomy 18. Oxford: Pergamon Press, 1975.

———. "The Exposure of the Fraudulent Address to the Reader in Copernicus' *Revolutions.*" *Sixteenth-Century Journal* 14 (1983): 283–91.

———. *Copernicus and the Scientific Revolution.* Malabar, Fla.: Krieger, 1984.

Rossi, P. "Galileo Galilei e il libro dei Salmi." *Rivista di Filosofia* 10 (1978): 45–71.

Russell, John L. "Catholic Astronomers and the Copernican System after the Condemnation of Galileo." *Annals of Science* 46 (1989): 365–86.

———. "What Was the Crime of Galileo?" *Annals of Science* 52 (1995): 403–10.

Sánchez de Toca Alameda, Melchior. "Un doble aniversario: XX aniversario de la creación de la Comisión de Estudio del Caso Galileo y X de su clausura." *Ecclesia* 16:2 (2002): 141–68.

Sciences et religions de Copernic à Galilée (1540–1610). Rome: École français de Rome, 1999.

Scott, John Beldon. *Images of Nepotism: The Painted Ceilings of Palazzo Barberini.* Princeton: Princeton University Press, 1991.

Schwedt, Herman H. "Das Archiv der römischen Inquisition und des Index." *Römische Quartalschrift* 93 (1998): 267–80.

Segre, Michael. *In the Wake of Galileo.* New Brunswick: Rutgers University Press, 1991.

———. "Light on the Galileo Case?" *Isis* 88 (1997): 484–504.

Shank, Michael H. "How Shall We Practice History? The Case of Mario Biagioli's *Galileo, Courtier.*" *Early Science and Medicine* 1 (1996): 106–50.

Sharratt, Michael. "Copernicanism at Douai." *Durham University Journal,* n.s., 36 (Dec. 1974): 41–48.

———. *Galileo: Decisive Innovator.* Oxford: Blackwell, 1994. Reprint, Cambridge: Cambridge University Press, 1996.

Shea, William R. "Melchior Inchofer's Tractatus Syllepticus: A Consultor of the Holy Office Answers Galileo." In *Novità celesti e crisi del sapere,* edited by Paolo Galluzzi, 283–92. Florence: Giunti Barbèra, 1983.

———. "Galileo and the Church." In *God and Nature: Historical Essays on the Encounters between Christianity and Science,* edited by David C. Lindberg and Ronald L. Numbers, 114–35. Berkeley: University of California Press, 1986.

———. "Galileo e l'atomismo." *Acta Philosophica* 10 (2001): 257–72.

———. "Galileo, the Copernican." In *Largo campo di filosofare: Eurosymposium Galileo 2001,* edited by José Montesinos and Carlos Solís, 41–59. La Orotava: Fundacion Canaria Orotava de Historia de la Ciencia, 2001.

Shea, William R., and Mariano Artigas. *Galileo in Rome: The Rise and Fall of a Troublesome Genius.* New York: Oxford University Press, 2003.

Simoncelli, Paolo. "Inquisizione romana e riforma in Italia." *Rivista Storica Italiana* 100 (1988): 5–125.

———. *Storia di una censura: "Vita di Galileo" e Concilio Vaticano II.* Milan: Angeli, 1992.

Soccorsi, Filippo. *Il processo di Galileo.* Rome: La Civiltà Cattolica, 1963.

Sosio, Libero. "Il copernicanesimo di Sarpi." In *Fra Paolo Sarpi dei Servi di Maria,* edited by Pacifico Branchesi and Corrado Pin, 153–86. Venice: Comune di Venezia, 1986.

Spruit, Leen. "Cremonini nelle carte del Sant'Uffizio Romano." In *Cesare Cremonini: Aspetti del pensiero e scritti,* edited by E. Riondato and A. Poppi, 1:193–204. Padua: Academia Galileiana, 2000.

———. "Giordano Bruno eretico: Le imputazioni del processo nei contesto storico-dottrinale." In *Cosmologia, teologia y religion en la obra y en el proceso de Giordano Bruno,* edited by Miguel Angel Granada, 111–28. Barcelona: Universitat de Barcelona, 2001.

Stabile, Giorgio. "Linguaggio della natura e linguaggio della scrittura in Galilei: Dalla 'Istoria' sulle macchie solari alle lettere copernicane." *Nuncius* 9 (1994): 37–64.

Stimson, Dorothy. *The Gradual Acceptance of the Copernican Theory of the Universe.* New York: Baker and Taylor, 1917.

Szilas, L. "Inchofer." In *Dictionnaire d'histoire et de géographie ecclésiastiques,* vol. 25, cols. 979–80. Paris: Letouzey et Ané, 1995.

Tanner, Norman P., ed. *Decrees of the Ecumenical Councils.* Washington, D.C.: Georgetown University Press, 1990.

Tedeschi, John. *The Prosecution of Heresy: Collected Studies on the Inquisition in Early Modern Italy.* Binghamton, N.Y.: Medieval and Renaissance Texts and Studies, 1991.

———. "Die Inquisitionsakten im Trinity-College, Dublin." In *Inquisition, Index, Zensur: Wissenkulturen Neuzeit im Widerstreit,* edited by Hubert Wolf, 71–87. Paderborn: Ferdinand Schöningh, 2001.

Torrini, Maurizio. "Giuseppe Feroni, gesuita e galileano." *Physis* 15:4 (1973): 411–23.

———. *Dopo Galileo: Una polemica scientifica (1684-1711).* Florence: Leo S. Olschki, 1979.

———. "La discussione sullo statuto delle scienze tra la fine del '600 e l'inizio del '700." In *Galileo e Napoli,* edited by Fabrizio Lomonaco and Maurizio Torrini, 57–83. Naples: Guida Editori, 1987.

Tramontin, Silvio. "Galileo Galilei nella recente storiografia." *Studia Patavina* 29(3) (1982): 159–67.

Università Cattolica del Sacro Cuore, ed. *Nel quarto centenario della nascità di Galileo Galilei.* Milan: Vita e Pensiero, 1966.

van Limboch, Philippus. *The History of the Inquisition . . . abridged.* London: Simpkin and Marshall, 1816.

Vawter, Bruce. *Biblical Inspiration.* Philadelphia: Westminster Press, 1972.

Viganò, Mario. *Il mancato dialogo fra Galileo e i teologi.* Rome: Edizioni La Civiltà Cattolica, 1969.

von Gebler, Carl. *Galileo Galilei und die römische Kurie.* Stuttgart, 1876. Translated by G. Sturge as *Galileo and the Roman Curia* (1879; reprint, Merrick, N.Y.: Richmond, 1977).

Walker, Daniel P. *Spiritual and Demonic Magic from Ficino to Campanella.* London: Warburg Institute, 1958. Reprint, Notre Dame: University of Notre Dame Press, 1975.

Wallace, William A. "Galileo's Early Arguments for Geocentrism and His Later Rejection of Them." In *Novità celesti e crisi di sapere,* edited by Paolo Galluzzi, 31–40. Florence: Giunti Barbèra, 1984.

———. *Galileo and His Sources: The Heritage of the Collegio Romano in Galileo's Science.* Princeton: Princeton University Press, 1984.

———. *Galileo's Logic of Discovery and Proof.* Dordrecht: Kluwer, 1992.

———, ed. and trans. *Galileo's Early Notebooks: The Physical Questions.* Notre Dame: University of Notre Dame Press, 1977.

———, ed. *Reinterpreting Galileo.* Washington, D.C.: Catholic University of America Press, 1986.

Wardeska, Zofia. *Teoria heliocentryczna w interpretacji teologów xvi wieku.* Wroclaw: Ossolineum, 1975.

Westfall, Richard S. "Galileo and the Jesuits." In *Metaphysics and Philosophy of Science in the Seventeenth and Eighteenth Centuries: Essays in Honor of Gerd Buchdahl,* edited by R. S. Woolhouse, 45–72. Dordrecht: Kluwer, 1988.

———. *Essays on the Trial of Galileo.* Studi Galileiani 1:5. Vatican City: Vatican Observatory Publications, 1989.

Westman, Robert S. "The Reception of Galileo's *Dialogue:* A Partial World Census of Extant Copies." In *Novità celesti e crisi di sapere,* edited by Paolo Galluzzi, 329–37. Florence: Giunti Barbèra, 1984.

———. "The Copernicans and the Churches." In *God and Nature: Historical Essays on the Encounter between Christianity and Science,* edited by David C. Lindberg and Ronald L. Numbers, 76–113. Berkeley: University of California Press, 1986.

Williams, Arnold. *The Common Expositor: An Account of the Commentaries on Genesis, 1527-1633.* Chapel Hill: University of North Carolina Press, 1948.

Wohlwill, Emil. *Der Inquisitions-prozess des Galileo Galilei.* Berlin: Oppenheim, 1870.

———. "Galilei betreffende Handschriften der Hamburger Stadtbibliothek." *Jahrbuch der Hamburgischen Wissenschaftlichen Anstalten* 12 (1894): 149–223.

———. *Galilei und sein Kampf für die kopernikanische Lehre.* 2 vols. Leipzig: Leopold Voss, 1910–26. Reprint, Wiesbaden: Martin Sändig, 1969.

Wolf, Hubert, ed. *Inquisition, Index, Zensur: Wissenskulturen der Neuzeit im Widerstreit.* Paderborn: Ferdinand Schöningh, 2001.

Wootton, David. *Paolo Sarpi: Between Renaissance and Enlightenment.* Cambridge: Cambridge University Press, 1983.

Zycinski, Józef M. *The Idea of Unification in Galileo's Epistemology.* Studi Galileiani 1:4. Vatican City: Vatican Observatory Publications, 1988.

INDEX

abjuration of Galileo, 282
   compared to sentence, 283
   doctrinal legitimacy of, 252–53
   text of, 140, 243
Accademia del Cimento, 289
Acquaviva, Claudio, 47, 155, 329
Adamo, ovvero il mondo creato, L'
   (Campailla), 298, 299, 310
"Ad lectorem: To the Reader on the
   Hypotheses of This Work"
   (Osiander), 14, 17
ad litteram interpretation of a text, 91
Against Impious Atheists (Fabri), 242
Aggiunti, Niccolò, 269
Alberi, Eugenio, 265
Alembert, Jean d', 308
   article on Copernicus, 306–7
Alexander VII (pope), 287
   Riccioli and, 289
Algarotti, Francesco, 302
Almagestum novum (Riccioli), 288–89
Almanac (Cagnoli), 312
Ambrogi, Paolo Antonio, 303–4
Anfossi, Filippo, 6, 279, 283, 312–13
Apes urbanae, 284
Apollonius, 161
Apologia pro Galileo (Campanella). *See*
   Defense of Galileo (Campanella)
Apologia (Riccioli), 290
Apostolici regiminis (Fifth Lateran Council),
   172, 239

archives of the Holy See. *See also*
   Congregation of the Doctrine of
   the Faith; Congregation of the Holy
   Office; Congregation of the Index
   history of, 194–96
   opening of, 191, 193
Aristotle
   Bellarmine's criticism of, 174–75
   cosmology, 160
   —1616 decree as defense of, 155–57
   —impact on theology, 183
   doctrine of the soul
   —Inquisition and, 236
   —Oreggi on, 251
   ideal of demonstration in natural
     philosophy, 162
   —taught at Padua University, 239
   —Tolosani on, 15
Artigas, Mariano, 213, 218, 220
   and EE 291, 287
Assayer, The (Galileo)
   atomism in, 287
   dedication to Urban VIII, 71
   denunciation of, 217–18
   engraved portrait of Galileo, 237, *238*
   as response to Grassi, 216
Astrologica (Campanella), 74, 75
astrology
   condemnation by *Inscrutabilis,* 77
   Galileo's accusation by Pagnoni, 66, 282
   omnipresence in Rome, 80

ERNAN MCMULLIN is John Cardinal O'Hara Professor Emeritus
of Philosophy at the University of Notre Dame.